WARNI

Those who believe the man Jesu years ago was God, should read no f being is God, those who disagree wil only find this book upsetting and disagreeable. This writing is not for those convinced they have the last word on Christ, but those searching for the real Christ. While I believe all Christians have the right Faith, I do not think all Christians have the right beliefs, right understanding or right views of Christ. Given all the Jesus-talk these days, Christianity comes across as a personality cult, the worship of a human being, which has nothing to do with Christ – it even turns people away. The reason for this writing, then, is my perception that the real Christ has been all but lost to Christianity.

Of first importance is to define the major terms used in this book, namely “Logos”, “Christ”, and “Jesus”. Those who think these terms are interchangeable, synonymous, or refer to the same Reality, will never understand a thing in this book. Indiscriminate use of these terms has already thrown people off track, thus it is of the utmost importance to define these terms from the outset. Those who disagree with these definitions will only become addled or irate and should read no further.

Because God is not a being, but Infinite Existence, we must be careful not to anthropomorphize the essence of God’s “triune modes of Existence” (the Trinity) as three beings or three entities – three gods, in other words. Also, because God transcends all gender, we have to be careful not to get caught up in the metaphors used for the Trinity as “Father and Son”. Since God is neither mother, father, son or daughter, these metaphors must not be taken literally or understood as God *ad intra* (God-in-Itself.) To avoid this pitfall, this book refers to God’s Triune essence as “Transcendent-Logos-Spirit”.

The Incarnation was God creating Its own human nature – i.e., man’s one universal human nature – eternally one with Itself. This is the oneness of God’s divine nature and man’s universal human nature that we know and call “Christ”. The term, word, or title “Christ”, is not the name of any human being, but refers solely to God’s eternal oneness with Man.

The Incarnation was not God uniting Itself to any particular human being or person. Christ is not the oneness of two persons, two individuals or two beings (a divine being and a human being), rather, Christ is the eternal oneness of two natures, divine and human. Thus the Incarnation was the revelation of Man (“Universal Man”) and

God's Plan for all mankind, and this Truth, this revelation, is everything we know as "Christ".

The purpose of the Incarnation was not to reveal the man Jesus – give us another god for the pantheon – but to reveal Man. Prior to the Incarnation Christ did not exist, nor did the man Jesus exist, only God, the divine Trinity, eternally existed. Thus neither as a human being or a human person was the man Jesus divine, or even Christ. It is solely the oneness of God with Its own human nature that is Christ, and it is this mystery of God's indivisible oneness with the essence of mankind we call the "Real Christ".

Since there is only one common human nature, not many human natures, different kinds, or particular human natures, one can count heads, but not human natures. As the "instrument" for revealing Christ, the singular man born into this world was given the common Jewish name "Jesus". It was not his *individual* person or particular human nature, however, that was Christ, rather, Christ is solely God's own human nature and not the human nature of any particular human being or person. So where the term "Christ" is a reference to the indivisible oneness of two natures, the name "Jesus" is solely a reference to a particular human being or person.

This book permits no anthropomorphic view of God (the Trinity) or Christ. Reference to the man Jesus is always to a particular human being and never to God. "Jesus" is the particular man of the Gospels, the historical person no longer with us. With his resurrection and ascension his human nature was totally transformed and glorified, thus he is no longer the historical figure of the past, but remains the example or icon of everyman's journey and eternal oneness with God. We must never, then, mix our terms – the Logos is solely God, Jesus was solely a distinct human person, and Christ, the eternal oneness of God and Man.

Those who disagree with these definitions should read no further, it would only confuse and upset them. Also, it would be useless to argue any of this since I've done my homework, am aware of all opposing views, and regard them as misconceived or wrong. Given the same Christian background and history as those who object, I already know where they are coming from, it is they, however, who do not know where I am coming from, and therein lies the difference.

THE REAL CHRIST

BERNADETTE ROBERTS

ContemplativeChristians.com

ContemplativeChristians.com Publishing
First Printing, February, 2017
Austin, TX

Library of Congress Cataloging-in-Publication Data

Roberts, Bernadette (1931 –)
The Real Christ
ISBN 13: 978-0-692-85115-9

1. Spiritual life – Christianity. 2. Christ. I. Title.

BT220.R55 2017

Printed in the United States of America

Cover Art
The cover picture was found in an old volume of the Catholic Encyclopedia many years ago at the library. Reminding me of the Trinity, I made a copy, blew it up and colored it. The center is reminiscent of the Eucharist in a beautiful monstrance. – B.R.

Cover design by Brian Burrowes.

CONTENTS

REASON FOR WRITING

As the title of this book implies, there is an "unreal" Christ, a Christ people think they know, but under scrutiny, do not know. The sole motive for this writing is based on my observation the real Christ has been all but lost to Christianity and replaced by what can only be called a "*Jesus cult*", the worship of a human being as God – or better, worship of a human being **mistaken** for God. As evidence of this loss, one need only listen to the sermons and sentimental hymns in the Churches, on radio, TV, in the literature and the language used, to realize Christ is not there. It seems people's understanding of Christ goes no further than the historical man depicted in the Gospels, a man many regard as a divine being who lived two thousand years ago, the same historical figure they worship today and expect to see in heaven.

While such a view may satisfy simple folk, it does not satisfy those seeking a more profound spiritual life, which seeking has led thousands out of Christianity to one or other of the Eastern religions. I have personally met hundreds of these people, all of Christian heritage dedicated to the spiritual quest, but who went East in pursuit of a spiritual life they did not find in their Churches. Apart from Jesus' ethical and social teachings, Christianity held nothing for them. Its sole focus on the historical Jesus seemed to go no further than sentiment, avoidance of sin and practice of virtue – no different from any other religion in the world. Jesus just doesn't do it for them, *he is not the God they have already encountered*, thus they have gone elsewhere – and are still going. As one gentleman put it to me, "I was raised and educated a Catholic, believed it, but eventually found it very shallow and dissatisfying" – so he went East. Although I could give pages of examples and quotes to illustrate this loss of Christ in Christianity, what follows are but a few different examples.

Several years ago there was a documentary of a young Catholic woman who converted to Islam. Asked what convinced her to become a Muslim, she said these people had simply asked her: "*If Jesus prayed to God, then how could he be God? Was Jesus praying to himself?*" Evidently the woman didn't know how to answer, but it seemed to convince her Jesus couldn't be God (she was right), and so she became a happy Muslim. But where did Muslims (and Jews) get the idea the man Jesus was God? Where else but from Christians themselves? Ask any Christian if they believe Jesus is God, and there you have the answer. That Christianity has been degraded to the worship of a human being not only robs it of its profound Truth and meaning, it is contrary to monotheism and totally incapable of promoting any true spiritual life with God. When the focus is solely on the human Jesus, people are kept from developing any true understanding of Christ, kept on the surface little better than the naive level of a five year old. Recently, even the Pope commented on the "disrespect" in which people, worldwide, hold Christianity these days. No wonder!

Everyone would do well to ask himself how he would respond to the Muslim – who thinks because Jesus prayed to God was proof he could not be God. People's answer could be a check-up on their own beliefs. Having put this question to at least a hundred Christians (mostly Catholic) everyone's reply was different – no one, of course, thought Jesus was praying to himself. Had the question been put to me, I'd have said immediately, "*The man Jesus is not God, no Christian believes a human being is God, Jesus was a human being, and like ourselves, prayed to God just as we all do.*" Since the Islamic view is that Christians believe Jesus is God, and since the Catholic woman did *not* believe he was (she was correct), she felt more at home in Islam. Does this example say anything to anybody?

Another example of wrong belief comes from an entirely different corner. For a long time I've known an old Catholic monk who, one day, when I mentioned the Eucharist as the "Way" we are transformed into Christ, suddenly turned to me and said, "*But women can't be transformed into Christ because Christ is a man!*" Oh dear, what do you think his problem was? Since I don't think he mistook Jesus' human nature for God's divine nature, he must have assumed there were *two kinds of human natures,* one male and one female. Obviously, he didn't understand that gender does not determine "human nature" or that there is no such thing as "different kinds" of human natures. At any rate, I reminded him of Paul's saying that in Christ "*there is neither male nor female*" – a good reminder, at least, to those who think Christ is a male man. Having said this, however, it is a good thing Jesus was a male, for had he been born a female, we'd never have heard of *"her"* or Christianity. There isn't a religion in the world not founded by a male, or where a female played any strategic part – and to think it is all about the "Y" chromosome, tsk tsk! This is all the more reason then, to get beyond the male Jesus and find the Real Christ whose eternal, deified *heavenly* body and soul is no *earthly* male torso, but as Paul affirms, a "*spiritual body" –* even, *"the summation of all creation."*

Evidently, some people think Paul's saying "in Christ there are no distinctions between male and female" refers solely to some form of social equality. That transformation *into* Christ implies Christ is genderless, and that *as Christ,* we too will be genderless, would not sit well with those for whom Christ is a male man. Perhaps this is why the Christian belief that salvation consists in being "transformed" *into*

Christ is rarely mentioned – women just don't fit the visual mold. Today, at best, it is only said we are transformed *in* Christ, never *into* Christ, yet *in* Christ what are we transformed *into* if not Christ? My impression is that Church leaders, theologians and writers, water down and eliminate anything profoundly spiritual or mystical – because they don't get it themselves and don't want others to get what they don't get.

Another example is that of a young child preparing for First Communion. Over and over he was told he would be eating the *physical* flesh of Jesus and drinking the man's blood. The idea so nauseated and disgusted him, when his "big day" arrived, he ran and spat it out. Jesus lost thousands of disciples over this very issue. And no wonder, he gave them no explanation whatsoever – just as no one explained to this child that the true nature of Christ's *heavenly* glorified "spiritual body" is *not* the *earthly* body of the man Jesus. (As Paul said, he saw the "*Resurrected Christ*", and "*never saw Jesus in the flesh*".) But these were not the only people Jesus lost, a recent poll of Catholics, asked if they believed that in the Eucharist they were truly receiving Christ, 70% said they only regarded this as a "symbolic memorial or ritual." Less than 30% responded positively. Those who think the real Christ has not been lost, had better think again.

For my contemplative friends, another example in this matter, is that of Mother Teresa of Calcutta, whose interior life was miserable (for 30 – 40 years) because Jesus wasn't there for her. Jesus, the love of her life from childhood – and seen in a vision prior to leaving her religious order – suddenly up and died on her, leaving her high and dry – seemingly, for the rest of her life. Seeing Mother Teresa lived Jesus' *same* God-centered life, how could she possibly suffer the loss of Jesus in her life? In my view, it was a failure to understand her human nature was *no different* from Jesus' human nature and that *her* oneness with God was *no different* than Jesus' oneness with God. Just like Jesus, she too was doing God's work in this world. As long as we think any difference exists in *man's common human nature*, so long do we fail to understand the Incarnation and the true Christ.

If one has God in their life, "who" (or "what") else is ever needed? Could it be Mother Teresa mistook Jesus for God? Evidently, this was much the same case with St. Therese of the Child Jesus. Toward the end of her short life, the man Jesus was no longer there for her either. Like Mother Teresa, she too doubted the existence of God and wondered if there was any truth in all she had believed. So what was all this about? People just have to be prepared for the shock that when they *see God*, they are *not* going to see the man Jesus – simple as that.

So what is wrong here? It seems Mother Teresa's view of "*Christ*" was *solely* the man Jesus, for which reason she could not identify her humanity as no different from his. Evidently, her interior oneness with God was not satisfying because it was *not* the man Jesus. (No one, of course, can be one with "another" human being because *human* is *what* he is already.) So, although one with God, Mother suffered because she didn't *feel* or *see* the man Jesus in this union, couldn't seem to personally communicate with this historical figure. This just illustrates how spiritually debilitating are the images, visions and concepts people cling to and rely on for Truth. This is why even some of the most saintly and spiritual people can suffer uselessly because they have wrong views of Christ – even though they have the right Faith. Since my interest is those seeking eternal oneness with God – transformation into Christ, no different from Christ – any clinging to the man Jesus can retard, even abort, their spiritual journey.

In some respects, I blame Mother's problem on her Jesuit confessors. The Jesuits are out to promote what is called *The Spiritual Exercises,* where people are to imagine some picture of Jesus in our heads, and then work up some kind of sentiment for him. Now who can doubt Mother was encouraged to do this by her Jesuit confessors? But what a mistake! These *Spiritual Exercise*s are not even regarded as a form of prayer, and for those who mistakenly think Jesus is God, they only promote idolatry. People who cannot let Jesus die, will not only have to go through his absence, but because of this, may even think they have lost the Faith. The truth of Christ, however, is beyond the man Jesus.

While nobody has to be Christian to do good works, yet considering what Mother Teresa accomplished, we can certainly see God at work in her – the real Christ, that is. That God never gave her to understand this, and that she suffered over what she mistakenly thought was a loss of the man Jesus in her interior life, seems incomprehensible. Even more so, in that every day she received the living, heavenly Christ in the Eucharist. Evidently the Eucharist did not match her childhood image of Jesus. Had she been able to let him die, she might have understood the Eucharist as the living (transfigured, deified, heavenly) Christ, and no longer the historical man or personality she (and everyone else) only depict in their minds. When all the visions or mental images and sentiments disappear – which is inevitable since they were not the truth anyway – there can only be a complete stalemate in one's spiritual development *unless* one has a correct understanding of the real Christ. People's understanding of Christ makes a huge difference in how they understand their interior journey and life with God.

The only reason for bringing up Mother Teresa is to point out how miserable life can be if we cannot relate our humanity to Jesus' same human nature and understand we can have Jesus' same experiences of God, even his experience of no-God – as he did on the cross. It is impossible to do this if we think the man Jesus is God – an error Jesus himself never made. The sole focus of his will, mind and heart was never on himself, but solely on God, which is exactly how it should be for everyone. It is because Jesus is the *example* of a human being who gave his whole life to God, it is such a terrible mistake to adore the man who gave his life to God, rather than adore the God to Whom he gave it. Just as the Spirit transformed Jesus' human nature, so too, the Spirit transforms everyone's nature – no different. Not to see and understand this is a failure to understand the whole purpose of the Incarnation. There is no authentic spiritual life so long as there is any focus on another human being – be it Jesus, some guru, master, or anyone but God alone. The revelation of Christ was for man to know and understand the true nature of his *own* spiritual journey and eternal oneness with God. This is the Christian goal or end – to be transformed *into* Christ, no different from Christ.

Without question, the historical man Jesus can get in the way of understanding the purpose and revelation of the Incarnation. People can get so caught up in the human personality of the man, they never get beyond it to the Truth God intended the Incarnation to reveal. People need to take Jesus' death seriously – the man of the Gospels, gone forever. The Logos' (God's) own *earthly* human nature, was transformed beyond itself, beyond everything we now think is human nature, beyond what could even continue to live in this world. And how this transformation went for the man Jesus is exactly how it will go for everyone. No question, having a right understanding of Christ makes a huge difference in how one understands his spiritual journey and eternal life with and in God.

My concern in all this – the loss of the Real Christ – is primarily for Catholics. In my own life, I never thought Protestants had Christ right in the first place, so there is no concern over this loss. As a child, going into Protestant Churches I found them empty halls, no God there; whereas going into a Catholic Church, I ever felt the warmth of God's *presence*. When I was older and realized Protestants got their view of Christ solely from the Bible, then I knew why they had missed Christ. Without the Eucharist, I hold it impossible to ever know the Real Christ.

The reason Protestants like to accuse Catholics of not reading the Bible – which is totally false – is based on their different view of Christ. Where they took their view of Christ solely from the Bible,

Catholics took theirs primarily from the Eucharist – the very heart and center of the Church from its inception. The Bible is but the story of Jesus, the man that *was*, whereas the Eucharist is the living, heavenly Christ that *is with us* now and forever. These two sources yield very different understandings of Christ – the historical Jesus that died, and the *living* Christ that ascended – i.e., Jesus of the *past* and the heavenly Christ *today*. These different views will also engender very different interior lives, spiritual journeys and goals. If people are ever to come upon the mystery that *is* Christ, they need only focus on the Eucharist because *this mystery **is** Christ*.

The best I can trace the loss of Christ in the Catholic Church is as one of the fall-outs from Vatican II and its attempt to Protestantize the Church. Gradually there came the tendency to substitute the proper name "Jesus" for the epithet "Christ" – as if they meant the same thing, which they do not. This "Protestantizing" is best symbolized by the decentralization of the Eucharist from the center altar of the Church to a side niche – or out the door entirely. In place of the Living Christ (Eucharist), we now have a bible on the center altar, signifying a switch from the Living God to a paper god. If this was not a Protestant move – substituting the centrality of the Eucharist for a book – what else can it be called? When the focus is solely on the life of the historical man Jesus – that St. Irenaeus (125 – 202) aptly called the "*Apostles' Memoirs*" – we miss the transfigured, glorified Christ whose ascended "spiritual" (invisible) body is the *living* Christ – otherwise known as the "*Eucharist*".

This is largely how (and why) the Catholic Church *changed* from being Christ-centered to centering on a dead biblical image – the man Jesus. With the loss of the Real Christ, however, comes the loss of Christianity. Although there will always be a handful to whom the Real Christ is revealed, this will not be enough to save Christianity as a whole. People today are too well educated and have too many choices of religions to stick with an *anthropolatric* Jesus-cult.[1] Without the knowledge of the true Christ, it will just be a matter of time before even this cult runs out of joiners and disappears. If it can be said Christianity will never be lost, it will only be because its essence and roots, being

---

[1] Anthropolatry is officially defined – "The worshipping or cult of a human being conceived as a god, and conversely, of a god conceived as a human being. The deification of individual human beings was practiced by most early civilizations and added much color to the folklore and religion of such countries as Egypt, Greece, India and Japan. The Shinto religion in Japan still considers the emperor as a "visible deity" and maintains shrines devoted to brave warriors or heroes. Monotheistic religions consider anthropolatry as a superstition". From a "Dictionary of Philosophy".

profoundly mystical, and its Truth transcending mere belief, it will belong solely to a few unknown Christian contemplatives.

Unfortunately, the Church I was raised in, is not the Catholic Church of today. And since there is no putting humpty-dumpty back together again, I shudder when anyone talks to me of becoming a Catholic. I can only warn them they will be disappointed. Where the Eastern Orthodox Church has kept its balance through its liturgy and adherence to the Early Fathers, the West has bogged down in all kinds of dictums and innovations, removing anything uplifting to the depths of Christ's mystery. Thus, the "sacred liturgy" has been replaced by services reminiscent of the old Southern Revivalists' tents – totally unexpressive of the *magnum mysterium* of man's profound life with and in God. Here too, we might recall the fact that one of the first acts of the Reformation was to disband, confiscate and burn down monasteries – for which no compensation has ever been forthcoming – highly symbolic of a particular fear lest others be privy to a deeper understanding of the mystery of Christ than themselves. Nobody wants their view of Christ to be challenged lest their view appear wanting or, possibly, not be true at all.

It is precisely because the **bible does not give us the whole story on Christ** that Christianity's "*tradition*" supersedes scriptures, its *focus* being on the mystery of Christ in light of the Trinity and the Eucharist – a focus ***not*** found in the bible. Without this, or based on the bible alone, there are many different views of Christ, all of them lacking the mystery of the true Christ. As to *who* sets the standards of *right belief* or "orthodoxy", is a good question. Christianity East and West consists of thousands of different sects all claiming to have right beliefs, but how do we know who has it right? To find out, we first have to *exclude* the bible since it has always been used as the proof-text for every heresy known to Christianity. Thus Docetism, Arianism, Apollinarianism, Monophysitism, Gnosticism, Messalianism, and many more heresies down to this day, all took their "proofs-of-truth" from the bible. Yet there isn't a single biblical quote one can give as "proof" that another quote cannot refute. If scripture proves anything, it is that it proves nothing – nothing but what is in the mind of the quoter.

The bible's potential is for divisiveness, not unity. Though historically valuable, it can never take the place of the specific revelation we know as "Christ". In this biblical matter, St. Maximus the Confessor (580 – 662) wisely cautions, "*It is necessary that one who seeks God in a religious way never hold on to the "letter" lest he mistakenly understand things said* ***about*** *God for God Himself. In this case we are unwisely satisfied with the* ***words of scripture in place of the Logos,*** *and* *the Logos slips out of mind while we thought by holding on to his garments (visible things) we could possess the incorporeal Logos,* ***thus mistakenly worship the creature instead of the Creator"*** – the very definition of "*anthropolatry*". Who could dispute this? St. Maximus considered the most outstanding Christian authority on the spiritual life, simply put it on the line.

The sole value of the New Testament is being able to glimpse the *interior* life of Jesus whose *human* spiritual journey we are called to "*recapitulate*". Thus, we too will know his oneness with God, his death, resurrection and ascension, and ultimately come to his same eternal oneness in the Trinity. The Incarnation revealed the "Way" it goes for every human being, thus the motto of this book is: "*as it goes for Christ's* **human nature** *so it goes for everyone".* St. Irenaeus said that in the process of the Incarnation the Logos *recapitulated* the whole of creation in Its cosmological descent to our humanity. Thus, the Logos (God) united Itself to man's universal human nature (a microcosm of creation) making all eternally one with Itself. This "descent" is also our path, only in reverse, we *recapitulate* Christ's *human* spiritual life by ascending the path by which Christ descended, thus making our way to God's singular oneness with man and all creation. Start off on a wrong foot, and one has not only lost years of the journey, but may have missed it altogether.

Another problem of adopting the biblical image of Jesus, is that people think they have pinned Christ down, know him, can tell us all about him. Yet no biblical view of Jesus has ever given us Christ. When Jesus said only God could *reveal* Christ, he was not referring to any *book* or mere *hearsay* – what someone else believes. All the bible can do is tell us *about* the historical life of Jesus; by no means is it the *revelation* of Christ.[2]

Even when God reveals the real Christ, until this revelation becomes one's reality, or until transformation into Christ is a *fait accompli,* one can never know the *fullness* of Christ, the *real eternal* Christ. Thus the unfolding of one's spiritual journey is equally the unfolding of the mystery of Christ. Apart from the Eucharist, there is no knowing Christ ahead of time, no knowing what we are being transformed into, not knowing the end for which we were created – until we get there. In short, there is no knowing the ultimate *reality of Christ* in the beginning, but only in the end – which end **is** *Christ.*

We do not, of course, recapitulate the *externals* of Jesus' life, but

---

[2] The true nature of "revelation" is *unmediated* – meaning, it comes directly from God alone and not *mediated through* any book or what someone *else* says or believes.

rather, share in the same mystery and grace of his human nature's oneness with God. Thus we are baptized into Christ's same mystery, receive the same Spirit, and above all, in the most blessed of Mysteries, the Eucharist, we receive the *living* eternal Christ. As Irenaeus put it, the Eucharist is "*just a continuation of the Incarnation*" – the Logos becoming incarnate in us, the Spirit transforming us into the same one Christ. Unfortunately, these Mysteries have come to be regarded as mere rituals. It is by the grace of these Mysteries, however, "*What he was by nature we become by grace.*" "By *nature*" is reference to the Incarnation – i.e., God creating *Its **own** human nature – which* nature we must *become* by "*grace*", by becoming *God's own human nature*, that is. (The difference between *becoming* Christ by "*adoption*" or grace, instead of by "*nature*" or "Incarnation", is that all have the *same ending* though not the same *beginning.*)

Some people may argue that what I call "the *Jesus-cult*" is just a matter of terminology. Thus they will argue the terms "Jesus", "Christ", "Logos", "God", "Word" all refer to the same divine one of the Trinity – all refer to "God", that is. Yet, if "*Jesus*" does *not* evoke the image of a *human being* or is not associated with the historical man by that name, then what else does it reference? If it is a reference to Almighty God (one of the Trinity or Logos) then it is sheer idolatry. Neither Christ nor the human being, Jesus, pre-existed the Incarnation. By no means is the "Jesus-cult" a matter of terminology! On the contrary, it is all those who believe the human being Jesus, is God. They are only *calling* it as they see it – believe it. Some people forget that "Jesus" (*Yeshua* in Hebrew) was a common Jewish name that had no connotation of a divine being or someone out of the ordinary. The term "Christ", however, was never the proper name of anyone, nor was it ever understood as a name for God.

"Christ" is solely an epithet or title like "holy" or "*anointed*" (in Greek, "*christos*"), the Judaic reference to some human being chosen by God for a special mission. Thus prophets were referred to as God's "anointed" ("*christos"),* a title the Apostles also took as reference to the Hebrew "*Messiah*" – "*the one born Jesus, **who is called** 'Christ'",* Matt 1:16. In time, however, this "Messiah" ("anointed" or "*christos*") went beyond Judaism's understanding of a Messiah who was to establish the "Kingdom of Israel" on this earth. Instead, "*Christos*" became a reference to the "*Incarnate* Logos (God)", understood *in Christianity* as the union or oneness of God and man's divine and human natures. It was this understanding of "Christ" that became part and parcel of the Church's traditional language. So where the name "Jesus" goes no further than an historical person or "*who*" someone *was*, "*Christ*" is reference to the *eternal* oneness of God and man – this alone is the "Real Christ".

The term "*Christ*", then, is not a reference to "*who*" some particular human being *was*, but a *title* referring to the mystery of God's eternal oneness with Man. This is why references to "*who*" one is – be it Jesus, Mary or Joseph – is not a reference to Christ because "*Christ*" is *not* a "*who*", but a *"what"* – *what God is, united to what man is.* This was the revelation of the Incarnation, of "*Universal Man*", and the *one* referred to as "*Christ*".

The other day, briefly opening the official *Catechism of the Catholic Church,* I read, *"Jesus united himself to all men through his Incarnation*". **Just a minute**! "*Who*" united Itself to all men through Its incarnation? **Jesus never even pre-existed the Incarnation!** The Incarnation was not *Jesus* creating *his own human nature eternally one with himself!* No human being can unite himself to God much less to "all men". The Catechism's statement is patently false. Innumerable quotes could be cited where the man "Jesus" has been substituted (mistaken) for references to Almighty God – in this case, the Logos. And like most books these days, looking in the index for "Christ", one will only find "*See Jesus*". Obviously, a wrong understanding of Christ is from the top down – those at the top being responsible for perpetuating wrong views. Either they know no better, or they deliberately foster what they think "simple-minded folk" expect to hear, i.e., take them for ignorant sheep – the herd mentality.

One senses a fear that the Truth of Christ's Reality might challenge the simple folks' belief system, fear it might go beyond what they learned as a child about "Jesus". Better, then, not to "question" lest Christian Truths go over one's head. There is also the fear of not being "dogmatically correct" lest one be censored and put down – God help those who stray from the proverbial "*party-line*"! Thus cautious, careful and restrained is how theologians and clergy come across – boring actually, same old, same old. Christians these days, however, are not those of yesterday, they are no longer satisfied with the simple platitudes, clichés, or childish naiveté of a Jesus cult.

Today, educated and free thinking, with instant access to information and communication, people are seeking Truth on their own with no reliance on clergy or church. Unless the Church can catch up to these sincere seekers of Truth and offer a deeper spiritual life, the Church will simply be left behind. Here comes to mind the parable of the Shepherd tending his flock (the *herd-mentality*.) When one of the sheep left to see what else was out there, the Shepherd went after him, and when the two finally met, the joy was such, they went off together and the Shepherd *never returning to his flock!* This is prophetic, people are leaving in search of Truth and God is going with them, the "Church" will simply be left behind.

In simple terms, those who believe the man Jesus is God, are *not* Monotheists, but *anthropolatrists*. Monotheism holds God is *Uncreated* and that everything God creates is *not, therefore,* God – not *Uncreated* that is. To hold the man Jesus, a *created* human being is God, is *anthropolatry* – another term for *idolatry.* It is because no Christian thinks himself an idolater, he needs to re-think his Christianity to be sure he has it right. Wrong views, after all, never led anyone aright.

To focus on Jesus as if he were God, misses the whole purpose and revelation of the Incarnation. Jesus was God's "*instrument*" for revealing *Christ*, an "*example*" of one who *became* the *eternal* Christ and whose *earthly* life with God all are called to *recapitulate* in their own lives. While as a human being, people can and should relate to Jesus' spiritual journey, even identify with many of his human experiences, yet the man, the person himself, was not God, but was as completely human as anyone ever born into this world. Focusing on God as a human being not only eliminates the human, but eliminates God – because God is *not* human.

In summary, my perception is that the Christians' usual view of Christ, especially in our day and age, goes no further than the individual man portrayed in the Gospels – the individual man Jesus. Since this book reflects the *Christ* that God gave me to know, it is primarily intended for those I already know and not for those it would be best not to know.

It is also written because, with few exceptions, I regard all man has ever known of Christ falls short of the mark. This book comes from nowhere but the conviction the Truth of Christ has become all but lost, and that unless people can recognize this fact, there can be no hope of turning the tide.

Jesus is reported to have said – "**I tell you the Truth which is why you do not believe me**". The reason Truth is *unbelievable* is because it transcends man's beliefs, and were this not so, there would be no need for *Faith.* There is no need, then, to *believe* anything said in this book, because where *Faith* is present, Truth will always be recognized.

THESIS

Because this book is premised on an understanding of Christ that may be unfamiliar to many people, it was suggested a brief summary of this understanding would be helpful from the outset. If a brief statement would suffice for this understanding, however, then there would be no use reading further. This book was written to clarify and meet the objections of those who do not share this understanding of Christ and not for those who do. So after reading the following statements, one can either put the book aside or read further.

Compared to all God's revelations to man, the revelation of Christ is the greatest. So God exists – what is that to man? Man dies and God goes right on without him. No revelation of God includes man, the only revelation that includes man is the revelation of *Christ*. So where God does *not* include man, *Christ* includes God. The revelation of *Christ*, then, is **not** the revelation of God, but the revelation of **Man.** It is the revelation of all man means to God and God's Plan for all men to be eternally one with God. It is this **eternal oneness with God that we know and call "Christ**". Christ, then, is neither God nor man, but the **eternal oneness of the two.**

What has been ineptly called the "In-carnation" – "inept" because man is more than "flesh" – was God creating ***Its own human nature*** eternally one with Itself. This was not the creation of any *particular* human being, but God creating Its *own* human nature that belonged to no one – not to Jesus, Mary or Joseph – but to God alone. God's plan and the goal (or end) of everyman's human nature, then, is to **become** God's *own human nature*, **and this *eternal* union of the *essence* of God's divine nature with the *essence* of man's human nature, this is the revelation of the "*eternal Christ*".**

Cyril of Alexandria aptly defined the Incarnation: "*The Logos* (God) *did not assume* (unite to Itself) *some particular human being, but universal man, or universal human nature, yet a nature that appeared as an individual".* Gregory of Nyssa also points out that scripture did not say the Logos became ***a*** man (some particular man), but became *man*, "*Universal Man*" – as Cyril put it.

The Incarnation, then, was *not* God creating *any particular* human being, but creating mankind's one common *human nature eternally one with Itself.* Just as the *essence* of God's divine nature is *One* and not "three ones", so too, the *essence* of man's human nature is "*one*" and not multiple "ones". There is ***One* God and *one* human nature, and the eternal *union* of these two *is* "*Christ*".** There is no such thing as different kinds of human natures, many human natures or even a "particular" human nature, for "*What is common to all is proper* (particular) *to none*". As Aristotle put it, "*It is the essence of human nature to be one*", thus man is multiple in number, but not in essence. Aristotle's definition of "*individual*" as an embodied "*numerical one*" means one can count heads, but not human natures. The fact every human being is created One-on-one does not make any "one" different from another "one". Commenting on "*the numerical unity of human nature*", Athanasius said, "*Just as the Trinity is a numerical unity in one essence so too man is a numerical unity in one essence*". We might compare this to the Eucharistic Christ being *one,* yet multiplied infinitely, is the *same one Christ.* So too, one human nature multiplied infinitely is the same one human nature. Obviously, the "mystery" of man and the *Eucharistic Christ* have much in common.

What accounts for *differences* is not human nature, but every one created with free-will, and how he uses this freedom – for good or ill – determines the "*person*" he *becomes*. All that makes for *differences*, then, constitutes what is called a "*person*". So while every *individual* human being is one in essence, no two *persons* can ever be the same. **Notice** – while God creates every human being One-on-one, yet **God creates no human *person.*** Thus God did not create a Hitler, a Mother Teresa, or even the *person* Jesus. God only creates "*what*" man is, not "*who*" a *particular* man or person *becomes*. Thus:

Human nature = **what** man is (universal)
Human person = **who** a man is (particular)
("Particularity" belongs to *person* and *not* to *human nature*.)

Because God creates no person, God is united to no person. God only creates human nature and is united to human nature. To understand the true nature of Christ, then, it is imperative to understand the difference between *nature* and *person* – they are not synonymous terms. Offhand, the distinction between "what" and "who" sounds simple enough, but since it is not, this is why these distinctions must be pointed out and stressed. Since an understanding of the Trinity and Christ depends on having a grasp of the difference between "nature" (essence or "what") and "person" (or "who"), we must go over the theological origin of the term "person" invented and defined by Christianity alone. Some fathers explained the difference between "who" and "what" this way:

Existence = "that" something is
Essence = "what" it is that exits
Person = "who" it is that exists.

The early fathers defined ***person*** as the ***agent*** *of the soul, the* ***sub-***

***ject**, the **I am**, one's **self-identity** or **"who"** one is* – which is not **"what"** one is, but **"who"** one is. Thus everyone, responsible for their own choices and behaviors in life, is the *person* he *becomes*. If Jesus had not been a *human person* he could not have functioned in this world, could not have been *fully human*. He had free-will, was his own free agent, subject, "I am", and had his *own* self-identity – this is clear from the Gospels. God, however, *creates no person*, not Jesus, Mary or Joseph – no one. So while Jesus was *his own person* or **"who"** he was, yet *what* he was, was a human being no different from any other human being. As Paul said, he was "*like us in every way but sin*". (God, of course, could never create a soul with sin – impossible.)

What all this means is that where God's ***own* human nature is *person-less* (God creates no person), yet every man born into this world becomes *his own unique* person.** Thus Jesus was his own unique *person* – until he died, that is. As Gregory of Nazianzus affirms, "*what God did not assume in the Incarnation, God does not save*", and since God did not assume (or create) any human *person*, then no human *person* is saved. The one "who" died on the cross was the human *person* (Jesus), died because all must be transformed into **God's *own person-less*** human nature – transformed into Christ, that is. The *eternal* oneness of God and man, then, is **"what"** Christ is (not "**who"** Christ is), and this oneness is *what* God destined all men to *become, **to be Christ – no*** **different.** As the **eternal union of *what* God is and *what* man is, Christ is the union of two "*what's*", not two "*who's*" –** as Gregory of Nazianzus points out, "*in Christ we have two "what's"* (natures), *not two "who's", two "I am's" or "two persons"*. Thus man is not transformed into "who" Christ is, but into "what" Christ is – i.e., **God's *own*** human nature beyond that of any *particular* human being or *person*.

As to the "way" God revealed Christ, Irenaeus (125 – 202) regarded the man Jesus as "*God's instrument*" for this revelation. This instrument or *particular person,* however, is *not* the revelation itself (*not* Christ), but solely the *medium* of God's revealing Man's ultimate destiny of eternal oneness with God. While Jesus was regarded as the model of the "way" to this end, Jesus himself was not the end – impossible in fact. No one is transformed into the man Jesus, rather, Jesus is the *example* whose spiritual life with God all are called to recapitulate. Thus, like Jesus, all are to *become* God's *own* eternal *human nature* – become ***Christ.*** Jesus, then, is the Christian icon ever pointing to Christ, pointing to *what* God destined all to *become*. And indeed, to follow Jesus' *interior life* with God leads all to Christ – to God's eternal oneness with man. As the model of man's ***spiritual life,* then, the**

"way" this went for Jesus is the same "way" it goes for every human being. As a model, however, Jesus is no object of worship – which belongs to God alone – but *like* Jesus, everyone must focus their life on God alone, must have Jesus' same faith, same love and *same* oneness with God – just as he prayed for everyone. "Christ", then, is a *reality* that transcends all historical persons and particular individuals.

Every reference to ***"Christ",*** then**,** *is* to *the eternal oneness of God's divine and human natures,* this alone is the "*Real Christ*". All references to "***Jesus"*** are references to the historical *human person,* the man Jesus. Is there a *difference* between the *Real Christ* and the *person* everyone knew as the man *Jesus*? Absolutely! Jesus was a particular ***person,*** whereas the Real Christ is no particular person – as said, God's human nature is ***person-less.*** (Remember, God does *not* create "persons".) So just as Jesus was transformed into Christ, so too is every human being. Thus the revelation of Christ is the revelation of the eternal life God destined for all mankind. Any reader who cannot grasp the difference between *human nature* as ***<u>what</u>*** man is, and a particular *human person* as ***<u>who</u>*** someone is, will not understand anything in this book. If the following definitions are not clear in one's mind, then it would be pointless to read further: In this book, use of the name "Jesus" is always reference to the historical, biblical ***person***, the human being given the common Jewish name, "Jesus".
– Use of the title "Christ" is always reference to the eternal oneness of God and Man, a union of ***what*** God is and ***what*** man is.
– Use of the word "God" is always a reference to "Infinite Existence", more especially, God's "*triune modes of existence"* – the Fathers' expression for the Trinity. (I also refer to the Trinity as God's immanent *triune* "*modus operandi*".) SO… reference to the man "Jesus" is **not** a reference to either *Christ* or to *God*

– and reference to "Christ" is **not** a reference to either *Jesus* or to *God*

– and "God" is **not** a reference to either *Jesus* or to *Christ.*

– "Christ" is solely a reference to the *eternal* oneness of God and man, more especially, God's oneness with Its ***own*** *human nature* and **not** the human nature of any *particular* human being or *person*.

When Paul said, "*No longer I, but Christ lives in me*", what did he mean?

Did he mean the man Jesus lived in him? Of course not.

Did he mean *he* (Paul) *was* Christ? No, as he said, "*No longer **I***".

Did he mean God lived **in** him? This was also not his specific reference.

So *what*, then, was his reference to "*Christ lives in me*"?

His reference was neither to *himself,* to the person Jesus, or even to God, rather, his reference was to the revelation that the ***true nature of his*** *(and everyman's)* ***oneness with God is Christ.*** **Indeed, *this "oneness" is "what" Christ is.*** So just as God's oneness with Jesus was "Christ", and Paul's oneness with God was "Christ", so too, the *true nature* of everyone's oneness with God **is** "*Christ*".[1] (We might add, Paul's same revelation of Christ has been given to Christians down the centuries and is by no means "*rare*".)

Besides pointing out the *universality of human nature* and the *particularity of person,* there is another important distinction to keep in mind. This is the difference between Christ's *earthly life* in this world and Christ's *eternal life* in the Godhead or Trinity. The difference is between being one with God *on this earth* and being one with God *in eternal life* – "heaven". On earth, man knows ***his own*** oneness with God – call it "*Theosis*" or "*Union with God*" – whereas his *eternal life* ***in*** God is a "*Hypostatic Union*", a union nowhere **in** man himself, but only **in** God. And being solely **in** God, this eternal union is known *only* to God.

The difference between these two unions is so great that no comparison is really possible. They belong to two entirely different dimensions of existence – one on this earth, the other, in God. One way to express this difference is that between the icon of the man Jesus as someone who lived Christ's life *in this world,* and the *Eucharist* as Christ's eternal life *in God.* In truth, anyone who thinks these are the same or no different, hasn't the first understanding of Christ. This is why one has to be careful when speaking of Christ – whether the reference is to man's oneness with God *lived in this world,* or to man's *eternal life in the Trinity.* Failure to keep this difference in mind has been the cause of much confusion and misunderstanding of Christ.

For now, at least, this understanding of the "Real Christ" is about as simple as it can be put. My finding, however, is that people have the greatest difficulty separating the two terms "Jesus" and "Christ". For most Christians, these are synonymous terms – for such is the inured mind-set created by the "party-line" presentation of Christ. To step outside this "box" and be able to have a different understanding of

---

[1] Because Jesus, Mary, Joseph, Paul (or *whoever*) is one with God, does not make *him, her* or *anyone* "*Christ*". Why? Because Christ is *no* ***particular*** *human being or* ***person***. Christ is solely the essence of man's one common human nature God created for *Itself alone* – and did not create for anyone else! It is God's *own human nature* all men are called to *become* – and not *their own* human nature. (No one can be transformed into what they are already.)

these terms, however, is for many people, asking too much. Not only does it require some mental exercise (a kind of de-programming), but there may be some fear attached to even trying to take this step. There is the fear of becoming an "outsider", of losing something, having to change, becoming confused – all kinds of fears.

This is why we say those who have no trouble with the above thesis or find it relatively clear, have no need to read further – in fact, reading further may only complicate matters. But for those, on the other hand, who cannot make heads or tails of what is meant by the "Real Christ", it would be useless to read further. Without a particular background, this book is not likely to clarify a thing, it may even prove too complex to stick with. Just as man has various ideas of God, so too, he has various ideas of Christ, yet, like God, Christ can only be *revealed.* For just as God transcends the created universe, Christ transcends every particular human being. Christ is no *particular* human being or *person,* but is everyman's *eternal* oneness with God in the Trinity.

End Note

Since throughout this book we emphasize the universal *essence* of human nature vs. a particular individual *person*, people are bound to ask "*What is the difference between God's* ***own*** *human nature and the human nature of particular individuals – more especially, the individual man Jesus?"* The attempt to account for this *difference* – the ***mystery of Christ*** – has been the bane of all Christian theology and, if nothing else, this book highlights the problems and points up the difference. The easy answer, of course, is that anything "particular" is **exclusive**, whereas anything universal is **non-exclusive**. Thus reference to any *particular* individual – say, Jesus, Mary, Joseph or *yourself* – is always reference to a "*person*" and always *exclusive*. Because God is not united to any *person,* but only to man's common human *nature,* means that God's *own* human nature is *person-less* (*universally* person-less), whereas all *particular* human beings are *persons* (*exclusive,* one-of-a-kind.)

So the *difference* is between God's *own person-less* human nature and a *particular* human being, say, Jesus – "*who*" is a *person.* While Jesus' human nature was no different than that of any human being, it was "who" he was that made him different from all others. **To become God's *own* human nature, however, means "who" you are must *cease* to exist**. (God, after all, is no respecter of *persons.*)

By and large the mystery of Man is bound up in the **true *essence* of human nature** – *"essence"* being a *universal* and never *a particular.* Though man has various definitions of *"human nature"*, he doesn't even know the true nature of *matter*, much less the nature of an *immaterial soul*. The bottom line – since only God knows the true essence of *what* God creates, then only God knows the true essence of human nature and "*what*" it is destined to become. Nobody, of course, waits for a definition before he starts to live, yet even in the living, man really does not know all there is to know.

In the long run, however, man's definitions are irrelevant because, as the early fathers held, **man was created to be *more* than he is now** – as the Apostle said, "we do not know *what* we are now, we only know *what* we *shall* be" – be Christ, that is. So no use getting stuck in what man is *now*, but keep eyes ahead to what man *shall be* – Christ, that is. This is why the revelation of Christ is the most meaningful of all God's revelations – Christ reveals that *whatever* the *essence* of God and *whatever the essence* of man, **the two will be united and one for all eternity**. Beyond this, what else does man need to know about God and man? Compared to the revelation of *Christ*, everything else is meaningless.

EARLY FATHERS

For purposes of this book, over five years were spent tracing the development of Christianity's original understanding of the Trinity and Christ. Though not unfamiliar with the history, this time, however, it was scrutinized with an eye to pinpointing where the early fathers could have unwittingly made a wrong turn or left a door open that could have led to the wrong views of Christ propagated today as a "Jesus-cult". To trace this development meant going back to ground zero, to the writings immediately following Paul and the Gospels, accounts written by those collectively known as the "Early Fathers of the Church".

Throughout this book "the fathers" is a collective reference to those who contributed to the development of the earliest understanding of the Trinity and Christ. References to one or more of "the fathers", however, is not intended to reflect any father's entire Christological paradigm, nor do any of the fathers reflect my own. While this book is not about the fathers, yet, like every author who quotes them according to his own understanding of Christ, so too, I quote them according to my understanding of Christ. Together, the fathers present such an invaluable variety that whatever one's personal view, it can always be found somewhere among the fathers. So agree or disagree, collectively, they are the enduring giants of Christianity.

The problem of researching the early development of Christian doctrine is that authors on this subject do so from a perspective that only *later* became acceptable orthodox doctrine. Thus they trace this development solely from a perspective of *present day* orthodoxy, which makes their accounts biased from the outset. Indeed, to be acceptable to their fellow theologians, no author would present this development otherwise. Reading the fathers themselves, however, gives us a different slant on this early development.

Basically, the fathers were *pre-orthodox*, it was their views and formulations that would ultimately determine what would later be regarded as *orthodox*. So there is a great deal the fathers wrote that authors either never mention, gloss over, or judge inappropriate, yet lend insight into their understanding of Christ. There was never a lock-step dogmatic adherence among them, they all had different views of Christ, and for this, many were exiled, their views anathematized or condemned, some denounced as heretics, a number besmirched for all time. It seems few totally escaped some form of ignominy – even Athanasius was exiled twice. This is why, taken collectively, the diversity of their Christologies is such that whatever one's particular understanding, it will surely be found among the fathers. This cannot be found, however, by casual reading, one must first have *his own* view before searching through the fathers – no use reading them to decide which view to pick! Rather, it is only if you are looking for *your own view* that you will find it there. But this is how it has always gone – every author's account reflecting *his own views.*

There exists no *single traditional* understanding of Christ that was handed down from the Apostles, nor does the bible provide any. While a great deal was handed down, the true nature of Christ was not one of them. From the beginning, it seems each of the fathers had their own particular Christological paradigm. Although all regarded Christ as God's unique revelation of the oneness of God and man, yet, as to the nature of this oneness, there was little consensus. What has come down to us today evolved through the first five centuries, evolved less by consensus than by disagreement.

All but one of the early Church Councils were called by the Emperor to find some peace in these matters – one or more ending in a riot. Yet the Councils themselves never decided anything, Gregory of Nazianzus put it this way, "*To tell you plainly, I am determined to fly from every convention of bishops, for I never yet saw a council that ended happily. Instead of lessening, they invariably augmented the mischief. The passion for victory and the lust of power are not to be described in words. One present as judge, will much more readily catch the infection from others than be able to restrain it in them. For this reason I must conclude that the only security of one's peace and virtue is in retirement*". As the story goes, Gregory Nazianzus, head of the Council of Constantinople, got up one day, walked out, resigned as Patriarch and went home. His ascetic lifestyle and writings are invaluable – the Trinity was the center of his life.

Despite his negative view of the Councils, however, everyone would enjoy reading about them, not to learn anything edifying, but for sheer entertainment – all the riots, shouting, anathemas and condemnations that went on. As to what was behind this enmity, it was simply articulating the Christian mysteries, a huge problem which none of the Councils actually resolved. Just finding adequate terminology in Syrian, Armenian, Greek, Latin and other languages was the cause of some dissension, yet even some of their agreeable terms haunt us today because they have lost their original intent and meaning. Thus Nicaea (325) was a major shift in the understanding of the Trinity that would never be recognized by many of the fathers, and though there was later a compromised agreement on the Council's final wording at Chalcedon (451), this did not mean there was the same understanding of its terms. Chalcedon was by no means the end of the issue, in fact, it caused a major rift among the Churches that remains to this day. So even after the early Councils, its stated views meant different things to different fathers. I do not think it could be said any of the fathers had Christological paradigms that were totally agreeable or the same.

Someone pointed out that the Christian understanding of Christ was not as developmental as "evolutionary" in that it had to be ever more finely honed to eliminate some of the wrong views that kept popping up. The fathers were not looking for pat formulas or a definitive creed, but taken up with discarding what they regarded as either inadequate or skewed understandings of Christ. Thus correct or "orthodox" views came about in the process of eliminating incorrect views. In some respects, this is how it might go in everyone's Christian journey. To discover the furthest reaches of Christ, we too should expect much the same developmental process by continually eliminating wrong views. To think we can fully know Christ ahead of time, or before we have completed our transforming journey, is a mistake. This is why any static preview of Christ pinned down to this or that formal view not only inhibits spiritual growth and frustrates spiritual expectations, but being *stuck* with one staid view, can abort any further progress.

One reason for my particular appreciation of the fathers' diversity, their various perspectives and debates, is because in my own life, Christ was a "problem". Although the specific revelation by which Christ was revealed to me was never a problem, it was its tenuous alignment with the Church's traditional understanding – that was the "*problem*". So if one gleans anything from the fathers collectively, it is that Christ was a "problem" for them as well. What made it necessary to formulate some type of agreeable understanding of Christ was due to their many different views, everyone with his own understanding and not many agreeing. Considering Christianity today, and its division into thousands of different sects, tells us there is still no consensus on Christ – possibly, there may never be one. About the only "end" of these early disputes that can be pointed to, is the onset of the Dark Ages. But if there was never any agreement across the board, these first centuries are pivotal. As a group, the fathers considered every possible understanding of Christ, almost as if anticipating all the views that would arise in the centuries ahead. In this respect, the fathers were ahead of themselves.

We have to admit there is something about Christ that refuses to be pinned down to this or that particular view, definition, doctrine, or any single Christology. Christ is multi-faceted and multi-purposed; in one form or another, Christ serves humanity's needs on different levels and in all ages. From the simple minded to the most learned, saints and sinners alike, there is something in Christ for everyone. Also, the greater the depths of Christian practice, the deeper and more expansive

Christ becomes, thus there is no one level of Christ, and nothing could be worse than being stuck at one level. Just as the fathers' view and understanding of Christ evolved, so too must our own.

So what were all their disputes about? What was there to resolve? Since most of the early fathers were Bishops responsible for the continuity of tradition and a right understanding of Christ, they had the daunting task of both articulating and defending the Christian faith, and doing so, in terms most suitable to its truth and understandability. To do this, however, they had to deal with a number of constraints that not only affected their works, but explains the particular predicament in which they found themselves. Since these constraints governed much of their thinking, they are worth going over and keeping in mind.

1. CHURCH REPRESENTATIVES

Since just about all the fathers were Bishops, they were always aware they were speaking and writing as representatives of the Church and its Faith – they were not writing opinion-pieces. This added to their sense of responsibility, knowing full well they'd be held accountable for everything they said. Any divergence from the expected norm and they would be reported and removed from office – which happened rather often. So this was one of the considerations hanging over their heads, they were by no means free to preach, teach or write without impunity.

2. TRADITION

As might be expected, the fathers were indebted to their predecessors. In passing on what they had been given, they were careful, even determined, to remain faithful to what they had been taught. They definitely had a sense of "tradition" and obligation, a vital part of which, they learned through their participation in the Church's liturgies, practices, prayers and so on. They were not merely obliged in this matter, but honestly desired to share with others what had been given to them. Thus being faithful to their "tradition", their predecessors, and the truths they had been taught, was a major consideration for all the fathers.

3. MONOTHEISM

The fathers' awareness of the boundaries of Monotheism, with its great divide between the Uncreated and the created, cannot be emphasized enough. This was no small issue, especially when it came to articulating the Trinity (i.e., avoiding tri-theism or three gods) and the dual nature of Christ (i.e., avoiding an anthropolatric deity.) That no human being could be Uncreated, and that the Uncreated could be no human being, was the rock bottom basis of their Christologies, there was no getting around it and remaining a Monotheist. So this was a major consideration ever in the background of their understanding and presentation of Christian truths.

4. SCRIPTURE

Another factor to contend with was the fathers' obligation to be faithful to scripture, to be sure they never went outside it or introduced anything new. Hence the pressure to back up their every view with some scriptural quote or other. As might be expected, strict adherence to the book was a major cause of dissension, each having different interpretations or presenting contradictory quotes. While the bible is innocuous in itself, its divisiveness is everyone's different understanding of it. So just as the bible has created thousands of different Christian sects, so too, it created divisions among the fathers. Actually, today's bible-thumpers would love the fathers, like themselves, they were always thumbing through the pages checking up on everyone else's views. Anyone who thinks the fathers were not "Biblical", has never read them.

An important note on the fathers' use of scripture, however, is that they never regarded the Gospel narratives and Epistles as "*sacred, holy*, or *inspired* scripture". This view of what later would be called the "New Testament" did not appear until after the sixth century or so. Instead, these accounts were regarded, as Irenaeus put it – the "*Apostles Memoirs*". While they believed these biographies to be true, they never carried the authoritative weight as did the "Old Testament". It was from the Jewish "book" they took their proofs of Christ as Messiah, the Trinity, the divinity of Christ, and much more. Just like Jesus, Paul and the Apostles, the fathers relied solely on the "Old Testament" as their authority. This explains why their earliest commentaries and quotes focused on the Old, and not the New, Testament. That today, people take the "New Testament" as the absolute or final word of God, was not the understanding of the early fathers.

5. THE FAITHFUL

Another of the fathers' constraints was having to consider how to make Christianity meaningful and understandable on the various levels of the people, some highly educated, others with little or no education. This is a two-pronged feat of sorts. On the one hand they had to consider the going philosophy of the educated, on the other, keep to simple terms and expressions in order to make it understandable to the "simple folk". Given the tendency to take words at face value (literally, that is), my impression is that the fathers never assumed much mental or spiritual profundity on the part of the "simple folk", people more attuned, perhaps, to a *polytheistic,* rather than a *monotheistic* mind-set. Yet even today, what Christian, for example, has ever heard of the difference between *essence* and *hypostasis*, between *nature* and *person*, or ever heard of the theological ruse called the "*Communication of Properties*"? Hardly anyone. So while the fathers passed on all the traditional language, they did not pass on their understanding of it.

The result, of course, has been a simplistic understanding on the part of the faithful which, over centuries, has become so inured and static that Christianity comes across as little more than repetitious clichés and belief-formulas that lack any transcendent profundity or personal meaning. Today, at least, rather than be stuck on such a simplistic level, some people have simply left Christianity in search of something more profound and meaningful – I know hundreds of them. (Actually, millions have left.) For sure, Christians today are not the "simple folk" of the first centuries!

6. POLITICS

Since there was no separation of Church and State, the fathers had to be careful with their every word lest it cause dissension and come to the attention of the Roman Emperor who, beginning with Constantine, acted as a kind of Pope to settle disputes. As said, the emperor was the one who called all but one of the Church Councils to bring some peace and resolution to disagreeing parties. This fact created centuries of court intrigue that made all Church business equally political matters. Some of the fathers jumped into this fray, others tried to avoid it like the plague. The Church had no way of exiling or banishing one of its own, the emperor did this. It seems it was also up to the emperor to either pass or veto a doctrinal belief before it could be propagated. This whole set-up had to be constantly considered by the fathers, the consequences of their views adjudged either favorable or unfavorable by those in power. There is a lot more to this type of constraint on the freedom of the fathers, but we needn't go into it.

7. LANGUAGE

Perhaps the most unfortunate restriction the fathers had to deal with was the traditional Church language and terminology. Although they were aware of this problem, they deliberately decided to stick with what they called the "traditional Church language", terms taken not only from scripture and used by their predecessors, but used in their religious liturgies and various professions of faith (later creeds.) This was done not just for the sake of continuity, but as *proof* of it. They did not want to be accused of introducing anything new. The use of the same scriptural, liturgical and catechetical language was very deliberate on their part and generally agreed on by one and all. So despite all the wrangling and bad feelings, from the beginning, the fathers all used the same terminology, the same that has come down to us today, and this, despite the fact they all had a different understanding of the same terms.

A number of the fathers commented on their use of traditional terms, sometimes in an apologetic manner. Thus Gregory of Nazianzus noted the tendency of scripture to "transpose" human terms to God – personify God that is – yet, for the sake of peace he writes, "*For those whose faith in God is pure, there is no greater **stimulus to unanimity than using the same words** when we speak of Him, nor is anything more conducive to division than disagreement on this score. A person who is extremely tolerant in all other respects, becomes quite heated when it comes to this matter, and the timid becomes a true warrior.*" But if sticking to the traditional terms was the only way to insure any peace and unity in the Church, we know everyone disagreed with the meaning and usage of these terms. Irenaeus also made some comment about accepting terms solely ***"as a formality and out of respect for tradition".*** Though he didn't care for the terms "Father and Son" implying any notion of God "begetting", yet he never changed his terms "out of respect for tradition". There are many examples of the fathers referring to certain terms as no more than "titles" or "metaphors".

The reason for noting the consistency of their language is because I found it disconcerting. The retention of traditional terms is problematic because it *sounds* as if everyone agrees, when, in fact, they do not. To think the traditional terminology meant the same to one and all, is not how it went – or has ever gone. There is also the problem that if terms do not mean what they say, and the reality is otherwise, then someone who hears and reads them is being deceived – because they do not mean what they say.

Thus to use anthropomorphic terms for God and then expect people to grasp this on some non-human, image-less or metaphysical level, defies common sense, it just doesn't happen. Given the human propensity to take terms literally is all the more reason *not* to promote this kind of naiveté. How can one ever reach "right-understanding" when all he has to go on are terms and concepts that do not mean what they say, terms that actually promote wrong images, ideas and understandings? If Christianity comes across sounding anthropolatristic ("worship of a human being as God") it is because it has taken as literal, terms that were never intended to be taken literally. This is why, on the surface, at least, Christianity can sound as profound as a fairytale.

In this matter, both the fathers and their commentators are keen on reminding us that some of the terms used for God, the Trinity and Christ, must not be understood in their *usual human way.* But then, with no further explanation or distinction, they go right on using these terms as if there were no differences. Here are a few examples:

1. We are told *not* to understand *hypostasis* as meaning an "individual" as a *human* individual (a being or entity), yet how is the human mind to grasp something "individual" that is not some being or entity? If God transcends all our human notions of "individual" then why use the term in the first place? The Trinity based on three "individuals" (as beings) is *tri-theism.*

2. We are told God is not three "persons" such as we think of human persons – distinct, unique individual beings. Yet how else are we to understand God as three "persons" but as three distinct beings? To do so is "*anthropomorphic tri-theism*".

3. We are also told *not* to understand the three "persons" of God as three "subjects" or "I am's" in any *psychological sense* of these terms, yet they go right on speaking and referring to God as a "subject" no different from a human subject or " I am". The only explanation given is that a divine subject *ontologically transcends* a human subject in the same way a divine person *ontologically transcends* a human person, and in the same way the Trinity as three individuals *ontologically transcends* human individuals! But how can the mere word "***transcend***" actually transcend man's understanding of these concepts and images? It can't, it doesn't! All it can do is promote God as some invisible *super-human being*. Obviously, there exists a fine line between Christianity and polytheism.

4. Then, of course, we are told God does not "beget" as humans do, told the Logos is eternal and that there is "*no **then** when He was not"* – Nicene Creed. Now to say the Logos (God) is *Uncreated* yet "*begotten*" is a contradiction of terms, so why hang on to this fallacy? Nazianzus' answer – *"Because it can be found in the scriptures!"* It just wouldn't do to quote the bible and then tell everyone "this is just a figure of speech, an allegory, so don't take it literally". Saying this, was not the fathers' style – although it should have been.

5. After affirming that both in essence and person God is absolutely *immutable* and *impassible*, we are then told God is "born, suffered and died" – this axiom called "*The Communication of Properties or Attributes*". Now how, in conscience, can we "attribute" human experiences to God when God has no human experiences? This is another contradiction.

6. In one sentence Gregory of Nazianzius refers to Christ's dual natures as "mixed" and "intermingling", and then stresses they are totally separate. Gregory of Nyssa says in the end, Christ's physical body is "transelemented" (totally spiritual), and later he reverts to a *physical* body. Maximus says in the end, there is a loss of one's individual self, yet later says there is no loss of one's identity. It would be possible to give hundreds of examples of the fathers dropping gems here and there – or sometimes, outlandish, false ideas – and then deliberately reverting back to iterate the "traditional party line". Do not think for a moment they were not cautious about staying within the boundaries of the traditional party-line, more especially, after the 3rd century and Nicaea.

There is no use going on with this problem, the point is this: we have been asked to accept as true what, in fact, is neither literally true nor its reality. And please note how *use of "analogies" for God invariably makes God into* ***man's own image***. The difference between truth and what is only metaphoric or analogous is enormous, and the failure to point out the difference is why Christians are educated with wrong views from the beginning. Although theologians and scholars warn us of these wrong understandings, they go right on using these terms, even *defending* them as if there were no differences at all. Either they never honestly grasped the differences themselves, or they regard common man as simple minded sheep. Or, perhaps, they expect people to be "orthodox" at the cost of their own intellectual integrity.

THE "PARTY-LINE"

One way to assess the early centuries of dissension among the fathers was their attempt to maintain a unified presentation of the mysteries of the faith, without, however, forfeiting their own intellectual honesty. Thus, after taking a stand intellectually warranted, they fall back on the usual clichés of the traditional language, terms cemented in the anthropomorphic and metaphoric language of the bible. Thus, by adhering to the expected usage, many of the fathers compromised their real views and understanding lest they be accused of straying from the faith. So instead of articulating the Christian mysteries as they saw them, they reverted to iterating the same proverbial terminology – the "traditional party-line", that is.

Since throughout this book there are references to the "party-line", we will define it as follows: *it is the terms, language and idioms used to express the Christian faith. It is how, for example, the Trinity and Christ are expressed and typically presented in speech and writing.* The "party-line", then, is how the truths of the faith are traditionally expressed in all Christian works, its doctrines, creeds, theology, teaching, commentaries, books, talks, sermons, etc. This "proverbial language" not only became a way of speaking, but governed a *way of thinking.* People take words *literally,* thinking they mean exactly what they say – after all, if word and usage is not true, then what is the truth?

Any deviation from the traditional way of expressing the truths of the faith is, of course, immediately "suspect". Adhering to this redundant use of language, however, has, down the centuries, created an *inured* Christian *mind-set* – every Christian with the same understanding, same way of thinking, speaking, teaching, etc. Not only can this become quite empty, but tends to inhibit people from questioning or thinking for themselves. This is why anyone who steps out of this line or thinks "outside-the-box", well, history tells us how they have been put in their place. As to the genesis of this *party-line*, it all came from adherence to *scripture* – as if God *had* to *adhere* to man's scripture and couldn't possibly reveal anything *outside* this box!

As we will see, Christianity took root in an age when the Gentiles' spiritual quest was seeking to be "one with the "One". The melding of Judaism with the Gentiles' more philosophical and mystical perspective, accounts for some of the differing views among the fathers. Keep in mind, all the fathers were not only Gentiles, but among the best educated of their time. Yet, after giving us some of their beautiful understandings of, say, the Trinity and Christ, they then couch their terms in the usual anthropomorphic *scriptural* terms – the same staid formulations found in today's creeds, doctrinal statements, theologies and teachings. So despite iterating the proverbial "party-line", the fathers retained their own profound understanding of these mysteries.

There is no telling all that was lost to Christianity for the sake of retaining the party-line as a form of continuity and unity – more verbal than anything else. Such a constraint, however, has only worked to the detriment of Truth. Thus to say "*Christ is God*" is party-line, but is it the Truth? No! Christ is the *Incarnation* of God (Logos) – God creating and *uniting* man to Itself. *Christ is not one of the Trinity, not God, but the oneness of God and man.* This is but one example of the traditional party-line falling short of the Truth. But whatever understanding this proverbial language may have had for the "simple folk" in the early centuries, it never worked to the good in the long run. Thus, in the seventh century most of these "simple folk" became "Mohammedans" anyway. The reason it has never worked is because it does not give a true understanding of the Trinity, Christ or the Incarnation. But so much for the traditional "party-line" verbiage.

TWO DIFFERENT CHRISTOLOGIES

Christianity began with no dogmas or doctrines. What made it necessary to formulate these were the many different views of Christ, everyone with his own understanding, and not many agreeing. There were views that Jesus only "appeared" to be human, that he was a prophet; that God "indwelled" in Jesus; even that he was an angel – and so on. Because these did not represent the true understanding of Christ, the fathers took on the task of articulating their understanding of the correct (orthodox) view of Christ. That Christ was wholly divine and wholly human was never the problem, the problem was the nature of the union between these two disparate natures. To give a correct understanding, and devise the terminology to articulate this mystery, this was the particular task of the early fathers.

If the fathers were never divided on the issue of Jesus' oneness with God, they were, however, hotly divided on the issue of Jesus' human nature – just how human was the man? Did the Logos unite itself only to human "flesh" – as it says in the bible "*He became flesh*" ("*incarnate*"), or did the Logos unite itself to a human soul as well? That the Logos only took on flesh is basically a Platonic view of human nature. For Plato, the "soul" was the "*divine form*" of man, whereas matter, or *flesh*, responsible for all multiplicity and individuality, was the human *predicament* – in short; the "body" was *not* good news.

The two main views on the issue of Christ's human nature have been divided into the Alexandrian school of thought, "*Logos-flesh*", and the Antiochene School, "*Logos-man*", the former adopting the more Platonic view of man, the latter, the more Aristotelian understanding. Where Plato regarded the soul as divine and flesh as the soul's unfortunate entrapment in matter, Aristotle regarded the unity of body and soul as the indivisible composite of human nature. So where, for the Alexandrians – for whom the soul was all but divine – God was only one with man's flesh (*God-flesh*), for the Antiochenes, however, God was one with a complete human being, body *and* soul (*God-man*.) It seems the origin of the Alexandrian school was a revolt against Origen's (185 – 254) view of the historical man Jesus as a *temporary* human being with a divine mission. Origen's "Jesus" was just too human for the likes of the Alexandrians. Also, Origen stressed the *soul* of Jesus as the *locus* of his union with God, which the Alexandrians absolutely denied.

It is said the difference between the two schools was the Alexandrian stress on the *oneness* of Christ's natures *over* the *duality* of natures. The Antiochenes, on the other hand, stressed the *duality* of natures *over* the *union* of natures. This assessment of the two schools, however, is much too simplistic. The differences were two totally different Christologies and understandings of Christ. For the Alexandrians, Jesus was ***no*** *human person*, for the Antiochenes, Jesus was a complete human being, a *whole human person.* If Jesus was just the "visible" appearance of the invisible God (Paul's view of "*the Spirit made visible*"), then all God united to Itself was the flesh, a temporal, *visible*, physical body. Thus, under the facade of flesh, Christ was totally divine – was God. Although this was basically the Alexandrian view (which some authors trumpet as the orthodox "winner" in the dispute between schools), it was this Alexandrian view that led to the heresy of *Monophysitism* ("*one divine nature*"), which, unfortunately, is the general view of Christ today – totally divine, that is. The extreme Alexandrian position adopted by the "Arians",[1] was that "*God only became **flesh**, not a **man**, for he did not take on a human soul.*" For the revered Alexandrian father, Apollinaris (330 – 390), on the other hand, the divine Logos ***was*** the *soul* of the man Jesus. In his view, the Logos had *replaced* (or taken the place) of the human soul of Jesus, thus the Logos (God) was the "*animating principle*" (or soul) of his humanity. This means the human faculties-of-soul – mind, will, intellect, consciousness ("I am") – were not *Jesus' own soul* (he had none), but were *God's own soul* – whatever that could be!? Even Jesus' flesh and bones were not *his* humanity – "*The flesh is not something added to the Godhead, but constitutes one reality or nature with It*" (Apollinaris.) In every way the man Jesus was God in that he had no human soul of his own, no use of his own faculties or even his own human body. There is no place for Christ's "dual natures" in this Alexandrian view, there is only place for Christ's *"single divine nature"*. Though later regarded as the heresy of *"Monophysitism"*, this never appreciably changed the Alexandrian view – a view most people today regard as the *orthodox* understanding of Christ.

It has been pointed out that the two different Christologies (Alexandrian and Antiochene) represent two different approaches to the mystery of Christ, the former a "Christology from *above*", the latter a "Christology from *below*". The "*above*" was primarily premised on Christ-as-God, the other, primarily premised on Christ as God-*and*-Man. Thus the Apostles' encounter with Christ was with the man Je-

[1] "*Arians*" – named after Arius (256 – 336) a priest of Alexandria – were condemned for their views. As to what Arius himself said and believed, this is another matter. In Chapter Seven we will go over his particular view or understanding of the Trinity and Christ.

sus, their friend and mentor. Paul's sole encounter, however, was with the heavenly Christ – the blinding Light that knocked him off his high horse. So where the Synoptics start from "below", Paul starts from "above". The challenge of the fathers was to find a middle ground that would include both approaches and meld them into a single coherent understanding of Christ. To do this, however, remains the challenge of every Christian. These two different views of Christ are as alive and dissonant today as they were in the earliest days of Christianity.

What ultimately got the Alexandrians to acknowledge a human *soul* in Jesus, was the dictum of Gregory of Nazianzius, an Antiochene, who won the day with "*What the Logos did not assume cannot be restored (or healed), it is only what is united with God that is saved*". In other words, any aspect of human nature the Logos did not assume or create for Itself, could not to be saved – and, of course, what could be more in need of salvation than the human soul? Gregory of Nyssa also said, "*By becoming **exactly what we are**, He united the human race through Himself to God*". Even for Origen, the soul was the "*seat of unity of God and man, the soul was **not** God (not Spirit or Logos)*".

But if the Alexandrians had to admit to a human soul, this is as far as it went. It is one thing to make a *formal* admission, but another for this to effect a change in one's view and understanding. Although authors like to vindicate the Alexandrians by giving quotes where they refer to Jesus' "soul", these admissions amount to no more than theological "lip-service", it never changed their Christologies one iota. Actually, all the fathers had a penchant for making "formal" statements about this or that (for the sake of peace no doubt), which never honestly affected their staid or personal view of Christ.

Although Cyril of Alexandria opposed Apollinaris' view of Christ's *"one nature"*, he nevertheless ended up defining Christ as the "*one incarnate nature of the Word"* – his oft repeated words. Both fathers had a horror of the slightest hint of any separation or differentiation between the two natures. But where Apollinaris outright said the Logos (or Spirit) **was** the soul of Jesus, Cyril explained this as the Logos' being the sole "subjective agent" of Its *own* human soul. For all practical purposes, however, between Apollinaris denying Jesus a human soul and Cyril's attributing all the soul's faculties (functions) to God, there is no appreciable difference. If God has all the experiences (mind, will, consciousness) of a human soul, then how is God not a human soul?

Obviously, the difference between the Alexandrian and Antiochene Christologies are totally different understandings of Christ. That Christ's human nature was only *flesh* gives the impression God's Infinite Existence was "enclosed" in the physical body of Jesus, thus, apart from the mere appearance of flesh, Jesus was God living this human existence. But is God **inside** the flesh – or *inside* anything that exists? The idea is ridiculous.[2]

The other view (Antiochene) is that Jesus was a complete human being, as genuine a human person as ever lived – body, soul, mind, will, subject (his own self-identity), human in every way. The incarnation was *not* God **in** (or inside) flesh, but God creating and uniting to Itself man's complete human nature, the *union* of these two disparate natures being "Christ". (It should be obvious which one of these two understandings of Christ would lead to *anthropolatry* – certainly *not* the Antiochenes'.)

Based on their different views of Christ, the two schools differed in another important way. Where the Alexandrians (mainly Athanasius and Cyril) attributed everything Jesus said and experienced to God (Logos), the Antiochenes had no problem attributing the whole human experience to the human Jesus. In their view, Jesus' soul was in perfect "attunement" with God – God had not "taken over" his human soul. Some authors regard this difference as the Alexandrians maintaining a closer oneness between man and God than the Antiochenes, who refused to allow Christ's human nature to be overwhelmed by the divine. And if we wonder what difference this makes, it is huge! Thus in the Gospels, "who" was walking, talking, suffering and dying? Was it the man Jesus or was it God? The answer to this question is strategic, it presents two totally different understandings of Christ. As said, although neither school denied the union or oneness of Christ's dual natures, they obviously had different views as to the effects of this oneness on human nature.

The reason reading the fathers is a relief from all the *Jesus-talk*, however, is because, as some authors noted, their focus was never on the biblical man Jesus – "*they evinced little interest in the Gospel figure*". Instead, they were preoccupied with the larger Christ-event, the Incarnation, its revelation as God's plan for mankind and how it worked

---

2 Man not only experiences his soul "within" himself, but experiences God "within" himself. Thus he tends to think his body "encompasses" a detachable immaterial soul – a ghost in a machine. Matter, however, cannot contain non-matter. The reason the Stoics were accused of "pantheism" was because they held there was no "disconnect" between the physical and spiritual, the material and immaterial were not "detachable". This is why, presented with the Christian understanding of "Resurrection" this seemed to verify their own beliefs – no disconnect. It goes without saying, while God "contains" all that exists, nothing that exists contains Infinite Existence – God. While the soul is "open ended" (created "theocentric") it certainly does not contain or enclose God. God is no human being walking around.

for everyone's eternal life in God. To narrow this revelation to a single human being, or limit its applicability to Jesus alone, never crossed their minds, this was not their understanding of Christ. If the incarnation was just about one human being's oneness with God, it would be meaningless to the rest of mankind. It was the *universal* implication of the Incarnation that consumed the fathers, not the individuality of one man. So a major value of their works is that they go right to the heart and essence of Christianity and never bogged down in any narrow understanding of Christ. Their main focus was on the union or oneness of the divine Logos with *all* humanity. Their motto "*Salvation is transformation*" meant, by becoming one with the Logos (which *oneness* **is** Christ), man's salvation **is** his transformation into Christ.

We suggest, however, there is another reason why the fathers never concerned themselves with the individual man Jesus. Taken solely from their writings, it seems obvious they never granted Jesus an "individual soul" – a human soul, yes, but not a true *independent* "individual" soul. No one could be steeped in the fathers and not notice the absence of recognizing Jesus as an independent human "person", seemingly, there was no clear grasp of human nature as an *independent soul.* Without an independent mind, will, and subject, however, there is no human "*soul*" to speak of. Even though denying God took the place of Jesus' soul, their understanding of Christ underwent no appreciable change because of this. It seems the soul as an *intermediary* between the body and God was a problem to be circumvented.

Instead of holding out for a human soul for Jesus, the Alexandrians made the divine Logos (God) the "subjective agent" of Jesus' soul, which "subjective agent" came to be called a "person". Thus ***instead* of Jesus as a human subject or person, the Alexandrians made God (Logos) to be the divine subject or person of Christ**. This way, by saying Jesus was *not* a *human* person, they could say the divine Logos was the sole *divine person* of both natures – human and divine. This meant everything Jesus said and experienced could be "attributed" to the divine agency or "person" of God and nothing attributed to the man Jesus (apart from flesh.) In other words, everything it means to be a "*human person*" the Alexandrians transferred to God – and did so with no authentic differentiation between a human and a divine person! Now if God can live, think and act as a *human person* then how is God *not* a *human person*? Theologically speaking, the Alexandrians regarded Jesus as "*impersonal*" (not a *human person*), a fact definitely reflected in their Christologies – regarded as "orthodox" we might add.

Cyril's "substituting" God as the *subject* of Jesus' soul, mind and will, however, is no different than Apollinaris' substituting God for

Jesus' human soul – a heresy. When a divine *person* (or subject) is no different from a human person (or subject), little wonder the fathers "*evinced little interest in the Gospel figure*" – the *individual* man Jesus. Apart from flesh, he was *not a true human being.* While Jesus, having flesh, "looked" human enough, yet under the facade he was really God – a view reminiscent of "Docetism", the heresy that Christ only "appeared" to be human. In truth, of course, God is no more a human soul and person (subject) than God is a divine soul and person (subject.) For the Alexandrians, however, to speak of *Jesus' "soul"* experiencing anything, would have amounted to a denial of Christ's divinity.

So what did they have against a human soul? According to Apollinaris, a soul for Jesus would have left him vulnerable to *doubts, 'enslaved to filthy thoughts'*, subject to passions of the flesh, fallible, liable to mistakes, in short, be plagued with everything that makes for a changeable, limited human being. Thus to consider Jesus with a human soul would only open up a can of worms. Although human vulnerability would not ruin the Logos' divinity, it would certainly cast a shadow on Its human nature, after all, if God cannot create Its *own* human nature any better than the rest of men, then where else are we to look for it? Or does it even exist?

For Apollinaris (and others) the *single divine nature* of Jesus eliminated any possible confusion of Christ having two wills, two minds, two subjects; it also insured his sinlessness and invincibility to death. In body and soul, then, Jesus was totally divine, and any talk of two natures was anathema to him. For Cyril also, to admit to any duality could only mean two Sons, two persons, Christ divided in two, or God merely "indwelling" in an ordinary man. Also, to ignore the oneness of the natures made it impossible to account for Christ as a *single composite being* – a **big issue** as we will see later. Cyril's thinking was that just as man's one human nature is a composite of body and soul, so too, Christ's *one divine nature* was a composite of God and human nature (flesh) – this is his *monophysistic* view. For Cyril to admit to any division between God and man, there would be no "Christ" at all. Whatever may be said for his view, it must not be at the cost of either ignoring the Logos' complete human nature, or making the Logos to be a *single being – which* is *tri-theism.* (The Trinity is *not* three beings!)

Although the Antiochenes insisted on the complete human nature of Christ – that Jesus had a human soul – yet their writings mainly refer to his "flesh" with little mention of anything we'd recognize as a human "soul". Also, the usual references to Jesus' *humanity* are interpreted as a "*concession*" God allowed for our benefit and example, *not* because the man was actually human. Basically, into the 5th century, all the fathers consistently referred to Jesus' "flesh", and while this can be laid at the feet of the Platonism of their day, it was not that simple. In their view, the soul of Jesus was so one with the mind and will of God, what else was there really to say about him? He willed nothing of his own, basically had the mind of God, and the few times he displayed any human vulnerability, this was given a physical explanation – due to his flesh – or it was excused as the Logos "*allowing*" Itself, momentarily, to "*appear*" human for our sake – Cyril's view, for one. Then too, since the soul of Jesus was regarded as sinless and perfect, who could imagine relating to such a soul? The up-shot of all this? That the man Jesus was *no human person – considered the present orthodox view of Christ.* This seems to mean that the ideal humanity is "impersonal" – which is not a bad idea when you think about it.

But there is a reason why Jesus was not regarded as an *individual* soul. Though it has never been recognized, one of the *revelations* of the Incarnation is that **God creates *every* soul One-on-one**, this was *not* just the case with the man Jesus. This understanding, however, was *not* the going belief is those days. The general belief was that there was only one "universal soul" handed down from father to offspring. Thus everyone inherited his father's same life – was a copy of his father's soul. In Judaism, of course, it was the first man's soul – Adam's – created by God, that was handed down from one generation to the next. It was because Jesus had no *human* father that his soul, coming directly from God, made it like no other soul of man. That Jesus' "father" was God, made his soul all but divine. They could not, then, connect Jesus' soul with their own or with that of any other human being. This belief – that males generate the souls of their offspring – is important to keep in mind when it comes to understanding the fathers' Christologies.

At first glance, the Alexandrians might be accused of deliberately robbing Jesus of his human personhood in order to make him a divine person, yet this is not what they did. They **only made the *Logos to be the divine person***, and **not** the man Jesus. Jesus was not a divine person, the divine person of Christ was solely the divine Logos. Thus, if one asks, "*Who* is Christ?" ("*who*" meaning *person*), the answer is "the Logos (God) is *Who* Christ is". The man Jesus is ***not*** "*who*" Christ is, rather, God is ***who*** Christ is. Solely as a *person*, then, Jesus was neither a divine person nor a human person – such is the *orthodox* understanding of the Alexandrian fathers, and one that remains *orthodox to this day*. Anyone who suggests Jesus was a "*human person*" will be axed as a heretic – a "Nestorian", to be exact. (Nestorius, of course, was an Antiochene.) Although later we will be looking into the whole issue of "person", here we only want to point out that the fathers' understanding and treatment of the man Jesus was never that of an *independent soul.* This is missing in all their Christologies, just as it has been missing in Christianity ever since.

Obviously, the complete human nature of Christ was not easy for the fathers to accept – as witnessed in their writings. Always, the Logos took on only "flesh", even the Eucharist is referred to as the glorified "flesh" or body of Christ; and in the end, all will be transformed into the *body* of Christ – so goes the "party-line" view of Christ. There is never any mention of being transformed into the glorified *soul* of Christ. By and large the fathers only gave lip service to the *individual soul* of Jesus. As said, even the Antiochenes, who insisted the Logos took on a human soul and was a complete human being, almost 100% of their references were to the *flesh* or *body* of Christ.

For the fathers, then, the imperative question was *who,* in the Gospels, experienced the human journey, *who* was born, suffered and died? According to the Alexandrians, it was *not* the man Jesus – he **was *not* a human person**, not the subject or agent of any *individual* soul, instead, it was the Logos – God Itself! While it is clear that scripture makes no division as regards any "person", yet, that God ate, drank, prayed and "grew in wisdom" is hardly Almighty God. Then too, no mere man worked miracles, forgave sin, or promised us his own divine Spirit. The debate over "*who*" said and did what, cannot be overlooked, the answer is strategic because it yields different views of Christ. Though, as said, neither school denied the oneness of Christ's dual natures, what differed were the effects of this oneness on human nature. If the divine simply overwhelms the human, then there was no authentic human being to speak of, no true Incarnation and no true *Christ.*

HILARY'S THREE STATES IN THE LIFE OF CHRIST

As regards the two different schools of Christological thought, one must always keep in mind Hilary of Poitiers' (300 – 367) wise counsel which he called "*the three states in the life of Christ":*

1. *Before* the incarnation there was only the divine Logos – no Christ and no man Jesus.
2. *With* the Incarnation there is the Logos *and* man, the union of the divine and human natures – and this is the *earthly* "Christ".
3. *After* the resurrection and Ascension, with the transformation and glorification of human nature – this is the *eternal heavenly* "Christ".

Speaking of Christ, Hilary says, ***"It is one thing that he was God before he was man, another that he was man and God, and another that after being man and God, he was perfect man and perfect God.***

Do not then confuse the time and natures in the mystery of the dispensation (incarnation), for according to the attributes of his different natures, he must speak of himself in relation to the mystery of his humanity in one way before his birth, in another while he was yet to die, and in another as eternal". Had all the fathers abided by Hilary's wise admonition – which is the theological gem of all times – there would have been far fewer dissensions, most of which were caused by basing their view of Christ on one or other of these stages and ignoring the others. Where Cyril based his Christology largely on Hilary's 3rd state of the deified heavenly human nature, the Antiochenes based theirs mainly on the 2nd state, Christ's human nature in this world.

Because of these different approaches, the face-off between Cyril and Nestorius (an Antiochene) became a genuine turning point in the development of the Church's Christology. After Athanasius and Cyril had declared the man Jesus was **not** a human person, Nestorius, then Patriarch of Constantinople, simply asked, "*How can you have a complete human being who is not a human person?*" The answer to this question would engross the fathers and medieval scholastics for centuries, but with no comprehensible answer forthcoming – why? Because after defining God as three *persons,* they had dug their own hole and couldn't get out of it. **God is no individual person**, no soul, no subject or agent, all this was the man Jesus, **he** was a *"person",* **not** God! To Cyril, of course, anyone who even suggested Jesus was *his own person* had to be thrown out. It simply flew in the face of his view of Christ as the "***one*** *incarnate nature of God the Logos"* – his own words, and the very definition of "*Monophysitism*".

As we will see, the fact Nestorius lost-out (was literally thrown out), was a major loss for the whole Church, a loss that could only lead to its losing hold of the real Christ. Had Jesus been understood as a complete human being – a "*human person*" – he could never have been *mistaken* for Almighty God. It was by making the Trinity three *persons* and the man Jesus *no-person,* theology made the union of two natures constitute *one divine person* – this one "person" being the Logos (God.) That the man Jesus is a *divine being either in nature or in person*, however, is the definition of *anthropolatry* – mistaking a human person or human being for God.

This could not have happened if Hilary's 2nd state had understood Jesus as a *human* person. If the incarnate Logos was not a complete human being or person, then there really was no "Incarnation" – no dual natures and no Christ. Furthermore, no heavenly, glorified human being could even live on this earth, much less Almighty God – who could regard the life of Almighty God as an "*example"* for everyone to *follow*? It makes no sense. It would seem the fathers took their understanding of Christ from two different "states" in the life of the incarnate Logos. While the Alexandrians all but eliminated the active role of Christ's human nature and merged it with that of the divine nature, the Antiochenes insisted on the full humanity of Christ – even Jesus as a human person. The difference between these two schools represents two different approaches to Christology – 1) except for the *flesh*, Christ is God, totally divine; 2) Christ is the eternal oneness of God and Man, a complete human being, body *and* soul – or whatever the essence of human nature may be.

In going over the development of the fathers' understanding of Christ, one lesson to be learned is that holding Christ as either totally divine or totally human, misses Christ completely. The whole mystery of Christ centers on the *oneness* of the two natures, divine and human, which brings up the question of how this "oneness" could have effected (or possibly even changed) the human nature so conceived. Altogether, there is no easy understanding of Christ, pat formulas and staid views can never do this.

One of the drawbacks of reading the fathers is that their original thinking and terms have been changed by various translators and commentators down the centuries. Every translator passes judgement on the work before him and should anything not be understandable to him (or perhaps unacceptable), he invariably puts his own spin on it – changing a word, inserting extra words, leaving out parts of sentences, in short, it is always the translator's version of someone's work and rarely the original. Comparisons have been made between some of the earliest translations of the fathers, and some of the differences are startling. I have also found quotes that cannot be found in their works today, not in English at least, but then, not all the fathers' works have been translated into English. Apart from this, is the well-known fact translating from Greek (especially the *old* Greek of the fathers) into Latin and other languages, can give a whole different meaning to the original.

My suspicion is that only those works judged agreeable with the *theology of the present day* ever got translated. After all, why translate anything that might counter the fathers' status as authoritative, or might counter the going theology of today's proverbial *party-line?* Then too, why translate anything judged too profound or "mystical" lest it be misunderstood or go over the heads of "simple folk"? There is a long history in Christianity of destroying the works of those who disagreed. At one time, anyone who copied the work of one regarded as having wrong views was ordered to have his hand cut off.

To take on the concerns of these fathers, however, one could only conclude that no other group in history was so occupied and dedicated to probing the deepest mysteries of God and man. They grappled with the great mystery of God as both One-and-Trinity, the true nature of the oneness of Christ as both God-and-man, these mysteries were the foci of their lives. To this task they brought every resource they had, scripture, philosophy, education, views of their predecessors, traditional terms and liturgy, to say nothing of their spiritual practices and personal experiences of God. Beyond their hot tempers and anathemas, we have to admit they were into the depths of God's mysteries well over the heads of most people. Even those with whom we do not agree, contributed, nevertheless, by expanding our minds with various alternatives while sharing the one same Faith.

Because each of their Christologies are premised on the truth of Christ, and each contributed in their own way to this understanding, it is a disgrace any of the fathers should come down in Christian history labeled a "heretic". Far from playing foot-loose and free with their Faith, their lives were literally consumed by it, one and all, their allegiance to God, the Trinity and Christ, was unquestionable. Once I wrote at length about Origen, not to defend his Platonic "theories" or his trying to make sense of Old Testament scriptures – where one absurdity only begets another – but to point out the genuine saintliness of his life and the enlightened contributions he made to the understanding of Christ. There is no history of Christianity without Origen's enduring presence, and so too, with all the fathers. Indeed, had it not been for Nestorius we might never have heard of Cyril. Even Apollinaris, of saintly life, contributed more profound insights into the true Christ than those who were not condemned. And as for Arius, we'll never know what he said because all his works were immediately destroyed after his condemnation – which works could not have been all that bad seeing that two-thirds of the Church (at that time) stuck by him.

But then, as in the case of a number of fathers, all that has survived are *accusations* hurled against them – all "hearsay" being heresy anyway. Obviously the Church would not want to preserve the works of anyone who disagreed with the traditional "party-line". Although we could go over each of these devoted fathers one by one, what is so blasphemous is putting any of them down as "heretics" – as if they did not affirm the truth of the Trinity, of Christ, of the whole Church in fact. In this matter, they were absolutely *one*.

Considering all the different views of Christ, we might ask if there was not some view or understanding the fathers held in common? For sure, all regarded Christ as the mystery of the oneness of God and man, there was no disagreement on this issue. So given all the rancorous disputes, anathemas, condemnations and exiles, there *was* indeed something that made for an undisputed continuity among them, and this was the continuous re-enactment of the "Lord's Supper", repeated down the centuries from the time of Pentecost. It was this continuity of belief and practice handed down from the beginning – and not the later creeds and doctrines – around which the Church would develop its understanding of Christ. This was the sole medium by which Christianity transmitted its understanding of Christ from one generation to the next, a heritage called "tradition", which, being prior to the written Gospels, took precedence over all else. It was the fathers' understanding of the Eucharistic-Christ that over the centuries was kept intact and has, ever since, yielded a true understanding of Christ.

Almost all the fathers left something in writing about the Eucharist. This was not just the mainstay of their practical lives and unshakable faith, this was the Christ they knew without question, the promised source of their own transformation. "*The Eucharist*", as Irenaeus said, "*is the continuation of the incarnation*" – Christ becoming incarnate in man, transforming all into Itself, this was the belief of all the fathers. No question, the Eucharistic Christ was "The Way", this is what the fathers not only believed, participated in, but *experienced* for themselves. In all of Christianity, there exists no other continuity as regards the mystery of Christ. Penetrate this Eucharistic mystery, and one holds Christ in his hand – as Irenaeus (125 – 202) summed it up, ***"Our way of thinking is attuned to the Eucharist, and the Eucharist in turn confirms our way of thinking".*** Indeed, to know the Eucharist is to know Christ, they are the one same *mystery*. Thus, any understanding of Christ apart from the Eucharist can never yield a true understanding of the Real Christ.

This is why, so long as one's understanding of Christ is premised on the Eucharist, all share in Christianity's earliest understanding of Christ. From the Incarnation to Christ's present heavenly existence, the Eucharist is not only the summation, but the consummation of the whole mystery that is Christ.

So despite all their differences, no father wavered from the truth of the Eucharist – Christ's presence among them. Of this truth there was never a single dispute. This was the sole traditional understanding of Christ that remained untouched, undisputed and accepted by one and all. Try to put your finger on any other source of continuity or agreement among them, and you'll find out there really is none. As to how to formulate the mystery of Christ for the sake of instruction, this was the problem, yet a problem they wouldn't have attempted had they not personally known Christ. As one theologian put it, "*What we must try to say in ever new ways is the whole task of Christology, which will never be completed.*"

What I have gleaned from the fathers can never be reflected in this book. Obviously, they never accepted any naive simplistic view of Christ, but on the contrary, their understanding of Christ was thought out and fought out. One could never say enough for the fathers, there is no lack of appreciation for all the ground they covered in these first centuries. They literally set the pace that no one in subsequent Christian history has ever caught up with, much less ever superseded.

Although this book makes frequent references to "the fathers", as said at the outset, these references should *not* be understood as representing any father's complete paradigm or understanding of Christ. **This book is not a commentary on the fathers**, nor a study of the theological complexities of their various Christologies. To do justice to all the fathers and the issues involved would take an entire library. Over the centuries, thousands of books have been written on the innumerable issues they raised, but as said, the sole purpose of this present writing is to *point out where a wrong turn* was made in the understanding of Christ that could have left a door open for Christianity to become a "Jesus-cult" – a form of *anthropolatry*. This is the sole concern of this book.

Dates of those Fathers referred to or quoted in this book:

Philo of Alexandria (25 B.C. – 50 A.D.) – The Jewish-mystic philosopher
Polycarp (69 – 155) – St. John's disciple
Justin Martyr (100 – 165)
Irenaeus (125 – 202)
Athenagoras (133 – 190)
Clement of Alexandria (150 – 215)
Tertullian (160 – d. 225)
Hippolytus (170 – 235)
Origen (185 – 254)
Novatian (200 – d. 258)
Methodius (d.311)
Arius (256 – 336)
Eusebius (263 – 339)
Marcellus of Ancyra (d. 374)
Athanasius (296 – 373)
Hilary of Poitiers (310 – 367)
Apollinaris (330 – 390)

The three Cappadocians:
– Basil (330 – 379)
– Gregory Nazianzius (329 – 390)
– Gregory of Nyssa (335 – 394)
Ambrose (340 – 397)
John Chrysostom (347 – 407)
Theodore of Mopsuestia (350 – 428)
Augustine (354 – 430)
Cyril of Alexandria (376 – 444)
Nestorius (386 – 451)
Pope Leo (391 – 461)
Boethius (480 – 524)
Leontius of Byzantium (6th c.)
Maximus the Confessor (580 – 662)
John Damascene (645 – 749)

PHILOSOPHICAL BACKGROUND

Based on the Gospel story, Jesus made it clear his particular mission was solely for his own people and not for the godless Gentiles outside his Judaic enclave. As we know, however, he was wrong, his mission was not for his fellow Jews, but for those who, in the Jewish mind, were pagans – because they did not know the one true God. Judaism had a long history of reformers, and in this matter, Jesus was no different. Yet, because he understood himself as having a particular relationship with God – even his being one with God – he was accused of being a blasphemer, a heretic, and was put to death – so much for his mission to his *own* people. But if his affirmation of being one with God was foreign to the Jews, it was by no means foreign to the Gentiles of his own day.

Following his conversion, Paul, a devout Jew, knowing his revelation of Christ would not be acceptable to his own people, never preached to them. He took Christ to the Gentiles who, as he affirmed, already knew God but did not know Christ – the only one who could fulfill their aspirations of being one with God. Judaism had no such aspirations, whereas the Gentiles of Paul's immediate world, had a long history of seekers, those looking for some path or way of realizing their relationship with the "One", the "All" – the "Source".

Interestingly, it was the Gentiles who regarded the Jews as pagans – people who worshiped some anthropomorphic "god". But where the Jews had only known the man Jesus, the one Paul took to the Gentiles was not the man Jesus – who, he says, he never "*saw in the flesh*" – but rather, his vision and understanding of the "resurrected heavenly Christ" – the blinding Light. So if the Jews were not ready for this revelation, the background of the Gentiles had, in fact, prepared them for Christ. And were it not for this particular Gentile background, the religion that came to be known as "Christianity" would never have existed.

By the time of Christ, various Greek philosophies had coalesced into an eclectic mixture of Platonism, Pythagoreanism and Stoicism, a mixture that formed the bases of numerous religious cults – said to be in the thousands at the time of Christ. This Gentile milieu was not, as some think, a pagan, polytheistic populace; not only did it believe in a transcendent "One", but even had the goal of seeking to be "one with the One".

By the time of the Incarnation, then, outside the Jewish enclave, there existed hundreds of practicing religious sects, each with its own disciplines, rituals, prayers, and paths of ascent to the "One". Not only were there groups living together (Pythagorean style), but individuals who had gone off to live in the desert to be "alone with the Alone"[1]. Christianity, then, did not come to life on barren ground, but occurred at the crossroads of reason and revelation. *Revelation* was Judaic monotheism poised and ready to break out of its small enclave, and *reason,* six centuries of Greek philosophy, developed to a point where it could go no further and was poised for its culminating revelation. Thus Greek philosophy – the "Mother of Western Philosophy" – was destined to meet up with the Truth it had already discovered – discovered not only through reason, but revelation as well. Had the Incarnation not taken place at this crossroad in history, there would be no Christianity, and no true understanding of Christ possible.

It is this monotheistic-philosophical background against which God intended Christ to be understood. Had the Incarnation taken place within some other religious or philosophical system – say, Hinduism, Buddhism, Taoism, Animism and so on – there would have been a totally different understanding of Christ, one in accord with their particular philosophy and religion, but none understood on the *grounds* God obviously intended. It is only at the pivotal intersection of monotheism and Greek philosophy – found nowhere else in history – Christ is a unique, one-of-a-kind revelation. With six centuries of philosophical development behind it and centuries of Judaic monotheism, this was the rich soil in which Christianity took root.

We know Paul was acquainted with the eclectic philosophy of his time, thus, dealing with this Gentile mind-set was all but inevitable. In its own way, Greek eclecticism became a vehicle for the spread not only of Christianity, but with it, monotheism. There is no question the Christologies of both Paul and John were highly influenced by their Gentile communities – particularly Stoicism. Whole books have been written pointing out Stoicism's influence in Paul's thought and writings. Thus his notion that all are one in Christ, that Christ is one Body, Christ is the sum of creation, that in Christ there is neither male nor female, Jew nor Gentile – this and much more that Paul preached, was *pure Stoicism.* We might also point out that the Stoic's view of love-of-neighbor, even love of one's enemies, went further than anything espoused in the Gospels. It is said the Roman Stoics found so little difference between their religion and the Christianity preached by Paul, their conversion was no great step.

The reason for pointing this out, is that when Paul and the Apostles went out to spread the Good News, they were not met by a world of pagans who didn't know God. On the contrary, Paul admitted they

---

[1] Basically, this is the background and origin of what would become the Christian *Monastic* tradition, both *cenobitical* and *eremitical.*

knew God, only they had not been faithful to Him and were wasting their lives going in a wrong direction. The eclectic Greeks were not mere rationalists, logicians or philosophers, prior to Christianity, they had a good grasp of the Transcendent Truth and Source of all existence. As said, by the time of Christ, many had dedicated their lives to seeking a "way", a path, to become one with the One.

Although the term "Neoplatonism" or "Middle Platonism" was only invented in the 18th century, the one credited as its founder was Ammonius Saccus (2nd c.), a renowned teacher of philosophy in his day. That it has been said he was an *ex*-Christian, may be why his two renowned pupils, Origen (185 – 254) and Plotinus (205 – 270), had remarkably similar paradigms of the Trinity. Although Plotinus was not Christian, he may have taken his Triad (emanations of the "One") from Christianity – possibly from Origen's works that preceded his own. On the other hand, Saccus' *Triad* may have inspired the two of them. No doubt it is due to their similarity that, down the centuries, if someone wanted to throw mud on a fellow Christian, he need only call him an "Origenist", a "Plotinian" or a "Neoplatonist". Some authors have even labeled the fathers as "Hellenizers" of Christianity. These authors, of course, seem to forget that without this Gentile background, there would *be* no Christianity. **Judaism did not spread the good news of Christ, it was the Gentiles. Those who eliminate Christianity's Gentile background could have no more understanding of "Christ" than Judaism has ever had.**

In the Jewish context, to be "anointed" ("*christos*" in Greek), never meant a man was "one" with God. It is when "*christos*" was transferred to Gentile soil, there was no problem with man being one with God. Indeed, this was the goal of the religious sects at the time of Christ. Thus Jesus' references to being one with God (his "Father") fit in with the spiritual aspirations of the Gentile world. Because Jesus was the model of someone who was one with God, the Gentiles' understanding of "*Christ*" was not the Jewish understanding of a Messiah, but rather, a reference to someone who was one with God. So this is how the term or title "*Christ*" became a reference to the oneness of God and man, a title that went beyond any Judaic understanding of some "*anointed*" human being. It goes without saying, those who choose to ignore the Gentiles' understanding of "*Christ*" and rely, instead, on the Judaic understanding of scripture's "anointed", are Jewish people and *not* Christians.

Obviously, the historical timing of the Incarnation was all in the divine Plan deliberately scripted and produced by God. Alone, neither monotheism nor Greek philosophy could give us the real Christ, it is only the point where these two meet that defines the dual natures of Christ – wholly God, wholly man. It can be said Christianity was a "third party" that brought together two different religious and philosophical systems (Jew and Gentile) taking the best from both, without adopting either system whole or entire. The Incarnation can be regarded as a seed planted in the very heart and core of Judaic monotheism, yet a seed that never took root there. This seed was destined to take root in the soil God had prepared through six centuries of the Gentiles' various and sophisticated philosophies.

Of itself, Judaic monotheism, with its great divide between the created and Uncreated, could not grant Christ any divine nature, nor could the eclectic philosophies grant any human nature to its absolute "One", "Unmoved Mover" or "Logos". It is because neither of these belief systems or paradigms could yield a true understanding of Christ, that Christ is a unique revelation, a paradigm unto itself, and why the Incarnation occurred when and where it did. Christ reveals how God and man can be eternally one without, however, one being the other. Thus the Incarnation revealed what every man was destined to be or become – *Christ.*

But if monotheism could not grant any divinity to Jesus, it alone granted him true humanity. Of all man's religions, none so valued what it means to be human as did Judaism. Next to angels, man is the greatest of God's creations, man "made in the image of God". Unlike many of their Greek counterparts for whom "the body was a sepulcher", the Judaic goal was to be what God created them to be, to fulfill His will and make themselves as desirable to God as God was to them. Thus Judaism could grant Jesus full humanity with none of its negative Gentile overtones. In contrast, none of the Greek philosophies placed any real value on human nature, in fact, the very idea of the eternal "One" taking on a body was unthinkable – "foolishness" as Paul put it. For them, matter or flesh was the lowest rung on the ladder of divine emanations, a terrible come-down reserved for some ignorant or fallen soul. Having a body was the cause of all man's problems. For the divine to take on flesh? Never!

It is a mistake, then, to think the Greeks could grant the transcendent "One" any *human nature* – a problem the fathers seem to have inherited. As we know, apart from giving lip-service to Jesus having a mind or soul of his own, their consistent reference to Christ is solely to his being "flesh". Since there was no mention of God becoming an "individual soul", the view that the *Logos* was the *soul* of the man Jesus, was perfectly Platonic – because the soul is divine.

As for a material body, most philosophies regarded matter as eternal, prime matter being either water, air, fire or earth, always changing and eternally in flux. For Plato – and others – matter was the *cause* of individuation and multiplicity. For him, individual material "things" were but dim "shadows" or poor copies of some transcendent divine Idea, Form or Archetype. As for the soul, its reality was the animating principle of the universe, a world-soul, its particular "forms" determining "what" a thing was to be an *image* of. So the only thing "individual" was the material body and not the soul. The ontological reality of the soul, then, was some universal Form which, for Plato – as well as for Cyril of Alexandria – was "Universal Man", an *image* of the "One". Since non-matter was not subject to space and time, then nothing "spiritual" could be "individual", only material things could be "individual". This meant that *what* things *really* are is *not* their material individuality, but some immaterial universal reality – call it *soul, form*, or whatever the term used by different philosophers. For the Stoics, of course, this reality was the "Logos".

Though much later, Christian theology would adopt the Aristotelian view of soul as "form of the body" – the soul being the *cause* of a physical "thing" being "what" it is – this understanding, however, had no impact on the early fathers' Christologies. (It is said Aristotle's "*metaphysics*" was virtually unknown at that time.) Thus we have Paul's reference to Christ as the "*Form of God*" and the "*Spirit made visible*". This is why, in part at least, the fathers regarded matter or "flesh" as the *cause* of Jesus' individuation (individuality), the embodiment of a universal soul – a divine Form or Spirit. One could even give a Platonic understanding to Aristotle's "form" (*psyche* or soul) as the body's "animating principle" in that, like Plato, he never espoused the idea of an *independent* substance that constituted an "individual soul". Where Plato's soul had ontological reality *minus* the body, for Aristotle, to be minus a physical body, was to have no ontological reality at all.[2] If the Antiochenes had this later understanding (of Aristotle), there is no explaining their consistent reference to Christ's humanity as *flesh*. Since Jesus talked about his *own soul* – sometimes a disturbed soul – the fathers put this down as a *disturbance of his flesh,* obviously, it could not be a reference to an *impassible* divine Logos or Spirit. As said, they seemed incapable of dealing with a soul "intervening" between God and the flesh – at least where Christ was concerned.

As for what constitutes an "individual soul", one thing we know,

---

[2] Although Aristotle granted body and soul ontological reality, he never granted it any *eternal life*. Even for Aquinas, without a body, man is incomplete and thus, not a human "*person*" – see Appendix I.

without awareness of one's own "*being*" ("*I exist*"), there could be no *individual* soul to speak of. Whatever the soul's immaterial substance, it is "that" which has a mind and will of *its own* and knows it – knows it is its own subject and not the subject (or self) of anyone else. The mind, after all, cannot conceive *its* existence without *awareness* of *its* existence. No philosophy or theology, however, has ever tackled the human *subject* as a "conscious subject or self", which illustrates how "self-awareness" is so taken for granted, no one could ever believe it was *not* as eternal as the soul itself. While Socrates' *Know Thyself* may sound profound, it went no further than Heraclitus (536 – 470 B.C.) telling people they already knew the truth, only they didn't know they knew it! Consciousness, or self-awareness, was never considered by the fathers, nor to this day has any Christian theology ever tackled the *subject*.

As regards the individuality of the soul, the Stoics are the only ones who denied any separation or duality of body and soul, which, for different reasons, Aristotle would agree – both affirmed "you can't have one without the other". So while the Platonic reality of Christ as the "Form of God" was not difficult for the philosophers to accept, yet granting Christ's human nature any ontological reality, was not part of the Platonic paradigm. For a Platonist to be confronted with a resurrected body could only be startling, whereas, for the Stoic, resurrection was a vindication of the non-duality of body and soul. Still, Paul affirms it was a "spiritual body" that arose, not a physical body – which resolves the Platonic dilemma at least. There is no mention, of course, of a *soul* rising from the dead because a *soul* doesn't *die* anyway – both Greeks and Jews assumed the immortal nature of the soul. So the marvel of the resurrection was simply the restoration of the "flesh" which, for a Christian Platonist, was *miraculous* enough – and for the Stoic, vindicating!

It is because there was basically nothing in Greek philosophy prepared to give human nature (an indissoluble unit of body and soul) any ontological reality of its own, that only Judaic monotheism gave us the true and complete humanity of Christ. So what the philosophers couldn't do, was the only thing Monotheism could do – grant Christ a complete human nature.

It was Greek philosophy, however, that, beginning in the 6th century B.C., literally sounded the death-knell of polytheism. Mythical gods played no part in Greek philosophy; the term "god" was never used to designate any transcendent Reality or Truth. To the philosophers, any reference to "God" was to some mythical "god" or some exalted human being, thus speaking to a Greek about "God" he might ask "Which one?" When Paul accused them of worshiping an "Unknown God", to their ears this could only have referred to some unknown polytheistic deity or other. Reference to the "God of Israel" was regarded as primitive, even pagan. Nothing could have been more foreign than the idea of worshiping the god-of-the-Jews. The personified god of Abraham, Isaac and Jacob, would be a tough sell to the educated Greeks for whom the ultimate "One" was utterly transcendent and not a personified being. And let's face it, the greatest misnomer of all times is the term "God" – of totally *polytheistic* origins. Certainly this was not the unnamable, un-pronounceable transcendent "One" that the Jews were forbidden to utter.

Jewish scholars tell us that Judaism actually developed from a polytheistic understanding of "god" – the god revealed to them was their *own particular* guardian or overseer. Just as other tribes and nations had their particular gods, so too, Judaism had its own, "the god of Israel" was their god, and not the god of other peoples. Basically, however, polytheism is not just the belief in multiple gods as transcendent "forces", but the "personification" of these forces. These were deities made in man's image, anthropomorphic beings with superhuman powers – fertility, war, victory, peace, just about anything. From these beginnings, however, Judaism would develop its more transcendent understanding of the absolute "One" from which we get the term "mono-theism" (one-god) as against "poly-theism" or many gods. No doubt Judaism's development of a transcendent One-and-Only, came about through its encounter with the Greek philosophers' non-personified "One".

It is said that centuries before Christ, Judaism had already absorbed elements from other religions and philosophical wisdoms. Those educated in Alexandria, or outside Palestine, were well acquainted with the Gentiles' religions and philosophies. Philo of Alexandria (25 BC – 50 AD), a Jewish mystic-philosopher who lived in Alexandria at the time of Christ, had no problem seeing the connection between his religion and philosophy. He affirmed that the God revealed to Moses was the same God revealed to the Greeks, only they developed this revelation along more rational, philosophical lines, whereas Judaism had the more "personal" understanding of God. Thus, where Judaism only gradually evolved from polytheism and its own "*personal*" god, Greek philosophy had no such evolution, but totally rejected polytheism. Indeed, Socrates was put to death for pooh-poohing the gods.[3]

---

[3] The purpose of government imposing a polytheistic state-religion was to keep a people unified, give them a common identity via its laws, rituals, celebrations and holidays. This helped to keep people in their place and above all, assure the emperor would be

This philosophical influence may just have saved Judaism – and even Christianity – from becoming a form of polytheism. For many people, there is a fine line between "god" and "God". So it may well have been the Greeks' philosophical influence on Judaism, that would eventually elevate its revelation beyond the anthropomorphic god depicted in its scriptures. We know that in time, Judaism's *Yahweh* would become utterly transcendent, and its scriptures, regarded as purely "allegorical". But if the philosophers' "One" kept Christianity from degenerating into anthropomorphism – a god, or three gods – Judaism's personal "One" emphasized man's personal experience and relationship to God.

It has been thought that one aspect of Paul's mission was to change what he regarded as the Greek's *impersonal* "One" to Judaism's *personal* personified One. Somehow this seemed necessary if they were ever to understand "Christ". The implication, however, is that the God of the philosophers is *impersonal,* and only the God of religion is *personal.* This dichotomy (between personal and impersonal), however, has nothing to do with God, but everything to do with man's different perspectives on *"God."* It goes without saying, were God-in-Itself *impersonal,* there would be no way man could ever know God existed. That God reveals Itself to every man, is all we need to know God "*cares*", and that the terms *"personal-impersonal"* are solely a man-made dichotomy.

Because the philosophers never personified the absolute – the "One", the "Good", the "Source", the "Uncaused Cause", etc. – does not mean the "One" was *impersonal* or a mere idea in their heads. Heraclitus, Zeno and Plotinus, to name a few, were so fired up about the Transcendent, they not only claimed to know It, to be one with It, but taught It to all who would listen. In fact, Philo's description of being united to God is not too different from that of Plotinus – who lived 200 years *after* Philo. But if Philo had a positive view of the philosophers "One" – which he nevertheless thought inferior to the Judaic revelation – the Gentiles, in turn, had no such positive view of Judaism. It regarded Judaism as the religion of some "barbaric tribe" – pagan, simplistic, childish. For them, it would have been unthinkable to *personify* the One as some god or other. The problem with personifying God is that it not only belies God, but throws people off track looking for some deity, image or idea, that does *not* exist. Either people will end up atheists or go to some "more advanced" religion that does not so mislead. The idea that only a personified, anthropomorphic image of **God *makes God personal,*** is clearly ridiculous. The truth is just the opposite, a

venerated as a kind of god – the purpose of any state-religion.

personified deity is what makes God a "god" – no getting around it.

It is not in the language of philosophy (or metaphysics) to "personify" the Transcendent Source, this is simply not its genre. The idea the Greek's "Absolute" was "impersonal" is pure myth. What is *true,* is that they never *personified* It – made It into man's image as did the writers of the Old Testament. Since the nature of this revelation does not remotely resemble a human being or anything in the existing world, the idea of personifying It would never have crossed their minds. It is a mistake, then, to think nobody *really* knows God unless their "God" matches the Judaic image of a personified ("personal") God, obviously, this is not the case. It could even be said, it is those who do *not* know God, who personify God in order to *make* God *personal* to ***themselves***.

People who think *only* monotheists know God "personally", must never have experienced the magnetic drawing power of God (or the One) present in every human being. This is a power ever drawing man up and beyond himself, longing to know and reach *that mystery* which transcends all images, names and definitions. Even Aristotle wraps up his metaphysics saying the ultimate "Uncaused Cause" is the "*One supreme object of all knowledge and the ultimate* ***object of all desire***". Indeed, God is the supreme object and end of all human desire, a striving toward *that* alone which can truly and eternally satisfy man. The Greek philosophers both recognized and spoke of this fact. Nothing is deeper in human nature than this incessant drawing power toward the absolute Transcendent, and not to recognize this fact is not to know "God" at all. Those who rest satisfied with their images, concepts and doctrines, live in complete ignorance of God.

And something else. The faculty of desire and longing is the soul's movement of *love.* Thus the *very desire* for the intellectually unknowable and imageless, is to *love* It. This type of *love,* however, is like no other; it is man's response to ***that alone*** which draws him beyond all *knowable* existence. Those who think that focusing on some particular knowable or circumscribed "being" is what makes God "personal", are polytheists.

Although God is revealed to everyone, the reason man does not recognize this is due to his *false* ideas of God, what he *thinks* God is or "should" be, more especially, according to some religion's idea of "God". Man picks up all kinds of concepts and images of God and then expects God to meet these mental demands – which cannot happen. (As someone said, *"Man creates God and then wonders why he can't find Him"*!) Something else to keep in mind: where "belief" is based on a "rational assent", with all its concepts and sensory input, the gift of "faith" (an "*unknowing-knowing*"), on the other hand, is beyond the intellect's capabilities and admits of no sensory images. Thus the true nature of *faith* is *always* non-personified and *never* depends on concepts or images.

There is no way a few pages could begin to recount the ingredients of the rich soil in which God planted Christianity. The term "Neoplatonism" is misleading because it only designates a particular era of religious zeal, one that took its lead not only from the ancients, but from contemporary philosophers, spiritual teachers and masters. Included in this era was a panoply of various mystical traditions and paths that would take many books to go over. On the one hand, this milieu could not help but influence the fathers, yet, only to a point. Where they drew the line was on Monotheism's Great Divide between the Uncreated and created. Their focus, however, was not on either side of this line, but on the *line* itself, for the question of Christ is ***how the line that divides is also the line that unites***. This is the mystery of Christ for which knowing both sides of the line is of no help whatsoever. Alone, neither philosophy nor monotheism has any answers. The great mystery of the line that both divides and unites, this *mystery is Christ.*

Without some background in the prevalent Gentile thinking of the first centuries, it may not be possible to fully understand the early fathers whose Gentile way-of-thinking was the foundation that not only gave Christianity its first intellectual understanding and expression, but lent it its mystical depths as well. While none of the fathers were beholden to any particular philosophy, or attempted to reconcile the two (with the exception of Origen perhaps), this was the background and mind-set of their times, a background that cannot be ignored without ignoring Christianity itself. Christianity never adopted anyone's philosophical system, and consistently drew a line on any philosophy that did not accord with Monotheism. No philosophy was prepared to handle the Trinity, the mystery of Christ, or as we have seen, even the full humanity of the man Jesus. So where theology employs certain philosophical ideas and dictums, no doctrine or dogma could be premised on any piece of philosophy – which is free of dogmas anyway.

As it happened then, those burdened with the task of bringing all this together were the first Christian Gentiles, the early fathers, who reflected the educated mind-set of their age. This was the Gentile milieu where the first Christians rubbed elbows with those of whom Paul said, "*for the Gentiles it* [Christianity] *was foolishness*". It behooved the fathers to use their best mental and educational resources in the interest of their Faith. They never tried to build a bridge between philosophy and monotheism, much less meld them. The Incarnation ushered in something so new and different it fit neither paradigm. So it was not a matter of integrating the two, but of making room for the *new*.

Apart from a few Apologists who were converts from the going philosophy, to my knowledge, all the fathers were raised in Christian homes, grew up amid the religious-educational culture of their time. Although few made a particular study of philosophy, they were products of the same Western philosophical heritage we have today, it was virtually in the air they breathed. One reason for calling attention to this historical fact, is to indict those authors who accuse the early fathers of "Hellenizing" Christianity. It is incredible anyone, after studying the first five centuries of Christianity, could ever think the fathers were "of one mind" on any single issue. Their disputes were never *philosophical*, but *theological*.

It is only in retrospect some authors point out – as we do here – the philosophical influence of the times. To ignore this, the historical facts of Christianity's background, can only be a matter of personal prejudice. Closing one's eyes on the earliest understandings of Christ is to close them on the understanding that God obviously intended Christ to be understood. Without this background, what is left is the Judaic understanding of the man Jesus – with no Christ or Christianity at all! As said, the time and place of the revelation of "*Christ*" was not mere happenstance. It was deliberately poised at the crossroad of Judaic monotheism and the Gentiles' philosophies so that "*Christ*" would be rightly understood. To dismiss this crossroad, is to miss the true nature of Christ so wonderfully reflected in Christ's "dual natures" – true man and true God.

As among the best educated of their time, the fathers' use of Greek philosophical terms and distinctions came naturally. They could not rely, of course, on philosophy for a correct understanding of Christianity. Although *revelation* may not be unreasonable, it also cannot be reached by reason. So when it came to using any philosophical terms in a Christian context, these terms took on a different meaning and understanding. Down the centuries, of course, language developed, new terms arose and old terms, honed to finer distinctions, were given different understandings. Thus a medieval understanding of the original doctrinal terms changed, and changed further with the Renaissance, and so on down to our own era. While the original terms remain, their original understanding and particular definitions changed – though not for the better.

Few people realize that given this philosophical background, when it comes to formulating the basic truths of Christianity, theologians have always found a way to "philosophically" cover their tracks. It could be said this fact actually reflects its dual heritage. The problem with this, however, is those the fathers called "simple folk", had no such philosophical background, but tended to take doctrines as "traditionally expressed" for the literal truth of things, the result being more naiveté than truth. Another problem is *whose* philosophy is used to ground one's theology? Even if this does not change the truths of Christianity, it can (and has) absolutely influenced the understanding of its doctrines and beliefs.

In this matter, we could even point out a "clash" between a Platonian and Aristotelian view of Christ. The point is this – where the eclectic philosophical background of the fathers unconsciously allowed for the diversity of their views, this diversity has been dearly *missed* in the centuries that followed, or once Christ was *dogmatically pinned down.* Over time, as the result of this stultification and staid dogmatism, the richness of Christ known to the fathers has not only faded, but degenerated to the point of becoming the most primitive of human beliefs – *anthropolatry*.

As the history of Christianity goes, the enormous contribution of the six centuries of Greek philosophy that preceded Christianity, can never be sufficiently emphasized. This is the soil God nurtured and in which the revelation of Christ took root. All was planned to give an understanding of Christ never intended just for Jews or Gentiles, but for every human being. By itself, neither monotheism nor any Gentile philosophy is capable of yielding a right understanding of Christ. As pointed out, while monotheism affirmed Christ's complete human nature, and philosophy affirmed Christ's divine nature, it was with the encounter of these two, the mind-set of both Jew and Gentile, that God intended man to understand the truth of Christ. As said, these are the two grounds of Christianity wonderfully reflected in Christ's "dual nature". Remove either one, and there is no Christ and no Christianity.

Christianity has always regarded Judaic monotheism as its "mother religion", yet there is no child without a father, and just so, the Greek philosophers can be regarded as the "patriarchs" of Christianity. Without the two meeting at the historical crossroads prepared by God, there would be no Christianity. Standing at this crossroad, Christ is not only a bridge between philosophy and revelation, between man and God, but would become the "oneness" of the two, the meeting place of the created and Uncreated, Jew and gentile, religion and reason, literally, a coming together of all dualities, *this is the true Christ*.

Seeing that the Gentiles already knew the ineffable transcendent One, what could Christianity possibly offer them? What Christianity came to give them was the "Way" to attain their goal, the way to fulfill their highest aspirations of being one with the One. Indeed, for this

Christ came, and came not only as the "way" and "means", but as the "end" itself. This is what Christ is all about and why Christianity took root in the Gentile soil God had prepared for six centuries prior to the revelation of Christ. This was God's way of preparing man for what can only be regarded as the most magnificent of God's revelations to man – the revelation of man himself, his "way" to God, and his eternal oneness with God. No question, were it not for *this* Gentile background, there would be no Christianity to speak of.

What we have wanted to point out here is that any understanding of Christ based on Judaic Monotheism *alone*, will never give anyone a true understanding of Christ. Nor will any understanding of Christ based on Philosophy *alone*, give anyone a true understanding of Christ. A true understanding is only possible at the **crossroad** of these two. No other background can ever yield a true understanding of Christ as God intended it be understood. It was at this crossroad God revealed Christ, intended neither for Jew nor Gentile, but for every human being who has ever lived, and will live forever with and in God.

LOGOS

"In the beginning was the Logos, and the Logos was with God and the Logos was God.....and the Logos became flesh."
(John's Gospel)

The writings of Philo of Alexandria (25 BC – 50 AD), the Jewish mystic-philosopher, were most appreciated by the early Christians, though not, it seems, by his Jewish contemporaries. It was his comparing the Gentile "Logos" with God's incarnate "Wisdom" – as personified in Jewish scriptures – that was carried forward as the prologue to St. John's Gospel, "*In the beginning was the Logos, the Logos was with God and the Logos was God*". One wonders how, without the long history of the "Logos" (six centuries), Christianity could have worked out the *divine nature* of Christ. As an understanding of the Logos is strategic for a true understanding of Christ, nothing could be more important than understanding the historical origin and meaning of the word "*Logos*". As it came to be understood by the fathers, any reference to the "*Divine Christ*" was a reference to the "*Logos*".

Paul, the earliest Christian writer, does not use the term "Logos" for the divinity of Christ. Instead, he refers to the divine Christ as the "*Spirit made visible*", "Spirit" being understood according to the Judaic use of the term. Until the end of the first century or until John's Gospel appeared, it was Judaism's understanding of the Spirit that was taken to be the "Divine Christ" – and *not* the Logos. Although Paul was familiar with the Stoics' understanding of "Logos", yet, like Philo, he regarded the Logos as only *comparable* to God's divine Spirit – "Wisdom" as understood in Judaism. It seems Philo himself was not totally clear as to the real distinctions between God's Spirit and God's Wisdom (or Logos), thus his biblical references could be understood as referring to either one – or both. For Paul, it was much the same. His understanding of "Spirit" in Judaism and "Logos" in philosophy, could be understood interchangeably as references to the divinity of Christ – "the Form of God", the "Sum of creation", or "Spirit made visible", etc. Basically, this is why it took another two centuries before the two, Logos and Spirit, were acknowledged as distinct "hypostases" of the Trinity – as stated at Nicaea and Chalcedon.

So this is why the earliest fathers, taking their cue from Paul, based their Christologies on the "Spirit" as the divinity of Christ, whereas later – after John's Gospel appeared (around 100 or so) – the divinity of Christ was based on an understanding of the "Logos". Thus it was the "Logos" that became the orthodox understanding of Christ's divinity. To my knowledge, none of fathers used the term "Wisdom" in place of "Logos" for their understanding of the Incarnation. Possibly, this was because it is more difficult to grasp how Wisdom or "God's own Knowing" could take on flesh, whereas the philosophical understanding of a *cosmic* "Logos" was ripe for an understanding of the Incarnation. This being the case, it is important to understand not only what "Logos" meant to the philosophers, but its understanding as used by the fathers in their formulation of the Trinity and subsequent Christologies. Without this understanding, it is unlikely anyone can grasp the true nature of the Trinity and the incarnation of the "Logos". So let us give some background to this particular understanding of what was meant by the term "Logos".

The 5th century BC has been regarded as an Axial period in the history of man. Overlooked in this axial line-up, however, is the revelation of the Logos. Far more profound and enduring than anything left to us during this period, the Logos is one of God's tri-fold revelations of Itself to mankind. Heraclitus of Ephesus (535 – 475 BC) is credited with making the Logos known. Considering its impact and enduring legacy to philosophy and religion, there is no reason to doubt it was a product of divine revelation. Heraclitus was not actually a philosopher or someone who happened to stumble upon a good idea, rather, he believed himself privy to a truth about man and nature that mere intellectual investigation (reason) could not discover or comprehend on its own. He claimed he alone was awake and knew the truth, while everyone else was "asleep". He claimed he knew "everything" and the rest of mankind, nothing. He would say, *"Listen not to me, but to the Logos, it is wise to agree that all things are **one**".*

Heraclitus regarded everything in existence as impermanent, changeable, in flux, yet, the principle *cause* or what determined the nature of this flux was the "Logos". The Logos was the "reason-for-being", it resided in all things and in all human beings, it literally made things "what" they are. The Logos was existence in itself, the purposive source that regulates all physical processes, animates all life, the source of all human law, it was the "law of nature" itself. Immanent and active in all reality, the Logos was the controlling principle of the universe together with "that" element in man by which this principle is perceived.

That "element" would later be called *logoi* by the Stoics, meaning, a "spark" or presence of the Logos in man and in all that exists. Though the Logos itself was One, yet it was inherent in everything that existed, its presence in the multiple being the "*logoi*". According to Heraclitus, and later the Stoics, man was to live in accordance with this interior *logoi* if he wanted to live a good and well-ordered life – live in *unity* with the Logos, that is.

As far as we know, Heraclitus coined the term "*Logos*", thus, what it meant to him can never be identified with any of its much later etymological definitions. In his words, *"It* (Logos) *is the power and knowledge that steers all things – the Logos* ***knows****". "There is but one wisdom to understand the knowledge by which all things are steered ("piloted") through all"* – the "pilot" he calls the *"intelligent helmsman". "This Logos is always existent, but men fail to understand it both before they have heard of it, and when they have heard of it for the first time. For although all things happen* ***through*** *the Logos, men seem as if they had no acquaintance with such works and words as I expound, dividing each thing according to its nature and explaining how it really is. The rest of mankind are* ***unconscious*** *of what they do when awake, just as they forget what they do when asleep."* "*When people make trial of my words they behave as if they had no* ***experience of the Logos*** *by which all things come to pass"*. Heraclitus blames people for not *experiencing* the Logos even before they had heard of It – *"****They are unable to understand their own experience of It****, for eyes and ears are bad witnesses to those who have barbarian souls". "Men are at variance with the Logos which is* ***their most constant companion****". "****Although the Logos is common to all, most men live as if each had a private intelligence of his own.*** *Although intimately connected with it, men keep setting themselves against it". "Listen not to me but to the Logos, it is wise to agree that all things in reality are one and one thing only".*

If we remember the saying, "*God is closer to us than we are to ourselves*" (Augustine), then we have grasped Heraclitus' understanding of the Logos as man's "*most constant companion* **beyond** *his own private intelligence"* or knowing. In Heraclitus' view, it is man's awareness of himself that precludes awareness of the Logos – because "*men live as if each had a private intelligence of his own*", thus they are *unconscious* of the Logos, not awake to it, but totally "asleep". To follow the universal Logos, was *contrary* to any form of individualism because, for Heraclitus, there was no such thing as a permanent ego or self.

Heraclitus was called "the obscure", not only because his teaching went over the heads of his listeners, but because his mannerisms and lifestyle were somewhat reminiscent of John the Baptist coming out of the wilderness with a mission declaring a great truth to all who would listen. From this date on, "*Logos*" would never lose Its immediate connection to nature (creation), to man, and even to matter itself. The term "Logos" was never used as a synonym for *human* reason or rationalization, quite the opposite, its reference was to a "knowing" (a "wisdom") *beyond* the intellect to the existence of the overarching source of cosmic unity pervading all reality, directing all toward the good. Man's soul is "naturally" one with the universal Logos, and the goal in life was to live in perfect harmony or *unity* with the Logos.

Down the centuries, this Logos assumed ever greater importance in Greek philosophy, until, it can be said, it reached full blossom with the advent of Christianity. Heraclitus has been called "The *Father* (or *elder*) of Greek Philosophy", and renowned solely for his *Logos.* Thus it could be said the "Logos" was the revelation that literally got Greek philosophy started. One would have to be blind (as Heraclitus said) *not* to see God's hand in this. The Logos is that "one" of the Trinity regarded as the Incarnation of God, and any Christian who does not know this, has missed the real Christ completely.

There is no use going over the little we know of Heraclitus' life and teachings – some of it may only be legend – there is only one interesting note to add. In his day, philosophers tended to identify one of the four elements, earth, water, fire and air as the founding bases of the cosmos – Aristotle's "first material principle" or "prime matter". For Heraclitus, the Logos was identified with *fire*, more especially a *thunderbolt* or *lightening*. This would remind Philo of Moses encountering God in a burning bush and on the mount. That the Logos was associated with light or lightning has a very mystical ring to it.

About two centuries after Heraclitus, the philosopher Zeno founded a school at Athens (308 BC.) Because he taught outdoors in a *stoa* or portico of some public building, his teaching was given the name "Stoicism". The Stoics developed a further understanding of "Logos" which not only found place in the whole of Greek philosophy, but was regarded as a "world religion" that had spread throughout the Roman Empire. It was a practical religion in that it brought the Logos down to its *presence* within man himself, a presence he must seek and be attuned to.

This was not just a philosophy of life, but a practice requiring great self-discipline, altruism, and concern for the community at large. (It is my view that, politically, they espoused the earliest form of *democracy* with their view of *equality for all.*) When Paul said that in Christ there is neither slave or master, Jew or Gentile, male or female, this is pure Stoicism. By the time of Christ, Stoicism both philosophically and practically, had been incorporated into the hundreds of religious and gnostic sects that existed at that time. Though never a cult or a mere philosophy, it was a practice of both interior self-discipline and exterior good works that emphasized the good of the whole rather than that of the individual. Its term for the One divine, of course, was "Logos".

The philosopher Zeno (340 – 265 BC), had been repelled by "Platonism" that had dissolved God into some universal "*abstract idea*". In his view, Platonism had banished God from this *material* world, leaving it a dark mass from which the soul must be detached if it would find God. According to Zeno, there was nothing that was not *in* its ultimate origin. It was, he said ***"He (the Logos) in whom man lived, moved and had his being"*** – does this sound like Paul or not? When Zeno would ask people where they could find God, he would strike his hand on the solid earth and answer, "*Here!*" He repeatedly affirmed "*God is Body*!", reminiscent, not only of the Incarnation, but of Christ referring to bread as his Body – the Logos being the very body of the universe.

The reason the Stoics were accused of pantheism was because they admitted no real separation between body and soul. They stood their ground, as did Heraclitus, to affirm that while the immutable and impassible Logos had an independent existence of its own, yet the "*logoi*" (plural of "logos") was present in all things and that matter "*participated*" in it. Like Aristotle, the Stoics denied the Platonic notion of independent "divine forms" existing apart from matter. Thus, like Aristotle, they denied the existence of an independent soul apart from matter (a body.) But where they were labeled "pantheists", Aristotle was never so labeled – obviously, some bias here!

By "*logoi*" (the Logos' omnipresence in all things), however, was not meant a "piece" of the Logos – as if it could be fractured – but rather, that the Logos as **the Ultimate *Cause, is in Its effect.*** Although the "effect" was lesser than the Cause, the effect contained as much of the Cause as possible. In other words, the limitations of human nature are such that it can only reflect as much of the Truth as its limited nature can bear. Basically, the *logoi* were regarded as God's ***existential oneness*** with creation, that like a *seed* ("*logoi spermatikoi*" they called it) could grow exponentially. (This "growth" is reminiscent of the parable of the mustard seed.)

The Stoics never denied the existence of a soul, they only denied it was a separate spiritual entity – like a ghost in a machine. They challenged people to see if they could possibly conceive of, or even imagine, the existence of anything totally *non-material* – i.e., something *not* connected to matter – literally conceive the existence of *non-matter*. Although people may believe the immaterial exists, the mind has no way of getting hold of anything it can verify as absolutely non-material.

Thus the existence of non-matter is a mere belief, perhaps, a matter of faith alone. This philosophy actually explains why people have to *see something visible* before they can begin to *believe* in anything *invisible* – if they can at all. According to Augustine, for some people to try to conceive of anything non-sensory, would be like asking them to conceive of *non-existence.*

For the Stoics, the "soul" in man was the "logoi's" *individual* manifestation. The body's *physical* oneness with the "logoi" lent an appreciation of the body not shared by any other philosophy. In like manner, St. John's prologue used the Logos to designate It as the divine that became *visibly manifested in a material body.* St. Irenaeus – perhaps the most enlightened of the fathers – commented that man was a microcosm of the universe, and that in the process of taking on human nature (the Incarnation), the Logos united Itself to the *whole cosmos.* Thus, along with Paul, Irenaeus referred to Christ as the "*Sum of Creation*".[1]

So if the Logos was the Source and Soul of existence, the cosmos was Its Body – Its "manifestation". Thus the Logos was the *soul of the universe* just as man's body is the visible form of his soul. This, it seems, was also St. Athanasius' (296 – 373 AD) view, "*Just as the Logos is the animating principle of the cosmos, it is of the rational soul of man. Christ's human nature was a part of the vast body of the cosmos. Logos, while present in the man Jesus, was simultaneously present everywhere else in the universe, vivifying and directing it with its life-giving power.*" For Athanasius, "*the Logos did not "enter" into a man, but became a man, took on flesh, it was his instrument*".

The Stoics' view was that while the Logos was immutable and not subject to change, yet Its manifestations were always changing, in flux. Solely in Itself, the Logos was dynamic, indeed, It was said to be "fire". The Stoics' goal was to find and attune their whole being to the unchanging *logoi* present in themselves. This goal, of becoming one with the immutable and impassible Logos, was called "*apatheia*", a goal attained by overcoming one's continually changing mental and emotional states. There was no egoic individualism (or "I am") in their practice. Christianity would inherit this discipline as well. This was the goal of reaching a state of *impassiveness* or "*apatheia*" in order to be-

---

[1] Maximus the Confessor noted that "*The divine Logos, in whom all things were created, contains in himself the diversity of creation*". He says, "*By contemplating that diversity, who will not perceive that the single Logos is the* ***multitude of logi*** *and that, conversely,* ***the multitude is one in the universal*** *return toward Him?" "This same Logos is manifested and multiplied in a way suitable to the Good in all the beings who come from Him according to the nature of each, and He Recapitulates all things in Himself. For all things participate in God by analogy insofar as they come from God.*"

come *one* with the impassible Logos. The fathers gave this state of oneness the name "*theosis*" and regarded it as man's "*deification*".

Needless to say, today's use of the demeaning terms "stoic" and "apathy" is a far cry from the Stoics' goal of "apatheia". To be one with the Logos meant becoming as impassible (or dispassioned) as the impassible Logos. To this we might add that the Stoic notion of "charity" and selflessness exceeded anything found in the Judaic or Christian Bible – but we needn't go over that here.

It seems the ancients regarded prime matter as eternal, yet none regarded anything *changeable* or *mutable* as divine, on the contrary, the One or Logos was immutable and impassible. So to say the Stoics took the ever-changing forms of matter **to be** the divine Logos is not true, what they held was that the Logos was the unchanging engineer ***underlying*** all flux and change. The Logos was the intelligent ***Cause*** of all impermanence, the *Eternal Form* underlying the multiple forms (*logoi*) created in the Logos, and their return, was to the one Logos. The Stoics were the first to use "*hypostasis*" for the Logos – meaning, the *real* that "*underlies*" the apparent (or manifest) cosmos as its Cause, the Cause of Its "eternal movement", change or flux. Since they believed the invisible Logos was *one with matter,* the Incarnation would not have been such a mystery to them – nor would the Resurrection. While matter or everything man knows of it, is *not* the Logos, yet the Logos is its underlying *invisible mystery,* which mystery constitutes the true *oneness* of all that exists.

One important feature of the *Logos* inherited by the fathers, was the understanding of God as "*impassible*" – meaning, God was not subject to passions, emotions, feelings, or human experiences of any kind. All the fathers took this as axiomatic saying that the idea of God as passible was "*madness*" (Cyril), "*an absurdity*" (Nyssa), "*atheistic*" (Appolinarius), etc. So while, like every human being, the man Jesus was *passible* – subject to human feelings and emotions – the divine Logos, however, experienced none of it. All held that the human experience, whatever it may be, was *not* God's experience. This was the understanding of all the fathers – and well worth keeping in mind.

God's impassibility, however, was never easy for the fathers to reconcile with the Old Testament view of an impassioned God – angry, demanding, punishing, even vengeful – subject to every kind of human emotion. Yet, all agreed God was *absolutely impassible* and that the biblical sayings were purely personified metaphors. Despite this fact, the Alexandrians, at least, hedged around this contradiction by inventing what came to be called "*The Communication of Properties or Attributes*" whereby Jesus' human passibility was "attributed" to the impassible divine "person" of the Logos. This way, they could *say* the Logos was "born, suffered and died", while, in truth, this could only be said of Its human nature and *never* of the divine Logos Itself. So despite all the protestation *against* the passibility of God, the "*Communication of Properties*" perpetuated the Old Testament's personified images of a passible, feeling God. No question, God's *impassivity* had great implications for the fathers' various Christologies and understanding of Christ.

Like people of any religion, however, where some find its value morally, socially and psychologically beneficial, there are others for whom only its deeper mystical implications of Truth are its real value. This was the case with the Jewish mystic-philosopher, Philo of Alexandria (25 B.C. – 50 A.D.) Convinced that Greek philosophy was grounded in God's singular revelation to Moses, Philo wrote a book correlating his Jewish monotheism with Greek philosophy. It is his comparison of Proverbs' personified "Wisdom" with the Gentiles' non-personified "Logos" that is his most outstanding contribution – to Christianity, at least. Right here we can put our finger on a strategic crossover of two different mind-sets – Judaism's monotheistic heritage and the Gentiles' religious-philosophical heritage. For Philo, the philosophical and biblical notions were not at odds, but complementary.

Philo was convinced the God of Moses had also revealed Itself to the Greeks, only they had taken it in a different direction, more rational and philosophical, while his people, of course, had the higher and more *personal* understanding of this as Judaism's particular *relationship* to God. In his view, the Logos was an *intermediary* between the ultimate divine reality and the sensible world. And though the Logos was not God, It was God's "first begotten" responsible for God's work in creation. Thus always and everywhere the Logos (or Wisdom) pervades the whole of creation.

Since in Ecclesiastics 24:3 "Wisdom" is identified as God's creative *Spirit,* for Philo, at least, there seemed to be no division between God's Wisdom and Spirit. Interestingly, however, God's Wisdom is not personified as masculine, but as feminine – "*Sophia*". It seems for the Hebrews and early Christians, God was always masculine, which is why only "sons" could be heirs or equals – that whole idea of "Father-Son". Philo makes absolutely clear the Creator (God) is masculine, and so too, God's Wisdom is masculine – he says, "*The feminine always falls short and is inferior to the masculine which has priority*". He even went so far as to say women had to *become* men if they wanted any spiritual status with God. Perhaps this is why he was never clear on the relation of the philosophers' Logos with his scripture's personified (feminine) Wisdom. But since the latter was scriptural and the former philosophical, he made Wisdom superior to Logos, telling us the *"Logos serves as God for the yet unenlightened"* – for the philosophers, that is. The philosophers, of course, would have scoffed at any idea of a "gendered" Logos. For them, the Logos totally transcended any notion of gender.[2]

For Philo, the Logos expressed creation as the thought and will of God, the cosmic governing and generative principle immanent and active in all reality. The Logos stands between and separates the creature from the Creator – *"And I stood between the Lord and you – neither unbegotten as God or begotten as you, but* ***midway between the two extremes serving as a pledge for both.****"* The Logos is also our *"heavenly nourishment, raining upon you* ***bread out of heaven****", "the* ***holy chalice of its own reason****, the Cupbearer of God and Toastmaster of the feast* ***who differs not from the draught he pours****, but is himself the undiluted drink, the gaiety, the effusion and cheer, the Ambrosian drug of joy and gladness."* These are but a few of the exalted views of Philo's *Logos* – right here, a beautiful foreshadowing of the Christian *Eucharist.* And just as the *"Shadow or Image of God is the instrument of creation, the Logos in turn is the Image and archetype of all things created"*. In all of literature, there is, perhaps, no more wonderful understanding of the Logos. Though this no doubt played a great part in the earliest understanding of Christ's divinity – "*In the beginning was the Logos ... and the Logos was God",* it was lost to the Christian public, obscured by the fathers' language, expressions and personified images of the Trinity as a "Father and Son" – two males, of course.

Without going into Plato's notion of "idea" or "image" – all creation being the image, idea, form, or "shadow" of some transcendent ideal – Philo regarded the Logos as God's *Image* and the medium of God's creation. "*The shadow of God is his Logos which he used like an instrument when he was making the world, and this shadow is as it were the model, the archetype of other things"*. Every man in regard to his intellect is connected with the divine Logos, being an *impression* of It, a fragment or *ray* of that blessed nature. "*The image of God is the Logos through which the whole universe was framed, the divine Logos is Himself the Image of God, chiefest of all beings intellectually perceived, placed nearest, with no intermediary distance to the truly Existent One. It well befits those who have entered into comradeship with knowledge to desire to see the Existent if they may, but, if they cannot,*

[2] Although Philo virtually condemns any anthropomorphic notion of God, he is sympathetic with man's anthropomorphic expressions for God, for "what else", he asks, does man have to go on? Language, after all, is only human, so no use apologizing for it.

to see at least his Image, the most holy Logos" – a quote from Philo. He speaks of "*suddenly*" seeing the Logos – the "*place*" of God, he calls it.

That the Logos is the Image of God, and that humans were "made in the image of God", means they are made in the Image of the Logos – "*when the divine Breath was breathed into his face"* – the very same understanding Christianity would incorporate as its own. It would be the *Incarnation* of the Logos, however, understood as "*Christ*" that would become the "Image" in which all men were created – created in the Image of "Christ" – the *oneness* of God and man.

Like the biblical account of God's Wisdom, however, Philo's Logos is utterly personal to God and man, not the more aloof-sounding Logos of the Stoics. So, in keeping with Hebrew scripture where God and God's Wisdom is consistently personified, Philo also *personified* the Greek Logos, all but "incarnated" it, which the Stoics would never have thought proper or possible. In its more philosophical setting, of course, the Logos was never personified. To the Greeks, this would have made the Logos a god – a myth, rejected by the philosophers. So there were differences in the understanding of biblical Wisdom and the more philosophical Logos. Yet the terms were close enough for Philo, at least, to use as an explanation for God's Presence and activity in creation – a reference that would speak to both Jew and Gentile.

Philo tells us the corner-stone of Heraclitus' notion of *unity "was the oneness of opposites, the* ***hidden harmony****"*, he says, *"is better than the visible, the fairest harmony results from differences. It is the tension of opposing forces that makes the structure one. The interchange of opposites with one another is itself proof they are only different manifestations of the same thing, the changeless unity in which all multiplicity inheres. Logos is the substance that creates, sustains, and in the end, perhaps,* ***reabsorbs into Itself****. The One is All and the All is one"*. Apart from this "*union of opposites*" being an apt definition of "*Christ*", his saying, "*The One is All and the All is one*" is no doubt the genesis of Paul's notion that in the end (after all is saved) "*God will be all in All*", meaning, all will *be* "One". As we'll see, however, this saying of Paul was the cause of division among the fathers.

Before moving on, it is worth going over Philo's remark that his Judaic Wisdom was superior to the philosophers' Logos – thus he says, *"Logos serves as God for the yet unenlightened"*. After his exalted and wonderful exposition of the Logos, this statement is curious. Obviously, he was not above adhering to the traditional Judaic "party-line", he does not want to be accused of adding anything to the proverbial Judaic understanding of God. His comment, however, serves the Logos in another way. In the history of religion, man's first encounter with God has always been through the cosmos or in nature, this is even true for most people today. Indeed, the cosmic Logos is God's first revelation of Itself to all mankind – the mystery of God in creation. While this is a piece of revelation in itself, it is not, however, the ultimate or final revelation of God. So in this matter, Philo had it right, there is more to God than the Logos' omnipresence in creation, which "*more*" is the Trinity – i.e., God's three major revelations to mankind. In Christianity, the Logos would be regarded as but *one* of God's triune "modes of existence" revealed to man, the Logos being *one* of the Trinity.

As we have seen, from Heraclitus to the Stoics to Philo, the "Logos" was well known for some six centuries prior to John's Gospel (written around 100 A.D.) which began "*In the beginning was the Logos...*" Where, for Philo, the Logos was *not* God, for John, the Logos *was* God. As to why John did not use the term "Wisdom" instead of "Logos", obviously the Greeks had long known the Logos, but had no idea of Judaism's personified "Wisdom".

Some authors think John did not use the term "Logos" as understood *philosophically,* but used it as understood in Proverbs as God's incarnate "Wisdom". John, however, was familiar with the Jewish understanding of Wisdom and could have used the term, but the fact he did *not* do so, means he deliberately chose "Logos" and not "Wisdom" as his reference to God. If one could fully grasp the meaning of "Logos" in the Gentile world of Christ's time, the Incarnation of the Logos had more meaning than the Incarnation of the Old Testament's "Wisdom" with which the Gentiles were not familiar. Then too, Wisdom could just be regarded as an "attribute" of God, whereas the Gentile *Logos* was never so understood. Though the term "Wisdom" is almost synonymous with Logos as God's transcendent "Mind" or "Knowing", yet even Irenaeus questioned, "*how can a quality* (or attribute) *of God be "hypostasized?*" – i.e., be made a distinct "one" of the Trinity?

This does not mean the Logos is not God's Wisdom, only that Its cosmic dimension is more understandable when it comes to grasping Its Incarnation – making itself one with man's human nature. Irenaeus is the one who succinctly pointed up the difference between God's Wisdom and Logos. He said, where Wisdom is the essence of God *ad intra* (immanent in Itself), the Logos is God's Wisdom manifested and revealed *ad extra* in creation. Thus Wisdom and Logos are just two sides of the same divine coin.

It is also worth noting, John never began his Gospel with "In the beginning was the Son, and the Son was with the Father, and the Son was God." The *Logos*, of course, had no "Father" and was never "begotten". John must have known the Greeks would never accept such metaphoric personifications. While some may think God as a personal "Father and Son" had the advantage over the philosophers' impersonal "One" or "Logos", matters were just the opposite. "Father and Son" made God two human beings, which the philosophers would only have scoffed at.

Although there is no proof John or Paul read Philo's works, we know Greek philosophy was well known to the Jews outside Palestine. Scholars, at least, have no trouble pointing out the Stoic influence in John and Paul, both, after all, were part of this culture. As already noted, few people realize that quoting Paul is often like quoting a piece of Stoic philosophy. This is why Christianity as presented to the Roman Stoics, at least, entailed no great leap of faith – because it made sense to them. We could take this to mean that Christianity was presented to them more *philosophically* than *doctrinally.* More, that is, in keeping with *reason* than reliant on Judaism's *personified* scriptures.

While some think John (or someone) added the Logos prologue "after" his Gospel had been written, there is no evidence for this. When the Gospel *first* appeared (90 – 110 AD or so), this prologue was *there*, in place, and so it remains. That John himself wrote it, makes sense when we consider he wrote from Ephesus, the city celebrated as the birthplace of Heraclitus, the "elder of Greek philosophy" whose statue was still in town in John's time. It is equally interesting that St. Paul was born in Tarsus, a city renowned for another Stoic philosopher, Zeno (not the original Zeno however.) So not only among the Gentiles was the term "Logos" a matter of common knowledge, but even among the educated Jews of Jesus' time. While it is easy to call this mere coincidence, who can say this was *not* all in God's plan? When it comes to a right understanding of Christ, God left nothing to coincidence.

Justin Martyr (100 – 165) counted Heraclitus as a Christian before Christ, *"They who have lived in the company with Logos are Christians, even if they were accounted atheists. And such among the Greeks were Socrates and Heraclitus."* Justin taught that divine truth appears in two forms: first, in man's power of reasoning; and second, in special revelation, such as given to philosophers, prophets – indeed, to all men. It is a pompous notion God is only revealed to certain people and not to others. That God revealed Itself solely to Moses and his people, but not to the Greeks, the philosophers or anyone else in the world, is ridiculous and not historically true. That there is a *god* for some people and not for others, is the essence of polytheism.

Given the long history and understanding of "Logos", we can now ask how this term was ever erased from John's Gospel and the term "*word*" substituted in its stead? As best I could research, it is said the Romans or Latins "*found it impossible to translate "Logos" by any single word, and therefore adopted the phrase 'ratio et oration' (reason and speech)*", and thus, the term *verbum* or "word" (in English) was substituted for the original "Logos". John, of course, never said, "In the beginning was the *word*", for him, "Logos" was not a reference to any written or uttered word, nor did any of the early fathers have this understanding. Even Cyril of Alexandria said *"the Logos of the Father of the universe is not the uttered word, but the wisdom and most manifest kindness of God, and His power too."* The idea the Logos is some kind of utterance, speech or word, is too *absurd for words*.

It seems that in the absence of the Latins having the Greek understanding of "Logos", they gave it their own etymological definition of "*utterance, sound, expression or word"*, which it never meant to the Greeks. For the Greeks, etymologically it was akin to "reason" or "mind" (*logic* being a derivative.) That the Romans redefined Logos as "word", is the ultimate ***etymological fallacy*** **(use of words to mean something other than their intended usage.)** The Roman's substituting "*word*" for "*Logos*" has to be the greatest etymological fallacy of all time – the ultimate *Christian fallacy*.

For any sound or utterance to be a "word", it has to have a *meaning*. Thus to say "In the beginning was the word" – well, *what* word? To be told it is a reference to God "speaking" can only be a reference to some anthropomorphic deity or other – and who ever heard of a word becoming incarnate? No one who has ever seen or known God's Omnipresence in creation would ever, in a million years, think to call God a "word". The utter impoverishment of the term ("word") could only have been invented by those who, in truth, do *not* know God. Indeed, Christianity has totally missed the Logos, missed God; missed the one of the Trinity that became "incarnate" and, consequently, missed Christ.

It has been pointed out that "Word of God" was a common Jewish reference to their scriptures as the "Law of God". In time, of course, Christianity adopted this same phrase ("word of God") for its own scriptures which, in neither case, was ever understood as "Logos". Interestingly, the Stoics regarded the Logos as the "Law of the Universe" or "law of nature", a natural law, however, very different from Judaism's understanding of the "Law of God". The bible or scripture is certainly not a reference to the divine Logos nor a revelation of the Logos, and reading it, has never given this revelation to *anyone*! This is why one can read the bible and completely miss the Logos – the divine one of the Trinity that became Incarnate. How is it possible for Christians to believe the bible true when they haven't the remotest understanding of the divine Logos? A true understanding of Christ totally depends on the Logos – on the whole Trinity, in fact. The term "word" has literally come to refer to a book – a "paper god".[3]

Today, few Christians have ever heard the term "Logos". For them, reference to "the word of God" is reference to a book, a piece of writing *about* God or about the life of the historical Jesus. The term "word" has no connection to John's "Logos" or the divine Christ. John did not say "In the beginning was the word", nor is the Trinity, "Father-Word-Spirit". The illicit change of "Logos" to "word" robs Christians of the true meaning of both the Trinity and Christ. These terms (*Logos* and *word*) have entirely different meanings that give entirely different understandings of Christ. This is but one example of how crucial terms can be when it comes to conveying any truth in this world.

I have not been able to find any date when this biblical switch from Greek to Latin ("Logos" to "word") occurred, probably it was earlier than Jerome's translation. For sure, reading the early fathers cannot give us a clue because their works have long been translated into the Latin's "word" instead of "Logos". (Translators have also consistently changed the fathers' original use of "hypostasis" to "person" – which also never meant the same thing.) The fathers' whole understanding of Christ was based solely on the original "Logos"; no Christology could ever have been based on a meaningless term like "word". Terminology can be crucial, not only because it changes meaning and understanding, but changes an entire paradigm, even changes what is true into what is false or misleading. A number of Christian terms have proved misleading, and use of the term "word" is first among them.

Since John's *Logos* has been so mistranslated, who knows what else he might have said that also has been mistranslated? Pieces of the oldest Syriac translations, for example, are quite different from the oldest Latin translations. At any rate, it could be said that substituting the term "word" in John's Gospel for "Logos", set Christianity off in a totally different direction from the "Way" *Logos* points out. People who want to be "biblically correct" would never substitute the term "word" for "Logos" ***because*** it is *not "what the bible really said!"* We can only imagine the surprise of Christians if *Logos* was restored to John's original Gospel. Should they inquire into its use and meaning, however, perhaps the Truth of Christ could begin to emerge.

---

[3] People who only know of God by way of words – either read or spoken – do not know God at all. This is why those who *experientially* know God will never find God in any book, bible or scripture. No "mediated" experience can compare with God's *unmediated* revelation – the difference is between Truth and fiction.

It has been said, one reason the term "Logos" was eliminated from the Gospel was out of fear it would be understood in the Greek sense (as *Logos*) and not in the Hebrew sense (as *Wisdom*.) No question, there was prejudice against the ancient meaning of "Logos" by those who looked down their nose at Greek philosophy as "pagan". After all, Christianity was out to convert others, not to agree with them, much less use any of their non-biblical terms. Although the fathers certainly used some philosophical terms, yet they tried to use only scriptural terms as "proof text" for their various views of Christ. Christianity, however, sanctified many a Greek philosophical term and notion – hypostasis, deification, gnosis, contemplation, essence, nature, the list goes on – so why not Logos? And who is to tell us the Logos was no less a revelation to the Gentiles than Wisdom was to the Jews? Philo certainly had no problem with this. Another mistaken excuse was the fear its cosmic meaning might be understood in some pantheistic sense – a view St. John obviously did not share. In truth, no one could see God and be a pantheist, God so utterly transcends creation that to sustain such a vision, man could no longer live on earth – which is why God has to keep a distance from man. There are those, of course, who absolutely disdain any notion of God as the Logos because it ruins their view that Jesus (and not the Logos) is God. No question, the term and meaning of "Logos" would find no place in the Jesus-cult.

As it stands, however, no term carried more meaning in the Gentile world at the time of Christ than "Logos", its reference backed by 500 years as reference to the divine transcendent One. Most authors, it seems, regard St. John's prologue as the sole biblical reference to the Incarnation, and if St. John deemed "Logos" the proper term to explain the Incarnation – Christianity's central belief – then *who* dared to change it? "Logos" is the point where monotheism meets the philosophical world of Christ's own day, and who is to say this was a mere coincidence and not exactly as God planned it? For someone to erase "Logos" and substitute "word", was either an act of sheer stupidity or a deliberate act of hostility toward the Logos and everything it means.[4]

Since an understanding of the Trinity depends on what the "Logos" meant to John and the fathers, without it, the Trinity remains little more than a dogmatic "formula" – which it is for most Christians. When the Trinity is understood as a mere philosophical or rational ex-

---

[4] Once in a group, going over this switch in vocabulary, the only theologian present suddenly got up in a huff and left for home. This bears out Gregory of Nazianzus' saying (quoted earlier) that "*nothing is more conducive to division than disagreement on* ***using the same words*** *when we speak of Him.*" No question, "terminology" alone, can get people hot under the collar.

planation for Christ, it loses its tri-fold *experiential* reality and is not recognized as God's on-going revelation to every human being. Thus man's first encounter with God is God-in-nature, an uplifting experience of marvel, beauty and mystery, all of which is the concrete manifestation of the divine Logos. There are many types of such revelations, none of them remotely reminiscent of some transcendent "word", but all of them, validating the ancient meaning of "Logos". For this reason, substituting "word", amounts to a denial of the divine Logos' revelation to mankind, virtually, a denial of God's *Triune* Existence.

Based on the term "word", the Romans would never be able to comprehend Paul and Irenaeus' view of the Incarnation as the *recapitulation* or summing up of all creation in Christ. With the loss of "Logos", the whole transcendent understanding of Christ is gone. In its stead we have terms like *Son*, *Person*, *Word*, that people mistakenly think refer to the man Jesus, whereas, prior to the Incarnation, there was neither Jesus nor Christ. It was solely the Logos that became Incarnate and solely the Incarnate Logos that was understood as the divinity of Christ. No definition of "word" could assume human nature, only the "Logos" has this necessary affinity with creation. Since the keystone of Christianity is the Incarnation, without an understanding of "Logos", there can never be a true understanding of Christ – never!

Having briefly gone over the Gentiles' philosophical contribution to Christianity's understanding of God and Christ, we must now to go over Judaic Monotheism, equally the premise of Christianity. Since the Incarnation occurred at the crossroads of Judaic Monotheism and Greek philosophy, to eliminate either one is to eliminate Christ and Christianity.

MONOTHEISM

Nothing is more important than starting out with a right understanding of the term "God", better provided, perhaps, by man's philosophies than his religions. Thus God is the Platonic "*One*", the "*Good*"; Parmenides' "***that which is*** *" or "the one real Being*"; Stoicism's "Logos", *"Source", "Immutable and Impassible*"; Aristotle's "*Uncaused Cause*" and "*Unmoved Mover*". These were some of the philosophical expressions to distinguish the Transcendent from the multiple and the mutable, a "One" never regarded as a "numerical one", an "individual thing" or "*a* being" among other beings, but rather, *Being* or *Existence Itself*.

The advantage of using philosophical, rather than religious, terms to define "God", is that they not only avoid all anthropomorphic images, but undercut the particular names and titles various religions use to refer to the "*One Absolute*" or "*Ultimate Truth*". As it is, the origin of the term "*god*" is basically polytheistic, and we want to avoid any such understanding of the term.

As already noted, Judaic *mono-theism* (*one-god*) developed out of a polytheistic belief system where the Jews regarded the "god" revealed to them as their own *particular* god. While other tribes and nations had their gods, Judaism had its own personal god – the god of Abraham, Isaac and Jacob. Jewish scholars have used the term "*henotheism*" to define the ancient Jewish belief in God. *Henotheism* (one-god) is the belief that *one particular god* is supreme over all the other gods. So while it could be said Judaism only worshipped "one god", it did not deny the existence of other or lesser gods. It took some time, however, before the Jews recognized their god as the One-and-Only. Prior to this recognition, the original meaning of *mono-theism* as "one god" designated a *numerical* "one-among-many" – i.e., a "particular" god set apart from other gods.

Given its polytheistic background, helps to explain the Old Testament's *anthropomorphic* portrayal of "god". Thus the "god of Israel" is a patriarchal "He", personified as a powerful invisible being, walking, talking, warning, punishing, blessing, angry, and so on. This was not just a matter of an occasional use of metaphor or allegory, but the provocative image of an anthropomorphic being. Although the Christian fathers, given their philosophical background were aware of scripture "*imposing human attributes on God*", yet, to remain faithful to *scripture,* they perpetuated much the same image, stuck to the same language, even treated as literal, metaphors of God as a father who "begets" a God – a son, that is. Thus, because Jesus, when expressing his personal relationship with God referred to God as a "Father", Christianity derived the anthropomorphic notion of the Trinity as two males – Father and Son. This, at least, is how Christianity inherited the Old Testament's anthropomorphic view of God as one absolute "Patriarch" – a view carried over into Christianity's *Monarchical view of "God-the -Father"* – one of the Trinity.

It might be said it was only when the Jews were "Hellenized" that, like the philosophers, they came to regard all anthropomorphic views of God as "pagan". Thus Judaism eventually came to understand the "God" revealed to Moses as the sole Transcendent "un-namable One". For Jews living and educated outside Palestine, then, the "God of Israel" was not only Transcendent to all other gods, but came to be identified as the philosophical One Transcendent of the Greek philosophers. But if the term "monotheism" sets it off from "polytheism", *mono* can never be understood as a *numerical* ***one*** such as "**one**" being or "**one**" individual. To think of God this way is to think of *a* god, *a* particular being. There is no revelation of God, however, as a numerical "**one**" – God can never be *circumscribed* as an "individual" – thus, God is not ***a*** being, but *Infinite Being*. So "monotheism", then, must be understood in its philosophical sense, and *not* in its original etymological sense as "one god" among or above other gods, nor even understood as "**one *individual***".

Perhaps what most sets off "monotheism" from other world religions is that being "Infinite Existence" having neither beginning nor end, God is *Uncreated* – the sole *Uncreated* Existence "*that is*". Since everything man knows has a beginning and end, it has only *created* existence. Thus no man brought himself into existence – in fact, no one even asked to exist. So the *Cause* of all man knows to exist is beyond man and all he knows to exist. This is why, if "something" exists beyond all man knows to exists, this can only be "revealed" to him. While he can theorize or rationalize to some ultimate Cause or Source, he has no verification or certitude of this, much less knows anything *about* this Cause. This is why "monotheism" holds that the Uncreated Cause can only be *revealed* to man and claims its religions are based on *revelation* – and not on philosophical speculation.

It goes without saying, authentic "revelation" has nothing to do with people's "paranormal experiences" – visions, voices, or any type of mental phenomena – erroneously labeled "revelation". The revelation of God is just the opposite. Not only is it *void* of any image or type of "mental phenomena", but it is not of the mind or intellect at all. Indeed, the revelation of God not only stops the mind, but blinds it to all else. (Elsewhere I've gone over the characteristics of authentic "revelation" and will not go into it here.)

Today, the term "monotheism", as used to define the religions of Judaism, Christianity and Islam, all share the understanding of God being "revealed" to man, and that as Uncreated, God is the Creator (Source or Cause) of all that exists. Though all three believe in God's revelation to Moses on Sinai, yet God has innumerable ways of revealing Itself to man, there is no *one staid* revelation of God.

Thus Judaism holds that with the creation of man ("*adam*" in Hebrew, "*mankind*"), man knew God. And indeed, every human being knows God, yet, as Heraclitus put it – *man knows **It**, but doesn't know he knows **It**.* Thus *"he is unconscious of it, unable to understand his own experience of It"*. In other words, God lets no man get away with the excuse "*Oh, if only I had known!*" Not only does every man know God, but everything created knows its Maker, for being "present" in all things, *God Knows.*[1]

But how is it man does not know he knows God? For one thing, he doesn't recognize "It" because intellectually, at least, he doesn't really know *what* to look for. For sure, God is no match for man's *ideas* and *concepts,* nor a match for what he has *heard* and *read about* God, much less, what other people *say* about God. Thus none of his images, even his beliefs, line up with anything man could even *think of* as "God". It is even fair to say, anything that matches up with man's *ideas* of God is *not* God.[2] It is only if man can get beyond his various beliefs he could then "see" God as all that's left when everything else is gone. So one way to understand "revelation" is that it is the recognition of *a Truth one already knows,* a Truth, however, that had to break through all man's concepts and erroneous views in order to *be known.* This is exactly why God has to be *"revealed"* or *breakthrough* all man's mental beliefs *about* God. Just the fact God *can* reveal Itself to man, however, tells us there is something in man receptive and capable of knowing God, of knowing Truth, and were this not so, no revelation of God would be possible. As to what "*that*" is in man that can know God, basically it is God Itself, a "knowing" that Heraclitus called the

---

1 By definition, an "*a-theist*" is one who objects to people's "ideas and definitions of *God*". No question, monotheism generally presents God as if God was some kind of invisible, judgmental Superman.

2 Once, at Mass, Fr. Charlie told us this story. In the middle of the night a young man banged on his door saying, "I don't believe in God anymore, God doesn't exist. I once believed, but I cannot believe anymore!" Fr. said to him, "Well, I don't believe in God either" – the boy was shocked. "But you're a *Priest*, how can you say such a thing?" Fr. replied, "***Well, I don't believe in the God you don't believe in***". This is a stumper everyone should ponder. (As a kid I was convinced everyone in Church had a different idea of God, was praying to a different God – and yet, God didn't give a fig.)

"Logos" (or *logoi*), literally, God's omnipresent "Knowing" in all things.

Perhaps nothing so defines Monotheism as its understanding of God as *Creator*, the sole Source of everything that exists – *everything **but** Itself.* Any notion the Uncreated could "create" Itself is not only a contradiction of terms, but results in *infinite regress* – the denial of an *Uncreated Source* of all that exists. As **Uncreated Existence**, God is the sole Existent that Exists of Itself. Nothing created has any existence of its own, but is totally dependent on God's existence for its existence.

The simplest way to illustrate Monotheism is to draw a horizontal line across a blank piece of paper, on top of the line write "Uncreated", and under the line, write "created", this is basic monotheism. **By definition, the Uncreated is "that" which cannot create Itself, thus, everything It creates is *not* Itself.** So the line between the two is the *Great Divide* between the Uncreated and the created. There is no crossing over either way, nor any admixture of the two dimensions, the Uncreated can never *be* or *become* the created, nor can the created ever *be* or *become* the Uncreated. This is "Monotheism", the fundamental belief of man's three major religions, Judaism, Christianity and Islam. This division – between the created and Uncreated – is the same *monotheistic* understanding adhered to by all the fathers and handed down in Christianity.

The *Great Divide,* then, is the line on which all man's mythologies, pantheistic philosophies, monism, and other beliefs *collapse*, collapse because there is no passing over the line or any admixture of the two sides. Do away with the line, and you have Monism, the belief that the Absolute is *everything* that exists. Thus Parmenides (6th century BC) held there was only one real Being, and that all particularity of individual things were "mere appearances and illusion". There are different brands of Monism – thus Plotinus' "One" was not a Creator but an Emanator whose emanations ("aeons", I think he calls them) keep getting less and less divine as they go out and away from the One – the last and least aeon being *matter*. Plotinus' goal, of course, was to go back up this ladder and disappear into the One – with no certitude, of course, that he might not just *emanate* out again! There is also pantheistic monism, matter itself is Absolute, all things being Its manifestations – no gradations of reality as in Plotinus. These are but a few examples of how things go when the Great Divide is removed. Obviously this removal makes a huge difference in one's understanding, not only of God and the universe, but man's understanding of himself and his own "finite" existence."

It should not be thought, however, the Great Divide "locks in" the Uncreated or that It cannot reveal Itself to the created. Being Infinite Existence, the Uncreated is not subject to space and time, has no parameters, no inside, outside, above or below, cannot be circumscribed or pointed to, thus God is neither near nor far. At the same time, however, It permeates creation, is everywhere, closer to man than man is to himself, and all this, without being any part of the created dimension. In truth, God transcends all man's notions of space and time – this whole created world.

Given that *true existence* is none other than *God's Existence*, we can understand the saying *"God is closer to us than we are to ourselves".* To see how this works, fold the paper on the line (on the *Great Divide*) and you will see how the created and Uncreated exist together, only on two totally **different *levels or dimensions of existence***. Because of the transparency of the Uncreated, it is possible to see how the created can exist *in* the Uncreated and how the Uncreated exists *throughout* the created while being *transcendent* to it. Not only can the Uncreated be glimpsed *through* the created, but the Uncreated can break though the created dimension to reveal Itself. Without this revelation or *breakthrough,* man could not know the Uncreated existed. This is why the monotheistic religions rely totally on this revelation for their Truth and not on any philosophical theory, mere belief, doctrines, books, or someone's theology. Indeed, it is because Truth is *unbelievable* man needs *Faith – that "truth-sensor"* in man – which is beyond all belief.

The idea all things came into existence from nothing *(creatio ex nihilo)* can only be the idea of an atheist.[3] **Existence, however, cannot come from non-existence.** To say existence comes from nothing makes "nothing" an *absolute* and postulates the existence of two absolutes – Existence and Non-Existence. (Thus, if God needed "nothing" to create, then without *nothing* God could not create.) In truth, however, nothing created has any existence *of its own,* only God has or is Existence. Thus, for the created to *exist*, its *true* existence can only *be* God – for what "other" Existence is there? This does not make anything created the Uncreated – impossible – it only means the created *depends* on God's existence for its existence. So while man *has* existence, he is *not* Existence Itself. So too, the soul *has* life but is *not* Life Itself. The soul can only "participate" in Life – as Aristotle affirms, "*that which* **participates** *in anything is distinct from That which is par-*

[3] *Creation ex nihilo* is what I call the "Magic Wand Theory" – god said "Let this be – or hocus pocus" – and there it was! This is the stuff of fairytales. God waves no wand, instead, God ***works*** it all!

ticipated in". And as Dionysius says, "*Everything participates in His Being, for the Divinity Which is beyond being is the being of all things*". And for Gregory of Nazianzus, "*For this* [God's] *divinity is the essence and subsistence of all things*". The soul, then, "participates" in Life – for as long as God wills.

From the atom, then, up the ladder of creation, everything has God for its true existence, otherwise it could not exist. It is because the ***Cause is in the effect*** that everything created is *existentially one* with God, a oneness sometimes called an "essential union" or "natural union", without which, nothing could exist. This is not an ***eternal*** *union,* however. Since nothing created has any eternal life *of its own,* should eternal life be granted to anything created, this can only be God sharing Its eternal existence with the non-eternal. **There is no other way anything could possibly be *eternal,* unless it were *united* to God's eternal existence – i.e., the created *participating* in God's own existence.**

Just as a babe in the womb gets its life from its mother yet is *not* the mother, so too, man lives on "borrowed" existence from God. There is nothing in a natural or *existential* union with God that necessitates or guarantees any form of "eternal" life, indeed, God can cut the cord at any time. But if there is to be any *eternal* life for the created, this can only be *God's own eternal life* in which man "participates" for all eternity.

Even though we can regard man's borrowed existence as his *existential oneness with God* – ***"existential"*** **meaning** ***"by reason of existence"*** – there is nothing about this existential union that is intrinsically eternal. Even if the Great Divide disappeared and the created gone forever, the Uncreated would go right on without missing a beat. Though we like to think more kindly of God, the truth is, God does not need creation at all. And something else to remember, only God is "perfect", and since God is "that" which cannot create Itself, then nothing God creates is perfect – simply because it is *not* God. By definition, then, creation is limited, impermanent, changeable and imperfect. If God could create anything ***perfect,*** **God would be creating Itself** – impossible. So for those who wonder why this world is so imperfect, they need only remember this world is *not* God, and that only God is perfect. Because man's soul is created and has no *eternal* existence or immortality of itself, then how could God grant it immortality? Although nothing created can pass over the *Great Divide* to *become* Uncreated, yet the soul, by becoming *eternally one with* the Uncreated can, in fact, *participate* in God's own Eternal Life. **There is no other way anything could ever be "immortal" or have eternal life without its *par-***

***ticipating* in God's own eternal life – after all, what other *eternal life* is there?** To think there is eternal life outside or apart from God's Eternal Life, is pure myth. It is only by God uniting man *eternally* to Itself man can ever have eternal life. There is no other way possible.

Centuries before Christ, God had established a long history with His Jewish people. They not only believed in an immortal soul, but in eternal life – a "world to come". They believed God forgave their sins and saved them, God was their "Savior" – as it says in the Psalms. They believed God's Spirit was present in the world, the same Spirit Who descended on good people, bestowed special graces, and anointed prophets with a mission on God's behalf. The Jews baptized their converts and believed in a bodily resurrection. Given these established beliefs, it is naive to think these were ever unique to Christianity! Sometimes the impression is given that Christianity has a monopoly on forgiveness, salvation, savior, eternal life, God's Spirit, grace, and so on, when, in fact, Christianity **took all this straight from Judaism! The revelation of "Christ" had nothing to do with any of this and changed none of it.**

It is because Judaic monotheism was the singular belief of Jesus and his apostles that these same beliefs became part and parcel of Christianity. Thus Paul's dual task was to present his Jewish monotheism and Christ at the same time. But instead of Yahweh as the Savior who forgave and saved, for the Gentiles, it became Christ – God's "anointed" *(christos)* – who forgave and saved. Thus one would be baptized *in* Christ and rise *with* Christ, in short, Paul simply transposed Judaism to Christianity. It seems Paul's view was that Christ was not just the promised Messiah sent to save Israel from its enemies, but sent to save *everyone* else as well!

For Paul, of course, Jesus was the pre-existent Messiah now "*made visible*". He was the "*first born*" – the first being God *created.* In time this "first born" of God would be sent to save Israel and establish a kingdom on earth, a kingdom where there would be peace for a thousand years followed by some cataclysmic event that would bring it all to an end. Not only did the Apostles believe Jesus was the promised Messiah, but according to some authors, Jesus believed this himself. Certainly the Gospels were written with this belief in mind for they iterated all the biblical events and sayings to show how Jesus had fulfilled the prophecies of the Messiah.

Paul's task, then, was to present Judaism in the light of a Messiah, a savior sent by God. Paul was perfectly aware he was introducing something new to the Gentiles, and if we asked where he got his dogged energy and certitude, we need only recount his conversion experience. As Paul tells us he never saw the man Jesus "*in the flesh*", what he saw was the heavenly *resurrected* Christ in a blaze of *light*.[4] After this, he went off to spend some three years in solitude, unknown and unheard of. With his return, however, begins the first Christian writings.

Though Paul's understanding and presentation of Christ was in the light of his Judaic framework – its tradition and scripture – there is no denying that his more mystical or *experiential understanding* of Christ was more understandable in light of the Gentiles' religious-philosophical framework. Keep in mind, the reason Jesus was put to death was for affirming *his oneness with God* and that Paul knew Judaism was not prepared to accept this truth – the truth of Christ. His synthesizing the two – Judaism and the Gentiles' religious framework – would create a certain dichotomy within Christianity itself, a dichotomy that would become part and parcel of its heritage. Thus we will always find in Christianity different perspectives on Christ: 1) the more *a priori* Judaic side with all its concerns with sin, sacrifice, redemption, salvation and so on, and 2) the more *a posteriori* side that goes beyond this to address the Gentiles' quest of "oneness with God". These and other trends are a result of Christianity's being at the *crossroad* of Judaic monotheism and the Gentiles' philosophical heritage.

Paul's synthesis of these two is quite evident to those who know both sides of the equation, a synthesis, however, that would never be wholly acceptable to one and all. Thus, the question is just how far can either side be stretched before they clash or contradict? One reason to emphasize Christianity's dual inheritance is to point out the extent to which it has been all but overwhelmed by its Judaic side – i.e., its view of sin, atonement, sacrifice and salvation – at the cost of de-emphasizing the more transcendent, transformative elements of its Gentile heritage. This is why the early fathers, in touch with this Gentile element, are of more value than all who came after. Those who came after would solely promote a Christ burdened with man's sins – the man Jesus specially created to be sacrificed (killed) to atone for the sins of man. For many Christians, this was the whole purpose of Jesus' life. Such a view, however, only meets the criteria of a crossover between monotheism and *myth*.

Although the Jews may have believed the Messiah pre-existed his coming into this world, this did not make him divine or God – the very

---

[4] Failure to understand that Paul's knowledge of Christ never relied on Jesus "in the flesh" is a failure to grasp the *real Christ*. While it is all very well to *relate* man *in the flesh* to Christ, yet no one "seen in the flesh" **is** the Eternal Christ. (There is nothing about "flesh" or "matter" as man knows it, at least, that is eternal.)

idea never crossed their monotheistic minds. Neither the Apostles or Paul believed Jesus was the "Transcendent One" or Yahweh – Whose name they were not even permitted to utter. So how did this "anointed" man, Jesus, ever come to be regarded as God? Since only God works miracles, how could this have ever been *proof* that a human being is God? (Then too, even though God raised the dead and cured the sick, in the end, they all died anyway!) The only miracle that counts is *Faith* – which is what Jesus actually stressed – Faith being the sole *purpose* of a miracle anyway.

The reason the Jews did not regard Jesus as the Messiah, however, had nothing to do with the question of his being divine or human. Rather, in their eyes, he did not fulfill their prophecies, did not save Israel from its enemies or establish any kingdom on earth. And as for bringing peace, well, who is not waiting for that to happen? As for Jesus fulfilling all their prophecies, let us just say the Jews had their *own interpretation of their own scriptures*. As said before, anything one wants to believe can always be found somewhere in scripture – which "proves" nothing other than what is in the mind of its interpreter.

So despite all the scriptural "proofs" that Christians have presented down the ages for the divinity of Christ, the one outstanding feature and *non-Biblical* mystery about the man Jesus was his repeated affirmations he was *one-with-God.* Though he called God "Father", he never claimed he was the "Father" – was God. What he claimed was that he was one with *his* Father, and given his miraculous conception, he did not object to being called his Father's "son" – God's "son". To the Jewish mind, however, the claim to be one with God was blasphemous, it fit *no Biblical* image or understanding. No one had claimed this before, and it was not their view of the Messiah. This claim was something totally new – and heretical. No question, Jesus' claim fell outside Judaic monotheism, yet this was the one *new thing* the Incarnation was to reveal to mankind – namely, *"Christ" being man's eternal oneness with God.* Indeed, **this is the sole *Good News* of Christ.**

Jesus could walk away from all other accusations but the Truth of his oneness with God. What his death was about was *not* saving man from sin, but **saving the Truth for man** – the *Truth of man's eternal oneness with God!* So, if asked how Jewish monotheism *differs* from Christian monotheism, we must go back to the *Great Divide* between the created and Uncreated. **In Christianity, the Judaic Line that *Divides, is* the revelation of Christ as the Line that *Unites*. If we put our finger on this Line we put our finger on *Christ*, because this Line is the *whole Mystery of Christ*.** That this Line both *divides and unites is a contradiction of opposites* and one not easy to reconcile.

Yet, this Line is the mysterious oneness of two disparate natures – divine and human – and the *mystery* of this "oneness" is everything God revealed as "*Christ*".

Christianity was literally founded on a contradiction. As Paul put it, Christ was a "contradiction" to the Gentiles (the oneness of opposites) and a "stumbling-block" to the Jews – who regarded oneness with God incompatible with monotheism. Yet, if we cannot first grasp the true nature of monotheism, we can never hope to grasp the tremendous mystery of Christ. In all their deliberations, the fathers strictly adhered to this monotheistic "line". As to how this line could *divide* and at the same time *unite*, this was the mystery confronting Christianity from the beginning. This was the *mystery* of Christ that totally absorbed the fathers.

It could be said, then, the sole difference between Jewish and Christian Monotheism is their different understanding of the *Great Divide*. Though Christianity was just as concerned as Judaism to preserve this division, Christianity was also concerned with the union of the two sides – the created and Uncreated. Along with Judaism, it held there was never any crossing over or admixture of the two sides – one side ever *becoming* the other, and vice versa. Although one of the fathers thought of Christ as the "bridge" between the two, this did not fit the reality of this *oneness*. A bridge, after all, implies a "crossing over", which is not, however, the way this *oneness* works. At any rate, we could say the development of Christology was centered on the attempt to explain this union of opposites – the *mystery of Christ.*

The reason this issue was uppermost, was because of its meaning for *all* mankind and not for just one individual – the man Jesus. Yet, despite the centuries of contention, there was not a single father who did not ultimately declare that the true nature of this *oneness* (of God and man) was not only the mystery of "Christ", but the mystery of *everyman's* eternal oneness with God.

Although the fathers and theologians down the ages have done their utmost to give this mystery of Christ a coherent intellectual understanding, they never succeeded and never will. With few exceptions, most seem to focus exclusively on the monotheistic "Line" as the *Great Unifier* rather than the *Great Divider,* the outcome being Jesus *falsely* regarded as totally divine.

With no dividing line, however, we not only have the heresy of "*Monophysitism*" (*Christ as "one-divine-nature"*), but we have *anthropolatry – worship* of the created mistaken for the Uncreated. Obviously a "fine line" exists between monotheism and polytheism. A fine line, it seems, Christianity has had a hard time walking.

When considering Christ, the reason we must always start at ground zero with basic monotheism, is because without this founding premise there can never be any true understanding of Christ or Christianity. What Christianity was to present to the world was *not* simply Jewish monotheism, but a *Christian* monotheism where "*the line that divides is equally the line that unites*". To explain how this works was the task of the earliest Christians – the fathers. One father put it this way, "*Being perfect God and now perfect man, brings about the greatest of all possible novelties, the only thing new under the sun*". Indeed, for Jew and Gentile alike, the revelation of "Christ" was absolutely *new, different, never heard of before.*

The reason the Incarnation took place within Judaism's established monotheistic revelation is because this is how God wanted Christ to be understood – understood against this particular monotheistic background with its Great Divide, and not against the background of any other belief system, philosophy or religion. The Incarnation was a deliberate revelation given to those who already knew the Uncreated – knew Yahweh or God, and all this meant. This revelation (Incarnation) was not a contradiction to Judaism, but a further extension of it. Only Judaic monotheism provides the necessary foundation for this further revelation of God in that it *expands* its monotheistic Truth to include *all mankind* – Christ *being* its *inclusive* revelation. This is why any attempt to understand Christ *outside monotheism* not only misses Christ, but can so skew this Truth as to be unrecognizable. For an understanding of Christ, then, one must begin with Judaic monotheism.

Given the fact all Christian beliefs were taken from Judaism, we might ask what, exactly, did Christianity add that Judaism did not believe already? Since Christianity did not add the revelation of God, the assurance of salvation, forgiveness of sin, God's presence in the world, grace, baptism, resurrection and eternal life, then what did the revelation of Christ add to all of this? As far as these truths are concerned, it added nothing. As to what Christianity did add, no one could have answered this more succinctly than St. Irenaeus (125 – 202 AD), "*The purpose of the Incarnation was* ***man's*** *deification*" – "deification" (*theosis* in Greek) meaning that man, as we know him *now*, must be transformed into what he is *not* now. Thus the motto of all the fathers: "*salvation is transformation*" – transformation into Christ that is.

Salvation, then, did not consist merely in believing, of being forgiven or doing this or that, but rather, in being *deified.* All the fathers subscribed to this understanding – their key reference being the saying, "*God became man that man might become God*" – *become Christ, that is.* As we will go over later, the term "*deification*" ("to become god") was never used in the monotheistic sense of *becoming* Almighty God, rather, it meant "becoming Christ". This is why the Incarnation was *not* the revelation of God, but the revelation of ***man***, of what *man* means to God, of *man's* "way" to God, and *man's* destiny of eternal *oneness* with and in God.

The reason this was to be a "further" revelation of Judaism is because of all man's religions, none had a greater value for *man*, for *being human,* than Judaism, which marvels at God's investment in man and God always *being there* for him. No question, Judaism best exemplified God's love for man – and even, man's love for God. That God wanted His people to know they would be eternally one with Him, is really all the revelation of Christ was about.

Just as Jesus' human nature was ultimately deified (transfigured, glorified) in its oneness with God, so too is that of every human being. One father (Maximus the Confessor) wondered why this truth, "*salvation as deification or transformation*", was never made a dogma of the Church, and indeed, had it done so, we'd have a different Church today, and a whole different understanding of Christ. This would have spared many a wrong notion of "salvation" and, consequently, wrong views of Christ. It is one thing to believe, as did Judaism, that God saves man, but quite another to know *how* this works, know it entails a radical transformation of man's essential nature. Man is not saved by faith alone, nor even faith and good works, but solely by *transformation* into Christ. This transformation has nothing in common with the naive notion of salvation as a sudden *fait accompli* or crying "Lord, Lord!" As Jesus said, this will get you no place. The purpose of the Incarnation was to reveal what man is to *become,* to know the way this works as the nature of man's eternal oneness with God – no different from Christ. Those who regard this as pure mysticism (*experiential*, that is) have it right, the very core of Christianity is mystical – the most mystical of all God's religions, in fact. Basically, there is no such thing as "*Christian mysticism*" because Christianity – transformation *into Christ* – is **the essence of mysticism.**

To understand the *why* of transformation, it is important to understand man is not created a static being. His creation is *not* a once-and-for-all act of God – **kerplunk**, here we are, stuck forever as we are *now* with no way out or up. On the contrary, **God's *dynamic act of creation* is not over until it is over, and it is not *over* until God's creative act has arrived at the destiny for which God created man in the first place**. Thus man is ever in movement toward his intended destiny, moving in circular fashion, as it were, back to the Creator or Source from whence he came, only now, *forever* what he *never* was at the beginning. Where he came from God *unknowing* he returns to God "*knowing*", it is all a process of transformation. At death, this process goes even further to resurrection and ascension, ending in an eternal oneness with God – "*Christ*". Thus we can understand the saying "*We don't know what we are now, but we know* **what** *we shall be – like him (Christ), that is*".

As to why Judaism, with its highly personified view of God – epitomized in its scriptures at least – rejected Christ, who never claimed to *be* God, but only to be *one with God,* it has been said that Christ was rejected not only on the grounds of the utter disparity of natures (divine and human), but on the grounds that such a "union" would undermine the *Absolute Transcendence* of God. In other words, there is no way the unutterable glory of God could ever have any *essential* union with man – impossible. In fact, it is *because* God is *so utterly Transcendent* to creation that God **created** his Spirit and/or Wisdom to be "*His medium*" in the world. Thus any view that God was in any way involved in the created would negate God's utter transcendence. (But that God needs "mediums" to create the world or to be *in* the world, speaks more of God's impotence than God's omnipotence.)

Once a Jewish Professor of Religion was asked why Judaism objected to the idea of God being *united* to man, since this union neither made man God nor made God, man. His reply, "*Judaism regards this as chutzpah!*" – Paul's same view that "*To the Gentiles, Christ is foolishness*" – *chutzpah!* Although no one can explain *how* God creates man, even though man believes it anyway, on what basis can he deny God could ever be *one* with man? Such a denial speaks less of God's "Transcendence" than of God's "limitations" – something God **could not possibly do.** But who can tell us what God *could never* do? Fortunately, Christians believe that with God all things are possible, and thus they stake their lives on God's *Chutzpah.*

But putting aside Judaism's anthropomorphic allusions to God, we can find in Judaism an exquisitely true understanding of God:

Shekhinah = the Glory of God, utterly Transcendent.
Wisdom = the All Knowing, Creative, Omniscience of God.
Spirit = the Pervasive Presence and Power of God.

So regardless of man's different *interpretations*, Israel indeed knows the One True God, the same God Christians know as "Trinity" – God's *triune modus operandi.*

Two Dimensions of Existence – Uncreated and Created

As noted earlier – when folding the paper of *existence* in half – there exists a Divide between the Uncreated and created, between two totally different *dimensions of existence.* To *maintain* this divide there exists a **tension** between the two, without which the created could not stay in existence – or exist at all. We might compare this **tension** to a magnetic attraction – God being the Magnet, creation being a vulnerable metal. So long as the Magnet maintains a distance, it can *cause* the metal to move, but should the Magnet get too close, the metal will leap up and snap on to the Magnet. This Magnet is the *cause* of the created being in a state of movement, flux and impermanence which, at some point, will be "snapped up" by the Magnet. Maintaining this *tension* (between created and Uncreated) is part and parcel of God's *modus operandi, a tension* that explains why God must maintain a distance from the created **in order for the created to exist!** Without this *tension*, the created could not exist at all.

Some people wonder why God "seems" so distant, yet it is this "distance" that makes it possible for man to exist – indeed, God's *first will for man* is that he exist. So this ***tension*** explains the *magnetic attraction* in every human being that draws him beyond himself, draws him *up* or *out* – call it an unexplainable *urge* or *desire.* And *what* is this *mystery* that draws him beyond himself? Somehow man knows that if he could ever reach it, be snapped up to It, he would be utterly and completely fulfilled, all his mysterious longings for *something he didn't know "what"*, would be forever satisfied.

Thus man's greatest longing is to be snapped up to the *Magnet* ever drawing him to *become one with It.* And the fulfillment of this eternal oneness with God is everything God revealed as "*Christ*".

THE MAN JESUS

Christians may never be able to understand Jesus as a man of his own day and age. To do this, they would have to take off the glasses through which they have seen Jesus for some 2000 years. These are glasses colored by centuries of Christian beliefs, doctrines and creeds, yet none of it actually true to the Judaic mind-set in which Jesus was born, lived and died. His mind-set was solely in accord with the religious beliefs and cultural setting of his Judaic surroundings, not in accord with Christianity's beliefs, cultural milieu and mind-set. Jesus has literally been buried under centuries of Christians' imposing on him their own views, ideas and beliefs. Because of this, it is worth the time to try to understand where this man was at in his own day, and not where we, today, think he was at. To best understand Jesus, a fervent Jewish monotheist, we would have to put on the Judaic mind-set of his day and leave aside the centuries of Christian overlay.

Jesus, of course, was not a Christian, knew nothing about Christianity. He never read the New Testament, didn't know a piece of Christian doctrine or theology, probably knew no Greek philosophy and never heard the terms "*Logos*", "*christos*" (Greek for the Hebrew "anointed") or "*Trinity*". For sure, he could not have told us what a "Hypostatic Union" was, and had he known the term "*person*" (only coined after his day) he might have been surprised to learn he was not (doctrinally speaking) a human person! [1]

Since Jesus neither knew Christ, nor understood himself in the light of later Christianity, his focus was never on some *other* individual person or human being, **much less on himself**. Jesus' focus was solely on God, who he sometimes referred to as "Father". So if people are to regard the man Jesus as a model for their *own* lives, like Jesus, they too would focus solely on God and *not* on any human being – and certainly never on themselves. That Jesus and his apostles were born into the Judaic belief system means that Jesus never saw himself as *Yahweh* or Almighty God, nor did his Apostles – or their successors – regard the man Jesus as God. There is nothing to indicate he ever thought he was God, on the contrary, he said many things affirming he was *not* God. It is incomprehensible anyone could think God talked, walked, slept, was tempted, etc. That he was an *instrument* of God, however, one with God from the moment of his conception and privy to knowledge only he could know, of this, there is no question. He was truly a one-of-a-kind *person,* and totally human.

---

[1] According to the Orthodox formula, Jesus was not a human person, he did not own *himself*, but was owned by God – was "God's slave".

About all we know of the religious mind-set of Jesus' immediate environment comes from himself and what his disciples wrote about him. Although no Jew could conceive of any human being as God, yet Judaism never denied man can have an intimate, personal relationship with God, even becoming God's instrument in the world, someone "anointed", such as the great prophets. Because of this intimacy, God was sometimes referred to familiarly as "Abba" or "Father" – all men being the children of God, more especially, God as the "Father of Israel". This use of "Father", however, was purely metaphoric, it never implied God actually "begot" human children – such an idea would never have crossed the Jewish mind. So although Jesus, in his more intimate settings, referred to God as "Father", he otherwise used the term "God" and repeatedly referred to himself as "son of man". The several references to him as "son of God", however, were true in that he had *no human, biological father.* In this sense, then, God was literally Jesus' biological father – supplying the Y chromosome for Mary's X. Thus he was truly the "*human* son of God". (In those days it was believed a child's lineage was *solely* from the father, the female *ovum* necessary for conception was only discovered in the 19th century.) God, of course, creates *every human soul* while parental genes only govern the physical body.

Dedicated to his Jewish scriptures and practices, Jesus' perspective and responses to the issues that came up in his life were governed by Judaism. It is because most everything he said and taught was taken from his scriptures, we have his Judaic notion of atonement for sin, sacrificial offerings, the idea of hell (*sheol*), baptism, resurrection, and much more, all of it perfectly understood by his contemporaries. Obviously, he understood his mission was to Israel alone, even referring to people who did not share his faith as "dogs". Although in sympathy with others not of his faith, his miracles were all performed that they might have faith – his own Judaic Faith, that is. That he had anything to do with God's Plan to save *all* mankind, seems never to have crossed his mind. Indeed, had the first Christians adopted Jesus' own views, Christianity would have remained part and parcel of Judaism. As said, without the Gentile influence, there would be no Christianity to speak of. Obviously, all that God intended to reveal through the Incarnation was even beyond the man Jesus.

It has been said Jesus regarded himself as the promised messiah, a view the Gospels support by making sure to cover those events in his life that accord with this prophecy. Jesus' understanding of the messiah was taken solely from his scriptures, he quotes them to his apostles and bases his fore-knowledge of events on them. Given this conviction, his goal was to *fulfill* these prophecies – to **become** the messiah.

In places he speaks of the "*anointed*" ("*christos*" in Greek) as one whose shoes *he must fill.* Thus we could say his goal was to *become* the "anointed one", and that his life was a process of ***becoming*** the one he thought God intended him to be – Judaism's messiah. God, however, obviously had other plans because Jesus would never fit the Judaic mold of the messiah. Just the knowledge and experience of his undeniable oneness with God – a truth for which he was put to death – fell outside Judaism; **this was *not* its belief**. That any human being could be "*one" with Yahweh* was blasphemous and heretical. This was not Judaism's understanding of the messiah. The lesson here, is that *God's "mission" for a man's life is one he'll never know, because God alone can carry it out and make it happen.* What man *thinks* is his mission, and all his striving to make it happen, will only come to naught.

Obviously God never intended this Judaic role for Jesus. As it turns out, the revelation of "Christ" was more than Jesus, more than "who" he thought he was. As to the true nature of "Christ", this had to be revealed to Jesus just as it had to Paul – and to everyone else! Jesus would learn "Christ" is far more than *himself*, learn that his mission was beyond that of a prophet, an anointed man or messiah. Once his mission had been fulfilled, he would indeed *become* Christ – just as God intends all human beings to *become.* The revelation of Christ is the resurrection, the nature of which was just as much a surprise to Jesus as it will be for everyone.

In Judaism, the term "*anointed*" ("*christos*" in Greek) was purely an epithet or title for an "anointed man", for which reason Jesus was called "the *christos*" or the "anointed one" – presently referred to as "*Jesus Christ*". To be an anointed human being, however, never meant one was God, and were this so, then Moses and all the prophets would be God. So the term "anointed" or *christos* was never, then, a reference to God. As already pointed out, the Gentiles' understanding of "christ" was not Judaism's understanding of the term "anointed". In time, the Gentile reference to "*christos*" would come to mean *more* than just the man Jesus. It would be understood as a reference to the *Incarnate Logos* – God's oneness-with-man. Thus following Jesus' death, "Christ" was always a reference to the heavenly *eternal* Christ – as someone put it, "Jesus died and Christ arose". There always remained, however, the division between a reference to the historical man as "Jesus" and reference to the glorified heavenly "Christ". So where "Jesus" was a common Jewish name referring to a particular *person, Christ* was *nobody's* name, but a *title* that came to be defined as the eternal oneness of God and man.

Given the belief that the messiah's heritage was to be traced back to David and Abraham, the fact Matthew and Mark traced Jesus' heritage through Joseph, implies no knowledge that *Yahweh* was Jesus' *human Father* – i.e., the Christian belief that the "Incarnation" was the human conception of the man Jesus. While it would have been clarifying had Jesus told the apostles the circumstances of his conception – as he learned it from his mother – this would only have questioned their belief he was the *messiah* – since the messiah was to *have a human father*. Considering the first Gospels were written 30 – 40 years after Jesus was gone, one wonders if Matthew and Mark still knew nothing about Jesus' miraculous conception. Perhaps they knew their fellow Jews would never accept a "miracle" like that.

But if Judaism never regarded the messiah as divine or God, it still had an exalted understanding of someone specially chosen by God for a special mission in this world. According to Jesus' biographers, there was never a doubt God was with him, in him, and certainly manifested **through** him – the general view of a prophet or "anointed" one. There was also the belief that the messiah was *created* and existed *prior* to being born into this world – which explains Jesus' saying "*before Abraham, I am*" – referring to his existence *prior* to any human lineage from Abraham and David. To explain why this statement was shocking to the Jews of his time, Christians believe it was his use of the sacred "I am" – an unutterable reference to God. Yet, this saying could only have referred to the messiah's *pre-existence* and *not* to God. The Jews also believed the messiah's mission was to deliver Israel from its enemies and establish the *kingdom of Israel.* Evidently, establishing this kingdom was a big concern of the apostles, because the last thing they asked as Jesus was about to ascend, "*Lord has the time come for you to restore the kingdom to Israel*?" to which Jesus replied, "*It is not for you to know the times and dates the Father has decided*". The subject has forever been left at that.

Since Jesus did not fulfill their expectations, the Jews obviously never regarded Jesus as the promised messiah. One thing they granted, however, he was as human as anyone else, something the Gentiles, with their various philosophies and mythical religions could never do – nor, subsequently, many Christians. Considering that for the first 30 years of his life no one heard of Jesus, had it not been for the miracles God worked on his behalf, no one would have known he even existed.

Sometimes we wonder about those 30 "hidden years" prior to John the Baptist's pointing Jesus out in the crowd. We can only assume this silence was because there was nothing unusual to report. He read scripture, went to the temple, worked at his trade and, no doubt, enjoyed family get-togethers. (The daily life of most people is not very elevating or inspiring anyway – it could even be boring.) But let anyone start working miracles, their private life is over and the crunch is on. Since what attracted followers were his miracles, they had no interest in his former mundane life at home – besides, had there been miracles, everyone would have heard of them already. The years of being relatively unknown, however, is one of the most overlooked aspects of his life, one that has more meaning to us common folk than much of what he (or rather, God) accomplished in the three years of his being known. These ordinary years of being unknown – or known only to God – dispel the notion those closest to God, the holiest of human beings, are immediately recognized or stand out in a crowd. Obviously, man's oneness with God is not for the looking, or even the knowing. The only one who knows this is God and oneself, no one else. Thus Christians who wish they had known the historical man Jesus – thinking "*Christ*" is a *visible human being – would* only be disappointed. "*Christ*" after "all, is but a "title" or term for man's oneness with God and *not a visible being.*

So what do these 30 years of Jesus' life tell us, what is the lesson here? For those who would deify the man, they might ask themselves how God or the *divine* Christ could walk on this earth and never be noticed as anyone other than a local carpenter? How is it no one thought there was anything special about him that might have drawn them to seek him out or have something unusual to report? What does this say about the divine Logos' human nature – God's *own human nature*? It tells us that even *God's* human nature (on this earth at least) is no different from the human nature of anyone else; it affirms that Jesus was, in every way, as human as anyone who ever lived on earth. That the Incarnate Logos could be among men and never appear or be known as any different from others, is the most outstanding lesson the Incarnation has to teach – indeed, it is a revelation in itself. Unless one realizes the enormity of the Incarnation, however, they cannot understand or appreciate this fact which should raise the status, spirit and insight of every human being. It is not a matter of just *accepting* one's humanity, but of realizing it is the greatest of God's creations capable not only of being one with God, but destined to participate in God's own eternal life – *no different from Christ.*

St. Paul, of course, never knew or *saw the man Jesus in the flesh*. His sole encounter was a *blinding Light* with the message that what Paul was doing to others he was doing to Jesus. But how was Paul persecuting Jesus? Clearly, the message was of Man's *one common human nature* and that what is done to one human being is no different than what is done to another human being. In other words, it doesn't matter ***who*** a particular *person* is – be it Jesus or Steven – what matters is *what* he is, a *human being* no different than Paul himself. Clearly, "*who*" someone is does not count with God, but rather, "*what*" one is – a human being. So Paul's encounter with the heavenly Christ was a *clear affirmation of the oneness of mankind* – a revelation that **is** *Christ.* Though Paul thought he was after those *who* believed in Jesus, he learned that the *eternal Christ* was not ***who*** the man Jesus was, but that the *eternal Christ* was *everyone's* oneness with God. Since Christ's *divine nature* is God – and there's no persecuting God – the only thing Paul was persecuting was Christ's *human nature* – no different than his own. So what Paul learned of the *resurrected Christ* is that "Christ" is more than one individual human being, more than just the man Jesus. Christ's *human nature* is "*what*" every human being is – more especially, his ultimate oneness with Almighty God.

Was this revelation to Paul merely *his own private revelation* of Christ? Or is it not much the same revelation God has given Christians down the centuries? Without these ongoing *revelations* of Christ, in truth, there would be no Christianity. No one can base their faith on someone else's revelation – mere hearsay – or even on Jesus' *own* revelation of God. Reading the Bible, knowing all the theology in the world and hearing *about* Christ, none of this can be counted as the *revelation* of Christ or the true life of Christianity. The only reason Christianity is a genuine *phenomenon* (and not some "institution") is because Christ has consistently been *revealed* to the common folk down the centuries. Without this, Christianity could never have survived, nor without this particular revelation of Christ, can it ever survive.

Any revelation of God to man is *someone's experience* – be it the experience of a Moses, Elias, Jesus, Mary, Paul – the list goes on and on. These people, of course, tell us about their experiences of God and what they learned from them, yet, no one can have the *experience* of another or give it to another. So while every religion is based on *someone's* experience of God's revelation, this revelation can only be verified when others have *experienced this revelation for themselves*. Thus if God were not *consistently revealing Itself to individual people,* no one's revealed experience of God could either *be verified* nor counted as a verification of any man's religion. This is why Jesus' *own* experiences of God (or Paul's experiences of Christ) work to *verify* other people's experiences of God and Christ, and why, *in turn*, everyman's experiences verify Jesus' experiences of God, and Paul's experiences of Christ. This is the circular way it works. Without this, Christianity could never have survived, nor without the particular revelation of

Christ, *can it ever survive*. (Of course, no revelation of Christ is someone's *sensory* vision of the man Jesus – God save us from the "paranormal" which is **not** "*supernatural*".)

But back to Jesus' historical life, 97% lived in total obscurity. No one (but his mother) knew him as other than the son of Joseph, the carpenter's son. Obviously, one can be as completely human and as one with God as the man Jesus and live totally unknown in this world. If genuinely understood, the lesson of these unknown years far outweighs Jesus' rather abrupt and dramatic ending. After all, a single day (or three years) in one's life cannot outweigh a lifetime. Failure to recognize the importance of living totally unknown to all but God, is one of the important "truths" the Incarnation revealed. Everyone lives out their lives totally unknown to all but God, and if God had not planned Jesus' life this way – to be a lesson for everyone – then this would not have been the case.

Seeing that Jesus neither preached nor taught anything new, or was not already part and parcel of Judaism, we might ask what was so extraordinary about him? As said, had God not worked the miracles, people would not have flocked to hear and see him. But is this all we know of him? What was new to his close friends, at least, was his claim to be one with *his* Father. Because he never actually said he was one with "*Yahweh*" but one with "*his*" Father, what he meant and understood by "Father" was obviously not its Jewish metaphorical understanding of God as the "Father of Israel". Instead, his reference was to his miraculous conception wherein God was, literally, his *biological father*. Jesus had no other way of referring to his oneness with God because this oneness is nowhere found in Judaism – no one had ever made this claim before. In this matter, Jesus was alone with his immediate experience and knowledge of his oneness with God. As said, it was for this very reason – affirming his oneness with God – he was put to death.

It is unthinkable that Mary did not tell him of his extraordinary conception. As the most spectacular event in her life, who could appreciate this more than the one so born? Even as a toddler Jesus knew the story, knew his *real* Father was not Joseph or any other man, but God Himself. Mary had simply told him the truth, and there was never a doubt. For Jesus, knowing the truth of his conception worked so that he could recognize and verify *his immediate experiences of God.* No doubt this was the main reason for the virgin birth – that Jesus would never be without the knowledge and certitude of his oneness with God, know that God alone was his true and only "father". It was as if God scripted the Incarnation so Jesus could *identify his experience of one-*

ness with God from birth onwards. And do not think for a minute God is not revealed to little children – there are numerous accounts – and such was the case with Jesus. So who is to say there was ever a time in his life Jesus did *not* experience and know his oneness with God? Nowhere are we given a hint he ever went in *search* of God, or sought out any human *insight* or *verification* in this matter. There is absolutely no account of his ever seeking answers or even questioning others about this. In this matter, his knowledge was absolute and assured.

As for John the Baptist knowing Jesus, remember, Mary and John's mother, Elizabeth, were cousins who shared their unusual pregnancies. Mary's confiding her story to Elizabeth was passed on to John. So it was through his mother John knew about his cousin, knew about his unusual conception and thus, deferred to him as the one who could baptize in the Spirit instead of water. Jesus' baptism was a major turning point in his otherwise obscure life, this was when Jesus' oneness with God was revealed *to others* – at least to John – *which* then began his public life. This was not God's revelation to Jesus, but God's revelation of Jesus *to others.* Those who think this was the moment Jesus "realized" he was one with God are *totally* wrong, there was no time in his life he did not know he was one with God. Born into what, in the Western tradition, is called a "unitive state" of being – and in the Orthodox tradition, "theosis" – Jesus was as aware of God as he was aware of himself, and this, from birth. He never knew any other *state of being* but what, today, is called "unitive or God-consciousness". It was at the time of his baptism, however, God "outed" him (if we may use that expression), thus making him known to *others.* This particular *experience* heralded the onset of his "Public Life". For the next three years, people would push and shove just to get near him – which must have been a nightmare.

Recently someone pointed out – an Italian Camaldolese monk, no less – that the numerous accounts of Jesus leaving or escaping the crowds and going off alone, was because "*he had to be saved **from** the people".* People wanted to "cage him", "box him in" as a miracle worker, a prophet, seer, messiah, make him an idol of sorts, which Jesus continually rebuffed. This was not a role he ever wanted to play, and never did. Jesus refused to have his identity pinned down or labeled in any way, always he pointed to God and never to himself. Christians, of course, have ignored this lesson – indeed, some idolize the man as if he was Almighty God. What is there about the human mind that *needs* some "idol" – be it an entertainer, athlete, public figure, guru, master, or even a saint? Maybe it's because people regard God as so utterly transcendent that they give up *knowing God* and settle, instead, for some idol. Obviously the "Golden Calf" is still around.

As for Jesus being "Christ" – as we would later understand his oneness with God-Jesus himself could not reveal this to others – as he said, *only* God could *reveal* this, not himself, and not someone else. Thus hundreds of people saw Jesus without either seeing or knowing the real "Christ". Those who think that to see Jesus is to see Christ either visibly or in their own minds, is not to see Christ at all. Neither Christ nor God can ever be seen visually or mentally, but only by a direct, unmediated *revelation* from God. And what, we might ask, could this specific revelation of Christ be? Since the oneness of God and man can never be an object of vision or capable of any mental imagery, the revelation to Paul is probably the most outstanding example, a Blinding Light, or even, "*No longer **I**, but Christ lives in me*". Yet however it comes, it is like no other revelation known to man; it is **not** the revelation of God, but of God's eternal oneness with man. Man can have all kinds of lofty revelations of God and still have none of Christ. This revelation is specific and one-of-a-kind, more in the order of enlightenment or a divine knowing, which may also be seen as *light* – as in the case of Paul. There are many such revelations and accounts. The point is that the revelation of Christ is not, as some think, the revelation of God, nor the revelation of the man Jesus. The revelation of "Christ" is a genre of its own.

So even though Jesus preached nothing new to Judaism, yet there was something very different he introduced into his world, which was his consistent assured knowledge he was one with God. Such an affirmation fell outside his monotheistic background – his Judaic belief system – which is why some regarded him as a heretic and blasphemer. It is one thing to be an anointed holy man or prophet, but Jesus' claim went beyond this. Although this oneness with God was never understood as making him God, yet the claim to be the "son of God" sounded exactly like it was – i.e., it meant God was both his true spiritual and biological "father". We can only imagine the predicament of God revealing something to a fervent Jew that was *contrary* to his own belief system and scriptures! (Compare this, say, to God revealing something to the Pope totally outside the Christian belief system and its scriptures.) It seems that if God revealed anything *not* in man's scriptures, or if God did *not* religiously adhere to man's scriptures, then this could only be judged as heretical and blasphemous – but so much for scriptures!

No question, Jesus' claim shocked the Jews, it was totally outside their traditional frame of reference. As to the true nature of his oneness with God, how it worked or came about, Jesus never told anyone. It was left to centuries of speculation and disputes to figure out the nature of this *oneness,* which even to this day, remains a mystery. All we know is that Jesus knew and affirmed this oneness, that his apostles were witnesses to the fact God was with him and worked through him. It is this revelation of *oneness* that constitutes the major difference between Judaism and Christianity. **In Judaism, the *Line that divides God and man* is, for the Christian, the same *Line that unites God and man,* and this oneness, this Line, is the mystery of "Christ".**

While we can understand what a stir Jesus made, sometimes we forget how offensive he could be to those he encountered. He constantly fought and argued with the rabbis – cursed them in no uncertain terms. He put people down (Gentiles were "dogs"), condemned all those who did not believe in him, insulted his own mother – "*Who is my mother*?" He never referred to her as "*mother*", but as "*woman*"! He wreaked havoc in the temple and so insulted the people in his own town, they tried to push him over a cliff – kill him. And there were others out to kill him, not because he was a kind, gentle person, but because he was a disturber wherever he went – indeed, at one point his family thought he had lost his mind. Yet nothing could be less excusable than his abruptly telling his disciples – without offering a word of explanation – that unless they ate his flesh and drank his blood they would not have eternal life. Now who can imagine suddenly being told a thing like that? It is disgusting! Jesus must have wanted to get rid of them, because it worked.

One reason Jesus only lasted three short years in public life is because he was so provocative and offensive. He even said he did not come to bring peace, but to bring division – which he certainly did. But such are the limitations of human nature – even God's human nature! It could be said Jesus actually revealed man's limitations and that, despite them, man is destined for a glorious and undeserved end. Although the fathers referred to Jesus as "the perfect man", yet it only took three years for this perfect man to engender such animosity and fear that he was put to death. Such is the destiny of a perfect man in an imperfect world where even God could not run a *perfect* human show.

Nothing created, of course, is *perfect,* only God is perfect, and seeing that Jesus was the best God could do, should give hope to the rest of mankind. Human nature being what it is, there is nothing perfect about it – until it reaches its eternal life in God. So one of the messages of the Incarnation is that despite being human, despite the imperfections and limitations of human nature, God nevertheless loves what God has created and intends to save and transform it into eternal life with and in God. This is why it is important to put on one side the human figure of Jesus with his transient characteristics (properties) and idiosyncrasies, to understand why, even the human nature of Jesus, was neither perfect nor unlimited. It is all these transient human properties, characteristics and accidents that must die (forever) so that, in the end, there is only *God's own* transformed, glorious *perfect* human nature.

Pointing all this out is by no means an attempt to take Jesus down a peg – it's all in the Gospels anyway – but to take down a peg those who put a divine spin on his every word and behavior, cover up his true humanity, that is. Those intent on deifying Jesus' human nature obviously don't want to admit he was as human as any other human being. For some, just admitting he was *totally human,* may seem to ruin their faith. Those, however, incapable of facing the *truth* that Jesus was as human as themselves, have missed the whole purpose of the Incarnation and all it was intended to reveal. What makes the Incarnation so unbelievable is just this: human nature is human nature, *even* if it is one with God. As to its final or glorious transformation, this is the eternal heavenly Christ – God's *own universal* human nature.

To understand Paul's notion that apart from Adam (the first human being God created) Jesus was the only one ever born "without sin", it behooves every Christian to know the genesis of this idea. The reason it is important to know its origin is because it affects the whole Christological and soteriological understanding of Christ. Centuries before Paul, the world-wide belief was that the male sperm or seed was the father's own life and soul that he passed on to his offspring. This was not a *new* soul, but the father's *same one soul* passed on generation after generation. While this was a universal belief, what was particularly Jewish, however, was the belief it was the seed of Adam (whose soul was created by God) that was passed down from father to son. It is because Adam fell, however, his offspring inherited his "fallen soul", and thus Adam's fallen soul was passed down the generations via the male sperm or seed.[1] This is the origin of the idea that all human beings are *fallen souls* and come into this world tainted by Adam's sin. This, at least, is the Judaic genesis of Paul's view that all men came into this world as sinners. It is ***because Jesus had no human father, however, that he alone was born "without sin".***

Obviously, at that time, there was no belief God created each indi-

---

[1] God, "*visiting the iniquity of the fathers upon the sons to the third and fourth generation*" (Numbers, 14 – 18.) "*The gods visit the sins of the fathers upon the children*" – Euripides (485 – 406 B.C.). "*Set us free from the sins of our fathers and from those that we ourselves have perpetuated*" (Rig-Veda, Prayer to Varuna.) In Hinduism it was believed the male seed also carried the soul's *karma* – no real difference between being born with karma or sin because either way, one has to get rid of it.

vidual soul One-on-one. Rather, the belief was that there was only *one original soul and* this *one same soul,* transmitted by the male sperm, was passed down the generations. This belief goes a long way to explain historical male dominance and patriarchal societies. Women, of course, had nothing to do with this. (That the female egg was equally necessary for human conception would wait thousands of years to be discovered.)[2] This was not just Paul's Judaic view and belief, this was Jesus' same belief! That God created *his* soul, however, meant *he came from God* and *not* from any human father – or from Adam. Indeed, God was his true *biological* "father", and he, Jesus, was his true biological "son".

It is in light of an erroneous world-view regarding conception that we get much of the Christian belief system – Jesus as God's sinless son. For some, Jesus' very soul or life *was* God's own *soul* or *life* passed on from his *divine* father. This view also accounts for why the early fathers never honestly granted Jesus an "individual" soul, and why they held God alone was the mind, will, subject (self) or divine *person* of the man Jesus. This and much more was premised on the belief in *one same soul* passed on from father to offspring. (An interesting sidebar – Philo of Alexandria said that only *unjust* and "*effeminate*" men created female souls, while it was the "*just masculine*" male that produced male offspring!) According to Aristotle, fathers hand down their souls from generation to generation ***"like candles passing on the same flame candle after candle"*** – his own words. The *flame* or soul is the same, it is only the candles (bodies) that differ. One way or another, however, the reason for male dominance – even God had to be a "*he*" – was not a matter of chauvinism, but the fact it was a universal *belief* that the male sperm was the genesis of all new life – the father's same soul passed along. Well into the Middle Ages there were disputes as to whether or not God actually created each individual soul, or if it came from the parents – "*traducianism*".

So Paul, like everyone else, believed man's fallen soul came from one's father – passed down the line from Adam. But since Jesus had *no human father,* meant Jesus, unlike anyone ever born before, *was sinless* – just like Adam was originally created. And since he took his *flesh* from Mary, it was also important she too be sinless – a virgin, that is – lest it be thought Jesus' flesh be contaminated by lust. (To read the fathers, just the act of conceiving a child was sinful. Quite a few wrote glowing accounts on the blessedness of virginity. After writing such a treatise, however, Gregory of Nyssa admitted that, unfortunately, he was no virgin.) So the fact Jesus had no human father and was thus

---

[2] For this discovery, see footnote 2, Appendix III, *Theotokos.*

born without sin, was not only a big issue for Paul, but down the centuries for all the fathers and theologians. It played a huge part in developing their Soteriologies – the doctrine of salvation. And, indeed, what would Christianity be without its "sin-business"? If man was *not* conceived in sin, then who would need Christ? If Christ did not come to save man from sin, then what was he about? For most people it seems, belief in Christ depends on Paul's belief that *everyone* inherited Adam's fallen soul. This is why he thought of Christ as a *second Adam* who had come to *restore* ("redeem") man to his *original sinless nature* – as if by just *believing* in Christ one could then, somehow, be saved and "inherit" the kingdom of God. Who can figure out how mere belief makes this so?

As one orthodox author pointed out, Paul's pointing out that Jesus was born without sin, was his way of making the "*diagnosis fit the cure*". Unless one could first be convicted of sin (diagnosed) what need would he have for Jesus as the cure? If Jesus only saves sinners, then in order to be saved, one must first be a sinner. Unfortunately, belief in Jesus never saved anyone from sinning – indeed, among believers, sin is as alive today as it has ever been in the history of mankind. Christianity never put a damper on sin. Like every good Jew, however, Jesus believed God both forgave and saved man, but what Jesus added to this was **the more important need for *man* to forgive *man* – forgive *one another*, that is. It isn't God that seeks revenge and satisfaction, it is *man*!** Heaping all this sin-business on Jesus, was Paul's way of presenting Jesus to a non-Jewish mind-set. Where, for the Jews, *God* was the Savior, now, for the Gentiles, *Jesus* was to be the savior. Paul made his own case for this transposition and it seems all the fathers carried through – kept to Paul's "party-line", so to speak. Some of the good fathers, however, believed Christ would have come even if man had never sinned – Duns Scotus put it best: "*Christ wasn't made for man, man was made for Christ*".

It goes without saying, those who believe only God can create an immaterial soul, could *never* believe God created a soul with sin – not unless they believed God created sin. No individual soul created One-on-one, coming from the hand of God, could have any sin at all. Although free-will allows for the potential to sin, this was never God's intention for human free-will. But this is where (or how) the whole idea came from – namely, that man somehow inherited Adam's sin and how his offspring were ever-after tainted with his fall – sin, passed along to others **via the *male* sperm *no less*!** This belief seems to validate the view there is only *one* original world-soul and that souls are not created *individually* by God, but rather, passed down from their fathers. This, at least, seems to have been the belief of both Jew and Gentile – as Aristotle put it, "*the soul a father begets*" is not a *different* soul, it only has a different body. This is the same view Christianity inherited, its Christology and soteriology *premised* on this belief. This is its view or understanding of mankind, of Jesus and even Christ – but is there any Truth in this? The truth is, God alone creates every individual soul, everyone with the same *original sinless nature* as "*adam*" (in Hebrew, "*mankind*".) There is no such thing as "inherited" souls or sins.

The miracle of the Incarnation was *not* God creating the soul of Jesus – God creates every individual soul – but God supplying the male chromosome and genes needed to generate a human body. Although the female ovum waited thousands of years to be discovered, conception of a *material* body (sperm and egg) is *not* the conception or creation of an *immaterial* soul – impossible! But then, "*Who*" could be less surprised or upset over man's sins than the *One Who* made them possible? **This is what free-will is all about.** Without this freedom, man would be no different from an animal governed by innate instincts. If God was so upset by sin, God could have given the planet back to the dinosaurs.

One reason some of the fathers were reluctant to grant Jesus a complete human nature was because they regarded it as fallen, prone to sin, thus God could never be one with such a man. Their idea of human nature was literally unredeemable, it had to be radically changed, a change only Christ's meritorious death could bring about. According to some of their writings, it seems they never adopted either the Jewish or Greek belief in the immortality of the soul. In their view, Adam's sin was the *death of the soul* – so obviously, it had not been created immortal – it was only the death of Christ that *conferred immortality* on man. This means that prior to Christ, no one was immortal, not Adam, Abraham, Moses – no one. Where the fathers were right to regard *Christ as the true nature of man's immortality*, they were wrong to think this was only because Jesus died to make it so.

For the Synoptics, Jesus was clearly a man set apart by his authority of speaking, miracles, prophecies and fellowship with God. Yet the Gospels give us few glimpses into his experiential life with God, for indeed, Jesus was the mystic of mystics, privy to the most profound knowledge and experience of God that we know of. He spoke of his experiences of the Spirit moving within himself, experienced transfiguration, experienced every one of God's miracles – walking on water, etc. Then there was his pre-knowledge of people and events, to say nothing of what he must have experienced at the resurrection and Ascension. If authentic mysticism is man's *unmediated experience* of God, then the man Jesus was the greatest of mystics and thus, Christianity was *founded* on Jesus' *mystical experiences* of oneness with God. Had he told no one of this oneness, and had God not backed up this truth with miracles, then no one would have ever heard of Jesus, of Christ, or Christianity. To regard Jesus' experiences *of* God as *God's own experiences,* however, is absurd. *God is impassible, has no human experiences – none whatsoever.* So beware of the theological switch from Jesus as a *human person* to a *divine person – it* is *not* God *who* experiences God (which makes no sense), it is *man who* experiences God.

One way to understand the Incarnation, is that with the birth of Jesus, God gave man an example of a human being who not only speaks from his living experience of God, but who *experientially* lived with God through all the major events in human existence, from birth to death and beyond. While we do not have to believe any of this man's *experiences*, yet we cannot complain that they were merely someone's philosophical or theological belief system. In fact, Jesus' experiences *contradicted* his belief system. Judaism recognized no true or eternal oneness of God and man – which is what Jesus affirmed even unto death. This truth was premised on Jesus' own personal *experiences,* what God gave him to know, his whole life an *experiential* working out of God's creative plan. His life, then, was the supreme example of God's archetypal Plan, not just for one human being, but for every human being. Human nature, being what it is, there is not one experience any human being can have that another cannot have. This does not mean everyone has the *same* experiences, it only means what is possible for one is possible for all.

What Jesus knew of God and God's ways with man, find no match in human history. Everything he knew, however, he never told others because, as he said, they would never be able to grasp it on its true mystical level. Thus he told the apostles he knew many things they would never understand – for which reason, he also said he only spoke in "parables". Those not privy to Jesus' experiential knowing and direct rapport with God, could never understand it on its true level, instead, they could only bring it down to their level of *misunderstanding* – which has certainly been its history. While the enlightenment of Pentecost turned the Apostles' lives around – more in the order of Paul's conversion experience – this did not come close to Jesus' intimate knowledge conveyed over a lifetime of living in oneness with God.

One author's explanation of why the early fathers never considered Jesus' *own* human *experiences* of God, is that *their own fallen* natures could never have conceived the experiences of a sinless *un-fallen* soul. This view, of course, is premised on the notion every human being (but Jesus) is a sinner. Yet, if everyone is a sinner, how could anyone know Jesus' experiences were any *different*? They couldn't! As sinners, they would have no way of knowing *any difference.* The idea everyone is a sinner only illustrates man's lack of faith that God truly *forgives* and that man can actually live without sin. For some of Jesus' worshipers, it seems in order to *divinize* Jesus, everyone else must be *demonized.*

While we can certainly relate to Jesus' humanity and its various predicaments, we also have to face the fact this historical figure died, his earthly personage gone forever, never to be seen or heard from again – heaven, after all, is not another planet somewhere. The man was totally changed, utterly transformed, taken up in the brilliant light of glory where he will never be visibly seen again. It was this Blinding Light of glory that struck Paul blind, yet for those still on earth, this Light of Glory may come as bad news – because this was not Jesus *in the flesh.* Heavenly life with God is beyond anything the human mind can conceive of; in fact, this "mind" will also be gone – as the Apostle said, "*We shall have the mind of Christ",* literally know as God knows. ("Divine Knowing" transcends everything man calls "knowing".) So people who are "waiting" to *see* Jesus, might as well be waiting for Godot.

What follows are some of the different early views of Jesus:

1. He was God's highest Angel made visible. **2.** For Paul and most early Christians, he was God's *created* Spirit made visible. **3.** He was the Father (God) made visible. **4.** He was God who only *appeared* to be human. **5.** He was a prophet commissioned by God. **6.** He was an ordinary man who, at some point, God united to Itself. **7.** He was the promised Jewish messiah, a *created* being and not divine. **8.** The Spirit *dwelled in* the man and was his divinity. **9.** The Spirit did not merely *indwell in* him, but *took the place* of his human soul. **10.** "*God dwelt in Jesus in the same way a man's reason exists in him*" – i.e., God's Wisdom incarnate in man. After John's Gospel appeared around the year 100, other views were added. So too, when it came to the Trinity as "persons", and Christ as a "person", the list of differing views goes right on. For all these views, of course, everyone had their *scriptural proofs!*

Following John, however, it was understood the *divine* Christ was the "Logos" – God. This understanding, however, was not limited to a "*cosmic* Logos", but also understood as God's "*Wisdom*" – God's own

Knowing. Although the incarnation of God's Wisdom is not as easy to grasp as the "cosmic Logos", yet one should never let go the understanding of the Logos as God's Wisdom or Knowing. The reason it was thought the Logos was the divine Christ is because only the *cosmic Logos* has an "*existential union*" with matter – with the flesh. (By "*existential*" we mean *by-reason-of-existence.)* This is why the fathers stressed that the body or flesh of Christ was one with the Logos (God) and *not* the immaterial soul. In contrast, however, the Incarnation of God's *Wisdom or Knowing* has its own unique Christology, one, however, that was never really developed by any of the fathers.

Obviously, there was no single or agreeable understanding of Christ handed down from the Gospels, Paul, John, the Apologists and on down the line. While all believed Jesus was a man with a mission specially sent by God, they believed that by the miracles God did on his behalf God was not only *with* him, in him, but that he was, indeed, *one with God.*

Jesus' "I am" sayings:

In Judaism, it is believed *"I am"* was the term (or name) God used to identify Itself to Moses. Thus it was a sacred epithet – God's own reference to *Itself.* To Jewish ears this sacred "I am" was never used to designate or point to any human being – to do so was as good as making oneself God. So in light of *Judaic* Monotheism – where nothing created is God – that a human being would think he was God, was heretical. So if Jesus honestly thought he was God – which he *did not* – then he was indeed a heretic. It goes the same way in *Christian* Monotheism – to think the *created* man Jesus is God, is also heretical. (The Uncreated can never *become* the created.)

According to Philo of Alexandria the answer given to Moses – "*I am he that is"*, is *equivalent to **"My nature is to be, and not to be spoken".** But that mankind not be in complete want of a designation for the Supremely Good, he allows them to use **analogically*** ("*I am"*) *as though it were his proper name"*. In other words, "I am" can only be understood analogically (as a human being might express himself), but not as a statement of God's existence. Philo also says, "*His Logos too, cannot be expressed by us through his own name, and indeed, if he is ineffable, he is also inconceivable and incomprehensible*". Maximus the Confessor understood God's "*I am who I am*" to mean **"*that which* IS**, *referring to the whole of being collectively*". (Once a young man, who doubted God's existence, told me of his confirming experience. Speaking of the Brilliant Light over his head he said, "*It was **as if** God said, "Here I am, I exist, this is me!*") God's saying "*I am*" is obviously man putting words in God's mouth – God, after all, doesn't "talk". But let us look over Jesus' "I am" statements.

1. Paul's conversion was a blinding light from which he heard the words, "*Saul, why do you persecute me?*" Because Paul saw no one, he asked, "*Who are you*?" "***I am Jesus***, *and you are persecuting me.*" Since Paul was not out to persecute Jesus, but only those who believed in him, how could persecuting others possibly be persecuting the dead Jesus? The message, of course, was that the human being Jesus was *no different* from any other human being, and that to persecute one is to persecute them all. This message was an eye-opener for Paul. Suddenly he understood what the revelation of "*Christ*" meant – i.e., it referred to **all human beings**. There would even come a day when he said, "*For* ***me*** *to live is Christ*". Paul would always refer to the "blinding Light" as having seen the "*resurrected Christ*" and *not* the resurrected "*Jesus*" who, he says, he "*never saw in the flesh*". Thus the resurrected Christ was a "blinding Light" in which Paul saw *no one,* not even the man Jesus. If this tells us anything, it is that a true *revelation* of Christ is not an image of the historical man Jesus. To say "I am Jesus", "I am Paul", "I am John", is always the identification of a human *person* and **not** the identification of Almighty God – or even Christ.

2. "*Before Abraham "I am"* – *but* who came before Abraham? There was Adam, of course (*adam* in Hebrew meaning "mankind") and why Paul called Jesus a "second Adam". It is also said, the Jews believed that the "created" messiah *pre-existed* his coming into this world. Thus "*before Abraham*" could be a reference to the pre-existed, *created* messiah. For sure Jesus did not mean "*I am Yahweh*".[3]

3. "*He who sees me sees the Father*" and "*The Father and I are one*". Jesus' saying harks back to the going belief that a father's seed or sperm generates the *soul or life* of the offspring. **Thus the father's *soul or life* was the *same* soul or life as that of his son.** So Jesus, having no human father, could say *his soul, his life*, was no different than that of his Father (God, that is.) To see *his life*, then, was to see *his Father's life.* That Jesus' soul was divine (God) was the view of some of the early fathers. His saying that to see him was to see God, however, contradicts his telling Peter that only God could *reveal* the "anointed one", the messiah or *christos*. Obviously, merely "seeing" the man Jesus is not to see "Christ" – much less see Almighty God.

---

[3] Jesus' saying he had been *sent* by God and was *returning* to God, assumes he existed *prior* to the incarnation. To explain this, Origen came up with the idea Jesus was one of those in heaven chosen for this mission *because* he had been the most faithful to God. This idea, of course, was *rightly condemned*! If Jesus existed *prior* to the *incarnation*, then there could be no "*incarnation*" of what was *already incarnated*!

God and Christ can only be *revealed* and never seen for the looking – as Jesus said, "flesh and blood" (both his and Peter's) could *not* reveal Christ.

4. The only passages in the Bible of more reference to Christ, are the two sayings, "*I am the Resurrection*" and "*I am the Bread of Life*". All other "I am" passages can be understood as references to himself as a human person. Thus "*I am the way*" was understood by his first followers as "the way" it goes for every human being. This is why, for the first century at least, those who followed Jesus called their group "*The Way*" – following Jesus was everyone's "way" to eternal life. (It was only later that foreigners began calling this group "*Christians*".) As a model of man's *earthly* life with God, Jesus is indeed the *earthly* human archetype – after all, no one can model their life on the life of Almighty God! *Christ* is *what* man is to *become,* and Jesus is the model of this "*becoming*". So one way to understand Jesus' saying "*I am the Resurrection*" is that this is the true nature or reality of *everyman's* eternal life. Just as there is only one Christ, so too, there is only one resurrection. So the saying "I am the Resurrection" can only be a reference to "what" Jesus would ***become after*** **his death and transfiguration** – "*Christ*".

Until the resurrection Jesus never knew the *eternal Christ* for the "*resurrection is the revelation of Christ.*" It was certainly *not* the revelation of Jesus or any particular person. No question, Jesus was in for the same person-less surprise of "*resurrection*" as it will be for everyone. (This is why Jesus was regarded as God's "*instrument*" for the *revelation of* Christ, but was not, *himself,* Christ.) The point is that there is no way these sayings can be understood as references to Jesus' earthly life – i.e., *prior* to his resurrection. His parting words affirm as much, "*I am ascending to my father and your father, my God and your God*" – obviously, Jesus was not ascending to him**self**!

"*I am the Bread of Life*" was Jesus comparing his messianic mission of saving Israel to the heavenly Manna (bread) God sent to save his people in the desert. Later, of course, this saying would be understood as reference to the "Eucharistic Christ" – reserved for another chapter.

Because Christians consistently impose their "Christian" views on the man Jesus, they do not see him in the light of his own beliefs and understanding of God – i.e., Jewish monotheism in his own day and age. People are always telling us what he meant and how he understood things, yet no one can speak for another human being! There can be no over-emphasizing the difference it makes if one sees Jesus in the light of his own times, culture, religion and *particular person,* as compared to how he has been seen in the later eyes of Christians. Only if one can understand Jesus *without* the overlay of 2000 years of Christianity is there any hope of ever understanding Jesus as a *bona fide human person* of his own times. Without this understanding – or *with* the idea he was Almighty God – there is no hope of ever understanding "*Christ*" – none whatsoever!

PREFACE TO THE TRINITY

"God –
the glorious Transcendent;
the powerful, illuminating and transforming Holy Spirit;
the divine knowing and intelligent Wisdom of the Creator and Logos,
each revelation being the fullness of God".
(Irenaeus, 125 – 202)

While the early fathers may have formulated the Trinity to fit Christianity, the Trinity, the eternal essence of God, is no prerogative of Christianity. Where the Christian development and understanding of the Trinity was centered on Christ, the Trinity, however, stands alone regardless of Christ, regardless had there been Christ or not. So while God is Trinity without Christ, there is no Christ without the Trinity. Strictly speaking, the keystone of Christianity is the Trinity, without It, no true understanding of Christ is possible. So any notion that one can know Christ apart from, or outside the Trinity, is not to know Christ at all.

In the history of the fathers, no one so accurately defined the Trinity as did Irenaeus – the quote above. The Church should have taken this for its formulation of the Trinity and never strayed from its truth and simplicity. As we shall see, however, in the formulation of the Creed, the Trinity is not there, in its stead, what is expressed is God as the biological "father" of the man Jesus (his "son"), which is *not* the Trinity. While the fathers started out with a true understanding of the Trinity, as we shall see, a transition took place about the time of Nicaea (325) that would forever obscure, if not belie, the founding Truth of Christianity, which is first and foremost, the Trinity. Christ only follows the Trinity and does not precede it, the Trinity does not depend on any Incarnation, but just the reverse, without the Trinity there could never have been an "Incarnation", no Christ and no Christianity.

Needless to say, the Trinity is not a Christian invention, only the term "Trinity" is attributed to Christianity – Justin Martyr (100 – 165) was first to use "triad", Tertullian (160 – 225) the first to use "trinity". Christianity merely gave a name ("*Trinity*") to God's discrete and different revelations, a name that aptly sums up all God's revelations to man. These triune revelations were known and in place long before Christianity – from the beginning of man, in fact. As each was independently revealed, It became the basis of man's various religions and beliefs, each with its own path and goal to be realized. For those who know the Trinity, it can be seen and found in all man's religions as the basis of all man knows of God. Thus the fathers saw the Trinity throughout the Old Testament – now in the cloud on Sinai, now the burning bush, now the Spirit descending on the prophets, now as God's Wisdom, and so on – each revealing a very different "aspect" of what the fathers called God's "*three modes of existence*". The term "Trinity", then, merely sums up all God's revelations to man. It is not unique to Christianity, but is God's continuous and ongoing revelation to man.

If there is any problem with the term "Trinity", it is that God cannot be known or "called" a Trinity unless one is first familiar with each of these three independent revelations. In other words, one must first know them independently *prior* to ever seeing their *unity* as constituting the One essence and existence of God. So prior to this revelation (of God as Trinity), or based solely on one of these revelations, no one would ever recognize or know God as a Trinity. In other words, *before* one knows the Trinity they must *first* know these three relatively independent revelations of God. Only then, when the three are seen *at once or as One*, man knows the fullness of the *Godhead* – the Trinity. Short of this, the Trinity remains but a theological formula in one's head – or as the doxology, "*Gloria Patri...*"

To give but one example of how this works, Judaism never understood the Spirit and/or Wisdom (Logos) as God, but only as God's created "mediators" in creation. But had they seen the three, Yahweh-Spirit-Wisdom together as One, they would have recognized this as the *unity* of God's *immanent modus operandi* and would have recognized the Trinity – even though they probably would never have called it a "Trinity". We could point this out in other religions as well, but since I have written of this elsewhere, we can move on.[1]

The reason for this preface is to start out on the right foot before launching into some three centuries of heated disagreements, mudslinging accusations, condemnations, exiles, and so on – and what was the issue at hand? Christ's relation to the Trinity both *before* and *after* the Incarnation. The upshot was the present terminology to express the Trinity as "Father-Son-Spirit", which is totally unrecognizable as God's triune revelations to man. As a consequence, the Trinity remains unrecognizable as man's triune (different) *experiences* of God. Thus there exists no revelation of God as the "father" of someone, or God as the "son" of someone, in fact, it makes no sense at all. There is no immediate revelation of God anyone would recognize or ever describe as

[1] My essay "*The History of Man's Religions Recapitulates God's Revelations to Man*" (found in my book, *Essays on the Christian Contemplative Journey*) is a summary overview of the Trinity as God's revelations to mankind. Also, my book *Contemplative* recounts the three-fold revelations on which my knowledge of the Trinity is based.

"Father", such a term would never cross one's mind. Anyone, of course, can always *think* of God as a "Father", but there is no such revelation as a "Father" – or a "Son". Those who think such a revelation exists, simply do not know God. Unfortunately, the Trinity as formulated in the creed and by some of the fathers, is experientially unrecognizable. So regardless of all the biblical exegesis, interpretation, metaphors, or philosophical reasoning, none of this verbiage is true to the Reality of the Trinity.

As for giving names to these three revelations, every religion has their own terms and definitions. God, of course, is not revealed as having any "name", nor can any descriptive experience convey such a revelation. The "knowing" so conveyed, however, is absolute and forever. Thus, for example, "Logos" is not a name for God, but a particular knowledge of God given in revelation, which knowledge has meaning for every man. Metaphors like "Father and Son", however, have absolutely no meaning beyond Jesus' reference to God as his "Father" – reference to the fact he had no other *biological father*. This is why it was a terrible mistake to define God's immanent triune nature in terms that only apply to Jesus' earthly reference to God as his "Father" instead of defining the Trinity as God's immanent *modus operandi* – or as the fathers put it, *God's triune modes of existence.*

As the experiential core of man's spiritual life, it is not possible to recognize or know the Trinity on any other than an *experiential* basis. God's immediate revelations can never be recognized on any doctrinal terms or by theological definitions, nor can the Trinity be known by mere hearing or reading – "hearsay". This is why, without some immediate encounter, the Trinity is but a doctrine given little more than lip-service that plays no part in man's spiritual life. So as long as the Trinity remains experientially aloof from man's immediate experience of God, it remains a mere belief with no intrinsic meaning for man's spiritual journey. Unless man *first* knows the Trinity (God), he cannot even begin to ponder the mystery and true meaning of "Christ". In fact, man had best know the Trinity like the back of his hand *before* he even thinks of Christ, for this is just how strategic is the Trinity to ever being able to have a true understanding of Christ.

While the fathers did, in fact, derive their understanding of Christ from the Trinity, yet the articulation of it in the creed, along with the theology that attempts to back up its view, is not the Trinity. What it is, is a post incarnational perspective wherein the divine Logos is presented as God's "Son", and the man Jesus made to be this "son" – be the divine Logos, **be God** that is – which is *absolutely incredible and false!* This is not the Trinity and, consequently, not the true Christ. So one reason for starting with this "preface" is when it comes to the creed's presentation of a "trinity", this is *not* It. And since we will be looking into how this tragic mistake came about, we wanted to start out with an understanding of the Trinity in keeping with Irenaeus' quote that begins this chapter.

Let us briefly go over God's triune revelations to man. 1) God *omnipresent throughout creation.* 2) God *immanent in* man. 3) God utterly *transcendent* to man and creation. Every revelation, and consequently every religion, falls into one or more of these three discrete revelations. Since God, being Truth Itself, cannot reveal what God is *not*, these three revelations are the Truth of God, which, when revealed together as One, is the *immanent triune nature of God's one essence.* One is not the other, each is discrete and infinite and can never be circumscribed – no inside, outside, above or below – and "*each*", as Irenaeus said, "*is the fullness of God*". Those who say the essence of God is "unknowable" do not know the Trinity. While the essence is "unknowable" in terms of something created – like "energy", "light", "power" or someone's experience – the Trinity is the essence of God not only *ad intra* (in Itself), but as revealed to man *ad extra* (in the created.) **God cannot reveal *ad extra* "what" God is not, *ad intra*.**

One way to symbolize the Trinity might be an equilateral triangle, a single essence with three sides or "faces" ("*prosopa*") as the Eastern fathers called it. (Somewhere Irenaeus refers to the Trinity as the "*three sides of God*".) In 3D, however, it could be said to be three dimensional, the Height, Depth and Breadth of God – dimensions wonderfully reflected in creation. These sides or dimensions are non-interchangeable, one side is not the other, and each is totally unique. Though we can define a triangle as a "unity" of three sides or faces, yet, there can be no division of its single essence. Take away any side and there is no triangle, no Trinity. There is no first, second or third, no one before or after the other, no one in or out of the other. There is no "begetting", no "emanation", no "source" such as "monarchial father", no "unoriginate" (Father) or "originated" (Logos) or "proceeding" (Holy Spirit) – in short, no tri-theism possible. Unfortunately, the way the Trinity came to be presented was as "three beings" – for who can think of a "father and son" that are **not individual beings**?

One cannot really grasp or take in the whole (of anything) without seeing its parts, sides or faces that constitute the whole or "One". Thus there would be no use thinking of God as an indivisible "unity" unless It is a unity of "something", which, in our analogy, is the unity of three sides or faces that constitutes the one essence of the Godhead. So too, it is only after seeing these faces singly and thus knowing their distinctions, that seeing them together as One, is the magnificent revelation of God's Triune *modus operandi.*

Although man has given various names to these different revelations, it is actually difficult to define them without some type of specific reference. Perhaps the most easily recognized would be the following three revelations based on *man's experiences* of God.

I. God has revealed Itself in and through nature – throughout the whole of creation as "omnipresent". This revelation is always external to the seer, even though it is no differently present throughout man himself than in everything else in creation, yet, this "omnipresent" can never be "localized" anywhere in "particular", not even *in* man himself.
II. God has been revealed "within" man himself, seemingly localized as the very Center of his being. This is a more "personal indwelling" because man himself is a "person", a personal self, and thus God is "personal" to him. So where the first revelation was more external, global and "relatively" impersonal, this *presence*, because it seems to be "within" man, is the most "personal".
III. God has been revealed as totally transcendent to all creation, including the seer. Though also relatively impersonal, yet whoever said, "See God and die", this would be the revelation. The reason it is the revelation to "die for" is because to sustain this vision, the seer would be dead to himself – and, ultimately, to this world.

So relative to man, we could say God is "Above", "Within" and "Without", these are God's triune revelations, and man's triune *experiences* of God. It is important to make clear, however, God is no part of creation. As previously pointed out, the two dimensions of existence are Uncreated and created, the Uncreated being *transparent*, the created being *apparent*. So although creation exists in God, it is no part or any aspect of God – do not forget the *Great Divide!*

Particularly noticeable about these revelations is that no One (of the Three) ever reveals "Itself", rather, *each reveals the Other*. This is because in the Godhead there is no self – no "I am me", or "I am this one", or "she/he is that one" – none of this nonsense. No "One" then, ever reveals Itself, but "each reveals the other", for in God there is no self, no "I am" to reveal.

It is God-in-nature, then, that reveals God "within", and God within reveals God-in-nature, and so too, the Transcendent is revealed by the others, and in turn, reveals the others. The reason this is the *modus operandi* of God's revelations to man, is because the Trinity is not only God "*ad intra*", or *how* God works in Itself, but is the same God "*ad extra*" and *how* God works in creation as well.

For each different revelation, man has innumerable experiential descriptions to report. The fathers did well, however, to express the Trinity as God's "*three modes of existence*" – as one in essence, but three immanent modes (or "how's") of existing. The only problem with the term "mode" is that it tends to limit the Trinity to separate "functions" which, though they are that, yet are infinitely *more* than that. Also, because every act of God involves all three, it could be said each contributes Its own part to every divine act. There are no separate acts, for where there is one, there are the others.

From the beginning, then, God has consistently revealed Itself to mankind in one of these three distinct ways: 1) through nature, 2) within man himself, 3) as utterly transcendent to man and creation. Apart from this threefold manner of revelation, we know of no other revelation of God – of Truth, of the Uncreated, the One Absolute, the Uncaused Cause – however one prefers to call "It".

All revelations of God, then, fall into one of these triune distinctions that coincide with God's threefold "modes of existence". Though three distinct and utterly different revelations, yet, because "*each is the fullness of God*", any single revelation can constitute a religion of its own – and, indeed, it has. From the beginning, then, all God's revelations fall into one or other of God's three-fold revelations, and apart from these, we have no other accounts of God's revelation to man. **It is because there is no revelation of God the Trinity does not include, the Trinity is the *summation* of all God's revelations to man.**

Those who truly know the Trinity will understand the tremendous difficulty of finding proper "names" or adequate terms to convey Its Reality to others. First and foremost we must avoid all metaphorical personifications which are not the truth and might only deceive others. We also cannot refer to the Trinity as mere "attributes" of God or limit them to functional definitions. "Attributes", after all, are not the *essence* of God, but only characteristics or properties of God – thus to say God is "one", "good", "true", these are "attributes" and very different from God as "Transcendent-Logos-Spirit". Because the Trinity can only be identified in the immediacy of Its distinct revelations, this experiential reality would never satisfy the theologically minded, much less, the scriptural exegete. Given the terminology of "Father and Son" is so remote from people's immediate experience of God, it makes the Trinity an incomprehensible belief, a doctrine largely excused as a "mystery". It is only a mystery, however, when it relies on the traditional terminology and its theological defenses. We don't want to come to the end of our lives and realize everything we thought we knew and understood as the "Trinity" turns out to be "straw"!

While we cannot, of course, envision God as a triangle – being infinite, God is not bounded by sides – yet the benefit of this analogy is to see how the Trinity constitutes the essence of God *ad intra* (as God exists in Itself) and that the Trinity is not merely three "ways" of God revealing Itself – now this way, now that way. **Because God cannot reveal what God is *not*, God's triune essence is abiding (always in Itself) and not merely some particular "way" God is revealed to man.** Being Truth Itself, God could never lie or deceive man into thinking God is "something" It is not, or *reveal "what" It is not.* Although some like to differentiate "God *ad intra*" (solely in Itself) from "God *ad extra"* (God revealed to man or in creation) the difference is not on the part of God, the difference is solely on the part of *man.*

In Itself, God is no different *intra* or *extra,* the difference is in man and how man knows God in this life (*ad extra*), and later, in eternal life (*ad intra.*) Thus where some like to say God *ad intra* is "unknowable" and that all we know is what God has revealed of Itself *ad extra,* this is *not* true. God cannot change, deceive, or reveal what God is *not.* **The difference is that *now* (on earth) man only knows as God exists *for himself,* whereas in eternity he shall know as God exists solely *in Itself* – and no longer in or for ourselves.** Between the two, however, there is no difference in God's essence, the sole difference is how man knows the Trinity *now*, and how man will know It for all *eternity.* No question, there is a difference. Beyond the grave man will eternally "participate" in the Trinity's "*modus operandi*" as he can never do on this earth. The eternal goal, then, is to know God-in-Itself and no longer in one's self.

It could be said, one reason man has made this division between God-in-Itself (*intra*) and God-in-man (*extra*) is to hang onto his *own* way of knowing God – hang on to himself, that is. After all – as the reasoning goes – who knows God like God knows God? This question, however, is facetious – God has no "God" to know. The only "God" that God knows, is the "God" that man knows. As for those who like to say God "knows Itself" – as if God were a self-conscious being – they are simply making God into their own anthropomorphic self-image.

To regard God as utterly transcendent and unknowable in-Itself, is the excuse of an agnostic – "*nobody really knows!*" For others, it is the excuse to claim their *own* knowledge of God is as far as any human being can go. Also, by denying man could ever know God-in-Itself, man hangs on to himself with the excuse that without himself, there would be nobody to know God. What man needs to realize, however, is "*that*" in himself that knows God is God, and that of himself, he knows nothing!

In Truth, man's true spiritual life is the Trinity, for:

– what is *that* in man that *knows* God? It is the Logos.
– what is *that* in man that *loves* God? It is the Spirit.
– what is *that* in man that *sees* God? It is the Transcendent.

Thus it is *God-in-man* that knows the Transcendent and it is the Transcendent that knows *God-in-man,* and between the two, Immanent and Transcendent, is the *Omnipresent* Logos ***throughout*** *man and creation.* These are God's Triune "revelations", *each of the Trinity revealing the other* because God is *no "I am"* – no *"me, myself or I"* to be revealed. So everything man thinks is *his own* spiritual life is not true – the **truth is that the Trinity *is* man's true "spiritual life"**.

This is why man had best know the Trinity first, before he ever begins to consider Christ. It is only *after* knowing and seeing first hand, God as Trinity, man then questions how he could possibly have any eternal oneness with this Infinite Godhead. It is in the *center* of the Trinity that the *real Christ* can be *revealed* (seen and known) as everyman's eternal oneness *with* and *in* the Trinity. As said, outside this revelation of **Christ *in* the Trinity, there is no true or real Christ at all. (Christ is not one *of* the Trinity, but one *with* and *in* the Trinity.)** It is by the failure to first know the Trinity that people fall into *anthropolatry* – mistake man's eternal *oneness with God as God* – or think some human being is God. If man does not first have a grasp of the Trinity – God's *triune modes of existence* – then they neither know God, man, nor the eternal oneness of the two – "Christ".

Although it is tempting to think the fathers somehow stumbled on the Trinity as a result of their inquiries into the mystery of Christ, or that the Trinity somehow developed of Itself due to these inquiries, this is not the case. Christ only made sense to them *because* of the Trinity, their whole understanding of Christ was based on It. Without the Trinity we only have the man Jesus and no Christ. There is no calculating the enormous difference between a Christology based on the Trinity and one based on the man Jesus. These are two totally different (even opposed) Christologies, two different understandings of Christ – and even of God. While it is nice to think these are just two different approaches to the same mystery, the truth is, they lead in totally different directions, one to Christ, the other to the Jesus-cult and anthropolatry.

With this bit of introduction my hope is that it may help explain the fathers' consideration of the Trinity as three distinct *hypostases* or *prosopa* (faces) of God's one essence (*ousia.*) It will be imperative to keep in mind that just as the existence of a triangle ***is*** Its three sides, so too, these sides, faces or *hypostases, can never be distinguished from the one essence of God.* **Differentiate these faces or hypostases from the essence by making them three "individuals", three "properties", or three "persons", and the Trinity is gone.** In Its wake we get either three individual beings (tri-theism), or the essence of God as some "unknowable monad".

While knowing the inner Trinitarian nature of God is wonderful in Itself, yet if man cannot somehow "partake" of It, see and know It for all eternity, then It loses all meaning for man. This is why Christ only has meaning *because* of the Trinity, for Christ **is** man's *eternal oneness* **with** and **in** the Trinity. Any consideration of Christ *outside* the Trinity and there is no *Real Christ*.

Conclusion: Always keep in mind: **1**.) Solely immanent *in Itself*, ***God ad intra*** refers to God's *triune-modes-of-Existence: the Trinity.* **2**.) God *in creation and man,* however, always refers to ***God ad extra*** – the *Trinity as revealed to man.* The difference between ***ad intra*** **and** ***ad extra*** **is solely on the part of man or creation** whereas **in God no such "difference" exists.**

TRINITY

"One is the might of my Trinity,
one the knowledge,
one the glory,
one the power.
The unity cannot be dissolved."
(From a poem by Gregory Nazianzus)

At the crossroad of Jew and Gentile was the agreement that the Source of all existence "transcended" the known world. As One True Existence, It was Absolute, Eternal and Immutable. There was also recognition of a divine creative Power and Intelligence "omnipresent" throughout existence (creation.) In Judaism, this creative *power* was called the "Spirit of God", for the Gentiles, this *Intelligence* was called the "Logos". So while both Judaism and the philosophers had come upon the one *Transcendent*, it was Judaism that defined the *Spirit,* and the philosophers that defined the *Logos*. It was these three different revelations of God that were duly recognized and understood by the fathers as **God's *triune "modes of existence"*** – their definition of the Trinity. Between Judaism and the Gentiles, then, what came to be known as the "Trinity" had been known (though given various names) for as long as man existed. By no means is the Trinity unique to Christianity, on the contrary, it is the *sum of all God's revelations to man.*

As to how the fathers came to refer to God's *"triune modes of existence"* as *"Trinity"*, this was all in the course of their grappling with the *mystery* of Christ. The revelation of Christ was not the revelation of God or the Trinity, nor is the Trinity the revelation of Christ. Christ is not the Godhead or Trinity, nor is Christ "one" of the Trinity. But if Christ never revealed the Trinity, yet without the Trinity, there could be no "*Christ*". So although it could be said the revelation of Christ brought the Trinity together for the fathers, yet, a true understanding of the Trinity has no need of "Christ".

In reference to the Trinity as God's *"three modes of existence"*, "*modes*" refers to the "way" or "how" God exists. Gregory of Nyssa put it this way, *"We must need in the first place believe that something exists, and then scrutinize the manner of existence of the object of belief, thus the question of existence is one, and that of* **mode** *of existence is another."* The Trinity, then, refers to God's *immanent modus operandi*, each mode with its own existential manifestation, each a distinct expression of God's one essence. The Trinity, however, is not just "that" God is, or the "way" God exists, but "what" God is in Itself – the very essence of God *that **is**.*

When it comes to the terms or names used for the Trinity, we must not get stuck as if these terms or names *said it all.* Terms are basically derived from man's descriptive experiences of God and what he learned (of God) from them. But if we put together man's accounts and descriptions, we can come up with *three* over-arching *truths* God has revealed to man:

1."*What*" is revealed in every experience is that "It" transcends everything that can be perceived (or seen) in this world – including the experiencer. In short, It is *Transcendent.*
2. "*What*" is revealed is totally immaterial or "spiritual" in nature, and thus It is *Spirit.*
3. "*What*" is revealed is "*un-circumscribed*" (not an individuated entity.) It is a *presence* either *within* one's own being, *throughout* all being, or *beyond* all being, thus It is *Omnipresent* – everywhere.

Given these basic aspects of revelation, we can sum up all man's experiences of God as *Transcendent-Spirit-Omnipresent* (*Everywhere*) and affirm *God is at once* ***above all***, ***within all***, and ***throughout all***. So the reason "Trinity" is a summary of man's triune experiences of God, is because this is a summary of God's *triune* revelations to man. And since God cannot reveal *what* God is *not*, these revelations and man's experiences of them, are a summary of *What* God ***is*** – Trinity. Apart from these discrete *triune* experiences, we know of no other account of God's revelations to man. Though given different terms, names, and a plethora of experiential descriptions, at bottom, all add up to what, in Christianity, is known as "Trinity" – "Godhead".

But if the fathers grasped the Trinity, there was the problem of trying to find It in scriptures that say nothing of God as Trinity. **Neither the New or Old Testament was premised on the understanding of God as Trinity, scripture takes no account of It or even hints at any recognition of It.** Although in ***retrospect*** one can see the Trinity in the biblical accounts – indeed, in all man's religions – still, trying to use the Bible as *proof* of the Trinity is no better than thinking the Bible *proves* God exists. Although, in truth, the Bible *proves* nothing, the fathers, however, had inherited the Judaic use of scripture as proof-text for its beliefs. But since neither the Judaic nor Christian scriptures were written with the understanding of God as Trinity, trying to use scripture as proof-text for the Trinity is merely "*forcing-the-fit*". But before launching into these scriptural battles, it is imperative to make clear, not one of the fathers ever denied the Trinity or even argued about it. As we'll see, at bottom, every one of their disputes centered on the *mystery of Christ,* and had nothing to do with God as Trinity.

As to the Trinity's relation to Christ, there were three issues:

1.) Which one of the Trinity was the "Incarnate Christ" – the Spirit or the Logos? Prior to the appearance of John's Gospel (in the early 100's), and based on Paul's understanding, Christ was the incarnation of the divine **Spirit**. Even after John's saying "*the Logos was God",* well into the 200's, numerous quotes could be given to show there was still belief the Spirit was the "divine Christ". To explain the background for this understanding, we might start with Philo of Alexandria (prior to Christianity) and his comparing Judaism's *Spirit* with the Gentiles' *Logos*. For Philo, of course, neither the Spirit or Logos was God, they were solely God's *created mediums* in creation.

Scripture makes pretty clear that *one* of these mediums was "begotten" (or *created)* by God to do God's work in creation. In Judaism, this Spirit was the intermediary between God and creation, everywhere present and active in creation. The Spirit enjoyed a certain divine status amid Judaism's angelic hierarchy. As a *medium*, however, the Spirit/Logos was *not equal* to God. Solely in Itself, God is *immanently transcendent* both to His *medium(s)* and creation. So given this *Judaic* understanding, the Incarnation of the Spirit (or Logos) was not the incarnation of God, but the incarnation of God's exalted *medium,* which for Paul was the *Spirit*, and for John, was the *Logos* – "*was God".*

For Paul and his generation, then, it was God's "begotten" (created) Spirit that was understood as God's "Son", the same divine Spirit-of-Christ. While the Spirit does not have a human life, It can *pervade* a human life, which it did in the man Jesus. For Paul, then, Christ was the "*Spirit made visible"*. There is no Trinity in Paul, nor any overt mention of the Logos. It has been said, however, for Paul, *Spirit* and *Logos* meant the same thing, which seems right, considering Paul preached to the Stoics and knew their belief in the Logos.

But this is why it was not until after John's Gospel appeared, the Logos was understood as the one that became incarnate and ***not* the *Spirit*.** That it was the Spirit that became incarnate and "indwelled" in the man Jesus, was a view, however, some of the fathers did not easily give up. But if neither Philo or Paul made clear distinctions between the Spirit and Logos, the Gentiles had no problem. Just about all of the early Apologists speak of the *Logos* ***and*** *the Spirit* – refer to them separately.

The question the Judaic view of the Spirit poses, is whether or not Paul had the same view of the Spirit/Logos as God's *created medium(s.)* For him, Christ as the "*Spirit made visible*" was not *Yahweh* or God made visible. He not only addressed all his prayers to God as "Father" (he never addressed any prayers to the Logos or Spirit), but said **the Spirit did not deem itself so "*equal to God*" that it could *not* become incarnate.** In other words, the Logos/Spirit was not "equal" to God because it was **not** God. Only the transcendent "Father" was God. So where Paul's Christ could be understood as the incarnation of the Spirit (God's *medium),* John states unambiguously, *"the Logos was God".* Though aware of the Judaic view of Spirit as "medium", none of the fathers shared this view. That God *needs* mediums only tells us what God *cannot* do, while the fathers believed in what God *can and did* do. They believed *God,* and *not* some *medium,* was truly Omnipresent in creation, truly "Indwelled" in man, and was truly, as Nazianzus put it, the Ground of All Being – *"For this divinity is the essence and subsistence of all things".*

These revelations were not "*mediated*" manifestations, but God's revelations to man from the beginning. Also, the fathers' interest was not simply the fact God revealed Itself, or that God *existed*, their interest was "*what*" God revealed of Itself – the nature or essence of God. As Truth-in-Itself (*ad intra*) God's revelation was not some *temporary* manifestation or *mediated* revelation "*ad extra*".

It seems the Judaic thinking was that by God having *mediums,* was a way of maintaining God's utter transcendence to creation. But since a *medium* cannot stand in the place of God (because it is not God), then how can it possibly reveal God to man? While a medium can reveal itself, how can it reveal something *not* itself – reveal God, that is? And why is it God cannot reveal Itself and needs mediums to do so? If God has no power to reveal Itself, then God is hardly "omnipotent". At any rate, given this Judaic view of "mediumship", there could be no dichotomy between God *ad intra* (*solely in Itself*) and God *ad extra* (*in creation*) because the Great Divide separating the Uncreated and created allows no such dichotomy. All God's *ad extra* revelations are only **"mediated" and are *not* God.**

2.) **So another issue was whether or not God, as revealed to man, is actually God-in-Itself, or just a particular "*way*" *or* "*mode*" God chose to reveal itself to man.** This issue – of God *ad intra* and/or *ad extra* – is where we meet at the "crossroad" spoken of earlier. Paul may have had the Judaic view of God *ad intra* (utterly transcendent), but the Gentiles had a different view.

For six centuries the Logos (the One Absolute) was not only the *soul* or essential *life* of creation, but its "body" as well – matter was the Logos' *material* manifestation and no "medium". That the Gentiles would relegate the Logos to being a "medium" of Judaism's personified "Father" wasn't going to happen, and it didn't. None of the fathers denied the Logos was Uncreated – was God.

3.) Another issue was the biblical notion of God's Wisdom and/or Spirit being "*begotten*". Now how could God *beget* God? Was this not a reference to God *begetting* the man Jesus? Whatever John's belief in this matter, he knew when he used the term "Logos" for the incarnate Christ, how the Gentiles would understand this. For the Gentile Christian, the understanding of God would not be Judaic – such was not their background or mindset. While scripture clearly states (in Proverbs) God's Wisdom was "begotten", this proved a problem even for the Jewish Philo. As already noted, Philo was not clear about the difference between God's Spirit and Wisdom, thus he compared Wisdom to the Logos and not to the Spirit.

As to how God could "beget" Its own Wisdom, or why Wisdom was not as Uncreated as the Creator, was a problem for Philo. Did "begotten" mean that at some point God *"created" Wisdom*? After all, is not *God in Itself Uncreated Wisdom?* Does it mean God had no Wisdom (or was not Wise) prior to His "begetting" or creating Wisdom? Since God **is** infinite Wisdom (divine Knowing) then how could it ever have been "begotten" or created? **Philo simply concluded that Wisdom was "*neither begotten nor unbegotten*", but "*like God, its true nature was an unknowable mystery*".**

But just as the biblical notion of a "begotten" Wisdom (or Logos) was a problem for Philo, this problem was carried over into the Christian understanding of God's *Incarnation* – **"who", exactly, was God's "begotten son", was it the eternal Logos (God), or was it the man Jesus?** Although the answer to this would become the key issue of what would become known as the heresy of "*Arianism*". This was precipitated by another so-called heresy, *Modalism* (i.e., *Sabellianism*). So called, because it was a heresy without any heretics. These issues, however, had nothing to do with the Trinity, but were a big **to do** over the true nature of *Christ.* Was God's "son" the divine Logos or the man Jesus? Did God *beget* God, or did God *beget* man?

The problem of how to interpret a biblical "begotten son" must have been a matter of dispute as early as Irenaeus (125 – 202) because, as a solution, he is the first (to my knowledge) to make a distinction between God *ad intra* (immanent in Itself) and God *ad extra* (as revealed in creation.) As *ad extra* referred *solely* to the revelation of *Christ*, he used the term "economy" to refer to the "economy of salvation" – i.e., the revelation of "Christ" as God's plan for man, or *how* God saves man. (Interestingly, he regarded the *how* of salvation as the "deification" of man – making man *what* Christ is.) From this time on, it seems, God *ad extra* was referred to as the "*economic Trinity*" where the terms "Father-Son-Spirit" **only** referred to the "how-to" (or *mode*) of man's salvation, **but did *not* refer to the Trinity *ad intra* (God-in-Itself.)** Irenaeus' "solution", of making a distinction between the "*Immanent Trinity" and "economic Trinity",* would prove invaluable to the future of Christian theology.

4.) The dispute for which Irenaeus sought a solution, was to find some justification for referring to the Trinity as "Father and Son", when this only referred to Jesus' references to God as *his* Father. After all, Jesus' reference to being one with *his* "Father" was *not* ***God's*** reference to being *one* with God. The Logos is not "*one with*" God, but **is** God. In fact, had Jesus known the Trinity, he would have known his human nature was one with the *Logos* and *not* one with the Transcendent "*Father*" – theologically, Christ is the incarnation of the Logos, not the Incarnation of the Father (or Transcendent.) It is because the fathers were aware of this, the "Father-Son" issue came up in the first place. Had they believed "Father and Son" was, in Truth, the true nature (or essence) of God's Triune existence, there would have been no dispute, no so called "*Modalism*". It is because they did *not* believe this, they had to find some way to justify referring to God as "Father and Son".

After Irenaeus came up with the solution – that the terms "Father and Son" *only* apply to the "economy of salvation" – from then on, the term used for the "economy of salvation" was "*soteriology*" – i.e., how the Incarnation worked to carry out God's plan for man's eternal salvation. The issue of *soteriology*, of course, has nothing to do with the Trinity, if anything, it escapes the whole issue of God *ad intra-extra.* In fact, one way to look at the *soteriological* presentation of Christianity, is as an *excuse* to avoid having to explain the Trinity. Just about every author who writes on the development of Christian doctrine tells us the fathers' *foremost concern* was the Incarnation's meaning for man's salvation as revealed by Christ. According to these authors, this is all Christianity and its theologies are about, that this was the *sole* concern of the early fathers. But there is no truth to this at all.

None of the fathers evinced any concern about the revelation of Christ being God's plan for man's salvation, this was a non-issue, and one of the few things on which there was unanimous agreement. Across the board, Christ as the "Way" of salvation was totally taken for granted. In this matter, all followed the traditional party-line, the **"party line" being exactly what "*soteriology*" is** – the traditional story of

Jesus dying to save man. But to say this was the fathers' sole or major concern, is unconscionable, and not true to the facts. Not a single issue the fathers fought over, had a single thing to do with man's *salvation* – thus Modalism, Arianism, Monophysitism and many other so called heresies, none were concerned with man's salvation.

Had the sole concern been man's salvation, there would have been no need for Christianity anyway. In Judaism, God was the Savior and Redeemer and Christianity changed none of this. Even belief in Christ as the promised Messiah, had no need for a Trinity. In truth, God as Trinity stands on Its own without Christ or any need for Christ. *The big question that confronted the fathers, was* ***how there could be Christ without a Trinity?*** This was the primary issue for the fathers – and so it should be for every Christian. Though the fathers never set out to define God as "Trinity", this became inevitable for a true understanding of Christ. As to *how* God saves, all the early fathers believed it was by being transformed into Christ – "*He became what we are that we might become what he is*" (Irenaeus.)

5.) The problem called "Modalism" revolved around the question: did the terms "Father and Son" refer to God *ad intra* or only to God *ad extra*? Is "Father and Son" a reference to the immanent Godhead (God-in-Itself), or only to God-in-creation – more especially, God revealed in Christ? Can we say God as "Father and Son" existed *prior* to the incarnation or only *after* the incarnation? **To say God as "Father and Son" only exist for man and his salvation, implies that after man is saved, there will be no Trinity at all! To think that beyond man's salvation, the Trinity does not exist, brings us back to the essence of God as some unknowable monad.** Novatian (200 – 258) and Tertullian (160 – 225), for example, held the distinctions of "Father and Son" (as "persons") would not last forever, that they were only temporary manifestations or "modes of God's external expression". While this may sound like "Modalism", neither denied the Trinity *ad intra*, they simply held that when creation ended (as many expected), God would no longer be known as "father and son" – or "persons". In the end, there would be no "Father-Son" (*ad extra*), but solely the Trinity *ad intra*. (In other words, once everyone is "saved", what need would there be for an "economic Trinity" anymore?) Many of the fathers shared this same understanding of the terms "Father and Son".

Irenaeus' solution, of explaining "Father and Son" as only referring to the "economy" of salvation, was no problem. It only becomes a problem when "Father and Son" are *mistaken* for a reference to the *immanent essence or nature* of the Godhead – the Trinity *ad intra* and *extra*. Unfortunately, it *has* been so mistaken! People actually believe the Trinity is a father with a son – the son being the man Jesus, of course. But is the man Jesus the Eternal Uncreated Logos (God)? Hardly! But, then, there exists no revelation of God as a "Father" or as a "Son". While people can think of themselves as a child of God and God as their father, there is no such *unmediated revelation* of God. The terms "Father and Son" solely point to Jesus' reference to God as *his* Father and goes no further than that.

6.) All references to the "economic Trinity", then, as the "economy of salvation", are *not* references to the Trinity *ad intra or extra,* but solely references to the historical revelation of Christ and how the Trinity works to bring about man's salvation. Because the Trinity (God's *triune modes of existence*) was revealed to man long before the Incarnation, any reference to an "economic Trinity" (*Father and Son*) is *not* a reference to the Trinity *ad intra or extra,* but solely a reference to the "economy of salvation".

So let us not confuse the theological notion of the "economic Trinity" with the *essential nature of God's immanent triune modes of existence.* In truth, what is called the "economic Trinity" is neither the Trinity *ad intra or ad extra.* **Reference to "Father and son" is solely a reference to the "economy of salvation", not to God *ad intra* (in Itself) nor *ad extra* (as revealed in creation from the beginning.)** The terms "Father and son" are Jesus' reference to God as his "Father", and "son of God" is the Apostles' reference to Jesus. Absolutely, "Father and son" are ***not* references to the Uncreated triune nature or essence of God.** As said, the Gospel writers knew nothing of God as Trinity.

To transpose a post-incarnate understanding of *Trinity* to a pre-incarnate understanding, is to transpose the so called "economic Trinity" to *being* God *ad intra* – ***which it is not.*** **It is because this transposition can never yield a true understanding of the Trinity, it also can never yield a true understanding of Christ.** Christianity is not premised on some passing revelation of God, but on the Infinite Existence and Essence of Almighty God – the Trinity.

7.) As regards the Trinity, the issue called *Modalism* can be defined as a *denial* that God-in-Itself (*ad intra*) is a "Father and Son", and that this only refers to the "way" (mode) God revealed Itself for the purpose of man's salvation.[1] By no means was this a denial

---

[1] Since the "Spirit" is not personified, it was not part of the "Father-Son" issue. Even as late as 325, at Nicaea, the Spirit was merely given "honorable mention". Also re-

of the Trinity, rather, it was a denial that the so called "economic Trinity" is the true nature or essence of God *ad intra.* There was not a single father who denied God was Trinity – none, ever. The whole issue called "Modalism" was whether the terms "Father and Son", used to refer to God as *Jesus'* "Father" and to Jesus as God's "Son", could legitimately refer to the eternal Uncreated Trinity *ad intra.* In other words, did the reference "Father and Son" go any further than the biblical figure of Jesus as the "son of God", and God, as his (biological) Father? Or was this a reference to the very *essence* of the eternal Godhead – Trinity? It has been said, those labeled "Modalists" were extreme *monotheists* in that they feared the Trinity, "Father-Son-Spirit", would be understood as three gods (*"tri-theism".*) And, indeed, as it turns out, Christianity would never escape the accusation of *tri-theism.* Due to the anthropomorphic way the Trinity came to be formulated, the tendency is to imagine or think of the Trinity as three embodied beings – the icon of an old man with a beard, a younger man, and a dove – which is a far worse *heresy* than "modalism" was ever said to be.

This fear of "*tri-theism*", however, explains why some of the fathers worked out a "Monarchial" view of the "Father" as the One Transcendent *Source* who "begot" or "generated" the divine Logos and spirated the Spirit. This way, they could say they were essentially "Monotheists" – having one Transcendent God (Father) as the **Source** of the Logos and Spirit. This "Monarchial view", however, is just another form of Modalism – the Logos and Spirit being "modes" of the Father's external *generation* and *spiration.* And do not think for a second this view was agreeable to one and all. No one was more against the view of God's "generating" or "emanating", than Irenaeus. He ranted against the view of the Christian *Gnostics* with their Platonic "emanation" theory. For him, the Trinity is the *"three sides of God*", not "emanations" *from* God.

One of the *accusations* (called "Modalism") was that some fathers held God was only a Trinity *ad extra* – just temporary "ways" God revealed Itself – and that *ad intra,* God is just a simple *monad* – whatever that is. This *accusation* (**that no father held**) implied that at one time God revealed Itself as Creator, at another as Savior, and at another time as Sanctifier – different *modes* of revelation, that is. This implies the Logos *really* **is** the "Father" that for a time became incarnate, and that the man Jesus was actually the "Father made visible". Thus the one

---

member, initially the "Spirit" was regarded (by some of the fathers) as the "Son" anyway. What is so interesting about the *Spirit* as the *non-personified* one of the Trinity, is that It is man's most "personal" experience of God, which is neither the Logos or the Transcendent.

who suffered on the cross was actually the Father (called "Patripassianism".) This accusation was called "Sabellianism", but if Sabellius wrote anything, his works were destroyed, so we'll never know what he believed.

So the accusation of being a "Modalist", was that God is essentially a *monad* that *temporarily expanded* into a trinity for the sake of creation, but when the work was done, retracted to its original monadic nature. (No father ever believed a thing like this.) It seems that as far as any father went, was to say the Logos and Spirit were *eternally* ***immanent in*** the Father and were only "brought forth" for creation. Once God finished creating, the Logos and Spirit would once more remain solely *immanent in the Father* and no longer *in creation.* This was basically the view of Marcellus of Ancyra (d.374), to name but one – who Eusebius *accused* of being a *Sabellian.* No truth to it whatsoever!

Basically, the terms "*Modalism*" and "*Sabellianism*" were mere *labels* used to *accuse* those who disagreed with a specific *interpretation* of scripture – as might be expected! Those who held "son" was a reference to the man Jesus were accused of denying the eternal Logos – denying the Trinity *ad intra.* And those who held the divine Logos was the uncreated "son" were accused of denying the created man Jesus was God's "son". At issue was not the Trinity *ad intra/extra,* but "*who*", in the bible, was the "*son*"? As said, the issue of Modalism had to do with the *true nature of Christ,* and not a thing to do with God as Trinity.

There is no use going over all the different *accusations* hurled at those who disagreed with someone else's interpretation of scripture and "formulation" of the Trinity. Although "Modalism" is defined as a denial God *ad intra* (in Itself) is a Trinity, not a single father denied this. The real issue was formulating God *ad intra* as either *Transcendent-Logos-Spirit*, or as the *economic Father-Son-Spirit.* So beware of the *accusative* label "Modalism", not a single father denied God was Trinity *intra/extra.*

8.) The *real* Modalists are those theologians who say the essence of God (*ad intra*) is "unknowable". Many theologians shudder when it comes to speaking of the Trinity as the *essence* of God. They regard God's *essence* ("*what*" God is) as totally "unknowable" and insist "Trinity" only refers to the "nature" of God, and not to the essence ("*what*") God is. Thus they agree with Kant that no one can ever know "*the thing in itself*". The reason this view is *true Modalism,* is because it makes *God ad intra* as some kind of an *unknowable monad.* It is a denial God can, and has, revealed Its very essence to man. That all man can know is God's plan of salvation makes the Trinity but a *temporary* manifestation of God, while God-in-Itself remains totally unknowable. If this division between *essence* and *nature* is not indicative of an agnostic, then it is indicative of a proverbial Skeptic, one who holds the mind can neither know nor affirm the truth of anything – which, without revelation, is true enough. For the skeptic, the best use of the *rational* mind is its *reason to doubt.*[2]

The positive side of skepticism, however, cautions man to examine his beliefs, question whether he only believes because he finds it intellectually satisfying, or if he knows something to *be* the Truth – a Truth on which he stakes his life. No question, without God's revelation, man couldn't know the truth of God, much less the truth of himself or anything else. It is because the mind can only go so far, "revelation" *cannot* be grasped by the intellect. But then, *revelation* was never intended for the intellect – revelation is beyond all *thinking.* Indeed, it is *because belief* relies on the *intellect* that *revelation* is also beyond all *believing.* The only reason man thinks God's essence is "unknowable" is because he expects to know "what" God is *on his own* intellectual terms, know God's essence as something he can intellectually grasp, define, or conceptually pin down. Thus he thinks God *incapable* of communicating Its true essence to man. Yet, there is an unaccountable aspect of man created *just* for God's revelation and nothing else – call it "spirit", a "truth sensor" or just the mystery of "Faith". Perhaps this is Aristotle's "other soul" which, he says, is "*that*" in man that eternally "*contemplates*" God – or better put by Irenaeus, "*The vision of God* ***is*** *the life of man*".

At any rate, the revelation of the Trinity is the revelation of the *essence* of God, and so too, Christ is the revelation of the *essence* of Man – man's eternal destiny or "what" he was created for. That God could reveal *what* God is *not,* means either God is incapable of revealing Itself, or God deliberately deceives man – what other option is there? Interestingly, those theologians who say the essence of God is *unknowable,* are the same ones who tell us God is two Gentlemen – a father and a son! Incredible! *They* are the deceivers, not God. There is no

---

[2] This book began by saying it makes no distinction between use of the terms "essence" and "nature" because it holds the true *nature* of something refers to "what" it is – its essence. The term "nature", however, can be used as opposed to "supernatural", and as opposed to "existence", it also opens the door to a monistic, even a pantheistic, understanding of "things" – more especially as it refers to God. This book, however, goes along with Aristotle's affirmation that "*what* a thing is, is *that* it is" – meaning, there is no separation of *existence* and *essence* as this refers to God and to all that exists.

such revelation of God as two male men, in fact, the very idea is silly. These people know nothing of God, what they call the *nature* of God (father and son) is no more than the **nature of man.**

It is *because* God cannot reveal *what* God is not, there is no difference between God *intra and extra.* This dichotomy, however, is all on the part of man and *not* on the part of God. It is because Man is a limited creature he receives God's revelation according to his own created capacity, **thus God *ad extra* is man's *limited* reception of God *ad intra* – as much as he can know or understand of God this side of the grave, at least.** Irenaeus pointed out a rare piece of enlightenment when he said God's divine *Wisdom **immanent** in God **ad intra,*** was also the *Cosmic Logos* (or *Intelligence*) manifested in creation ***ad extra***. Thus, the Logos known in creation to man is the Intelligence of all creation, whereas solely **in Itself**, the Logos is God's divine Knowing – Wisdom. Thus Irenaeus brought together Judaic *Wisdom* (***ad intra***) and the philosophers' *Logos* (***ad extra***), a profound **Truth** for which we could never say enough.

So all that is meant by "God *ad extra*" is how *man* knows God *in creation,* knows God *in and for himself,* which knowledge, however, is not God solely ***in Itself*** – i.e., beyond man and creation. Once transformed into Christ, however, man will indeed know as God knows (*Wisdom*) because he will "*have the mind of Christ*". *Outside* the Trinity, as said, there is no Christ, for Christ exists eternally *in and with the Trinity.* It could even be said *Christ is the oneness of man and God **ad intra** – one* in the very *essence* of God, that is.

9.) The problem with the term "Trinity" is Its being mistaken for *three* individuals, three entities, beings or even, *persons.* God, however, is not even a *numerical* "one" – as one among others, but is solely *one in essence* and **not** "three" *in existence.* Though God is three distinct and different *modes of existence,* it is the one essence that constitutes the oneness and unity of God's Existence. So just as God is one in existence and not one in number, so too, the Trinity is one in essence and not three in number. Maximus the Confessor put it most succinctly – "*We say: that the same God is truly Unity and Trinity – Unity according to the **principle of essence,** and Trinity according to **mode of existence.***"

10.) To grasp the father's understanding of the Trinity we might consider some of father's *non-personified* analogies of the Trinity. While their most often used expression or definition was "*three modes of God's existence*", they also used a variety of analogies.

a. We might start with Paul's reference to the *height, depth and breadth of God* – a three dimensional view of God. The Spirit = the *depth* of God; the Logos (throughout all) = the *breadth* of God; and the glory of the Transcendent = the *height* of God. Though relational and interdependent, each is distinct and not the other.
b. For Cyril, the perfect reflection of the Trinity was man himself, "*body, soul and spirit*", each distinct, yet composing one essence.
c. Others compared the Trinity to the *faculties of the soul functioning* together as one.
d. A favorite of the fathers was the *sun, its rays, and the heat so generated.* This was Athanasius' analogy – it is said he nowhere ever mentions "three hypostases" – or *persons*.
e. The triune modes of being were also described as three distinct *powers* – 1) creating, 2) divine knowing, 3) transforming and sanctifying – each a distinct *expression* of God and often referred to as the three "faces" ("*prosopa*") of God, each with its own existential manifestation.
f. Tertullian, scholar of Roman law, even compared the Trinity to one imperial government exercised by three coordinate branches – reminiscent of the American democratic set up.
g. There were numerous analogies taken from nature – root-trunk-branches; watershed-river-stream, and so on.
h. But no one had a more unique analogy than Origen's comparing God to a "*centrifugal force*" – "*an outward inclination of superabundance*". Those acquainted with a "centrifuge" will appreciate this way of "distilling" the basic elements of a single compound – distilling the Trinity, as it were, from God's infinite essence, the Trinity being the immanent composition of God.

Origen's *dynamic* analogy has got to be the most compelling understanding of almighty God as Trinity. God is not some "unmoved mover", some stoic "still point", Elias' "gentle breeze", some staid *immovable* monad, or an introverted "I am". For Origen, God is Eternal Movement, an absolute Dynamo. From this dynamic view we get his understanding of the Logos as being "*eternally generated*" as "Light from Light". (Origen is also the one who referred to the Trinity as three "*hypostases*", a term that caused a lot of controversy.)

It seems Arius objected to Origen's analogy of the Logos "*eternally generated*" as Light-from-Light, saying that anything "eternally generated" could never be "finished" or a complete *being,* thus, how could one regard God's Logos as *not* a complete *being?* Arius' concern is reminiscent of Parmenides who accused Heraclitus (both of the 6th century B.C.) of saying the Logos was a *"becoming"*, which, for Parmenides, was as good as saying it had no *being* – did not actually exist. He said, *"Unless something* ***is,*** *it cannot even be thought, and, therefore, cannot be"*. For him, *being* fills all space, whereas non-being is empty space – a void. Parmenides is the one who defined God as *"what Is"* – an enduring phrase to this day. On these same grounds, Arius objected to Origen's dynamic Logos as "eternally generated" as if the Logos was not ***a being.*** **And, indeed, the Logos is *not* a being, nor is the Trinity three beings!**

Origen's dynamic view of God as *eternally creating,* alerts us to the fact "creation isn't over until it's over", that it is an on-going process and not limited to some point in *time*. That creation is a process of "becoming" is, indeed, the dynamic transformative movement of man's life. This view – of the Logos as God's *eternal generation* – was not only the keystone of Meister Eckhart's mysticism, but in one form or another, the keystone of all the fathers' understanding of Christ. This was God *eternally generating the Logos* ***in*** *man* so all would be transformed into Christ. This was Eckhart's "***Birth of God in the Soul***" that he took from the fathers. Irenaeus regarded the Eucharist as the *Incarnation* of the Logos *in* man – the "Eucharist", no different from the Logos "generated" (or *incarnated*) in the man Jesus.

All the fathers had their favorite analogies, ***none*** **of them *personifying* the Trinity as individual beings or entities.** Their views were anything but the human image of a "Father and Son" – as the traditional language might lead us to believe. They all pointed to *distinctions,* and none to separations, divisions or individual beings. The Trinity was not a "numerical unity" of three "ones", but a unity of essence. Unfortunately, the fathers' terminology was highly constrained to using Biblical language *despite* its anthropomorphic images of God. As St. Augustine notes, the Biblical personification of God *"was the language of analogy and an accommodation to the childish understanding of men ....Scripture rarely uses terms which are not spoken metaphorically about God and which are not found in any creature"*. In another place Augustine actually apologizes for use of the terms "Father and Son" as "*persons*", this was due, he said, to a "*deficiency in human language"*.

If we wonder, then, why the fathers were so intent on finding some way or some terms to express the reality of God's triune modes of existence – such as "hypostasis", for example – it was to eliminate the purely anthropomorphic images inevitably attached to "Father and Son". Had they been satisfied with the usual understanding of "Father and Son" as individual beings or persons, they would have left it at that. After all, what need is there to make a "distinction" between a father and son when everyone takes their relationship for granted anyway? Who doesn't know a father is *not* a son, and who doesn't know a father and son are of the same ontological nature? So what was there about the terms "Father-Son-Spirit" that was insufficient to express the triune essence of God so that the term "*hypostasis*" was used instead, as a better way to express the reality of the Trinity? "Hypostasis" was a philosophical term, and like all philosophical terms for the ultimate "One", it carried no anthropomorphic overtones. So while they stuck to the traditional *soteriological* language of "Father and Son", they obviously had no anthropomorphic understanding of this as God *ad intra.* But if they did their best to get this across in their *Chalcedon* statement of God's triune "*hypostases*", this was lost on the public for whom "Father and Son" retained its usual *Nicene* anthropomorphic understanding.

11.) It has been pointed out there was a difference between the Eastern (Greek) and Western (Latin) Church's approach to understanding the Trinity. Where the East first considered the "particularity" of Father-Son-Spirit and *then* God's one essence, the West first considered the one essence and *then* the particular "inter-relations" of the three. So where the East gave priority to the "particular", the West gave priority to the one "essence". In retrospect, it could be said the East espoused the more Aristotelian view of the particular or "individual" as the ontologically real, while the West espoused the Platonic view of "essence" as the ontologically real. The difference, however, is largely a matter of priority – do we give priority to the essential nature of something, or to the *particularity* of some "thing"? According to some authors, where the West recognized the essential *unity* of God over the personal diversity, the Eastern tradition recognized the personal *diversity* over the essential unity of God. So where in the East, the Trinity is *one essence in three hypostases,* in the West, the Trinity is *three hypostases in one essence.*

As it turns out, those who stressed the one essence of God over God's triune hypostases were sometimes called "Modalists", while those who stressed the three hypostases over the one essence were called "Tri-theists". Thus some Eastern authors regard the West as "Modalistic", while some Western authors regard the East as "tri-theistic" – but such is the nature of theological mud-slinging.

12). It seems East and West had different views regarding the inter-Trinitarian *relationship* of "Father-Son-Spirit". While it can be said God's modes of existence are "interrelated", this has nothing in common with any notion of "relationships". The notion of "relationship" is purely a sociological analogy only comprehensible in human terms. Thus to speak of any kind of relationship of father-son, parent-child, siblings, friends, spouses and so on, not only requires individual beings, but demands a totally anthropomorphic idea of God, i.e., Trinity. The sole Father-Son "relationship" that existed, was Jesus' own *human* rapport with God. Jesus always referred to God as "other" than himself, his personal "relationship" to God being the example of everyman's relationship to God. Jesus was *not* an example of God's "relationship" to God – which makes no sense. So beware of ever imposing any notion of "human relationship" on the Trinity *ad intra or extra.*

As for the Eastern fathers' way of expressing the Trinitarian *ad intra* "relations", Gregory of Nazianzus (329 – 390) is reported to have said the Father was the "*Unoriginate*", the begotten Son, the "*Originated*", and the Spirit "*Proceeded*" from the two. (The Spirit could not be "begotten", of course, lest it make two Sons.) Yet nothing that has an "origin" (or is *originated*) **is Uncreated**. The idea of the Uncreated "begetting" the Uncreated is not only a contradiction of terms, but implies "*infinite regress*" – God having a father, a grandfather, a great grandfather – *ad infinitum.* To define these "relations" as *cause-and-effect* – "*unoriginate, originate*" and "*spirated*" is hardly a definition of the Trinity's immanent life or God's *modus operandi.*

This Monarchial view is obviously premised on the Father as the "principle" of a Trinitarian "ordering". That only the Father is "unoriginate" makes the Father the *one essence, Source* or *Fountainhead* of the Logos and Spirit – these being Its "*effulgences*" or *emanations*. But if the Unoriginated is prior to the Son, then the Unoriginated could not have been a "Father" *until* it "emitted" (or begot) a son – as we'll see later, this implies there was a *time when there was no son,* no Logos or Spirit. Due to this view – found in a number of the fathers – the Logos would be regarded as "*secondary*" and the Spirit as *third,* both being *subordinate* to "God" – the *Father*, that is. Here we must interject – along with Jesus and Paul, the fathers almost consistently refer to God as "Father".

Thus we will find reference to the Trinity as "God (Father) *and* his son *and* his spirit" as if Son and Spirit were "other" than God and not equally as "unoriginate" (Uncreated) as God – or "father". Even the Creed reads, "**We believe in God the Father Almighty *and* in His Son**…" implying the Logos is a *subordinate,* whereas the Logos is no less "Almighty God" than the Transcendent and Spirit. In truth, **in the Trinity no "one" is subordinate to the other, there is no *line-up* as first, second and third, no source, no "originator" no begetter, no**

emanating. The reason every act of God requires the three act as one, is because they do *not* act *independently.* Though each has distinct prerogatives, they are not three independent, individual spirits, entities or beings. Any attempt to "circumscribe" God or *God's triune modes of existence,* is so much *tri-theism.* Though each can be revealed *individually,* this does not mean they are *individual spirits or beings.* It seems the only reason for pointing to the Father-God as the One Unoriginate Source of the other two, was an attempt to affirm the Trinity was totally *monotheistic* and not *tri-theistic,* i.e., three gods. But if the Logos and Spirit had a "Source" or "Cause", then they are **not** Uncreated and eternal – not God, that is. Thus any "Monarchial" view of the Trinity inevitably leads to the view the Logos and Spirit are *secondary or subordinate deities.*

Although it is said the term "monarch" meant the same as "monotheism", this "monarch" was a reference to the Father as the **sole *essence* of God from which the other two "originated" or "proceeded".** This view, however, is not appreciably different from Plotinus' "One" as the *Source* or origin of the Godhead, eternally generating the *Nous* (demiurge, divine mind, or Philo's Logos), which, in turn, eternally generates the *Spirit* (Universal Soul.)[3] Both the fathers and Plotinus used the same analogy of the Sun as Source eternally "generating" rays as the *Nous* or *Logos.* As for why the fathers called the Nous or Logos "*begotten*" and not "*generated*" it is because "*begotten*" is the *Biblical* term! Obviously, this tri-part understanding of the Trinity not only creates a ranking system, it is virtually Gnostic *emanationism* so condemned by Irenaeus. It implies "subordinationism", an inequality, to say nothing of its patriarchal "*Monarchianism*" (another form of Modalism.) Frankly, there is no authentic Trinity here, it is a piece of "*emanationism*" that belongs to the Gnostics and Plotinus. While adopting the notion of the Father as the One *Source* was intended to counter the accusation of *tri-theism*, in doing so, the Truth of the Trinity was completely skewed. What we have instead, is *Plotinism* clear and simple. This could even be regarded as a form of Modalism in that God is only a Trinity *ad extra* – having *emanated* the Logos and Spirit. **This is *not* the Trinity *ad intra or ad extra.***

There is another problem with the notion of Father as the *Source* of the Godhead. If the goal is to be one with the Source, or to "get back" to the Source, one would have to go *beyond* Logos and Spirit,

---

[3] The works of the philosopher Plotinus (205 – 270) greatly influenced the religious thinkers of his day, especially the Greek fathers. Though he was not Christian, one can point out similarities that may have originated with Ammonius Saccus, the reputed founder of *Neo-Platonism* and the teacher of both Plotinus and Origen.

leave them behind, in which case, there would be no Trinity to speak of. Since this was the Plotinian goal (to return to the Source) why settle for anything less – like the Logos or Spirit? Forget the Trinity! The Trinity may not be an equilateral triangle, but it is also not a ladder of emanations, generations, processions, begettings, or any of that business.[4]

Perhaps the sole notion of an intra-Trinitarian "relationship" with some meaning to mortals is that articulated by Augustine. This was the Spirit understood as the love between the Transcendent and Logos, which, in its mystical sense, means "that" in man that loves the Transcendent **is** the Logos, and "that" which the Transcendent loves in man, **is** the Logos, with the **Spirit being the union of the two *in man* – the whole Trinity present in man!** The only reason this is "mystical", however, is because there is *no human being* involved in this love, there is no "other", no *human relationship* with God to speak of. This is a love beyond anything man could ever generate, be it for God or another human being. For this type of *love*, no human comparison is possible, it is indefinable. It is interesting that the philosopher Empedocles (495 – 435 B.C.) held that the One Existent was *Love*. *Love* was the genesis of the universe, the first principle or cause of all existence, the *unity* and oneness of all things. Without it *(Love)* nothing exists. Aristotle, after affirming this, Empedocles' view, then proceeded to debunk it as so much poppycock. Too bad for Aristotle!

If one can look beyond the *accusations* labeled "Modalism" and "Sabellianism", get to the bottom of the issue, he will find it had nothing to do with the Trinity, but with what can only be called "*the father-son problem*" – the subject of the next chapter. Basically, this was taking the "economic Trinity" (Father and son) and treating it as if it was reference to the Trinity *ad intra.* With this "switch" from the Trinity *ad intra/extra* to an *"economic"* Trinity – two males, no less – the Trinity was totally left behind, Its reality unrecognized, Its Truth, merely labeled an "*inscrutable mystery"*. That the fathers' original understanding of the Trinity was formally replaced by an anthropomorphic image of a "father and son", is one of the most disastrous wrong turns in the history of Christianity. But let us end this with Irenaeus' (125 – 202) understanding of the Trinity:

"God – the glorious Transcendent; the powerful, illuminating and

---

[4] This was the whole problem with Eckhart's "*Breakthrough*". He tried to get to the *Source* – beyond "Father and Son" – which only landed him in a "*wasteland", a "desert"* – no God, no nothing. But since the Trinity **is no "father and son"** anyway, there is no use trying to get *beyond* what does not exist in the first place. In truth, the only thing man can go *beyond* are his own wrong ideas of the Trinity – of God.

transforming Holy Spirit; the divine knowing and intelligent Wisdom of the Creator and Logos; each revelation being the fullness of God".

In the history of Christianity, no one articulated the Trinity more beautifully than this.

FATHER-SON PROBLEM

*"It is one thing that he (Logos) was God **before** he was man, another that he (Christ) **was man and God,** and another that **after** being man and God, he (Christ) was perfect man and perfect God."*
– Hilary of Poitiers (310 – 367)

After defining these "**three states of Christ**" Hilary goes on to say, "*Do not then **confuse** the time and natures in the mystery of the dispensation (Incarnation), for according to the attributes of his different natures, he must speak of himself in relation to the mystery of his humanity in one way **before** his birth, in another while he was yet to die, and in another as eternal*".

Had the fathers heeded Hilary's admonition – which is the theological gem of all time – one of the most momentous and disastrous wrong turns in Christian history could have been averted. Just about all the major dissensions in the first five centuries can be traced to having based an understanding of Christ on one or other of these states and having ignored the others.

It is said that for the first three centuries, the fathers understood the terms "Father and son" as solely a reference to the man Jesus. We have already gone over how Jesus knew of his birth, understood God as his sole natural (biological) father, and how all references to Jesus as "son of God" were references to his miraculous conception and ***not*** references to Almighty God or the Uncreated Logos. The synoptic writers knew nothing of a Logos or a Trinity. So, obviously it was not God who was *conceived* by God, or God who called God "my Father", this was solely the human being – the man Jesus.

There are numerous biblical references to God's "sons", specific "sons" being the patriarchs – Abraham, Isaac and Jacob – as well as "anointed" kings, prophets, and holy people. For all these "sons", God was their "Father", and as such, God was the Father of all Israel. This was the understanding of the biblical writers, the understanding of Jesus and his apostles. Jesus' reference to "his" Father, however, was different in that it implied or affirmed his miraculous conception by God, a meaning it never had before – or since.

So prior to the formulation of the Trinity, all references to "son of God" found in the Gospels were understood as reference to the man Jesus, not references to God. Even centuries later, after the Trinity had been formulated, the man Jesus was never understood as the Uncreated Logos or one of God's *triune modes of existence.* While Jesus was the human "person" of the incarnate Logos, prior to the incarnation the man Jesus never existed.

Knowing this, it seems incredible the question of "*who*" God's son was, could ever have become the pivotal issue for promoting a true or false understanding of Christ – and of Christianity. Was "son" a reference to the Logos *prior* to the incarnation or a reference to the man Jesus *after* the incarnation? How this question is answered yields not only different Christologies, but different understandings of the Trinity and Christ. All the major disputes, at least by the time of the third century, centered around this particular "Father-Son-Problem". Had there been some agreeable definition or understanding from the outset, this might have been prevented, but there was no such agreement, not even after the Council of Nicaea (325) was specifically convened to settle the matter. Thus, where some of the fathers' references were to the incarnate *human* nature as the son, for others, it was reference to the Logos' *divine* nature as the "son". What hung in the balance, of course, was a true understanding of the Trinity and Christ – as said before, failure to get the Trinity right is a failure to get Christ right.

No author seems willing to point out or even admit, the drastic "switch" that came about from the initial understanding of the man Jesus as the "son of God", to the declaration that the "son of God" *was God* – specifically, the Uncreated Logos. This was a transposition from a human being as "son of God" to God as the "son of God"; a switch from a human being as *son* to one of the Trinity's immanent *modes of existence* as *son*. **With this *switch,* the "son" Jesus became God (Logos), and God became the "son" Jesus.** We can easily understand why scholars and theologians do not like to point out this *switch*. To do so, they would have to account for the reason behind it, a reason that would only open up a can of worms and jeopardize the present "party-line" rendition of the Trinity and Christ. The sole reason for this switch was to **avoid the accusation of *anthropolatry* – the worship of a human being as God.** If people are going to worship a human being, then the only way to justify this worship would be to *deify him* – make a human being God.

But rather than get into the reason behind this *switch*, authors skim over it by making the case that the Apostles and Paul had *always* believed the man Jesus was God, that reference to him as "son of God" was always a reference to God. While this is the view they would *like* everyone to believe, **it is patently false** and totally misleads. **The transposition from Jesus as "son" to Jesus as Almighty God (Logos) as "son", was the genesis of the single most egregious error in Christian doctrine.** There is not a single father of note that ever believed Jesus was God – none. That any of them ever adopted what came to be the "traditional party-line" in this matter, was either out of coercion or solely for the sake of "peace" – lest Christianity implode and be lost forever.

By the early 300's the issue of "*who*" was the "son of God" became so explosive the emperor called for the first Church Council to settle the issue. So it was at Nicaea (325) this transposition was pinned down. From then on, the biblical "son of God" was to be a reference to one of the Trinity, the Uncreated Logos, Almighty God, and no longer a reference to the created man Jesus. From this time forward, this switch has been responsible for a totally *mistaken*, if not *false*, understanding of Christ, and indeed, the whole Trinity. Thus, in the Creed for example, *who* does "Son of God" refer to? Is it God, the eternal Uncreated Logos, or is it the created man Jesus? Since few people actually know the eternal Logos, yet everyone knows the man Jesus, everyone *mistakenly* takes Jesus, the biblical "son of God", for Almighty God. This is how it goes, this is what became the traditional "party-line". Those who truly know God, however, know God is neither a human being nor the "son" of anyone.

As to giving any particular date for the onset of this Father-Son-Problem, or even giving a name to any particular father who inaugurated it, this cannot be done. All we know is that this transposition came about in the early 300's when the fathers were still formulating the Trinity. Clearly the New Testament references to Jesus as "son of God" were to the historical man Jesus and not to the Uncreated Logos. Even if the references were to the preexistent messiah, the messiah was never regarded as God. The Gospels made no division between "who" was speaking, all references were to the single person Jesus. It never occurred to the writers they were writing about Almighty God or Yahweh, nor did they know anything about the Trinity. No question, Jesus was a specially anointed human being, and this is "who" they wrote about.

The fact the Gospels only speak of Jesus as a single person, attributing both miracles and crucifixion to him, became a problem for some of the fathers. Thus "who" said, *"I am the Way, the Truth and the Life*", and who said, "*My soul is sorrowful unto death"*? If there was any debate involved, it could not have been over **who** said it – obviously, Jesus *said* it. The debate was who these sayings *referenced* – God, Messiah, Christ, or only the man Jesus? As to the status of *who* was speaking and acting, this became an issue, for as soon as the voices are switched from Jesus speaking to God speaking, there is a different understanding, not only of *who* said it, but of *what* was meant.

While in the process of formulating the Trinity, with no agreement on the proper reference of "Father and son", the fathers were always talking past one another. Thus if one said "the son was created" (referring to the man Jesus), he was accused of denying the divine Logos – as "the eternal and only begotten Son". Then another would say, "the Son was begotten and not made" (referring to the Logos) and he would be accused of denying Jesus was the "son of God". And so goes centuries of disputes and anathemas over "who" the son was – divine, human, exactly "who" – or "what"? Pages and pages of sayings of the fathers could be quoted where their references to "Father and son" could be interpreted as either references to the man Jesus or to the divine Logos. This was also the crux of the whole issue of "Modalism" – was the Logos God's "son" (*ad intra)* **before** the incarnation, or just God's "son", Jesus, (*ad extra*) **after** the Incarnation?

As best I can make out, it was the priest, Arius of Alexandria (256 – 336) who seems responsible for bringing this issue to a head or at least drawing a line in the sand. By no means did he start this dispute, in fact, he would have been the last to even propose such a "switch". For him, only Jesus – not the Logos – was the "son of God". It seems the central issues were based solely on two biblical references:

1. In Proverbs, God's Wisdom is personified, "*Before the ages, in the beginning he created me, and for all ages I will not cease to be"* – or *"The Lord possessed me in the beginning of his ways, before he made anything from the beginning. I was set up from eternity, and of old before the earth was made"*. (These are two translations of Proverbs 8:22-23 that Judaism understood as God's creation of the Spirit/Logos to use as an intermediary in creation.)

2. *"The Lord hath said to me: thou art my son, this day I have begotten thee"* – or *"Let me proclaim Yahweh's decree, he has told me, 'You are my son, today I have become your father'"*. (Two translations of Psalm 2:7.)

It is hard to believe that due to two lines or so in the bible, Christianity would be stuck forever with the idea of God (Trinity), as a "Father and a Son" – **incredible**! If this isn't an indictment of scripture, it is certainly an indictment of those who take its personified anthropomorphic deities literally. For sure, should man experience a true revelation of God, he'd be hard put to find it in scriptures – with all its anthropomorphic personifications and images it conjures. To interpret metaphors and personifications of God as Truth, is literally the death-knell of any authentic revelation of God. While metaphors and analogies have their place, people must be warned not to take them as the literal Truth of anything – this is how people make God a god. The problem with personified metaphors is their becoming so mentally concretized and imbedded in people's minds, they are virtually handed down from one generation to the next like original sin.

God, of course, does not *depend* on scripture for the Truth of anything. For some people, however, God *has* to be in accord with their scriptures, otherwise, God doesn't exist – because God could *never* reveal anything outside or apart from the "book". If people thought God actually revealed what is *not* in their "book", they could *never* believe it. This is how scripture works not only to box God in, but to box people in. An authentic revelation of God, however, is solely *unmediated* and can never be *mediated* by anyone's writings or mere hearsay. This reminds us of Jesus' saying, "*It is because I tell you the Truth you do not believe me*". That he was one with God was the Truth, and yet, it was a Truth **that fell *outside* his own Judaic scriptures, his own belief system!** For what other reason was he, a human being, put to death but for affirming he was *one with God*? Such was *never* in the Judaic belief system, ***never in its scriptures!***

Because no author points out this rather abrupt transition in the Christian understanding of the Trinity – from "Transcendent-Logos-Spirit" to "Father-Son (Jesus)-Spirit" – yet, by connecting the dots, it becomes obvious this switch was the whole issue that came to a head with the "Arian heresy". What is inconceivable, however, is that some unknown priest, Arius, ever said or wrote that the divine Logos and Spirit were just "created" creatures (i.e., were not God), and that this statement would have caused such a radical split in the Church: the first "schism" in Christian history. This report is just not credible. Any priest in the early 300's who said such things – denied the Trinity – would have been dismissed by his Bishop as a fool and we'd never heard of him again. But that the majority in the Church at that time sided with Arius, gives us pause to discover and know just what the man was saying.

Although Arius' works were destroyed, yet given his position as stated by others, there is no evidence he denied the Logos and Spirit were God. On the contrary, what he denied was that God's "begotten son" referred to the Logos (God), but instead, referred to the man Jesus as God's "begotten son". The dispute, then, centered on the issue of just "who" was the "begotten son" – the Uncreated Logos or the man Jesus? Thus, if **one worships the "son", is this the worship of God or just a man?** Accusations flew back and forth in this matter depending on one's understanding of "son". Because the Arians regarded the "son" as the man Jesus, they addressed their prayers and worship of Christ to the Logos (God) and not to the "son" Jesus. Any notion the "son" Jesus was the Uncreated Logos or God, could only lead to the worship of a man as God. In their view, to address prayers to Jesus as the "son" would have been "*anthropolatry*", the worship of a man. **It was Arius' accusation of *anthropolatry* that was the issue at hand.** So the whole issue, then, of what became known as the "Arian heresy" was the issue of *anthropolatry*.

While no father worshiped a human being as God, yet they knew other people did so. By far, the majority of uneducated Christians were the "simple folk" but a step from the polytheistic system from which they had emerged. For them, Christianity offered something new and special. This was the combination of the lofty philosophical belief in *One* utterly transcendent invisible *Source* of creation, with the *One* God that so loved man as to take on a visible form, literally, come down to man's level to save him and show him the way of salvation. When the incarnation is stated "*God **became** man*", to take this *literally*, means the Uncreated "*became*" created – God literally "became" a human being. Thus it could be said that in Christ, Christianity fulfilled both man's loftiest philosophical aspirations and, at the same time, fulfilled his polytheistic need for some tangible "deity" on which to focus his worship of God.

Because of Jesus' miraculous conception, it could rightly be said he was the "son of God" – even, "begotten" by God. This was the reason Jesus called God his "father" and did not object to being called "son of God". But if the Uncreated Logos is God, how could it be said that God "begot" God? – some of the fathers scoffed at the very idea, indeed, it makes no sense. Jesus, of course, never understood himself as God or the divine Logos – he was raised with no Trinity and no Logos. If one wanted to be *theologically* correct in fact, Jesus, as the Incarnation of the *Logos*, was *not* "one" with the *Father*, but "one" with the *Logos!* So if Jesus had been truly "orthodox" he would have said "*the Logos and I are one*", **not** "*the Father and I are one.*" But then, Jesus was *not* orthodox, he was made to *fit* Christian orthodoxy, and not the other way around.

It seems early on, liturgical prayers were addressed to "Jesus Christ" as prayers to God. (The Jewish reference to God as "Lord" was also used to refer to "Jesus Christ" as "Lord and God".) But just as Christians were accused of tri-theism, so too, they were accused of *anthropolatry*. The fathers understood this perfectly. They knew the difficulty of formulating the mystery of the Trinity and Christ that might lead to the false conclusion that a human being was Almighty God. Thus they had to find some way to justify people's worship of Christ as God – specifically, how they could say, in truth, "**Jesus Christ is God".** Since neither scripture nor philosophy provided any solution in this matter, they came up with an *interpretation* of scripture that would justify reference to "son of God" as a reference to God and not just to the man Jesus. Thus, the Uncreated eternal Logos was to be understood as "son of God" and it was this "son" that *became* the visible man Jesus.

By switching references from Jesus as the "son", to the Uncreated Logos as the "son", it could then **be said** that worship of the "son" was *not* the worship of the man Jesus, but the worship of God – the divine Logos. But to think this transposition from the human to the divine could resolve the problem of *anthropolatry* is naive, all it did was **promote** it. The only "son" people know is the man Jesus, and to now say this *son is God,* is the ultimate definition of *anthropolatry*. Needless to say, the attempt to make this switch created a furor – anathemas, exiles, and accusations of heresy that ended with the first schism in Christianity. Obviously, when it comes to an understanding of "Christ", it makes a great difference "*who*" can be referred to as "son". While some fathers may have thought this switch – from the human to the divine – resolved the issue of anthropolatry, it totally skewed the Trinity. Father and Son" is no longer reference to just an "economic Trinity", but a reference to the Godhead, the Trinity "*ad intra*" – that whole "Modalistic" issue. **Needless to say, make a *human being* Almighty *God* and there is no Incarnation, no Christ, no Trinity, no Christianity, and no Monotheism.**

To think the anthropomorphic biblical interpretation of God "generating" or "begetting" an Uncreated "Son" could have justified a transition in the Church's whole understanding of the Trinity and Christ, can only be put down as the most flagrant wrong turn in the entire history of Christianity. That because of this, the fathers' original understanding of the Trinity and Christ would be gone forever and replaced by a totally skewed paradigm of the Faith, is indeed a tragic error, and one perpetuated now for over 1700 years.

Although the "Arian heresy" takes its name from the priest "Arius" – because he was the one who drew the line in the sand – he, himself, was perfectly orthodox. Arius held that the human being Jesus and Almighty God "*were not of the same substance*". For him, "son" was a reference only to the man Jesus, because, as he astutely points out, to say the divine Logos was "begotten" implies *there was a time when the Logos (God) did **not** exist*. Thus the one "begotten" in "time" could only be the man Jesus. He held that since God (Logos) existed eternally, there was no "time" when the Logos did not exist or was ever "begotten".

Because the Logos is eternal, "**one substance with the Father**"

(Arius' own words), then "only-begotten son" could only refer to Jesus, the post-incarnate Logos. For Arius, the man Jesus was the Incarnate "son", and as a created human being, he was not divine – in his own words, "*Jesus and God were not of the same substance*". He understood the quotes from Proverbs and Psalms as references only to the Incarnate "son" Jesus, and not to the divine Logos. What follows is his argument against those who regarded the "son" as the eternal Logos:

1. To say the Logos was the "begotten" son means there was a time when the Logos did not exist and that the son was not eternal. So if the Logos only came into existence when "begotten", then how could the Logos be "eternal"?

2. This also means that until God "begot" the Logos, God was not yet a "Father" and thus, God could not be called a "Father". Only *after* the incarnation can God rightly be called a "Father" – the "father" of Jesus, that is. (Keep in mind, no man can be called a "father" *until* he has a child.)

His thinking made perfect sense, to say the Eternal Logos (God) was "begotten" is a contradiction of terms – how could the Uncreated "beget" the Uncreated? Either we must re-define "God" or put this notion aside as nonsense.[1] Since the term "begot" implies there was a "time when the begotten did not exist", why use the term at all? As one father scoffed, "*Who ever heard of God 'begetting'?*" Transposing the human event of "begetting" from man to God, is the ultimate anthropomorphic understanding of a "god". This is why Arius held the term "son" could not be a reference to the eternal Logos *before* the incarnation, but only *after* the Incarnation or when Jesus, "the son", had been "begotten". It is said Arius presented more Biblical proofs for his views than could be countered by any biblical objections – which must have enraged his opponents no end. All that has survived of his position, however, is mainly what his accusers said he said, but as we know, all "hearsay" is heresy anyway.

It seems there has been some scholarly concern with use of the term "***only** begotten son*", which they say is not in the original Greek or Hebrew bible. But **if** "son" refers to the Logos or God, then it would be *true* because there is ***only one*** **Logos** – nobody denies this. And as for the man Jesus being the **only** *human* son for whom God was his biolog-

---

[1] To say the Uncreated can "beget" the Uncreated is a case of "infinite regress" diametrically opposed to monotheism. If "God" can beget "God" where does it stop? If god can have a "father" then god can also have a grandfather, a great grandfather – *ad infinitum.* This view denies the existence of One Uncreated Infinite Absolute – the whole meaning of "monotheism".

ical father, this is also the *Truth*. Even if Mary had 50 kids, ***only one*** *was conceived (or begotten) by God* – otherwise, one might as well believe *everyone* is the Incarnation of God. But what did Jesus say about this? He said – "*My father and your father, my God and your God", "**I say you are all sons of God"***. This common metaphor, however, has nothing to do with the issue at hand. The issue here is "who" the biblical "son of God" referred to, was it a reference to God (Logos) or to the man Jesus? **The problem is not man as a "son", but God as a "Son".**

When Nazianzus was questioned why the term "begotten" was ever used, he tells us he is only "*quoting scripture*". "*Everyone knows that in practice we very often find tenses interchanged when **time** is spoken of, this is the custom of holy Scripture, not only in respect to past tense and of the present, but even of the future*." This is reminiscent of Hilary's admonition quoted at the beginning of this chapter. In short, where time is involved, count God out, this is just human talk. In the end he says, "*the begetting of God must be honored in silence, anything more than this is hidden by a cloud and escapes **your** dim eyes.*" (And probably escaped his eyes as well.)

The fathers left numerous apologies assuring us the Logos was not "begotten" in any human sense of the term. One excuse was that, for the fathers, "begotten" meant "of the same nature" whereas anything "created" or "made" could *not* be of the same nature. Another excuse was that it was not a reference to God *ad intra*, but only God *ad extra* – that it referred to the *incarnate* Logos and *not* the *eternal* Logos. The problem with this latter excuse, however, is that by their own definition, Jesus was "created" and not "begotten" – the incarnation was not understood as God "*begetting*", but rather as God "*creating*" human nature *for Itself*.

Yet, after denying that God's "begetting" was in no way similar to human begetting – which is the sole reason for using the "analogy" – they go right on using the term! After all, if *scripture said it*, who are we to question? It would not do to suggest the bible might "beget" false ideas – like taking its anthropomorphic description of God as the truth of God. Too bad the fathers didn't rely on John's "*in the beginning was the Logos"*, it would have eliminated the whole problem of "begetting".

An example of one who took the opposite line from Arius was Nestorius, later Patriarch of Constantinople – the highest position in the Eastern Church. Before being assigned to this office, Nestorius had been a monk well-known for his wise counsel and, more especially, for his *orthodoxy*. His understanding was this: since *prior* to the incarnation the man Jesus never existed, then he could *not* be the *eternal* "begotten Son of the Father". **Since Jesus was a *created* being, and not "eternally begotten", then it was *only* the Logos *who* was "the only begotten Son" and *not* the man Jesus.** He said referring to Jesus as the "Son of God" made Jesus God, whereas Jesus was only a human being and not a divine being – he was *not* the Uncreated Logos, not God's "begotten Son". Like Arius, this too, made perfect sense, yet he and others were accused of positing "two sons", one *before* the incarnation (Logos), and one *after* the incarnation (Jesus), thus he too was duly anathematized. What is so interesting about both their views, however – seemingly reached from two different positions (or interpretations) – is that *both* agreed Jesus was not God, not the Logos. Indeed, not a single father held, or ever said, the man Jesus was God – **none**!

Later, when we take up the issue of "Theotokos" – a reference to Mary as "Mother of God" – we will recall an observation made by Nestorius. He pointed out that the way the Creed was worded led people to think that the "Son begotten of the Father" was the *same* son "born of Mary" – for which reason, Mary was regarded as "Theotokos" or "Mother of God". In his view, this was due to a mistaken understanding of the Creed, i.e., the one "begotten" of God was equally "begotten" of Mary, which meant **Mary *and* God "begot" God** (the eternal Logos) – thus she was "Mother of God". Either this, or there were "two births" – one of God and another of Mary which, for Cyril at least, would make "two different sons". Nestorius, of course, believed none of this, he never believed Mary conceived the eternal Logos and never believed in "two sons" – as he was *accused* of doing. He also pointed out that if Mary is the "Mother of God" this means she was *hypostatically* one with the Father – absolutely, a marvelous understanding of Mary!

Nestorius is right about the Creed. It states "*We believe in one Lord Jesus Christ, the only Son of God eternally begotten of the Father...true God from true God...came down from heaven.... and became man*". This makes "Jesus Christ" "*eternally begotten*" and **not** the Logos. According to this, it was "Jesus Christ" who *pre-existed* the incarnation that came down to become incarnated! Now, who can fathom *incarnating* one who is already *incarnated*? Evidently the man "Jesus" existed *prior* to the incarnation – *true God from true God,* one of the *Uncreated* Trinity, a "*mode of God's eternal existence*". Is this what Christians are taught to believe? In truth, this is not Christian at all. No father believed the man Jesus was "eternally begotten". Clearly the creed is a *post incarnate* statement of Christ with no reference at all to the *pre-incarnate Logos.* Strictly speaking, the Creed makes no true reference to the Trinity – the Logos is totally missing. Instead, it clearly states Jesus is the one "eternally begotten". And then we wonder why few people understand the Trinity, or even have a true understanding of Christ!

When it comes to the Truth of Christ, the formal Christian Creed is no help, it may even be a hindrance. When people confuse the two (as Nestorius pointed out) and take the created Jesus for the Uncreated Logos (God), the real Christ is gone. There has to be God (Logos) **before** there is any incarnation of the Logos – before there is any Christ and before there is the *created* man Jesus. No question, the Creed must be totally restated, Christians today are not the semi– polytheists of yesterday. Without a clear distinction between the eternal Uncreated Logos and the created man Jesus (son born of Mary), there can be no honest understanding of Christ or the Incarnation.

So the real question was whether or not "son" referred to the pre-incarnate Logos (before Jesus ever existed) or if it referred to the post-incarnate Logos and the miraculous way Jesus was "fathered" – created or conceived – by God. The answer to this question would be the cause of untold confusion, disagreements and battles that went on for centuries, a confusion that persists to this day – though who in the Church would admit it?

We have only given two well-known examples of this Father-Son-Problem – Modalism and Arianism – but there are many more. A number of the fathers regarded "father and son" as just honorary or transitory "titles", while others only went along with the "traditional" terminology out of "respect" and not because they agreed with it. For Tertullian (160 – 225) and Hippolytus (170 – 235), "son" was only a reference to the incarnate man Jesus – *"The Logos cannot be called 'son' until the incarnation"* (Hippolytus.)

For the Apologists, prior to creation there was only the eternal Logos **in** the Father – "*the Father's intelligence, mind or knowing*" – that only "*came forth*" as the agent in creating and ordering the universe. Prior to creation, the *Logos was immanent in Him as His "potential" for creating things*. Only for creation the Logos came forth "*spirit from spirit, rationality from rationality*". Thus the Logos was only distinguished from the Father when required for the work of creation. For these Apologists, the term "Son" was a "title" that only had to do with creation, revelation and redemption – God *ad extra* as the "economy of salvation". The Logos, however, was eternally immanent in the Godhead – *ad intra*.

For Athenagoras (133 – 190) the Logos never "*came into being, for God from the beginning, being eternal intelligence had His Logos in Himself being eternally rational. In time He issued forth into the world of formless matter as the archetypal idea and creative force. The son being in the Father and Father in the Son by the unity and power of divine spirit".* Origen also did not hold to the Logos as "begotten", instead, he held the Logos was "eternally generated" from the Father – i.e., neither begotten nor generated at any point in time. His was a widely held view among the fathers. Arius, however, objected to Origen's view of the Logos as "eternally generated", saying it meant the Logos was not yet complete, was never finished – not a "being", that is. And indeed, until all are transformed into Christ it can be said the "*Incarnate* Logos", at least, is not finished, not complete. As "eternally generated", the Logos has meaning for everyone as God's on-going incarnation in all men. The notion of the Logos as "begotten", on the other hand, is not only an anthropomorphic idea unworthy of God, it has no meaning for man whatsoever.

For Irenaeus, the Logos was never "begotten", "generated" nor even "preexisted" in the mind of God before it came forth. On the contrary, he said "*the Logos was as eternal as the Godhead and never 'left' the Father, the Logos was God as He is in the beginning, is now and ever will be.*" For Irenaeus, "Son" was just a "metaphor" for the Logos, and his reference to Christ was to "*God and his man*". It was out of "respect" for tradition, however, he continued to use the terminology of "Father, Son and Spirit" – as did all the fathers. Also, where other fathers ranked the Trinity as First, Second and Third (as Source, Begotten and Spirated), Irenaeus insightfully stressed that each of the Trinity was the "*absolute fullness of God, thus the Father was fully God, the Logos fully God, and Spirit fully God*".

Perhaps one of the most outstanding opponents of the "Father-Son" depiction of the Trinity was Marcellus of Ancyra (d. 374.) While "Father-Son" was Jesus' expression of his human relationship to God, it was *not* an expression of the relation of the eternal Logos and "Almighty God". He refused to use the terms "Son", "Jesus", "Christ", "Firstborn" and the like, for the pre-incarnate Logos. This is what he is reported to have held: "*The notion of Sonship **was improperly applied** to the divine in Christ, it referred only to the person incarnate as the use of the term in scripture showed. Of the eternal, **divine** element in Christ there was one term only used: **not "Son", but Logos**. The Logos is the eternally immanent power of God, dwelling in him from eternity, manifested in operation in the creation of the world and, for the purpose of redemption of mankind, taking up a dwelling in Christ and so becoming for the first time in some sense personal. The God-man thus coming into being is called, and is, the Son of God; but it is **not** accu-*

rate to say the Logos was "begotten", ***nor was there any Son of God until the incarnation.*** *The title Logos is the title which must dominate all others, expressing as it does the primary relation. The relations expressed by the other titles are only temporary and transient. When the work which they indicate has been effected the relations will cease to exist. The relationship of Sonship will disappear; it is limited to the Incarnation and the purposes for which the Logos became incarnate, and the Logos will again become what he was from eternity, immanent in the Father."*

Marcellus never accepted the Creed's statement, *"We believe in God the Father Almighty and in his Son, our Lord Jesus Christ"*, instead, his creed read, *"I believe in Almighty God, in the Logos and in the Spirit"*, etc. Since Marcellus was never docked for his creed, one can assume it was also the view of many of the fathers, it was never anathematized, no one raised an objection, not even the presiding Pope at the time. His close friend of many years, St. Athanasius, refused to utter a word against Marcellus – ever. This is because many of the fathers agreed the terms "Father and Son" were only applicable to the **post** incarnational Christ and not applicable to defining the essence or nature of God as Trinity. Later we will go over Marcellus' last sentence in the quote above, it was due to some objection to this, there was added to the Creed, "*And his kingdom will have no end*" – so remember Marcellus when you hear it. [2] (Anyone who thinks "the kingdom of heaven" is on this earth will be in for a big surprise!)

We could go on and on quoting the fathers to affirm that none ever regarded the man Jesus as the Uncreated Logos, none. Well into the fifth century the debate continued as to whether or not "Son" only referred to the man Jesus or to the Logos. This is how Gregory Nazianzus put the dilemma, *"It is this that has taken the one Church and split it into many parts, and also many – I shudder to pronounce the word –* ***'Christs'.*** *Not just 'one' (Christ); we have the 'generated' Christ, the 'created' Christ, the one who 'originated' with Mary, the one resolved 'back into the source' of his being, the 'mindless' human, the one with 'real' and the one with 'phenomenal' existence."* Many fathers pointed out that referring to both the Logos as "Son" and Jesus as "Son" only "*confused*" the two disparate natures, divine and human, which is exactly what it did – and still does.

What we have been pointing out is how the initial understanding of "son of God" was transferred from the human being, Jesus, to the eternal Logos (God), and how reference to the Trinity as a "Father and

---

[2] For this addition to the creed see the chapter 26, "God Will Be All In All".

Son" came to be. That one honestly believes God literally "begot God", is a concept only a polytheist could wrap his mind around. To resort to such an obvious contradiction, the fathers got themselves into a corner. Yet the mental imagery evoked by Father and Son is now so imbedded in the minds of Christians, they are unable to grasp the fact God is Pure Spirit with **no gender** and could never "beget". Use of the terms "Father and Son" automatically evokes images of individual human beings – how else can one conceive of a father and son but as two Gentlemen? No question, this issue of the Uncreated "begetting" the Uncreated, is a contradiction that has plagued Christianity ever since.

Some people, of course, will simply skim over this whole issue holding that reference to "Son" was to the *same* one Son both *before* and *after* the Incarnation. To hold this view, however, implies the son was born twice – once from the father and once again from Mary. It also implies two different sons – one divine *before* the incarnation, and one human *after* the incarnation. Also, if the same one son is Christ, the implication is Christ was the one that became incarnate, which makes the Trinity *Father-Christ-Spirit,* with no divine Logos and no true Christ. **Christ is the Incarnation of the *Logos*, Christ is *not* the incarnation of "Christ",** much less the incarnation of the man Jesus! It seems even those who know better, are unwilling to point out these distinctions lest they cause confusion to the misguided and end up being accused themselves. Those who make no distinction between Logos, Christ, and the man Jesus, are *monophysites* anyway – "one divine nature" across the board. They do not deny two natures, they simply ignore them, give them mere lip-service, it means nothing to them. This is how one author summarized this whole problem: "*The transfer of the concept "Son" to the preexistent Christ* (Logos) *is the most significant factor in the pluralistic distortion of the Christian doctrine of God...and the monstrosities of Monophysitic christology".* He had it right! Later we will look into how Cyril of Alexandria tried to resolve this whole issue by merging these "two sons" into *one divine hypostasis or person* – that whole *Monophysitic* heresy, which is the general belief of Christians today.

As to why Christian theologians or scholars fail to point out this transposition or *switch*, is because they have already *assumed* the "present orthodox position" and wouldn't dare present it in any other than a positive light. Thus we will always get a totally one-sided view where those who oppose this switch are maligned, and those who approve it are canonized. In anticipation of this notorious and decisive transposition, every author will start out quoting from Paul and the earlier fathers to make a case this understanding of the Trinity (God as "son" of

God) had always been the belief of the Church – which is absolutely false. Authors do not want to admit to any "switch" in the understanding of the Trinity and Christ lest they have to explain the reason for it – which reason, was the attempt to *avoid anthropolatry* – which might not be to their in-house advantage. On the subject of the Trinity and Christ, there is no such thing as an "objective" scholar or researcher. As a crucial subject matter, this switch or transposition from the original understanding of the Trinity and Christ to what, in time, would degenerate into *anthropolatrism* can be spotlighted as a major turning point in the history of Christian doctrine – a major wrong turn.

As to the reason for this transposition, one scholar put it this way, "*The controversy on the relation of Jesus to God involved the question of the divine status of Jesus. If he were* ***not*** *divine, how could the church justify him as an object of worship, of trust and adoration? If he* ***is*** *divine, how could such a belief square with the doctrine of one God (monotheism)?*" In other words, because to worship a human being as God is anthropolatry, the problem was to find a way to justify this worship within the confines of monotheism.

Another Christian scholar put it more succinctly, "*Jesus had become the object of Christian worship and the revealer of God, thus it was felt necessary to establish his Deity along with the monotheistic belief...to avoid the pitfalls of polytheism.*" Thus he says the doctrine of the Trinity "*was formulated to make religiously valid the belief in the complete Deity of Jesus.*" So there you have it! The reason or purpose of this "switch" was to deify Jesus, to make him God! And how was this done? According to this same author, the fathers devised the Trinity as ***three individual persons*** – understood as three "beings" no less. By switching the reference from Jesus as the "son of God", to God (Logos) as the "son of God", this is how it was done. So now, when speaking of Jesus as the "son of God", the reference is *not* to a human being Jesus, but to almighty God – the Logos.

So one way, at least, to avoid the accusation of *anthropolatry,* was to declare "son" was *not* a reference to the man Jesus, but to God Himself – the Uncreated Logos as the true "Son" of God. It was this same divine Son that *became* the man Jesus. Apart from flesh Jesus was God, the eternal Uncreated Logos. So now, with this switch of sonship, worship of Jesus could be regarded as the worship of God – the eternal Logos.

People, of course, want to worship somebody they can see or imagine in their minds, and since they cannot "imagine" a genderless invisible, infinite God, if told, however, some man is God, then this works! But that a mere switch of biblical interpretation could somehow make a human being God – what fool would think this could work? Certainly the fathers never did. Every father knew that the moment he declared a human being to be God, he would be out of monotheism, out of Christianity entirely. No father denied the humanity of Jesus, or ever made his human nature divine – none! For them, his humanity stood for all human beings, this was the wonder of the whole revelation of Christ. None ever denied Christ's dual nature, to do that would have been to deny the incarnation. To make a human being "god", however, never crossed their minds – they were no dummies.

Although Nicaea did little more than stir the waters of discontent, no author pinpoints the major issue involved here – which was the switch from understanding Father-Son as a reference to the *post incarnate* Logos (Jesus as "son") to the *pre-incarnate* Logos (God as a "son".) This was an unwarranted leap from a *post* to a *pre* incarnational understanding of Christ, one that was bound to change the original Trinitarian and Christological paradigms. To my knowledge, no author on the development of Christian doctrine ever highlights or even discusses this disastrous "switch" in the understanding of the Christian faith.

Although there is no question this "switch" was made by a handful of "enforcers" – those backed by the emperor, who alone had the power to exile and punish – still, the question is whether the fathers' intention was to deify the man Jesus – to make him God? While this switch may have satisfied the belief of many a "simple folk", or those still held in the grip of polytheism, this was not, however, the fathers' understanding of either the divine Logos or the man Jesus. To deny Jesus' complete humanity was to deny the Incarnation – deny the true Christ. As said before, none ever held the man Jesus was God or was one of the Trinity – not one, ever.

To overlook this switch from Jesus as "son", to the Logos as "son", is to miss the most strategic turning point in the development of Christian doctrine as regards the Trinity and Christ. For 1700 years now, Christianity has been stuck with this skewed understanding which, slowly but surely, has taken its toll. A few centuries later these so called "simple folk" would go over to Islam anyway – which holds no human being is God. The faith also never made in-roads in India or the Far East; and down the road, most of Europe would be lost to Christianity. Obviously, "simple folk" grow up! To think that "Christ", the greatest Truth God ever revealed to mankind – become lost to Christianity... what can be said of this?

The cause of just about all heresies – Modalism, Arianism, Apollinarism, Monophysitism – can be traced to this Father-Son-Problem.

All were issues of *who* should be referenced as "son of God" – the man Jesus? The eternal Logos? The Incarnate Christ? None or all of these? There was never a concern or question of the union of natures, *always* it would be the question of "*who*" was the individual "*person*" – was it God or the man Jesus?

It would be a mistake to think this transposition was brought about by anything less than a major upheaval in the entire Church. By no means did the majority of the fathers agree to it. This not only changed the understanding of Christ, but the understanding of the Trinity to "Father-Jesus Christ-Spirit". To my knowledge, this is what brought on the first major schism otherwise known as "Arianism" – named after Arius, the most vocal opponent of this switch. No single priest, however, could cause a major schism had not the majority of bishops also opposed it. It is said that Arius' understanding was so widespread – accepted as orthodox – that there were few Churches that did not embrace his views. Someone estimated two-thirds of the entire Church agreed with him, which means two-thirds of the Bishops agreed that Jesus (not the Logos) was the "son of God". The *minority* who disagreed, of course, blamed Arius for having caused the schism, which is not true, he simply brought the issue to a head. By definition, however, schismatics are never those in the majority, but those in the *minority* – which was certainly the case here. It seems that after some eighteen Councils (or synods) had been convened to consider this whole question, for the sake of peace in his realm, the Emperor called for a Council to settle the matter, and thus the Council of Nicaea (325) came about.

We know at this Council no one representing Arius' view was present. This means that those who espoused the Logos as "Son" – and not the man Jesus – wielded the greater political power which, unfortunately, is the way all Church Councils work. Arius was condemned on the grounds of denying the eternity of the Logos as "Son" and for saying the "son" (his understanding of *Jesus*) was created – **which is not what Arius held!** This schism is one of the most outstanding examples of the "Father-Son-Problem", even though the heresies of Modalism, Sabellianism and Monophysitism can be traced to this same problem – even to the accusation of *tri-theism*. There is no underestimating the confusion of usage when the same terms "Father and Son" are applied to Christ both *before* and *after* the incarnation, more especially prior to the incarnation when there was no "Christ" or the man Jesus, and only the Trinity – God.

Let us end this by once more going over Hilary of Poitiers' (310 – 367) wise counsel regarding the three "states" in the life of Christ – "*It is one thing*", Hilary says, "*that he was God* ***before*** *he was man; another that he was man and God; and another, that* ***after*** *being man and God, he was perfect man and perfect God".* This statement tells us that Jesus was not "deified" until **after** his resurrection and ascension – the accepted view of all the fathers. Hilary is warning us not to confuse the times and natures – "***because sometimes Jesus speaks of his earthly humanity, and at another, of his exalted eternal humanity, we must be careful not to mix this historical line and speak of Christ existing before the incarnation, nor as an exalted human being prior to resurrection and ascension".*** Had the fathers adhered to this rule-of-thumb it would have saved centuries of misunderstandings, disputes and anathemas. But since this was not the case, however, we have inherited no true understanding of the Trinity and, consequently, no true understanding of Christ.

NICAEA AND CHALCEDON

The Council of Nicaea (325) met to put an end to Modalism and condemn Arius' understanding of the "Son of God". The intent was to so formulate the Trinity *ad intra* as to knock down any modalistic interpretation and, in doing so, formulate the divinity of Christ as the "Son of God". Unfortunately, its Creed accomplished neither. This is what it said:

"We believe in one God, the Father almighty, maker of all things visible and invisible, and in one Lord ***Jesus Christ,*** *the son of God,* ***begotten from the Father****, only-begotten, that is, from the substance (or being) of the Father, God from God, light from light, true God from true God, begotten not made, of one substance (essence or consubstantial) with the Father, through whom all things came into being, things in heaven and things on earth, who for the sake of men and for the purpose of our salvation came down and became incarnate, becoming man, suffered and rose again on the third day, ascended to the heavens, and will come to judge the living and the dead. And in the Holy Spirit."*

The understanding of Christ presented here is not based on the Trinity. Instead, we have the biblical figure of the man Jesus Christ "*of one substance (essence) with God (Father)"* as one of the Trinity – the one who became incarnate. That Jesus Christ *pre-existed* the Incarnation is inexplicable. Evidently the Incarnation of Jesus Christ was nothing more than Jesus Christ becoming *"visible"* – appearing on earth as a human being. This view of the "Incarnation" is about as close to the heresy of *Docetism* as one can get.[1] If the traditional understanding of "*incarnation"* is that *God became man*, and yet this creed states it was Jesus Christ that *became man,* how are we to understand this? Evidently, he was already incarnated prior to his "appearance" on earth. One thing this creed makes clear, however, is that Jesus Christ is Almighty God, eternally Uncreated, one of God's *triune modes of existence* – one of the Trinity.

Although everyone knows Jesus "the Christ" as the historical gospel figure of the man Jesus, here now, we are told this man existed from all eternity – "*true God from true God"*. The incarnation, then, was no more than Jesus Christ being made "visible". Needless to say,

---

[1] *Docetism* was the belief that under the *facade* of being human, in *reality,* Jesus was a divine being, a spiritual being, and as such, was incapable of suffering. This view, of course, cannot explain the suffering and death of a *divine being* or a "*spiritual body*". Basically this was a denial Jesus was as human as anyone who ever walked this earth.

there is no real "incarnation" here, no union of the divine and human natures, no real "*Christ*", and no Trinity.

This document, of course, was deliberately worded to knock down Arius' view that Jesus as God's "son" did not always exist, or was not eternal. It was also to knock down the views of Sabellius and the Modalists that "Father and son" only referred to the revelation of God *ad extra* – the "economic Trinity" – and not God *ad intra*. As can happen, however, condemning false views can end up promoting views more false then those that were condemned – usually the case with "dogmatists" bent on slaying all who disagree with them. As history has it, Nicaea alone caused a big split in the Church. Offhand we would think opposition to the Nicene formula would be its reference to the *incarnate Christ* as the one that *became incarnate* – which puts the cart before the horse. Oddly enough, however, opposition centered on the term "*substance*" – meaning, *being*, *essence*, *hypostasis, ousia*, *nature, consubstantial* (one with) or *homoousios* (same as.) The fight over this term, its meaning and usage would only last about two centuries, or before there was some agreement on use of the term "hypostasis".

When the creed states Jesus Christ is of the same *substance* (same essence, nature or being) as God, what we have is a "*Monophysitic*" belief system. *Monophysitism* (or "one-nature") is the belief Jesus Christ is of one divine nature – "*of the same substance*" as God. This is the way the creed establishes Jesus' divinity. Although this *Monophysitic* belief is regarded as a heresy, it shouldn't be. Given that the Nicene Creed is to be taken as the last word on the Christian faith – for some 1700 years now – no one would call all Christians "heretics". The problem, however, is not Christian people, the problem is the "Creed", it is clearly *Monophysitic*. Yet, this is the revered creed that made Jesus Christ God.

The head of this council was bishop Alexander of Alexandria, along with his deacon, Athanasius – his secretary and right-hand man. The creed was obviously a product of the Alexandrian school of Christology (God-flesh), which school never developed the Trinity as fully as the Antiochenes – more especially Gregory of Nazianzus for whom the Trinity was the center of his life and being. Almost by definition, a "God-flesh" Christology allows no true human nature – but only flesh – which, of itself, promotes *Monophysitism*. The Nicene Council clearly reflects this Alexandrian domination, it is the supreme example of why, if one gets the Trinity wrong, he gets Christ wrong.

That all but two bishops ratified this document can be put down to the political milieu of the time and the ramifications if one did *not* sign on. To go against the powers that be (i.e., the head of the powerful Alexandrian See and the Emperor), could be intimidating, if not coercive. To be labeled "on the wrong side" was a threat to one's good name and position. To think this was *not* the case is to turn a blind eye, not only on this Council, but all Church Councils. On the other hand, we know people sign with the intention of giving a document *their own* interpretation – just as happened this last century at Vatican II. [2]

It is a mystery, however, that Marcellus of Ancyra, a close friend of Athanasius – with him at the Council – could ever have sanctioned this creed. His stated view – "*The notion of Sonship was **improperly applied** to the divine in Christ, it referred **only to the person incarnate*** (Jesus) *as the use of the term in scripture showed. Of the eternal, divine element in Christ there was one term only used: **not Son, but Logos**.*" For both Marcellus and Athanasius the "son" was the incarnate "person" Jesus, *not* the divine Logos. While Marcellus may not have regarded his view as anti-Nicene, it was obviously not in total accord with it. No doubt this is why his name has come down in history besmirched to this day. That Eusebius of Caesarea tried to accuse him of "Sabellianism" was a laugh – not true. The only explanation for Marcellus' signing is that, like so many of the fathers, he went along with the wording for the sake of unity, but retained his own interpretation of it. While Creeds may dictate what can be officially taught, they cannot dictate what people actually believe. Even today, for people in the pew, Christianity means "whatever works for them".

The only good thing to remember about this creed is the furor it unleashed. Don't think for a minute the fathers were happy with it, the same dissensions went right on and even got worse. Some 126 years later, however, we get to the 4th Church Council of Chalcedon (451) where there is finally a bona fide statement of the true nature of Christ, one however, not without its problems. This is what it said:

"In agreement, therefore, with the holy fathers, we all unanimously teach that we should confess that our Lord Jesus Christ is one and the same Son, the same perfect in Godhead and the same perfect in manhood, truly God and truly man, the same of a rational soul and body, consubstantial (of one essence) with the Father in Godhead, and the same consubstantial (one in essence) with us in manhood, like us in all things except sin; begotten from the Father before the ages as regards His Godhead, the same in the last days, for us and our salvation, begotten from the Virgin Mary, the Theotokos, as regards his man-

---

[2] See: *The Rhine Flows Into The Tiber, A History of Vatican II*, by Ralph Wiltgen, Tan Publishing Co.

hood; one and the same Christ, Son, Lord, only-begotten (or "unique"), made known in two natures without confusion, without change, without division, without separation, the difference of the natures being by no means removed because of the union, but the distinct property of each nature being preserved and coalescing (combining or concurring) in one prosopon and one hypostasis – not parted or divided into two prosopa, but one and the same Son and only-begotten ***God the Logos,*** *Lord, Jesus Christ, as the prophets of old and Jesus Christ taught us about Him, and the creed of our fathers has handed down".* [3]

As we can see, the fathers had come a long way from Nicaea. Chalcedon's presentation of Christ is remarkable. With the exception of a few terms, it is the last word on the true nature of *Christ: fully divine and fully human.* If this could have been kept just as it is, nothing further was really needed for a true understanding of Christ. But as it goes with these Councils, everyone has their own interpretation, to say nothing of those who were dismayed by it – in this case, the Alexandrians. This was no "God-flesh" Christ, but a true union of "God-Man" such as the Antiochenes had insisted.

If we could leave aside everyone's "interpretation" of this document, if rightly understood, what we have here is the one single unifying document in the history of Christianity, a true understanding of Christ. By the time we get here – to Chalcedon (451) – however, all those fathers who made this understanding of Christ possible, were long gone. They were the ones who did the ground-work, made it possible to ultimately articulate a true understanding of Christ. From here on, however, these fathers' understanding of Christ will be left behind and a totally new and different understanding of Christ would take its place. But before moving on, it is important to point out the most important points of the Chalcedon document.

1. It clearly affirms a **union of the essence of God with the essence of human nature** – "Consubstantial (in essence) with the Father in Godhead, and the same consubstantial (in essence) with us in manhood".

---

[3] *Prosopon* literally means "face", the Trinity sometimes referred to as the "three faces of God". This was solely an Eastern term, however. In the Western Church, the term was "*person*", thus the Trinity as "three persons". As best I could research the original Chalcedon document in Greek, there is no mention or use of the term "person". Translators, however, almost always use "person" instead of "*prosopon*" and "hypostasis". The Greeks, however, never accepted the Western term "person" unto well into the 6th century, and even then, never referred to "hypostasis" as "person" – because they do ***not*** mean the same thing!

2. "The difference of the natures being by no means removed because of the union" – means **the divine did not become human and the human did not become divine**. "Each nature being preserved and coalescing in one *prosopon* and *hypostasis*", (**in** the Logos, that is.)
3. That the union of essences is united ***in*** *one prosopon and one hypostasis* (the Logos), means **the *locus* of the union (of God and man) is *in* God and *not* in man.** (The Trinity defined as "*three hypostases in one essence*") refers to the "distinctions" or "triune modes of existence" in one essence. Thus, the *union* of natures or essences (God and man) is ***in*** the *particular* hypostasis of the Logos.
4. Also note, the union of two disparate natures (or essences) is "*in one prosopon and one hypostasis, not parted or divided into two prosopa" – meaning* there is *no union* of two "*prosopa*" (plural of "*face*"), two "sons" or two "persons" (one divine and one human.) Rather, Christ is the union of natures ***in*** *the one same Son and only begotten God the Logos.*
5. That this union was "*in one prosopon* ***and*** *one hypostasis*" implies a distinction between *prosopon* and *hypostasis*. As we will see, this distinction came to be understood as a distinction *between* "person" and "nature" (or essence.) One of the most important facts to keep in mind for a true understanding of Christ, is that **there is *no* union of persons, but only a union of essences – or "natures".** Chalcedon does not say there is a union of nature **with** a person, but only a union of natures **in** a person. Although it is assumed the Logos was the divine person of both natures, still, there is **no union** of a divine person **with** *human nature.* This means that Jesus' human nature was not united **to** or **with** the divine *person* of the Logos, but only united to the divine *nature* of the Logos.

This Chalcedon statement is as good as Christianity gets. Like the fathers, everyone would like to change a few words here and there, but be that as it may, there is no other document like it in the history of the Church. Everything that went before and after can be erased.

Later we will take up the issue of the difference between what is meant by *nature* and *person*, but first we have to find out how the term "*prosopon*" – along with the term "*hypostases*" – came to be *changed* to the term "***person***", a term *not* used in the original Greek Chalcedon document. In this matter, keep in mind it was not until sometime in the 6th century that the Greeks (Eastern Church) agreed to the West's understanding of *persona* as synonymous with their understanding of *prosopon*. To my knowledge, however, the Greeks never agreed *hypostasis* meant *persona – and* indeed it does not. In time, however, in the

West at least, *hypostasis* and *person* were used as synonymous terms. So due to this *error,* **there occurred another switch from the original *hypostasis* to *person* – a monumental wrong turn** as regards a true understanding of the Trinity and Christ.

Where the Eastern Church was mainly responsible for Modalism, Arianism, and the "switch" spoken of in the previous chapter, now it was the Western Church that would be responsible for not just "another" wrong turn, but worse, responsible for the most blatant **error** in all of Christian theology, which was **making God *three persons* – that's** it! Now there is no true Trinity, no real Christ, and no real Jesus – making God three persons made Jesus *no person* at all – *unbelievable*!

In the development of Church doctrine there is, perhaps, no more crucial term than *"hypostasis"*, used to define both the Trinity and Christ. **The classical definition of the Trinity was "*one essence in three hypostases*" (or "*three hypostases in one essence*"), and the classical definition of Christ as – "*two essences (natures) in one hypostasis*".** It thus behooves us to understand the fathers' use of the term "hypostasis". Since there were many other terms that could have been used, it is important to understand, not only its literal meaning, but how it was used in its particular context – or what it was originally intended to express. Since usage governs meaning, we are not interested in the numerous philosophical uses "hypostasis" had for the old philosophers, all that matters is what the fathers wanted to clarify by their particular use of this term.

Although etymologically "*hypostasis*" means "under-stand", it actually means the opposite – to "*stand under*". Used as a verb, it meant "standing beneath" or "underlying" the essence – "supporting" the essence to make it "what" it is. It was also a reference to action, function, or *mode of existence*. Used as a noun, however, it meant the *real* underlying the existence of "something", the *essential foundation* of a thing and the vehicle of all its qualities.

Based on this definition, hypostasis is a "support" without which, nothing holds up or has any permanence. (Interestingly, Irenaeus referred to the Trinity as "*The sides that support the essence*" – an analogy of the Trinity as "sides" of a triangle.) As the foundation of God's essence or "what" God is, *hypostases* designates the three pillars of God's single essence. As opposed to the Trinity being only the attributes or powers of God, *hypostasis* designates "*that*" which gives something its *reality*.

It is said the term is Stoic in origin – "*hypostasis*" designating the One Reality (Logos) that underlies (stands-under) the cosmos and its multiple manifestations. To my knowledge, neither Plato or Aristotle used the term "*hypostasis*", yet its meaning as "real being" or the "essence of things" would align with Plato's universal divine "substance" underlying the ever changing multiple "things" that appear. This would not be true for Aristotle, however, for him, real being did not "underlie" anything, rather, ***that** a thing is, is **what** it is.* For Aristotle, if anything exists that is *not embodied*, it has no true being – indeed, if not embodied, how would anyone even know something existed? He is speaking, of course, of material "things" – yet: it is because God is *not* some material "thing" that God can only be *revealed.*

It seems Origen (185 – 254) was the first to use "hypostasis" to define God's immanent triune realities. Although his was the first attempt to give a more philosophical understanding of God as Trinity, even the earlier fathers expressed a Trinity in their writings. But if, like Philo and Paul, they were not clear as to the distinction between Spirit and Logos, Origen, on the other hand, made clear distinctions and referred to these distinctions as God's triune "hypostases".

To express the Trinity as the essence of God *ad intra,* the term "*hypostasis*" affirmed the eternal *reality* of the threefold *distinctions* of God's non-exchangeable "modes of existence". The Trinity was not just three temporary manifestations of God or different revelations at different times, but the eternal, immanent, infinite, immutable, impassible, indivisible one essence of God *ad intra.* "Hypostasis", then, asserts the abiding reality of the threefold distinctions in God's essence, each unique in its own right, yet working in unity, each contributing its part to every act of God. **So "three hypostases" was reference to God's triune "modes of existence", not only *distinct* in their revelation, but distinct in God's immanent *ad intra* existence.**

Part of the dispute caused by the term "hypostasis" was whether it was to be understood as a reference to the essence of a *universal* or to the essence of a *particular or individual.* Thus some argued Origen meant three "individual essences", while others said his reference was to the "one" universal essence. Origen, however, used hypostases to point up the reality of God's triune *distinctions* as being the distinct or particular modes of the same one universal essence. At no time did hypostasis mean the Trinity was three individual essences (or substances), nor did hypostasis mean the "composition" of three different parts of a whole.

If anything, Origen's use of hypostasis was indicative of his aversion to any anthropomorphizing of God – which fact turned many against him. Obviously, the notion of Father and Son evoked no such images in his mind. Also, it has been said, no one before or after Origen so stressed the human soul of the man Jesus. The soul was the "intermediary" between the Logos and the human body, for him, soul was the *locus* of the union of the two natures: "*The soul was the iron, the Logos the fire, and Christ was the union of the two*". The work of the incarnation, he said, was a work for all mankind: "*The Logos is ever being born in the soul, and as each reflects this, each becomes Christ. The union of God and man was to be fulfilled in each one of us, the soul having the same possibility of glorification as that of Christ*". These are words to remember! Origen held the same one "son of God" was the same "son of man" and that the only difference was a "*distinction in thought*". An interesting idea.

Interestingly, this was also Cyril of Alexandria's *Monophysitic* idea of Christ's *one divine nature,* where the distinctions in Christ's *one nature* are only distinctions "in thought" or in one's mind, though *not* in reality. This, unfortunately, became the popular defense that the man Jesus *was* the divine Logos. At any rate, Origen held that once everything had been saved, there would be no further need for Christ, his mission having been fulfilled, in the end, there would be only the Logos – the view of many of the fathers. This only makes sense, however, **if** the sole *purpose* of the incarnation of Christ was to save man. But if we go with Irenaeus' view – the purpose of the incarnation was man's "deification", all being transformed into Christ, then the end of Christ would not only be the end of all that were saved (transformed into Christ), but the end of all creation.

Considering all the misunderstandings, contentions and condemnations that arose over the term "*hypostases*", why didn't the fathers stick with the terms "Father and Son" which are already self-defining? Since everyone knows a father and son have the same nature, yet are two different "individuals" distinct from one another, what meaning did *hypostases* add to "father and son" that these terms did not already convey? Obviously, they were not satisfied "Father-Son-Spirit" were adequate expressions of the Trinity *ad intra*. For one thing, the Trinity was not *three individuals* such as "father and son" suggest. They had to avoid the impression the Trinity was three individual "beings" – which is how most people think of the Trinity anyway.

While each of the Trinity has its own distinct revelation, all that is "singular" is the difference between these revelations and not **what, in essence,** is revealed – each being the "fullness" of God. There is no revelation of a "particular being", entity or individual, **not even the revelation of a "one"**. And as said before, there is no revelation that could be described as a "Father" or a "Son" – the very idea would never strike the mind. Referring to God's triune modes of existence as "*three hypostases*" does not mean God is three *discrete individuals*, it only means God has three *distinct revelations according to Its mode of being,* each different, each revealing a great truth of God, and each playing Its part in the life of every human being.

Basil of Caesarea explained hypostasis this way: "*The indefinite concept of essence, which, because what it signified is common to all, finds no fixity; but that which by means of special characteristics or properties which are made apparent, give fixity and circumscription to that which is common and uncircumscribed*". Again, he says, "*Essence has the same relation to hypostasis as the common (universal) has to the particular*".

He makes the point "essence" refers to what is *common*, and "hypostasis", to "what" (of the same essence) is *distinct*, different or "particular". Hypostases had to be "*that which is spoken of* ***distinctively****, rather than the indefinite notion of ousia* (essence)". Thus *hypostases* expresses God's triune distinctions and not God's one essence. According to Basil, while God's essence cannot be "circumscribed", there are particular "characteristics or properties" of God that have been revealed and can be circumscribed – his reference, of course, being to those "characteristics or properties" we call "Father, Son and Spirit".

What is interesting about Basil's explanation of the Trinity, is his division between essence (nature) and "*property*" – which later became understood as "*person*". What he is saying is that while we cannot think of the infinite essence of God (or Trinity) as some individual being, the mind, however, can have some idea of the *property* of God "*made apparent*" (or revealed) as *circumscribed* individuals. Since the mind demands some concrete "thing" to focus on, for Basil, this seems to be its focus on the Trinity as three *particular* ***circumscribed*** *individuals or beings – later*, "*persons*". The question this poses is not whether God is three beings, but rather, is God (or has God) three *properties*, *characteristics* or *attributes* that can be regarded as *circumscribed individuals* – or three *persons*? To satisfy the human mind and meet the demands to envision **a Father and Son** as individual beings, he may be just taking God's three *properties* as three *circumscribed* individuals for granted. To think of the Trinity as three "*circumscribed individuals* or persons", however, is *not* in keeping with the "*revelation*" of God as Trinity. The Trinity is not *three* balls of fire – or whatever.

No question, there was confusion as to whether *hypostasis* was a reference to God's *one essence* or to *three "particular ones"* of the same essence. It seems for some, "hypostasis" referred to a "numerical *one*" (one anything) and always designated some individual "thing" or entity. This reference, however, could only be to *material* things, and as such, was not suited for the Trinity – God as three individual things? *What* things? As it turns out, three individual "beings" – that's *what*! Incredibly, this became the general understanding of "*hypostases*"– three *individual,* "numerical ones". What had been intended to designate the reality of the triune ***distinctions*** of God's one essence, came to be understood as three numerical "one's" – basically, three individual, but equal "beings". Putting aside all the good intentions, the denials, excuses, and endless explanations, the fact remains, theology promotes the Trinity *as if* they were three individual beings, there is nothing in its language that would lead one to think otherwise.

Use of the term *hypostases*, of course, was specifically used to avoid any view of the Trinity as three individual beings, yet it always has a way of slipping back to being three discrete beings. Having to keep denying this is why the Trinity is usually put aside as an inconceivable "*mystery*". Actually it is the technical theological language used for the Trinity that makes it a "mystery". On an *experiential* level, nothing is easier to understand and grasp than the Trinity. Indeed, without this *experiential* understanding, man would have no way of ever having a true understanding of his spiritual life with God. This is why it is so unfortunate the Trinity as three particular "ones" or individuals is most people's understanding of the Trinity – "unfortunate", because as *individual ones,* no such revelation of God or the Trinity exists.

Trying to divide God into essence, nature, hypostasis, individual, person, properties, and all the rest, indicates no honest understanding of the Trinity. This is why the Trinity became no more than a philosophical-theological construct, one that has lost Its reality as the Godhead present in everyone's life.

It is good to remember, however, that many, if not most of the fathers, objected to use of the term "*hypostases*". Irenaeus made the comment, "*We ought not to hypostatise qualities*" (attributes or properties.) He also said that each distinction was the absolute fullness of God – meaning, one cannot separate the fullness of God's essence from God's immanent distinctions. So too, Marcellus held out for these distinctions or hypostases being part and parcel of God's single essence and not "individual" hypostasis – or numerical ones. Gregory of Nyssa objects, saying that "*strictly speaking, just as it is inaccurate to speak of Peter, James and John as 'three humans' – since 'human' was the term they had in common – so too, it was just as inaccurate (even 'dangerous') to speak of the Trinity as three* ***hypostasis or 'individuals'*** *since they had a common nature. Thus, where no one could conclude from 'three humans' there were 'three humanities', yet people could* *conclude from God as three individual hypostasis – three gods".* He was right! This is just what people have concluded. No one wants to admit it, but the theology of the Trinity is worded such that It comes across as three individual entities or beings – of the same divine nature, of course. So while the fathers all held to the existence of God's triune distinctions, they did not agree they were separate individual hypostases.

Maximus the Confessor regards "hypostases" as part and parcel of God's essence or nature. He does not divide God according to hypostases and/or nature. But then, he was obviously a man of experience and knew better. He says, "*The Unity is not distinguished from the Trinity as common and general considered only* ***by the mind*** *as distinct from the parts (hypostasis) which make it up, since it is an essence which exists properly by itself and a force which is absolutely mighty. Nor as one* ***through*** *the other, for there is* ***no mediation of relation*** *as from effect to cause, nor from* ***between*** *what is completely identical and absolute. Nor is one* ***from*** *the other, for the Trinity is not a derivation of the Unity, since it is without origin and self-manifesting".* He is saying, 1. The single essence is not distinct from its parts (hypostases.) 2. Since one is not *from* the other, there is no *begetting.* 3. One is not *in* the other. 4. They are *not a relationship.* 5. Hypostases (or persons) are not as the mind supposes – the parts are *not distinct from the whole* – i.e., the hypostases are not distinct from their common essence. Thus, in the Trinity there are no "relations", and the unity cannot be *divided* by hypostases – or later, "*persons*". Maximus pretty much threw out all the erroneous views of the Trinity!

So long as hypostasis retains its original usage and understanding as pointing up the "distinctions" of God's *triune mode of existence,* it is on the mark. But when *hypostases* is taken to mean three "individual, numerical ones", or to mean, as in the West, "three persons", then it is *pure tri-theism.* One author says well, "*The fact hypostasis is irreducible to the concept of a* ***particular*** *nature or to the notion of* ***individuality*** *is crucially important, not only as regards Christ, but the Trinity as well.*" Since God is immaterial, not subject to space and time, God is not an "individual" or a "numerical one", nor the Trinity, a "numerical three". The term "individual" can never be applied to God as if God could be divided into three individual "ones" – individuals, entities or beings. It is hard to get away from a "numerical three", but **God is not a *quantity*, has no quantitative dimensions.** While everything created comes in "ones" and is thus quantifiable, yet quantity, even "one", cannot apply to the Uncreated in any respect. God is infinite and has no boundaries, nor can anything created "contain" God. The Logos is not an "individual" or a "being", and in the Incarnation, the Logos never *became* an individual being, but rather, created man's *one* human nature, *uniting* it eternally with Itself. Neither Jesus or Jesus Christ "contains" or "circumscribes" God. Impossible.

A hypostasis, then, cannot be reduced to, or equated with, either "a particular nature", an "individual numerical one", nor any notion of "individuality." Only *created things* are "individual", never the Uncreated. Where essence or nature refers to the *universal* – or what is held in common – hypostasis only refers to *distinctions* inherent in the universal. This is somewhat reminiscent of Origen's analogy of a centrifuge distilling the trinity as the immanent composition of God's essence. Hypostases are not the "composition" of God. The essence cannot be divided, it is not a *unity* of three "ones". God's threefold modes of existence are not distinct from the essence, not something over and beyond it, not anything "other" than it. In short, God cannot be divided into essence *and* hypostasis because hypostasis is **of** the essence and cannot be designated or distinguished as anything else or "other" than the essence of God.

In the history of Christianity there is no term or word that has been the cause of more errors, heresies and dissensions than the term *hypostasis*. As a mere word it is innocuous, yet everything depends on the purpose for which it was originally used, what it was intended to mean. Whole books have been written on the different meanings and various usage of "hypostasis" without providing a single definitive definition. That at one point the problem was thought to be solved by using the term "person" instead of "hypostasis", this substitution was the final blow to the development of any authentic Christology and the Trinity. Hypostasis may have been problematic, but "person" threw Christianity off track completely.

If what we have been going over seems complex, well, it gets ever worse. From here on – and **forever** – a distinction must *always* be made between whether one is speaking of the *essence* or *hypostasis* (*person*) of God, the Trinity, of Christ, the man Jesus or, basically, every human being. While initially intended to point out the reality of the triune *distinctions* in God's essence, in time, however, hypostases became a hard and fast line that amounted to a **division between essence and hypostasis**. **Thus one has to be careful to point out if his reference is to the *essence* of God, or to the *hypostases* of God as a particular *person,* any confusion in the reference became a cause of dissention and cat-calling.** While this confusion was a major cause of contention among the fathers, today, however, people make no distinction at all – in fact, don't know a thing about it! Thus when thinking or speaking of God, who distinguishes the essence of God from God's triune hypostases? Who distinguishes the *essence* of the divine Logos from Its *hypostasis* (or *person*)? Above all, who distinguishes Jesus' human nature (or essence) from *his* human "hypostasis" or *person* – much less, distinguish his *hypostasis* (or *person*) from the Logos' divine hypostasis or *person*? **No one!** If Christians are even aware of these distinctions, certainly they never make them. The traditional Christian language nowhere makes these distinctions clear, not in its creeds, teaching, catechisms, prayers, religious literature, or even most of its theology. How important are these distinctions? They can make the difference between a true or false understanding of the Trinity and Christ, even a true or false understanding of Jesus – and mankind in general.

The point is this: as later defined, *hypostasis* ended up just as some of the fathers feared, creating a division between essence and hypostasis. Instead of affirming "distinctions" in the essence of God, *hypostases* came to mean "particular individuals" – three "numerical ones", the Trinity, spoken of as if It was three individual "entities". For those who read theology and wonder at its complicated terminology, this is due to having to point out which of its innumerable divisions of God and man it is speaking of – essence, substance, nature, hypostasis, property, characteristic, attribute, person, personality, supposit – a list of terms would fill a page. Thus the constant need to parse, to make clear distinctions between terms, especially if one is referring **either** to the divine *essence* **or** to a *particular hypostasis*. **Thus, hypostasis was no longer a distinction *within* the immanent essence, but a distinction *between* the essence and hypostases – between God's one essence and God's triune modes of existence.** The upshot of this division was that the whole focus was on the *individuality* of the hypostasis at the expense of God's essence. This resulted not in just the image of three beings, but all the human language, theology and anthropomorphism that goes with it. It could be said this division created *tri-theism* for the Trinity, and *Monophysitism* for Christ.

But this is why, when using this term "*hypostasis*", we have to be careful to distinguish its *original meaning* and use from how it *later* came to be understood. Authors of the history of doctrinal development usually give us the *later* understanding of hypostasis as "person", while others neglect the term "*hypostasis*" entirely. By and large the term came to be more a philosophical concern then anything strategic to theology, but this is only because it lost its original intent – which was to affirm God is **not** three *individual beings*, and that as Trinity, God is beyond the names, terms and images of "Father and Son" – beyond all such impoverished metaphors and images.

Despite the centuries of disputed explanations for the use and meaning of *hypostases*, the Christian Creed retains the same modalistic terms, "Father-Son-Spirit", with no more explanation than they implied from the beginning – namely, three individual entities of the same divine nature. Unfortunately, this does not avoid tri-theism – even gods have the same divine nature. So why didn't the Creed stick with the term "three hypostases" to define the Trinity? Apart from the fact few Christians ever heard of the term, much less knew what it meant, it had no single definition, its philosophical usage and meaning differed widely. What matters, however, is how the fathers used it, the meaning it had for them to express **the Trinity as "*one essence in three hypostases*" (or "*three hypostases in one essence*"), and the definition of Christ as "*two essences (natures) in one hypostasis*".** Properly understood, these are *classic* definitions!

As far as the original intent of using the term "hypostases" is concerned, as long as it points out the immanent, abiding, real **distinctions** in God's one essence, this term is acceptable – after all, some term has to be used, and since *hypostasis* served its original intent and understanding, the term well serves its purpose. Carry its definition any further, however, and its original intent is gone, and there begins the slippery slope that ends with no true understanding of the Trinity and, consequently, Christ. This is what happened when "hypostasis" was changed to mean "*person*" – the most horrendous misnomer ever applied to God. As to how the original term *hypostasis* ended up being replaced by *person*, we will examine next.

THE PERSON PROBLEM

If we ask how the term *hypostasis* was ever changed to "person" – which it never meant – we learn its genesis is uniquely Christian. "Person" is nowhere found in the bible – new or old testaments, Hebrew or Greek – nor is it found anywhere in Greek philosophy. All we know is that it came from the particular use of "*persona*" found in Roman Law. It is said the Latin fathers' translation of the Greek "hypostasis" meant "substance" – the Platonic understanding of essence – which would not do to express the *triune modes* of God's existence. Since God is not three substances or three essences, the Latins decided to come up with a different term to express the Trinity.

This Latin "excuse", however, is problematic. First of all, etymologically *hypostasis* (*under-stand or stand-under*) means the same as *substance (under-stand or stand-under.*) Secondly, since Roman Stoicism was the going religion of the day, both the Latins and Greeks knew the Stoic background of Origen's use of the term *hypostasis* – so who cares what "Plato" would have thought of hypostasis or substance? Since usage governs meaning, there is no excuse why the Latins did not adopt the Greeks' use of "hypostasis" – after all, the meaning of "hypostasis" was no clearer to the Greeks than it was for the Latins. As it turns out, of course, the Latins rejected *hypostasis* as an expression for the triune distinctions of God's singular essence.

African born Tertullian (160 – 225), before his conversion to Christianity, had been a scholar of Roman Law and, most likely, a Stoic as well. In Roman Law, "substance" meant "property" as when speaking of a "man of *substance*", thus substance referred to what a man *possessed* or *owned.* So in the Law, *persona* ("person" in English) was the legal reference to "ownership", something an individual *owned*, a piece of *property* that belonged to him and to no other – such as a slave, money, land, etc. A "person", then, is something an individual *has, possesses, or owns;* "person" does not refer to "***what***" one is (in essence), does not refer to "*being*" or to *what* an "*individual*" being ***is***. It is important, then, to keep in mind – **"individual" refers to "*what*" one is, while a "person" only refers to what an individual *owns* or *possesses*.** (It is because a slave *owned* nothing he was someone else's "property" – whereas, in truth, he *was* a slave *because* he was someone else's property.) Thus, for example, Nero owned slaves (among other things), thus *he* was a *person*, whereas slaves, *because* they owned nothing, were not persons – did not ***own themselves***! Slaves were regarded as *human*, but not *persons*. But putting "*person*" aside, all human beings are "**what"** they are, yet, this is not "***who***" they are. So what an "individual" human being *is,* is "*what*" he *is* and **not *what he owns* – *which*** is first and foremost, ***his own person***. So a "person", then, is "*who*" one is, and not "*what*" one is.

As this understanding of *person* was used in the West (by the Latins) to define the Trinity, God's one nature *owns* three distinct *properties*, which properties are God's "persons", namely: "Father-Son-Spirit". These "three persons" do not, however, refer to the *nature* or *essence* of God, but only to *what* God *owns* or *possesses*. Just as a human being is not *what* he owns, but *what* he *is*, so too, God is not *what* God owns, but *what* God **is. This means God is the *owner* of a Trinity (three persons), but is *not* Itself (in essence) a Trinity**. So right off, the term "person" has to be rejected. It does *not* define the Trinity, or align with the purpose for which It was defined as *three hypostases* – namely, the three distinct modes of God's Existence. **God does not *own* a Trinity, God *is* a Trinity. While the** term "persons" makes *no* distinction in God's essence, it does, however, make a distinction *between* God's essence and God's persons (or properties.) Thus in essence, three persons is *not what* God is, but only what God *owns*. **So God owns three persons, Father-Son-Spirit, but God is *not* in essence three persons.**

This use of the Latins' "*persona*" was rejected outright by the Greeks. For them, *persona* meant "a mask" such as actors wear in Greek dramas – one individual playing several roles and switching masks accordingly. The Trinity, of course, was not three different masks or roles God was playing, this idea is even worse than "*modalism*". So the next term suggested was *prosopon,* literally "*face*", a term found in the Bible no less. While this was accepted by the Greeks as the best the Latins could do, it *never replaced* their understanding of *hypostasis*. In Hebrew, *face* was "*panin*" and generally referred to an *external* presentation of God, a mode (or way) of being apprehended. Thus to see someone face to face was to see the *outward presence* of an otherwise hidden reality. *Face* (*prosopon*), then, referred to the *external presentation* of God *ad extra,* which did not, of course, express God *ad intra* – as did the term "*hypostasis*".

To express the Trinity as God's *three faces or prosopa,* however, is well taken. Just as there is no triangle without its "sides" or "faces", so too, there is no God without Its triune sides, faces, or distinct "modes of existence". Similar to the Greek *persona*, however, *prosopon* could also be given a Modalist or Sabellian interpretation, which brought matters back to *hypostasis.* For the Latins, however, once they came upon *persona* (its Latin understanding as a "property") they held on to this understanding of the Trinity. From here on, it would define the Trinity as "*three Persons in One God*", or "*One God in three persons*". It seems it was only sometime in the 6th century, the Greeks accepted the Latins *persona* (person) as equivalent to their term "*hypostasis*".[1] This, of course, was a huge mistake, person *never meant* "hypostasis", nor vice versa.

What might be of interest today, however, is the original Greek understanding of person *(persona)* as a temporary "role" someone plays. In today's psychological context, a role or mask is a "put-on" that can legitimately be called a "*false self*". *Person* is all on the outside, an external presentation of someone, which is *not,* however, his *true nature*. Even today, "*persona*" means some fictitious character, a role "consciously" put on by an actor – yet, "unconsciously" put on by many people! While no one would admit this definition of "persona" (ownership) is what the Latin fathers had in mind, it is difficult to escape this same conclusion.

While *hypostases* was to signify God's immanent Triune "modes of existence" – of the very essence of God – it never signified God's *ownership* of three persons! Unless "person" is of the "essence" of God, then a "divide" exists between essence and person, between the *owner* and the *owned.* Theologians do not like the notion of any "divide" between the essence (nature) of the Trinity and the "persons" of the Trinity, but there is no other way to put it. As we'll see, **when speaking of the Trinity and Christ, whether the reference be to *nature* or *person* makes for a totally different understanding of the Trinity and Christ – which can be orthodox or heretical.** For example, to say, "*Jesus Christ is God*", is this a reference to Jesus' nature and/or person? Or is it a reference to God's nature and/or person? Is it a reference to the union of both natures and persons? Or does it reference none of these? Since it references none of these, what exactly is "*Jesus Christ*" a reference to? (Watch out for your answer!)

Since it was obvious that something *owned* did *not* define the true

---

[1] In the mid 500's at some meeting, the Eastern Church officially accepted the Western use of "persons" for the Trinity. It was not clear, however, if they accepted this as equivalent to their "*prosopa*" or "faces of God", or as equivalent to "*hypostases*" as well. One thing is sure, however, the West has consistently used "persons" instead of "hypostases", used them as if they were synonymous terms. Eastern theology, however, has never used them as such, but sticks with Chalcedon's statement that Christ's natures are united *"in one prosopon **and** one hypostasis"*. Thus today they will simply say "in one *person* and one hypostasis" – meaning, in the one person of the *Logos' hypostasis (essence)* – a union *in essence* and not just *in* a person. Chalcedon explicitly references the union of natures *in* the particular *prosopon* or person of the ***Logos' hypostasis,*** and not *in* or *with* the persons of the Spirit or Father. Jesus, however, only spoke of being one with his Father.

nature of the *owner,* and that "*persons*" as mere "*properties*" only spoke of God *ad extra*, the Latins eventually came to recognize the importance of *hypostasis.* By itself, "*persons*" did *not* define the Trinity – because **God is not the *owner* of a Trinity (or three persons), rather, *God is Trinity*.** So recognizing the need for the term "*hypostasis*", from then on, ***person* meant the "property" of *each hypostasis,* and *not* the properties of *God's one essence.*** In other words, it is not God's essence that *owned* or had three properties, rather, it was ***"each hypostasis"* that had its *own particular property* or was its *own person*.**

Later we will see how this plays out when it comes to understanding Christ. For right now, what we have is God's *essence*, God's *hypostases,* God's *prosopon* and God's *persons,* all meaning something different. If anybody wonders why the Trinity is a "mystery", it is because theology made it so. Of Itself, nothing is easier to understand and recognize *experientially* than the Trinity, few people with any sense of "spirituality" could miss it.

So let us be clear, **God as three *persons* cannot and does not, refer to God's *essence*.** At best, it can only refer to **"properties" of God's triune hypostases.** In essence, God is three distinct *hypostases* and ***not*** (in essence) three persons. So remember then, *person* does *not* define the *owner or God.* Before there can *be* a *person,* there must be *someone* to whom it belongs – there cannot be a *person* if there is no one there! **So the two terms, *hypostasis* (owner) and *person* (owned) are not synonymous or inter-changeable terms.**

Since *person* has to refer to "someone" – some "individual" entity – this is fine as far as man is concerned, but unless the Trinity is three "individual entities or beings", how could they be "persons"? Based on Aristotle's definition of *individual* as a *"numerical one",* how could God be an "individual"? much less *three individuals!* Despite this fact, however, God was held to be three *persons,* and *hypostases* re-defined to refer, primarily, to *autonomous individuals* – little different from "persons".

By no stretch of linguistic subterfuge, however, does "person" mean "hypostasis", neither etymologically nor in its original intent and usage, yet, authors continuously use them as synonymous terms. All the Latin (Western) translations of the early fathers will use the term *person* instead of *hypostasis* – totally deceiving the reader. Not only did the early fathers not think in terms of "person", they would never have used *persona* as "mask" with its *modalistic* understanding of the Trinity. So anyone who thinks the early Greek-speaking fathers used the term "person" must be disabused of this notion, none of the early fathers accepted it. Western authors, of course, want to make it sound as if the early fathers all agreed with use of "person" – not true at all. And while we are at it, there is a quote from Paul, "We are all *one person in Christ*", which Paul could never have said because the term "person" wasn't even coined in his time. Also, having gone over many different translations of Chalcedon and becoming familiar with the Greek writing for *hypostasis* and *person*, the term "*person*" was not used at Chalcedon – and certainly not at Nicaea. "Hypostasis" and "*prosopon*" are there, but not "person". The very idea of God as a "person" is a disaster, and that God is "three persons" is pure *tri-theism.*

As reference to the abiding triune **distinctions** in God's essence, *hypostases* is as far as the term can legitimately go. Taking it beyond to mean three *individuals*, three *persons*, three *subjects,* three "who's", which the mind can only grasp as *three beings,* there is no getting around "*tri-theism*". It is one thing to deny *tri-theism*, but another to remove the possibility of it. As soon as God is made to be a person, the Trinity is personified, *anthropomorphized as three individual beings*. The term "*person*" cannot escape *tri-theism* – the worst of all Christian heresies. If language is not honed to the truth, the result can never be the truth.

Since it is not possible for the human mind to think of a "person" other than as a concrete embodied individual being or entity, the notion of God as three persons has to be thrown out. While promoting this kind of polytheism is wrong, the problem is, people do not recognize it as "polytheism". Like the fathers, Christians would be horrified to think they were polytheists or believed in three gods. But this is why the Trinity is kept at a distance, declared a "mystery" incapable of the human mind to grasp. This is also why the Trinity means relatively nothing to the average Christian and plays no part in his spiritual life. To their credit, however, and despite their constantly being presented with three deities or individual persons – Father, Son and Spirit – somehow, Christians know God is not three individual beings. To be a Christian, one has to *ignore* the traditional theological tri-theistic presentation of the Trinity – as found in the creed, prayers, doctrines, and so on.

This is why Christians focus solely on the historical figure of Jesus, because Jesus is the only "*person*" that makes sense to them, the only "person" they know. And indeed, Jesus *is a person*, while God is **no person(s.)**

Though the meaning of *person* would change, it continued to be regarded as an incommunicable "*property*" distinguished from the individual "who" *owned* it. Thus an *individual* is **not** a "property" or *person*, and a property or *person* is **not** the *individual* that owns it. While you own your own person, yet in essence, "what" you are is *not* your person, on the contrary, you are "*what*" you are ***minus*** your property or person! **Thus, "*what*" you are is distinct from "*who*" you are**. And not only is "person" to be distinguished from "what" you are, but to be distinguished from "*that*" you are (*that you exist.*) **In short, *that* you are and *what* you are is not "*who*" you are!** Do not, then, mistake an *individual* for a *person*, they are not the same thing. Neither theologically nor philosophically were the two terms (*individual* and *person*) regarded as the same reference or used as synonymous terms. *Person* is *premised* on their first *being* some "individual", even though "individual" is **not** a *person.*

So here is the first problem with the term "person". As it entered the world's common language understood as a "property" of nature – both God and man's – *person* does not define the nature or essence of either God or man. It does not define *what* God is or *what* man is, all it defines is what these natures *possess* or *own*. *Person* has been called a "property", an "attribute", even an "accident" "*that follows necessarily from nature*". Thus God and man's essential nature "necessarily" *has or owns* this property called "person". An official rendition is this: "*The person must be defined as a basic principle endowed with no less intrinsic value or ontological content than nature, profoundly **distinct** from nature although intimately **united** to it"*. According to this, *what* you are and *who* you are is a *union – but what* does this union form*?* If it forms some entity or being, this brings us back to an individual "*what"*. But if *what* refers to the essence, and *who* to person, *what* exactly is this "*who*" that nature owns and is united to? Interestingly, "*who"* is said to be the soul's mover and shaker – one's own **self**, no less! Thus nature *owns* its **self**, self is its *own* property, its *own* person. So *who* one is, then, is his very own(ed) **self**!

As to how human nature – body and soul, will, mind, psyche – could be *united* to its own self, is either a piece of nonsense or a profound mystery. The only reason theology regards *nature* and *person* as a "**union**", is to make the case Jesus' human nature was ***united*** to the divine *person* of the Logos. This way, it can say Jesus was *not* a *human* person, but a *divine* person – God-*in-person*. Without postulating nature and person as a "**union**", they would have no way to explain why (or how) Jesus was **not his own person**, but was God's own person instead. So by saying nature and person is only a "union" they could dis-unite the two (nature and person) and *substitute* God for the divine person of Jesus. This way, Jesus was no longer to be regarded as a **human** person, but as a **divine** person! Now, if God (as a divine person) can be the person (or self) of *man's human nature*, then God can be the person (or self) of every human nature. After all, anything *possible* for one human being – say, Jesus – is possible for every human being. That everyone can **become** God-in-person or God's own Self, is, indeed, the belief of some *Monistic* religions. So if one wants to find out how all this works, they'd best go to India and Hinduism because it holds that one's True *person* or *self* **is** God.

That nature is only "united" to person (or self) sounds as if *person* is some independent substance (some "thing") that can, or cannot, be *united* to human nature. This, at least, is the theological notion that God's person *took over* for the *human person* of Jesus – a genuine case of divine "possession". **This is justified by saying God was not only the *owner or person* of Its *own divine* nature, but owner or person of Its *human* nature as well.** To make this claim, of course, not only depends on the assumption God **is** a *person*, but that God as a person is not of the essence or existence of God, but only a "property" of God. It also assumes that God can *act* like a human person as well as a divine person. It is one thing for God to *own its own incarnate human nature*, but quite another for God *to act the part of a human person*. These are radically contrary views and later we will be pointing out why this is so.

For now, let us apply this divide (between essence and person) to God. Does *person* refer to God *ad intra* or only *ad extra*? To be told God as persons "Father-Son-Spirit" is **not** a reference to God in *essence*, but only to God's "*properties*", does this mean God as persons only refers to the *economy* of salvation – the "economic Trinity"– but *not* to the *essence* of God-in-Itself? A true understanding of the Trinity stands or falls on the answer to this question. Are we to believe God is three persons only *soteriologically* – economically *ad extra* – but not in Reality, not in essence and existence? Either person is of the very essence (nature) of God or it is *not*. If *essence* and *person* is only a *union*, then these can be separated such that *person* (God's own self) is not the essence of God – nor the essence of Man. This means that if "person" (one's own "self") was *eliminated,* this would not change the nature (essence and existence) of either God or man.

Theologically, then, since nature is not a person, and person is not nature (or essence), to be without the *owned* or *person* would not change the essence or nature of God or man. So *person*, then, is **not** of the essence (the "nature") or the abiding Reality of either God or man. "Who" (person) you are, is not "what" you are, because "who" is not the True nature or essence of either God or man.

To give some idea of the difference between Trinity as three *hypostases* and three *persons*, John Damascus (7th c.) gives the following explanation of *person* that he called "*hypostasis*":

Existence = "that" something exists
Essence = "what" it is that exists
Person = "who" it is that exists
Hypostasis = "mode of existence".[2]

Where essence is *common* or *universal*, *hypostasis* refers to God's distinct triune modes of existence. "*Who*", however, always refers to a "*particular individual.*" How a division between essence and person could be justified without making **God three particular individuals or beings** is inexplicable – it is a prescription for polytheism.

As we will see, this division between essence ("what") and person ("who") went so far as to redefine the "ontology of being". There was a shift from *essence* as the *reality* of being to *person* as the *reality* of being. Thus real being is not *what* you are, but *who* you are! Where a few theologians admit to this shift, others simply "assume" it – unknown to the unwary reader, of course. This shift, however, is all too obvious in the proverbial formulations of the Trinity and Christ. The theological excuse, of course, is that God's essence is *unknowable* and all man knows is God revealed as three persons – absolutely, **false!** There is no such revelation of God that could remotely be defined as a "person or three persons", people who think so, simply do not know God.

But this is how the original "*hypostasis*" used to point out the *real and eternal triune "distinctions" of God's modus operandi,* was shifted to God's properties or persons as *real being.* Although there is no reference to God as three "beings", **yet what *person* exists *who* is *not* a being?** While beings exist who are *not* persons, no person exists who is *not* a being. This is why using the term *person* for the Trinity is a prescription for tri-theism, polytheism.

So what exactly is this property or person *owned* by God and man? "Person" is defined as the *subject* or *agent* governing the nature, it is its mover and shaker, the one *who* runs nature and determines all its thoughts, words and behaviors. So, "lo-and-behold," the *owned* becomes the *owner*! **While nature *owns* the person, yet the person *governs* the nature, literally, runs the show. Incredible!** While

---

[2] While "Father-Son-Spirit" references the "economy of salvation", the Reality of God's essence or nature, however, is not Father-Son-Spirit (three "*who's*"), but God's triune hypostases or "modes of existence" – "*three hypostases in one essence*", this is God *ad intra*.

body and soul have all their faculties in place, yet it is the "person" or "subject" who uses or governs them, is totally responsible for them. The soul may be one's "life", yet this "life" is governed not by *what it is*, but by what it *owns* – a person! Body and soul, then, cannot function without its *person.* In itself, nature is just a "potential" waiting to be activated by its *owned* person. To define person as a "property" of nature (something *nature owns)* and then make this person totally responsible for its nature – as *if it owned the nature* – is an odd twist of definitions. That nature owns a property that owns the nature is like a Japanese Kōan – how can *you* own a property when **you *are* it?**

While there is something schizoid about this division (*nature* and *person*), on the other hand, it is not without its rationale. Certainly it lends insight into the difference between ***who*** you are and ***what*** you are, between the *essence* of one's real nature and its *person.* It also poses the question of what would happen to the essence of human nature if it was without a *person* – without *a "who"?* Could it *function* at all? Could it be that "death" is not the demise of nature (body and soul), but rather, the death of a *person,* "who" you are? No question, this is something to think about!

Since one can only *own* something he is *not* already, then whatever he can *own,* is *not what* he **is** already. To say, then, God *owns* or possesses three persons (or properties) means God *owns* what God is *not already – meaning, person* is **not** *what* God is. Indeed, it is because God *owns* creation that God is *not* creation, and creation is not "*what*" God is. So to call God a "person" is solely a reference to God as the owner of "what" God is *not.* **Thinking God is three persons, then, is not "what" God truly is.** Neither the nature of God nor man can be defined as what it *owns*, but only as *what* it **is**. Just as God is *what* God ***is*** and not what God *owns*, so too, man is *what* he **is**, and not what he *owns*. **In short, a "*person*" is not *what* man *is*, and is not *what* God *is*.**

A further problem is that there exists no definition of "person" that distinguishes a divine person from a human person. The definition of *person* is the same for both man and God. Telling us God transcends all our ideas of a human person, defeats the purpose of using the term in the first place. If there is no understanding of God as person any different from a human person, then why use the term at all? When the excuse is given that one is only speaking "analogously", notice how the use of "analogy" always makes God into *man's* image and likeness – it never fails! As to how this notion of the Trinity as three "persons" affects one's view and understanding of Christ, it means the difference between a Christianity centered on the Real Christ or a Christianity that can only be defined as "*anthropolatry*".

There is one contemporary writer (a theologian) who owns up to the fact there is no other definition of God as person than that of a human being as a person. He says – "*Admittedly God's person infinitely transcends human persons, we cannot transpose divine person to a human person, a veritable chasm lies between. Yet there are similarities – the principle of "analogy" applies to person. Created in the image of God we are also a reflection of God's persons. So we cannot define them "persons" as completely different.... we can only speak of persons in God only by a likeness stamped in the human person. Without this likeness we could not apply the term person to God.* ***Thus we have to start with the human person to have any idea of a divine person".*** And there you have it. Unless you can conceive of an *anthropomorphic deity*, you will never understand God as a *person!*

This is the whole problem with "theology" – its propensity to makeover God into the image of man. This, of course, totally discounts God's revelations to man. It is *because* God is in **no way** like man, that a revelation of God will stun his mind, stop his brain, all his ideas, concepts and images – gone forever. The reason "person" is such a deceptive term for God is that people have no other way of thinking of God except as a *human* person! This is why people think of God as a kind of super-human being – only a bigger and better *person* of course. But this is the way with many terms used for God. The saying "*man made in the image of God*" cannot be used to justify personifying God "*made in the image of man*". The Truth is, **God has no *image – none!*** Apart from a direct revelation of God, everything man thinks and knows of God is always "analogous" – like this or *like* that – but is this the Truth of God? Why promote *analogies* (like *person)* when they only promote human images of God that totally mislead and are not the Truth of God? There must be some other way to grasp the one triune essence of God than promoting God as three beings, three persons – three gods. (Someone once said, "*Man creates God, and then wonders why he can't find him*" – how true!)

Although thousands of pages could be written in refutation of tritheism and the consistent attempts to legitimize use of "person", this only digs the hole deeper. There is no use adding to the already confused, complicated theology of the Trinity and Christ with its philosophical terms and scholastic definitions. What makes all this necessary, however, is theology's need to consistently "cover its tracks".

With no definition of person capable of distinguishing a human from a divine person, the concept and image of God as three beings or gods is inescapable. Nobody has the slightest idea what a non-anthropomorphic, non-embodied "person" could be, none whatsoever!

Another excuse given for use of "person" was that it made God "personal" – an idea that could only come from someone who honestly didn't know God. To think that personifying and anthropomorphizing God makes God "personal" is not only absurd, it works *against* knowing God. The only reason man thinks God is "personal" is because he, himself, **is** a person – a "personal being"! As long as man thinks God is anything like a human person or being, however, he'll never know God because no such "God" exists. For one who truly knows God, it would be a contradiction of terms to say God is "**im**personal" – if God were impersonal how would anyone know God exists? The fact God reveals Itself to man, nullifies any notion God is impersonal. **It is those who do *not* know God who have to personify and anthropomorphize God in order to have "someone" to believe in.**

Possibly, use of the term "person" was a deliberate personification of God to accommodate the "simple folk" barely converted from polytheism. When we think of the polytheistic state religion of the early centuries, the image of God as three beings (or gods) would fly rather well with the politicos and common people. As already noted, Christ had the advantage of uniting the lofty philosophical Transcendent One with the polytheists' image of a human deity.

No question, the fathers were ever concerned with how the common people – uneducated by most standards – could understand God as Trinity. Origen, Augustine and others, mention this issue and referred to these people as "simple folk". The fathers went as far as they could to accommodate them without forfeiting their monotheism. Thus Augustine (354 – 430) says, "*When it is asked what the 'three' are, human utterance is weighed down by deep poverty of speech. All the same, we say three* ***persons****, not that we wish to say it, but that we may not be reduced to silence. For the sake of speaking of things that are ineffable, that we may be able in some way to say what we can in no way say fully, the terms* (one essence and three persons) *are* ***permissible****.* ***The persons are*** **not** ***the Trinity****, but* (what) *the Trinity can be* **called** *– also the Holy Spirit, because all three are God, and Spirit and Holy"*. (Note: the *Spirit* always escapes "personification" – escapes the term "person".)

When it comes to explaining and defining God as "three persons", three individuals or subjects, every author warns us not to think what the fathers meant by "person" is what, today, we think of as a "person". The implication is that if we can just let go all definitions, ideas and images that we *think* is a person, *then* we will understand what the fathers meant by "God is a person(s)". So let us say we did that – let go of everything we think is a "*person*" – and now what's left? Nothing, not the slightest idea! **Obviously, God is *not* a person, and negating all definitions of *person* is all the proof we need.**

Still, how is one to consider a "Father and Son" as anything but two individual "persons"? With no ability to differentiate between a human and a divine person, people are left with no other way to consider the Trinity but as two *human-like* persons. Granted, no Christian regards the Trinity as polytheistic deities, but to get Christians beyond these images and ideas, Christian theology is a failure. It not only reinforces false images and ideas, but seems to rely on them for its own understanding. No question, use of traditional terms, language and images holds people back from the Truth, and many who have come to realize this, have simply left and gone elsewhere.

The theology of the Trinity can become so complicated it is no wonder people dismiss it as a "mystery" and focus, instead, on the man Jesus. And who does *not* regard the man Jesus as a "person"? Everyone does! The only problem, they think Jesus is a "divine" person even though they couldn't tell you the difference between a divine and a human person. Unknowingly, people merely capitalize the "p" in "person" thinking they know a divine person when all they *really* know is a *human* person.

Aquinas tries to explain this, he says, "*Our human intellect cannot attain to the absolute simplicity of the divine essence considered in itself and* ***must, therefore, apprehend and name divine things according to its own human mode, i.e., in so far as they are found in sensible things from which it derives its knowledge.***"

What he is saying, is because we have no other way of knowing divine persons apart from knowing human persons, this leaves no other way to know the Trinity but as *human* persons. And indeed, that is exactly how theologians present the Trinity – as three human persons. While we are warned they are not the same as human persons, yet to *say* one is divine and the other human, defines no difference whatsoever. If man has no other way of knowing God as persons than knowing *human* persons, then the whole concept of person should be scratched, it only deceives and promotes wrong views, gives a false understanding of the Trinity and Christ.

As to why anyone would stick with the term "*person*", obviously, it was because it served his purpose to do so. The purpose here, of course, was to make the Logos a person in order to define Its incarnation (Christ) as a *single* ***divine*** *person*. This, in turn, either consciously or unconsciously *implies* the man Jesus was a divine person. Yet, if the *Logos is the sole divine person* of Christ, then it was not Jesus **who** was the *divine* person, but solely God (Logos.) So if one asks, "**Who** is Christ?" the answer could never be "Jesus is **Who** Christ is", it could only be, "the Logos is *Who* Christ is". Of himself, Jesus, a human being, was never understood as the *divine person* "Christ", it was solely the Logos (God) who was the divine *person* of "Christ". So as a *person*, then, "*Who*" Christ is, is God (Logos), even though in *essence or nature* Christ is neither God nor man, but the oneness of the two *natures* – God *and* man.

As to how it happened the term "person" became the keystone of all Christian theology, let us go over the rationale for its use of the term "*person*":

1. The term *person* was invented to avoid the accusation of *anthropolatry.* They had to find a way to explain the man Jesus that would justify him as the "one Christ" worthy of worship. Keeping in mind Christ's dual natures as the *union* of God's divine nature with man's human nature, and that Jesus was, indeed, united to God, yet how can this *union* (which **is** Christ) be understood as the *single human being, Jesus*? (As we'll see later, the *real* problem was that the union of natures does *not* constitute one individual ontological being.)

2. By giving God's *triune modes of existence* – or three hypostases – the **property** of "persons" (each being their own independent agent and subject), then it could be said the two natures were united **in** the one hypostasis (or person) of the divine Logos. The Incarnation, then, was not the *essence* of God's divine nature "born" into this world, rather, it was only a divine "person" *who* was born into this world. So while Jesus had no divine nature, God, however, as the Owner, was the divine Person of Its own human nature.

3. So while Jesus was a human being, he owned no property of a human person, but was the *property* (or person) of God alone. God, then, as the "owner" of Its created human nature was *not* the man Jesus. God alone was the sole *owner* (or person) of Its own human nature. **It was not Jesus, then, who was the divine person of Christ, it was solely God (Logos.) Jesus had no divine nature and was no divine person. God alone is *Christ's* divine nature and person.**

4. This means that while Jesus was *not* a divine person, God (as a person) took the place of Jesus' human personhood and acted in his stead. God was the agent and subject of Jesus' whole life and being, God ran the show. This is why it could be said, "God (*as a person*) was born, suffered and died", all referring *not* to Jesus as a human being or human person, but instead, all referring to God as a *person – the owner of Its **own** human nature.*

5. So now we have the theological formula, "**Christ is one divine person with two natures**" – or Christ is the *union of two natures* ***in*** *one divine person* – the divine person of the Logos. The worship of Christ, then, is not the worship of a human being, but the worship of a *divine person.* **The one divine *person* of "Christ" being the divine Logos (God) and *not* the human being (or human person) Jesus.**

6. It is because God (and not Jesus) was the owner of Its own human nature, **Jesus was not a human person.** Jesus' human nature was not *his* own property, it was *God's property.* To say Jesus was "God's property or person" means Jesus was not God in *nature*, but God in *person*.

7. It works out, then, by making the Trinity three *persons,* all references to the Incarnate Logos or "Christ" – even references to the man Jesus – are references to ***one*** *divine* **person and *not* a reference to either a divine or a human *nature.*** The word "*Christ*" is *not* a reference to either the essence of God or man, but solely a reference to a divine "person" – Logos (God.)

8. With this understanding, no one could accuse Christians of *anthropolatry.* People do not worship the man Jesus or any *human being* as God, rather, the one people worship is a *divine* ***person***, and this ***person is*** not the human person Jesus, but Almighty God as a "person".

This, then, is the way the theology of Christ works to avoid any form of anthropolatry. If a division had not been made, however, between *nature* (*essence*) and *person* – or between "*what*" and "*who*" – this scheme could not have worked. This division with its definition of *person* is totally a Christian invention, and now we know why and how it came about. While there is some truth in this Christology, its problems, however, all but overwhelm what truth it contains. Before pointing out the problems, however, let us first point out its truth.

The Incarnation was, indeed, God creating *Its own* human nature, uniting it eternally with Its divine nature. God did not, however, create the human nature of this or that individual human being or particular *person.*

In fact, God never creates *any* human person – a person is what man makes of himself, makes of his own free-will and determination. Christ's human nature, then, *belonged* to no particular human being or particular *person*, but belonged to God alone. So yes, indeed, **the human nature of the Incarnate Logos is God's *own* human nature, and this is the truth.**

Also, that **the source and locus of the union of natures is *in* God, *in* the Logos** and *not* **in** *human* nature or **in** any human being,

this is also the truth. But now for the problems with this theology:

1. **Who** is Jesus?

As soon as God was made a "person", Jesus became a non-person – impersonal. (Somewhere Cyril says Jesus' "*humanity is impersonal*".) Remember, God was made to *take the place* of Jesus' human personhood – i.e., God acted as the agent and subject of his soul and all its faculties. So Jesus was *not* his *own* person, instead, God was substituted for the human person Jesus. But because Jesus was not a human person, can we say he was, therefore, a *divine person* – say "*who*" *he* was, was God? If so – if Jesus is "who" God is, how is this not *anthropolatry?* Human nature cannot **own** a divine Person. While God can own Its human nature, no human nature can own a divine Person. Strictly speaking, however, God did not "*take the place*" of Jesus' human personhood because it was never "his" human nature in the first place! At any rate, keep in mind that neither in nature or person is the man Jesus, God.

No one explains why Jesus is not a human person better than a contemporary Orthodox author who says, "*One person cannot be identified with another person without ceasing to exist as a personal being – that would mean the annihilation of human persons in the unique Christ, an impersonal deification, a blessedness in which there would be no blessed*". He is so right! If a human person was one with the Logos' *divine Person,* he would *cease to be* a human person, but would **be** Christ – who was *not* a *human person.* So this is exactly how it goes – "*an impersonal deification in which there would be no blessed or blessedness*". But without a *person*, however, "**who**" would there be to *miss* being *blessed or blessedness?* **No one**!

Like Jesus, man can only be united to the Logos (God) and not to another human being or person. Since Jesus was not a human person, then **to be united to God means there is no human person in this union.** Like Jesus, then, everyone must become no-person – become Christ. **Man's oneness with God is neither a oneness with the man Jesus nor a oneness with Christ, but solely a oneness with God. Just as the human being Jesus was one with the Logos, so too, all must be one with the Logos, a oneness that *is* Christ.**

2. **Was Jesus a divine person?**

Since *person* is a possession or property of nature, a *divine* person can never be the *property* of *human* nature – no *man owns a divine person.* The theology is this: while human nature cannot possess or be a divine person, yet a **divine person can own or possess *two natures,* thus a single divine person can act (or serve) as the *single person* of**

both* natures, divine and human**. That the divine person **acted** as the person of Its human nature, however, does not make Its *human* nature a divine person. To make God and Jesus *both* divine persons makes Christ the union of two persons – **unorthodox**. It is because God took the place of a human person that, theologically, at least, Jesus is to be regarded as *not* a human person. Basically, then, **the man Jesus was *neither* a human person *nor* a divine person.** ***God alone was the one divine "person" of Christ, and this one person was God, not the human being or person, Jesus.

So the definition of "person" as property or ownership worked well to define Christ. Since **Jesus is not a divine person, Jesus is not "who" Christ is. "Who" Christ is, is solely the divine Person (Logos) and not the man Jesus.** It is a mistake, then, to think because Jesus was not a human person he was, therefore, a divine person. This is false – and unorthodox. Christ is two natures **in** the one hypostasis or person of the Logos – "person" being a reference to the Logos and not to the man Jesus. So as long as person means nothing more than "ownership", it serves its purpose to affirm that the human nature the Logos created was Its *own* human nature and not the human nature of any particular human being – not even **Jesus' own** human nature.

The problem, of course, people assume because Jesus was not a human person, *therefore,* he was a divine person. Human nature, however, cannot *own* or *possess* a divine person. ***Only God was the divine person of Christ.*** While Jesus' human nature was *possessed* by God's divine person, yet **the man Jesus *owned* no person at all.**

As a human being, then, Jesus "*owned*" nothing, he was neither a divine or human person, thus, he was "impersonal". One can only imagine the surprise of Christians to learn Jesus was neither a human or a divine person – learn that he was totally *impersonal*! Who could believe it? Not a single Christian! So just *who* was this man Jesus? Theologically, at least – nobody! Neither according to his nature or person was Jesus divine. Imagine the Pope on his balcony telling the crowd, "The Church teaches that Jesus was not a divine person and not a human person – he was nobody!" While this is perfectly orthodox, they'd lock him up!

3. **How is a divine person different from a human person?**

Given the fact the definition of *person* is the same for both God and man, who honestly knows the difference? Basically, the only difference between God and man is whatever the difference between the Uncreated and created, the Infinite and finite. **In the absence of knowing this difference, and taking Jesus for a *divine person,* people are mistakenly taking God for a *human person*.** As said, all one has to do is capitalize the "p" in person to get a *divine person* – and why not? **If God can *act* as a human person, then how is God *not* a human person?** If a divine person can live on earth for 30 years and not stand out from the crowd, than how is a divine person any different? (Indeed, who has ever seen a divine person stand out in a crowd?) **No one knew Jesus to be anything but a *human* person**. If all human experiences are those of a divine person, then *how* are the experiences of a human person any different from those of a divine person? With no ability to define any difference, merely to "call" one *divine* and the other *human,* defines no difference whatsoever. This is merely **attributing to God what is human.** To make a human person a divine person – or vice versa – is the simple definition of "*anthropolatry*".

This could not have happened had God not been made to be a *person* (or persons), and Jesus not robbed of being an authentic *human person*. Any attempt to deify Jesus does away with the whole purpose of the Incarnation and the revelation of Christ. **Christ is the revelation of everyman's eternal oneness with God, *a union of natures* that has nothing to do with any *persons* – divine *or human.***

4. **Is Jesus "one being" with God?**

According to the present Nicene-Constantinople Creed, "*Jesus Christ*" is "*one in Being with the Father*". How are we to understand this? Since "*One in Being*" refers to the nature or essence of God, is this a reference to the man Jesus being of the same Infinite Essence as God? We know the Logos (God) is "one in Being with the Father", but prior to the incarnation did Christ – or even Jesus – exist? If so, then *who* or *what* was Incarnated? (Can't incarnate what is already incarnated!) Was **Jesus Christ** born "*before all ages, God from God, Light from Light*"? If so, then "who" was incarnated in Mary?

It seems the Creed has assumed the *Monophysitic* position – namely, that the incarnate Logos or **Christ had *one divine nature* (*Monophysitism.*)** The thinking must be that because **a divine person is of one divine nature, Christ as one divine person is of *one divine nature*** – this was Cyril of Alexandria's thinking. How else are we to account for the saying, "*Jesus Christ is one being with the Father*"? (Actually, Jesus is *supposed* to be one with the divine "Logos" and *not* one with the "Father"!) But as said, the whole Creed needs to be redone, it promotes *Monophysitism* – one divine person understood as one divine nature. There is no Real Trinity here, no True Christ, no affirmation of a union of two disparate natures, and thus, no authentic Incarnation.

The few problems we have gone over are but the tip of the iceberg. There is no end of problems engendered by the *division* between God's *nature* and *person,* between the owner and owned, between the **what** and **who of God**. Few people realize how utterly dependent Christian theology is on the term "person" for its understanding of the Trinity and Christ. This dependency is such that if "person" (*who*) was removed from the mind-set and language of its theologies, all its Christologies would fall like a row of dominoes, fall all the way back to before Nicaea, where it would have to start all over again. Thus, if God is *not* a person, then *who* is the man Jesus and *who* is Christ? Without the division between God's divine *nature* and *person*, there would emerge a different understanding of the Trinity and Christ, one more in keeping with its Truth.

Over centuries the Christian mind has become so inured to the view of Christ based on "person", that to present an understanding of Christ *not* based on "person" is sure to be dismissed as either unorthodox or so challenging to the inured mind-set, the brain will simply give up and go back to its usual wrong views. It is because "person" can only be understood as a *human person* that the Logos (God) is *mistaken* for a human person and a human person *mistaken* for a divine person. To merely capitalize the "p" in person does not make a person "divine". To right this wrong, the notion of "person" can never be applied to Almighty God or the Trinity – never.

The huge mistake, of course, was **making God a person *instead* of Jesus** – which totally defeats the whole purpose of the incarnation. There is no place in this Christology for a *genuine human being.* Jesus, after all, is the sole historical *person* of the Gospels – somebody or some *person* died on the cross, and it was *not* almighty God! It was the ***person*** Jesus "who" died, and the *person-less* Christ *that* arose. Obviously, **the *union* of the divine and human natures does *not* constitute *one single ontological being* either divine or human.** This is why the true **mystery of Christ is an "ontological problem".** Because the union of natures is not a single embodied being, Christ fits no ontological reality we know of. **In truth, God creates no person – because *God is not a person(s.)*** The eternal union of natures has nothing whatsoever to do with any person, divine or human.

Because the term "*hypostasis*" served both to affirm the abiding *distinctions* of God's triune nature and to *ground* the *oneness* of Christ's natures ***in*** the divine Logos, no division was ever needed between nature and person – between owned and owner or *what* and *who.* Had *hypostasis* been retained, there would have been no need to deny Jesus was a human person – a *complete human being,* that is. The only reason for substituting *person* for *hypostasis* was to **substitute God as a person for the human person Jesus in order to say *Christ was one***

divine person **– implying one divine being. The divine Logos, however, is not a divine "being"** (the Trinity is not three *beings*), **nor was Jesus one *divine* being.** It is because Christ, as the oneness of divine and human natures, *does not constitute a single ontological being* that "*person*" was **invented** to refer to Christ as *one* single *person* – with two natures, of course.

But if the Alexandrians excluded Jesus from being a human person, this was not the case for the Antiochenes. Maximus the Confessor (580 – 662) would say that Jesus, created in the image of the Logos, is the "model" of every *human person* – not the model of a divine person. He says, *"Each human individual, fully* ***consubstantial*** *with his fellow men is, and nonetheless, radically distinct from them in his unique, unrepeatable, and unassimilable* ***person*** *or hypostasis, no man can be* ***in*** *another man. But Jesus' hypostasis* (*human* person) *has a fundamental affinity with all human persons, that of being their* ***model****. All were created according to the image of God, image of the Logos. When the Logos became incarnate the divine stamp matched its imprint, God assumed humanity in a way which did* ***not*** *exclude any human person, but which opened to all of them the possibility of restoring their* ***unity*** *in Himself"* – be one with God, that is.

The Antiochenes, of course, did not go along with the Trinitarian distinction of *hypostasis* as "*persona*". For them, this would have meant God (the Logos) was the one (persona) born of Mary, the one ***who*** suffered and died, which was totally contrary to God's *immutability* and *impassibility*. Gregory of Nazianzius regarded the term "persona" for God (or three persons) as merely a "metaphor". Another regarded "father and son" as "*nominal attributes*". Augustine apologized for using "person" saying it was an inadequate term. Even Tertullian avoided the term "persons" and referred to the Trinity as "the Three". For his part, Athanasius never mentions three *hypostases*, much less *persons*. Aquinas referred to *person* as a "metaphor", and the contemporary theologian, Karl Rahner, suggested it should be eliminated altogether.

While the fathers held the Logos to be the *divine hypostasis* of Christ, when *hypostasis* was taken to mean the one "person" of Christ, Jesus could not be considered a human person lest this make Christ the union of "two persons". When speaking of Christ as *"one person"*, however, "*who*" immediately comes to mind, the Logos or the man Jesus? And who, after all, honestly knows the Logos? Anyone who has truly *seen* the Logos knows it is nothing comparable to anything in this world and could never be regarded as a "person" or "who" someone is. (The revelation of God is not the revelation of "who" somebody is!) Thus, because God is *not* a person or three persons the only "*person*" that comes to mind is the human person Jesus. This is why those who think Jesus is a divine person mistake God for a *human* person and mistake the *human* person Jesus, for God.

The best way to understand "Christ" (and not *God*) is to think of **Christ's *human nature* as *belonging* to the Logos,** but Jesus' ***person belonging* to *himself* – which is the meaning of "person".** Because God is *not* Jesus' human nature, Jesus was his *own person*. The reason people find it difficult to separate human *nature* from *person* iterates Nestorius' question to Cyril, "*How can you have a complete human being who is **not** a human person*?" Like Nestorius, most people cannot separate the two – human person from human nature – and yet, there is no other ***theological*** way to understand "*Christ*" as a divine *person*. What Nestorius *should* have asked Cyril – "*How can you have a human being that **is** a divine person?*" It is because this is impossible, Jesus was robbed of his personhood and held to be *no* human person at all. Such a view totally misses Christ's *earthly* existence, misses the Incarnation, and skewed Christianity ever since.

PERSON AS SELF

As theologically defined – "*Person is a self-conscious entity, it is the thinking, self-conscious and free subject of the soul*". "Person", then, is everything man calls "self", and every definition given for *person* **is** a definition of *self.*

While essence or nature is a *universal*, "person" is a *particular,* an incommunicable one-of-kind ("*incommunicable*" means "one cannot be the other".) Where *hypostasis* pointed up the reality of God's triune incommunicable "modes of existence", *person* points up a particular subjective identity that answers the question "*who* exists?" The answer, of course, is **"I exist", "I am myself and no other", "I am who I am".** Person, then, is always a reference to an individual subject or "I am", and as an individual's identity center, it is the "agent" of its own thoughts, words and deeds. A person, then, is a being *in itself,* possesses its *own* being as the subject of consciousness, is the one who determines his *own* life and behaviors. As we have seen, the origin of the term "person" was to define God as "three persons" – God's single nature possessing (owning) three distinct incommunicable properties or separate identities. **The Trinity as three "*persons*" literally makes God *three subjects*, *three divine selves*, *three "I am's"*, *three "consciousnesses"*, *three independent agents* – basically, *three individuals.*** If an "individual", however, is understood as a *person* or an independent being, then, of course, three *persons* make the Trinity three individual beings – *tri-theism.*

Some authors have said "person" as we understand it today, is not what the early fathers understood by "person", but there is no truth to this. The entire understanding and definition of "person" came from the fathers, no one else in history coined and defined the term. They used its definition to rationalize and explain their theologies of the Trinity and Christ – the same as today. Trying to tell us the fathers did not mean what we mean today, is just another example of theologians trying to cover their tracks – dodge the real issues, that is.

From the start, "person" meant exactly what it does today – a discrete autonomous being, its *own* independent agent or subject. "*I am*" is a statement of *being* ("*I exist*"), of self-awareness, a conscious being that indicates reflexive-consciousness and everything man knows and calls his "*self*". The early fathers defined it thus and we have been stuck with it ever since. Referring to the state of *theosis* or *unitive* state in which Jesus was born, I believe Clement of Alexandria (150 – 215) was the first to say God was the *true subject* of the man Jesus. Later, Cyril of Alexandria (376 – 444) tells us, "*The identity of the person of the God-man was that of the Logos. His* (Jesus'*) person* (self-identity*)* *was constituted by the Logos. In this union the Logos is the* ***personal subject and directive principle*** *of the man Jesus,* ***the soul of Christ does not retain any of its natural powers*** *".*

Cyril built his whole Christological paradigm on the premise God was a *person* or subject that knows Itself as "me, myself and I", and that, just like **man's** self-awareness, God can say "*I am, I know, I suffer, listen to me*", and so on. Cyril (and some others) not only assumed this kind of human self-knowing as *God's* self-knowing, but said this divine knowing was Jesus' same *divine knowing*. Evidently, the only difference is where man knows himself as *man*, God knows himself as *God*. Making God the "person" of Jesus, then, means that Jesus never *knew himself* as a human being, he only knew himself as God! That Jesus knew *he* was the Creator, Omniscient and all Powerful, etc. is incredible – incredible that anyone can believe it. That Jesus never knew himself as a human being and only knew himself as Almighty God, and that his self-identity was "I am God and no other", or that "I am the Source of all that exists", is nothing more than someone's demented idea. Jesus knew he was one with God ("*the Father and I are one*"), he never thought **he** was God – Yahweh or his "Father".

What is so unfortunate about this idea, is that it indicates one has never had a true revelation of God – not even a glimpse. It only takes a glimpse to let man know God is nothing in this created universe – and is certainly *not himself*. To intellectually believe in God is one thing, but to see God is enough to nullify all man's *ideas about* God. Right here we have a good example of the absurdities that ensue when transposing anything created or human to Almighty God – in this case, human consciousness, self-awareness, self-identity or self. This is the last word in making God in *man's* image, the last word in polytheism and anthropolatry.

As the thinking goes, although Jesus was a human being, yet because it was not *his* humanity, but the humanity of the divine Logos, the Logos was made to be the sole *divine person* of Christ. Thus God was Jesus' *self-identity, subject, "I am"*, along with all his words and deeds – his whole life, in fact. There is no place here for any true human being, a robot maybe, but no authentic human being. To hold God was the sole subject and *agent* of Jesus' human nature, of his mind and will, is no different from Apollinaris' view that the Logos *took the place* of Jesus' soul – regarded as a heresy. To avoid this heresy, Cyril did not *replace* Jesus' soul, he only replaced its *functioning or faculties* – as he says, "*the soul of Christ does not retain any of its natural powers*". This is really no different from Apollinaris' view – after all, why have a human soul if you can't use it?

If God can "possess" a human soul, can live, walk and talk like a human soul, then how is God *not* a human soul? This is exactly why the Alexandrians regarded Jesus as so much *flesh* and not a genuine human being. They never gave Jesus' human soul more than lip-service, it played absolutely no part in their Christology. Yet, having no free will or mind, is the definition of an animal, not a human being. In this scenario, Jesus is a *possessed body*, but not a human soul. And what is behind this insistence on making Christ a divine *person* if not to somehow deify the man? It seems the more Christianity tries to deify the man, the more it diminishes him – and all men – and the further it strays from the truth of the Incarnation. Unfortunately, it was this same Alexandrian Christology that has come down to us today and is largely responsible for *anthropolatry*.

First, by making God a *person* – a self, subject or "I am" – and then transposing *God's self-identity* to be the acting principle, subject or "I am" of Jesus' human nature, one could then say "*Jesus is God in person*". This, of course, is solely a reference to God as a "*person*", with no reference to either God's *divine nature,* Jesus' *human nature – or a union of natures.* Still, by making God to be the one divine ***person*** of Jesus (and of Christ), the accusation of *anthropolatry* could be avoided. Worship of Jesus – or of Christ – then, was not the worship of either a divine or human being, but the worship of a divine *person* – the Logos (Almighty God.) If any reader does not understand this "trans-position" of person or self from man to God, then he has missed the whole Christological problem, which, by the end of the 5th century, became the proverbial "party-line" – with us to this day.

Few people realize the Christian affirmation "*Jesus is God*" or "*Christ is God*" is *solely* a reference to God (Logos) ***as a person*** with no reference to **the divine or human natures.** Alone, Jesus is not God, nor is Christ (dual natures) God. From here on, however, "*Who*" God is, who Christ is, who Jesus is **as a person,** is the sole Christian criterion for all references to God, Christ and the man Jesus. Thus, "*person*" – one's *self-identity* – is the *foundation* of the entire Christian party-line presentation of the truths of Christianity. As said before, remove the whole notion of God (Trinity) **as "*person(s)*",** and this whole party-line goes down like a row of dominoes. Without the notion of God as a *person(s)* the party-line presentation of Christ has not a leg to stand on.

A well-known theologian defines **man** thus – *"regarded as a **person or a self**, metaphysically as an autonomous subject, that is, a self-existent **being** who has dominion over his own actions so that **self** is the ultimate center to whom these actions are to be attributed. Directly we* *apply this definition to Christ's human nature (Jesus) we find ourselves confronted with the whole mystery of the* **hypostatic union***, the Word of God took to Himself a complete and perfect human nature, and yet there was* ***no human person in Christ****. ... the human actions of Christ belonged to and are attributed to the* ***Person*** *of the Word as their sole responsible agent. There is* ***no human self*** *in Christ to perform human actions, nor a human self to be regarded as responsible for these human actions. Thus the Councils of Ephesus and Chalcedon taught that* ***Christ had no human personality*** (was not a human person)*, and thus the medieval theologians had to show that though he had no human personality* (was not a person)*, Jesus was nonetheless a complete and perfect man".*

That theologians had a problem with Jesus as a *complete human being*, is obviously a problem of their own making. First they switched the reference from Jesus as God's "son" to God as God's son. Then they switched Jesus as a *person* to God as a person, and then switched the *ontology of being* from *what* human nature is to *who* someone is. When it comes to deifying the man Jesus, theology never misses a trick. For sure, the first thing on the Christian agenda was *never* to *humanize* Jesus. And after all this, they wondered how Jesus could possibly have been a true human being?! Theologians are like a man who digs a hole so far over his head he can't get out, yet, he would rather die than admit he had dug his own grave.

In the history of Christianity there is only one person who stood up for the full humanity of Jesus as a *human person*. This was the Patriarch of Constantinople, Nestorius (386 – 451), an Antiochene, who dared to correct Cyril. All he asked Cyril was, "*How can you have a complete human nature that is not a* ***human person****?*" This so flew in the face of Cyril's Christology that, using all his political power, Cyril promptly had Nestorius dismissed, condemned and exiled. All this, because of Nestorius' common sense question that Cyril could not answer – **a question that has never been answered**! (As said, what Nestorius should have asked, was "*How can you have a* ***divine nature*** *that is a* ***human*** *person?*")

Many of the fathers, the Antiochenes especially, did not understand the term "person" to mean the *sole* subject of the incarnate Logos. **For them, "person" was a term for the *unity* of the two natures and did not mean the Logos was the *sole* subject of Christ.** Thus for Theodore of Mopsuestia, *"The "I" in Christ was singular and a* ***product*** *of the union"*. This "I", however, did not belong to the Logos (God), but to Christ as the "*singular product of the union, a subject who could now be addressed as God, now as man"*. The Antiochenes argued that Jesus' human *subject* acted in *unison* with the divine subject, but was not itself a *divine subject.* They had the right understanding of *theosis* (unitive state) in which Jesus came into this world, a "unitive state" that did not rob him of personhood or his own self- identity, rather, it was perfectly *in tune and* one with God. Even Cyril admits *"Jesus is the example of one most perfectly aligned with God's will as any human can be".* Another said, "*Logos was the active agent or subject, humanity was the passive agent or subject*" – an interesting way to put this union, only he had it backward. Even as a "person", God was understood as *impassible,* thus it is the human person or self that is the *active agent* or subject.

Though the Antiochenes regarded Jesus as a human person, they never said or held Christ was the union of two persons – none, ever! They never took "hypostasis" as reference to a "person". They adhered to Chalcedon's affirmation of Christ as the union of two disparate natures – not two disparate persons. **It was precisely this truth – union of natures – that left Jesus free to be his *own person.*** As a human person, Jesus was perfectly aware of *his* union or oneness with God – he never said or thought **he** was God. Also, Jesus, as a human person, the Holy Spirit "indwelled" in him, he knew this, *experienced* it. None of this was *God's* experience – the idea is absurd. This was the scenario of a true human being, a *whole human person.* So, in affirming Jesus as a human person or self, the Antiochenes are actually pointing out the difference between Jesus' *earthly state of theosis* or union with God, and *the eternal* **person-less** *estate of Christ.* The only name we have for the heavenly or *eternal* (non-earthly) estate of Christ, was coined by Cyril as a "*hypostatic union*" – to be discussed in another chapter.

No question, the Antiochenes understood Jesus to be a genuine human person – a self-conscious subject. With the condemnation of Nestorius, however, they lost their best opportunity to affirm this. With a single blow – the condemnation of Nestorius – Christianity forever lost the opportunity to affirm Jesus as a complete human being. After this condemnation, no one in the history of Christianity ever stood up for Jesus as a **human person – lest** they get the same "Nestorian treatment". And please note, *even today,* no theologian will dare say Jesus was a *human person,* all they will say is that he was a *"personality"*! Theology does not regard a "personality" or "psychological subject" as a *person.* Since, theologically, God is the divine person or subject of Christ, the human being, Jesus, was solely the ***external expression* or presentation** of God's divine person. Thus Jesus was *not* a human *person* (the orthodox belief), but only a *personality.*

Note the theological definition of Jesus as a "personality". Since theologians cannot say Jesus was a *human person*, they cover their tracks by saying he was a "personality". As to how there can be a *divine* person with a *human* personality – who can figure this out? But then, theology is not really the study of God (how can God be *studied*?), theology is the attempt to make its own absurdities, rational. (Tertullian once said, "I believe because it is absurd" – an apt definition of *theology.)*

What the medieval theologians had to figure out was how to answer Nestorius' question – "*How can you have a complete human being that is not a* **human** *person*?" The reason theologians have never been able to figure this out, is **because Nestorius was right, Jesus was a complete *human person.*** The day Nestorius' "human person" was thrown to the lions, is the day a true understanding of Christ was thrown out as well.

But let us go over a list of categories of *person* or *subject* that theology would have us differentiate:

1. Ontological person (subject) – God.
2. Metaphysical person (subject) – man.
3. Epistemological person (subject) – the knower as a *subject* knowing itself.
4. Psychological person (subject) – a "personality" or how a *person* is expressed to the outside or seen by others.

Having given us these divisions of person or self, all we need now are comprehensible definitions to explain their differences, explain them, however, where one definition is not used to define another – which is always the case. Basically, these distinctions are all in one's head, for without making clear **experiential** distinctions, it all boils down to theory and no substance. Actually, they could be put down as no more than different levels of "*Know Thyself*", all belonging to *man*, however, and *none* to God. One can define and speculate no end, yet, in truth, God transcends all man's notions of person, subject, self, consciousness, identity, and so on.

Ontological Subject

One renowned theologian tells us – *"hypostasis responds to the question 'who' and indicates an 'I'*, but adds, *'this 'I' must not be understood as a psychological or existential 'I', the patristic notion of personhood is* ***strictly ontological,*** *it is not the unity of consciousness"*.

So here comes the *ontological switch* from *essence* ("***what***" something is) as the ontological criterion of being, to *person* ("***who***" someone is) *as the criterion of ontological being*. "Ontology", however, deals with universals, whereas "who" deals with *particular* individuals. To say the *real being* of God and man is not *what* they are (in essence), but *who* they are (unique *particular* individuals) defies the whole notion of "ontological being". But not only is God beyond all man's categories of "ontological being", but strictly speaking, Christ – man's eternal oneness with God – also transcends all categories of ontological being.

That for the first thirty years of his life, Jesus was regarded by his peers and contemporaries as just another human being, another *person*, does not say much for God as an Uncreated ***ontologically Transcendent person or subject***! That God could walk, talk, pray to God, shop in the supermarket, and no one recognize "him" as *God*, is pretty absurd. On the other hand, perhaps the lesson here is to treat one's neighbor as if he were God – because he just might be!

If a *divine subject (God)* can be the *same subject,* agent, *who,* or "I am" of a *human being* – such as we are told is the case with Jesus – then what is the difference between an *ontological* and an *existential* subject – "I am"? That **the divine can *act as a human subject, and a human can act as a divine subject, who can tell us the difference?*** When the one subject is the same for both natures – as in Christ – there is no difference to speak of. Thus, all this does is affirm God **is** a ***human subject!*** If God can *replace* or *substitute* the subject of one human being, then God can replace the subject of any human being. This, at least, was the view of Maximus the Confessor (580 – 662), who is considered one of the greatest authorities on the spiritual life. He said that in the **end "*God takes away the ego and replaces it with His Person*"** – in his day "ego" meant "self". Thus God replaces man's human person, self or "I am" with Its own divine person – no different from Christ. On the other hand, however, Maximus tells us, "***God has no consciousness, his knowing is not relative or dual like ours (subject-object)***". Obviously he did not equate "consciousness" with *person.* But to claim there is no *ontological* difference between God's "I" and man's "I", can never span the chasm between man's way of knowing and *God's Divine Knowing.* Divine "Knowing" has nothing in common with any form of human "knowing" – be it consciousness, person, self, intellect or whatever. The idea God knows Itself as "God" is absurd anyway. God has no "God" to know, only man knows "God".

The reason people think of person or self as an "ontological being" is because all reference to "one's self" ("me, myself and I") is a reference to *one's whole being* – body, soul, psyche, everything he is. **Thus**

to affirm "*I exist*" is a statement of ontological *being* – existence. Who makes a distinction between *his being* (*human nature)* and *his self* – or *person?* No one regards *self* or *person* as a "property" of his existence, or something he *owns.* Rather, he takes "I exist" or "I am" as referring to his entire ontological existence – being. As defined, however, *person* is **not** one's *being* (nature or essence), rather, person or self is a "property" of *being* – i.e., "accidental" to it. Thus "who" you are is accidental to "what" you are – certainly something to think about!

Metaphysical Subject

It was either one of the fathers or a later theologian who said, *"A* ***human*** *person requires an ultimate* ***metaphysical*** *subject. What constitutes His* (Jesus') *Person is the metaphysical subject of his being, the hypostasis of the Logos was the unique metaphysical subject in Christ*". (Note his reference is to a "metaphysical" subject and not an "ontological" subject.) *Meta* not only transcends a physical body, but the intellect as well, thus a person, subject or self, is nothing the mind can grasp, seemingly it is the mystery of one's *true being* – or one's *true self.* Basically, this would not define person or self as a "property" of nature, but equates one's *true self* with one's *true being.* This is not all that different from the notion of God as an "ontological subject", only in this context, it must also account for *God as* ***man's*** *true metaphysical subject,* which is *not* ***God's*** metaphysical subject!

But once God was made the sole *person* or self of Jesus, if one asks "***Who is God?***" Can the answer be "***Jesus is who God is*"?** If so, it indicates no true knowledge of God, not even as a *person.* Strictly speaking, "*who*" is not a reference to God, to Infinite Existence, but only a reference to one of those three *properties,* subjects or selves of the Trinity. It is because a *divine* person **cannot** be the "property" of *human* nature that a divine person had to ***act instead of*** **– or *as if* – it** was the human person of Jesus. This means that any reference to "who" Jesus was, or Christ is, is solely a reference to one of God's *properties* or *persons* (subjects or selves), and not a reference to either the nature (essence) of God or man. So, even if God was Jesus' metaphysical subject or person, Jesus, however, was *not* God's metaphysical subject or person! **While God may be *Jesus'* true subject, Jesus is not *God's* true subject.** That God is the true metaphysical subject of *every human being*, in no way makes a human being God. As said before, God is man's *true* being or existence, but man is *not* God's true being or existence.

Epistemological Subject

Basically this is the question of *how* one knows "*I exist*". The concern here is human *consciousness* – how it knows what it knows. Though it could be said "how" one knows himself or *his own* existence is due to the mind's autonomous **reflexive** mechanism, yet this goes no further than a *mental* construct, which by no means is all there is to "self" – subject, agent, or person. If someone did not first *exist,* there would be nothing and no one (no *who*) to "know". It could be said epistemology deals with the *true nature* of subject and/or object. It could even be considered the question of "non-duality" – whether or not the subject *is* the object. Some would identify an *epistemological subject* as man's existential "i", as differentiated from man's *metaphysical subject* as "I". In the case of Jesus, then, he was never an "i" (epistemological subject), but always an "I" (metaphysical subject.)

Aquinas tells us, "*Person and the subject of action belong together – no* ***nature works*** *unless it subsists* (exists) *as a person".* Nestorius would agree with this completely! No *human* nature "*works"* without some agent, subject or person to run the show. This is why, without a subject, agent or person, human nature would be *dysfunctional* – could not function in this world, at least. But note, Aquinas does not specify "*what*" kind of nature he is speaking of – he cleverly leaves this out. Since we assume, however, he is not referring to plant or animal, we take his reference to *both* God and man's nature – natures he obviously *assumes* are alike because both exist as "*persons*". Based on this assumption, he can then make the case God's person was *substituted* for the human person of the man Jesus. Although this contradicts his own dictum – i.e., "*no nature works unless it subsists as a person*" – he obviously makes Jesus the *exception* to his own rule, because Jesus is *no human person.* It was God's person that acted as a *human* person.

To say God was the single subject of Jesus, leaves no room for an independent human being, Jesus was just a robot, a puppet – an *ontological anomaly.* That God *possesses* or takes over a soul is no different from making God a human soul. That Jesus was not a human person or subject, makes him no better than an automaton with no mind or will of *his own.* In refutation of this, Gregory of Nazianzus (an Antiochene) wrote, *"If anyone has put his trust in Christ as a* ***man without a mind,*** *he is bereft of a mind and quite unworthy of salvation. For that humanity which he (*God) *has not assumed, he has not healed, but that which is united to his Godhead is also saved."* In other words, whatever in human nature God did not unite to Itself – in the Incarnation – is not saved. To deny Jesus a soul, a mind and will of his own, was to deny the *salvation* of every man's human nature.

In the eyes of the Alexandrians, however, to attribute anything to the man Jesus, made him a *human person,* which, in their view, was a denial Jesus' human nature was God's *own* human nature (belonged to God and not to the man Jesus.) This is why any reference to *Jesus' own* human nature, and one would be accused of saying Christ was the union of "two persons" – one divine, one human. Basically, then, for the Alexandrians, the man Jesus was neither a human *or* a divine *person – God* ***alone*** *was the divine person of Christ.*

By himself, the human being Jesus was *not* a divine person; rather, it was the *union of natures* ***in*** a divine person that made Christ one divine person. So *who,* then, really was this human being Jesus? Apart from flesh – nobody! It seems the man's flesh was so "possessed" by God, that as a human being, he was no more than a dead man walking.

The principle stated by Nazianzus – "*what the Logos did not assume* (or unite to itself in the Incarnation) *is not saved"* – was accepted by *all* the fathers. Even Cyril had to admit this truth. The issue of *salvation* was premised on the union or oneness of God with man's *complete* human nature. To take away Jesus' full humanity (or anyone's) and what is there to *save?* Whatever constitutes human nature, must be united to God, otherwise, *what* is there to save or *transform*? Even Jesus' death, resurrection and Ascension were regarded by the fathers as Jesus' *own* transformation into the *heavenly, deified, glorified Christ.*

Something else to keep in mind about Nazianzus' dictum. Since the Logos never created or united to Itself *any particular person,* but only united Itself to man's common human nature, this means no person (or self) is saved. God did not unite Itself to the particular property, person or self of Jesus – or of any particular human being.

God only assumed or united to Itself man's common essential human nature – this was Cyril's own understanding of the Incarnation. Obviously, then, man's earthly *properties* needed for *earthly* existence were never intended or destined for eternal life. Indeed, man's final and glorious estate (*hypostatic union)*, cannot be lived on this earth. This eternal *oneness* belongs to an entirely different *dimension of existence*, a glorious eternal estate in which no man could even *function* on earth.

That God never created any person, and is only eternally united to man's human nature, has to be the last word on human personhood – because no person, subject or self **is either created or saved.** So what does it matter what definition is given to *person* or *subject* when, in the end, it has no eternal life? What is saved is no *particular* human person or "*who*" one is, rather, **it is human nature transformed into the**

***Logos' own human nature,** this is "**what**" is saved for eternal life, and not "**who**" is saved.*

If, however, man came into this world *person-less* (or self-less) he would be totally dysfunctional, could never function as an independent human being. This was why there had to be a *kenosis* (an *emptying*) – because no human being can *function* in God's glorious eternal life and live in this world at the same time. We are talking here about *two entirely different dimensions of existence.* Thus *kenosis* was **God's human nature** having to forfeit Its eternal estate in order ***to be*** a human ***person*** *in this world.* Without human self-awareness or self-identity, without a subject *who* is the "agent" of his **own** free mind and will, we are not talking about a human being at all. Jesus, of course, was all this, *a* genuine *human person.* God could no more function as a human person in the world than God could function as a rock, a plant or an animal. Only human beings can ***be*** *persons*, this is what makes man unique in all creation. Only man has the freedom of being his own agent and subject. In fact, the fathers regarded *free-will* as the meaning of man "*made in the image of God*" – virtually, a mirror of God's *own* free will.

Knowingly, however, theology has a penchant for predicating of God everything that can be predicated of man, none of it, however, derived from any authentic revelation of God. There is no revelation of God as "person" or as a "subject" – nothing that even remotely could be defined as such. If God had been revealed as a "Who" or "I am", Moses would not have asked God, "**Who** shall I say you are?" The only answer to the question "who?" of course, is "me, myself, I" – man's *understanding of himself,* but certainly **not** God's understanding. Though Moses knew God instantly, the problem was how to convey this Reality to *other* people. He did this, of course, in terms they would understand. Since the only answer to his question "who?" is "I am **who** I am", this is the answer he gave them – and they understood. So although there is no revelation to back up any revelation of God as a "**Who**", there is obviously a great deal of human *psychology* behind it.

Another problem inherent in switching the meaning of "hypostasis" to "person" is how two natures can be united *in* a property, a subject, or *in* an "I am". As stated in the Chalcedon formula, the dual natures are united **in** the Logos' *hypostasis* – nature (essence) – but as to how two natures could be united in a *property* – *accidental* to nature – is anyone's guess. To be united **in** a person (self) implies ***a union in the mind or consciousness of God,*** **instead of in the hypostasis – nature or essence of God.** Union **in** a *person* or *subject* makes it a union *in* the mind – the mind of one of God's three consciousness's, subjects or "I am's". Such a union, however, goes no further than a *mental construct – the* ***reality*** **of the natures being of no account.** Do not think for a minute this false understanding of Christ is not the view of many people. Based on the notion of God as a *person,* subject, or "who", the conclusion is that oneness with God's "who" is man's true *self-identity – "who" he really is.*

Based on the ontological switch from "what" to "who" – in order to make Jesus a divine person – we now get the notion of God as an "*ontological person or* ***self***". So **"who",** then, is the *real* subject of Christ? Is it God or man? According to Cyril – *"the identity of the person of the God-man was that of the Logos.* ***His*** **(Jesus')** ***person (self-identity)*** *was constituted by the Logos."* That Cyril made God the divine *person* or *subject* of Jesus is actually a piece of *orthodox Hinduism.* People familiar with Hinduism may recognize theology's divine "ontological Person or Self" as Hinduism's divine ontological Self or "Atman" – "Who" Brahman is.

Hinduism's definition of *Brahman* (the One Absolute) as "Being-Consciousness-Bliss" refers to an *ontological consciousness* wherein "self" is the non-dual subject called "*atman*". As best I understand it, when an adept discovers Brahman (in himself) to be the Ground of his (and all) Being, he regards this "God-consciousness" as Brahman's *own* consciousness. Thus the answer to the Hindu question "*Who*" one really is, is the proverbial Judaic answer, "*I am Who I am*" – God, that is. Though I do not want to misrepresent Hinduism, there obviously exists a comparison between the theological notion of "*Who*" God is, or "*Who*" Christ is, and the Hindu belief that God (*Brahman*) is "*Who*" everyone really is. The theological "switch" in the *ontology of being* (from **what** to **who**), explains why Christianity never made in-roads in India – because Hinduism already believes this, had it down pat before Christianity ever came on the scene! As one Hindu said, "*Christianity has Christ, we have Krishna*" – so what else is new? This also explains why Christian "adepts" are finding their *true selves* in Hinduism's teachings, yet regard themselves as perfectly Christian – and why not? Since "orthodox" Christianity (the "party-line" at least) boils down to "orthodox" Hinduism, what is the difference?

Another interesting comparison. Just as Christian theology points out that man's epistemological "i" is *not* God's ontological "I", so too, Hinduism points out man's "jiva" (ego or "i") is not Brahman's "Atman". Carl Jung also pointed out the difference between the *ego-self* and man's metaphysical, *numinous* self – which he compared to the Hindu view. Today, one way to express these levels of self (theology's *person)* is as an *existential* "ego-self" and a *metaphysical* "true-self".

As far as man is concerned, a legitimate distinction can be made between an *existential* or phenomenal "lower" self (i), and a *metaphysical* "higher" *true self* – a "*whole person*", that is. But to think any of this defines God's divine *Knowing* or constitutes *God's self-identity*, is nothing more than man making God into his own self-image. **In truth, if man had no self, it would never occur to him to regard God as a *self, subject or person!***

While in Hinduism one's "True Self" **is** Brahman – the absolute Subject or divine "I am" – in Christianity, one's "true self" accords with Paul's death of the "old *person*" (egoic "i") and the birth of a "New Person" – Christ *in this world,* at least. This is the "unitive state" (or *theosis*) in which the man Jesus was born *into this world* and which man attains with the death of his old "i" or person. The arising of the New Person (Christ) is man's oneness with God ***in this world.*** **It is the death of this New Person (Christ or True Self), however, that ultimately dies in order to enter *eternal life in God – and* no longer in this world.**

Paul's "*No longer I*" affirms there is no longer any I **to be** God, or *to be* Christ. Thus Paul discovered that **neither Christ's human or divine nature is "I am", myself – subject or person.** But then, anyone who believes he is "*who*" God is, belongs in an asylum. Not for a second did Jesus ever believe or think he was God, and those who think he was, also belong in an asylum. The point is that theologians who think the *ontological reality* of **who** God is, is a *person, subject or "I am"*, are in perfect agreement with *orthodox Hinduism*, but they are not, however, in accord with the revelation of God or Christ. Due to this wrong ontological idea of God as a "who", many people look to Hinduism to find themselves, find "who" they really are – find out they are really God! **Incredible!**

So much for basing the ontology of being on *person* or *self* instead of on *nature* or *essence*. By making a division between nature and person, and then substituting God's person for Jesus' person, one can now declare *person* and not *nature* as *real being*. Thus one can *ignore* Jesus' *human nature* because the real *being* of Christ is **Who** Christ is – a divine person, a divine *human* individual, no less, literally, *God in person.* Since there was no way of making Christ's **dual natures one ontological *being,*** theology came up with the term "*person*" to *make Christ* ***one ontological "person"*** **instead.** So where Christ's *natures* are *dual*, Christ's *person* is *singular,* and as such, *person* constitutes God's divine ontological reality (being.) This, then, was the reason for the *ontological switch* from *nature* (**what**) as one's ontological reality, to *person* (**who**), as one's ontological reality. So God and man's *real* *being* are not their natures or *what* they are, but rather, their persons or *who* they are.

The problem with this solution – making Christ one person – implies Christ is one individual being. But is this the Truth, is Christ *one individual **being***? The Alexandrian view of Christ as *one* divine *person* leads to the view of Christ as one *individual being,* implying one divine nature – Monophysitism. Given this understanding of Christ, is why they had to figure out how Jesus could possibly be a *complete* human being but *not* a human person. The reason this can never be resolved is because Jesus ***was* a human person**. Christ as a union of two disparate natures (divine and human) had nothing to do with any "person", divine or human. Had Jesus been recognized as a genuine human being – person and all it means – this would have eliminated centuries of useless disputes, wrong views and understandings of Christ.

There is no way of understanding the Gospel *person* but as a genuine self-conscious, independent, willing, thinking *human person.* In fact, no one can even conceive of any "person" **but** as a *human person.* To think of God as a *person* is to conceive of some polytheistic deity. While "*person*" has something to say about man, to think it has anything to say about God is false. Unfortunately, theology's attempt to make Jesus a ***divine*** person only succeeded in **making God a *human* person.** In fact, it is *because* no human being can *be* a divine person, they had to say Jesus was **no** person at all – in order to make God a human person instead. This way it could be said the worship of Jesus was not the worship of a human being, but the worship of God as a *person.* Though denying Jesus was a human person was a denial of Jesus' true human nature, for the Alexandrians, he was only *flesh* anyway.

It was by denying Jesus was a human person, that Christianity became stuck with the Alexandrian view of the Incarnation as God only uniting Itself to *man's flesh.* That everything but Jesus' material body was divine, is the epitome of a Platonic belief system. For the rest, God was the person and self-identity of the man, he had no functional "powers of soul", he was not a human person or self, indeed, he was not what most people would even think is "human". He was literally God in sheep's clothing – the "lamb of God". Jesus' human nature could be ignored because nothing he said or did was human anyway, it was all divine, all God. One wonders why, if Jesus could neither say or do anything human, he was ever regarded as human in the first place. But this is the Alexandrian Christology, and the same that has been handed down to Christians, taught to this day, and considered the epitome of orthodoxy.

The later scholastics would define a person as one who exists in and through itself or has its *own* existence – a curious statement in that only God is *self-existent*. Thus Aquinas says – "*person signifies a certain nature with a certain mode of existence... the mode of existence which the person enjoys is the most eminent of all – which is that something **exists of itself**.*" Since human nature, however, does *not* exist of itself, neither does a person or subject – nothing exists *of Itself* but God. His reference must have been to the Cartesian *cogito ergo sum* – the one *who* exists because he thinks he exists.

Descartes gave priority to the ontological reality of person – *who*, or "*I am*" – and not to *what* exists. This is exactly why people think "*I am*" is a statement of their *whole existence, their very being,* and that without an "*I am*" (person or self) they would not exist at all. The Cartesian fallacy, of course, is the notion "I am" is prior to *existence* – or the equivalent of it. The truth is, however, if existence and essence were not prior to a conscious, thinking "*I am*", there would exist **no one** to even think "I am". But this is Descartes putting "de-cart" before the horse – i.e., if *he* didn't exist, he couldn't *think* he did! Anyone who gives priority to "I am" as an ontological reality has been sold a bill of goods.

In keeping with this, one theologian says only persons and *not* natures can *be conscious*. He says "*any view that associates consciousness with a person's **nature** or **faculties** is mistaken.*" I agree! Nature is not conscious of itself, only a *person* ("who") is conscious of himself. Man's common human nature is not "*who*" anyone is! Human nature is void of consciousness or self – remember – nature **is not person and person is not nature.** Take away person and nature does not change, but goes right on without it. Thus, since person is not of the essence, it has no eternal life, it was but a temporary ownership needed to function in this world. To live eternally, however, man can take nothing with him from this world – not even his very self! Absolutely, God is no respecter of "persons".

This is why, to say the man Jesus was a divine person, means he only knew himself (personal identity) as God and never as a human being. So how could he be aware of oneness with God if **he *was* God?** *Anybody there?* ***Flesh, that's all!*** (That God is aware of oneness with Itself makes no sense.)

It has also been explained that Jesus saying he was one with God, was actually the Logos saying He was one with His Father – God referring to oneness with God, *incredible!* This means all Jesus' references of being one with God were **not** references to any **human being at all! Instead, this was God referring to being one with God!** Hands down, **there is no "*Christ*" here at all!** It is also said the understanding of the Logos as *subordinate* or *secondary* to the "father" was based on Jesus' saying "*The father is greater than I*". This is how the "father" came to be regarded as the *Source* of God (of Logos and Spirit), a totally Plotinian view of the Trinity. This is Plotinus' "One" (Father) *emanating* the Nous or Demiurge (Logos), that in turn *emanates* the Universal Soul (Spirit.) Anyone who bases their understanding of the Trinity on this Plotinian scenario has missed the Trinity completely – and, consequently, missed Christ. God neither *emanates* nor are the Logos and Spirit *immanent in* some "One". But so much for theology's need to keep covering its tracks – digging itself into ever deeper holes.

It is curious that "consciousness", "self-awareness", "self" (or "ego") was never of particular interest to the ancient philosophers. Even though the Greek term for "soul" was "psyche", there are no specific references to consciousness or self-awareness as a faculty or function of the mind, soul or psyche. Only in modern times do we have a distinction between *psyche* and *soul,* or the Latin "ego" and "soul". Sometime in the Middle Ages, however, a distinction was made between "*pure ego*" and "*empirical ego*", sometimes referred to as a "*higher and lower self*". The "pure ego" was regarded as ordinarily inaccessible to direct introspection and only inferred from introspective evidence. The ego (or self) was also regarded as a *permanent* spiritual *substance* underlying the fleeting succession of conscious experience. For Kant, of course, it was an inscrutable (transcendental) *subject presupposed* by the unity of empirical self-consciousness. We are not going to go into the various theories of consciousness or self, we only want to point out this has never been part of Christian theology – ever. As much as can be found, is the theological notion of *person,* which, for theology, is literally the end of the *subject.*

Just keep in mind the Greek term for "soul" was *psyche* or *mind,* and that it was the fathers who defined the *subject* or *agent* of this psyche or mind as *person* or *self.* Christianity not only gave us the term "*person*", but its definition as *subject or self ("I am")* – the *agent* (doer) *of psyche or soul.* Sometimes we wonder how Western civilization ever became so *self* oriented compared to other civilizations that were more oriented to the benefit of everyone over their individual selves. Well, who invented the individual and particular "person" or self, and who gave it ontological priority over everyman's common human nature? Christianity! It was all wrong of course, because the Incarnation had nothing to do with any *person* or *who*, but solely to do with *natures* – the union of *what* man is and *what* God is.

The *true nature of self-awareness* was never given any consideration in the formulations of Christian theology, in particular, its Christologies. Even today, the theological outline of the faculties of the soul gives no consideration to man's self-awareness, consciousness, or "self". This goes to show how taken for granted is self-awareness or consciousness, it seems to be an unquestionable "given", as unquestionable to the mind as the body is to the senses.

Theologians have never understood (or wanted to) that **the only way a subject knows itself ("I am") is as *object to itself.* Take away self as object to itself and there is no subject or "I" to speak of.** The term "I" or "I am" indicates reflexive self-awareness – "reflexive" being subject as object to itself. The sole *object* of consciousness **is** *its-self.* **With no *object* of consciousness there is no *subject* of consciousness – and vice versa**. And let us not mix up sensory "objects" with the *object* of consciousness. Material things are only *objects of sensory perception,* **not** objects of consciousness. **No *material* object is an object of consciousness, the sole object of consciousness is always *itself.*** Thinking God is an "I" or "I am" is just another of man's anthropomorphic attempts to make God into man's self-image. Consciousness, subject, self, mind, intellect, reason, these are all *human ways of knowing,* ***none*** are God's *divine Knowing* – none!

To dismiss the philosophical-theological division between *nature* and *person* would be fine had the whole Christian paradigm of the Trinity and Christ ***not* been premised on this division.** Ignore this division, however, and one could never understand any Christian doctrine – its formulations or use of terms. No question, the term "person" could be regarded as the *keystone* of Christianity's whole theological paradigm. Remove it, and this whole structure collapses.

Just keep in mind, self is what man owns, but is not *what* man is. Thus person (or self) is something man can live without, something he can give to God – and God can take – while the essence of God and man go right on without change. Since person is not of the essence then it obviously has no eternal life – was never, in fact, even created by God. So what nature owns **in this life** – person, self or property – has no place in God's eternal life – couldn't even function in God. (As a priest once reminded us – "*there are no U-Hauls behind the hearse*". Can't take anything with you, not even your self! Obviously God is no respecter of "persons".)

The Last Word on This Whole Issue – according to the fathers

When all is said and done, every father believed and affirmed that not only in *essence* (*nature*), but also in *person*, God is *immutable and impassible.* Where everything created is changeable, in flux, impermanent, God is none of this. As *impassible*, God neither lives nor experiences created existence, thus **God *experiences* no human existence**. While God *knows* all that exists – better than man even – yet God experiences none of it. God does not even experience "I am", "I think", "I want", "I say" – *ad infinitum*. This is neither God's experience nor God's way of Knowing. How, then, could anybody believe Jesus' experience of all this was the experience of a ***divine immutable, impassible person?*** Not one of the fathers believed this – none! While such experiences may define a mythical deity, none define Almighty God or Christ's divine nature. All biblical references are to the life and experiences of man's totally human way of knowing God, all belong to the human *person* Jesus, no more, yet, no less.

So if anything points up the **error** of Jesus as a divine *person* – agent, subject, self, with its ever changing experiences – it is the **Truth that God is *immutable* and *impassible.*** This means that in *essence and in person,* God is incapable of any human experience – including its way of knowing. So after all the dissensions (between the Alexandrians and Antiochenes) over trying to make Jesus a *divine* person, it never worked – couldn't work. Realizing this, what did the Alexandrians do next? Well, they invented what is called the *"Communication of Properties"*, an invention that can only be regarded as the greatest conspiracy ever foisted on Christian believers. Just what this means, we will go into later.

In summary: every notion of "person" is premised on an understanding of man and not God. It is premised on the Christian definition of *person* that has no philosophical foundation – if that even matters. **First** it is agreed person is but a "property" of human nature and not human nature itself. **Then**, by separating nature and person, these can be spoken of separately as meaning different things – "what" and "who". **After that**, one can argue over which has *real existence, nature* or *person.* One resolution, suggested by Boethius (480 – 524), was to equate *person* and *nature* so that *both* would refer to a *single individual ontological being*. This way, all theological references to *Christ* could be understood as reference to a *single individual being.* But is this the truth of Christ? Is Christ a single individual being? This is the question we will examine next.

PERSON VS. INDIVIDUAL

In any discussion of the term "person" it would be remiss to omit the name of Boethius (480 – 524), whose inept definition of "person" became a Christian dogma. While it has been said "person" never became acceptable to the Greeks or Eastern fathers until Boethius came up with his definition, this is inexplicable because his definition has nothing to do with God, the Trinity, Christ, or the person-less Jesus. At any rate, "person" was given its formal entry into scholastic philosophy, defining ***person is "an individual substance of a rational nature"***. "*Individual substance*" refers to the material body and "*rational nature*" to the soul. Although it is said this definition is taken from Aristotle, there is no *person* in Aristotle, nor anything equivalent. What Boethius defined as "person" is Aristotle's definition of *human nature* – a single "*unit*" (Aristotle called it) of a *material* substance and an *immaterial* rational *psyche* (soul.)[1]

Interestingly, the Greek for "soul" was *psyche,* and the term for "rational" was *logos.* Thus we could define a "rational soul" as a "*logos – psyche*" – a far more profound understanding of "human nature" than the trite theological "rational soul". To my knowledge, none of the Greek philosophers showed any interest in what accounted for differences among human beings or why one human being was not another human being. It seems "who" one was, never struck them as a profound inquiry. As said before, the whole notion of "person" is purely a Christian innovation, all definitions and usage are solely its own.

As originally intended, hypostasis – defined in the Western Church as person – was to distinguish God's triune modes of existence, point up these distinct realities of God's one essence. Needless to say, "person" defined as "an individual (material) substance of a rational nature" can never define God, the Trinity or Christ. It couldn't even define the man Jesus who, theologically, was held not to be a person, yet a complete human "individual". Also, everything meant by person is a far cry from the meaning of "hypostasis", they are not synonymous terms and can never be interchanged – they are even at odds. So as far as Boethius' definition having any theological meaning to Christianity, it can be scratched.

The reason for not ignoring Boethius, however, is because of the damage he unconsciously wrought. This damage is people mistaking an individual (human nature or a being) to mean person. They equate the two, treat them as if they meant or referred to the same thing.

---

[1] For Aristotle's understanding of man, see "*Christian Ontology*" – Appendix I.

These two terms – individual and person – however, are as different as night and day, it can even be said they reference two different realities. "Individual" can refer to any human being, whereas "person" refers only to "who" a particular individual is. Where "individual" is a universal – everything in creation is "some" material, individual "thing" – "who" an individual is, however, is a one-of-a kind, unique human being. That everyone is an individual entity is a sensory "given", but "who" someone is, can never be a "given", in fact, the "real person" is the next thing to "unknowable". We are speaking here of every human person and not, of course, of Almighty God – by no definition can God be called a person(s.)

While Boethius' definition defines man's common human nature, it does not allow for any differentiation between human beings. To define "person" as "human nature" and "human nature" as "person" is a vicious circle – goes no place. His view implies that since every human nature is the same, and every human nature is a person, then every person is the same person. Also, because his definition of nature includes properties, accidents and all, it allows for no distinction between individuals – which is what "person" signifies. If person is defined as a "property" of human nature, then according to his definition, "property" is human nature and human nature is "property" – no distinction. To do away with the definition of person as a "property" of nature pulls the rug out from under "essence" (what) as the ontological reality of human nature. So given his view, if person defines who a man is and human nature defines what a man is, then who a man is, is what a man is – another vicious circle. For Aristotle, of course, "that" a man is (exists), is "what" a man is – there are no "who's" in his equation. So, as far as Boethius' definition of person serves to distinguish between individuals, it doesn't.

That every individual *is* a person, makes both *individual* and *person* universals, whereas no incommunicable person or "who" someone is, can be a universal. Nor, for that matter, can any material individual thing or "numerical one" constitute a universal – it takes *many individuals* to extract a common or universal nature. It is not, then, "individuals" that account for human differences, rather, it is "who" a person is that makes for multiple differences.

Like Jesus, everyone is an *individual*, but it is "who" he is (the person) that points up his difference from all others. Jesus was different **not** because he was an *individual* human being, but because, like everyone else, he was an unrepeatable *human person.* Among human beings, Jesus was just one of the many, but as a "person", he was like no other. Thus no one could ever be the human person Jesus, nor, for that matter, be Mary, Paul, or be anyone "other" than *who* he is.

The philosophers' concern was the true nature of what man is, not who some particular man was. Who someone is, was purely a Christian concern – its obvious concern being "who" Christ was. So philosophy was no help when it came to considering what made one individual human being different from another or what accounted for everyone's "incommunicable uniqueness". According to Plato, the only difference between individuals is that, unlike spirit or soul, individual material bodies could not occupy the same space at the same time. Aristotle defined "individual" as a "numerical one", some individual material thing.

When he said it is the essence of man to be a "numerical one", his reference was to an embodied individual. For him, then, the reason an individual was "incommunicable" was because it was not some other individual material thing. So while universally, every human being is a material individual or a "numerical one", it is person that distinguishes one individual from another. Person, however, is not a material body, not even "a being". Just as one can add up individuals but not human natures, so too, one can add up individuals but not persons. Between individual and person is the difference between "that" some individual exists and "who" it is that exists. It was to account for differences between human beings (numerical ones), that person (who someone is) came up for consideration. In particular, it was important to answer the question "who" was the individual man Jesus, how was he different from all other individual human beings?

Every human being born into this world will *become* his own independent *person,* and just as Mary, Paul and David became their own person, so too, Jesus became his own independent person. Although God's *own* human nature is person-less, yet being incarnated in this world, it could not have functioned if it had not been a particular person. Obviously, what man needs to function in earthly life is not what he needs to function in God's eternal life. We must always, then, keep Hilary's admonition in mind – Christ's life on earth is not Christ's eternal heavenly life in God.

So although Jesus was his *own* person, yet **w*hose* human nature was it?** Since the Incarnation was God creating man's common human nature one with Itself, this was not the human nature of any *particular* human being or one especially created for Jesus – *who* never existed prior to the Incarnation. **So while the Incarnation was God's *own* created (*common) human nature*, yet we could say Jesus was the Logos' *earthly human person.*** Since *person* is said to be a "property" of human nature and *not* human nature itself, **it** could be said **Je-**

sus was the property or *human person* of the *Logos' human* nature. It is because human nature has no "property" of a *divine* person, and a divine nature has no property of a *human* person, that Jesus was his own *human person,* whose common human nature was one with God. Though his human nature was no different from any other individual human being, yet, as a human person, he was indeed unique and like no other.

For a true understanding of Christ, perhaps nothing is more important to stress than the difference between God's **own common** human nature and Jesus' **own** *individual* human nature. Where reference to God's *own* human nature is a reference to man's **universal** human nature (the human nature of Christ), reference to "Jesus' human nature", however, is solely to one ***particular*** individual human being – to a "person", in other words.

Thus *"Jesus' human nature"* refers to a *particular human being or person,* whereas theologically, at least (according to all the early fathers), God's **own** human nature is **not** that of any *particular* individual human being or *person.* So where reference to God's (or **Christ's)** human nature is *universal*, reference to Jesus' human nature is solely to one *particular* human being or *person.*

It should be noted that all the fathers – those we know of, at least – believed and affirmed that "what" God created and united to Itself in the Incarnation was man's *one common, universal human nature.* None believed that God only united *one particular individual* human being to Itself, this was not their belief or understanding of "*Christ*". No one denied the man Jesus was Christ, but the understanding of "*Christ*" was not limited to one individual or particular human being. On the contrary – "*He became what we are that we might become what he is*", this was the belief of one and all. That God is eternally united to *only one particular* human being is impossible anyway – *for* ***"what is common to all*** **(human nature)** ***is proper*** **(particular)** ***to none*"**. So never look to the early fathers for this narrow view of Christ – i.e., that *only* the particular man Jesus was (or is) Christ.

As to whether God's *own* human nature was somehow different from everyone else's, according to Paul, Christ's human nature was "*like ours in every way but sin"* – we've already gone over the myth that human fathers pass on their sins with their sperm– souls. But if neither Paul nor any of the fathers thought there was any difference – between God's *own* human nature and everyman's human nature – yet, who really knows the ultimate *essence* of *human nature?* More especially, who knows its bare *essence* ***without*** the **potential** of ever *becoming* a "*person*", i.e., human nature with *no self-identity* – which is the case of God's *own* human nature.[2] For sure, only God knows the *true essence* of human nature and *what* it is to *become*. While the absence of person would not change the *essence* of human nature, it would certainly make a difference. If one erases everything they know as a *person* or ever thought was a *person* (their self-identity, that is) ***there's*** the difference! Indeed, until he died, Jesus was the *human person* of the Logos' *common human* nature, but this *human person died,* and the one that arose was the eternal *person-less* Christ – which is the definition of "*hypostatic union*" to be gone over later.

For now, we only need remember a "person" is *not an individual human nature*, but only an earthly "property" of human nature, and, evidently, a *temporary* property – after all, it was some person *who died*. As a *person*, then, Jesus was the "property" of the Logos' *human nature,* but *not* the "property" of the Logos' *divine nature*. Like everyone else, Jesus was the *owner* (person) of his *own* human nature, it was only after it died that he found out otherwise. And just as it was the *person* Jesus *who* died, and the *person-less* "Christ" that arose, so it goes for every human being. So where the man Jesus was a particular *person*, *Christ's* human nature, however, is *no particular* human being or person. **Big difference here – where Christ is a *universal,* Jesus was a *particular.***

It seems that referring to "*Christ*" simply as the *oneness of God's divine and human natures*, is just too difficult for some people to get hold of. Apparently, people were worshiping Christ as God in the iconic figure of the man Jesus – which is why Christians were accused of *anthropolatry*. To resolve this dilemma is why the fathers came up with the term "*persona*" or "*person*" as reference to ***Christ* as *one divine "person"* and *not* as *one divine "being"***. If, however, should **"one divine person" be understood as "one *individual being"*,** then the Trinity as three persons would be understood as three *individual beings – tri-theism!* So a further solution was to affirm that *person* neither refers to *individual beings* or to *natures*, but only to what a nature *owns* (a property, that is) and does not refer to *what* beings or natures (in essence) *are*. So *person*, then, does **not** refer to individual beings, but only to what a being *owns* (a property.)

So now, with "person" defined as a "property", it could be said

[2] According to Duns Scotus (1266 – 1308), the great Franciscan theologian, the universal has the *potential* to be *actualized* as an individual. Thus the individual *actualizes* man's *common* potential. He calls this actualization a "contraction" (a "mode" or "instantiation") of the real nature or essence, but one, however, that does not differentiate the nature or essence. *So "individual", then, does* ***not*** *differentiate the nature or essence, what differentiates individuals is* "**person**".

God *owns* the human nature It created and united to Itself. As *owner* of Its *own* human nature then, God is the sole divine *person* of Christ. Since, theologically, Jesus was not the *owner* of *his* human nature – God alone *owned* it – thus the man Jesus was ***no person at all*** **– neither a human or a divine person. God alone is the *one divine person of Christ.***

This solution – of making God a person (or three) instead of three *beings* – seems to avoid *anthropolatry.* By declaring God a *divine person* and Jesus *no human person,* people would then ***not mistake*** **the *human person,* Jesus, *to be* God – to be the *divine* person of Christ.** (Only God is the divine person of Christ and **not the man Jesus.)** It should be obvious, however, that making God a *person* never worked to avoid anthropolatry, if anything, it only made matters worse. Anyone to whom God is revealed will never see, know or refer to God as some *person* – by *any* definition of the term. All people honestly know are ***human persons,*** *not divine persons.* So thinking that by declaring God a *divine person* would eliminate people thinking the human being (Jesus) was God in person, this, however, never worked. Instead, it *justified* taking an *individual* man for Almighty God in "*person*", when, in truth, all man knows is the *human person* – the man Jesus.

The problem, then, created by Boethius' definition, was equating "individual" with "person", a tautology incapable of accounting for distinctions of any kind. Any theology of the Trinity and Christ based on this tautology is obviously fallacious. Apart from *person,* there is no distinction among *individual* human beings beyond mere physical appearances. The problem, however, is that like Boethius, most people identify the individual ("a numerical one") with *person.* The best example of this is **not** taking the *individual* man Jesus as a ***human*** person, but taking him instead, as an ***individual person of the Trinity*** – as God, that is. (*Anthropolatry* and *tri-theism* really amount to the *same heresy.)*

Although Boethius' *definition of person as an individual substance* was his definition of man and not *God*, by putting God into the equation as three persons – and thus three individuals – totally skewed the truth of the Trinity. The Trinity – three individual beings? **Tritheism**! It was only because Jesus was an *individual* human being that God was defined as a *"person"* in order to make Christ a divine *person* and not *just* the human person Jesus. This seemed to justify the man Jesus as *God-in-person***,** a view that skews the truth of Christ – ***Monophysitism*!** By the time Boethius' definition came on the scene in the 6th century, the *Alexandrian* view of Christ – already considered *orthodox* – was as follows:

1.) Jesus was *not* a *human person.* God as a *person* had taken the place of Jesus' human *personhood.*
2.) Since God's *divine person* acted as the "*person*" of the *individual man Jesus,* then God was the divine person of *Christ* and *not* the man Jesus. Thus Jesus was neither a divine nor a human person.
3.) Although Chalcedon holds ***Christ is two natures united IN the one divine hypostasis or prosopon (person) of the Logos,*** it never affirmed human nature was united ***to*** a divine hypostasis, *prosopon* (or person.) But whether Jesus was *united* to God's person or God *substituted* for his person, either way, he himself was not a divine person, only God is the divine person of Christ.

Evidently, it was thought that by making Christ *one divine person* – and not just a union of natures – *Christ* could then be understood as a **single individual being.** Though Jesus was not himself a divine person, theologians continually refer to his human nature as *united* **to** God's person – even make an elaborate case for this. Though his human nature was not divine, yet, by uniting it to a divine person, they could justify referring to Jesus as "God-in-person". (Not God in nature, mind you, but only *in person.*)

If one could honestly understand the *difference* between an *individual* human nature and a *person,* it would be easy to understand how Christ is ***God's*** *human nature*, but ***Jesus'*** *human person.* In other words, **the human nature was God's, but the human *person* was Jesus'.** And let us be clear – since God is *no person* and Christ is solely the *union of natures*, the fact Jesus was a *human person* in no way makes Christ the union of *two* persons. The reason Cyril ranted against the union of two persons is *because* he regarded God as a person! It is because there is **no such thing as a *union* of *two incommunicable "who's",*** that, for Cyril, Jesus could *not* be a *person.* While he was right – Christ is *not* the union of two persons – **he was wrong to make God a person instead of Jesus!** At any rate, the *person* who died on the cross was the human ***person*** Jesus (it wasn't God ***who*** died), and the one that arose was the **person-less Christ (and not God.)** How and why this is so will be better understood when we go over the true nature of "*Hypostatic Union*" – the *person-less* oneness of two natures. For now, we only want to establish the *universal* fact that every human being is ***an individual,*** while ***person*** is the *particular "who"* that every individual *becomes* or *is*. Just keep in mind – "***Person***" **is not *individual* "being", but the "property" of individual being.**

For right now, however, let us assume Christ is the Logos' divine *person*. Since every question "*who*?" requires a subject for an answer, then asking "*Who is Christ*?" – is to say that the subject (identity) is that of a *divine person* and **not** the *human person* Jesus, nor any human person. Thus, since Jesus, an individual human being, is *not* a *divine* person, then Jesus is not **"Who"** Christ is. Keep in mind, the reason for denying Jesus was a *human* person was to *avoid* making a human person a divine person! People were to worship the divine Christ – the divine person being *God* and not the human *person* Jesus. Another reason to avoid the notion that the *particular person* Jesus was Christ, was to avoid the idea that God only picked out some pre-existent (already existing) man to unite to Itself. Still another reason was to affirm that the union of essences or natures was *not* the union of two persons – because persons are ***not*** of the essence or nature. (Every father down the line affirmed Christ as the *union of natures*, none even *suggested* Christ was the union of two persons.) Christ is the duality of natures, not the duality of *ownership* or persons. As said, the official statement of Christ as a *union of natures* ***in*** *the divine prosopon of the Logos,* did not state that the natures were **united *to*** the *hypostasis* or *prosopon* (later, "*person*") of the Logos.[3]

The fact Christ is the union of natures does not preclude Jesus from being a human person. Certainly everyone who knew Jesus regarded him as a *human person* – as he said, apart from a specific revelation from God, no one knew him otherwise. So he, the human person Jesus, was no "revelation", neither a revelation of God nor "Christ". Even Peter, who regarded him as the *Messiah,* never regarded him as God-in-person – in Judaism, the Messiah was *never* understood as God. The revelation of Christ, then, is not the revelation of any particular *person* – **who** some particular *individual* is – but the revelation of man's oneness with God.

While we cannot blame Boethius for loss of a true understanding of Christ, yet his definition – equating *individual* (human *nature)* with *person* – certainly contributed to it. Based on his definition, theologians not only give ontological priority to person as the divine Christ, but make the case ***only*** Jesus' "*individual*" human nature is God's own human nature – whereas we know "*What is common to all is proper* (particular) *to none"* .

Another problem equating *individual* and *person* is that "per-

---

[3] To say *nature* and *person* are a ***union*** means that man and God are only *united* to their self-identities or persons, and that, **in essence (nature) they are *not persons at all*!** This being the case, why, then, divide man and God into *nature* and *person*? By uniting human nature **to** a divine person, reference to Christ could be understood as *one individual person.* What other way could it work – different natures, different persons, how else can we envision them as "one" – one what?

son(s)" applied to the Trinity, makes the Trinity three *individual* "numerical ones", three individual *beings* – the definition of "*tri-theism*". The Logos is *not* "an individual being". Only *created things* are individual beings. Unless one can understand the *difference* between *individual* and *person,* he can never understand the Trinity or Christ – because neither are *individual embodied beings or person(s.)* Though Christ's *universal* human nature is a "numerical one" or *individual,* yet it is only *person* that differentiates – and not the fact every *individual* is the same "numerical one". From all this it should be obvious the importance of understanding the difference between *individual* and *person*, especially as it applies to the individual man Jesus and to the divine Christ – they are **not** the same. All reference to the *divine Christ* is to the divine Logos (God) and is not a reference to Jesus or to any individual human being. All references to the man "Jesus" are solely references to a particular **human *person*** and **not** to an **individual** *human being* – that could be anybody.

It is because all this may sound too complex for "simple folk" – and to some extent it is – that people just skip it and say "*Jesus is God"*, *Christ is God* – end of ***subject.*** And indeed, end of ***subject*** is the **end of person** (a "subject".) It is this failure to know the difference that has led to *Monophysitism* – a *heresy.*[4] How many people, for example, when they think of the Trinity, the Logos, Christ, or even the man Jesus, actually divide them into their *natures* and/or their *persons*? Because few people have ever heard of such a division, they have no idea how these differences could change their whole understanding of these Realities. Who, then, grasps the difference between the *essence* (or nature) and *person* of God, as well as the *essence* and *person* of the man Jesus? And who grasps the difference between the *dual essences* of Christ and the *divine person* of Christ – knows that the *person* of Christ is *not* the man Jesus but is solely God? In fact, whoever thinks of the difference between ***who*** and ***what***? If they did, they would realize the orthodox position that Jesus is not "who" Christ is – sole *divine person* is the Logos, this is *who* "Christ" is. (Theologically, at least, the man Jesus is no *who* – no person at all.) Although this is "orthodox", it is nowhere articulated in the proverbial party-line presentation of the Trinity and Christ. Thus when it says "*Jesus Christ is God*", is this a reference to a divine or human nature? Or to a divine or human person? For those who do **not** know the difference, this statement ("*Jesus Christ is God*") is a piece of *anthropolatry* – i.e., a human being is God. Needless to say, had God not been made into three *persons*, this

[4] See chapter 14 on "Monophysitism".

mistake could never have arisen and a true understanding of the Trinity and Christ could have been maintained.

While it was a terrible thing to make God a "person", it was equally terrible to *deny* Jesus was a *human* person. This caused an uproar among the fathers, especially the Antiochenes (God– man) school. Because of this uproar, they were accused of making Christ the union of two persons – which none ever did. While they upheld the union of natures **in** the Logos' divine hypostasis, this was no reason to deny Jesus was a human person – a *complete* human being, that is. Remember, the term "person" was not used by these early Greek fathers, the whole notion of *persona* (*mask*) applied to the Trinity was anathema to them. It was the *hypostasis* of the divine Logos that was the sole divinity of Christ, while the Logos' human nature – being no different than that of any other individual human being – was, indeed, its own unique *person,* the man Jesus.

Since the fathers never believed God created a human person or was united to a human person, Christ as a union of *natures* had nothing to do with either a *divine* or a *human* person. It is *because* Christ is solely a union of *natures* that Jesus was a *whole person* – a *complete* human being. (Reference to "*whole person"* is to the "unitive state" in which Jesus was born, for no one is *wholly human until* he is as aware of God as he is of himself.) The incarnation never needed or *required* God be a person, but it *did* require the one born into this world be a *whole human person.* If the fathers (*some*, at least) had *not made* God a divine person(s), there would have been no reason to deny Jesus was a human person. It was denied so "*Christ*" could be regarded as one *individual ontological being* – and right here is the *big* problem. **The union of two disparate natures neither constitutes one *individual* ontological being, nor constitutes one ontological person.**

No man is created a *particular person* or "who" he is – after all, God does not create a *person* "*who*" lies, cheats and murders, nor creates one "who" is honest, generous and devout. God determines none of this, it is man himself "who" determines his *own person* of his own free-will. The idea God creates persons either good or bad is the fallacious notion of *predestination* – totally false. *Person* is what each man makes of himself, how he exercises his freedom for good or ill, it is all up to him. So too, in the Incarnation, God did not create a particular *person*, not even the person Jesus. Let's give Jesus some credit here!

It is because the Incarnation was not God creating and uniting to Itself a human person, that Christ is solely the oneness of natures and not the oneness of persons. A person, after all, is not some discrete "being" or entity that can be united to some other "being" – "persons" are incommunicable. This is why, to deny Jesus was a human person, is basically to deny Jesus was a complete human being. It was this denial that forever left Nestorius' unanswered question in the air – "How can you have a complete human being that is not a human person?" What Nestorius really should have asked is "How can you have a divine person that is a complete human being?" If Aquinas is right, and "person (or a 'supposit') only concretely exemplifies some nature or essence", then he agrees with Nestorius – the person Jesus concretely exemplified some human nature or essence. It goes without saying, God as a person does not concretely exemplify a divine nature – God is not a material reality or an individual being.

Since God is *never* united to a person, but only to human nature, those who think God is united to their "*self*" or *person*, have it wrong. God is solely united to their "*being*", to their *human nature* and *not* their *particular person.* **It is because people tend to think of "their being" as "their self", they equate being with *person or self.*** The revelation of God's oneness with man, however, is *not* the revelation of any "self" united to God, but the revelation of one's very being – existence or nature – united to God's *Being, Existence or nature.* Thus God is Man's *true eternal being – though* **man is *not* God's being. Were God not the Source of man's being united to God, there could be no such thing as "eternal life" – because man has no eternal life *of his own.*** There is **no union, then, with "who" one is (person or self)**, but only with "**what**" (in *essence*) one is. This is a oneness of being with Being, not a oneness of person with person or self with self – which makes no sense anyway.

Were it not for making God a person and then denying Jesus a person, it would not be so imperative to grasp the difference between an *individual* human being (no different from others) and a *particular human person* (unlike all others.) That "*Christ is two natures in one hypostasis – prosopon (or person)*" – does *not* mean God is an *individual* being (or the Trinity three beings), nor that Jesus is a *divine person.* Referring to *Christ* as a *divine person,* cannot be a reference to any *individual* being because God is *not* an individual being(s.) Nor can reference to the "*divine Christ*" as a divine *person* be a reference to the *individual* man Jesus, because Jesus *was* an individual being whereas a *divine person* is *not* an *individual* being. Simple as that.

As to how any of this fits into Boethius' definition of *person,* obviously it doesn't. To define a *person* as an "*individual*" and then say Jesus was *no human person* would mean he was no "individual" human being! Also, to say the Logos (God) as *person* is an *individual* being is pure *tri-theisim.* This is why any attempt to use Boethius' definition to say anything about God, the Trinity, Christ, Jesus, or anybody, for that matter – doesn't work. His definition of *person* as an *individual* defines no one and no-thing. To point out all the wrong implications of Boethius' definition we could just keep going, but all we want to point out is the fallacy of equating "individual" human beings with "persons". Merely for an *individual* to *exist,* does not account for his being his own unique *person*.

If anyone finds this difficult to follow or understand, they need only put their finger on the theological notion of God as a divine person -- or three persons. To follow all the ruses invented to justify this **wrong turn,** is what has made theology not just complicated and difficult to follow, but made it an illogical mess. Although to ignore this wrong turn (God as a person) would certainly simplify matters, yet it is too late to ignore it, one can only point it out and deal with it as best he can. After all, the whole of Christianity since about the 5th century has been premised on God as a person (or three), and unless people can see how this leads to *tri-theism, Monophysitism* and *anthropolatrism,* the Real Trinity and Christ are gone forever.

View of the Early Fathers

Fortunately, long before Boethius appeared the early fathers had a beautiful understanding of what accounted for differences between individuals. Let us go over their understanding.

1. First, all agreed there was only "one" human nature, not many human natures or different human natures, thus every human being was identically the same human nature, everyone an individual "numerical one".

2. What accounted for differentiation was that every human being was created with free-will, and what he does with his free-will determines the *person* he *becomes*. Thus nobody is created or born a *person*, no one created a "particular" human being or person, rather, person is what every human being makes of himself of his own free-will. Maximus the Confessor expressed it well – "*person is the* ***mode*** *of our existence or what we make of ourselves*".

3. The fathers were also convinced every human being is created "theocentric", everyone "made in the image of God." Generally, they regarded man's free-will **as** the image of God in man, *free-will being a reflection of God's free-will.* Created theocentric, this "center" of human nature (or being) was a "*reflection*" (image) of God, which they also regarded as the image of Christ – God's oneness with man. Thus man was made in the image of Christ (some said "*sealed*" with Christ.) For Origen and others, this "theocentric" (divine center) was the center

of the human soul where man is one with God – a center or "space" in man that *only* God can occupy.

God's image in man is not the image of any *person* or "individual being" – certainly not some sensory or sensible image – but an image that transcends all man's images and ideas of created "things". This image, as a reflection of God, the goal of life was to bring the will in conformity with God's will in order to *become* not only a perfect reflection of this image, but *become* "this" image itself. "***Thus we must become that of which we are only now but an image***"– says Irenaeus. God, then, is the only one that knows the *true* person because only God knows Its own image.

While some focus their will-on-God, and others, only on themselves, yet whatever the degree, determines the *true* difference between *individuals.* Although "*person*" is what man makes of himself, yet a "***whole person***" is what only God can make of man. Person is developmental, a process of becoming "**whole**" – a full complete human being God intended everyone to *become* (or *be*) in this world. **No one is really a "*whole person*" until he is one with God because only God is the completion of man's humanity.** Until *completely* human, man is incomplete and *divided* in himself – recall Irenaeus saying of the Gnostics, "*They seek to become divine before they have even become human!*"

As for the *whole person* being a true image of Christ, this is known only to God and if God should reveal it to the person himself. Because this person is totally incommunicable, however, it can never be known to others. All other people know of a person is what they judge from the outside, "personality" perhaps, which is neither of the essence nor the *true* person. If "personality" is thought to be an external expression of the person, then when a person is *not expressing himself* there is no "personality" at all – in truth, the notion of "personality" goes no deeper than that.

In order to become a "whole person" or a *complete* human being, one must strive for this wholeness because it is not something that happens automatically. Only by aligning the will with God can one overcome the conflict between body and soul with all its moral and emotional friction. It is by conforming the will to its *divine center* it becomes one with God's will. This *whole person,* then, is the indivisible unity of body, soul and spirit – the *whole* undivided person at one with himself and at one with God. This *wholeness* is the "new person" Paul speaks of – the old divided person (old "I am"), dead and gone. This *new person* is now a true reflection of Christ – as Paul says, *"No longer* ***"I"***, but Christ lives in me". So the notion of *person* to define a *whole* or *complete* human nature is well put, but it is also basically mystical – which is why it is **not** the "theological" understanding of "person". (Theology has nothing to do with man's spiritual life, in fact, this is how theologians define '*mysticism*' – "*the term begins in 'mist' and ends in 'schism'*" – so much for the crass mentalities that Heraclitus rightly called "*barbaric souls*"!)

In the fathers' view, what it meant to be a *whole person* was to be the perfect reflection of the image **in which** man was created – Christ, that is. In the end, however, that image, *mirror* or *reflection* will disappear (be "*broken*" according to Maximus) when man *becomes* the image itself – which he was created **to be.** Note the difference between created ***as*** an image and created **in** an image – meaning, the true image of Christ is solely **in** God and not actually **in** man himself. Since outside the Trinity there is no Christ, no one should expect to see or know Christ other than **in** the Trinity.

Actually, we come upon a whole different view of man when we say "person" is the image of God in man. The "image of God" transcends everything we know as a human "individual" or "person. The fathers' understanding of *person* transcended any idea of individuality and particularity, for them, the ultimate "person" as the "image of God" in man ***is*** **Christ.** If, then, we give *person* the lofty definition of *Christ* as "God's image" in man, we can understand why **God is *not* a "person", because *in Itself* God *has no image.*** It is the **"image of God *in man*" that is man's oneness with God – is *Christ,* that is.** To become this image – the fathers' stated goal – was to be a *whole person*, a true, complete human being in oneness with God *in this world* – we should add. When this *earthly* image of Christ dies, however, this image is no more, for now there is *only* Christ and no "one" (individual or person) left *to be* an image of Christ.

The only thing left to point out is that this *becoming* or transformation, no man can achieve without God's help – "grace" it is called. This is because man can only change himself to a point beyond which he cannot go – a point he does not even realize is "himself". Thus he cannot change his intrinsic human nature or effect any permanent change, God alone can do this because God alone knows the true essence of man. Man, of course, thinks *he knows himself*, knows the "*way*" and the "*how to*", but in truth, no one knows ahead of time *what* he is *becoming*. He can only know this in retrospect. Thus he must leave himself in God's hands, give God free reign to accomplish in him the end for which he was created, an end no one can envision ahead of time. To think man can accomplish this by himself is foolishness, it won't happen.

Although every individual human being is created the same, and free-will accounts for the unique person he becomes, there may be another intrinsic **cause of differentiation.** Heraclitus said, "*You can never put your foot in the same river twice*" – because it is not the same water that has already gone by. So too, one can never see the same person in the mirror twice, since one image is not the other. Given that everyone is created in the image of God and that no two images can ever be the same, ***each man's image is a different reflection of God,*** each unique and like no other. So there is *one* God and *one* human nature, each *individual* being a unique reflection of God.

The uniqueness of each individual human being, then, is that he is created One-on-one, each reflecting God in a special way – **everyone the same image, only different reflections.** The fact every created "thing" is "one", is a wonderful reflection of "One" God, and the fact that created matter is *three dimensional*, is a wonderful reflection of God's immanent "Triune" nature. Now then, if we compare this – the fathers' understanding of a *whole person* as the image of Christ in man, with Boethius' definition of *person* "*as an individual substance of a rational nature*", his definition is vacuous. Anyone who equates "individual" and "person" has not yet attained a "rational soul".[5]

[5] There is little evidence man is, in fact, a "rational soul". As a *self-conscious* being, all man's responses are too *subjective* (self-governed) to ever be purely rational. Man's behaviors are more governed by how he *feels* (his emotional apparatus) than how *un-self-consciously* he can think or reason. It is because the Stoics realized this, that their ideal was to get beyond the emotional self to *become* wholly *rational* in order to become one with the *Reason for being* – the divine Logos, that is.

CYRIL'S CHRISTOLOGY

No view of Christ should overlook the particular understanding envisioned and articulated by Cyril of Alexandria (376 – 444.) It is important for a number of reasons. First, it is regarded as perfectly orthodox; and second, it could be said his views had a more profound impact on the Church's Christologies than any of the other fathers.

The rock of Cyril's Christology is: ***Christ is God's own human nature, it is not the human nature of Jesus or any human being, but God's alone.*** While this was the belief of one and all, yet no one hit it home with the force of Cyril. For him, Irenaeus' reference to Christ as "*God and his man*", was improper, there was no "*and*". His was no Antiochene Christ as "God-Man", other than "flesh", *Christ **is** God.* Christ is no mere "union" of two disparate natures, rather, Christ is a *oneness* incapable of a separation or division into divine *and* human. Christ is an indivisible "*oneness*", a singularity and wholeness which, while a mystery, can never be thought of as *one and/or the other.* In Christ there is no "other" or "otherness", God and man are not "other" to one another.

No question, Cyril's understanding of the incarnation as *God's **own** human nature,* and **not** the human nature of any *particular being or person,* was his ace in hand. For him, Christ must not be separated into "God **and** a particular man", Christ is the "***one incarnate nature of God the Logos***". "*We say there is one Son* (Logos)*, and that he has one nature even", "the same **one** is at once God and man".* Although he had to admit to Christ's dual natures, yet, in his own mind, Christ would always be "one nature", one person, one being, and this *one nature-person-being* was the divine Logos-the-Son.

Now try to get around Cyril's basic Christology. Try to make a case the Logos created **Jesus' particular** humanity, or united Itself ***only*** to Jesus' human nature, and you will totally miss his Christology. **God was solely united to Its *own* created humanity and not to this or that particular human being.** For many, if not most, his was the last word in "orthodoxy". But if he got the Incarnation right, his Christology raised serious questions.

"If" he could have gotten away with it, he would never have referred to "*Jesus*" being born, living, saying or doing anything, always it was the *one divine Christ,* not just some man that was born, lived, spoke or did anything. He had no tolerance for any reference to *Jesus' human nature*, or Jesus doing this or that, it was not the man Jesus, but the one divine Christ – ***God's humanity.*** This was not just his powerful Christology, but his powerful position to fight anyone he thought disagreed with it. He enjoyed the prestigious position of Patriarch of

Alexandria, the oldest, largest, most populous See in Christendom. (The tiny See of Jerusalem has always been given precedence as the *first* Christian See.)

Perhaps the best way to grasp Cyril's Christology is by way of the analogy he used for the union of the two natures of Christ. He compared this to human nature as a union or "composite" of body and soul. Thus, for him, the union of *two natures* was the union or "composite" of Christ's *one nature.* Any hint of a division between Christ's two natures was as good as having no Christ at all. Yet, body and soul as a composite of human nature, is hardly a proper analogy for Christ as the composite of two *disparate* natures. While body and soul make **one being**, the union of such disparate natures as Uncreated and created, does **not make one being,** yet, for Cyril, it made ***"one incarnate nature of God the Logos"*** – his oft repeated phrase.

In Cyril's view, **since both natures *belonged* to God's one divine nature, therefore, Christ was one divine nature,** this was the basis of his Christology. While no one could dispute this understanding of **Christ's *divinity*,** or that Christ's humanity was God's *own* humanity, nor that they were united **in** the one divine hypostasis, yet, how does this make Christ's humanity divine? For Cyril, however, any notion that the *one divine Christ* was not of one divine nature, was anathema.

We can imagine what the Antiochenes (the God-man people) must have thought of Cyril's Christology. Where was God's *human nature* in all this? That God's humanity was no more then a temporary *appearance* of flesh, was anathema to them. If Jesus' life-experience was solely that of God (the Logos), then the man Jesus only "appeared" to be human – "*docetism*" (a heresy.)

That the natures were *united **in*** the divine essence or nature, did not make *both* natures divine. Although this union excludes *division* – as Chalcedon put it – this does not exclude the *differences* of the natures. If both were divine, there would be no *union* to speak of, no Incarnation – no Christ. For Cyril, however, to speak of any differences or hint of separate natures, was "*dangerous*" he said, "*because it threatened their unity*". Any separation of this union, instead of "Christ", there would only be "*God **and** His man*". As far as Cyril's "man" is concerned, nobody could possibly relate to Jesus' human nature – because there is none to speak of – apart from "flesh". It was not that he tried to deify Jesus, it was that there was no genuine "man" to deify.

No one adhered more strictly to the indivisibility of Christ's single nature than Cyril. "*The one born of David is the same one (Logos) begotten of the Father*". Thus the divine Logos (or Son) who was born, prayed, was tempted, suffered and died, this was the one divine Logos. Should anyone hold to any difference between the Incarnate Logos and the man Jesus, for Cyril this meant "two sons" (two different "births") instead of one *divine* Son. Nothing whatsoever can be said separately of the man Jesus. To divide the two natures was "*blasphemous and proof of complete madness.*" Those who "*split up and completely divide his words and acts, attributing some things as proper solely to the Only Begotten, and others, to a son who is different to him and born of a woman ...have missed the straight and unerring way of knowing the mystery of Christ clearly*".

Cyril's saying Christ had *one divine nature* was no slip of the tongue – as some authors would like us to think. Cyril built his whole Christology on this understanding, an understanding basically in line with the Alexandrian school of thought – the "word– flesh" people. Read his essay "On the Unity of Christ", the man Jesus was a mere puppet whose humanity was no more than his en-fleshed appearance. Because the Logos *owned* Its own humanity, for Cyril it was a case of "possession", not a "union". The Logos so possessed Its human nature that it had no human autonomy, no mind, will or consciousness of its own – as he affirmed, the man **Jesus was *not a human person.*** This, of course, makes Jesus an ontological anomaly – not genuinely human. Cyril carried the notion of the oneness of divine and human so far, the human all but disappeared into the divine.

One author noted, "*Cyril easily leads to the view of Christ as a composite being – a confusion of God and man – the Logos having absorbed humanity resulting in one person and one nature*". Indeed, it was this "confused" view of Christ that would ultimately lead to *Monophysitism* – another heresy. The union of natures does not make a "single being", nor is Christ a "composite" of the two natures. When a divine person replaces (or acts as) the human person, the dual natures cease to exist and there is no Christ at all.

Cyril's view of Christ was obviously Platonic, only the flesh was responsible for man's earthly existence, man's soul was a *form* of the divine. For Cyril, in the Incarnation the flesh is all the Logos really assumed or united to Itself. The reason he thought the Logos governed the soul of Jesus was because Jesus himself was *no human subject or person.* Instead, it was God (Logos) walking, talking, suffering and dying. Although, reminded of Nazianzius' saying "*what Christ did not assume is not saved*" he was forced to formally admit Jesus had a human soul, yet the soul played no part in his Christology, he gave it no more than lip-service.

It is one thing to acknowledge a union of natures, but another, to treat this union as "one composite nature". Even while admitting the Logos (God) was impassible – and thus, never *experienced* a thing – Cyril insisted it must be "***said***" the Logos experienced everything, for this was *Its* human nature and not the human nature of the man Jesus. No division could be drawn in Christ's actions between those that were divine and those which were human – "***The subject or acting agent of his human experiences was the Logos***".

Difference between *God's* human nature and *Jesus'* human nature.

If one asks, "What is the difference between *God's* human nature and *Jesus'* human nature?" he would put his finger on the single most Christological *problem*. How this question is answered, however, is strategic for a true understanding of Christ. For the Antiochenes (God-man school), it was Jesus' oneness with God (*theosis*) that made him a *whole human person*, thus they saw no disparity between *God's* **human nature** and *Jesus'* **human nature**. It was *God's* human nature and *Jesus was its* ***human*** *person* – no problem. The union of man and God, after all, is a union of *natures (essences)*, **not** a union of *persons*.

The Alexandrians (God-flesh school), however, would say the man Jesus was only the *physical (or external) appearance* of God, he was the human *body* of God, thus he was God-*in-person,* **not** *a human person.* Jesus could **not** be a *human* person because it was not "*his*" human nature, but *God's* human nature. So where, for the Alexandrians, *God's* human nature is **person-less,** for the Antiochenes, the union of natures (theosis) made Jesus the perfect example of a ***whole human person.*** Obviously, the Antiochene understanding of *theosis* did not preclude Jesus as a human person.

So we have two different answers to the question of differences between God's human nature and Jesus' human nature. For the Alexandrians, ***God's*** humanity is ***no*** human person, for the Antiochenes, ***Jesus'*** humanity ***is*** a "whole" human person. For the latter, those who held Jesus was *not* a human person, flew in the face of the very revelation and meaning of the Incarnation. For the Alexandrians, however, to say Jesus *was* a human person, was a denial God was the *one divine* person of Christ. A major difference between these Christological paradigms, is that the Antiochenes never accepted the definition of *hypostasis* as a *person (*defined as the *agent, subject or self* of God's divine nature), nor accepted that God was the subject or agent of Jesus' human nature. Even though **it was *God's* human nature, yet it was *Jesus* – not God – who was its *human person.*** Obviously, these are two different Christological paradigms, each a different understanding of Christ, and each leading in different directions. The Antiochenes, of course, accused Cyril of denying Christ's human nature, and ignoring the ***unity*** of the two disparate natures. As for attributing "human life and experiences" to the Logos, this was absolutely **contrary to God's *impassibility***.

It could be said Cyril guarded Christ's unity like the Antiochenes guarded Christ's humanity. So while Cyril had the right understanding of the Incarnation (the Logos creating Its *own* human nature and not that of any particular person), his notion of the unity of natures was one of "possession", a divine "take-over", God's literally possessing Its own human nature. In this Christology, Jesus had no genuine humanity. Cyril's Christology also implies Christ had always existed, and that the Incarnation was just Christ taking on a human body. Thus, one place in his writing he said that if people wanted to think Jesus had always existed, that would be fine with him. He really didn't care "who" Jesus was, he only cared "*who*" Christ was. For him, Christ was the revelation of "**Universal Man**" (his very words), and not **a** man.

Every author excuses Cyril's understanding of Christ – "*one incarnate **nature** of God the Logos*" – telling us what he really *meant* to say was "*one incarnate **person** of the Logos*", and not "one incarnate *nature*". They say he mistook *hypostasis* to mean "nature or essence" *instead* of its meaning as "*person*". Thus, *we are told,* what he *really* meant to say was that Christ was the union of natures ***in** one divine **person*** and not ***in** one divine **nature***. But what kind of excuse is this? If Cyril believed *hypostasis* meant *nature* and he said "*nature*", then *nature* is exactly what he meant! The inseparable unity of the two natures he called a "hypostatic union", by which he *originally* meant the union of natures *resulting* "*in one divine **nature***", which later, however, someone else changed to mean a union "*in one **person***".

While the hypostatic union did not *result* in one divine nature, Cyril, however, was absolutely correct to say the *natures were united **in** the one divine **nature** or essence of the Logos.* That he was corrected to say "*united in the **person***" of the Logos (instead of *in the nature*) is false, because God is no "person". Cyril had it right, not those who later corrected him, determined to fit him into **their own party-line rendition** of the Trinity and Christ.

Making "person" the essence of being, is contrary to Cyril's understanding of what he called a "hypostatic union" – i.e., a *union of two natures **in*** **God's** (Logos') **one divine hypostasis,** which is perfectly correct. (*Hypostasis* is the nature or essence of the Logos, it is not a *person*.) The *locus* of the union is *in* the divine nature and *not* in any *person* – human or divine. But to regard this union as constituting *one divine nature* is *not* correct, and was never acceptable. Unfortunately, this was the excuse given for changing Cyril's *original "union of natures in one divine* ***nature****"* to read a *"union of natures in one divine* ***person****"* – another example of the "ontological *switch*" from essence to person.

When it comes to God's *human nature*, however, it doesn't matter if Cyril never *meant* "one nature" or someone later changed his mind, the fact remains, he only gave lip-service to Jesus' human soul. He insisted it was only the Logos who was born, and not some "other" being or *person*. For him, admitting to two natures was a mere formality, his vision of the "whole Christ" was of *one complete divine being.* In his view, the *result* of the union of natures was the *one nature of Christ* – **the one "object of perception"**, the one external undivided appearance that is *"Jesus Christ in whom God is invisible and whose humanity is deified in God".*

In defense of Cyril, someone pointed out, while he regarded the **single *person*,** Jesus, as an "*objective reality*", the natures, however, are distinct from the person. Thus, as a *human person* Jesus was an "objective reality" which was *not*, of course, his *true nature or person.* **But this could be said of anybody!** Everybody is an "objective reality", which is neither their *true nature,* or their *true person.* To make "person" no more than a material "objective reality" is just another case of *Docetism* (*appearance*.) Jesus *appears* to be human, *looks* and acts like a human person, but *really* he wasn't, under the skin he is really God. The bottom line in all this is that God alone knows the *true essence of* man, and God alone knows the *true person* as well. The mere "objective reality" – of anything – nets us absolutely nothing!

Another excuse for correcting Cyril's *original* Christology is that he thought he was only correcting the wrong view of Apollinaris – the revered bishop who thought the Logos had *replaced* the human soul of Jesus. Both their views, however, amount to the same thing – one would be hard put to find any soul granted the man Jesus in either of their views. Although Apollinaris was later branded a heretical *Monophysite,* yet, like father like son, Cyril was also branded a *Monophysite.* Some authors, however, go to great lengths to champion Cyril as the "victor" of orthodox Christology. Some even say Chalcedon and *Leo's Tome* merely hawked their Christology from Cyril. (Obviously, there is no such thing as an *unbiased* author.)

But let us say something about the good bishop Apollinaris (310 – 390.) His idea of the human soul, was that it was so inherently rotten, it was just not suitable for the good man Jesus. **All Apollinaris ever saw in Jesus was God** – the ideal vision for sure. Besides this, however, he was only articulating what most people regard as the "divine" in

Jesus – his soul, that is. For Paul and others, Jesus was "*the **form** of God*", and what is this "form"? For Plato (even Aristotle) *form* was the ***soul***! Apollinaris' "mistake" was merely putting into words what everyone believed of Christ anyway. When Apollinaris said God took the place of Jesus' human *soul* (**form** of God) this is people's general understanding of Christ's divinity – nothing divine about his body or "objective presence", his soul was his divinity.[1]

For the less Platonically minded, however, saying God took the place of Jesus' soul sounded like a denial of Jesus' humanity. Because few regarded Jesus' humanity as more than a physical body, Apollinaris' *mistake* was only saying it aloud – admitting it. No question, the fathers' view of the human soul was so negative, they had a hard time burdening Jesus with it. Vilifying Apollinaris, however, never restored Jesus a human soul. He was no more a heretic than any other Alexandrian. In my view, none of the fathers were *ever* heretical, in fact, they represent just about every view and understanding of Christ the human mind can come up with. Their diversity and genuine insights, indeed, their love and dedication to Christ, is unparalleled in Christianity.

To avoid Apollinaris' view, Cyril of Alexandria came up with a slightly different view. While Jesus had a soul, yet God took over its *functions* (or faculties), became its sole agent, the one who ran the show. God was the soul's "I am", subject or self. To say Jesus *had* a soul was just a formality, after all, it was not *Jesus'* soul, but ***God's*** **soul anyway.** This is why God was responsible for its every thought, word and deed, even its conscious "I am". It is *because* the man *owned* no soul of *his own,* he was *not* a human person – *this is the orthodox belief.* Obviously, it is one thing to **say** Jesus was a human being, but another to honestly *believe* it – teach it.

Cyril's view can be summed up in his tenth anathema – Jesus "***was not a man distinct from the Logos,*** *but was the incarnate Logos Himself*". Jesus was God in person, it was God who was born, learned to walk, talk, etc. There could be no speaking of the Logos *and* the man, or the "*one who assumes* ***and*** *the one who is assumed*". He, Jesus, is the Logos – is God.

Of all the brands of "Monophysitism", Cyril's Christology was the most disastrous – why? Because it was taken as the most definitive view of orthodox Christology – provided, that is, the term "*hypostasis*",

---

[1] As a kid trying to figure out what was divine about the man Jesus, I decided it could only be his invisible soul. Thinking this over, however, since souls are *created,* they couldn't be divine or God, so that was the end of that. I can see, however, how people could think, with Apollinaris, that Jesus' soul was divine.

meaning "*nature or essence*", is changed to mean "*person*".

To show up (up shore up) Cyril's accepted orthodoxy, every writer on the subject pits him against his major Antiochene opponent, the Patriarch of Constantinople, Nestorius (386 – 451.) Nestorius was not the only Antiochene against Cyril's view, in fact, there immediately comes to mind more outstanding fathers (including the Cappadocians) on Nestorius' side than on the Alexandrian side. No one in the history of Christianity, however, ever stood up for the full humanity of Jesus as did Nestorius. He was an ascetic monk, renowned for his wise counseling, and a stickler for orthodoxy who, overnight it seems, was elected Patriarch of Constantinople in 428 – to the political chagrin of Cyril, Patriarch of Alexandria. At one point Nestorius asked Cyril, ***"How can you have a complete human nature that is not a human person?"*** Cyril couldn't answer this – nor has anyone ever done so. That Jesus was *not* a *human person* is just one of those doctrines left dangling, lest one be accused of denying the man Jesus was God. Just for the asking, however, Nestorius was accused of believing Christ was the union of two persons – which he never said and never believed. On the contrary, Nestorius wrote, "*The natures must remain* ***in their own properties*** *and so one Glory must be understood and one Son confessed in virtue of the wonderful union which transcends all reason. We do not make two persons one person,* ***but by the one name "Christ", we denote the two natures together."*** Beautifully said!

Nestorius was right, "*the natures must remain in their own* ***properties***" – meaning, there can be no switching properties or persons, no granting human nature a divine property or divine nature a human property. Chalcedon states this Nestorian principle clearly – "*Christ exists in two natures, each complete and* ***each retaining its distinctive properties and operation unimpaired in the union.***" This is why attributing all **human** experiences to the "property" or *person* of the divine Logos *instead* of to Jesus, is a *switch* of properties (*persons*) that can only lead to *Monophysitism* – whether the reference be to an *individual* nature or *person* makes no difference.

Cyril, however, never "switched" properties, he simply eliminated Jesus' human property (person) in order to regard Christ as *one divine person with one divine nature.* Both terms "*person* and *nature*" came to serve the same purpose – Christ as *one* divine *person* with *one* divine *nature,* and Jesus, of course, was this one divine being.

Nestorius did not regard the Logos as the *person* of Christ "*lest it be said the Logos suffered, and lest it jeopardize the full humanity of Jesus*". He maintained that the fusion of the divine and human in Alexandrian Christology not only jeopardized the ***impassibility*** of the

Logos, but made meaningless the passibility of the man Jesus. "*Thus the account of the Angel strengthening Jesus in the garden could not have referred to the divine Logos, for He had no need of anyone to strengthen him. It was the humanity that needed strengthening.*" The fact Nestorius could not identify Christ with the Logos as the "person" of the union means – like many of the fathers – he did not buy the notion God acted as Jesus' human soul. The sad history of the early development of Christian doctrine is that so many compromised under pressure to adopt the party-line of the few who wielded the political power to enforce it. While some may have compromised for the sake of peace, and others out of "respect" for the "traditional language", there was also the fear of losing position, being exiled and besmirched for all time – Nestorius being one outstanding example.

After Nestorius was shot down by Cyril – condemned and exiled – no one after him ever dared stand up for the full humanity of the Incarnate Logos – lest they too be shot down, unjustly accused and defamed. To this day, the fear of *Cyrilian reprisal* remains intact in the whole theological field of Christianity. Anyone who dares to oppose Cyril's view of Christ or stand up for the full humanity of Christ – i.e., affirm Jesus was a human *person* – will be accused and vilified as a "Nestorian". [2]

Somewhere Nestorius told Cyril he had put too much trust in his "philosophical" thinking – which was obviously Platonic. This is reminiscent of Averroes' "*double-truth-theory*" – a proposition may be philosophically true, but theologically false.[3] This seems to be what Nestorius was pointing out to Cyril. His position sounded "logically" defensible, given his premise that a "*person* is an *individual being*", but does not hold up as theologically true.[4] To say or imply the Logos (and, consequently, *Christ*) was an "individual being" is clearly tritheistic. Although Nestorius' statement in this matter is not as clear as it should have been, nevertheless, he pointed out that Christ's manhood – the individual human being – **was the sole "being" of Christ,** and *not* the Logos (God.) The union was not **in** an *individual being* – either divine or human – rather, the union was **in** the "*prosopon*" or "hypostasis" (essence) of the Logos. As said before, the Incarnation as the un-

---

[2] For the "*Theotokos*" issue between Cyril and Nestorius see Appendix III of this book.

[3] Averroes (1126 – 1198) was a Muslim theologian whose commentaries on Aristotle greatly impressed Aquinas and his teacher Albert.

[4] Several of the fathers cautiously pointed this out – i.e., some distinctions and differences were only ***mental***, but not ultimately real or true.

ion of *two natures* had *nothing* whatsoever to do with any *person or persons,* human or divine. This is why it matters not if one regards God as a divine person and Jesus as a human person – because the Incarnation is solely a **union of natures and not persons.** What does a union of natures have to do with any *person* – human or divine? Nothing!

Merely doing away with Jesus as a human person, did not, of course, make him a divine person. Besides, there is no way anyone can *think* of Jesus but as a *human person.* Nestorius was not just holding out for Jesus as a complete human being, he was articulating the only view of Jesus anyone can have – that of a human person. That one *believes* he is God, doesn't make it so. Since no one knows what a *divine person* is, just capitalizing the 'p' in "person" won't do it. All Christians really know is just the *human* person, Jesus – mistakenly thinking, however, they are focusing on God, a divine person. But as we know, Christ's divinity was never for the looking, never a sensory being, which is why the divine Christ can only be revealed. Revelation transcends all visible forms and images, transcends the mind and intellect as well. (Today what people call "revelation" is a sham – paranormal experiences, visions, voices, mediumship, etc., none of this is genuine "revelation". The supernatural and paranormal are light years apart.)

Since the definition of "*person*" is no different for God than for man, there is no need to "switch" *persons.* Though one can ***say*** God acted the part of a human soul, how is one to know the difference? How can one ascertain if God is acting or the man Jesus? To **say** God acted *instead* of the person Jesus, doesn't say much for Jesus! If God did not trust Jesus with Its human nature, then God can trust no one with it. But whether one *substitutes* a soul (Apollinaris' view) or God *acted* as a human soul (Cyril's view) makes no difference. Both views make an *individual human being* a divine person, and in so doing, make God an *individual human being.* They did not make Jesus God, but instead, made God, Jesus.

Although Cyril verbally granted a union of two disparate natures, this was inconsequential. It was God, the divine Logos, who had the whole human experience. God was the divine person – agent, subject or self – the sole *human* "experiencer". This, at least, was Cyril's "*Christ*". To say it was the human being Jesus who knew the human experience, was anathema, it flew in the face of his whole Christology.

Something else Nestorius said that Cyril used against him was that the Spirit "indwelled in Jesus". Cyril accused everyone who disagreed with him as holding the unity of natures was just an "indwelling" he called "adoptionism". Nestorius' reference to the indwelling of the

Spirit, however, was not a reference to the *unity* of the two natures, but to the *presence* of the divine Spirit *in* the man Jesus – just as the Spirit indwells in all good people. Even the Gospels speak of the Spirit's movement in Jesus. After John's Gospel appeared, none of the fathers thought it was the Spirit that became Incarnate, or that the nature of the union was with the Spirit and *not* with the Logos. It would seem, however, Cyril did not honestly know the difference between Spirit and Logos. It is one thing to philosophically think one knows the difference, but another to experientially know it firsthand. Cyril gives no evidence for this latter knowing.

But this was Cyril's Christology, one not only regarded as orthodox, but taken as a dogma to be imposed on all who disagreed. Only those who can grasp his Christology could ever understand why Nestorius' question to Cyril – "*How can anyone be a complete human being who is not a* ***human person****?*" – was like throwing a bomb on his whole Christological paradigm.

So it is thanks to Cyril, then, one whole door on the development of Christology and understanding of Christ was closed and sealed **forever**. Where, for Cyril, it was God who really lived this human life, for Nestorius, it was the complete human being, Jesus. What is so inexplicable is that Cyril, with a history of tyrannical persecutions and despicable behaviors, is called a "saint", while Nestorius, whose life is impeccable (to my knowledge, at least) *continues* to be maligned. (Recently I discovered the Nestorian Churches continue to revere him, his *feast day* celebrated Oct. 26th.)

So what is the matter with Cyril's Christology? Strictly speaking it cannot be called a "Christology". Human nature is not just flesh. Without a human soul with its *own* free human agent, subject and self-awareness, there is no true "human nature", and with no true human nature there is no "union of natures" and **no real "Christ".**

Once God was made three persons, the Christological problem was how to affirm God as the sole divine *person* of Christ without, however, making a human being God. Thus, if a divine person is God, and Jesus is a divine *person*, then how is Jesus (a human being) **not** God? That Jesus, however, is *not* God, indicates something is terribly wrong in the thinking here.

Making God a "person" required dividing God into **nature** (essence) and **person,** two very different references to God. Reference to the Trinity as three *persons* is **not,** of course, reference to three *natures* or three individual beings, **yet, who can possibly think of a "person" that is *not* some individual being?** Nobody! And there's the problem. How can God as three "individual persons" not be three beings? To say Jesus is a divine person, not only makes an individual *human being* God, worse, it makes God an individual being, a *human being* – the very definition of *anthropolatry.* God, of course, is not even ***a*** being – much less a human being. Neither in *nature* or *person* is God an "individual being".

It was by *denying* Jesus was a human person, however, Cyril could make a divine person **act** as a human being – literally, **make a human being, God.** This error could never have happened had he, and everyone else, adhered to Nestorius' "wise counsel" – namely, **the man Jesus was a *human person* and not a divine person.** All references to Christ as a *divine prosopon* or *hypostasis* are references to God alone, not to any *individual* being or person – divine or human. Making a *human being God* – whether in nature or in person – can be laid at the feet of Cyril and his Alexandrian cohorts, which is one way, at least, to account for *anthropolatry.*

In Cyril's mind, somehow this *union* created a single being, a single nature, a single person – totally divine of course. But there is no truth to this. While the *locus* of the union was **in** the divine nature (the Logos' distinct hypostasis), this union did not make Christ a "single divine being" not in *nature* and not in *person.* Evidently, it was to make his case for God as a human being, Cyril said God was the sole agent, subject or self-identity of Its human nature, thus God *acted* the *human being, the human person.* Now if God acts like a human person and looks like a human person, **then God is a human being.** What other definition is there for *anthropolatry*?

Trying to make this view *orthodox*, several scholars and theologians have said the human nature was not actually *united* to the divine nature (or essence), but *united* solely to the divine person. In this view, Christ is not the union of two natures – as Chalcedon affirms – but the union of *human* nature *and* a divine "person". But if *nature* and *person* (the soul and its agent, subject or self) are only *united* to one another, then ***what*** one is, is only "united" to ***who*** one is. (This idea opens up the possibility these two, *nature* and *person*, can live without one another – something to consider seriously.) The only reason for "uniting" *what* to *who*, however, was to throw out Jesus' "*who*" and insert God's "*who*" instead. Still, union of human nature with a divine person would not make human nature a divine person. All this notion does is open up another can of theological worms.

Actually, Cyril never made Jesus a divine person, the Logos was the sole divine person of Christ. The divine person only *acted* (or functioned) as the soul of Jesus, which is why Jesus had to be canceled as a human person – can't be a divine and human person at the same time.

All this switching around of persons, however, only illustrates how theology is always trying to fill in the holes it has dug. "Orthodoxy" has a strange way of changing whenever it meets something deemed threatening to its proverbial party-line.

When all is said and done, however, to my knowledge Cyril never used the term "person". As already noted, he understood "hypostasis" as the *nature* of God – which is absolutely correct. He never understood "hypostasis" as "person", and indeed, God is no person(s.) Thus his understanding of "Hypostatic union" was also correct – a union of natures **in** the divine nature or "*hypostasis*" of God, the Logos. Keep in mind, the term "person" was never acceptable to the Eastern fathers until sometime in the 500's *after* Cyril and all the early fathers were dead. **So be wary of authors' changing the fathers' actual terms and language, more especially re-wording "*hypostasis*" to mean "*person*"!**

Considering that Cyril and Nestorius held more in common than they disagreed with, one way to account for their dispute can be traced to ignoring Hilary's warning about mixing up the three states in the life of Christ: Where Cyril seems to have based his Christology on the deified human nature *after* the Ascension, Nestorius based his on the human man of the Gospels *prior* to his transfigured, glorified human nature. In the light of these different states, we can understand Nestorius as speaking pragmatically – and rationally – of the second state, Jesus as a complete human person such as the Apostles and all his peers knew him. Cyril's approach, on the other hand, was decidedly from the third state, his view of Christ's deified, glorified humanity. The two men were obviously talking past one another.

When all was said and done, and all the acceptable Christologies ratified, every one of the fathers affirmed that the nature of the *oneness* of God and man **was a mystery**, Christ the very essence of this mystery. Even Cyril wrote: *"Godhead is one thing and manhood is another thing... but in the case of Christ, they came together in a* ***mysterious*** *and incomprehensible union without confusion or change. The manner of this union is entirely beyond conception"*.

A Postscript

The Third Council of Constantinople in 681 declared Christ possessed two wills and two minds, not opposed to each other, but cooperating in such a way Christ's human nature was of one mind with God and willed according to God's will. Finally, the Antiochene understanding of Christ's human nature triumphed. This union of natures accorded with their understanding of "*theosis*", the state in which Jesus lived out his *earthly* life. While this basically affirms Jesus was a complete *human person* – was fully aware of his own being, own mind and will – yet Christ would still be referred to as a single *divine person.* So even though this Council basically affirmed Jesus was *his own person,* no one would ever dare stand up and say as much lest he be given the "Nestorian-treatment". So how Jesus could be *his own human person* while Christ is *one divine person,* remains the theological problem (a union of persons?) and another example of theology digging its own hole.

MONOPHYSITISM

The term "*Monophysitism*" or "*one-nature*" is not just the name of an ancient heresy, it is a particular Christology that, today, best represents the Christian understanding of Christ. Thus Christ is a divine being, a divine person with a divine nature who, apart from his external appearance in the *flesh* of Jesus, is God. Jesus, then, *is* Christ, and since Christ *is* God, then Jesus is God – in the flesh. This pretty much articulates the Monophysitic belief and understanding of Christ, an understanding in keeping with the traditional party-line presentation of Christ.

The reason this belief was called "*Monophysitism*" is because it implied Christ was of one divine nature, even though no one denied Jesus' physical body. The Bible, after all, says "God *became* flesh" – no more and no less. For a Platonist, of course, "flesh" was good enough to account for "human nature". So Monophysitism is not the denial of Christ's physical body, but holds that apart from his external appearance, Christ was totally divine – was God. Thus to say "Christ is God" both affirms and implies *God's one divine nature.*

As we might expect, the genesis of this Christology (*Monophysitism)* came from the Alexandrian "God-flesh" school of thought. Though we are told Cyril was only *accused* of Monophysitism in his lifetime, the fact is, he was not only a monophysite, but more responsible for its survival in Christianity than any other person in its history. Though "*Monophysitism*" is sometimes referred to as "*Eutychianism*" – named after the Abbot Eutyches (378 – 454), an avid disciple of Cyril – he was only promoting Cyril's view, but was not its originator.

Some point to Apollinaris (310 – 390) as the originator, after all, he denied Jesus had a human soul and plainly refers to Christ as "*the one incarnate nature of the Logos*" – the *same phrase* used by Cyril. While Cyril gave Jesus a human soul, yet Jesus was unable to use it – use its faculties of mind, will, consciousness, etc. – instead, God used these "faculties", God was sole "agent" and "subject" of Jesus' human nature. So, although Jesus had a soul, it was *humanly* dysfunctional. After this, his disciple Eutyches comes along with the declaration, "*I confess that our Lord was of two natures* ***before*** *the union, but* ***after*** *the union, I confess* ***one nature***."

The reason Cyril is not nailed for this Monophysitic Christology, is due to a theological bias that favors his view. This is why, after his view was amended by a switch of terms – *nature* to *person* – he has come down in history as a champion of *orthodoxy, his* is the proverbial "party-line" presentation of Christ. Apart from flesh, Christ is totally divine, is God. In light of this fact, it could be said "*Monophysitism*" is just another "so called" heresy without any heretics. Because none of the fathers denied the union of two natures, strictly speaking, none were *Monophysites,* not, at least, in this sense of the term.

What some of the Alexandrians believed was that *after* the union of the two natures, Christ's nature was a *single composite* of two natures – a kind of *third nature* if you will. (Even Aristotle referred to the composite of body and soul as a "third substance".) So the thinking was *because* the union of natures is **in** the ***one*** hypostasis or *nature* of God (Logos), it can rightly be said Christ is **one** divine person of ***one*** divine nature, and that, as Incarnate, Christ is **one** divine being. Whether this single *being* refers to Christ as a single person, a single nature or both, makes no difference because Christ is all this – but flesh. There was also the view that because of the union, not only Jesus' soul, but his *body* was also *deified* – made God, in other words.

Seeing no father denied the *union* of natures, the obvious problem was the *true nature of this union.* The fathers did not merely have a "problem" with Cyril's Monophysitic Christology, it was the cause of one of the hottest dissensions in the history of Christianity, one that bordered on the fear of physical violence between parties.

There were several brands of Monophysitism, the extremists even called a council or synod to *condemn* the belief Christ had two natures. This was aptly called a "*robber council*" – the "robbery" of Christ's *human nature,* that is. In their view, given the *disparity* of natures, the divine basically "over-shadowed" the human. This view is reminiscent of Aristotle's list of possible results when there is a *union* of any two "things". The *most extreme* result was that one thing would so "*predominate*" the other as to *transform it into itself.* Some of the fathers seemed to share this view. Thus Gregory of Nyssa thought that in the *end* – when all were deified in Christ and God would be "*All in All*" – the divine nature would "*absorb*" human nature "*like the sea absorbing a drop of honey*". Nyssa's view of the ***end,*** however, had nothing to do with "Monophysitism" – few people think as far ahead as he did. The issue here was the nature of the union effected by the Incarnation. If human nature was "transformed" into divine nature, there was no Incarnation to speak of.

Cyril's union of natures allowed no genuine duality and, consequently, no genuine human nature. It was his overstress on the unity of natures that was the genesis of *Monophysitism.* Though regarded as a heresy, it shouldn't be, because this is the belief of most Christians, more especially, theologians who promote it – as reflected in their proverbial party-line. **No question, theology speaks of Christ as if he was a single being – one divine person with one divine nature – which is not just a matter of language, but the whole Monophysitic**

belief. Yet, it is this belief, this view or understanding that became acceptable *orthodox* Christology. What Christian, for example, does not regard the individual being, Jesus, as the **divine Christ?** And what Christian does not regard Christ as God? Well, this belief is the definition of "*Monophysitism*".

Obviously, the etymological term "*Monophysitism*" as "*one nature*" implies far more than it means – which is *why* no Christian regards themselves as an "heretical Monophysite". The term, however, is deceiving. While it does not deny the dual natures of Christ, it nevertheless posits **Christ as a *single being.*** Christ, however, is not a "single being", but the *union* of God with *man's being*, a union with man's complete *non-divine, created human nature* – warts and all. Monophysitism blocks the ability to grasp God's oneness with man's common human nature, which is what the revelation of Christ is all about. Christ is not the revelation of God, not the revelation of some individual being, but the revelation of Man's eternal oneness with and in God.

Any Christology that does not clearly articulate the **union** of two disparate natures does not define Christ according to the revelation of the Incarnation. The Monophysitic mistake is making **Christ a single *being* – a single *divine* being – whereas Christ is the union of God with *man's being.*** God is not **a** Being (or three beings), and God's union with a human being does not make God or man "one being" – one entity. Since Christ, then, is *not* "one divine being", then how did this Monophystic mistake ever come about? How did theology justify this error?

To answer this, we need only put our finger on the term and meaning of "*person*", not as it applies to man, however, but as it was foisted on Almighty God. Cyril's original thinking went like this: since the divine Christ or Logos **is** a divine ***person*** of *one divine **nature**,* then all references to "Christ" are to the **one divine *person*** (Logos) of **one divine nature**. This was Cyril's Monophystic thinking, the one divine nature of Christ – but is Christ one divine nature? Of course not. Although God could never become a human person – or, for that matter, *become* a human being – God can, and did, unite human nature to Itself and *this **union** is the dual nature of Christ in God.*

When speaking of Christ as a "divine person", what *person* or *individual being* comes to mind, who else can one point to but the image of the man Jesus? But can anyone point to God as a *person* or *individual being*? If so, then God is some individual sensory *being* and the Trinity three beings – **tri-theism**. To say Christ is "*one divine person*" not only implies one divine "nature", but implies **one divine being** – after all, how can there *be* a *person* if there is no *individual* being? And how can a single being have two disparate natures? **Merely changing the references from *nature* or *person,* is no more than theological parsing.** It does not change the view of Christ as a single being or entity. The ordinary Christian, of course, knows nothing of the theological division between *nature* and *person*. Thus, to speak of a *person* is to speak of *somebody* – some individual *human being,* which, for Christians of course, is the individual human being Jesus – **but is a divine *person* an individual being?** If so, then the Trinity is three beings – tri-theism!

"Person" always denotes "***who***" *someone* is, some *particular being,* entity or embodied individual. Thus to say the incarnate Logos or Christ is a divine *person, who* do people think this divine *person is*? **The only *person* people know is the human *being* Jesus.** So based on this image, God as the *person* Jesus is taken to be a *particular being,* and based on this, the three *persons* of the Trinity are regarded as three *individual beings*! (Indeed, Jesus is taken for one of the Trinity!) **No question *tri-theism* and *Monophysitism* go hand in hand – get the Trinity wrong = get Christ wrong.**

Now if an individual human *being* is a *divine person*, it follows that this *divine person* has a *divine nature* – *Monophysitism* in a nutshell, Jesus, of course, is neither a divine person nor has a divine nature. The unity of man and God does not constitute a single being. Christ is not a *single being* with dual natures, but solely the *union* or oneness of two natures. It is because the only "person" man knows is some *human being*, that calling God a *person* (or three) is not just misleading, it makes it impossible to ever have a true understanding of Christ. That Christ is one divine *person,* not only implies *one divine nature,* but implies Christ is one *divine being.* Had Jesus been understood as a genuine *human person* as Nestorius and the Antiochenes affirmed, no divine *person* could have been substituted for a *human person,* and the *error* of Monophysitism avoided.

Since the only "being" we know called "Christ" is the man Jesus, and since Jesus had no divine nature and was no divine person, then how could he be divine in any sense of the terms *nature* or *person*? To *fit* him into this equation, he was robbed of his *human* personhood, denied he was a human person in order to make God *instead*, the sole divine person of Christ – the ***one person*** *of both natures.*

God, of course, was not **both** a divine and human person – was not a *dual person* or a *duality of persons.* Even theologically, God was the *one divine person* of Christ, not the person Jesus. So, basically, the man Jesus was neither a divine or human person, he was no person at all – and this is *orthodox*!

The error of Monophysitism is thinking Jesus, an *individual* human being, was a *divine person* with a *divine nature*. Christ, however, is not a divine being nor the union of two *beings*. It is solely Christ's *human nature* that is *man's* being, which is not God's being. While we can *individualize* man's one common human nature into billions of individual *beings*, God is **not** *"a being"* and can never be *individualized*. **Yet, the view Christ is a single embodied divine being, is the essence of Monophysitism and the belief of most Christians.** Responsible for this view, however, is no naive Christian, but theologians, teachers and scholars who have promoted it for centuries. It is all in the proverbial Christian language – the traditional party-line. Though Christ be defined as one *person with two natures,* this does not alter the consistent reference to Christ as an *individual divine being, a single embodied entity*. But then, how could one think of Christ as *one divine person* if Christ was *not one divine being*? Since no theologian can answer this, neither can anyone else.

Although theologically, referring to *Christ as one person,* does not mean *Christ is one individual being,* yet how many people – theologians especially – do *not* equate an *individual person* with an *individual being*? One would be hard put to find any theologian telling us *person* is **not** a reference to an *individual being*. Like everyone else, they take for granted *person* is a reference to *individual being* – a fact certainly reflected in their language. Obviously, the whole problem is the term ***person*** applied to God as if God was a being and the Trinity, three beings. Unless *person* can be eliminated, thrown out, it is impossible to ever have a true understanding of Christ.

Monophysitism stands (or falls) on the premise that *person* refers to some *individual being – a "numerical one"* as Aristotle defined it. *Person* is always a reference to a particular being, a concrete, embodied *being*. Who, after all, thinks of an individual nature and person that is ***not*** one being? This is why referring to Christ as a *divine person* or *being* is generally understood as God's *one divine nature*. Christ, however, is *not* just the divine nature of the Logos, Christ is the *union* of the Logos' divine nature with man's human nature. While Christ's *human* nature was "one being", this human being had no dual natures – **Jesus has no dual natures, God has no dual natures, only Christ has dual natures.** It is just as Chalcedon affirms – Christ is not the union of two *beings* or two *persons,* Christ is solely the *oneness* of two *natures*.

The whole Christological problem was to find some way to justify Christ as "one" *individual being*. After all, if people could not think of Christ as the individual being Jesus, then how were they to think of

Christ? They couldn't! But is the man Jesus a *divine person, a divine being?* No. The one divine nature of God is *not* an individual being, nor are the distinct hypostases of the Trinity three beings. That God is united to an individual human being neither makes God an individual being, nor an individual being God. Monophysitism was just another attempt to resolve the problem of how to think or speak of Christ as "a single being" a concrete human-divine entity. Whether one thinks of Christ as "one nature" or "one person", both presuppose an *individual being* – and therein lies the problem.

Christ is not the union of natures *in* one individual being, but a union of natures *in* God – and God is not an individual being. The union of natures is not a union **in** some individual being or person. To define *person* as an agent, self, subject, "I am", and then say the union of natures is *in* a divine agent, subject, "I am", etc., smacks of some kind of *psychological* union, certainly not one grounded in the being and essence of God. How the union of natures can be grounded in a "who" (a person or self) and not in the very *nature or essence* of God, is pure rhetoric with no substance. It doesn't even make sense.

For most Christians, however, a Monophysite understanding of Christ as **one divine being** is par for the course. If this Monophysistic Christology was not the present day (21st century) Christian belief and understanding of Christ, it would have been pointless to spend any time on this subject. The thinking is this: *Jesus is Christ, and Christ is God,* ***therefore****, Jesus is God,* this is not just *Monophysitism*, this is *anthropolatry* – what else can it be called?

It is very possible people love God, and love the man Jesus, yet do not know Christ at all!

COMMUNICATION OF PROPERTIES

There is no greater Christian conspiracy than what is called the "*Communicatio Idiomatum*" (*Communication of Idioms*), also known as "*Communication of Properties*" or "*Communication of Attributes*". It is the ultimate theological cover-up for the whole language of Christianity's reference to God, to Christ, and to the man Jesus. The "*communicatio*" is the language or "*idiom*" of the proverbial Christian "*party-line*". It is a "conspiracy" because few Christians have ever heard of it.

Before anyone can understand how this "Communicatio" works, however, it is imperative to understand the difference between *person* and *nature,* understand one is *not* the other. Thus to speak of God as a *person* is not a reference to God's divine *nature*, and to speak of a human being as a *person* is also not a reference to man's human *nature*. Once this is clear, it is necessary to understand the following premise on which the *communicatio* is based:

1. The Incarnation was the divine *person* (Logos) creating and uniting Its divine nature to human *nature. God did* **not** *create a human person or unite any human person to Itself, God* **only** united human *nature* to Itself.
2. So the Incarnate Logos or "Christ" is the union of two *natures* **in** the one divine hypostasis (or *person)* of the Logos.
3. Thus the **sole *person* (or *subject*) of "Christ" *is* the divine Logos – God.**

Based on this understanding, this is how the "Communication of Idioms" works. Because the sole "*person*" (or *subject*) of Christ's dual natures is God, then all references to *both natures* (divine and human) are references to the *one divine person* (or *subject*) – *God.* Thus, anything that can be *attributed* (predicated or *said)* of either Christ's divine or human natures, this can be *attributed* to the *one divine person* – God. Thus *Christ* is God in *person*, but dual in *nature*.

So referring to Christ as a divine ***person*** (and not to God's divine **nature**) one can **say,** "God *was born, was thirsty, tempted, suffered and died",* and at the same time, say God is *creator, omniscient, omnipresent, dwells in unutterable glory, etc.*, all these human and divine *properties* attributed equally to the one divine person – God.

Thus the *person suffering* on the cross at the same time *dwells in unutterable glory*. That God *suffers* is *not,* of course, a reference to God's *divine nature*, nor to say God *dwells in glory* is a reference to God's *human nature*. The sole reference to *both natures* is a reference to "God" alone as a divine ***person.***

In a nutshell, then, anything *said* of either nature, divine or human, can be *said* of (or attributed to) the *one divine* **person** – *God (Logos.)* Since God's human nature was given the name "Jesus", then anything Jesus *"said" or "did"*, means *"God said it", "God did it"* – God being the one *"person"* of Christ. Thus all reference to "Christ's" *dual natures* are references to God as their sole divine agent, subject, self – or *person*.

Since *"Christ"* is the union of two natures and **not** two persons, all references to *"Christ"* are to God (as a *person*), and **not** references to the man Jesus, who was neither a divine person or a divine nature. Obviously, the *Communicatio* is totally dependent on the premise God is a *person* (or three persons), otherwise, it loses its whole rationale, wouldn't work. **So too, if Jesus were regarded as a *human person* the *Communicatio* wouldn't work.**

It is because Christ cannot be two persons at once that for the *Communicatio* to work, Jesus as a *human person* had to be nullified, discounted, and declared *not* to be a *human person.* God, after all, cannot be *two persons at the same time* – human and divine. Christ's dual natures can only be that of *one person – God.* This is why switching properties, making God a *person* instead of man, robbed Jesus of being a human person. It is this "switch" from human to divine that *"communicatio"* expresses. With this "switch" it became perfectly permissible to **say** one *worships*, adores and glorifies the "Lord Jesus" *because* this is the worship of a *divine person,* of Almighty God, and not the worship of a man. Some Council in 553 even states, *"The Lord Jesus Christ is one of the Trinity"*, the reference, of course, is not to the man Jesus as one of the Trinity, but to Christ's divine *person* as one of the Trinity.

Using the "Communicatio", we could give hundreds of "official quotes" all *implying* Jesus was God. What people do not realize is that **the entire *language* (*idiom*) of Christianity, its proverbial *party-line* or "way of speaking", is all premised on the *"Communicatio Idiomatum".*** The way of expressing the man Jesus as if he were God, can be found everywhere – creeds, doctrines, catechisms, theology, all Christian literature – all referring to Jesus as if he was eternal, had always existed, was (or is) God. By *attributing* all the events and experiences of the Logos' incarnate humanity to *God as a person,* the life of Christ – everything Jesus said and did – could be attributed to God as a *person.* With the few exceptions that could only refer to the flesh – its growth and physical needs – all the experiences of Christ's (or Jesus' human nature) were *those* of Almighty God, a divine *person,* ***not*** those of *any human person* – not even those of Jesus.

According to the "*Communication of Idioms or Properties*", however, all references to "*Christ*" are **not** to any *human person* or human being, all references are to *Almighty God* ***as a "person"***. So what is the matter with this? When people think of "*Christ*" as a divine *person, who* do they think of? Hands down, they think of the man Jesus. Anyone who tries to think of God as a "person", will only come up with some anthropological individual being. The "common folk" know nothing about dividing *nature* from *person* and *person* from *nature*. Instead, they automatically think of a *person* as an "individual being" and thus, regard the individual man Jesus not only as a divine *person*, but as a divine *being* – totally unorthodox, of course. It could be said, the C of P ("communication of properties") *depends* on people ***not knowing*** the difference between *person* and *nature* (or *person* and *individual*.) And do not ask to define the difference between a human and divine person, because none exists. It is *because* no one really knows the difference, that what the C of P *calls* a divine person is, in truth, only a *human person*. As to the difference, one could only **say** one is eternal and the other, non-eternal. (To say a human *person* is "non-eternal", however, would surely raise some theological dander. Only Jesus is *no-person,* nobody else!)

The reason this is a Christian "conspiracy" is because few Christians have ever heard of the C of P or know anything about it – and all should be outraged when they learn of it. The C of P merely capitalizes the "p" in *person* and expects everyone to think this refers to a divine person. The whole ruse was a way to legitimize speaking of the man Jesus as if he was a *divine being* or *person* – which he was not. By making God a *person* and the man Jesus *no-person*, **the C of P was a way of referring to a human person as a divine person without, theologically, at least, having to declare the man Jesus a *divine* person** – which it could not *rationally* do. The human being Jesus is *not* God's divine *person,* one of the Trinity, or the *divine person* of Christ (God, not Jesus, was the *divine* person.) To think God is a human person or a human person is God, is the definition of "*anthropolatry*". Far from denying *anthropolatrism,* however, the *comunicatio* not only promotes the worship of a human being, but justifies it! The problem, of course, is that people take all this *idiomatic jargon – the proverbial "party-line" – as Gospel truth,* ***and it's not the truth at all!*** This kind of language has to be thrown out, condemned, because it does *not* articulate the Truth. To *attribute* to man what is God's and what is God's to man, is the essence of *anthropolatry*.

Nothing so promotes and abets a totally erroneous and false understanding of Christ, of God, and of the man Jesus, than the C of P. One could say the C of P was one way, at least, to answer Nestorius' question, "*How can you have a complete human nature that is not a person?*" The answer was to make Jesus no-person, and God a *person* instead – that's how it works! For the Antiochene, of course, Jesus was a "**whole person**" ***because*** **he was *one with God* and not *because* he was God!**

It is said, initially the C of P was supposed to eliminate all the bickering over "*who*" in the Gospels *said* and *did what*? Who was tempted, Jesus or God? And who worked the miracles, God or Jesus? To think the solution was ***saying*** God was the "*person" who* was responsible for it all, was naive at best, and at worst – totally false. It simply eliminated the man Jesus as a human person, and so doing, missed the whole purpose of the Incarnation – the revelation of *man.* The C of P was one way, at least, to relieve theology of having to deal with Jesus' *human nature,* now all Jesus' thoughts, words and deeds could be attributed to the divine *person* – God. Jesus' human nature was only "flesh" anyway. To justify this *ruse*, it was pointed out the Gospels made no distinction between God and man; and indeed, the Gospels made **no** such distinction ***because*** their reference was solely to the *human person* Jesus, and **not** to Yahweh, Almighty God – never! Remember, "Christians" never wrote the Gospels or Epistles, their Jewish writers were totally of the Judaic mind-set that made no human being God.

As we know, "*idioms*" are just a "way of speaking", the use of terms in a certain way to mean certain things. What few people realize, however, is that the official Church or Christian language is totally premised on this use of *idioms* ***instead*** *of on the* **truth of Christ.** Since the traditional party-line is premised on the C of P it is important every Christian understands what this means, understands the reason for its use, its premise and conclusions, above all, understand its repercussions as regards a true understanding of Christ – and, indeed, the whole of Christianity. So let us go over the C of P step by step to be sure everyone honestly understands it.

This is the way it works:

1. *First*, one has to mentally make a division between *nature* and *person* – must understand that *person* does not mean *nature* and nature does not mean person.
2. *Then,* one has to regard the Trinity as three *persons* – not three *natures*.

3. *After this distinction* is made, one has to understand it was the specific *person* of the Trinity, the Logos, that became incarnate by creating and uniting Itself to man's human *nature*.
4. The Incarnation **was not the creation of any human *person*,** only the creation of a human *nature*.
5. *Thus*, the *sole* **person** *of Christ* (the union of natures) was the divine Logos – God in person.
6. *Since* only God was the *person* of Christ, the human being, Jesus, was *no human person.* Jesus' human nature was **not that of a divine person**, rather, the sole divine *person* of ***both natures*** was God.
7. *This means* that anything ***said*** of either natures (divine or human) can be *attributed* to (or *said* of) the one divine *person* – God.
8. *What is not permitted*, however, is any crossover between *natures*, such as attributing to the divine *nature* what only belongs to human *nature* and vice versa.
9. *But as long* as both natures are *attributed* solely to **God as the *one divine person of Christ***, then just about anything one could ***say*** about the divine and human natures can be *attributed* to God or *said* of God – **as a person**.
10. *In short*: the *Communicatio Idiomatum* (or "attributes") means anything *said* (or *attributed*) to either God's divine nature or man's (Jesus') human nature, is a reference to the **single divine person of Christ,** Christ being the eternal *person* of God – the Logos.

God, then, serves as the person of both the divine and human natures, the divine "person" or Logos, regarded as the "site" or "locus" of union of these two disparate natures. Thus the natures were united **in** God, in the divine person of the Logos. This way, everything that belongs to both natures can be attributed to the divine person of Christ – to God. So all the attributes, properties and experiences of human nature belonged to the divine agent, subject or self of God alone, and none to the human person, Jesus.

Although it is said "attributing" Jesus' words and acts to God went back as far as Ignatius, Tertullian and Origen, yet the "Communication of Idioms" was only officially recognized and sanctioned by Pope Leo in his document called *Leo's Tome (in 449.)* In this he says, Christ "*acknowledged in two natures without confusion, without change, without division and without separation, each nature was assured its own ontological distinction, even though* ***verbally permissible*** *to predicate them of one and the same Christ".*[1]

---

[1] I was called on this quote. Several versions of the Tome do not say "verbally permissible". Because I compared three different versions, this one must be somewhere in the

The problem with "verbally permissible", however, is the tendency to take words at face value as literal truth. It is one thing to *attribute* human experiences to God, but another for God to *have* human experiences. While the C of P does not outright make Jesus a divine person, it makes God a *human person* instead. To substitute everything meant by a "human person" to refer to God, literally makes God a human person. If God *can* take the place of Jesus as a human person – which is the belief – then how is God not a human person? If God thinks, speaks and acts like a human person, then God *is* a *human person.* The C of P legitimizes referring to a *human being* as God in *person.* This way, everything Jesus said and did, it could be *said* God is the one *who* said it, did it – and then we wonder how Christianity could ever have degenerated into *anthropolatry?*

Theology's most egregious wrong turn was making God a *person* in the first place. Because of this, a division had to be made between *nature* and *person(s)* in order to *attribute* the life and experience of man's human nature to God's person – **even though God experienced none of it.** Obviously, the consequences of this split between *nature* and *person* proved a disaster, one resulting in an understanding of Christ that has misled the faithful ever since. People do not think in terms of "who" or "what" (*person* or *nature*) when speaking of a human being or of God. What Christian constantly makes a mental distinction between God's nature and God's persons, or constantly makes a distinction between Jesus' nature and person? Apart from a few theologians, it would not occur to anyone. Unfortunately, even theologians do not separate a human from a divine person because, in truth, they, themselves, do not know the difference. If they did, if they really knew God, they would never have labeled God a "person" – or three persons. Their view of person is no different from the man in the pew, like everyone else, they merely capitalize the "p" and then *think* this a *divine* person.

No one regards **human nature and person** as a reference to anyone other than some individual ***human being or entity*** – while God, of course, is neither. Thus people do not realize when *saying* God was born, suffered and died for them, this is mere *verbal jargon* and not the truth – God was never born, suffered or died. "Attributing" to God what is *not* God's is false – really a sin.

While God certainly orchestrated the events in the human life of

---

Bibliography. If someone had *inserted* these words (not me), this at least was its "proverbial" understanding, otherwise, I would not have quoted it here. My discovery is that translators and authors *insert*, *change* and *delete* with impunity.

Jesus, God never *experienced* any of it!

To think it is ***not orthodox*** to regard Jesus as a *human person,* yet ***perfectly orthodox*** to regard ***God* as a human person** is absolutely **incredible**! Since neither philosophically or theologically can a *divine person* be the property of human nature or a human being, the C of P was a way to at least *imply* a human being was a divine person without, however, having to *declare this outright* – declare Jesus a divine person, that is. But this is all part of the conspiracy. When people think of Christ as a *divine person "who" are* they thinking of? They are not thinking of God – nobody knows God *as a person* – they are thinking of the man Jesus as a divine *person!* So even though Jesus was *not* a divine person, the C of P promotes this misunderstanding, even justifies *thinking* and *speaking* of Jesus as if he were a divine person – God.

Does the C of P convey any truth at all, or is it all a conscious ruse of rhetoric, words used to justify and impress? Since idioms are mere figures of speech, are Christians expected to take these metaphorical predicates, epithets and idioms as expressing the *truth* of anything? One early father said of the C of P, "*it just manipulates words*", another said, "*it only confused and intermingled the natures*". Although Nestorius was against the C of P, he admitted it was not inappropriate, at times, to refer to the man as God, or God as man, as long, he said, as it was a matter of "*mere words*". In his view it was used more to accommodate the "*simple folk*". He also said, "*As for the Logos suffering, this could be said in the sense in which a monarch suffers when, for example, his statue is dishonored.*" Hard to believe Nestorius made such an inane remark! On the other hand, it affirms his belief it was the human being who suffered and died, not God – the whole idea, he said, contradicted the ***impassibility* of God.** To think the Uncreated is changeable and passible would change the whole understanding of God to "god". This is why to say God is the *subject* of human experiences, not only makes God a *human being*, but opens the door to all forms of pantheism, monism, polytheism and anthropolatry. Any implication God is *passible* – as implied in the C of P – falls right outside monotheism. God's *impassibility* nullifies and pulls the rug out from under the whole idea of the "*communication of idioms*" – it is really a "communication of errors".

But knowing this, why didn't the fathers blow it off as so much rhetoric? Since the Logos had no need to experience Jesus' sufferings to know them, why did the Alexandrians think it necessary to ***say*** God suffered and died? The reason is this: in their view, since the death of a mere human being could not merit redemption for mankind, they had to find some way to justify **saying** God was the one who suffered and died. The C of P worked to at least verbally *attribute* Jesus' death to God's *person.* Because God cannot suffer or die, however, this obviously didn't work – because its premise was wrong to begin with. First of all, to hold a *man's* death cannot merit anything for anybody, should not be a hard and fast rule, if God so willed it to be meritorious, then it will be. We cannot dictate to God what is meritorious and what is not.

For another thing, the idea *God dies* to atone for sins *against God* makes no sense whatsoever – how can *one* atone to *oneself* for a sin against *oneself*? No rational mind could come up with a cockamamie idea like this. It seems for some of the Alexandrians, it would have detracted from God to *attribute anything to the man Jesus* – a view that totally contradicts the whole purpose and revelation of the Incarnation. Yet it was **Cyril's idea of *Theopaschism*** ("God suffered") that was ultimately vindicated by the "communication of properties" – to the horror of just about everyone but the Alexandrians.

So for the Alexandrians, at least, the C of P served its purpose as a way to **speak** of Jesus as a divine *person,* even though the divine *person* of Christ was solely God and **not** the man Jesus. Still, referring to "*God suffering*" implies God experiences everything a human being experiences – and Jesus experienced everything a divine person experiences. But as we have seen, there is no truth to this either – who honestly knows what God "experiences" anyway? If we can presume the Logos as person can suffer, then so can the Spirit and Father, and who knows, maybe they also died.

To think the divine Logos (God) was subject to any human experiences is contrary to the monotheistic understanding of God as unchangeable, impassible (unmoved), insensate, emotionless, imperturbable, not capable of human qualities. God has no need to *experience* anything – joy, bliss, ecstasy, glory, etc., it's all totally human. This is why attributing these human experiences to God makes God a *human being.* The truth, however, is that only the human being, Jesus, was subject to the panoply of *human experiences*, from its ups and downs to its most intimate experiences of God. Indeed, it is because of this we can relate to him and his ungodly predicament. We cannot relate to any changeable, suffering or ecstatic God; in fact, we cannot even comprehend such a thing. Those who think this way obviously do not know God.

But let us be very clear, the C of P is solely a reference to the one "***who***" was born, suffered and died, it is **not** a reference to "***what***" was born, suffered and died (human nature, that is.) The C of P is solely premised on "***who***" Christ is, not on "*what*" Christ is. Its reference is not to *what* "being" or *nature* (divine or human) is, but to "*who*" a *particular being is,* to a single, personal identity – a person, that is. But is "*who*" God is, a *particular individual being* – or three beings? If so, this is *tri-theism.* If, however, "Christ" as a divine person is an *individual being,* this *individual being* can only be the man Jesus "*who*", however, was *no divine person.* So, if God is not individual being, and Jesus is not a divine person, then how do we get Christ as *the one individual being of one particular divine person?* We don't! Not unless God as a person is one individual being – tri-theism.

What is interesting about the theological division between *who* one is and *what* one is, is the implication *nature* does not suffer, rather, it is the *person,* the subject or self *who* suffers. Applied to Christ, this means God as a *person* is the one *who* suffered and not Its divine or human *natures.* But if Jesus' human nature did not suffer, and God as a *person* cannot suffer, than *who* or *what* actually suffered? Is it possible that *nature* itself never suffers and that only a *person* suffers? Think of it this way: nature is always in the process of being transformed toward a higher end, which end is all to the **good of nature.** Yet, it is the *person* (agent, self or subject) **who** suffers this transformation and not, actually *nature* itself. This is an interesting scenario, and the bit of truth in it may be worth thinking over.

While it may be comforting to think God has undergone the human experience, yet God "experiences" none of it. God actually knows the human experience far better than man. God knows the *truth* of it all, the whole human experience, while all man knows is his *human experiences* from which he derives all kinds of ideas, theories and conclusions. Man really doesn't trust that God knows, instead, he wants God to know the same as he knows and *how* he knows. But to think any of man's experiences are God's experiences, requires a totally anthropomorphic view of God. In truth, however, if man knew what God knew, he wouldn't like it a bit, couldn't take it, because all his ideas, concepts and experiences would become exactly what Aquinas said – "*straw*".

Needless to say, the C of P couldn't work if Jesus was a *human person,* it only works if he is *not* a human person and a divine person *substituted* in his stead. Strictly speaking, the C of P is just another form of *Monophysitism* where a divine person eliminates a human person, and thus, with no distinction between persons, there can be no real distinction between natures – apart from mere lip-service. If a divine and human person are *not* as *disparate* as their divine and human natures, then why not equate their natures as well? What does it say for human nature when its human experiences are attributed to God? Nothing! If *person* is the sole experiencer and knower of both natures, then where is there any real difference between *saying* Christ is *one nature and one person*? Actually, the C of P is not only another term for *Monophysitism*, even worse, it could be another term for *anthropolatrism.*

Certainly it would be a big a mistake to think the majority of fathers went along with any of this. On the contrary, this must have been one of those issues the good fathers rioted over. In fact, a good portion of the Church at this time split apart – after Chalcedon. Obviously, this whole issue of the true nature of the *unity* (God and man) was a major issue, the major problem of Christ. While all agreed on the unity of natures, the issue of "who" was born, suffered and died, was an issue from the beginning. The C of P resolved nothing, it only made matters worse. Applying the properties (persons) or attributes of God to the man Jesus – i.e., beatific vision, omniscience, omnipresence and all the rest – virtually does away with his real humanity, closes the door on any understanding of Jesus as a complete human being. All the protestations that Jesus was as complete a human being as the rest of mankind, goes out the window. And by the same token, applying human attributes to God, and God goes out the window.

The bottom line: the C of P as a "way of speaking" defines no reality or truth at all. People do not understand this rendition of Christ and Christianity as *mere words*, idioms or metaphors, but instead, take this for the Gospel truth. The C of P is little more than an excuse for *calling* an orange an apple, a conspiracy because "simple folk" are not only in the dark about it, but the C of P **depends** on people being in the dark about it. The C of P is not taught or ever spoken of, never called to one's attention or pointed out. Even when mentioned in passing by a few scholars dealing with Christ, it is so taken for granted they never bother to go into it. No question, the C of P is the most deceiving ruse in all of Christian history, a ruse responsible for totally wrong views of Christ, the Trinity and the man Jesus.

It is not necessary to posit the Logos as a "person" in order to define the oneness of Christ's divine and human natures. We need only affirm the locus of their union *in* the Logos, in God – and not *in* the man Jesus – a oneness "without separation, division, change or mixture of their disparate natures". As the *point,* site or locus of this union (in God), the term "person" is not needed, in fact, it only confuses. Since the term *person* is not needed to affirm this union, the term *person* was obviously used for an entirely different reason. This devious reason was to attribute the life of the man Jesus to the life of God – attribute what is God's, to a man. A real disgrace.

While we can *attribute* human life and person to the Logos' *incar-*

nate human nature, we **cannot** *attribute* human life and person to the divine Logos or God. Yet the whole purpose of making the Logos a *person* and Jesus a *non-person* was to do just that – to attribute *human nature* to the divine Logos as a divine "person". The "Communication of Properties" was the last ditch to make Jesus a divine being. Yet the more divine one makes the Logos' human nature, the more Christ fades from the picture and the more Christianity deteriorates to a Jesus-cult.

The C of P was basically a product of the *God-flesh* idea of Christ – the Alexandrians. Most certainly, no Antiochene went along with this. But how is it that the views of a few can dictate what everyone else is supposed to think, understand or believe? A hard fact to face, this has always been dictated by the Church power-brokers, the politicos who hold the most power. Cyril was right in there, a frightening man of power. After swiftly getting rid of the Patriarch of Constantinople, (who the Emperor initially supported), no one has ever dared go against him. Had Jesus been understood as a human person – *"like us in every way"* – there could **never** have been any C of P. The *Communicatio* articulates the difference between understanding Jesus as a human person, and making God a *human person instead.*

This is why the "Communication of Idioms" is *literally (*and not just "idiomatically") the *authorized* genesis of Christian *anthropolatry* – the worship of a human being as God. This particular *use of language* for Christ is heavily imbedded in all Christian literature – its theology and creeds, one hears it everywhere – references to "Jesus" as if he were Almighty God. **This is what people *believe*, never realizing it is only a "*way of speaking*" and not, in fact, the truth!** Does or does not the C of P work to *deceive* people and *promote* wrong views of Christ, of God and of Jesus? **Absolutely**! At bottom, the C of P was a ruse to make it *sound* as if the man Jesus was a *divine being,* which is the very genesis of *anthropolatry* and the final nail in the coffin of the Real Christ.

So the solution, how to make Christ's dual natures *one* individual, *one* being, *one* entity, was to make God a *person(s)* and then attribute or "predicate" all the properties and attributes of both natures to this one divine person. Everybody believes this, and yet it is only an *idiom*, a way of speaking, **with no Truth in it at all.**

In conclusion: if anything blows the whistle on the whole notion of the C of P it is the fact *all the fathers* believed and affirmed that both in *nature and person, God is impassible* – could never be the subject of any created life's experiences, could not have man's changing ideas, emotions, feelings, passions, ups and downs – in

short, God could not *experience* human existence. (Unlike man, God is not subject to "*experiences*".)

THE PROBLEM OF CHRIST

Because the "problem of Christ" is endemic in the revelation of Christ, it is a problem endemic in Christianity itself. In a nutshell this is the problem: God is Infinite Uncreated Existence, whereas Man is finite created being, and the *union* of these two – Infinite and finite, Uncreated and created – does not result in *one individual being*. Thus the union or oneness of God and man does not constitute a *single being,* nor does it make two beings. So...

– **God is not an *individual being;*** nor the Trinity three individual beings. God is Infinite Existence, Uncreated Being, the Source of all created being.
– Man, however, is a **created** being.
– God's **own** (created) human nature is "one Universal" human nature, not one *particular* human being. (A universal is not quantitative, it is not a numerical or particular "one". A "numerical one" is one among many.[1])
– Because the **union** of God (Infinite) and man (finite) does not constitute one individual being, **"Christ" is not *one* individual being.**
– The **oneness** of two disparate natures does **not** constitute either ***one divine being* or *one human being*.**
– Neither God nor man has *dual natures.* Of all we know that exists, *only Christ* is (or has) dual natures.
– Christ, then, is neither **one** Uncreated being, nor **one** created being, rather, Christ *is* the eternal *oneness* of two *natures* – Infinite and finite – the *eternal oneness of the two – God **and** man.*
– Since no one can point to the Uncreated, but only to the created, how, then, can one point to the ***union*** or oneness of the Uncreated and created – point to Christ, that is?

– **So the problem** is how to think of Christ, image Christ, speak of Christ, or even point to Christ when **Christ is *not one* individual being?**

---

[1] God did not unite Itself to one among many, but created Its own human nature. For God to unite Itself to one particular man, that man would have had to exist already. Cyril's big fear was that people would think Jesus was just one out of many people that God could have chosen to unite to Itself – a view that totally negates the "Incarnation". God's Incarnation was creating Its *own* human nature, not of a particular human being. While God can unite Itself to those who already exist, they are not, however, God's *own* universal human nature. The Christian goal, of course, is to be transformed into God's *own* eternal human nature – transformed into *Christ,* that is. (The idea God has multiple human natures is absurd.)

– Christ, then, is no *individual being – divine or human* – but the inseparable oneness of Uncreated and created being, the ***unmixed*** union of divine and human natures.
– How is one to present and speak of Christ when Christ is neither one human being or one divine being?

This is the problem endemic in the Incarnation, yet a "*problem*" *that is the true mystery of "Christ"*.

A Question: "Because the man Jesus was an *individual being* and was one with God, is *he,* then, *not Christ*?"
– While Jesus was certainly one with God, he had no dual natures – nor, for that matter, does God (Logos) have dual natures. So, "*No, the singular man Jesus is not God's union or oneness with man";* he had a human nature, but no *divine nature.* So while every man is an *individual* being, Christ, however, is neither ***one*** individual *human* being nor **one** *divine* being.
– Just as Jesus, Mary, Paul (and a host of other human beings) are one with God, yet *they, themselves,* are *not* Christ. Like Paul, Jesus could have said, "*Not **I**, but Christ lives **in** me*" – a truth that does not, however, make "**me**" (be it Jesus, Paul or whoever), "*Christ"*. Christ is the true nature of *every man's* eternal oneness with God, which oneness (Christ) is ***no particular human being***.
– So the problem is that the union of God and man – **which is Christ** – does not constitute *one* single being – not a single human being or a single divine being. Thus, Christ is not a **single *individual* human being.**

The Reality of Christ was not only a "problem" for Jew and Gentile, but a problem for all the fathers, and so it remains to this day. The problem is not God or the man Jesus, the **problem is "Christ"** – neither God nor man, but a union of the two that neither makes man God, nor makes God, man. The eternal oneness of these two disparate natures is the *magnum mysterium of Christ,* indeed, there is no greater mystery on earth or in heaven than the *Real Christ.* As the *oneness of two natures,* Christ is a unique, one-of-kind Reality, a *mystery* not only for the philosophically minded, but above all, for the theologically minded. In Truth – "*Being perfect God and now perfect man, brings about the greatest of all possible novelties – **the only thing new under the sun!**"*

The fact there is no *ontological category* for the *oneness* of two disparate natures, can be regarded as the "*problem"*. The early fathers wanted to find a way to make Christ's dual natures a **single ontological being** without, however, making God a human being or making a human being, God.

The problem was to find a way to **conceive** two natures as *one,* but *one what?* One hypostasis, one nature, one being? It was to resolve this problem that the term "*person*" was invented and defined to become the *keystone* of the *proverbial party-line Christology.* This is how it went:

a) "Person" was regarded as a "*property*" of human nature – or something human nature *owned.*
b) This "property" was the *agent*, *subject* or *self* that governed its human nature.
c) So while "person" defined "who" someone is, it could not define "what" he is.
d) By transposing this same notion of *person* to God, the Trinity became three "*who's*" – three *agents*, three *subjects*, *selves* – persons "*who*" *governed* God's one divine nature, yet were not Its true nature or essence.
e) This way God (Logos) became the *one divine person (owner) of two disparate natures,* and thus it could be said – Christ is the divine *Person* of the Logos (God) with **two natures.** (Keep in mind, the Logos (God) is the divine *person* and **not** the man Jesus.)

So this is how the problem of Christ's dual natures was resolved – by making Christ *one ontological divine person,* making God (Logos) one ontological being! (The term "ontological" refers to the reality of "being".) This resolution, however, assumes a "person" is an *individual being,* yet God as three persons is not three individual beings. **So any notion of *person* premised on "individual being" can never refer to the Trinity. Since the Trinity is *not* three individual beings, God is *not* three "*persons*".** If "*person*" is not reference to a particular *individual being,* then it references no being at all. Those who hold the Trinity is three "*persons*" can only regard the Trinity as three individual beings (*tri-theism.*) God, however, transcends all categories of "ontological being". Not only did making God a person(s) *not* solve the problem, but ever since, has promoted totally wrong views and understandings of both the Trinity and Christ. That the term "person" ("*who*" someone is) was ever applied to the Trinity, is a Christian disaster. God is not even ***a*** Being, much less three Beings – three "who's" or three individual persons. As the Source of all being, God (Trinity) is Infinite Existence.

Strictly speaking, Christ is not the "union" of two different natures, but a "oneness" of the two – just as Chalcedon said, "no separation or division possible". So Christ is more than putting one-and-one together – such that they can be divided into two discrete *beings.* Rather, Christ is the inscrutable "oneness" of Man and God **in** God's one divine essence or nature. Obviously, Christ is not the revelation of God, but the specific revelation of ***man*** whose whole purpose in life is to *become* eternally one with and in God. The revelation of Christ was *never* that man ***becomes*** God or that God ***becomes*** man – which amounts to the same thing. (The Uncreated can never *become* what it is *not.*) The revelation of Christ reveals that God destined man to become **more** than he is now – and what is this **more**? This ***more*** is everything we know and call *"Christ".*

To have an honest grasp of this "problem", is to understand all the centuries of dissensions, accusations, synods and councils that went into developing a Christology that would both solve this problem and be true to Christ. There was never a question of Christ as man's eternal oneness with God, the problem was how to present this, make it understandable when it neither pointed just to God nor just to man. While Jesus was an earthly example of someone who was one with God, yet Christ is **neither one individual *human* being nor one individual *divine* being**. In simple terms – Christ is beyond any and every individual human being. As **more** than Man, yet **less** than God, Christ is the oneness of the two.

Just as the term "God" is **not** a *name* to designate *who* someone is, so too, the word "Christ" is not a proper noun that designates *who* someone is. Christ is not the union of two "who's", but the union of two "what's" – *what* God is and *what* man is. The term "Christ" is no mere *linguistic* problem, but the word for a Reality the mind may never be able to grasp. Throw away all names and titles, the reference ("Christ") is solely to the *mystery of God eternally united to man.* Because no one man is Christ and no one of the Trinity is Christ, the term was *never used for God* ***or*** *man,* but solely to express the Truth of the oneness of God ***and*** man. "Christ", then, is not just a handy word for this oneness, but, on the contrary, points up the greatest of great Realities – man's eternal life in God.

We know the word "Christ" (or "*anointed")* was an honorific Jewish title or someone specially appointed by God for a particular mission. For neither Jesus or his Apostles, however, did this term mean "God" or "Yahweh". (Indeed, even used in its most Christian sense, "Christ" is not another term or title for God.) For Jesus' followers, "*christos*" referred to their belief Jesus was the promised Messiah, his mission being purely *earthly*. As regards immortality, Jews believed God alone was their *eternal* "savior" – only God could grant them *eter-*

nal life. In like fashion, Paul would regard Jesus not only as an *earthly messiah* or savior, but *unlike* the Jews, would regard *Jesus* as the "medium" for God's saving man. So putting together the Jewish belief only *God* saved man, and Paul's belief *Jesus* saved man, it seems the conclusion was that "Jesus" had to be God because only God saves man.

Had the fathers believed Jesus was God, however, they would have had no problem with people worshiping Jesus as God. As it happened, however, they were not *polytheists*, but *Monotheists* – nothing created is God. All believed only God could save man, but along with Paul, believed God *used* the man Jesus as God's "instrument" for doing so. Since the messiah was God's *anointed* emissary for this mission, Jesus was called "the Christ" – or "*Jesus the Christ*". So "Jesus Christ" was solely a reference to *a man* sent by God to save man, and **any worship of "*Jesus Christ*" – the man sent by God to save man – is *not* the worship of God,** but worship of *a man* sent by God**.** While Jesus can certainly be revered, yet as a man sent by God – *christos,* messiah or savior – this does not make him God. The fathers, of course, never believed any human being was God. So how did it ever happen that *Jesus Christ* ever became understood as a reference to God?

The answer to this question was all part and parcel of the *development* of "Christology" – the theology of Christ starting with Paul and the fathers. How to have a *right* understanding of Christ was the major concern of the early centuries. The term "Christ" had to mean **more** than just a man (messiah or savior) sent to save man. And, indeed, because the revelation of Christ is so much *more,* Christ is a problem. Needless to say, the idea of god sending a man to be murdered so he could forgive Adam's sin, can only be put down as pure myth – such a "god" is the definition of an "*ogre*". As already noted, many of the fathers and their successors believed Christ would have "come" or been revealed had man *never sinned.*

The fathers based their whole understanding of "Christ" on the *Incarnation* – "*God became man that man might become God*", "*the Incarnation was the deification of man*", "*salvation is transformation into Christ*" – and so on. For Paul and the fathers, "Christ" was the revelation of God's "plan" for mankind. The Incarnation was not the meaningless revelation that only *one* individual man was one with God – what would be the point of such a revelation? Christ as "*universal man*" did not mean only one man, rather, "Christ" expressed a great Truth revealed for the whole of mankind. With Irenaeus, all believed the man Jesus was "God's instrument" for revealing the *eternal Christ.* So as a term to designate the oneness of God and man, "Christ" was not the name of any *one* particular individual. "*For Christ did not become a mere man, nor is it orthodox to say that he assumed a* **particular** *man, but rather, that He (God) assumed man-in-general, or the whole human nature".* (Theodore the Studite, 759 – 826.) This is the belief and understanding of "*Christ*" espoused by all the fathers.

While intellectually and spiritually, the fathers had no problem understanding the truth and reality of Christ, it was how to present this mystery to others **that** was the problem. How to get this profound understanding of Christ across to the "simple folk" remains, to this day, the biggest problem in all of Christianity. As said, had the fathers thought the man Jesus was God, they would have had no problem with people worshipping Jesus Christ as God. It was the fear that people did, in fact, worship Jesus as God that was the *big concern.* It seems from the beginning Christians were accused of *anthropolatry* – worshipping the man "*Jesus Christ*" as God. As to why anyone would worship Jesus as God, it could only be **because they did not honestly** ***know God.*** No one who knows God could ever think God was a human being – or anything created, for that matter. And as for the human mind needing some *image*, this is the whole genesis of "polytheism".

It was to resolve this "problem of Christ" the fathers sought some way to present "Christ" as not just another human being nor as Almighty God. As the Incarnation of God's *own* humanity, Christ was at once God **and** man. Anyone who thinks this is easy to grasp, however, had better think again. Were it easy to understand, there could never *be* any "Christian *anthropolatry*" – that insidious plague of Christianity. Indeed, if the truth of Christ was easy to grasp, there would be no need for *Christ* to be "*revealed*". No *vision* of *Jesus* is the "revelation" of Christ – in fact, no *image* in the mind is the true nature of *any authentic* "*revelation*" from God. It is *because* ultimate Truth is *beyond* what the mind can grasp, that Truth can only be *revealed.* All the mind can grasp is what's *in* it already.

So it is one thing to *know* and *understand* Christ as the oneness of God and man, but quite another for the mind to be left with **no image of this union or oneness** to focus on. This is why, to the human mind, Christ is a mystery – because it cannot grasp or hold on to Christ as if Christ was some particular individual *being* or a mere mental image. What the mind can hold on to, of course, is the image of Jesus – the *example* of one who knew first hand, *his own personal* oneness with God. But if Jesus is the *earthly* icon of someone "who" was one with God, still, the fathers believed his human nature was only "deified" or transformed *after* his death – which means he is only the image of Christ on *earth*, but not the image of the *eternal* Christ in God. Like Jesus, every man is created in the image of Christ – the image all are to *become*. And just as Jesus ultimately *became* that of which, on this earth, he was but an image, so too it goes for every human being. (It goes without saying, the idea people are to *become* the man Jesus, is absurd.) But if Jesus was the image of Christ in this world, he was neither the image of God or the image of the "eternal" Christ in God. The eternal Christ refuses to be an image because **Christ is not one individual *being*** – just try to make an "image" of the **oneness or union** of God and man and the mind is left blank. This union or oneness is incapable of being *seen* or becoming a mental image. So if one wanted to understand the fathers' problem, he need only try to present and explain to others **an image-less Christ**! Anybody who tries this will immediately understand the "problem of Christ".[2]

The reason Christ cannot be identified as either a single divine being or a single human being is because neither God nor man has *two natures*. Even though the term "Christ" always referred to the "oneness" of the natures, yet early on it seems, the catechetical and liturgical use of the word "*Christ*" referred to God as the ***divine*** *nature* of Christ, while the name "Jesus" referred to the ***human*** *nature* of Christ. Thus putting the two together – "*Jesus* and *Christ*" – the reference was to man *and* God. Yet referring to Jesus as *"the Christ"* ("Jesus-the-Christ") changes the meaning of "Christ" to refer to one particular individual human being – the man Jesus, of course. But are prayers and adoration addressed to "*Jesus Christ*" addressed to God, to the man Jesus, or to the union of two natures – Christ? Can we say the terms *God, Christ, Jesus,* all mean the same thing and can be used interchangeably? That they can, seems to be the proverbial assumption, an assumption, however, that totally skews a true understanding of Christianity. If prayers and adoration addressed to "*Jesus Christ*" are addressed to *God, Jesus, and Christ* without differentiation, this is not a mere *linguistic* problem, this is a matter of a *true* or *false* teaching. But who knows what people think they are praying to or worshiping? We can probably say for certain they are *not* praying to the dual natures of

---

[2] The *Iconoclastic controversy* (725 – 843) banned the "veneration" of Christian icons as "idolatrous". It was not that people worshiped some material icon as God, rather, they took the *one* represented – the man Jesus – as God. Since Christ's *divine* nature is God, and God could not be depicted, then icons of Jesus (as Christ) had to be banned. It is one thing, however, to ban man's art-work, but who can ban the human *mind from forming images?* There is really no *difference*. The defense was that the *incarnate* Christ – the man Jesus – could, in fact, be circumscribed and therefore, symbolically depicted. **Obviously, the *iconoclastic controversy* merely reflects the "*problem of Christ*" as a single discrete "being"**. Interestingly, however, the one exception made by the Iconoclasts was veneration of the *Eucharist*, this was the only "Christ" man could venerate – the *image-less* eternal Christ.

Christ! The problem with the proverbial reference to "Jesus Christ" is that it neither points to Almighty God nor to Christ. Instead it *falsely* points to the individual man Jesus as if he was God and Christ.

To think of Christ as totally divine is to think Christ has one divine nature – the definition of "*Monophysitism*". And to think the *divine* Christ or Logos (God) is *one individual being* is "*Tri-theism*". (God cannot be circumscribed as an "individual", nor the Trinity as three individual beings.) While the *divine nature* of Christ is God, the *human nature* of Christ is *not* God. Not only is the man Jesus not God, but Jesus is not Christ – because no human being has *dual natures*. Even God (the Logos) is not Christ – because God also has no *dual natures*. Of himself, no man is Christ, nor of Itself, is God, Christ. In short, Christ is not *who* God is or *who* Jesus is. As Chalcedon affirms, Christ is not the union of two *"who's"*, but two "*what's*" – *what* God is and *what* man is, their union being eternally one ***in*** God.

So the problem was how to answer the question "***Who*** *is Christ*?" Since everyone knows "who" Jesus is, and everyone knows God is *not* "who" any human being is, how, then, is one to answer the question "***Who*** *is Christ?*" Obviously, merely asking "*who*?" implies the answer must be some *particular individual being or* **person**. Yet, since God is not an individual being or person and Jesus **is**, then the only understandable answer is – "Jesus is *who* Christ is" which, for most people, is the end of the subject. But if "*Christ*" is a reference to *who* the *person* Jesus is, this is not a reference to *who* God is. We know, of course, how this problem was solved. By making God "three persons" it could be said "*God* is **who** Christ is". So the *person* Jesus is not "who" Christ is, rather *God is* ***who*** *Christ is.* **Without making God a *person,* however, the question "*Who is Christ?*" has no answer at all – none!** Obviously, how to answer the question "***Who*** *is Christ*?" has always been a problem for Christianity – even to this day. Because, in truth, God is no *person* – no *who* or three *who's* – the only way to solve it is to admit Christ is ***not*** a "**who**", but a "**what**" **– the eternal oneness of *what* God is and *what* man is**.

Nothing so attests to this "problem of Christ" as the party-line statement "*Christ is God*", or "*Jesus is God*" – neither of which are true. Christ is neither God nor man, but their eternal oneness. As pointed out, the union of God and man does *not* make *one individual being,* and to think it does, is either *Monophysitism* or *tri-theism.* So how, then, is the mind to grasp this union or *oneness* when it can have no "image" of it? Strictly speaking, it cannot. That no one can point to Christ or even be *one with* Christ tells us why man can only be *transformed into Christ – Christ being every man's eternal oneness with*

God, and not just *one particular individual created human being.*[3]

With the inability to point to Christ, people simply take Christ as the single person Jesus, thinking, of course, he alone is Christ. That God went to all the trouble to reveal that only **one** human being could ever be eternally one with Itself, is an idea that defeats the whole purpose and truth of the Incarnation – no father believed this. God never created any "particular" human nature for Itself **because there is no such thing as a "particular" human nature!** (*"What is common to all is proper to none".)* It is because the oneness of two disparate natures does not meet the mental demand of Christ as one ***visible ontological being*** that the fathers had to find a way to make Christ *one,* if not one *being*, then one *nature*, one *hypostasis,* one *prosopon* – **one** *what?* Well, we know exactly what they did.

The term "*person*" is totally a Christian invention, invented to serve one purpose and one purpose alone. Though initially defined as a "property" of nature ("*persona*" or "*person"),* it was used to refer to the Trinity as **three particular individuals,** thus, the Trinity's triune distinctions or *hypostases* became three individual "ones" or *persons*. By making the Trinity "persons", it could then be said the Logos (God) was the **one individual divine *person "who" was Christ.*** Thus we have *Christ as two natures* ***in*** the *one divine person of the Logos.*

Of all the theological problems – and solutions – this is the worst. Making God a person(s) only created a bigger problem. Since everyone regards a *person* or "*who"* someone is as an *individual being,* then the Trinity, as three "who's" is three discrete *individual beings* – **tri-*theism.*** If, on the other hand, person is ***not*** an *individual* **being**, then Christ (*as a divine person)* is ***not*** one *individual being* or entity. So either way, making God a divine *person(s)* has never worked – the Trinity is neither three beings, one being, nor Christ.

Yet this is how the party-line understanding of Christ is presented – God (Logos) is the divine *person* of Christ taken to be *one individual being.* But if one of the Trinity is ***not*** an **individual being, then "who" is?** The *only individual being*, of course, is the *human person* Jesus. In fact, it is because God as a person is **not an individual being** that Jesus had to be removed from the list of *human persons* – lest this make Christ the union of two persons and not two natures.

It is defining Christ as two natures *in one divine **person*** that threw both the truth of the Trinity and Christ off track. The Logos is not *one individual being*, yet, how is one to think of a *person* that is *not* an individual being? If Christ is **one being** (which is how Christ is always

[3] That man can never be *united* to Christ, see Chapter 28, "*Eucharist"*.

spoken of) then Christ as one being would be either God or man as one being – both wrong views. This, however, is how most Christians understand Christ and what Christian theology leads them to think – no doubt *intends* them to think. This is how ***"person",* used to define Christ as a single being,** ends up promoting *tri-theism* (three beings) and *Monophysitism* (one nature) and *anthropolatry* (God, a human being) – all *wrong* views of the Trinity and Christ – and even, a wrong view of the man Jesus (regarded as *no* human person.)

This, at least, is how it came to be that when people think of Christ they think of ***a single person as a single being,*** which *single being*, of course, they can only regard as the man Jesus. It is *because* no one has a clue how God could be an **individual person but *not* an individual being,** that Jesus is mistaken for a divine *person* – for God. Although it is tempting to think the use of *person* was just an attempt to deify the man Jesus, this is not the case. It was how to "simplify" Christ in order to present Christ's dual natures as a *single divine being* – this was the problem to be solved. **Thus everyone can grasp a "*who*" as some individual *person,* but who can grasp a "*what*", i.e., the oneness of Christ's dual natures?** "Simple folk" could never grasp this latter understanding of Christ.

The fathers were fully aware that people not only regarded the man Jesus as *Christ*, but took "*Christ*" to be God. The thinking was this: because "*Jesus is Christ*" and *Christ is God in person,* **therefore**, "*Jesus is God*" – absolute *anthropolatry.* Offhand we would think the simplest way to deal with this anthropolatric problem would be to make it perfectly clear to people that no human being is God, that God's human nature was not divine, and that the word "*Christ*" means the *eternal union* of God's divine nature and man's human nature – *simple as that.* But no, instead of continually reminding people of this **Truth**, centuries of theology were spent determined to justify the worship of God as "*Jesus Christ*" – literally, justify *anthropolatry,* whereas "Jesus Christ" is not even a reference to God. Neither Jesus or Christ is Almighty God. *Christ is solely Almighty God's oneness with man.*

Theology has gone to all possible lengths to justify the proverbial party-line presentation of Christianity as "*Jesus Christ is God*". But what intelligent scholars and theologians do about this "problem of Christ", however, is to ignore it. They go right ahead speaking of the human being Jesus (or *Jesus Christ*) as if he was a *divine being,* one of the Trinity – for such, at least, is the traditional language. Of course it is not orthodox, not what the fathers taught, not what Chalcedon said, and yet, they consistently get away with it and nobody objects, everybody believes them – and no doubt they believe it themselves. This is false teaching for which the only polite term is "*Monophysitism*" – or worse, "*anthropolatry*".

Perhaps all this really attests to, is the human mind's discomfort with the idea of *dual natures* – the inseparable oneness of two. The mind tends to reduce this duality to a single individual thing or being. This is why, when speaking of "Christ", people can only think of one single individual person, the individual man Jesus – what other *individual person* is there to think of? Though God (*Infinite* Being) is ***not a being,*** yet God's *own human nature* is, indeed, "created being". By themselves, however, neither God nor man **is** Christ – only the oneness of the two is Christ. But since no one can see or point to this *union* (a duality), the mind is satisfied to focus on the *one being it knows* – a *human* being.

Paul, John and all the fathers, had their own Christologies to explain this "problem" (or *mystery)* of Christ, and all the early synods and Councils were called to resolve it. It could be said the development of all "doctrine" is simply the mind's attempt to grasp the *mystery* that can never be *intellectually* resolved. The reality and truth of Christ is beyond the rational mind to pin-point or ever get hold of. This is why Christianity is the most mystical of man's religions – because **Christ can only be *revealed* and never *mentally* grasped or *imaged.*** Also, since Christ is *what* man is to *become*, until this is a *fait accompli*, the Truth of Christ can never be fully known.

The bottom line is that the human mind cannot *conceive* or grasp the reality of the "*oneness*" of two disparate natures. It will either make these natures "one" or sandwich the two together. **It is because the *oneness* of the natures neither constitutes a numerical "one" nor a numerical "two", that the mind is at a loss.** To collapse everything into *one something* seems to be the way the mind works. The philosophers had this same problem – the mental necessity of reducing the multiple to some ultimate "one", some individual thing or numerical one – be it divine, a genus or species. But what is responsible for this mental demand? The culprit, of course, is the senses. The senses are only capable of apprehending individual "ones", of perceiving only discrete material "things"; they are incapable of apprehending any *oneness* – more especially in this case, *the dual natures of Christ.*

Since all knowledge enters through the senses, the mind is prone to consider everything accordingly – as sensible *singular* things. Thus the mind ponders how, despite this multiplicity, things could be boiled down to one something – one category, one essence, one being. It is due to this obsession with "one" – thanks to the senses – the mind has never been able to grant any true reality to *oneness* – because *oneness* is not a "thing", not some discrete individual being. In fact, the mind tends to judge *oneness* to be *no thing,* no individual one, no discrete being – pretty much "nothing". It is because the mind cannot grasp the truth of *oneness* that it remains a complete mystery to the mind – and probably always will be. As said, to the mind, *oneness* has no *concrete reality, no sensory reality*, and yet, ***oneness* is the greatest of great realities, indeed, it is the whole mystery of the eternal Christ *in* the Trinity.**

For the moment, then, putting aside the various attempts to resolve this "problem of Christ", we need to ponder why this need arose in the first place. For one thing, given the mind-set of the earliest Christian converts, many born and raised in a polytheistic belief system, Christianity brought together the philosophers' Transcendent *One* whose *incarnation* as a human being gave them a God that incorporated the best of their mythical deities. Thus "Christ" united the Transcendent and the human to fulfill the need of a polytheistic mind-set, which is to have a god to worship. For the fathers, of course, this presented the problem of *anthropolatry.* It was not only Jews that railed against this, but the educated Gentiles scoffed at it as a piece of paganism.

For Paul and the fathers, of course, Jesus was the "**way**" God revealed Christ to mankind, he was the "model" and "exemplar" whose spiritual life of oneness with God all are called to recapitulate. Thus, if the iconic figure of the man Jesus does not point to Christ, or is not the medium of revealing Christ to man, then forget him. As a particular human being or person, Jesus himself is not God's eternal oneness with mankind. (As said, man's transformation into Christ is *not* transformation into the man Jesus!) It is because the fathers knew all this, we question their effort to find some way to *present Christ* as a single ontological being. Seemingly, this was to find some way to justify the "simple folk's" understanding (or worshiping) the man Jesus as the one and only Christ. For these people, because Jesus was an individual ontological being, so too was Christ – Christ being the one ontological being of the man Jesus, no difference whatsoever.

But does Jesus' union with God make him *one being with dual natures?* While there is no question Jesus was an ontological being, but is God an ontological being? The simple answer is "No". Were the answer "Yes", would this make the union of two disparate natures one ontological being? If it does, then this is a Monophysitic view of Christ (one nature.) As said, the whole problem can be traced to the mind's need to focus on some "being" or "image" as the object of its prayers, love, worship – indeed, its deepest desire to know. And we are not just referring to polytheists or to Christians, but to all man's anthropomorphic ideas of God. The mind all but has to make God into the image-of-man. The need for someone to worship, however, is not merely a prerogative of man's religions, but society as a whole. Society is full of hero worshipers, people constantly chasing after someone to cage, follow and glorify. This is a human phenomenon, a fact of life, and by no means just a prerogative of people-of-religion.

The mind's need for some *form* of an image brings us back to its sensory apparatus. We are all familiar with the philosophical dictum "all knowledge begins in the senses". All objects of the senses being concrete material "things", their images are stored in the mind as its database. The intellect depends on this data to formulate ideas, concepts, or reasoning – basically all intellectual functioning. To *reason* to the existence of something *not* in this database, is not only possible, but innovative. The point is – the mind not only requires its database, but even depends on it for something to be believable, or even possible. Thus "man believes because he sees" and tends *not* to believe what he cannot see or what is not, first of all, in his database.

So as the pre-school of the intellect, the senses only perceive *individual* material things – multiplicity a plethora of "*ones*". Since the intellect bases all its knowledge on these perceived individual realities, it can never "make sense" of anything the senses cannot perceive. The point is that because the senses can only perceive *individual things,* the human mind cannot grasp the *ultimate truth and reality* of *eternal* "*oneness*" – in this case, *the eternal oneness of God and man.* If the tendency is not for the mind to make everything an absolute "One", then it makes the *union* of any two "things" the union of two separable *ones* or two discrete *beings*. But since God is not **a** being (or three beings), man's union with God is not a union of two discrete "beings" or entities.

Given this "problem of Christ" is why, to resolve it, some of the fathers thought it important to ***ground*** the ***unity*** of Christ ***in*** the "*one*" divine hypostasis (or person) of the Logos (God.) As said, the whole notion of "person" was invented to serve this very purpose – to make Christ "one something". Since "*person"* is not a reference to "being" (existence and essence) but solely to "*who*" an *individual being is,* this provided an individual "*who*" people could consider, think about, focus on, point to, or image. And "*who*" is this "one person" people know to focus on? It could only be the historical man Jesus – *who* else is there to see, image, focus on, or even think about? Certainly no one is thinking about the Logos' invisible, unknowable *divine person* that is *not an individual being* and can never be seen. People focus on the *only person* they know that they can see and verify for themselves –

Jesus. If they *mistakenly* think he is a divine person or a divine being, well, we can always blame this on the *Communication of Properties*. The true Christ, however, can never be "imaged", but then, no "mental" image is the *truth* of anything anyway. For Truth, no one can depend on their mental images or senses for anything.

All this is pointing out is why, in order to believe something, the mind requires some sensory image, something it can focus on, even if just a *symbol* or *concretized* attribute of something – there are all kinds of possibilities. So when it comes to the mind's need, not just to believe or understand something, but its need to "see to believe", this explains the need for some concretized symbol, icon, image – or whatever. Even when God is revealed, the mind will conjure up and associate all kinds of different mental images (or linguistic metaphors) to express this revelation. But even when "concretized", these images – a stone, the sun, figure of man, or even a snake – all represent God in some way. What man worships, of course, is not some concrete sensory thing or mental image, but rather, the mystery it represents, the mystery that *transcends* any material object of vision and every possible mental *image*.

When it comes to Christianity, the human mind did not change in this matter. While everyone knows God transcends all man's material and mental images of God, yet **Christ was *not* a revelation of God, but the revelation of Man – God's eternal oneness with Man.** Thus the *icon* of this oneness of God-and-man was focused on Man, more especially the man Jesus, a focus utterly satisfying to the mind's need for an image of this *mystery*. We might add that the mind's need for some image is better known to God than it is to man himself. Indeed, one wonders *how* God could have revealed *"Christ"* without *using* an earthly concrete human being to do so. It is not for nothing (or no reason) God gave man an icon (Jesus) as representative of everyman's eternal oneness with God. This is why Christianity is **not** an iconoclastic religion, its stress is on Man, on human nature, on all man means to God and God's eternal plan for man. Even though Judaism has the same referendum on man and human nature, it missed out on man's *eternal oneness with God,* which is all Christianity is really about – "Christ", that is.

So the icon of the man Jesus is not a problem, the problem is "who" this man *was*. Is Jesus an icon of Almighty God or just the icon of one particular man? Although in neither case is this an icon of an *imageless* "Christ", yet if this icon of Jesus does not uplift one to the real mystery of **Christ**, then he can find some other icon that will uplift him to his eternal oneness with God – the *Eucharist*, perhaps. Christianity has no apologies for its iconic figure of the man Jesus any more than man can apologize for the way his mind works. The meaning and reality of all images, after all, transcends the mind's figurative representations of this Reality. In fact, after his own *earthly* oneness with God, what Jesus *became* with his glorification is *what* every human being is to become – Christ.

Like nothing else in creation, Christ as the *oneness* of God and man constitutes an ***ontological genre of its own.*** As man's ultimate reality, Christ is a Reality no one can grasp intellectually or imagine ahead of time. As the oneness of two dimensions of existence – divine and human – Christ **is** the Line uniting the two. The best definition of the oneness of Christ is Chalcedon's definition of "union" – "*without confusion, without change, without division, without separation, the difference of the natures being by no means removed because of the union*". Thus no mixture, no half-and-half, no absorption, no over–shadowing, no "one being" and no "two beings", ***Christ's oneness is literally numberless –*** not one, not two, not many – but a "oneness" known only to God. So while God is *infinite being* (not **a** being) and *man is* a microcosm of creation, Christ is "*universal being*" – the *summation* of all *being* **in** God.

Third Man

Use of the term "*person"* to *ground* the oneness of Christ's dual natures *in God* is reminiscent of what is called the *"Third Man*" in philosophy. This is how it would go: since God as a "divine person" is *impassible* (can't experience anything), and since (theologically speaking) Jesus was *no "human person"*, then "***who"*** really experienced human existence? If it is not the person of God and not the person of the man Jesus, then it can only be some *other person* – some "*Third Man*".

In philosophy "*the third man*" was a term or phrase to point out some fallacy or other. I do not recall if Plato spoke of a "third man" or if he was only accused of it, but Aristotle used it to point out the fallacy of Plato's idea that all forms (or souls) "participate" in a divine Form – which Aristotle debunked. Thus Aristotle said, *"If man participates in divine Form, then neither the form nor some* ***particular*** *man can be, by participation,* ***in*** *the Form, therefore it must be a "****third man****"*. In other words, if a particular form or soul (man) "participates" in a "divine Form" (God), then a "particular form" (soul) is neither God nor some particular man, but must be some "third man" – *one that is neither a* ***particular man nor God.*** Using this same idea, we might say that since Christ is not *just* God nor "*some particular man"*, then Christ is a

Third Man. So besides Christ being "Universal Man", Christ is also an unspecified "*Third Man*".[4] We might also think of this "*third man*" (Christ) as the *bridge* uniting God and man.

Aristotle also said if there is anything eternal about man, it could only be a "*third soul*". He also posited human nature as some kind of "*third*" substance – matter is one substance, the soul is another substance, and the two together is a *third* substance – which alone is *true being*. Not only do several other philosophers mention the "third man" fallacy, but it seems the number "three" had some relevance for the philosophers, from the constitution of the universe to man as a composite of three – body, soul, spirit – having three faculties of the soul and so on. Philo of Alexandria also speaks of true being as a union of opposites (a contradiction) and posits this union as a "whole" – something over and above the opposites, some "***third***" thing that constitutes real being. Then again, he says three things are required to know God – 1. God, 2. The breath of God, 3. Man's "*in-breathing*" God's breath – "*for*", he says, "*of itself the mind could never know God unless God himself had drawn it up to himself*". Thus, he says "*the* **third** (man) *to reach perfection (in-breathing) is the "Man of Practice" who received as his special reward the vision of God"*.

For Maximus the Confessor, to say Christ is two natures *in* one divine person, posits a "third" "something". He says while Christ is identified as two *what's* (natures), yet Christ cannot be reduced to them – the Logos (God) as the personal hypostasis "*cannot be reduced to the sum of Its natures*". In other words, two natures do not add up to one person and person cannot be reduced to the sum of two natures. He put it this way, "*Christ is a Whole, and his dual natures, the parts*". This holistic view eliminates the concern of what belongs to which nature, all that is relevant is the *Wholeness*, the *Oneness* of Christ.

While how to define Christ as "one being" was the *ontological* problem the fathers tackled, this "problem" has no resolution. The mystery of Christ encompasses not only the whole mystery of man and God, but the mystery of their eternal oneness. The saying "*man was created to be more than he is now*" means there is an ontological transformation of what man is *now* to what he *will be or become* – Christ. This transformation does not *replace* man's initial ontological reality, but goes beyond it to the destined end for which it was created – whatever the "ontological reality" of Christ may be. There is no need to ground the oneness of two natures **in** any "being" or individual person,

---

[4] For more on the "Third Man" – or how one gets from a "universal" to a "particular" – see Appendix I, "*Christian Ontology*".

it is grounded **in** God (the Logos according to the fathers), by which and through which, the two natures (God and man) are eternally united. No need to make the Trinity three individual *beings* or *persons*, for such an understanding is contrary to the revelation of the Trinity.

Perhaps we can now understand what the fathers were up against and understand centuries of their disagreements – accusing and anathematizing each other's views of Christ. Nothing could be more naive than to think the True Christ is not a problem, not only "back then", but, obviously, to this day. The Christian *party-line,* however, goes right on spreading its totally misleading understanding of Christ – presenting Christ as a single being – when, in truth, the union of God and man does not constitute a single being. While every man is a single being, yet his oneness with God does not make this *oneness* (Christ) a single being – or "*himself*". Whether "man" as a created being is understood universally or singly makes no difference, for either way, Christ is not "one being". Also, since how it went for Jesus in this world and in the next (in God) is how it will go for every human being. It makes no difference whether the man Jesus or the eternal Christ is regarded as "Universal Man", for in either case, the meaning is "*universal*" and not *particular*.

So where did all the centuries of dissensions end up? What came of all this? Based on the ensuing theology we have today, it is the Christian's view and understanding of Christ that "Jesus is God!" That it would all end up as *anthropolatry* – the worship of a man as God – can only tell us something went very, very wrong. If one can understand, however, Christ is not a single being, he will have put his finger on the most enduring problem in all the Christologies down the centuries. This is virtually the "Christ problem" inherent in the Incarnation itself. Because the divine Logos is not a "being" (only Its incarnate humanity is a being), Christ can never be a single being. Though Christ is always and forever God's oneness with **man**, still, because Christ is not *just* a man (**or a human being**) Christ is not a single "being". It is the *oneness* of the two natures, divine and human *that is the true Christ.* Should all this boggle the mind, then one is that much closer to understanding the real Christ.

A Solution

Perhaps the only solution to the quandary of how to understand the dual natures of Christ as "**one**", is the ***Eucharist.*** (One wonders why the fathers did not think of this in the first place)! The Eucharist is the only *image* the mind can have of the *one* eternal *Christ*. To grasp the *oneness* of Christ, there exists no other reality, theology or icon that embodies the true mystery of Christ other than the Eucharist. The entire mystery of Christ is bound up in It – One Eucharist = One Christ. And please note, no one refers to the Eucharist as "*who*" someone is, the reference is always to "*what*" it is – to Christ – and not "who" it is. As one author notes: "*The* ***truth*** *encapsulated in the statement of Gregory Nazianzius that in Christ we have two 'what's', but not two 'who's' or 'I's* – namely persons – *seems to have escaped attention".* The Eucharist perfectly encapsulates the *oneness* of "*what"* Christ is and *what* man *will be.* For Irenaeus, the Eucharist was the only basis for a true understanding of Christ – ***"Our way of thinking is attuned to the Eucharist, and the Eucharist in turn confirms our way of thinking".*** **So** if one's whole understanding of Christ is bound up in the Eucharist, he will know the Real Christ.

Conclusion

According to the proverbial presentation of Christianity, only the man Jesus is Christ, he alone was God's "incarnation" – God in the flesh and in-*person,* this is the thinking:

1. Thus, because God creates every human being One-on-one, then every human being is a "numerical one".
2. In the incarnation, God created *only one* human being *eternally* one with Itself, and *only* this one individual was the man Jesus.
3. Jesus, then, is the only human being that can ever be eternally one with God and no one else – ever. Because only Jesus is God's incarnate human nature, **only** he is Christ.
4. Since God is a divine "person" and Jesus was *no* human person, then Jesus is God-in-person.

This is the theological premise of the proverbial party-line – in force now for over 1500 years. At first glance this seems to be fairly reasonable – makes sense to most Christians at least. So what is objectionable? If one starts with a *wrong premise* he ends with a *wrong conclusion.* As Athanasius says, *"Just as the Trinity is a numerical unity in one essence, so too, man is a numerical unity in one essence".* So too Aristotle – "*It is the essence of human nature to be "one"*, be a "*numerical* one" – every *individual* having the same one essence or nature. There is no such thing as a "particular" human nature – "*what is common to all is particular to none".* So just as the essence of God's divine nature is One and not "three ones", **so too, the essence of man's human nature is "one" and not many "ones".** That God creates every human being One-on-one does not mean "**different ones**". As said, "person" alone differentiates "individuals" – and God creates **no** persons.

1. It is a fallacy, then, to think God united Itself to *one particular human nature when* ***there is no such thing as a "particular" human nature!*** That God could unite Itself with a "*particular*" human being *prior* to the existence of a *particular* human being, makes no sense. In fact, one of Cyril's big fears was that people would think the Incarnation was God uniting Itself to **some *already existing* human being – some *particular* human being, that is.** He called this union an "adoption" which was *not* the Incarnation.

2. Any reference to "*Jesus' human nature"* is reference to a particular **person – to "whose" human nature it belonged to.** Because Jesus' human nature was no different than that of any human being, reference to ***his*** human nature is reference to Jesus as the ***person,*** the owner or agent of *his* personal humanity. The orthodox teaching, however, is that in the Incarnation **God did not create any *person.***

3. The human nature God created as Its *own* can *never* be the human nature of any *particular* human being or *person.* This means **God's *own* human nature** was not that of Jesus any more than it was that of Mary, Moses, or any *particular* human person.

4. To think, then, God created *only Jesus' human nature* one with Itself, **is clearly false**.

Since Jesus was the human *medium* God used to reveal *Christ,* one way to understand *Christ* is that **Jesus was the *human "person"* of *God's own human nature* –** while on this earth, at least. Unfortunately, orthodoxy holds Jesus was *not a human person* – so there goes that understanding of Christ. In truth, **Christ is no man's particular human nature or person. Christ is solely *God's one and only universal personless human nature.*** [5]

[5] For the "person-less Christ", see Chapter 21, "*Hypostatic Union*".

SUMMARY SO FAR

To trace the development of Christianity's earliest understanding of the Trinity and Christ, two contrasting features stand out. One is the ease with which the Trinity came to light almost as if a foregone conclusion. While neither Jesus nor the Apostles knew any Trinity, yet as soon as the Judaic view of God touched ground in the Gentile world, there was the Trinity all but plain as day. There were no disputes over the Trinity, all believed the Logos was God, the Spirit was God, and the Transcendent (Father) was God.

Although prior to any formal statement of God-as-Trinity (Nicaea) there was no clear cut distinction between Logos and Spirit, still, the earliest writings contain references to both Logos and Spirit, each used in their own specific contexts. So even before there was any "formal" declaration of the Trinity, the fathers had an intuitive grasp of God's distinct, immanent *"modus operandi"*. The Trinity was not some idea the fathers put together or "decided" on, but on the contrary, it emerged as an inherent necessity for a true understanding of Christ – for indeed, outside the Trinity there is *no Christ at all.*

But if there was no dispute regarding the Trinity, this is in sharp contrast when it comes to a *right understanding* of the true nature of Christ. Indeed, Christ would become *the* great problem, a problem that remains to this day.

Who was the "son"?

It could be said *Modalism* merely spearheaded the issue of "*who is the 'son of God'?*" Can we say the Trinity is a "father-Son" *ad intra* (*before* the incarnation) or only a "father-Son" *ad extra* (*after* the incarnation)? It seems prior to this dispute, for the first three centuries (so it has been reported) the general understanding was that "son" referred to the man Jesus, and not to Almighty God – the Uncreated Logos. Because Jesus and the Apostles knew no Trinity they could not have understood "son" as the Uncreated "Logos". Jesus never understood his reference to God as *God's* reference to God – or the Logos' reference to the Transcendent (father.) On the contrary, Jesus' reference was to God as both his heavenly and "natural" (or biological) "Father".

As miraculously conceived by God and Mary, Jesus was God and Mary's "son". Prior to his conception, Jesus never existed. Since the eternal Uncreated Logos is God, then how could it ever be said God *begot* God or that God *eternally* "begot" a son? (The idea God "begets" God is the notion of "*eternal regress*".) Furthermore, how could "God" ever be *humanly conceived, be born, suffer and die*? Impossible! Obviously the issue called "*Modalism"* had nothing whatsoever to do with God *intra* or *extra*, rather, it was solely the issue of "*who*" the term "*son*" referred to – was it God or the man Jesus?

The so called "heresy" of *Modalism* and *Sabellianism* is presented as if there was a dispute over whether or not God was *only* a Trinity *ad extra* (just different *ways* of God revealing Itself), or if God-in-Itself (*ad intra*) was a Trinity. This, however, was never the issue at hand. **The real issue was how God's immanent essence (God-in-Itself) could be called a "father and a son".** *"Modalism*" was an ***accusation*** leveled at those who *disagreed* that the eternal Logos was a "son". Was Jesus' personal reference to God as his "father" to be understood as reference to *himself as God* – to himself as the pre-incarnate Logos? In short, can it be said God is both a "father and son" ***before*** the incarnation (*ad intra*), or is this only a reference to God as the father of Jesus ***after*** the incarnation?

All recognized a difference between God's immanent Existence (*ad intra*) and God's *ad extra* revelation in creation and man. The difference, however, was not on the part of an Immutable God, rather, the difference was on the part of mutable man and creation. Thus the sole difference was between *as God exists–* ***in-Itself*** and *as God exists–* ***in-man*** *and in creation.* No father disputed this difference (*ad intra* and *ad extra*.) At bottom, the whole issue called "Modalism and Sabellianism" was a "Father-Son-Problem" – how it could be said God *ad intra* was a *father-and-son* when this was solely a *post* incarnational reference to the man Jesus as God's son.

To resolve the issue, Irenaeus proposed "*father and son*" as reference to the "*economy*" of salvation – i.e., God's plan for man according to the "mode" of its Incarnational revelation. This plan is called "*soteriology*", and the Trinity on which this is premised is called the "*economic Trinity*". So the terms "*father and son"* were solely references to the *economy* of salvation and ***not*** **references to either God *ad intra* or ad extra*.***

It would seem that until the mid-200's, no one had a problem understanding the man Jesus as the "son" of God. This was reference to his miraculous conception by God "who" he rightfully called his "father" – not just his heavenly father, but his "natural" (biological) father as well. For Origen, all references to "son" were to the man Jesus, for him, Jesus was totally human. After Origen's death (254), however, it seems there arose a backlash to his understanding of "son" as solely a reference to the man Jesus. This backlash is said to be the origin of what is called the *"Alexandrian school of thought*", a *God-flesh* understanding of Christ. For these fathers, the "Incarnation" was God only uniting itself to *flesh,* for other than this, Christ is solely divine.

For the Alexandrians, then, it was God's *divine son* – the first begotten by God – that took on flesh (incarnated) and was born of Mary. So apart from his body, Jesus was the Uncreated "son-of-God" – the Eternal Logos. There was tremendous opposition to this view. Jesus was not *just* flesh, nor can God's Infinite Existence be *encompassed* in the flesh. As Paul affirmed, Jesus "was like us in every way but sin", and the absence of sin does not make one God. Accusations flew on both sides of the aisle – "two births", "two sons", "ignoring the union of natures", "Jesus wasn't completely human" and so on.

The whole dispute was the issue of just how human or divine the "son" was. Taking it from Judaic scriptures, was the "*begotten* son" a *created* being or *Uncreated* – eternally **in** God as God, that is? What brought this issue to a head was Arius, an Alexandrian priest accused (falsely) of holding that the divine Logos was a *created* being. He was only pointing out the absurdity of saying God was "begotten" by God – i.e, the Logos was begotten. The term "begotten" could only refer to the man Jesus as the "son", not to the Uncreated Logos – after all, the many biblical references to "begotten" were to *biological* generation, certainly not to God "generating" offspring. At any rate, this issue – "*who*" was the "son" – erupted into the so called "Arian heresy" that split the entire Christian Church. So do not think for a second "it makes no difference" what one believes in this matter, on the contrary, we have two totally different Christologies, and one of them is wrong.

The "switch" from Jesus as "son" to God as "son"

The outcome of this dispute was the most strategic and radical "switches" ever made in the history of Christology and the understanding of Christ. From here on, all references to God's "son" were to be solely to God – the Uncreated Logos – the same "son" begotten by God, and later, born of Mary. To make this understanding official was the purpose of the first Church council, Nicaea (325.) In one stroke, **God** (Logos) became **Son of God,** and Jesus *was* **God** (Logos) *in the flesh.* Apart from his human appearance, **Jesus** was the eternal **Uncreated Logos,** one of God's *triune modes of existence omnipresent in all creation* – and later called the "**second person of the Trinity**". So now the Trinity is "Father-Son-Spirit" or "Father-Jesus-Spirit". Could anyone think of a more efficient way to divinize the man Jesus than to switch the created to the Uncreated?

Since Jesus knew nothing of the Trinity or Logos, his understanding of being God's "son" was obviously *not* that of the Council. The consequence of shifting Jesus' *own* understanding of "son of God" to this being a reference to one of the Trinity, had no good outcome. It gave rise to heated dissensions and animosities that seethed for centuries. Far from solving any Christological problem, the **switch** from a human son to *God* as a *"son"*, threw Christianity off track of any true understanding of the Trinity and Christ. God never *begot* God; God was never born, suffered and died, and the man Jesus was as completely human as any man who ever walked this earth.

Stemming from the switch of "son" from human to divine, the next wrong turn or major issue was how God's immanent essence or "*triune modes of existence*" could be referred to as two *individuals* – "a father and a son" – clearly, anthropomorphic terms applied to God. But before we come to this, a major development that bears on this issue was the fathers' affirming the Trinity *ad intra* as *"three hypostases in One God"*. The term "*hypostases*" was used to underscore the immanent *essence* of God's *triune modes of existence* as not only **distinct *ad extra*,** but *immanently* **distinct *ad intra*.**

Division of Trinity into three *individual* "numerical ones"

Many of the fathers were against referring to the Trinity as *three hypostases*. There was the fear lest these *distinctions* be understood as "separate" or "individual" entities or beings – i.e., *tri-theism.* As we'll see, this fear was not unfounded, for as "three individuals" is just how they came to be understood. Also, while the fathers had no intention of making any "division" between God's one essence and Its triune *distinctions* or *modus operandi*, still, this too, was another unfortunate outcome of speaking of God as *three hypostases in one essence*. Where three hypostases was to be understood as the immanent *ad intra* **distinctions** in God's one *essence,* now it was also to be understood as God's *ad extra* "external presentation" as three *prosopa* (*faces*) or *persons.* These "persons" came to be understood as three "individuals" – three individual "*what's*"? Three individual "**who's**" – that's *what!*

As long as *hypostases* is reference to the triune *distinctions* **in** one essence, no problem, but when understood as three *particular individuals or "numerical ones",* there is no escaping tri-theism. Philosophically speaking, every "individual thing" (a "numerical one") is always a reference to some *material* or *embodied* "thing" – be it an individual atom, rock, plant, animal or man. Given the multiplicity of "individual things" is why the philosophers sought out the *non-individual,* the *immaterial* "One" that transcended all multiplicity – the One reality underlying all "individual" things. **This is why the Trinity, understood as three *individual numerical ones* implies three *embodied* beings or entities** – tri-theism, if not polytheism! Indeed, any understanding of the Trinity as three "individual ones" or three individual *persons* implies three beings – all protests to the contrary.

<u>Trinity divided into *essence* (nature) and *persons* (individuals)</u>

To make matters worse, the next understanding given *hypostases* – by the Western Church – was "*person*". The excuse was that in Latin, *hypostasis* was Plato's meaning of "*substance*" – basically no different than the Greek *hypostases*. This, however, is not a believable excuse. Since *hypostasis* had different uses in Greek, the Latins could have adopted the same Greek understanding. Yet, according to how *some* evidently regarded the Trinity, it came to be defined as three individual "*persons*". By using the otherwise unheard of term, "*person*", they defined the Trinity as some people, at least, must have understood it. Thus *hypostasis* was changed to mean *an individual person* – with all its human, anthropomorphic definitions no less.

Although *person* was said to be a "property" of nature (something nature or essence *owned*), it turns out, *person* is the *one who* acts as the owner (agent) of its own nature. So *person* does not refer to the essence or nature of either God or man, rather, it refers to a "property" of the essence (or nature) of God and man. **Right here we have a major *divide* between *essence* (*nature*) and *person*.** While one may presuppose the other, yet *nature* (*essence*) and *person* are ***not*** one another. From here on, however, all references to God (or man) had to be constantly *divided* between whether one is speaking of the *essence* of God (or man), or was speaking of the *person* of God (or man.) Given this division between ***what*** God is (essence) and ***who*** God is (person), if one does not make absolutely clear whether his reference is to *nature* or to *person*, then he'd best say nothing at all. This *division* would be the genesis of mass confusion and misrepresentation that promoted totally wrong understandings of the Trinity, Christ, and even the man Jesus.

<u>Trinity as three individual self-identities, three "I am's", three subjects – three *who's*</u>

The definition and understanding of "person" was a reference to one's self-identity – to "**who**" one is. Person was regarded as the "agent", the mover and shaker of the nature or essence, it is the incommunicable "subject", "I am" or "self" that runs the whole show. This made the Trinity three individual self-identities, each its own independent agent and incommunicable subject – "I am" or self. This understanding of the Trinity is obviously *anthropomorphic* and **admittedly** premised on man as *human persons*. Because the human mind, however, cannot possibly conceive of a *non-anthropomorphic* "*person*", reference to God as "person(s)" is nothing more than literary "*personification*". (Who can think of some "person" that is *not* some being?) Yet this is how the Trinity is consistently, theologically portrayed and spoken of – as if the Trinity were three individual **beings or entities.** The term "*person*" not only promotes anthropomorphism, but tri-theism as well.

Although Clement of Alexandria (150 – 215) referred to God as the *true subject* of Jesus, this was not a reference to **God as a subject**, but to the subject Jesus, whose deepest (subjective) experience of "*being*" *was God.* (This was Clement's reference to Jesus' unitive state of "*apatheia*" or *theosis.*) Of course, Jesus was *not* God's *being*, rather God was Jesus' personal *experience* of God's being. God is the *true being* of all that exists and the "unitive *state of being*" is this experience of being one with God's being. The big mistake, of course, is concluding that because God is one's deepest *true being* this makes the *experiencer* himself *to be* God's own being or self – makes him Almighty God! Transposing man's knowing and experiences to be God's, however, is just another attempt to make God into man's image of himself.

The Antiochenes regarded Jesus' "unitive state of being" to mean his *whole person* was in accord with God's will and mind. They *never* agreed God *replaced* Jesus' own will and mind, replaced his own subject or personal-identity. Cyril of Alexandria is the one who *substituted* Jesus' *human subject* or *self* for God – **as if God was a subject or self**! He was absolutely **wrong in this because God is *no person*, no subject or self.** Yet, this is the present orthodox view – namely, that God's own self-identity ("I am"), person or subject, was Jesus' sole self-identity ("I am".) This, however, is a piece of orthodox Hinduism – *who* you *really* are is Almighty God! So let all those who believe this go East where they too, can discover, like Jesus, they are God.[1] This, at least, is Cyril's Christology considered totally orthodox. Thank God for the Antiochenes who never countenanced his erroneous Christology.

---

[1] When those who go East discover they are not God, they will either come back or resign themselves to the belief they must be re-incarnated 10,000 times before they can discover they *really are God.* The reason this belief is incompatible with Christianity is because *to be Christ* is not *to be* God, but to be *eternally one with God.* People who think they should be God (or realize they are God), do not know what they are saying. A genuine revelation of the *Transcendent* is all people would need to flock to Judaism because they'd know they are "*not that*" and could never "*be that*". Where, by itself, the *Logos* can tend to pantheism (being Omnipresent in creation), and the *indwelling Spirit* in man can tend to the belief one's own being is God, the *Transcendent,* however, blows these wrong beliefs out of the water. This is just another example of how the Trinity – God's *modus operandi* – exists in divine *equilibrium* that not only keeps man *in balance,* but keeps him on the right path of Truth.

It is because Cyril denied Jesus was a human person, Nestorius asked, "*How can you have a complete human being* (an individual) *that is not a person?*" In other words, if God was the *person* of Jesus, then how is **God *not* (like Jesus) an individual *being***? To believe God is *some individual being* (or three beings) and there goes Monotheism! What we have instead is some form of monistic pantheism.

Making God a human person called for a "*Communication of Properties*"

The reason that substituting one of God's divine persons (Logos) to be (or act as) the *human* person of Jesus did not work, is because all the fathers held God to be *impassible* – i.e., not subject to *human* experiences with all its changes, ups and downs. Thus thinking everything Jesus said and did from birth to death was God-in-person doesn't work **because it is not the truth**. To take care of this problem, they came up with the *Communication of Properties* which holds that even though God did **not** experience anything (birth, walking, talking, suffering and dying), yet *because* Jesus' human nature *belonged* to (or was the "property" of) the divine *person* of the Logos, then everything experienced by *God's own human nature* could be ***attributed*** (or said **to belong)** to the Logos' **divine *person***. This way, though God experienced *nothing*, yet all Jesus' human experiences and sayings could be ***attributed*** to God **as if** they belonged to God or were God's own words and experiences – which, of course, they were *not*. (Even as a divine "*person*", God is *impassible*.)

A Monophysitic Christ

The understanding that because God (Logos) as a "*person*" has one divine *nature*, t**herefore Christ, as a *divine person,* has one divine nature – this is *Monophysitism.*** Since Christ's *body* (or flesh) was one with God, then Christ is one divine en-fleshed ***individual being.*** And *who* is this divine *being*? It is the Logos, one of God's eternal *modes of existence* – God's *immanent modus operandi*. But where is the man Jesus in this? He was flesh, a *material* being, a human *person,* the only one "*who*" could be **seen** at least.

But even if Jesus' human nature was only flesh, and the natures were united **in** a divine person, this does not make "Christ" *one being* – much less, of *one divine nature*. To say Christ is one "*person*" is solely a reference to *"who"* some *individual being* is, it is not a reference to "what" that individual being is. Thus, Christ is not *one individual being,* not one God, not one hypostasis, not one nature, not even one human being. To think a divine person is one *individual* ***divine being*** is *tri-theism*, and to think a divine person is an *individual* ***human*** *being* is *Monophysitism.* Yet this view of Christ as one divine person, one divine being, one divine nature (minus the flesh), is the proverbial party-line's *Monophysitic* presentation of Christ. No one denied Christ a physical body, yet even granting Jesus a human soul, never changed the view of Christ as *one divine being.*

Switch in the ontology of being

The *ontological* problem of Christ is that the union of two disparate natures does *not* constitute a single individual *being*. The only way Christ can be understood as a single ontological being is as a single *person* – even though, by definition, person is *not* the essence or nature of being. **Still, it was by making Christ *one individual person* that Christ came to be understood as one individual *being*.** Where philosophically, the reality of "ontological being" is based on the *essence* or nature of "*what*" something is, now, however, this had to be **switched from *what* being is, to *who* a being is.** One excuse for this switch was because no one knows *what* God is in the first place – or even *what* man really is – thus the ontology of being had to shift from "*what*" is ***not known*** (essence) to "*who*" ***is known*** **(**person.**)** As one divine *person*, then, this is not only *who* Christ is, but *who* God is – *one* of the three divine persons. Another excuse for this switch: since the Trinity is *not* three ontological *beings*, then referring to the Trinity as three "*persons*" *avoids* referring to them as "beings". Yet *who* does not understand a "person" as some particular individual being? Without some *individual being,* "who" is there *to be* a person?

Since God is not an individuated embodied being, then God is *not* a "who", and not who Jesus – an embodied being – is. It is because he is *not* God that the term "person" was used. It was used ***not* to refer to *Jesus* as a divine person, but to refer to *God* as the divine *person* of Christ.** In other words, Christ as a divine person was not the man Jesus, rather, the divine person was solely God (Logos.) Yet, as an embodied person, can we now point to the man Jesus as *who* Christ is? Is he a divine person or is only God the divine person? This is the whole problem with the "ontological switch" from essence (nature) to person – it *can't* work.

The twisted thinking was that because there is no *human* nature without its property of *person*, so too, there is no *divine* nature without its property of person. The primacy of *being,* then, is not some *unknowable* essence or nature, but rather, a *knowable* individual person – *who* someone is. *Without this switch in primacy from nature to person, how is one to give Christ any ontological reality?* If the ontological reality of Christ cannot be the union of natures, then it can be **one ontological *person* – a divine person.** This, of course, only promotes a *Monophysitic* understanding of Christ – since one divine person implies one divine nature. But as said before, the *problem* of a union of *two natures* is that it *does not, cannot,* constitute *one ontological being.* It was because it *does not,* that "*who*" one is, became the ontological (and theological) reality of Christ.

It is ironic, however, that this ontological understanding of Christ was premised on the view that Jesus was **no** human person – thus Jesus' human nature was *not* his *real being,* rather, his *person* was his real being! (In other words, if real being is a *person,* and Jesus was not a person, then he had no real being – who can figure this out?) According to the Christian ontological view, the *real being* of Christ was neither the human being Jesus nor the divine being of God, but **was Almighty God *as a divine person.*** So forget the "*hypostatic union*" of Christ's dual natures, in *reality* Christ is one *divine individual person* and "*who*" this *person* is, is Almighty God. If this is not the orthodox teaching, this is certainly its formal presentation of "Christ".

When all is said and done, however, this ontological *switch* (from nature to person) is **null and void,** because both the Godhead (Trinity) and the Real Christ ***transcend*** **all man's ontological categories of "being" – absolutely!** Making the Godhead three *ontological* persons, and Christ one of these "persons", so skewed the Trinity and Christ that a true understanding became impossible – virtually lost. This was more than just a "wrong turn", it was the most egregious error in the history of Christianity.

No use going over the repercussions of this **switch** of *real being* from ***what*** to ***who.*** It may be interesting, however, to point out one of its more social fall-outs. People have often pondered how it happened that Western civilization came to stress and emphasize the importance of the ***individual self*** when the mind-set of other civilizations emphasized, first of all, the needs of **others** – tribe, clan, family, kingdom, group or whatever. How it is Western civilization is first of all mindful of the *individual person or self, before* concern for the larger good of society? ***Who*** **invented, defined, and gave priority to "*person*" as an *individual subject, self, "I am",*** *one's* ***personal identity?*** **Who made "*who*" *you* are of more importance than "*what*" you are?** Christianity! While this has its pros and cons, to think this "mind-set" is a Christian legacy, well, it is a legacy that ultimately bears *no fruit* – which may be why Jesus cursed the barren fig tree.

But this is the theology of the proverbial party-line that Christians are expected to believe without question. The only good thing to say about it, is that many of the fathers fought it tooth and nail, for which many were condemned, exiled, unjustly accused and besmirched for all time. Indeed, this was the cause of the first (though not the last) big schism in the Christian Church. It is difficult enough to articulate the truth, but to so complicate, twist and convolute it to a point that defies all logic, only makes the truth more unbelievable, and deservedly so – a leap of faith based on this party-line may only end in disillusionment. To put a finger on the most egregious error in all of Christianity, it is the idea of the Godhead or Trinity as "persons". There is no truth to it at all. Because of this, however, Jesus was robbed of ever being treated or thought of as a human person, no different from anyone else who ever walked this earth. Nobody can relate to God as a person, but everyone can relate to the man Jesus as a human person – like themselves. **People have to understand Jesus' life with God is the same path as their own life with God, for as it went for him so it goes for everyone – which entails being both loved and despised to death and beyond.** Jesus' *human experiences* work spiritually in everyday life to verify everyman's "way" to eternal life with and in God.

Dependency on "person"

What would the centuries of Christology do without the term "person"? Without it, how could Christ ever be *misunderstood* as one being, one entity, one single individual? Impossible. Unless the three persons of the Trinity are beings or entities, and the *person* of the Logos understood as an individual "being", no one could envision Christ as a single being or entity. All Christologies that envision Christ as a single individual or "*being*" depend on "*person" understood as a single divine "being"*. Eliminate the term "person", and how is Christ to be envisioned as a single being? Without theology's absolute dependence on *person* as an individual being, its Christologies would go down like a row of dominoes.

Because everyone knows a person as a distinct individual being, the term "person" is a way to think of Christ as a single individual, a particular human being. Unless Christ, after all, is a fixed entity, how could people even "think" of Christ? Since people couldn't begin to imagine "what" a divine person is, or how it differs from a human person, all they do is capitalize the "p" in a human person and there you have *Christ*, when, in truth, it is only the *human* person people actually know. Use of the term "*person"* certainly illustrates how convenient it is to *make God a* ***human*** *person.* While this may *not be* theologically correct, this is, in fact, how people think of Christ – the *human* person Jesus as one individual *divine* person. They know nothing at all about any *transcendent*, *invisible*, *impassible* and *immutable* "person" (God), which, obviously, was not the man Jesus. Had it been stressed from the beginning Jesus was a *human person* there could be no mistaking him for a divine person – which theology obviously intended people to do.

As matters stand today, the duality of Christ's natures is totally subsumed under the umbrella of Christ as one divine "person", a divine being, which leaves the union of two natures *a mere doctrinal statement.* In truth, that is all it really is, just a *doctrinal statement* with nothing more to back it up.

While no one in town gives "person" a thought, a theologian stakes his life on it. Apart from him, few Christians know anything about this division between *nature* and *person* or could tell you a thing about it. Yet use of "person" on which every Christology came to depend, totally derails the truth of Christ. The real Christ is no person at all, human or divine; Christ is the eternal union or oneness of divine and human natures. If people could understand this, know about it, how might this affect their understanding of Christ? If the truth of Christ does not have a profound spiritual effect on people, then they belong to a different religion – like the Jesus-cult.

PREFACE TO THE INCARNATION

There is a reason for waiting this long before going over the key Christian revelation – the "Incarnation". Before anyone can begin to understand it, however, we first have to clean house – i.e., throw away the notion of the Trinity as three *persons;* get rid of the idea of God "begetting" God; clear up the "son" problem; sweep away the myth of males begetting souls and everyone born with sin; burn the "Communication of Properties"; toss out Boethius and all the mental gymnastics of the Scholastics that Aquinas aptly called "straw". Get rid of all anthropomorphism, polytheism (tri-theism), anthropolatrism, Monophysitism, and other misleading views. This list is not complete, but it is the reason for delaying the Incarnation. Just as Mary's house was clean of all this debris, so too, it is important to clear out all erroneous ideas of Christ.

Unfortunately, the term "*Incarnation*" is inadequate to articulate a soul's "enfleshment" or what it means to be a complete human being. The term "Incarnation" solely represents a Platonic idea of a *divine* world – soul becoming "individuated" by matter – becoming "enfleshed", that is. We have already pointed out the problem with the traditional Christologies based on this belief – that Christ's human nature is so much flesh, with no indication of an authentic human soul or of being a complete human being. So although "In-carnation" does *not* express the whole truth of the revelation of Christ, nevertheless, we use this term with the understanding that every human being is first and foremost a human soul, for without a soul what is there to "enflesh"? "Incarnation", then, means God creating for Itself a *complete* human nature eternally one with Itself, and only this eternal *oneness* of divine and human natures, is the "real Christ".

INCARNATION

"Everyone acknowledged this truth:
Logos' oneness with all creation
Holy Spirit's presence in all
All are in the Father".
(Theodore of Mopsuestia, 350 – 428)

From the beginning, God has revealed Itself to every human being the world over. Man may have different terms, names and reports of this revelation, he may even draw different conclusions from it, yet God allows no one the excuse "*I didn't know*". Yet no revelation of God, however subtle or sublime can ever satisfy man. So God exists – what is that to man? Or better put – what is man to God? Before man existed God didn't miss him a bit, and even *after* man exists, God wouldn't miss him. Considering the Infinity of God, what could man possibly mean to God? Does he honestly mean anything at all? So the whole universe can blow up and God goes right on without it! (The Stoics thought the Logos would burn it up and then recreate it.)

The reason God's revelations are not humanly satisfying is because they reveal nothing about man himself, they do not reveal man's life and ultimate destiny, do not answer his perennial questions – what is the real purpose of life? Why death? What happens when he dies? Does man have any "afterlife" or eternal destiny? If so, what could that be? These are not questions of God's existence, but questions of Man's existence – more especially, his eternal existence. For answers, nobody is interested in formal philosophical or theological rationalizations, doctrinal formulations or what somebody else believes. The mind can find no definitive satisfaction or fulfillment with mere concepts and hearsay. What man is seeking is the **living experiential reality of the Truth, his own immediate experience of this truth.** Until he does, he will go right on questioning and being dissatisfied. Even if man knew the truth, he could never be fulfilled by merely "believing" it. He is only fulfilled by *experientially living it* – knowing it firsthand.

God – knowing man better than man knows himself – had a way of answering man's perennial questions. This was not, however, by giving the answers to some great individual – a Moses, Heraclitus, Buddha, Jesus or Paul. Since God cannot reveal what is not the Truth – and if the Truth is man's *eternal* life in and with God – then how else could God make this a reality but by creating Man's human nature eternally one with Itself? Since, of itself, nothing that exists has any life of its own, then *only by God uniting man eternally to Itself could man have eternal life.* Thus, the *true nature* of man's "*eternal life*" is his oneness with God. **There is no "other" *eternal life* possible than man's existence being eternally united to God's Existence.**

Because God is beyond *time*, there is no use guessing *when* God decided to grant eternal life to man. It makes sense, however, that it was when God first created man – this, at least, was the view of Paul and the fathers. This being the case, from the beginning then, mankind was destined for eternal life with God. It would be facetious, however, to think some human being had the *power* to *ruin* God's divine plan for mankind or that any man could alter or abort God's will in this matter. There is no need to be concerned for the "undeserving" – since no man "deserves" eternal life anyway – nor can any man "make it happen". That this was God's "plan" from the beginning, however, may account for why all human beings (with few exceptions) believed there was something immortal in man that did not die and would go on living. As to "what" this something was, everyone had different ideas. That this was a universal belief, however, indicates that the truth of eternal life lies hidden in every man. Were this not so, man would regard death as no more than a flower or weed returning to the soil. That somehow, someway, man moves on to a better life seems to have been a universal belief – if not, the "great hope".

Of course, how all this could be so, was the perennial question. Though history accounts for a number of enlightened individuals whose works and words are revered to this day, God had a more *universal* way to enlighten man, which was not by words, writings, or anyone's personal enlightened experiences, but rather, by simply revealing *Man* to himself. Seen in the light of all God's revelations, what makes this revelation so unique is that it was ***not* the revelation of God, but the revelation of Man.** This was not, of course, the revelation of "**a**" man, but the revelation of "*Universal Man*". **While every human being is "a" man, no *particular* individual is "*universal man*".** It was the revelation of every man's eternal oneness with God that would be called the "Incarnation", a revelation that would become known and called "***Christ***". Indeed, it is because the word "*Christ*" stands for *everyman's* eternal oneness with God, that Christ **is** called "Universal Man".

We usually think only God needs to be "revealed", but not man himself. While everyone knows human nature as it exists on earth, what he does *not* know, however, is human nature as it does *not* exist on earth. Christ is not the revelation of what *man is now* – nobody needs that to be revealed – but *what* man *is to become* – *become* Christ, that is. Man's earthly existence tells him nothing about his *eternal existence.* He may think he knows, but until it is a *fait accompli*, he doesn't know. All he has is hope, ideas and various beliefs. With the revelation of Christ, however, God has revealed what *more* man is to be – *Christ, man's eternal oneness with God.*

Though God could have revealed this Truth without any *earthly* Incarnation, it would never have had the meaning and impact of its immediate (earthly) manifestation. Greater than words or merely telling us, God demonstrated this Truth by manifesting it in body and soul, not only informing man he comes from God and is one with God, but also, to reveal the true nature of his death and what becomes of him – i.e., his resurrection, ascension, and, in the Eucharist, his glorious eternal life in God. The purpose of the Incarnation, then, was not to tell us *about* the truth, but to ***manifest*** it, *be the living proof of it,* not by anything said or done, but by *being* the Truth of God's oneness with man. Thus, as the concrete manifestation of Man, the Incarnation is the answer to everyman's perennial questions. This is not *just* the revelation of God **or** man, **but God *and* Man as one – this is the revelation of the *Real Christ.***

What is called the "Incarnation", then, was first and foremost, God's creating and uniting man's universal human nature to Itself. Next, was God "revealing" this Truth via the historical event called the "Annunciation". This "announcing" was God *manifesting* this Truth in the life of a single created human being, God literally *demonstrating* the "way" man was to live his life with God, how to recognize and know it, and to realize its destiny of eternal oneness with God. There is nothing greater God did for man than creating an eternal union with him, and there is no more meaningful revelation than this Truth. There is no other recorded revelation like it – as one father put it, "*Being perfect God and **now** perfect man, brings about the greatest of all possible novelties – the only thing **new** under the sun!*"

For a true understanding of what is called "Incarnation", we have to refer back to Monotheism and its *Great Divide* between the *Uncreated and created,* a Line there is no passing over one way or the other. By definition, God is *not created,* and man is *not uncreated,* thus God is not *what* God creates, and what God creates is not *what* God **is**. The "Incarnation", then, was not the Uncreated *becoming* some created being – impossible – but God creating Its *own* universal human nature, uniting it eternally to Itself. Given this revelation, we learn that the "*Line*" that *divides* is *also* the *Line* that *unites,* this Line being everything that would become known as "Christ". "Christ", then, is a term for the eternal union or oneness of the Uncreated and created. This *Line* does not mean God *became* a human being or that a human being *became* God, rather, **the revelation of Christ is simply the eternal one-**

ness of the two – God and man.

So the event Christianity calls the "Incarnation" was God creating and uniting to Itself **man's common human nature.** This was not the creation of *just another* human being, but **God creating Its *own* human nature *prior*** to its being any ***particular*** **human being.** Because this union was *prior* to all possible human distinctions and differences – prior, that is, to its becoming a particular "*person*" – no particular human being could ever identify ***his*** *human nature* as ***God's*** **human nature –** ***because*** **God's is universal and not particular.** Christ is called "*Universal Man*" *because* Christ is no single or particular individual. Although we can say everything that exists "belongs" to God, this is not, however, a reference to God's *own incarnate human nature.* This *Incarnational union* is no *existential union* – i.e., all things united to God by reason of their mere existence. Man's *eternal* union with God is of a totally different nature, a union that would be called a "*hypostatic union*" – to be discussed later. The Incarnation, then, was God **creating Its *own* human nature.** The oneness of these two natures – divine and human – is "*Christ*". This means that for man to *become* eternally one with God (be "transformed into Christ"), is to *become God's own* human nature, one that is neither his own nor that of any *particular* individual or *person.* The mystery of Christ, then, *is* the mystery of *God's one universal human nature,* and **not** the mystery of any man's *particular* human nature or *person.*

The second meaning or understanding of "Incarnation" refers to that particular event in history when this eternal union was *revealed* as God's destined plan for all mankind. While what is called the "Annunciation" can be regarded as this "*revelation*", this is generally celebrated as *Mary's* Feast and *not* a Feast of the "Incarnation" – a fact I always found curious. In this matter, however, it was interesting to learn from a Jewish scholar that Judaism does not regard a child *in utero* (womb) as a "*person*". Only when the child is born and can live on its own – its *life* no longer *dependent* on the mother – it is regarded as a "person". **So *birth,* then, is the celebration of the *human person.*** Prior to this, human nature (*in utero*) is in the process of developing into what will *become* an independent human *person.* So this is why, in Christianity, **"Christmas" – the *birth* of Jesus – is the celebration of Jesus as an independent *human person.*** Absolutely, Judaism has it right. Jesus was as independent a *human person* as ever walked the face of this earth. Had he not been *aware of himself,* of **his own personal identity**, he could not have functioned in this world.

The point is that neither the conception (*Annunciation*) or birth (*Christmas*) of an individual human being is the true nature of "Incarnation" – God creating and effecting an eternal union with man's ***universal* human nature**. These historical events were the ***revelation*** of the "Incarnation", but not the "Incarnation" itself. The Incarnation took place solely *in* God's divine nature and not *in* this world. God's eternal union with man's common human nature was not God's union with any **individual** human being nor with any "pre-existing" individual, but a union with the human nature *God created for Itself* alone, and *not* for anyone else.

The purpose of the Incarnation, then, was not to reveal the man Jesus – who never existed prior to the Annunciation – but to reveal *Christ as everyman's* destined oneness with God. As the fathers said, Jesus was the *instrument* of this revelation, a living *example* of it, yet, beyond his individual life, "Christ" is the eternal Archetype of every man's "way" to eternal life in God. The Incarnation, then, was not the revelation of ***a*** man, but the revelation of "**Universal Man**". If all God had to do was unite Itself with one human being, no incarnation would have been necessary. Christ, however, is more than God's oneness with a *particular* human being. *The Incarnation was God creating* ***Its Own human nature****, uniting* ***Its one essence*** *with the* ***one essence of mankind****, and it is this* ***eternal union of essences*** *we know as "****Christ****".*

According to Paul, from the creation of the first human being, God had a Plan for mankind, a particular path and final destiny for every human being. The Annunciation was the *revelation* of this Plan and how it works out in the life of everyone. "Christ", then, as the True Life and Way of mankind, reveals *how it went for Christ (God's* ***own*** *human nature),* ***both in this earthly life and in eternal life,*** *is how it goes for everyone.* Thus "Christ" is *God's Archetypal Plan for mankind.*

"Archetype" means "*first form*", "*the original pattern of which actual things are copies*". To my knowledge, Plato was the first to propose the *real* as the *archetype* ('forms' or 'ideas') and it was in this sense of *archetype,* Paul and others referred to Christ as "*Adam*" (the Hebrew term for "*Mankind*") as the first or original human being. As the theory goes, the first human being was created perfect, but not being able to sustain this perfection, he fell. As a fallen human being, then, the individual man, Adam, could *not* be the ideal archetype of humanity. Thus Paul regarded "Christ" as the *original Adam* (mankind) who never fell, and who came to restore mankind to its original perfect nature. Once *restored* ("redeemed" was the fathers' term for "restoration") man could then go forward to complete his ultimate destiny – i.e., his eternal oneness with God. For Paul, then, the Incarnation was God's *revelation* of this universal Plan, Christ not only the archetype of "universal man" and man's "original nature", but everyman's *true life* and eternal destiny with and in God.

This archetypal view was the basis of much of the fathers' thinking. This is why, along with Paul, they held that with the advent of Christ, man was no longer held down by Adam's sin, but could now go forward to fulfill God's original plan. They believed the man Jesus was born in a perfect state of oneness with God, and this same oneness was now within the reach of every human being. As God's archetypal plan, "Christ", however, was not some Platonic "idea" in God's mind, on the contrary, this archetype is the living Reality God not only carried out with the Incarnation, but continues to carry out in the life of every human being. Nothing idealistic about this plan, on the contrary, this is the Spirit's carrying out God's transforming plan in every human being, a plan only God can fulfill and no man can bring about of himself. Christ, then, is the "Way" this plan works, the end being man's eternal oneness with and in God. Another way to put it, this archetype (*Christ*) stands for human *potential* – what human nature is to *become.* As the fathers would say, "*man was created to be* ***more*** *than he is now",* more, that is, than even his *original nature.* Another way to put it – *man's creation is not over until it is over,* or until it has reached its destined end in God.

The mistake of Christian thinking is that Christ is just one "particular" human being – the person Jesus. That *only* the man Jesus is Christ, however, shreds the whole purpose and revelation of the Incarnation. To think God went to all the trouble of eternally uniting Man to Itself *just* to reveal one particular human being, is too naive for words. Prior to the Incarnation there was no man Jesus, in fact, prior to the "Incarnation" there was no "Christ", there was only God – the Trinity. The ***essence*** of human nature, however, is *no particular* being, but ***what* all human beings *are***. People, however, get so caught up in the historical *dramatization* of the life of Jesus, that the *real* Christ is lost. People reverence the story, love the leading man, and forget the Truth it was intended to reveal – namely, God's *own* human nature as *Universal Man, not* some *particular man.* To mistake the messenger for the message misses the message completely.

Everyone, of course, needs an icon, someone to exemplify the ideal, someone who sets the bar or acts as the standard against which others can be measured. Thus, the man Jesus is the central icon of Christianity. *God's common human nature,* however, *is not that of any* ***particular*** *being or* ***person****,* not even the man Jesus. Still, Jesus was God's example of someone who, with his death, Resurrection and Ascension, *became* Christ, became God's *own* human nature. So while the particular man, Jesus, was certainly the *earthly example* of one who lived in union with God, yet, the mystery of Christ is not the man Jesus or any *particular* man or individual. The **mystery** of **Christ is *beyond both* the *individual* (particular) and the *multiple.* The mystery of Christ is *Universal.***

It is generally accepted that no one had the clarity or unambiguous understanding of the Incarnation as did Cyril of Alexandria. This was what he said, ***"The Logos did not assume some particular human being, but man's common human nature, yet a nature that appeared (was seen) in one individual"*** – by "assume", of course, he meant "become one with". Cyril's use of "*appeared*" did not mean God's human nature only *looked* or *appeared* to be human (the heresy called "*Docetism*"), he was only pointing out that every human being is *an embodied "individual" being.* For Aristotle, and even the fathers, an "individual being" is a "*numerical one"* – one in *number,* but *universal* in *essence (nature.)*

Although, fittingly, this understanding would be the rock of all orthodox understanding of Christ, yet, this is not easy for most people to get hold of. In simple terms, Cyril affirms God (the Logos) never created any ***particular human nature*** – there is no such thing anyway. As said, there is only *one* "human nature", not many, different kinds or *particular* one's – "*what is common to all is* ***proper*** (particular) *to none*". So let us make clear:

1. God is one essence.
2. Human nature is one essence.
3. The eternal union of these ***two essences* is** "Christ".
4. This **union** of essences, does not constitute any one "individual being". God is not one individual being, the essence of human nature is not "one" individual being, and their union does not constitute *one individual being.*
5. The *mystery* of Christ is bound up in the truth that *what* God united to itself was *not* just one particular human being, but Man's one common human nature.

Although Cyril's reference to man's "*common"* or "*universal"* human nature may sound Platonic – and it probably was – this does not negate the fact God only created **one** human nature. There is no "quantifying" a *universal*, there are only quantities of "*individuals*". Neither a divine or human nature is "quantifiable", only *individual beings* are quantifiable. Thus billions of people have "one" same human nature, and in this respect, Jesus was no ontological anomaly. This is why there are not *multiple* Christs, but only *one* Christ – *one* common human nature *one* with *one* God.

In this matter, Cyril couldn't tolerate speaking of "*Jesus'* human nature", simply because it was *not his*, but God's. **To speak of *Jesus'* human nature made Jesus a human "person"** – considered unorthodox, a theological no-no. So, theologically speaking, the *human person,* Jesus, was *not* Christ. Christ is not the oneness of *who* God is with *who* some man is; rather, Christ is the eternal union of *natures,* not a union of *persons*. This means that no *person* – Jesus, Mary, Paul or *who*ever – is "*who*" Christ is. The human nature God created for Itself was *nobody's* human nature, but solely **God's human nature** and not that of any *person* or *"who"* someone is.

In this matter, Gregory of Nyssa points out that scripture did not say the Logos became ***a*** man (some particular man), but became *man* – "Universal Man", as Cyril put it. The Logos' oneness with man was solely with his bare essential nature *prior* to its becoming a *particular person.* The *essence* of man, then, is prior to taking on all those particular characteristics, properties or "accidents" necessary for man's *temporary earthly* existence, an earthly existence, however, never intended for *eternal life in God.* While these *individualistic* properties and accidents enable man to live on earth, they are incapable of living a *glorified eternal life in and with God.* Those who think otherwise, might heed one of the fathers' major dictums – *"What the Logos did not assume in the Incarnation is not saved"*, and since the Logos assumed no "person" – ***person* defined as what makes one human being *different* from another –** then whatever makes for differences is not saved. God's oneness with man is only with what all have in common and *not with* anything that makes for differences.

The sole reference to "Christ", then, is to the *dual natures of God and Man,* an eternal union created *in* the very essence of God. That Jesus' common human nature was one with God does not make *his human nature* any different from that of any other. This is why, if one asks "**What is the difference between *God's* human nature and *Jesus'* human nature?" the answer is simple: "*God's* human nature is *universal* and *personless*, whereas *Jesus'* human nature is that of single individual, a particular *person".*** This is exactly what Cyril was pointing out – i.e., God's common human nature "***yet a nature that appeared (was seen) in one individual".*** It is because God's *universal* human nature could never be just *one individual* human being, everyone's *eternal* union with God **is** Christ. That Jesus was a particular *example* of one human being united to God, there is no question. Indeed, it was ***his, and every man's, eternal union with God that is "Christ".*** Christ as "Universal Man" means that no single human being is Christ or ever could be Christ. God's *own* human nature is *universal,* it is not the human nature of any particular individual or person.

Failure to grasp this truth is why people think only *one* ***particular*** *human being is Christ* – the man Jesus, of course. Like everyone else, Jesus "appeared" or "was seen" as an *individual* human being, yet God's union with man's *common human nature* was not with just one individual being, nor, for that matter, a union that can ever *be seen as* an "individual". Indeed, the bare *essence* of human nature cannot be "*seen*" at all. In fact, God is the only One that even knows "*what*" the *essence* of man really is – more especially, its eternal or heavenly estate in God.[1] Because Christ is no particular individual person, means that no man's oneness with God makes *him* (*her*, *me* or *you*) *"Christ"*. To understand this, we need only think of the Eucharist – One Christ, and everyone transformed into the same One Christ.

So Christ, then, is *no particular individual or person,* not even the unique man Jesus. And since no one can point to either the *essence* of God or man, so too, no one can point to *Christ.* People who think it is *they, themselves, who* are one with God, have it wrong. God neither creates a person, nor is one with any person; God is solely one with man's common human nature. So it is not the *person* Jesus *who* is one with God; the **bare essence of human nature is no "who" (*me, you, etc.*), but a "what" – *what* man *is*.** This essence is *prior* to being an individual "*who*". Paul knew this when he said "it is not **I "*who*"** lives, but Christ". He never said, "**I** am Christ", or "**I** am one with God", or even, "**I** am one with Christ". Simply put: Christ is not "*who*" someone is, rather, Christ is the *mystery* of everyman's eternal *oneness* with God.

So, when Cyril said "***a nature that appeared (was seen) in one individual***", the reference was to the fact every human being comes into this world one embodied *individual* being. That every human being "*appears*" (is seen) as one "*individual*" (defined by Aristotle as a "*numerical one*"), means one can *count* individual *beings*, **but can never count *human natures*.** So any reference to a *particular* human being would *not* be a reference to his *common* human nature, but solely to his

[1] The implication of Cyril's saying Christ was "seen **in** one individual" and not "**as**" one individual, is rather telling. It means people can not only *see* Christ **in** the man Jesus, but can *see* Christ **in** other people as well, and, if God so reveals it, even *see* Christ **in** themselves. But to see Christ in a St. Francis, a Mother Teresa or whoever, does not make *them* Christ – there is no such thing as "*many* Christs". So too, to see Christ ***in*** the man Jesus, does not make *him* Christ. Seeing Christ in others or in one's self, is not, of course, to *see* the man Jesus – a human being *inside* another human being? Ridiculous! Indeed, to see and know the *real Christ* is to be confronted with the greatest *mystery* God ever revealed to man. Why? Because Christ is neither one's "self" nor some "other".

being an individual *person.* God, however, creates no human *person.* It is by the exercise of his own free-will man becomes his *own* unique person. God, after all, did not create the *persons* Hitler or Mother Teresa, it was they, *themselves, who* were responsible for the unique *persons* they became. (The idea God creates particular persons is the notion of "*predestination*" that totally robs man of free-will.) It is because there is only one human nature and no *particular* human nature, all references to the man "Jesus" are references to his unique *person* and *not* references to his human nature – which was no different from that of any other human being.

One reason Cyril emphasized Jesus was *not* a *person,* was to avoid any notion Jesus *pre-existed* the incarnation – as if God had merely "adopted" him as His special "son" – that whole "adoptionist" theory. At the same time, however, Cyril left the door open for a false understanding of Christ. **Instead of considering the man Jesus as his *own* unique *human person*, he made Almighty God (Logos) a *human "person"* instead!** That God is the *person who* Jesus is (God's own self-identity, subject, etc.), is a piece of orthodox Hinduism. The idea God is a *person*, a subject, self, *who,* "I am" – and all the rest – is simply making God into man's own image, and any Christology based on this idea, is false. To think God is a human person or that man is a divine person is the definition of *anthropolatry* – idolatry. In all man's Christologies, there could be no greater error than thinking God is a "*person*" or *three persons.* And do not think for a minute this notion – the Trinity as three persons – was the view of all the fathers. Certainly *not* those in the "Antiochene" school of thought.

A unanimous understanding of the fathers, however, was that the Incarnation was God creating *Its own* universal human nature and no one else's. This was basic to their Christologies, and any other understanding of the Incarnation can be dismissed out of hand. The Logos did not create or unite Itself to any "particular" human being or "person", but created *Its Own* human nature eternally one with Itself. On this score, at least, the fathers were in total agreement.

Although everyone expects God's *own* human nature to be vastly different from the rest of mankind, the fact is, since there is only *one human nature,* God had no choice. Either God creates some *other kind of "being",* or sticks with the human nature God created in the first place. Not only did God stick with it, but united it to Itself in order to live with it forever! Human nature, then, could not be all that bad, indeed, this is exactly what the Incarnation is telling us: not only is mankind not that bad, but rather, it is of greatest worth to God. Still, for some people, accepting their human nature is not always easy, which is why God's taking on human nature should raise one's optimism to the heavens, appreciate what a marvel man is, and how loved he is – despite it all. Somewhere Irenaeus said of the Gnostics, "*They seek to be divine before they have even become* ***human.***" Had the Alexandrians understood this, they would not have spent so much time trying to divinize the human being Jesus.

While all the fathers adhered to the universality of human nature, the problem remains – "who really knows the *universal essence* of human nature?" As Origen pointed out, man doesn't even know the true nature of matter (the physical body), much less know the true nature of the soul. This is why no one can really point to man's bare human nature or essence, all he can point to is this or that individual *person,* point to *who* someone is – some particular subject. God, however, assumed none of this. We are given nothing to suggest that Jesus did not regard his humanity as his own – he had his own will, mind, awareness, actions, speech, all the human faculties, along with every kind of human need. There is nothing "divine" about human nature or a human person.

It is because the Alexandrians shared Plato's view of man as an unfortunate *embodied* being, they regarded "*incarnation*" as God only uniting Itself to a physical body. For them, this was the sole nature of the "*in-carnation*" – God only assumed "flesh". The literal meaning of "*in-carnation*", after all, is John's understanding "*the Logos* ***was made flesh***" (or "***became flesh***".) But, obviously, this was not the true nature of the Incarnation. What God created for Itself was a *complete* human nature, not just "flesh", but a human *soul* as well. In this respect, John's Platonic notion of "in-carnation" is misleading – or let us say, *incomplete*. The term "*Incarnation*" does *not* really define "Christ".

To think that God could *become* flesh – or even *become* a human being – is also *not* the nature of the Incarnation. God can neither "*become*" what God is ***not,*** nor "*become*" what God **is.** In truth, God cannot *become* anything. Needless to say, the term "*became*" is a problem in its own right. How could the Infinite, Immutable and Uncreated *change* to *become* something it was *not*? If taken literally, "*became*" meant God became something created, something *other* than God – an impossibility and totally outside *monotheism*. For the fathers, God could not be subject to change, impermanence or "*to anything that had a beginning or had changeability implanted in it*", rather, "*God, whose existence transcends all beginning and passing away, is superior to change*" (I do not recall which father said this.) Only *created* existence, given over to time, was subject to change and impermanence. "*Thus the* *divine Logos was not transformed into the nature of flesh in such a way that the divine immutability was impaired, the oneness of the two could never compromise the impassible nature of God".* "*If human qualities and experiences were ascribed to the Logos who transcended all things, this would be blasphemy*" – sounds like Cyril.[2] So we have to throw out any notion God *became* flesh or *became* a human being. It is proper, however, to say God *created* and *united* flesh to Itself, this was the fathers' understanding of John.

It goes without saying, God's Infinite essence cannot be *contained* in the flesh, or even in a soul. The incarnation was not God putting on a human body as if it were a coat, or God being enclosed *inside* some physical body. God can never be *circumscribed* or *contained* **in** anything. God can, however, be united to body and soul, and this union of man and God *is* Christ. The true nature of the Incarnation, then, was not God merely creating *another* individual human being, rather, it was man's universal human nature *conceived in* God as God's *own* human nature, this is the "Incarnation". It was for the sake of *revealing* this eternal union that God's *common human* nature had to *become* (*be seen*) *in* an individual being. So while God's *eternal* oneness with man (conceived in God) was *prior* to its *earthly* revelation, yet, to *reveal* this Truth, God's human nature *became* an individual *person* on this earth. It was **"***becoming" an individual being *in this world* that necessitated what is called a "***kenosis"*** *(emptying)*, the end result being the conception and birth of the individual person "Jesus". So we might think of the Incarnation this way:

I. Man's common human nature ***conceived in, for, and eternally one with*** **God's divine nature, this** is the *eternal, heavenly Christ.* Christ is thus the Archetype and image in which all men were created, the same image God destined all to *become.* As archetype and image, Christ is not the revelation of what man is ***now*** on *this earth,* but what man is to ***become*** eternally in God.

II. In this Incarnation, **what** God *eternally* united to Itself was solely the *essence* of man, this alone is destined for eternal life. God did not unite Itself to all those properties, attributes or "accidents" (non-essentials) of human nature – why? Because they are ***incapable*** of eternal life in God. While these *non-essentials* are needed for *earthly* existence, they were never created to be (or to become) *eternal*. So God

[2] That God could *become* a man was a notion Cyril regarded as "*stupid and altogether wicked*". For him, the notion of "*became*" was "*nothing other than sheer sophistry and trumpery, the fabrication of a deranged mind*".

never united Itself to any human properties *(persons),* attributes or accidents.
III. To reveal the eternal Christ, God's common human nature had to *become* an *individual person* in this world – this historical revelation being the conception and birth of the man Jesus. Although not the *eternal Christ,* Jesus was nevertheless born into this world *one with God,* a union called "*theosis"* – an *individual's earthly* oneness with God. While this union *(theosis)* was Jesus' *personal* oneness with God in *this world,* this was not, however, the *personless* "*hypostatic union*" of the *heavenly* Christ *not* in this world. In this matter, the fathers agreed Jesus' human nature was only "deified" (transfigured and glorified) *after* his death and not *before*. This is why Jesus is the *example* of one who *became* the heavenly, eternal Christ. His *earthly* oneness with God *("theosis")* was *his own individual* oneness with God, whereas, following his death, it *became* God's *universal human nature* – Christ.
IV. God's *eternal* oneness with man's universal nature is called a ***"hypostatic union****", a union solely* **in** *God and nowhere* **in** *man.* It was to **reveal** this eternal union **in** God that God's ***human*** *nature* had to undergo a ***kenosis*** to *become* a human person ***in*** *this world.* The reason this human person was born in the unitive state of *theosis,* is because this is as far as man can go ***in this world*** and be one with God.[3] *Theosis,* however, is not Christ's eternal *"hypostatic union",* a union not humanly livable *in this world.* This is why the fathers believed Resurrection and Ascension was the "deification" of Jesus' human nature to *become* God's *own human nature (a "hypostatic union")* – the same God destined every man to *become*.
V. What this means is that Jesus is the example or icon of someone who lived in this world one with God (*theosis*) – an example of *Christ-in-this-world.* It was his resurrection and Ascension, however, that revealed the *eternal heavenly Christ – i.e., Christ* as **no particular human being in this world, but Christ as the *true nature* of God's *eternal* oneness with mankind.** There is a great difference, then, between Jesus as the example of an ***earthly Christ*** **in this world, and the *eternal Christ in* God *– not in this world.*** This is the difference between man's *individual* union with God *(theosis)* in this world, and the heavenly *hypostatic union* that is *no individual* and not in this world. Unfortunately, the difference between these "unions" has never been given any consideration. Not only is there a difference between Christ-

[3] There are different definitions of *theosis* – "*made godlike*", "*deified", "the ultimate absorption of the soul into Deity",* sometimes just "*a state of union with God".* (See Chapter 25 on *Deification*.)

-in-this-world and the heavenly Christ-in-God, but a huge difference exists between man's earthy union with God or "*theosis*" and his *eternal* "*Hypostatic union*" in and with God.

The "difference" we are pointing out, is reminiscent of Hilary's three states in the existence of Christ. We have put the last estate (the *eternal* Christ) *first,* however, in order to explain the reason for the "*kenosis*" Paul speaks of – to be gone over next. Hilary, however, says nothing of what it took for God's common human nature to *become* a particular person in this world. Since the "Incarnation" was man's *essential* nature created in God's glorious dimension, this heavenly condition in God had to be forfeited (be *emptied*) in order to become an individual person on earth. This was Paul's "*kenosis*", *a* forfeiture or emptying required *prior* to the earthly birth of the individual person "Jesus". The temptation to avoid, is to think it was the heavenly man Jesus *who* came down, lived this earthy life, and then went back again. **False**! Prior to his conception and birth from Mary, Jesus never existed. The human nature God created for Itself was *no individual particular person* – as said, the *eternal Christ* is no *particular* human being. There is no great mystery about the man Jesus, the mystery of Christ, however, is something else entirely. In fact, it is a mystery that can never be grasped *intellectually.* Those who think the *real Christ* is easy to understand, or who have relied on the naive presentation of the proverbial party-line, will have missed this *mystery* completely. Actually, the **mystery** of Christ is not on the map of man's ordinary thinking abilities – which is *why* Christ can only be "*revealed*".

Before there can be any understanding of the true nature of the *kenosis* necessary to reveal Christ to man, let us go over the historical event by which this revelation came about. The *miracle* of this revelation – referred to as the "*Annunciation*" – was not God creating a human soul – God creates *every* soul – but the miracle of God taking the place of a *natural father's* contribution to human conception. **If God had not provided the male sperm or chromosomes, the child born of Mary would have been her "*clone*".** In those days, of course, they knew nothing of the female ovum necessary for conception. They thought only the male sperm was responsible for generating offspring – the womb was only a receptacle for the child's physical development. Mary knew, of course, that without a man she could not have a child. So, for the conception of the man Jesus, God miraculously supplied the male counterpart to Mary's equally necessary contribution – the female ovum.[4] For God, however, miracles are nothing, they are simply God's *ordinary modus operandi.* It was because of this *physical* miracle of God providing a natural father's genes and chromosomes, however, that this event was called an "*in-carnation*" – the *physical* "*embodiment*" of Jesus by his divine Father – God.

The only description we have of this event is Luke's account. His depiction is remarkable in that it was long before there was any acknowledged "Trinity"– nearly two hundred years before there was any full recognition or formulation of God as Trinity. His account, however, wonderfully illustrates how an understanding of Christ totally depends on God as Trinity. The account is also interesting because it could only have come from Mary herself. Thus she learned that:

I. – "*The Holy Spirit will come upon you*". For the Spirit to *come upon one* is the definition of what it means to be "*anointed*" (*christos* in Greek) – i.e., one specially chosen by God. (Where people called Jesus the "*anointed*", it was God's angel that informed Mary she was *anointed.*) To be *anointed*, of course, does not mean hearing words in one's head, rather, it is God's divine Spirit entering the soul to make Its abode in the center of man's being. (This does not mean the Spirit can be "circumscribed", rather, it means the soul being "*opened*" onto the Infinite.) – *"She conceived by the Holy Spirit"*, a human soul was created in Mary's womb by the Spirit. Thus the Spirit created a soul one with Itself from the moment of its conception.
II. – "*And the power of the Most High will over-shadow you*" – (or "*will cover you with its shadow".)* This is reminiscent of Moses' encounter with the *Most High* (the Transcendent) on Mt. Sinai. The term "shadow" or *over-shadow* has tremendous significance in mystical lore. We need only be reminded that to *see* God in this life always *over-shadows* the intellect or mind. Thus the saying, "*See God and die*" means no man can continue to live on earth and see God face- to-face at the same time. So a "shadow" is literally a "cloud of unknowing", the "darkness" of the soul's faculties due to the *excess* of God's *Light.* And, indeed, this is the Unknown "*Light" that "came into the world.*"
III. – The Spirit's creating a human soul in Mary's womb, however, is *not* an "in-carnation" – because the soul is *prior* to the body. It is the soul that will *cause* or *form* a human body, which is the part the divine

[4] Those who deny God supplied the Y chromosome, or deny the human XY, can only believe Jesus appeared out of thin air – as if God was a fairy and only had to wave a wand.

Logos plays in this event. Only the Logos has an *existential union with matter,* thus only It could supply the *body* or flesh to be *in-formed* by the soul. The "miracle" of supplying a natural father's chromosomes, then, was the "miracle" provided by the divine *Logos – "and the child will be holy and be called the Son of God"*. (Note: it was the "*child*" Jesus, conceived by Mary and God that would be *called* the "Son of God" – certainly it was *not* God that would be called the "Son of God". As noted, the New Testament writers knew nothing of a "Trinity" or "Logos".)

What is called the "Incarnation", then, was not an independent act of the Logos, but like every divine "*Act*", required the entire Trinity – God's "modus operandi". No *one* of the Trinity was more involved than the others. Christ is not *just* the oneness of man with the Logos, but the oneness of man's human nature with the whole Trinity. To think man could *only* be one with the Logos' divine nature, but *not* with the divine Spirit and Transcendent, defies the *single essence of God.* **As Trinity, there cannot be one without the others.**

The only reason the Logos is strategic to the "in-carnation", is because only the Logos has an *existential union* with matter – no use creating an *immaterial* soul if there is no "*matter*" for it to "in-form". Also, because the Spirit and Transcendent have no *existential connection* to creation, they could never have been *incarnated.* It is only ***through*** the Logos anything created can be "*embodied,*", only *through* the Logos can there be an *eternal* body, and thus, an *eternal* human nature. Confronted with the mystery of the Annunciation or Incarnation, Theodore of Mopsuestia (350 – 428), had no problem understanding it, he said,

> "*Everyone acknowledged this truth*:
> *Logos' oneness with all creation* – already one with Mary
> *Holy Spirit's presence in all* – already present in Mary
> *All are* ***in*** *the Father"* – because God has no "outside".

Since the Logos was *already* present in Mary, at the Annunciation it was by the "power" of the Most High the Spirit created a human soul to *in-form* the body fashioned by the Logos. Thus it was the Logos, already present *in* Mary that became the flesh of this human soul. Obviously, the Incarnation was more than a *body's "existential union"* with God (Logos), even more than a *mystical union* (*theosis*) of the *soul* with God (Holy Spirit.) Above all, it was *God's own human nature* created **in** the very essence of God that, from the moment of conception, was eternally one with Itself. It is this ***eternal oneness*** that defies the rules of ordinary creation. Clearly, the Incarnation was *not*

God *becoming* a human being, not God *conceiving* God or being *born* into this world. The one born was a human being that, like everyone born in this world, is one with the Logos, but *unlike* everyone else, was born one-with-the-Spirit (*theosis*), which is why he was aware of his oneness with God from birth.

It could be said, the "Way" the Incarnation was revealed is the *reverse* of man's *ascent* to God. Where man's ascent or journey *ends* in God, this is where the Incarnation *begins*. Thus the point where God's humanity *began* its journey to human existence on this earth, is the point where man's journey to God *ends* in God. Keeping in mind, man is a *microcosm* of creation, we can see how Christ is the Alpha and Omega of man's eternal oneness with God, and how the *incarnate Christ* is the "Way" between the two. Maximus put it this way: "*what he underwent in himself through the incarnation as man, is our future destiny*". Thus we ascend not only as the earthly Christ ascended, but ascend in the reverse of the eternal Christ's *descent*. If rightly understood, the Incarnation is the most momentous event in human history.

The eternal union of two disparate natures cost God nothing, it was solely an act of divine Goodness. If there was a problem, however, it was how to *reveal* this Truth to mankind for all time. Those already one with God (in heaven) knew it, but what about those on earth who did not know it? As already said, no one can *see* man's common essence or *see* its oneness with God – this union is not some individual "thing" or a being one can point to. This is why, to reveal this Truth to those on earth, required God's own human nature to become one of the "multiple" here on earth, one individual indistinguishable from others, yet, one that would forever be known as a unique *human person*. To understand why this involved what Paul called a "*kenosis*" (or *emptying*) is because from the moment of its conception **in** God, man's common human nature *participated* **in** God's divine nature – God's Knowing and Glory. For God's universal human nature to *become* a single earth-bound human being, *necessitated* a *kenosis,* a forfeiture or "coming out" of life in God to life in this world. **This *kenosis*, then, was on the part of God's *own* universal human nature, a *forfeiture* of its glorious life in God in order to become *its "own individual person"* on this earth.**

But before going on to consider Paul's understanding of "kenosis", we might go back over the fathers' understanding of the Incarnation as God uniting Itself to man's *universal* human nature (*Universal Man),* yet "***a nature that appeared (was seen) in one individual***" (Cyril.) **There is no greater philosophical question than how *to get from a universal to the particular*** – or to the individual. There is not a philosophy in the world for which this is not its key problem – everybody, of course, having their different theories or paradigms. Of all man's religions, none, however, so depends on the answer to this philosophical conundrum than Christianity. This is the difference between Christ as just one *individual* human being or Christ as "*universal* man" – i.e., all mankind eternally united to God. As we know, the proverbial Christian party-line presents the *individual* man Jesus as the one and only Christ – one *individual* human being. This, of course, not only skips the whole philosophical and theological problem, but promotes a naive, if not false, understanding of Christ. The only theologian who actually took on this problem was the great Franciscan theologian, Blessed Duns Scotus (1266 – 1308.)[5]

Scotus is very clear that it is man's universal *essence* or "***quiddity***" that *becomes* ***"haeccity"*** (literally ***thisness***), meaning, it is man's universal human nature that *becomes* an *individual* human being. Thus it is ***what*** man is (essence), that *becomes* **who** some *individual is.* Scotus further points out, "*Christ's* ***human nature*** *is the same as every other human nature. Christ's* ***human nature*** *has a passive potency for assumption* (that is, being united to God.) *The passive potencies and liabilities of a nature are* **essential** *features of it,* **not** *accidental features. The passive potency for assumption had by Christ's human nature is thus* **essential** *and therefore shared by all human natures."* In short – man's *essential* (universal) nature has the *potential to be* Christ, to *become* God's *own* human nature, to literally ***be God's incarnation***. This also implies, of course, that God's divine nature has the *potential* to assume (be united to) man's human nature. And as to *how* God *actualizes* this *dual potential* – divine and human – all this is bound up in the ***mystery that is Christ.***

Scotus opined that the process of moving from man's *universal* nature to *becoming* an *individual* human being is what he calls a "*contraction*", a *reduction* in scope as it were – the antonym of "contraction" being "expansion". He referred to the "individual" as a "modification" (or *mode*) of man's universal nature. As to *how* this actually

---

[5] Unlike Plato for whom *matter* was the cause of "individuation", or Aristotle, for whom the *soul* or psyche was the primary cause of "individuation", for Scotus, "individuation" was the process of man's universal essence *becoming* an individual being. Thus neither body or soul accounts for an *individual* human being, rather, it is the essence of man (whatever God's knows it to be) that *becomes* an *individual* human being. For Scotus, then, **what Man is,** is *prior* to his **becoming** any *individual* human being – prior to being any particular man or **"who" someone is.** Without an "individual" man, of course, there would be **no "person"** to talk about, for the ***essence of man is no person***.

works – going from a universal essence to multiple individuals – only God knows.[6] Though Scotus may not have connected the universal "becoming" an individual with Paul's "*kenosis*", yet this is one way, at least, to understand it – i.e., understand God's *universal* human nature having to forfeit its eternal life in God to become an *individual* being in this world.

Given the essence of Man's "human potential" *to be* Christ, explains why God *never* creates any particular *person.* As Scotus affirms, God did not unite Itself to any of man's *accidental properties,* or *individual* characteristics – all those extraneous attributes *not* of the **essence** of human nature. All differentiation adds up to a *person* "who", as we know, God *never* created in the first place. The reason these properties were never united to God is because they were solely intended for *earthly* life and would be of no use (couldn't even function) in *eternal* life. So while these *accidental* properties are useful for earthly existence, they are of no use as regards man's eternal life in God – a life not remotely akin to earthly existence.

In Summary – The real *mystery* of Christ is that Christ is *not* one individual being, but God's oneness with man's *universal* (or common) human nature. The reason this is difficult to grasp is because of the difference between man's human nature as he knows and lives it *on earth,* and the bare essence of human nature destined for an eternal life *not* on this earth. There is nothing eternal about this world or man's life in it. It is because only God knows the true *essence* of man that man cannot imagine his destiny of eternal life in and with God. So the difference is between man's short earthly existence, and his *eternal existence in God.* Man's mistake is to premise his understanding of *eternal life* on what he knows of his *present* earthly life. He cannot conceive how his eternal life in God is *nothing* like his present life. As the fathers said, *"Man was created to be* ***more*** *than he is now*" – *now* on this earth, that is.

We are not going to spend time going over all the myths man has created about *eternal life* premised on his present understanding of man on earth. Even the best of theologians are reluctant to admit any radical existential change in human nature – much less an *ontological* change. Instead, they assure us everyone will go on just the same – only better,

---

[6] It is my view that *self is the cause of individuation* – the cause of every individual becoming *his own person.* What Scotus calls a "contraction", I call a "reflex-action" – i.e., the soul being aware of its own existence, "*I am*", *I exist*", "I *am myself and no other*". Where man's *universal* nature is *personless*, as an *individual,* however, he is a *person* – his own *self.*

of course. After all, nobody would want to alarm the "simple folk" or imply they will have to "lose" anything – much less *everything*. Other than being "perfected" whatever that means – their present life will go right on. This, of course, is pure myth and wishful thinking. Heaven and earth are two radically different dimensions of existence, one in this world, the other solely in God. For man to be able to "partake" or "participate" in God's dimension of existence requires such a radical change in his human nature that everything he knew and experienced on earth is wiped out completely – and forever. To "gain eternal life" is the loss of everything man ever knew about himself and life on this earth – even, perhaps, everything he knew about "God".

KENOSIS

"Jesus Christ, who being in the ***form of God****, did not count equality with God a thing to be grasped, but* **emptied himself (kenosis)**, *taking the form of a servant, being made in the likeness of men, and in habit found as* ***a*** *man, he humbled himself, becoming obedient unto death*".

It would seem Paul not only regarded "Jesus Christ" as equal to God, but that he *pre-existed* his appearance in the world. While the Jews (including Jesus) believed the *messiah* (*christos)* pre-existed, they did not, however, believe the *messiah was* God. As for thinking Jesus *pre-existed,* this would make Luke's account of Jesus' miraculous conception (Annunciation) his "re-appearance" in this world, a "second coming", or maybe, a "re-birth". But if Christ's *Incarnation* – defined as the union of God and man – *pre-existed* the Annunciation and birth of Jesus, then Luke's account is *not* an account of the "*Incarnation*" – since Christ *pre-existed* the birth of the man Jesus. The implication is that since Christ's *human nature pre-existed,* then the birth of Jesus was its taking on the *form of* ***a*** *man – an* individual man, that is. Thus Paul made it clear it was the *pre-existent* Christ (or messiah) and *not* God who "*emptied himself*". There is no way Paul, a devout Jew, believed God could be *emptied* or forfeit (be *emptied* of) any aspect of Its divine nature.

Like many others, Paul mixed up his time-frame – such as Hilary warned us not to do. He *begins* with a *post-incarnational* view of Christ (as God) and *then* explains Christ taking on the *form of man* (Jesus.) As John would later testify, however, *prior* to the "Incarnation" there was neither Christ nor the man Jesus – "*In the beginning was the Logos*" – only God existed. There was as yet no "Christ" and no man Jesus. But putting aside Paul's skewed time-frame, his understanding of Christ is on the mark. His understanding hinges on his meaning of "***Christ***" as the ***"form of God"*** *taking* on the ***"form of man".*** Thus God's ***divine nature*** took-on (*assumed* or united) to Itself the *form of man,* a union that **is *Christ*.** This union, of course, involved no *forfeiture* on *God's* part, and as for man, this was his ***gain*** *of eternal life*. The Incarnation, then, was no forfeiture of God's *divine nature*, but God creating and uniting man's *human nature* to Itself – the definition of "Christ".

Paul's use of the term "**form**" seems strategic to his understanding of Christ. That Christ is *both* the "*form of God"* and "*the form of man",* is on the mark. The term "*form*" is a Platonic term for some divine archetypal image of God, and no doubt this was Paul's reference to Christ as the "form" or "image" of God. The Platonic use of *"form*", however, was also a reference to the **essence of a thing as *distinct* from matter, a** reference to the ***real*** as **distinct from the *apparent.*** For Aristotle, on the other hand, "form" was a reference to some individual "soul" ***in-forming*** a physical body – hence the definition: "the *soul* is the *form* of the body". For still others, however, *form* had the connotation of an "*external presentation*" of the *real,* which seems to be Paul's understanding of Christ as the "*Spirit made visible*" – an "*external* (or visible) *presentation*" of the *Spirit.* This understanding, however, raises the question of Paul's Judaic understanding of God's "*Spirit*" – Judaism recognized no "*Logos*" per se. Once again, it is important to remember that none of the New Testament writers understood God as a "Trinity", none premised their understanding of Christ on God's "*Triune Modes of Existence*". Also, by the time John's Gospel appeared and referred to the "*Logos*" as "God", Paul was long dead.

If, then, for John it was the *Logos* made flesh, for Paul, it was the *Spirit.* Note, however, neither said it was **Yahweh** or the "**Father**" (their usual reference to "**God**") that was *made* flesh. Granted, it was forbidden for Jews to utter the *name* of God, yet many other names were used to refer to God, but *Spirit* and *Logos* were **not** among them.[1] Also, as noted earlier, there had not yet been a clear distinction between the Spirit and Logos anyway. According to the *Judaic* understanding of *Spirit, he* was the "exalted one" God *created* to be *His* medium in creation. Thus, since the Spirit was *not* God, "*he thought it not robbery to be equal to God, but emptied himself taking the form of a servant.*" For Paul, then, the Incarnation was the "*Spirit made visible*", *not* "God" made visible. Obviously, it would have made no sense to say "*God was equal to God*".

Paul's reference to "*kenosis*", then, had nothing to do with God (the *Father or Yahweh) emptying* itself. Paul's implication is that it was the *Spirit* who did not think itself so equal to God that it could not *empty* itself to take on the form of man. It was the Spirit, then – God's created *medium* in creation – that *forfeited* its glorious existence with God to take on the form of man. This is reminiscent of Paul's fellow contemporary, the Jewish mystic, Philo of Alexandria, for whom the Spirit (or Logos) was a lesser being than God. Philo put the Spirit be-

---

[1] While the term "God" is used throughout scripture, this was not regarded as God's "personal name". As to who gave God a "name", it was Moses' "I am who I am" – the same any human being could say *about himself.* In truth, however, God has no "*name*". To truly see and know God it would never cross the mind to give God a "name", a gender, nor any "I am" – me-myself- or-I. God has no need to *identify* Itself to anyone, for no *authentic* revelation of God could be mistaken for something else.

tween the "Uncreated and created" as a *bridge* between the two, even suggesting in his mystical way, an Incarnation of the Spirit *in man.* So too, for Paul, the Incarnation *was* the "*Spirit made visible*" (in the flesh), this was "Christ". That the Spirit was *not* God, but a lesser spiritual being, may explain why Paul always addresses his prayers and worship, not to Christ or even to the Spirit, but to God – who he addresses as "Father". Even the early fathers, despite their affirmation of the Trinity, always referred to God as the "Father", as if the Spirit and Logos were once or twice removed – "secondary" and "third" *persons* – as they were eventually called. That today, liturgical prayers still reflect this kind of *hierarchy*, illustrates the difference between the Trinity as a mere concept or formulated figurehead instead of the experiential Reality of God's ongoing *Triune* revelations to man.

As said, however, neither Paul or John's Christology was premised on the *Trinity.* Their understanding of Christ was based in part on the Judaic (*Spirit*) and in part on the philosopher's *Logos.* As for their understanding of "human nature", clearly this was Platonic! For both, the Platonic notion of man's "human nature" as a "visible body" seemed enough to define their understanding of "*in-carnation*". What is significant, however, is John's linking the flesh with the *Logos.* That the Stoics believed matter was united to the Logos, explains why the fathers always linked the Logos to Christ's *body* or *flesh* and *never* to his soul or divinity. It is man's link with the Logos, however, that is the meaning of an *"existential union" – i.e., all things united to God by **reason** of their mere existence* – divine ***Reason** being the Logos.*

Though Paul certainly knew the real Christ, he had to meld his understanding with the Judaic belief in a "messiah" – someone sent to save Israel and establish a kingdom on earth. Given his Judaic Monotheism, however, Paul certainly never believed the Uncreated could *become* the created, or that God could "empty" Itself of Its divine nature to become anything. As said, for God to create and *unite* Itself to man's human nature cost God nothing; this was solely an act of God's good will – even, God's esteem for the marvel of Its own creation – man. But since God cannot *become* anything or be *emptied* of anything, "**what", then,** *emptied* itself?

Based solely on his own experience, Paul knew enough about God to know that no human being could remain on this earth and exist *in* God's glory at the same time. As someone "*rapt to the third heaven*" who didn't know if he was "*in the body or out of the body*", **he knew man's heavenly and earthly existence were incompatible.** So based on *his own experience* of being rapt to the third heaven, and then having to *return* to ordinary earthly life, this "come down" was literally, a *kenosis*. Being *emptied* of a glorious existence *in* God can only be called a "let-down", a "descent" from a taste of glory to an inglorious existence in this world. Thus he relates his *own* experience to the necessity of man – or Spirit – being *emptied* of "*God's glory*" in order to live on earth, live as one of the multiple. No question, Paul based his whole understanding of *Christ on* ***his own*** *revealing experiences*. His problem was trying to make it suit the Gentile mentality and, at the same time, fit into his Judaic belief system. Better had he stuck *only* with what God had *revealed* to *him*.

The *feat* of the Incarnation, then, was not God creating Its own human nature or effecting an eternal union with man. To reveal this truth, however, **the feat was God's *own human nature* forfeiting its glorious life in God to live an inglorious life in this world.** This *kenosis* (*emptying)* was solely on the part of God's *universal human nature,* certainly *not* on the part of God's divine nature, nor on the part of any individual or particular person. The feat, then, was God's universal human nature having to become an individual being in this world and, consequently, to become its *own person*. This *descent* from God is actually the *reverse* of man's *ascent* to God. Where this *descent* was *taking on* the life of an individual *person,* man's *ascent* to God is being *emptied* of this individual *person* – emptied in order to *become not his own,* but become God's *universal humanity*. This latter kenosis was the very nature of Jesus' death – death of the *individual person Jesus.* And so it will go for every human being.

"Kenosis", then, was God's ***universal*** *human nature becoming* an **individual** being – one of the multiple, its *own* person, a relative nondescript in this world. So a *kenosis* is what it took for God's universal human nature to "leave" its *eternal life in* God and take up an indefinite life in the world. To be an *individual* in this world means, of course *becoming one's* ***own*** *person* – *i.e.*, being aware of one's **own being** – "*me, myself and I"*. So where *God's* universal human nature (*in* God) is *not* aware of its *own being* – no "me, myself and I" – yet to be an *individual in this world* requires one to be aware of his *own* being, his *own* independent existence. Just to *function* in this world, every man has to be free to be his *own* self, his *own* individual *person* – such, at least, did God ordain it *to be.*

The reason for this kenosis is that man's common human nature, conceived **in** God's divine *modus operandi* (the Trinity), is not remotely prepared (or equipped) to live under any *earthly* conditions. Those who think earthly existence is *compatible* with life **in** God's heavenly dimension, will never understand the eternal Christ. In fact, the sole reason for speaking of "*heaven*" (man's eternal life in and with God) is because it is **not** life on *earth,* nor even remotely *like* earthly existence. It is because these two "lives" have little in common that there is the phenomenon called "death". There is no other reason for death than entrance into *eternal life* in God. The more people think these two existences (heaven and earth) have in common, the less they know God and Christ – we'd even say, the less they know human nature and themselves.

Kenosis, then, actually affirms the tremendous difference between the *essence* of man's *eternal union with God* and an *individual person's* union with God. Kenosis was a descent from participating in *God's* heavenly existence to participating in *man's* earthly existence. **No *individual person* underwent this kenosis, rather, it was "what" man is (the essence of man) that underwent this kenosis to *become* "who" some individual person *was.*** This ordeal, then, was not on the part of any individual human being or person, but solely on the part of God's common human essence *prior* to *being* an individual person. Thus because it was *no one's* "experience", it can best be regarded as an "*inhuman event*" – "inhuman" because it was *not* the experience of any individual human being. Rather, *kenosis* was man's universal nature *becoming* an individual *person.*

It is *because* the human nature God united to Itself was *not* that of a particular human being or person, that in order to reveal this union it was necessary man's universal nature *become* an *individual* person in this world. How else could God reveal this eternal (heavenly) union to man in *this* world? *Kenosis,* then, was the forfeiture of man's *eternal* life *in God,* in order to take on life *in this world* as "one of the many". This meant coming-out of (or down-from) man's glorious existence in God to being an individual man in an inglorious world. This, however, was not some instantaneous or over-night miracle, but the most terrible *ordeal* human nature could undergo. It might be compared to crossing over *a chasm – no-man's land* – between the Uncreated and created. To put a finger on this *God-awful* ordeal, one can put his finger on the *Line* (*Christ)* and then move it down into the world of multiple beings. This descent falls outside anything man could experience or compare it to. It is beyond all man's notions of "suffering", spiritual and physical, even beyond his worst notions of hell. Because it was *not* the experience of any individual person, it can only be called *inhuman and ungodly.*

The fathers were right to understand this "come-down" or kenosis as Christ's true "sacrifice" – and *not* the crucifixion and death of Jesus. In truth, the *sacrifice* was God's *own* humanity putting off its glorious life in God to become an individual human being – a particular person.

This was not the experience of any *individual person,* but of the essence of man *prior* to *being* an individual person. This was not, then, the experience of Jesus or any *individual person* – prior to his conception and birth "Jesus" never existed. No question, to reveal the "Incarnation" was a *divine* feat, *God's own doing and knowing,* compared to which, creating the whole universe was as nothing. As said, compared to this *kenosis*, Jesus' crucifixion was a blessed *release,* for death begins the *ascent* to God. This kenosis, however, is what it took to reveal man's destiny of eternal oneness with God.

The ending of this kenosis (or descent) is generally regarded as the miraculous conception and birth of the *individual* man given the name "*Jesus*". Since it was not Jesus "*who*" underwent (or experienced) kenosis, if he ever knew anything about it, this would have been the same as Paul's experience – rapt in the glory of God and having to come back to ordinary life again. This experience, however, has absolutely nothing in common with the reality of "kenosis". Kenosis is not a "coming back" or re-adjusting to ordinary life again, rather, it is *prior* to there being any individual rapt to the third heaven. Kenosis was *no one individual's* "experience", rather, it was the terrible ordeal of *becoming one individual*. **Kenosis was God's own common *undifferentiated* human nature – "what" man is – *becoming* an individual *differentiated* being, which means becoming *its own person*.** To think it was the *individual* man Jesus who underwent this ordeal negates Luke's account of Jesus' conception and birth. If Jesus *pre-existed* his own birth, then Luke's account is no more than Jesus being "re-incarnated" or re-born into this world.

As to how someone already incarnated can be "re-incarnated", this is best left to those who believe in "reincarnation" – *the fallacy of all fallacies*! While the fathers held Jesus was God's "instrument" for the revelation of Christ, yet "*Universal Christ*" is man's *universal eternal oneness with God* and *not* some individual's oneness with God. **It was not the *particular* man Jesus "who" was God's human nature, rather, God's *undifferentiated* human nature is *no* particular individual person.** Human nature is ***what*** man is, Jesus was ***who*** an individual man *was*.

Needless to say, no man can *empty* himself of anything – even if he wanted to – much less empty himself of God! Kenosis was solely God's *doing,* done once, and done for all mankind. Man had no say whatsoever. Although kenosis was *how* God revealed the Incarnation, this was certainly not the way every human being comes into this world. Although we can say every "individual" is "one instance" of man's common human nature, yet there are "instances" of "individuals" that are *not* so common, and in this matter, we think of the individual man Jesus.

Probably everyone has heard stories, legends or myths, of someone's unusual or "miraculous" conception and birth into this world. To find out if there is any truth in it, all we have to go on is the *evidence.* Just because somebody "says so", doesn't make *anything* true. So given the data on the life of Jesus, is there any *evidence* he ever went in *search of God?* Did he look for a teacher, a rabbi, a holy man – or whoever? Any evidence he joined a sect or spent time as a desert hermit? Apart from knowing his Judaic scriptures and living up to its practices, we have no other *evidence* whatsoever. After he became known, of course – some three years before his death – there is overwhelming *evidence* of his life with God. That *he knew he was one with God* may be *why* he didn't appear in public until shortly before he died – since Judaism did not believe in man's eternal oneness with God. While he did not broadcast this knowledge, he made it known sufficiently to be put to death **because** of affirming he was one with God. But we need not go over the wealth of evidence provided during Jesus' public life – of his being one with God – there are thousands of books on the subject.

Here the focus is on what it could mean for someone to be "conceived", as he was, by God and Mary. How might this make him different from the rest of mankind? As just another *individual* human being, he was no different. According to the fathers, however, Jesus came into this world in a *state of union with God,* which state or condition they called "*theosis*". So where every human being born in this world becomes aware of his *own* being, his *own* existence or *own self,* this was *not* the case with the man Jesus. He came into this world with what can best be described as the awareness of being a **"Whole Person" – defined as one who *is as aware of God as he is of himself.*[2]** It is *because* Jesus came into this world a **"Whole Person" he was *more fully* human than others. After all, man is not *fully* human until he comes to a state of an abiding oneness with God – indeed, one cannot *afford* to be fully human until he does!** (Recall Irenaeus' saying – the Gnostics were "*striving to become divine* ***before*** *they had even*

2 This does not mean one is merely conscious **of** God, rather, it means that the single *awareness of one's own being is, at the same time, the* awareness *of God's Being.* While God is man's true being, man is not God's being, yet the *dual* awareness of this union is such that no line can be drawn between the two – as regards where one begins and the other leaves off. This is not a *union* between two individual beings, but a *oneness* of two *totally disparate beings – Infinite and finite.* (Anyone who thinks *he* is God is clearly insane – he couldn't create an atom or alter a thing in the universe.)

become human".) Although the fathers believed everyone is created "theocentric", yet where most people have to search this out or have it revealed to them, Jesus never lived without the immediate *experiential* awareness of God as the Center of his being – his True being. It could be said he was *deliberately* born of a "Virgin" so he would know from birth he had no other "Father" but God. That his mother informed him of his miraculous conception, only worked to verify and recognize (or explain) his personal experiences of God – and this, from infancy. Of his oneness with his Father there was never a doubt; as said, he was put to death *because* he could never deny this. For an ordinary Jewish man, however, to claim he was one with God, well, this was not something ***new,*** this was *blasphemous*.

What this suggests is that there is a link between "*kenosis*" and the state of "*theosis*". One way to think of kenosis is as a gradual *descent* from Man's eternal **life with and in God, t**o becoming an *individual person* in this world. A descent that, at the same time, was also a gradual development of all the requirements necessary to live man's earthly experience in this world – a "gradual accommodation" to this world, we might say. **That the end of this *kenosis* was the birth of an individual in the state of *theosis,* means that God's common *human* nature only came *down* to that "*point*" where, as an individual person, it could function in earthly life and, at the same time, be fully aware of its oneness with God.** So the *point* at which *kenosis* came to an end, was the moment its human nature became aware of its *own* union with God and could *function perfectly as a human "person"* in this world. **It is *because* the Incarnation was solely a union of *natures* with *no persons* involved, that *Jesus was free to be his own person.*** He did not think he was Yahweh (Almighty God or "the Father"), nor did he think he was God's helpless *puppet* – with no mind or will of his own.

The state of *theosis,* then, was as far "down" as God's human nature could come without totally losing its original "Hypostatic Union". In modern terms, Christ's human nature came into this world "egoless", a state not unknown, however, to the Stoics as their "ideal" goal in life – called "apatheia". Christians, however, believing every man is created *theocentric,* to experientially realize this earthly union is what they called "*theosis*". This is not the place to go over this "unitive state" (or *theosis),* we only want to point out the difference between the "way" Christ's humanity came into this world and the way the rest of men came into this world. The *revelation* of the Incarnation was not just the birth of *another* human being in this world, if anything, its focus was on the *unique person* this human being *became* – i.e., the life of the man Jesus. God's whole purpose of revealing "Christ" was to give man an example of "how it went for one human being (Jesus) is how it will go for every human being". In some fashion, every human being should be able to relate to the historical *person*, Jesus. It is not for nothing he is the icon of Christ-on-earth.

Although man's earthly state of *union* with God is not his *final* estate, yet it is the true state in which every human being was intended to live on earth – or *should* at least. Because this is purely an "earthly" estate, however, there comes a turning point when there will be another type of *kenosis (emptying.)* Where the initial kenosis of God's universal humanity was its "individuation" (or *descent)* into this world of individual *persons, a reverse kenosis* will be an individual person's *ascent* to God. This latter kenosis is the complete loss (emptying) of one's own *individual personhood* – i.e., his own identity, "*who"* he is (or was.) Resurrection is the revelation of the "*Eternal Christ*", God's *own* person-less common human nature. So even the *human person,* Jesus, had to undergo this final kenosis to *become* the *eternal Christ.*

It should be obvious that to understand the true nature of the Incarnation, it is necessary to make a division between *what* in man is to *become* eternal, and what in man is non-eternal. By "non-eternal" we mean anything solely necessary for *earthly* life that can never be *eternally* one with the divine nature of God. Thus God is not eternally united to one's personality or temperament, to his genes and their variations – race, appearances, gender, characteristics, etc. Whatever goes into making one human being *different* from another are the *non-essential properties* of human nature. While these may be necessary for earthly existence, in God's eternal life, however, these do not exist. They are not – and never were – the e*ssence* of man's human nature.

All those distinctions that define "*who"* one is, can never be eternally united to God. This is why ***who*** one is, is not saved, but only ***what*** man is. This is a hard saying, but in truth, God cares nothing for persons or *who* they are – there is no "*Who's-Who"* the other side of the grave. God creates no "person" and is united to no "person". Sharing in God's eternal life, of course, nothing is wanting, all is perfectly fulfilled with no need for all those accidental properties that made earthly life possible. Absolutely, Christ levels the playing field – no one greater or lesser than another. After throwing out every distinction, **what** is left is every human being's bare essential nature created and transformed by God. To be transformed into Christ means to become God's *own* human nature eternally one with God. This is the transformation from one's *own* human nature into God's own universal human nature – *sans* any person. In the final analysis, then, no one can claim

"*I am one with God*" because in the end, *only* God's human nature is one with God – not *mine*, *his, hers* or *yours*. This is not a matter of terminology, but of *transformation*. The essence of human nature is beyond person. In the Trinity there is no place for any *person* – divine or human.

INCARNATION II

"On account of His infinite love he became what we are, in order that he might make us what he himself is". "Thus we must become that of which we are only now but an image".
(Irenaeus, 125 – 202)

A Gentile view Paul picked up, was the old philosophical tenet of man as a "microcosm" of creation. Thus Paul would refer to the Incarnate Logos (Christ), not only as the "*first born of all creation*", but the "*sum of creation*" – Christ, the Alpha and Omega of all creation. This is reminiscent of the Stoic view of the Logos as not only the *soul* (life) of the universe, but the material body of the universe, Its manifestation as well. For Philo, the Logos' *omnipresence* in creation was not appreciably different from Judaism's "Spirit". Thus Paul, assimilating this understanding, presented the Incarnation as the *embodiment* of the Logos or Spirit, and referred to Christ as the *summation* of all God's creation.

Irenaeus, however, is the one who picked up on Paul's reference to Christ as the *sum of creation.* In his view, the "way" the divine Logos *became* Incarnate (assumed human nature) was by "*recapitulating*" the whole of creation, uniting all to Itself, atom by atom, cell by cell, passing through all stages of human life, sanctifying each in turn. The Incarnation, then, was God's *recapitulating* the whole history of creation from the beginning so all things could be "*summed up in Christ*". Irenaeus' understanding of the Incarnation as a process of God's *recapitulation* of the whole of creation, was not only the *process* by which the Logos created Its human nature, but the process by which the Logos *saves* all creation – by uniting all to Itself. And just as man is a *microcosm* of creation, so too, Christ as "*universal man*" is the *sum* of creation – a *"cosmic Christ"* as some refer to this.

Reference to a "Cosmic Christ", however, is not a reference to any human being, but solely a reference to the Logos' *existential* oneness with *all creation.* It goes without saying, neither God nor any human being is the *sum of creation.* Reference to a "Cosmic Christ", then, is to creation's union with the Uncreated by reason its mere *existence*. Of the Trinity, only the Logos is *Omnipresent,* and not some man. The reason for pointing this out is to counter the false idea that because the man Jesus was one with God, therefore Jesus is *omnipresent* in creation. This is absurd, of course. Only God (Logos) is *omnipresent*, whereas "Christ" is a reference to God's oneness *with* creation, not God's eternal oneness with anything (or anyone) in particular. So where "Cosmic Christ" refers to God's *existential* union with *all* that exists, "*Incarnation*" refers solely to **man's** eternal oneness with God – Christ as "Universal Man" *beyond* a mere existential union.[1]

In this matter, Irenaeus noted that the Logos ***ad extra*** was Its *cosmic* manifestation, while the Logos ***ad intra*** was God's *Wisdom.* Thus, like two sides of a single coin, the Logos is both God's Wisdom *ad intra* and God's existential oneness with creation *ad extra.* The reason this is such a profound insight or truth, is that, in the end, God's Wisdom or Knowing will have more meaning for man than the Logos' connection with creation. Where the created is not forever, God's Knowing or Truth is eternal. This is why, in the end, it will be more important to have the "Mind of Christ" (God's Wisdom) than even the "Body of Christ".

One reason the "in-carnation" is usually linked to the *cosmic* element of the Logos is because this is easier to understand than how God's Wisdom could possibly be "incarnated" – *be made flesh.* More important than any physical (cosmic) oneness with God, however, is man's oneness with the Logos' *divine Wisdom.* While all of creation is ever changing and in flux, it is God's Knowing and Wisdom (Logos) that is *eternally* united to man. No question, God's Wisdom and Knowing totally outweighs any other connection God has with creation or man. Far more wonderful than a "cosmic Christ" or God's oneness with the "body", is man's ultimate oneness with God's Wisdom. To participate in God's own Wisdom and divine Knowing is the last word on the *Real Christ.* This totally overshadows any oneness with *Christ's body* – consistently talked about and stressed. Union of a *body* with God is nothing compared to sharing in God's divine Knowing or Wisdom!

It would be hard to find a more comprehensive understanding of the *Incarnation* than Irenaeus' "Christ". The process (or way) by which God united man to Itself entailed a *recapitulation* of the whole of creation – beyond a mere "existential" union. He based his understanding of Christ on his view that the ***"purpose of the incarnation was man's deification"***. That man is *saved* by this same *incarnational* transforming process, shifts the whole import of salvation from the cross and Jesus' death, to the Incarnation and *eternal* life – God's "coming" for man, not God's leaving man. This was also the meaning of the fathers' dictum *"salvation is transformation"* – literally, the **Logos *recapitulating* Its Incarnation in man making it eternally one**

---

[1] Those who think Jesus was God, or that he alone was Christ, are bound to mistake the epithet "*Cosmic Christ*" to mean the man *Jesus* is *omnipresent* in creation – Martin Luther, to name but one.

with Itself. This is how "Christ saves", this is the "Way" of Christ. By becoming incarnate in all men, man returns to God the same way God came to man. Here again, we have Christ, not only as "*Universal man*" but the "*Sum of creation*" being the "*Sum of mankind*".

For Irenaeus, the *Logos* was the *"Form in which the Godhead manifested Itself"* – implying, the immanent *Transcendent* was *formless* and *unmanifested*. Also, his reference to Christ was "*God and His man"*, implying the man Jesus was *his own* independent *person* – which indeed he was. Of all the fathers, Irenaeus seems to have had the most astute and unfailing understanding of the Trinity, Christ, and the true meaning of the Incarnation – even the Eucharist. When asked where he learned all this, he said from Polycarp, the disciple of St. John and friend of Irenaeus' parents whose home he visited. To my knowledge, Irenaeus is the only one of the fathers who had any direct contact with one of the Apostles' immediate disciples, yet, it is what God gave him, personally, to know, that truly counts.

In keeping with the Incarnation as the Logos *recapitulating* creation, this has implications for man's spiritual journey as a *recapitulation* of Christ's human journey from birth to death – and beyond. This means going through the whole incarnational process of transformation necessary to *become* Christ. Thus, if we think of this as *recapitulating* Jesus' own *interior* life with God, then *recapitulating* his spiritual life is the "way" man *becomes* Christ, becomes God's own human nature. If someone thinks of Jesus as Almighty God, then of course, there is no human model or spiritual life to recapitulate. To be transformed into Christ does not mean transformation into God, or transformation into the man Jesus. Rather, transformation is man's earthly human nature *becoming* God's one and only eternal, universal human nature – Christ, that is.

It is one thing to "relate" one's life with God to Jesus' historical life with God, yet it is quite another to know his *human experiences by way of one's own.* While we cannot verify Jesus' experiences or particular states prior to encountering them ourselves, yet, when, and if we do, then there is the marvelous recognition of the *Truth* of Christ, and we begin to understand *how it went for the earthly incarnate Christ, is exactly how it goes for every human being.* Thus we literally "recapitulate" Christ's human earthly, *spiritual journey* and ultimate transformation. In this way, our experiences not only verify Christ's human experience, but at the same time, Christ verifies our own. Mere belief cannot verify the Truth of Christ, it is only ***in our own life* with God that the Truth of Christ can be verified, known and lived.** We are not transformed into some other human being nor transformed into

God, but transformed into "Christ" – God's *own human nature* eternally one with Its divine nature.

Although some people think this "process" of incarnation started at the moment of creation and not at the historical time of the man Jesus, yet, imposing "time" on God's *doings* is always a fruitless speculation. What God can do in a second, can seem like thousands of years to man. All we know is that "Christ" was *only revealed* at a particular *time* in human history, not before and not after. As to *how long it took* God to create and unite man eternally to Itself – what could be a more inane question? All we know is that at some point God ordained man's ultimate destiny, and at some point revealed this to all mankind. This knowledge was the major purpose of the revelation called "the Incarnation" – the revelation of God's plan for man, revelation of the "way" it goes for all men, the end being *"Christ" – the* eternal oneness of God and man. This is the meaning of Christ as the Alpha and Omega of man and all creation.

It seemed to be Paul's view that when God initially created mankind (*adam* in Hebrew), the Logos was, from the beginning, incarnate in man or one with man. This is what was meant by man being created in the "image of God", which image was the incarnate Logos – the same Image that, for Paul, was "*the Spirit made visible*". That mankind (*adam*) was created without sin, Paul likens to Jesus, who, because he had no *human* father, was born without sin – "*like us in all ways but sin*". The basis of his understanding, however, was the widely held belief there existed only *one original soul* handed down – via the male seed – generation after generation. Thus the Judaic belief was that man's (*adam's*) *one original soul* was handed down one generation after another, a soul, however, tainted by Adam's fall – his sin. So given Paul's Judaic belief that the male seed generates the soul of the offspring explains why he and others believed because God created the soul (or life) of Jesus (one *not* handed down from a human father), this made Jesus the only sinless man (apart from Adam) God ever created. No question, one of the most overlooked revelations of the Incarnation is that God alone creates *each soul,* a soul just as sinless as the first human being ever created. God, after all, cannot create sin or a sinful soul. So the fact God creates every individual soul as innocent and sinless as Adam, negates Paul's view that only Jesus was born "sinless". Since the world at large had this same view – fathers handing down their soul (or life) to their offspring – this was man's long held *world belief* – Jew and Gentile alike.

But what if Paul had understood that **God alone creates every individual soul, a soul no different than the innocent sinless soul of**

Adam? What, then, would have been Paul's understanding of Jesus' "messianic" mission? In light of this truth, what becomes of the Christian paradigm based on Jesus' mission to redeem, restore, atone – all this Christian *sin* business? Absolutely, it would make one look further to understand the revelation of *the* Incarnation and Christ. **In truth, the Incarnation had not a single thing to do with *sin*.**[2]

So one totally overlooked revelation of the Incarnation is that *God alone creates each human soul* – and that no soul is a hand-me-down from any natural father. Furthermore, to create the body of a human being, the mother's genes and chromosomes are **equally** as necessary as the father's, thus it was not just Mary that supplied the *flesh* of Jesus, but God as well. So the notion that Jesus' human nature *only* came from Mary and that his divine nature (or soul) came from God, is a Platonic notion that can be dismissed out of hand. Although the fathers consistently say Jesus got his **human nature** from Mary, obviously this view is not true. **Human nature is *more* than a body, God alone created the individual soul of Jesus' *human nature – not* Mary!** Also, had God not supplied the male counterpart to her ovum, Jesus would never have been *conceived.* (Had Mary not been needed, then Jesus could just as well have appeared out of thin air.) It was by having no *natural* father, Jesus would know he came from God, was one with God, and without God, could not have existed. So Jesus' human soul came right from the hand of God – as does every soul.

It was Paul's belief, because Adam did not live up to the "image of God", he lost this image – fell. And since his fallen soul was passed on to his offspring, the purpose of Christ's coming was to restore man to his original sinless nature – restore the *image* of God in which he was created. This was not just Paul's view of sinful (or tainted) souls, it seems this was Jesus' same Judaic belief. Thus, since his soul, like Adam, was created by God – and not some hand-me-down, he could align his Messianic mission to restoring man to his original nature – the "*image of God*", that is. Where Adam's fall had closed the gates of

---

[2] Judaism never regarded its "Messiah" as a man sent to redeem man from sin or die to atone for them. But if Judaism believed God forgave sins, there was still the problem of "atonement" – i.e., making good one's injuries to his fellow man, requiring some form of "restoration" – "redemption". *Undoing* a wrong against one's fellow man, however, is rarely possible *even* if one regrets his actions. Since an *exact* "repayment" is rarely possible, for Paul at least, Jesus' death was this *exact* repayment on behalf of *all* offenders. So for Paul, the solution of "restoration" was God sending his son to "pay the price" (atone) for all men. While this vicarious atonement cannot do one's neighbor any good, it may, however, relieve the perpetrator of his guilt. All we can say is that Paul's notion of *Christ* as man's "atoner" has never sunk-in – "pay back" is the cause of all wars.

heaven, Christ came to open the gates for everyone.

For Paul, then, "redemption" meant the "restoration" of man to his original sinless nature, which *original image is Christ*. Thus Jesus, as a "*second adam*" (*mankind* in Hebrew), was a reproduction or restoration of the first Adam. And just as Adam "*contained all his descendants in himself*", so too, "Christ" *contains all humanity in itself.* Thus just as the Incarnation recapitulated the genesis of mankind – a whole *new creation* of man – so too, this same incarnation is recapitulated in every human being in order to become the true "image of God" – *Christ.* Man's redemption, then, was not achieved by Jesus' death on the cross – none of the fathers believed this – but rather, by the recapitulation of Christ's incarnation in every man. For Paul, it was by being "baptized" *in* Christ, that man was initiated *into* this "new creation".

Though baptism was regarded as the means of this restoration, unfortunately, even after baptism man goes right on sinning. Like the original *adam,* having free-will, man falls. Indeed, as long as man has free-will he is almost sure to fall, it is only when he has **no free-will** (in heaven) he can never fall. Obviously, there is no such thing as a *perfect* human being – only God is "perfect". So whatever may be man's perfection or "original nature", it awaits its heavenly destiny eternally in God.

The fathers, however, did not believe this "restoration" was all Christ was about, or that this was the end of man's journey. On the contrary, they believed man was created to be *more* than he is now, created, that is, to become the image in which he was created – become Christ, that is.[3] In their view, Resurrection and Ascension was the ultimate deification, not just of the man Jesus, but of all mankind. Christ, then, is what makes this final deification possible, man's final destiny being far *more* than man is *now*. So the human nature man begins with, is *not* the human nature man ends with. Man is radically changed, transformed, even *recreated,* into what God destined him to become from the beginning, this Omega point being everything we know and call "Christ."

As should be expected, the Gentile fathers who came after Paul, did not make the same connection with the incarnation and revelation

---

[3] Since most of the early fathers' references to "Christ" were references to God, they believed man's transformation into Christ was transformation into God. *"He (God) became **what** we are in order that he might make us **what** he himself is. Thus we must **become** that of which we are only now but an image"* (Irenaeus.) So what is this image in which man was created? God! Anyone who has a problem with man's transformation into "*Christ*" – God's eternal oneness with man – might have a bigger problem being transformed into Almighty God! (Later we will say more about this.)

of Christ as did Paul. From the first, everyone agreed salvation meant "deification" – as Irenaeus put it, "*The purpose of the Incarnation was man's deification.*" This was the one sure tenet the fathers never debated. Deification never meant mere belief, or some kind of experience, rather, it was the graced process of transformation, even an ontological transformation in which human nature was changed, a change made possible, in their view, by the grace of the Incarnation. The day Christianity lost this understanding of *deification as the* ***way*** *man is saved,* is the day it lost Christ. All the faith and good works in the world won't save anyone, only God's dynamic transforming grace can do this, and until completely transformed into Christ, no one's salvation is complete.

The Apostolic Fathers were not occupied with sin. Though they believed Christ came, lived and died for man, it had no *atoning* value. Between their Christology and soteriology, there was no overriding connection that later became the view Christ only came to die for man's sins, **this was *not* their view.** For Ignatius, the essence of "*salvation consists in union with Christ through whom new life and immortality flow in. He dwells in us and we become his temple, thus Christ is our true life, our inseparable life*". For Clement, "*the Logos became man so that you may learn from man how man may become God.*" The function of Christ's humanity, he said, was to serve as a "model".

It is the failure of man to understand Christ as *their own ultimate mystery,* that makes Christ little more than a symbol of forgiveness, atonement, redemption, a victim, whose sole purpose was to be sacrificed and killed because of man's sins. That Christ is all about sin or man's fallen nature and depravities, is the greatest insult to Almighty God man ever invented. What could be more offensive to God than heaping man's degrading sins on the greatest of God's revelations – Christ? Christ has been literally crucified by man's horrendous views and wrong understanding – the glorious truth of Christ literally buried under man's sins! **If people were asked what else Christ could have been about, most couldn't tell you.** The cross Christ carries is not man's sins, but man's complete and absolute failure to understand the true nature of Christ and what the Incarnation actually *revealed.*

To live a sinless life in this world was never the destined end for which man was created. Indeed, "*man was created to be more than he is now*", which "more" of course, is to be eternally one with God – be Christ. No father understood redemption or restoration as an end in itself or the whole purpose of the incarnation. On the contrary, everyone held "*salvation was transformation*" – transformation into "what"? Into Christ! As the principle of transformation, Christ was the "way" it worked, the alpha and omega of "deification" – as the fathers called it. Thus to be redeemed or restored (saved) was only the beginning of man's journey to God, the *alpha* being man's natural *existential* oneness with the Logos, and the *omega* being his *eternal* oneness with God – Christ. So while all are one with the Logos *naturally*, the incarnation went beyond to reveal a greater truth, which is man's eternal destiny in and with God. Those who find the scenario of sin, sacrifice and atonement comforting and reassuring, are simply beneficiaries of their own beliefs. As one author noted, "*To a considerable degree the definition of sin in church doctrine appears to have developed* ***a posteriori****, by a process which, proceeding from the salvation of Christ and from infant baptism,* ***made the diagnosis fit the cure****"*. In other words, what else is a messiah or savior about if not to *rescue, ransom and save* man from his evil ways – or from some devil?

If Paul had *not* assumed *everyone* was a sinner, what need would they have for Christ? This is why Paul (and others) first had to convince people they were sinners *before* they could promote Christ as their "savior". Paul made Christ dependent on sin, thus no sin = no Christ. It is because Christ made no sense without sin that Augustine and others decided everyone is *born in sin* – Adam's same "original sin". So man, born totally corrupt, had a strike against him *before* he even exists in this world! Augustine even referred to Adam's sin as a "happy fault" *because* it brought Christ into existence – the most obnoxious idea in all of Christianity. The truth, however, is that the revelation of Christ stands on its own with no connection to sin, to Adam, to the devil, to Jesus' death, or to any of the other negative ideas man has hung on Christ.

What could have been less of a surprise to God than man's "sinning", after all, God is the one who created man with this possibility – with free will, that is. As Tertullian said, "*Sin is man's second nature*". Actually, no one can *offend* God, man offends himself and his neighbor. And who can make sense of the idea God must "atone" to God? – i.e., the Logos (God) atone to the Father (God)? Did God atone to Itself? (If someone offended you, how could *you atone to yourself?)* The notion one god atones to another god is mythical polytheism. The incarnation was the most gracious act God ever did for man, and to connect it to sin, evil, God's wrath, God's need to be pacified or atoned to, is an abominable myth. This is not the good news of Christ, this is *blasphemy*.

The only people who had it right are those who affirmed **Christ would have come whether man had sinned or not**. To make the Incarnate Christ dependent on man's sins, as if Christ were an "after-thought", is man taking credit for Christ. To make Christ dependent on Adam's fall or man's sins, means that if man had *not* sinned there would be no Christ. According to Duns Scotus, to make Christ totally dependent on Adam's sinning is to reduce Christ to the servant of fallen man. For Scotus, the purpose of the incarnation was **not** as a means to redeem man from sin, rather, Christ was the *bridge*, the *medium* between the created and Uncreated, revealed so all would know the Lord of all creation. He said, ***"Man was created because of Christ, Christ was not created because of man"***. ***"We were made for Christ, Christ was not made for us...the Incarnation was not God's "after-thought".*** Gregory of Nazianzus also points out "*if Christ was only incarnate for our sake, then we are greater than he, more important to God than He, because Christ would only exist for us*", he scoffs – "*who would maintain such a thing?*" "*If the Logos was only brought forth so God could create me, then I am of more worth to God than the Logos", "that would make me far worthier than the celestial Christ – if Christ were made for me."*

Hilary of Poitiers – "*He had no need of becoming man, for it was he who made man. But we had need that God should become flesh and dwell in us, that He should assume one body of flesh and thus dwell in all flesh. Since he is God in the flesh, we are renewed from the flesh unto God"*. Like Athanasius, Hilary makes scarcely any distinction between what is true of Christ and what is true of all Christians – "*God gains nothing by our assumption (taking us into Himself.) God loses none of his divinity while man is enabled to become God". "What is essential is the continuity that joins the head and the members, causes the glories of the Head to pass into the members and effects the collective divinization of human nature by virtue of the* ***singular union of the Logos with Its humanity.***" That Christ would have come even if man had not sinned, was also the view of Clement of Alexandria, Theodore of Mopsuestia, and, I believe, Methodius. Irenaeus sums it up – "***Christ came out of love, not out of pity, mercy, sin, or any other reason".***

As noted previously, Duns Scotus held that human nature has always had the capacity to be *assumed* by the divine Logos, and that everyone's human nature can be *united to* (or "*assumed*" by) the Logos – become Christ, that is. Thus, "*Christ's human nature is the same as every other human nature. Christ's human nature has a passive potency for assumption* (being united to God.) *We know this, factually, since Christ's human nature is assumed. The passive potencies and liabilities of a nature are essential features of it, not accidental features. The passive potency for assumption had by Christ's human nature is thus essential and therefore shared by all human natures. All human natures have a passive potency for assumption, thus no human nature can possess a feature that is sufficient to block assumption.*" In short – every human being is *potentially* set up to be assumed by the Logos, become the Logos' *own* human nature no different than Christ.

The Truths that the Incarnation was intended to reveal far outreach any narrow dogmatic interpretation. Man may never be able to fully understand or fathom all it was intended to reveal. For sure, its purpose was never to reveal the person Jesus – who never existed prior to his birth in Bethlehem. All that God intended to reveal *through* him, was *beyond* him completely – indeed, God's plan for one's *own* life is *never* what he thinks it is. Not only is God's plan beyond man's comprehension, but God is the only One that can carry it out anyway – despite man. The Incarnation, then, was not God creating some human being, but God creating man's common human nature *for Itself alone*. God did not "become" human, but without any change in Its Uncreated existence, God established a *unique* eternal union between Its divine Essence and the *essence* of human nature. We stress *unique,* because it was a *oneness* utterly different than anything God had created before – or after. This is a *oneness* beyond creation's natural or *existential* oneness with God, and beyond any union with God man can experience in this life – such as a "mystical union" or *Theosis*. As to the true nature of this unique *oneness*, or how God brought it about, that *mystery* ***is*** *Christ.*

We might summarize the purpose of the Incarnation as God's revealing the Truth of Man to man. While every revelation of God is the revelation of Truth Itself, in the annals of human history, however, the Incarnation is the sole revelation of God that *includes man,* thus, its primary revelation is all *man* means to God – his ultimate destiny and eternal oneness with God. It is also the revelation of the true nature of man's death and what follows – resurrection and ascension into his glorious life in God. This is what the incarnation was to reveal, a truth that, unfortunately, most people do not believe is the way *of their own life*, but instead, only the life of one man – Jesus. This wrong view, of course, totally misses "Christ" – Universal *Man.*

While nothing is effected in a day, we can nevertheless point out many consequences of the Incarnation that have gradually seeped into society. The real influence of Christianity has never been by "conversion", but by osmosis – comparable, perhaps, to the subtlety of a genetic mutation. The riches of the Incarnation have yet to be realized, uncovered and articulated. As one father remarked, the incarnation was the "*pivotal axis of the whole history of mankind, past and future*". So we have a ways to go before all its implications are fully realized. As much as we know at present is the tip of the iceberg.

Obviously, the incarnation far outreaches the narrow meaning given it by most Christians. In some cases, it was an extension of the truth of Judaic monotheism, as well as a correction of many false beliefs. Thus it verified belief in resurrection, and eliminated belief in *metempsychosis* – the Greek belief, today pared down to "re-incarnation". It also eliminated most people's belief in the efficacy of human and animal sacrifice. It has even been said the incarnate Christ fulfilled some of man's compatible myths – Christ giving some myth its reality and not vice versa. Above all, the incarnation did away with the notion of some "universal soul" handed down by the male species. That God alone creates every individual soul *One-on-one,* is one of the revelations that has been totally overlooked. What today we may take for granted, was not the belief of the world at the time of the incarnation, not among the philosophers, not in Judaism, and to my knowledge, no one in the world at that time.

In light of the incarnation, then, erroneous beliefs have fallen away and those that were true, have been seen in a new light. In this way, the Incarnation was intended to either rectify, extend, or verify man's beliefs whatever one's religion. The intention was not to start a new religion, but give meaning and truth to one and all, regardless of their religion. What the Incarnation was about was people knowing the *Truth*, recognizing it wherever it exists, and replacing their erroneous *beliefs.*

The Incarnation also gave man a concrete archetype or example on which to model his own earthly life of oneness with God. It could be said the good done by every believing Christian comes directly from the Incarnation – thus he asks himself "What would Christ do?" Even though the man Jesus had a different (miraculous) beginning, yet his ending is the same for everyone. In truth, man's life is one of being transformed into Christ and all this means. As someone said, we do not know "**what**" we are now, "*we only know **what** we shall be, we shall be like Christ"*. No one, of course, is transformed into "*who*" some other human being is, but rather, into "*what*" Christ is. (Remember, the Logos' human nature was never "*who*" some *particular person* was.) So too, man's *heavenly or eternal* existence is not *his own,* but the Logos', God's *own*. Thus it is not we, *ourselves* "*who*" are eternally one with God, rather, it is God's *own* (essence) of human nature that is eternally one with Itself. Whatever makes for individuality and particularity (differences) has never been one with God. As said before, if God had only wanted to be united to only one individual or a particular person, there would have been no "Incarnation" whatsoever.

None of the fathers thought the revelation of Christ was about just one man's oneness with God. This would have made the Incarnation pointless, its revelation meaningless to the rest of mankind – why reveal a thing like that? It makes no sense. Why reveal one man is united with God if no other man could ever know it, have it, or *be it* as well? **If God can be eternally one with one human being, God can be eternally one with every human being.** Absolutely, the incarnation was not the revelation of some lone individual's oneness with God. "Christ" is not a reference to either God or to a *particular* human being, but to *everyman's* eternal oneness in and with God.

Centuries before Christianity came on the scene, man was seeking oneness with God, a oneness every man could realize. Had Christianity come on the scene and taught *only one man* could ever be one with God, "Christianity" would never have gotten off the ground or made any inroads into the Gentile world. Fortunately, as Gentiles, the fathers were totally in tune with the Reality of Christ within their own culture, understood it as utterly relevant in the context of their background and surroundings. That down the road, Christianity was turned into the narrow, naive and childish view we have today – i.e., *only* the man Jesus is Christ, *only* Jesus could ever be eternally one with God – is the inevitable loss of the whole revelation of the Incarnation, and, consequently, of Christ and Christianity. This is exactly why, today, Christian people – numerous Catholic Priests, Monks and Sisters – have turned to the Eastern religions for a deeper understanding of their life with God. Consciously or unconsciously, they may, in fact, be searching for the *Real Christ*. At any rate, the Eastern religions certainly offer a more democratic understanding in that *every* human being is eternally one with God – can become a Buddha, whatever that means. **Christianity's *exclusive*, *boxed-in* view of Jesus and Christ, not only aborts man's spiritual journey, but will be its own undoing – why? Simply because it is *not* the Truth of "Christ".**

Because the man Jesus was the example (*exemplar*) of everyman's oneness with God, *how his spiritual journey or life with God went for him* – including not only in ***this earthly life****, but above all, man's* ***eternal life*** *– is exactly how it will go for every human being.* The fathers believed Jesus' human nature was not *deified* (ultimately transformed) until *after* the resurrection and ascension, which means that the man Jesus only reached the *final destiny* of God's incarnate humanity at the *end* of his earthly journey. Obviously, man's *creation* is not over until it is over, or until it has reached its definitive end in God. In the end, however, all those human properties that made earthly life possible, will fall away (die) because they are not compatible with man's eternal heavenly existence in and with God. With his death, then, the man Jesus as a particular human "*person*" died – *person* meaning "*who*" he was – and thus *he* no longer exists. "*What*" ultimately exists, however, is God's *own* glorified human nature created solely for Itself. While people may think of this glorified human nature as solely that of the man Jesus, yet remember, *his* human nature was no different than that of any other human being – not on this earth and not in heaven. In the end, all are transformed into **God's *own one* human nature – whether his earthly name be "Jesus", Mary, Joseph – Dick or Harry. God cares absolutely nothing about this.**

The sole divinity of Christ is the Logos, and the sole humanity of Christ is the Logos' own human nature – and *not* the human nature of any *particular* human being. This is why *only God can reveal Christ,* and not any human being. Just as Jesus said – only God could reveal "Christ" – because he, Jesus ("*flesh and blood*"), could *not* do this. Jesus could not reveal *himself* as Christ because as a *particular* human being or *person he, himself,* was *not* Christ. While *Christ* was Jesus' oneness with God, no one can ever see or point to this oneness, a oneness that is neither God nor one's self, but the oneness of two disparate natures – God and man. Christianity would never have survived had God not continuously revealed the *real Christ* to individuals down the centuries. No mere belief, doctrine or bible story, is capable of *revealing* Christ. Christ can only be revealed to someone *directly* by God. God alone is the sole *source* of the revelation of "Christ", and apart from this direct revelation, there is no other way Christ has ever been (or could be) *revealed* – for sure, no one will get Christ from a "book" or mere "hearsay". In other words, without God's direct revelation of Christ to an individual human being, Christ has no honest reality and can never be truthfully understood.

Some Questions

As to the mystery of the true nature of Christ, there is probably no end of questions that can be asked – in Truth, there is no end to Christ. The issues gone over in this book are but the tip of the iceberg, below the surface, however, exists the unfathomable mystery of the eternal Christ. As said before, Christianity is the most "mystical" of man's religions *because* it is so profound and un-obvious, this is why it poses questions only answerable by Faith alone. As Jesus said, "*I tell you the* ***truth,*** *which is why you do not believe me*" – meaning, because Truth is *unbelievable,* it *requires Faith.* ("Belief" is *not* Faith, the two are even opposites. Where "belief" is all in the mind and what one chooses to think is true, "Faith", on the other hand, is that "Truth Sensor" in every man, the Truth that turns out to **be** God in man.) But since we cannot go over all possible questions, we might go over those, perhaps, most asked.

I. Timing of the Incarnation – did Christ pre-exist the Incarnation?

A legitimate question regards the "timing" of the incarnation or when it actually occurred, Paul raises the question himself. As God's *plan* for all mankind, did this *plan* begin with creation itself (the *recapitulation* theory), or with the creation of the *first* human being (say, Adam), or was it some ten thousand years later when the man Jesus was created? This is also tied to the question of whether or not Christ "pre-existed" from the beginning and was only *revealed* at the time of Jesus' birth? Seeing that innumerable human beings – Abraham, Isaac, Jacob, Moses, among others – were already "saved" or in heaven with God, were they not transformed into Christ? While indeed they were, yet none were **God's own humanity from the moment of its conception *in* God.** So whatever the "timing" of the incarnation, we only know that *prior* to the incarnation there was no "**incarnate"** Logos or "*Christ"*. Thus, those already in heaven prior to the birth of Jesus, knew nothing of "Christ", yet were as one with God as what would later be *revealed* as "Christ". At no time, however, were they (or anyone) God's "incarnation". What they attained was the "Omega point" (end) which **is** Christ, certainly, however, they were not the "Alpha point" or *Christ* from the beginning.

In this matter, a distinction can be made between 1) the "Incarnation" as that point *outside time* when God united Man eternally to Itself, and, 2) that point *in time* when this eternal union was **revealed** to man. Since we really cannot say ***when*** God decided to unite man eternally to Itself, what we mean by "Incarnation" then, is *both* a reference to its Reality *outside time* and its Reality *revealed in time – as* with the conception and birth of the man Jesus. Thus we have the view of "Christ" as the "*summation of all creation*" – the Incarnation being God's "*recapitulating*" the whole of creation in the process of uniting man to Itself – a view not incompatible with the simple story of the "Annunciation" as Christ's revelation to man.

The party-line presentation of Jesus Christ – as "God" no less – certainly says Jesus Christ "pre-existed". If Christ is "God", then God certainly *pre-existed* any incarnation. If Christ pre-existed the conception of Jesus – by God and Mary – then this event was *not* the "incarnation". John, however, tells us it was **God (Logos) that became incarnate, it was not "*Christ"* nor the man Jesus that became incar-**

nate. In truth, **it was *God* that assumed human nature, not Christ or Jesus**. If Christ is the union of natures, then Christ could *not* have *pre-existed* the Incarnation – after all, there is no *incarnating* ***what is already*** *incarnated!* (It also goes without saying, the man Jesus did not create and unite man to himself!) So whatever the "timing" of God's uniting man's human nature eternally to Itself, all we know is that prior to this union, there was no "Christ".

One thing we can count on, however, is that God's *Plan* for man must have been in effect – a reality – *before* Christ could have been *revealed.* That this *Plan* for man and creation was in effect from the beginning, means it never *depended* on ***how*** or ***when*** it was *revealed.* Basically, the *timing* of the Incarnation or "when" God united man's common human nature with Itself, is really a useless question, for who, after all, can put a "timer" on God? For man in space and time, a second or a thousand years has no meaning for God.

II. Is everyone saved?

Since God's *Plan* was for all men is to be transformed into Christ, does this mean every human being is transformed into Christ – is everyone saved?

The fathers had different answers to this question. Some definitely believed all would be saved – Origen believed even Satan would be saved. Some, of course, thought no one had ever been saved (or were in heaven) prior to Jesus' death and resurrection. Others tended, with Paul, to believe that in the end "God will be all in all". To my knowledge none stressed that in order to be saved one *had* to believe in Christ – but, then, perhaps they took this for granted. Perhaps the real question is: "Is there anything God cannot transform into eternal life? Is there any man that can ruin God's destined plan for mankind?" Since nothing can exist that does not depend on God's Existence, then God, of course, can always "cut the cord", in which case, people would simply cease to exist – there is no such thing as "eternal garbage". That God would "hang on" to anything that could *never* be transformed makes no sense. So who, then, is to say there is anything or anyone God could never transform or never save? No one!

III. That God united Itself with man's one universal human nature, does this mean every human being is the "incarnation" of God (Logos)?

Interestingly, somewhere Methodius exclaimed, "*We are all Christs!*", implying, of course, there are "*many Christs*". No one, however, held there were "*multiple Christs*". Yet Duns Scotus was on the mark when he said we are all *potential Christs* – meaning, because we all have the same human nature, we all have the *potential* to *be* Christ. There is only *one* Incarnation, *one* human nature created one with God, and this *one* is the *eternal Christ* – the same all are destined *to become.* No *individual* human being is God's *own universal* human nature, which is why, to become Christ, every individual man must be transformed into God's *one and only human nature*. But if all are to *become* Christ, no man comes into this world as "Christ". Even Jesus, born in a state of *Theosis* – an abiding union with God – had a ways to go. Those who regard him as the *sole* Christ, have to admit he had to go through death and resurrection *before* the real Christ could be revealed. This revelation was *not* that *he* was Christ, but that "Christ", *God's own human nature* – belongs to no *individual* man, not even to the man Jesus. Needless to say, anyone hung-up on *different or particular* human natures won't get this at all. But think of the Eucharist, billions of Hosts (wafers of Bread), yet one single Christ – every "one" transformed into the one same Christ. Just as one can count heads but not human natures, so too, one can count Hosts, but not "Christs". The Incarnation was no quick-fix for humanity.

For many people, a true understanding of Christ is not easy to grasp. Of the obstacles that stand in the way, first and foremost is thinking the man Jesus (or Jesus Christ) is *God-in-person,* which is, indeed, the proverbial party-line presentation of Christ. Even for those who understand that God is invisible, and that the oneness of man and God (which **is** Christ) is equally invisible, yet to say the *person* Jesus is *not* Christ, might seem to rob them of their icon of Jesus **as** Christ, or as *God in person*. The *fact* there can be no true image of man's eternal oneness with God, however, in no way diminishes the iconic figure of the man Jesus as a *model* of God's *earthly* humanity – we cannot be reminded enough that the man Jesus was as human as ourselves. If Jesus does not uplift one to God, at least he should uplift one to the marvel that is Man. **Iconoclasm, after all, is only a problem for those who think God is a human being, not for those who know no human being is God.** Remember, the Incarnation was *not* the revelation of God, but the revelation of *Man* – his eternal destiny **to become** Christ.

IV. After all that has been said here, one might ask – **"If God's common human nature is not *Jesus'* human nature, then did God's *own* human nature actually experience life in this world – had the whole human experience, went through it all?"**

The answer is "yes" as regard the bare *essence* of human nature, but "no" as regards all those properties, accidents or attributes of human nature – more especially "*person*" and all that means. We might put it this way, the *bare essence of human nature* was God's universal human nature, but all the accidentals or properties were that of the *individual person* Jesus. Remember, God never united Itself to any *person*, or to any purely *individual* properties or accidents of human nature, these were never destined for eternal life, but were only necessary for man's earthly existence.

To understand how this works one would have to know the unitive state of *theosis* in which Jesus was born. The essence of his human nature was rooted in God, but outside of this (man's divine Unitive Center), he had his own thoughts and emotions, experienced all the ups and downs of the human condition which, as we know, were considerable. The *essence* of his human nature, however, was stable and right "on the Line".

Differentiating between what is eternal (or of the essence) and what is *not*, really requires some understanding of the unitive state of *theosis*. In this state it is not difficult to differentiate between *that* in man that is God, and *that* in man that is *not* God. Anything man can call "*himself*" is obviously *not* God. In truth, however, "***that***" *unknown essence in man* that is *one with God, this* is a *mystery* – really, the mystery of Christ.

The bottom line is that only God knows the *real essence* of man. So despite being in a state of *theosis* (here on earth), Jesus' journey was not yet complete. The true nature of his death would be not only the end of his earthly journey, but the end of *his own earthly oneness* with God. It is important, then, to grasp the difference between "*Christ on earth*" and the "eternal or heavenly *Christ in God*". Those who think death, resurrection, ascension, transfiguration – even transubstantiation – makes no difference, are only fooling themselves.

One last thing. A number of the fathers regarded man's spiritual journey as *not just* a process of "*transformation*", but a process of "*incarnation*", of man becoming as one with God as the *incarnate* Logos (Christ.) Speaking of man's *deification*, Maximus the Confessor reminds us that this (deification) "*demands the kenosis and self emptying of the adopted sons in order to lay hold of the divine* ***to the same degree*** *as that to which the Logos of God truly became man*".

HYPOSTATIC UNION

Earlier we said that if one put their finger on the Line between the Uncreated and created, he would put his finger on Christ. This Line is the reality of the Incarnation, God's creating man eternally one with Itself. Prior to the revelation of this union or oneness, man had two primary views of God and creation, 1) God was all that existed, was all of creation, a belief known as "*monism*" – *one* form of which, is "*pantheism*". 2) The other view was that God so utterly transcended creation that everything could only have come from "nothing". God simply said "Let man exist" and that was it. Basically, this is Judaic "*monotheism*", the belief that by abiding by God's *laws*, man would be rewarded with some form of eternal life. In neither of these two views, however, is there any eternal "union" or oneness with God. In the first view, there is no Line at all – because "all is God" anyway. In the second view, the Line indicates an *absolute* separation between the two, with a chasm of "nothingness" between them – i.e., the "nothingness" from which God creates all things.

With the revelation of "Christ", however, a whole new understanding of God, of creation and man, opened up. More especially, the revelation of man's ultimate destiny, his eternal oneness with and in God. As the revelation of "Christ", the Incarnation was not God uniting Itself to some already created human being, rather, the Incarnation was **prior** to the creation of any individual human being. The fathers liked to point out Genesis saying, *"Let us create man"*, it did not say, "Let us create ***a*** man". Also, the Hebrew word "*Adam*" meant "*mankind*", and was not a reference to one particular human being. The Incarnation, then, was not God deciding at some point in time to make Itself one with existing mankind, but was prior to the creation of a single man. This means the Incarnation did *not* take place in *this world* or that God's *own* human nature was conceived ***in*** any human being, on the contrary, *God's* human nature was conceived and created **in** God alone. Whatever the *created* essence of man, God united it eternally to Its *uncreated* essence, and the *union* of these two essences is what Cyril called a "*Hypostatic Union*", a union of two disparate natures created and united *in* God – and *not* in man. **Strictly speaking, Christ is not God-in-man, but rather, *man-in-God.***

It was Cyril who coined the term for God's *eternal* oneness with man. By "*Hypostatic Union*" he meant a "union of natures" (or essences), a term that remains Christianity's sole reference to this *particular union* effected *in* God (and not in man.) Since, for Cyril, *hypostasis* meant *nature,* then his reference to this as a *union of two natures* is on the mark. For two reasons, however, he has been continuously corrected. First, the term "hypostasis" *only* refers to the Logos' *divine* nature (which is basically what he meant) and not to the Logos' *human* nature, for which reason he was accused of "Monophysitism". Second, the more correct definition given was the union of "*two natures* ***in*** *one hypostasis*" (a union **in** the divine Logos, that is), which would become the Chalcedonian formula.

But if there were objections to the use of "*hypostatic union*", it still remains the *only term* Christianity ever reserved for the particular type of "Incarnational Unity" of God and man. Since *hypostatic union* means the union of the divine and human natures, it could just as well be another term for "Christ". As long as "*hypostases*" retains its original definition as the "*distinct modes of God's triune nature (essence or existence)*", the term "*hypostatic union*" well serves its purpose to define Christ as Man *conceived in* God's *own* divine *nature* (*hypostasis)*, making it eternally one with Itself.

That the oneness of natures is ***in*** the particular *hypostasis* of the Logos, affirms the natures are united *in* God and not ***in*** any human being or human person. A "hypostatic union", then, is *not located* in any human being, but only **in** God. Thus Chalcedon defines Christ – "*made known in two natures without confusion, without change, without division, without separation, the difference of the natures being by no means removed because of the union, but the property of each nature being preserved and* **coalescing in one prosopon and hypostasis***, not parted or divided into two prosopa, but one and the same Son...*" ("*Son*" being reference to God (*Logos*).)

We have already gone over the Western Church's switch of definitions for *hypostasis* to mean a particular *person.* As to how two *natures* can be united **in** a mere "*property*" *of nature* (in some subject or self), who can figure this out? This is one of those theological bugaboos put down as a "mystery". We know, of course, why hypostasis (essence) was defined as a "person". It was an attempt to resolve the problem of Christ as "*one individual being*" – which Christ is *not.* It was by making the divine Logos *one person* it could then be said Its incarnation was that of *one* divine *person.* **Thus *Christ is one divine person* and *not* one individual *being* – divine or human. All references to "Christ", then, are *not* to one *individual being*, but to one *divine person.*** (To have made Christ one individual being would have made God an individual being – and the Trinity three individual beings.) The problem with "*person*", however, is that it *assumes* it is a reference to a *particular being,* whereas God (Trinity) is *not* a particular being – or three beings.

The importance of the term "*hypostatic union*", however, is that it *solely* defines the *Incarnate* Logos or Christ. This term sets it apart from other types of union with God that man can have. Thus, in order for anything to exist, man has an "*existential union*" with God sometimes called an "essential union" or "natural union". There is also a "*supernatural union*", a union by *grace* (usually associated with the "sacraments") that the fathers regarded as a form of "*adoptionism*". This was God effecting a union with a particular individual and often regarded as the Spirit's "*indwelling*" in man. Then there is "*theosis*", a "*mystical union*", variously regarded anywhere from a "union of wills" to man's nature radically changed or made godlike – "*deified*" as some of the fathers put it. Apart from these three established types of union – well known in Christianity – there are other passing experiences regarded as "union-with-God". None of these states, experiences or types of union, however, define "*hypostatic union*", that alone defines the eternal Incarnate Unity of God and man – Christ. **This union is God's *eternal* (or heavenly) oneness with Its *own* human nature, and *not* God's union with the human nature of any *particular* human being or *person.*** Basically, there exists no comparison between anything man regards as "union with God" and what is meant by "*hypostatic union*", they are of an entirely different nature. Where *hypostatic union* was *conceived* ***in*** God from the *beginning*, all other unions are states or stages on the way to this hypostatic *ending,* for it is where Christ *begins,* that man *ends*.

What most sets off *hypostatic union* from all other types of union is the *locus* of this union. Where all man knows of "union-with-God" is *in* himself, by contrast, the *hypostatic union* is nowhere in man at all, it is solely **in** God. And given that God is Infinite, means that this *hypostatic union* has ***no point of locus even in God.*** The reason man knows and experiences a "union" or oneness with God is because *he* is the locus, he is the *experiencer,* he is the site or point of reference for his own personal union with God. "*Hypostatic union*", on the other hand, has no place in man whatsoever. Man has no point of reference for this union, interiorly, exteriorly – anywhere. It is because this union is beyond any "experience" man could possibly know or verify for himself, its true nature can *only* be ***revealed***. Strictly speaking, this union has nothing to do with man, but everything to do with God.

To define God's oneness with *Its own* human nature as a "*union*", however, is not really an adequate term. More in keeping with the true nature of Christ, the more accurate term is "*hypostatic **oneness***", instead of "***union***". Where a line can be drawn *between* a "union" of two things, *no such line can be drawn between* "oneness". Like two sides of a single coin, there can be no separating the two sides – because no matter how the coin is sliced, there are always two sides. So, as a single coin, Christ is the inseparable *oneness* of both sides, God and man. Earlier we said that if we could put our finger on the Line between the Uncreated and created – a single line with two sides – a single coin is another analogy for the oneness of Christ's dual natures – the only problem with this analogy is that one side is *Infinite*, the other is *just Man*. The best analogy, however, is the Eucharist – one Eucharist, two sides. No question, t**he mystery of Christ is a veritable oneness of opposites**.

If there is a problem with the term "*oneness*", it is the tendency to reduce it to a *numerical* "*one*" – *one* being, *one* person, *one* nature – the Alexandrian and *Monophysite* problem. Reducing *oneness* to *one,* however, merely illustrates the mind's need to focus on, "***one** something*" or "*some **one***", the mind is really not equipped to grasp the **reality of "oneness"**. To some extent, however, this is its *advantage.* Where people can get some idea of "one" or a "union of two", the mind can never grasp the "*oneness*" that is the *mystery of Christ.*

So where a "*union*" is putting one and one together, "*oneness*" is neither one nor two. The true nature of the Incarnation was not God *joining* Itself to human nature, but creating human nature *from* Itself and *for* Itself alone. This is no type of "union" man knows of, much less, could ever attain of himself. In fact, because it is not man's and solely God's, only God *knows* this *hypostatic oneness.* It could even be said "**only God knows Christ"** – which is why *only God* can *reveal* Christ. Left to himself, no man really knows Christ.

All the fathers believed Jesus was born into this world united and one with God. Prior to Cyril's coining the term "hypostatic union", however, the fathers called this union "*theosis*". (Although Clement gave this state the Stoic term "apatheia", for sure, Irenaeus called it "theosis".) Its reference was to a state of being united to God, a kind of "deification" of one's human nature, of being made "godlike", that is. Today we would call this *theosis* a "mystical union", which was not, however, Cyril's understanding of "*hypostatic union*". *Theosis* (man's union with God in this world) and *hypostatic union* (that is not in this world) are so totally different they really have nothing in common. Where the man *Jesus* was born into *this world* in the state of *theosis*, yet, God's human nature conceived **in** the essence and glory of God, is *not theosis.* Theosis is the *experience* of a *person (self)*, whereas the hypostatic union is not an "experience" because it is *person-less*. Indeed, it is because a *hypostatic oneness* is *not* compatible with earthly existence that there had to be a **"*kenosis*" – i.e., God's *human nature***

emerging from its glorious estate *in God* in order to exist as a particular person *in* an in-glorious world. Thus God's human nature, conceived in God's glory, could only be born into this world in the inglorious *unitive* state of *theosis.* As said elsewhere, *"theosis"* means one is just as aware of God as *he* is of *himself,* and in this way is aware of *his* own personal oneness with God. This was Jesus' awareness of *his own* individual oneness with God, *his* personal life and experiences, *his* knowledge – and so on. The reason he was a "whole person" is *because* he was as one with himself as he was with God. **This, of course, did not make him God – or make God *himself!***

While we like to think of this type of union (theosis or mystical union) as a *foreshadowing* of a *hypostatic* union, and may even think it is the *same* union, only more glorious, this is *not* so. While theosis can be regarded as a "preparation" for man's final union with God, the *hypostatic union* is of a totally *different nature,* so different, it is one of those *Truths* the mind cannot even grasp. No individual man or person is "glorified", only *Christ* is the glory of God-and-man's eternal oneness. Christ, as the true nature of the *hypostatic union* is man's *only* eternal oneness with God, there is no other *eternal union* possible, no other *form of eternal life possible.* Yet, this is the eternal life God destined for every human being – the **same *hypostatic oneness* that *is* Christ.**

It goes without saying, the most naive notion of the Incarnation is that all God did was *become a visible man,* or somehow enclosed Itself in a physical body. God, of course, never became *visible* – like some *god*, or someone's *sensory* vision – nor can God ever be enclosed in matter or "circumscribed". Taking a clue from Paul's reference to the Logos/Spirit as the *"Form of God"*, we might think of the Incarnation as God's *human form* "emerging" directly from God's *divine Form – from the Logos,* that is. Thus God's human nature was conceived **in** God's immanent essence, but had to "emerge" to take on earthy existence. **This "emergence" from life in God is the "*kenosis*" of God's universal humanity becoming an individual human being – *becoming its own human person.*** If God's *human nature* had *not* emerged from its glorious existence in God, it could never have entered into man's earthly existence. **So it was this *emergence* from being God's *own* "universal" human nature to being one's *own individual* human nature, that was the true nature of *kenosis.***

For Cyril, the *hypostatic union* of God and man was so completely inseparable and indivisible, he basically granted no real human nature to Christ – for him, Jesus was not even a human person. Anyone who disagreed with him would be accused of postulating no *real* union –

maybe a "moral union", one of "likeness" or some other shallow idea. The standard accusation against the Antiochenes was they held this union to be God's "*indwelling*" in Jesus – to which there are a number of biblical allusions. Although no Antiochene (apart from Eutyches or someone) regarded this "indwelling" to be the *union of natures*, they did, however, refer to God's "indwelling" in Jesus – which is absolutely true. Even though this was not the "hypostatic union", the Spirit certainly "indwelled" in Jesus. In fact, born into the "Unitive State", this "indwelling" was Jesus' most immediate experience of oneness with God – after all, neither the Transcendent or Logos "indwells". **The *hypostatic union*, however, was *not* Jesus' experience – as said, the hypostatic union is *no one's experience* – which is why its very existence can only be revealed.** At any rate, "hypostatic union" was the meaning of "Christ", defined as the "oneness of two natures ***in*** the Logos" – "*en-hypostasis*" ("**in** God"), as Leontius put it.

It is important to understand the nature of the Spirit is to "indwell", whereas the *omnipresent* Logos does *not* "indwell", nor does the Transcendent. Though we say the Spirit "indwells", this does not mean the Spirit has any "place" in human nature or is any "part" of it. To be born "theocentric" means God is the empty space in the center of man's being – comparable to a hole in a donut. Nothing created can possibly contain or circumscribe the Infinite, in fact, one of the fathers noted that no man could "*contain God lest he explode*". So while man *experiences* God *within* himself, this Spirit does not "indwell" as any part of man or anything created. But even if God is not *in* man, God can be *united to* man. As for the Logos' oneness with man, this presence is too pervasive (*throughout all creation*) to be localized anywhere **in** man. Thus the saying, "*God is closer to us than we are to ourselves*" is reference to the Logos' *existential* union with *all creation*.

Although the only one of the Trinity *existentially* or *essentially* one with human nature is the Logos, yet Its omnipresence is as *dispersed* as is the soul throughout the body. Thus It can never be localized anywhere in man – as Athanasius says, "*The Logos did not* ***enter into*** *a man*". Indeed, the Logos is *already* present. So where the Spirit may be *localized* (even "enter into man") – revealed as man's divine "Center" – the Logos can never be localized *in* man. Strictly speaking, the divine *hypostasis* that man often calls the "*Ground of Being*" is neither Spirit or Logos, but the Transcendent. Indeed, if man truly understood his experiences of God, he would know the Trinity first hand, and not as an incomprehensible theological doctrine or dogma.

As to how the *hypostatic union* affected the human nature born into this world, this has always been a matter of speculation, if not contention. We know for several of the fathers, this oneness all but swamped the Logos' entire *human* nature, thus they regarded Christ as *totally* divine. For others, however, there was no crossing over the line, each nature forever distinct from one another, their oneness, however, constituting "one" Christ. Jesus, of course, never specified his immediate experience of God. Though he spoke of the "spirit" within himself, the early fathers were not sure if the reference was to his own personal spirit (maybe his soul) or to God's divine Spirit. (Remember, the fathers had no clear idea of an "individual soul", and that the Platonic notion basically made it divine anyway.) Jesus' sole reference to being one with God was with his "Father". He never said he was one with the "Spirit", and most likely, never heard of the "Logos". Due to these different understandings, it was not until the third century the "Spirit" was formally recognized as a divine hypostasis (one of the Trinity) and not just Jesus' personal spirit. The point, however, is that while the divine Spirit did indeed "indwell" in Jesus, this was not the true nature of his *eternal oneness* with God – nor, theologically speaking, was this his oneness with the "Father" or the Transcendent. According to the fathers' understanding of the Trinity, Jesus' human nature was solely one with the divine Logos, *not* one with either the Spirit **or** the Father (Transcendent.)

To understand why Jesus' human nature was said to be united *only* to the Logos and *not* to the whole Godhead or Trinity, keep in mind the "switch" that shifted Jesus' reference to himself as "son of God" to this being made a reference to God (Logos) as "son of God". Thus it was not the *man Jesus* who was one with the Father – as *he* thought he was – but instead, it was the **Logos (now made the "son") that was one with God (Father.)** This switch made *God* the "son of God" **instead** of the man Jesus. From here on, all Jesus' references to the "Father" were to be understood as **God's** references to *God* – i.e., the **Logos'** (Son's) reference to the Transcendent (Father.) Thus Jesus was regarded as the "incarnation" of the Logos, his human nature was not – as he thought – one with the Father, but one with the Logos (the son.) Jesus, of course, never heard of the Trinity or the Logos, his reference to be one with the "Father" was simply his being one with "God" – simple as that. *Theologically*, however, as the *incarnation of the Logos*, Jesus' human nature was *only* one with the Logos (Son) and not one with the Father. Now either Jesus was mistaken or those who made the "switch" were mistaken. (To say Christian theology is "complicated" is the understatement of all time. It is an unadulterated *mess.* It so defies common logic as to require man to forfeit his intellectual integrity in order to "believe".)

It goes without saying, "hypostatic union" does not refer to any *union* of "Father-Son-Spirit" or the Trinity. While God's "*triune modes of existence*" are profound "distinctions" (*hypostases*), they are *not* "*united*", not a "*union*" or even a "*oneness*", but rather, *one indivisible essence*. "Hypostatic union" *only* refers to *man's* eternal oneness with God, it has nothing to do with the immanent Triune nature of God. **Thus the Son (Logos) is *not hypostatically united* to the Father (Transcendent), this is *not* the meaning of "hypostatic union".** Though sometimes the Trinity is called a "*unity*", this is not an adequate term, the **Trinity is One Essence with three modes of Existence**. **The Logos, then, is *not united* to the Transcendent or Spirit,** and any talk about a *union* of the Logos (son) with the Transcendent (father) is *not* a reference to the Trinity at all. The Trinity is not a *united* threesome – three individuals, three persons or three entities.

Although *theologically* speaking, the man Jesus was *not* "hypostatically one" with the "Father" (Transcendent) and only "hypostatically one" with the Logos (Son), does this mean Christ's *humanity* is *not* one with the Transcendent and Spirit as well? This question is what the "*Father-Son*" dispute was about. Is it possible to be united to only *one* of the Trinity and not with the *others* as well? **In truth, it is *not* possible to be united solely to one and not the others.** The Trinity is one essence, man is one essence, and Christ is the oneness of these two essences or natures. John of Damascus said this: "*We declare that the **entire** and perfect nature of the divinity in one of its hypostasis* (Logos) *was united to the **entire** human nature, **not a part to a part***". The only reason Christ is regarded as the "**in-carnation**" of the *Logos* is because *only* the Logos has an *existential union with **matter*** **– the physical body.** But what of the Spirit's union with the soul, and the fact all "being" is grounded in the Transcendent? Without the whole Godhead or Trinity there is no *whole* Christ, all there is, is flesh. At least we can't say Christ is no-**body!**

Something else important to point out. Once the "hypostatic union" was eternally effected **in** God, it was not *forfeited* by human nature taking on *individual* existence. What was forfeited was not the *immanent oneness* of the two natures, but only human nature's *participation* in God's immanent and glorious divine nature. As said, this forfeiture or *kenosis* was necessary for human nature to live an *earthly* existence as an individual human being. Following its earthly existence, however, God's human nature returned to its glorious estate conceived **in** God. Thus the *beginning* was the same as the *end* – the Alpha **is** the Omega. Between the two, however, the man Jesus was born into this world a "whole person" – defined as the "unitive state" of man's **earth-**

ly oneness with God. The difference, of course, is that a "hypostatic oneness" is *person-less*, while the "unitive state" is that of an individual *person* – a *whole person* united to God. Another way to put the difference – on ***earth God is In man,*** **whereas in eternal life,** ***man is In God*** – big difference!

Because God is no "person" and God creates no *person*, God's *hypostatic oneness* with man is *person-less*. Nothing so defines "*hypostatic union*" as its being "*personless*". This is not a union with an *individual* human being or *person*. *Hypostatic union* is solely *God's* oneness with Its *own* universal human nature, not a union with any particular human being. That this union is personless is what distinguishes it from all other types of union with God man can have or ever experience. The reason this union is not an *experience* is because there is no person to experience it! Experiences belong to individual persons, whereas man's universal human nature has no *personal* experiences. As said, in God, man *participates* in God's own dimension of existence.

So where ***God's*** *universal human nature* is personless, **Jesus'** human nature *was that of an individual person*. (This is what the Antiochenes, Nestorius, Boethius, and others held – every individual human being is a *human person* and thus, the individual man Jesus was a person.) The true nature of Jesus' death, however, was the loss of *his personhood*, and the Resurrection is the *revelation* of human nature's *hypostatic "person-less" oneness* with God. If this truth is difficult to grasp, this is unfortunate because how this went for the man Jesus, is how it will go for every human being.

Because Christ reveals the truth of Man, the **difference** between *God's own person-less* human nature and *everyman's unique person,* is imperative to understand. This is not only necessary for a true understanding of Christ, but for an understanding of everyone's eternal life with God. So let us go over the Incarnation as succinctly as possible.

1. What is called the "Incarnation" was God conceiving and creating man's universal human nature one with Itself, and this ***"hypostatic union" or oneness is the true nature of the eternal Christ.***
2. By "hypostatic union" we do not mean God's union or oneness with any individual human being, but solely the *eternal* oneness of God's divine nature with God's *own universal* human nature.
3. For the sake of revealing this eternal *oneness* God destined for all men, God's universal human nature had to undergo "*kenosis*" – that is, had to become an individual human being capable of existing in this world – of living everyman's ordinary life on earth. Thus we have the

earthly incarnate Christ, and though *not* the *eternal* Christ in God, this was not, however, a forfeiture of the eternal *hypostatic union*, but a forfeiture of human nature's *participation* in God's eternal divine nature.

4. Just to live the human experience, to even function in this world, it was necessary to *become* an individual *person,* a *particular* human being – as is everyone else on earth.

5. ***Kenosis*, then, was the transition from God's own *person-less* human nature, to becoming one's *own* individual person.**

6. The one born into this world, however, was not *just* one particular individual, but a *whole person* – defined as *theosis* (a unitive state) and all this means. This unitive state of being was as far down – or *out* of God – as human nature can go without forfeiting the *hypostatic union*. **Thus one could say it was God's *own universal* human nature that was born into this world, yet, the individual man, Jesus, was the *human person.***[1]

7. It was not, then, the individual person Jesus *who* was Christ. Christ is solely the oneness of two *natures* and not a "*person*" or "*who*". The man Jesus had no dual natures and God has no dual natures, *only Christ is the dual natures of God and man.* Christ's human nature is *undifferentiated (person-less),* whereas Jesus, an individual human being was *differentiated* – a human person. Obviously, for an understanding of Christ, it is imperative to distinguish "*nature*" (***what** one is*) from "*person*" (***who** one is)*, for they are not the same.

8. Using the past-tense, we say Jesus ***was*** a person, because the true nature of his death was the death of his *whole person,* the *whole state of union* in which he lived out his earthly life with God. **Thus we can say the *person* Jesus *died,* and the *person-less* Christ *arose.***

9. To be transformed into Christ, then, requires *loss of person* – because God neither creates a *person* nor is united to any *person*. There is no person *in* the "hypostatic union" which is solely God's oneness with the essence of Its *own* universal human nature.

10. Keep in mind, Christ is not the union of two "*who's*" or two persons. Christ is the union of two "*what's*" or natures – i.e., the union of

---

[1] Born into this world, man's natural or original state-of-being is "I am", "I exist", etc. If someone does not first know "I exist", there is no way he will ever know "God exists". Without his natural "I am" man could never come to the supernatural *unitive* state-of-being – *"we are"*. For the revelation of the Incarnation, however, the *kenosis* – coming out of a *hypostatic* oneness in God – the one born into this world was solely in a "we are" *unitive* state-of-being from the beginning. The "*hypostatic union",* of course, is neither the state "I am God" or "we are one", rather, it is totally *person-less* – no "I", "we", "union", or even a *numerical* "*one*".

what **God is and** ***what*** **man is.** In the end, then, Christ is not *who* some*one* is, but *what everyone will be* – eternally one with God.

Those who cannot grasp the difference between ***nature*** and ***person*** will never be able to understand the real Christ. Jesus' human nature is that of one individual human being, a *particular person,* whereas God's human nature is **no** particular human being or person. "Person" has nothing to do with the Incarnation, it is solely the union or *oneness* of *natures.* There is no union of "persons" nor one person united to a *different* nature, or a union of one person with *no person.* As said many times, God creates no person – nor is God a respecter of persons. God's concern is not "who" one is, but "what" one is – a human being, that is.

The real Christ, then, is not a *who,* but a *what.* As expressed by Irenaeus, "*Christ became* ***what*** *we are, in order to make us* ***what*** *Christ is*"– notice, he did not say "*who*" Christ is. In many quotes from the fathers, Christ is referred to as *what* we shall be transformed into – no one, after all, can be transformed into *who* some other *person* is. And just as the *person* Jesus died, so too, when man's transformation into Christ is complete, *he* too (the person) will die. Christ is neither a separate divine being or a separate human being, rather, Christ *in* the Trinity is God's eternal oneness with mankind. And so too, when man has been completely transformed, his place in the Trinity **is** Christ – no different. In God there is *only* one Christ, not trillions of human beings, *persons,* or "other Christs". The reason Gregory Palamas and Maximus insisted on the uniqueness of the *hypostatic union* was "*so that deification could not be taken as a potential multiplier of Christ*" – there are no "other" Christs. In heaven, all **are** the one body of Christ, all **have** the one "mind of Christ", and all **in** the one glory of Christ – this is the end God destined for all mankind.

Obviously, there is no such thing as being one ***with*** Christ or one ***in*** Christ. Since there is only one human nature, how could human nature be *united to another* human nature? Impossible! All human nature can ever be united to is Almighty God. Other than God, what else exists man can be eternally one **with and in**? Nothing! The idea of being one *with* or *in* Christ assumes every man has a *different* human nature. If people cannot grasp the fact there is only *one common human nature,* there is no way they will ever grasp the *Hypostatic Union* or the reason for "*kenosis*". *Christ* is God's one and only eternal human nature, and since there is no "other" human nature, there is no other way man could ever be eternally one with God.

"Hypostatic oneness with God", then, belongs to no single or particular human being. There is no individual person or self "*who*" is transformed into Christ, rather, it is **man's common human nature** that is transformed into *God's own human nature.* Only God can transform human nature, man neither knows how this works or how it actually ends. Man only knows the **end** once he gets there, which ***end*** is everything we know and call "**Christ**".

In summary

Hypostatic union is not God's union with a single individual human being, but God's union with the *essence* of man's universal human nature. As a union made solely in God, it cannot be accounted for anywhere **in** man, nor even be described by man. (Besides, since this union is *person-less,* **who** is going to tell us about it anyway?) The true nature of this union is known only to God, and if God did not *reveal* its reality and truth, no one could know that this **hypostatic oneness with God even exists.** When the *real Christ* is truly known, however, this knowing is solely due to *participating* in God's *own* Knowing – regarding which, we might recall Irenaeus' distinction between the ***Logos* as "*God-in-creation*", and *Wisdom* as *God-in-Itself.***

DEATH OF CHRIST

With full deliberation this chapter is entitled "death of Christ" and not "death of Jesus". There is no mystery in the death of Jesus, his death was no different from the death of any other human being. The real mystery is the *death of Christ,* a mystery, however, that cannot be grasped without an understanding of the *real* Christ. For people who think Jesus was God, then of course, the death of Jesus would be the *death of God* – not a bad idea since Jesus was **not God anyway!**

The death of Christ is premised on the definition of Christ as *man's eternal oneness with God,* a oneness not only **in** this world, but more importantly, **in** God's eternal life **not** in this world. Death of the earthly-Christ is the death of man's *earthly* oneness with God, a death necessary to *rise* and *ascend* to his *eternal* (heavenly) *life **in*** God. So where man's ***personal,*** individual union with God in this world is "***theosis***", his final *eternal* oneness in God is the undifferentiated (*personless*) "***hypostatic union***". Thus *Jesus'* death was the transition from *his personal* earthly union with God (*Theosis*), to God's eternal "*Hypostatic*" union with man's universal human nature.

Just as "Christ" was Jesus' oneness with God on earth, so too, Christ was Paul's, Mary's, and everyone's union with God on this earth. There is no mystery, however, about the physicality of death – every *body* dies of something – the real mystery is the loss of "**person"** along with its experience of *oneness with God.* For Jesus, it was his *personal* oneness with God that died – i.e., his earthly unitive state-of-being (*theosis.*) To understand this particular death, however, it is imperative to know the *experiential reality* of man's earthly *unitive state-of-being.* This is not a state with two *different* experiences of *life* and *being* – *God's* being and *my* being – on the contrary, there is but ***one simple abiding experience of life and being,*** and it is the death of this unitive experience that is the death of the **earthly** Christ.

Given the reality of the unitive experience, to take it away, is to rob one of his *experience* of *Life and Being* (God) – a "*death experience*" like no other! This death, however, has nothing to do with the physical body, indeed, the death of "Christ" is far *more* than the physical death of the man Jesus – more, even, than the physical death of all who know Christ as the true nature of *their* oneness with God. The death of man's oneness with God ***in this world*** is the death of the *person* or *self who* experienced God as **his** true Life and Being. Thus, with the sudden falling away of the *"experiencer"* ("*person*" or "*self*"), the body is left without the slightest experience of *life* or *being.* This is the end of the *person or self **who*** experienced oneness with God – and for the man Jesus, the end of *his* oneness with God *on this earth.* **In that**

"*Christ*" was the true nature of Jesus' oneness with God, the true nature of his death was the "*death of Christ in this world*" – *literally* the end of Jesus' *personal* experience of *theosis.* This death of *self* or *person* is the end of the "*experiencer*", its *experiences,* and the *experienced* – God!

To grasp the ***true*** nature of Christ's death (or even *Jesus'* death) requires a certain understanding:

First – it was certainly not God who died.

Second – even though Jesus "physically" died, this was **not the true nature of his death.**

Third – death of a *person* is not the death of human nature – we've spent a long time going over "person" as a *property* of nature and not nature itself. So the *one* that died was the *person (or self)* ***who*** **experienced oneness with God – but *not* human nature.**

Fourth – whether one knows the Unitive state of *Theosis* or not, he still may never be able to grasp its abrupt falling away and leaving the body with no experience of life or being. That the body goes right on with no experience of life can only be called a state of the "*walking dead*".

Fifth – unless one can grant a difference between the **earthly *incarnate* Christ and the eternal (heavenly) Christ,** there is no possibility of understanding the true nature of Christ's death – or even Jesus' death. Everything needed to function in earthly life will be left behind because it cannot exist in God's eternal life. But then, the sole purpose of transformation and death is to enter into God's own *eternal life.* And for this, man even has to leave *his self* behind.

Without the above understanding, it is not likely anyone can ever grasp the true nature of Jesus' death. Since Christ was Jesus' oneness with God (*theosis*), the *death of Christ* ***on this earth*** is (like Jesus) the death of everyman's *personal* oneness with God. This is the death of the one (*person or self*) "*who*" knew and experienced his oneness with God. This is the death of his entire *earthly identity.* Though a body remains, in truth, it is "nobody". All this means is that the *eternal Christ* is no *particular* individual *person* or "*who*" someone is. To *become* God's *own universal* human nature and participate in God's divine nature, every *particular person* has to die. To *become* Christ means to become God's ***own*** human nature and **not** the humanity of this or that person. As noted before, God neither creates nor saves persons. They are incapable of eternal life.

This understanding of Christ's death, however, flies in the face of Cyril's view that it was **not** the *human person* Jesus who died, but a *divine person – Almighty God died,* **the "one divine *subject*" of Christ.** Cyril could say "*God died*" because he (and others) had **made God a "*person*".** Thus it was neither a divine or human nature that died, but one of the Trinity's three persons. Off hand, we would think the idea that as a *person,* God could either live or die, should have been enough to put an end to this absurd notion. **Yet, it was because Cyril and his cohorts made God, *instead* of Jesus, a *person,* they totally missed the true nature of Christ's death!** This was the death of Jesus' *whole person,* a death that left him with no personal identity – no person, self, subject or agent. Without this identity there is no person or self left **to be** Christ. **It is because the *eternal (heavenly) Christ* is no *particular* human being or *person* that the *person,* Jesus, had to die in order for the *eternal* Christ to be revealed.**

This death was the end of the unitive state in which Jesus lived his earthly life, the end, as well, of the incarnate Christ manifested in this world. This was not just the death of Jesus *who* was one with God, but the death of God *who* was one with Jesus – God being his *experience* of Life and Being. Since God is no person, and now the person Jesus is dead, Christ, the eternal oneness of two natures, is obviously no person – *and never was.* Indeed, God creates no person, is united to no person, and saves no person.

With the death of the particular *person* Jesus, we can now understand the true nature of *Christ* as "*Universal man*" and not a *particular* man. God's oneness with man's *universal* human nature is not God's oneness with any *particular* human being or person. Absolutely, the Truth of Christ is beyond the man Jesus, and, like Jesus, everyone will come to this same (seemingly unbelievable) Truth. The death of Christ is not the death of "I am", but "We are", the whole experience – "*God and I are one*". This was the *theosis* that defined Jesus as a "*whole person*" expressed by Paul, "*No longer I, but Christ lives in **me***". But here now, take away "**in *me***" and *where* is Christ? "*Who*" is left for Christ (or even God) to **be in?** Indeed, with no "**me, myself** or **I",** "*Who*" is left to be one with God? **No one!** The death of Jesus' *personal identity* is the end of man's *earthly* oneness with God, and the end of the "earthly" Christ as well. With this death there is no *person* left **to be** Christ – "*It is finished!*"

Without the *revelation* we know as "*resurrection*", this would be the end of the story. Man's *earthly* oneness with God, however, is not his *eternal* oneness. On earth man only knows God as God exists for himself – in *man* and *creation (ad extra)* – but does *not* know God as God exists solely-in-Itself (*ad intra.*) It is this transition from his *earthly* oneness to *eternal* oneness **in** God that **defines** the mystery of *death-resurrection*-and-*ascension*.

Apart from the "original kenosis" necessary to reveal the Incarnation, the fathers recognized another "kenosis" required for the "final deification" of human nature. This "emptying" was their understanding of the passion and death of Jesus, prior to his "*deification*" – Resurrection and Ascension. **In this final kenosis human nature had to forfeit all it had taken on to be an individual *person* in this world** – forfeit all the properties, accidents, attributes, characteristics of human nature that were necessary to live on earth. Thus God's *own* created human nature had to forfeit its earthly life in order to return to the glory in which it was conceived in God. So Christ's two *kenoses* are the reverse of one another. Where the kenosis necessary to reveal the Incarnation was "*inhuman*" – i.e., forfeiting the glory of God to take on individual personhood – this second *kenosis* was a return to the glory whence it had come. Although these two different *kenoses* have nothing in common, yet they wonderfully represent the dual natures of Christ – the first, inhuman or divine, the second, totally human.

The *true mystery* of Christ's *death,* then, had nothing to do with Jesus' physical death – even though he certainly died. Those who think this was merely the death of Jesus' *ego* or "*I am*", don't know what they are saying. Even Paul's *"No longer I...."* affirms Paul was already beyond any egoic or subjective **"I".** Yet beyond this subjective ego-loss ("I"), the next unsuspected event would be the disappearance of the objective "***in me.***" With the disappearance of the divine *Center* (*Ground* of being) there is no **"*within*"** anymore – for without a Center there can be no circumference, no *within* or *without.*[1] The demise of the Unitive state leaves no person, divine or human – but then, God created no person and united Itself to no person. So now, with the death of the particular person (Jesus), we can understand the true nature of Christ as *Universal man* and not a *particular* man. Absolutely, the Truth of Christ is not only beyond the man Jesus, but beyond every **person**.

While a person can experience his oneness with God in this life, he cannot, however, experience it in God's life. While the union of

---

[1] The two poles of consciousness are the subjective "I" and the objective "me". Because the subjective only knows itself as object-to-itself, take away the objective pole and there is neither "I" nor "me" – no self at all.

natures remains, it is no longer (in this case) ***Jesus'*** human nature, but *God's human nature.* In God, no one has or owns a human nature, its eternal life belongs to God alone. Where *theosis* served its purpose in man's earthly life, this will not work *in God's eternal life* – a radically different dimension of existence. So death of a person or self is the end of man's earthly oneness with God – *"It is finished".*

Since beyond this death (of person or self) all that remains is a body with no experience of life – of soul, energy, mind, will – the sole question that can arise is *"What is the true nature of* ***'what'*** *remains?"* Because its true nature remains unknown, all that can be done is to await some resolution to this *mystery of mysteries.* Its resolution will be the revelation of the *Eternal Christ – the* true nature of *"resurrection".*

Obviously, there is more to "death" than organ-failure. "Death", after all, is just a medical term for as much as most people know of it. There is probably no greater mystery in life than the *true nature* of death. Apart from its inevitability, man has always tried to give it some **meaning.** Down the ages man has come up with numerous theories, yet nowhere in history has its *meaning* and true nature been a greater mystery – or *revelation* – than the death of ***Christ.*** No other event has so endured to confront man with the mystery of death than the iconic figure of the man on the cross. This was not just the death of the man Jesus, but the death of *Christ – every man's* ***earthly*** *oneness with God.* This is the death of everyman's *person or self-identity* in order to become **God's own eternal, universal human nature – Christ.**

It was not for nothing God so dramatized the death of Jesus that it would become known the world over. The man on the cross, the *major icon of Christianity,* forever links Christ to the mystery of man's *death.* Like the dual natures of Christ, there is sadness on the human side, glory on the divine side, yet, **hidden in the event of *everyone's death* is the unbelievable truth of Christ**. "Unbelievable" because the true nature of Christ's death, while the same for everyone, cannot be grasped *intellectually.* Its true nature can only be known *experientially* – which means everyone will just have to "wait and see".

To *explain* Christ's death was a problem for the Apostles, Paul, and all the fathers. Paul's view of Christ's death as a "sacrifice" was his *Judaic* interpretation. The whole notion of sacrificing something or someone (Jesus in this case) in order to merit or atone for something, can be traced to pagan beliefs and the bizarre myth of "appeasing" the gods. No need to waste time on this idea, it totally demeans God's revelation of Christ and degrades the Incarnation. As noted earlier, Paul's explanation for Jesus' death was his *making the cure (Jesus) fit the di-*

agnosis (sin.) Given his view that everyone but Jesus was a born-sinner, Jesus died so everyone could become as sinless as he was. This is why one can hardly think of Jesus without the cross, his death being more the focal point of Christianity than the Incarnation itself. (There is not even a "feast day" in Christianity for the "Incarnation", instead, death and resurrection is its central focus and liturgy.)

But what if Jesus had died of old age, some accident or disease, what would Paul and others have made of his death? Would this have nullified the revelation, and changed the whole understanding of Christ? What would have happened to the idea of "sacrifice" and "suffering to save mankind" – and who would believe "God" died of old age? Certainly it would have robbed Christianity of its major icon – the man on the cross. God's forgiveness and salvation, however, have nothing to do with the Incarnation or Christ's death, and to link the two, misses the whole revelation of Christ.

The fathers, however, never connected the purpose or meaning of the Incarnation with Christ's death. If there was any salvific purpose in the revelation of Christ, it was the Incarnation itself – Christ's coming for man – and not leaving man. Alone, the Incarnation was redemptive; and the *inhuman kenosis* required for its revelation, a million times worse than anything man could call "suffering". Jesus' death could add nothing to this wondrous gesture of God to man. The fathers regarded Jesus' death and resurrection as his humanity's *transformation* into God's *own* glorious *human* nature. They were of one mind that death and resurrection brought about a radical transformation of everyman's nature – "*Man was created to be more than he is now*", this "more" being his transformation into Christ. Yet the dilemma Paul bequeathed to them was how to explain the death of Jesus as the means of salvation for all mankind.

Of utmost importance to interject here, is the fact that anyone in the Unitive State (Theosis) is **incapable of any interior "suffering".** Because the Divine Center of their being is God, and not their own self, they are incapable of "suffering" – God cannot "suffer". Jesus' "suffering" on the cross was purely *physical pain* with no "interior" spiritual or psychological "suffering" at all. As long as the body exists it "suffers" bodily neurological ***pain***. This "physical pain", however, is totally divorced from man's *interior* life with God. There is a tremendous distinction between *interior spiritual and psychological "suffering"* and *physical pain*. This fact, however, can only be known to someone in the Unitive State *(Theosis)* and not by those who are **not** in this state.

In this state, the slings and arrows of life simply disappear into the Divine Center – God that cannot suffer. That interiorly Jesus did **not** suffer, however, is a fact – ask those who know the Unitive State. While confronted with many trials, the Divine Center of Being is not merely "peace" but the abiding joy of life, a joy nothing in this life can ever match nor alter, this Center is untouchable. That Jesus was in this unitive State is something to keep in mind when considering his "suffering and death". The Center of his being was in peace, he knew his death as God's will – "So Be It!" This is why the idea that man's salvation hangs on the physical *pains* of Jesus – or any man – makes no sense at all. This can only be some pagan idea of a vengeful deity demanding satisfaction for the sins of bad apples.

Since the Judaic belief was that only God can save man – a belief held *long* before Jesus ever appeared – then how was it possible to believe the death of a human being could ever save man? The simplest answer, of course, would be to say "God ordained it that way and so be it – amen to the subject." But evidently this was not deemed a sufficient explanation. What, after all, made Jesus so special that his death could link all men eternally to God? For the fathers, the problem was how to forge a link between God saving man and the death of the man Jesus, somehow, this had to be explained – made reasonable and thus believable.

To resolve this, it might be well to remember both Greeks and Jews believed in the immortality of the soul. Though the philosophers may not have called it a "soul" (the Latin "*anima*" or Greek "*psyche*"), yet they believed there was something eternal in man that did not die. Given this belief, the only "thing" that could die was just a material body. So if God did not die, and the soul did not die, then death is just the cessation of the body's functions – generally, everyone's view of death. For the fathers, however, the whole mystery of Christ's death came down to one question – "***Who*, exactly, died on the cross?"** Anyone capable of grasping the *true* answer to this question is automatically guaranteed to know the Real Christ – because no simplistic answer is possible. This answer is so strategic that, from Paul onward, the true nature of Christ's death was a pivotal consideration of every Christology – Christ forever linked to the mystery of death.

There is only one answer to the question "*Who?*". It solely refers to some *person,* a particular human being – and what is the definition of "*person*"? It is the soul's agent, its *subject,* "I am" – self. The question "*who* died" is *not* a reference to the death of human *nature*, but to **the death of someone's *personal identity.*** And what was Jesus' personal identity? "*The Father (*God*) and I are one*". This is not God's identity nor merely Jesus' self-identity, but the identity of ***Christ*** – man's oneness with God. Since man's oneness with God (*Christ*), however, is not a "*who*" – not a particular human being or *person* – *the* real issue is not *who* died, but *what* died? Here again we are confronted with the *mystery* of Christ as neither God nor man, but the eternal oneness of the two – God *and* man.

In order to forge a link between Jesus' death and God's saving man, we know how some of the fathers arranged their theology to be able to **say** "*God died*" – "*theopaschism*" was Cyril's term for this. As to how it could be said "*God died*", well, we know how this was manipulated:

First, the terms "*hypostasis*" and "*prosopon*" ("face") were defined as "*persona*" or *person* in order to make God three *different persons.* To do this, of course, a division had to be made between God's *essence* (or nature), and God's *persons.* (Keep in mind *essence* (*nature)* is **not** *person* and person is **not** essence or nature.)

The next step was to declare Jesus the embodiment or incarnation of a divine *person* – the Logos (God), thus, making Jesus "God **in person"** – not in *nature*, but only *in person*. So to see God-in-person (but not in nature) was to see the man Jesus. (If people think that ***as a person*** God is an *embodied being,* then this is the definition of *anthropolatry.* And that the Trinity is three embodied ***persons,*** is the definition of *tritheism.)*

After this, since God *took the place* of the human person Jesus, then Jesus could no longer be regarded as a *human* person and, thus, could *not* be regarded as the *person who* died on the cross. **To ensure Jesus was a *divine* person, the understanding of Jesus as a *human person* had to be *condemned*** – Cyril's condemnation of Nestorius, who regarded Jesus as a *whole human person.* So, by robbing Jesus of all human personhood and making God a human person instead, this is how it worked to be able to say "*God died*" – though only **God *as a person.***

This, then, was the "theology" worked out to link Jesus' death to *God's* dying to save man. Although *by definition,* human nature cannot be a *divine* person, yet, using the conspiracy of the "*Communication of Properties*" it could at least be **said** the one who died on the cross was *God-in-person.* So today, a Christian who believes God died to save him, is *unknowingly* putting his faith in the *"Communication of Properties*" that ***says*** God died, when, in Truth, God did not die – impossible!

Since the idea God *could die* makes no sense, it seems eternal life had to be *limited only* to those who *could believe* such a thing. Making this belief a *prerequisite* for "salvation", however, smacks of coercion – the fear of *not* believing. We must not forget the background of most early Christians. For many, the only religion they knew was an imposed *polytheistic state religion,* they had no Judaic or philosophical background. For these to believe a god could become human and then die for them, was not too difficult. If we wanted to analyze this particular mindset, we could show how, for these people, Christianity was a kind of "life-saver". It not only gave practical meaning to their myths, but injected a kind of climactic Truth to them all. And do not think for a minute the fathers were not aware of these "simple folk", nor think these folks were aware of the fathers' theological dilemmas and much fought-over conclusions.

What is somewhat mind boggling, however, is that having lived 30 years unknown and unrecognized, it only took three short years after entering the public market-place, for Jesus to be condemned as an **un-**orthodox Jew. He was a blasphemer and heretic, to say nothing of his ability to stir up controversy wherever he went. To say he was a "controversial figure" is to put it mildly. So what was his heresy?

Although Jesus never said he was "*equal to God*" he was accused of this when he affirmed he was one with God, and was, in fact, "*God's son*". This truth, of course, fell outside Judaic monotheism that held nothing created could ever be, *in essence,* one with God. How *oneness* with God, however, would make someone "equal" to God is not really explainable, yet, this was the accusation for which he was condemned. That Jesus was one with God, however, was the truth, God was his most profound *experience* of *life* and "*being*". From birth, he had always known and experienced his oneness with God, he never knew any "other life", and it was for this Truth he gave his life. There is nothing in existence more powerful than Truth – because *it is eternal.*

If anything gets in the way of a true understanding of Christ's death, it was the condemnation (thanks to Cyril) of Jesus as a *whole human person* – a "whole person" defined as "man's *earthly* oneness with God". There is no such thing as a "whole person" or a *complete* human being without an *abiding awareness* of his oneness with God. (Some have ineptly called this "God-consciousness", which does not define the unitive state, which is a *state-of-**being**,* not an altered state of consciousness.) Without this *wholeness,* man is divided in himself, unfulfilled, incomplete, is left searching for something that will totally fulfill himself. Jesus, however, knew no life apart from the *experiential* reality of God as his deepest experience of *life and being.* Indeed, the true nature of his *death* was the *loss* of this *experiential reality.*

For those who rightly understand this "*unitive state of being*", no one could be more nonplussed with Jesus' cry, "*My God, my God, why have you forsaken me?*" Who could believe "death" is the loss of a man's *experience of God as one's true life and being?* The death of this experience leaves Jesus in no-man's land. It is not that God had abandoned Jesus, but that God had taken from him ***his*** whole experience of life and being, which was not, of course, *God's* experience of life and being, but Jesus' *own personal experience.* That God could leave (abandon) Jesus, is so unbelievable, all kinds of explanations have been substituted for the true nature of his death. That he cried this experience aloud to be heard the world over, echoed down the centuries, means God intended this truth for everyone to hear and know. The cry itself is a *revelation*, a mystery, the truth of *Christ and death* forever bound together.

Jesus was obviously articulating his *immediate experience,* and not, as some would have it, merely saying a prayer from Psalm 22! To connect physical pain with the *experience of losing all experience of life and being* is absurd, there is no connection. Besides, if his words did not express his *experience* or mean what they said, then why believe anything he said? It is the reality of his *experience* that needs to be rightly understood. On the cross his deepest experience of ***Life*** (God) left him – even physically "went out of him". This was his *experience* of *death,* and to miss it, is to relegate his death to nothing more than the cessation of his bodily organs. Whatever else man thinks is "death", it cannot be compared to losing the entire *experience* of Life and Being – the ***divine and human as one.*** **Just as they had lived as one, so *they died as one*.** This is why it is the "death of Christ" and not just the death of the man Jesus.

With this *experience,* Jesus' *earthly* life of oneness with God was over – *"It is finished!"* The death of this union was not the death of God or man, but the death of the two as one. While the Alexandrians insisted this was the *death of God,* the Antiochenes – who never bought this idea – stressed it was the death of *God's* ***own*** *humanity* – the death of *Christ in this world.* The Antiochenes (God-man school) had little problem understanding this as the death of the *Logos' incarnate* ***human*** *nature,* thus "*Christ* died", **not** "*God* died". The Alexandrians (God-flesh school), however, could never be satisfied with anything less than saying "God died" – which is why they made God a *person.* **There is a certain irony in their making God "*a person*" *only* to have this divine *person* die!** In truth, however, the epithet "*God died"* was the *horror* of most the fathers.

No father, of course, believed "God died", not one. As *immutable* and *impassible,* God is not subject to *change* or any "*experiences*". God is not only beyond all man's experiences, but beyond anything man *can* experience. Indeed, God's immanent nature – glory, omniscience, power, etc. – can never be called an "experience". To impose human experiences on God is the definition of a "god". **If anything points up the error of thinking Jesus is a divine *person* it is God's *immutability* and *impassibility*.** Neither in *essence and/or person* is God capable of any human "experiences". This is why the idea that Jesus' experiences – thinking, speaking, praying, suffering – were those of God, not only contradicts the Truth of God, but is no more than someone's idea of a mythical *god.*

The *experience* of union or oneness with God belongs solely to *man*, to human nature, certainly it is *not* God's experience. To be one with God is the *experience* of a *human person,* not the *experience* of a divine person – that God *experiences* oneness with God makes no sense whatsoever. Those who think a divine person is *passible* would have to think that on the cross "God" experienced being abandoned by "God" – absurd!

The fathers, however, actually faced Jesus' death squarely and never beat around the bush – for Ambrose, "*Obviously God left him! Life is the divinity, and his divinity withdrew*". Another said, "*Jesus died because he was* ***human***" – indeed, what *greater proof* that Jesus was a human being? It is because the Antiochenes believed Jesus a *whole human person* they came closest to a true understanding of *Christ's* death. They believed Jesus lived in a unitive state of being (*theosis*) in *this* world, and that this *earthly* estate was the prelude to Christ's *eternal* existence **in** God – and no longer **in** this world. So the "one" that died was **"Christ" in this world,** the "*whole person*" Jesus. On the cross, his *earthly* unitive life with God was over, "*finished*", and here begins his ascent to eternal life **in** God.

It is because the Alexandrians robbed Jesus of all personhood, they were left without a clue as to the true nature of *Christ's* death. Still, it is probably fair to say, of all the fathers, the question "**Who died?**" was of more concern to Cyril than all others. One Eastern Orthodox scholar – for whom Cyril was the last word – put it this way, "*The pre-existent Word* (Logos) *is the* ***subject*** *of the death of Christ, for in Christ there is no other personal* ***subject*** *apart from the Word (Logos), only* ***someone*** *can die, not* ***something****, or a nature, or the flesh.*" This is exactly Cyril's view. God as the *true subject* (or "*true self*") of Christ's *human nature,* is the subject or self that dies – not some psychological "me-myself-and-I" that dies. This is a **divine metaphysical subject *who* died,** this is Cyril's "*theopaschism*" ("God died"), considered perfectly orthodox to this day.

No question, there is some truth here. It goes without saying, God did not die, rather, it was man's *experience* of God as *his own* true being or *true self* that dies – leaves him and is never experienced again. But if God is the *true subject* **in man,** solely in Itself, God is **no subject** at all. God is no *person* (or three) and has no *self-identity* such as "I am God", "this is me", "I am myself" – all that subjective business. God is not a *subject* or a self-aware being, **this is *man*, not God!** God's *Divine Knowing* is of a totally different nature; in fact, God knows no "God", only man knows God. As said, making God a *human* person in order to make Jesus a divine person is the most egregious error in the history of Christianity, it is *not* the truth of God, of Christ, nor even the truth of the man Jesus.

But if the Alexandrian premise is false, what is the other side of the coin – the truth of it? In *theological* language, God was Jesus' "**true divine self**", and it was this, ***his divine subject* or *"true self"*, that died.** While this is true, yet theology is incapable of logically following through with this truth. It could never admit that God as *Jesus' own* ***true self*** **or subject (*person)*** actually died. Following through with this ***truth*****, the rational conclusion is that *this leaves no divine "person" (self or subject) at all – and thus, "Christ" is no person, divine or human.*** This *rational conclusion* **is** the Truth – Christ is no person, no "*who*", yet theology could never follow through to this Truth. The eternal oneness of two natures is "*what"* Christ is, not "*who"* Christ is – some particular person, that is. As Gregory of Nazianzus reminds us, "*in Christ we have two "what's"* (natures), *not two "who's", two "I am's" or "two persons"*.

Many people are familiar with the saying "God is **my true self**" (***true subject***) – meaning, "God is **my** *true* life", "**my** *real* existence", "**my** true being" – an articulation of the *experiential* reality of the *unitive state of being.* It is the one "***who"*** **experienced this reality that dies, the *whole person*** *(God and man as one)* taking with it all possible **self- identity.** Thus the particular **person – Jesus' self-identity –** died and no longer exists. But his *human nature*? It is totally transfigured and transformed into God's **own** glorious human nature. No "person" is transformed, only man's common human nature – created by God and destined to be eternally one with God – this alone is transformed.

Where Cyril and the Alexandrians made a huge mistake was their ignoring Jesus' *unitive condition,* which condition was Christ's *earthly life in this world,* but *not* Christ's eternal or heavenly life *in* God. Any failure to *differentiate* between Christ *in this world* and Christ *in eter-*

nal life, not only leaves one without any true understanding of Christ's death – in this world – but without any true understand of the "Real Christ". Christ in this world and the eternal Christ in God are both *realities*, but totally different dimensions, different states of existence – "different forms" of reality. The *earthly* condition of *theosis* is not personless, whereas the *eternal* condition of *hypostatic union* is absolutely personless. No authentic Christology can be premised on any heavenly Christ *prior* to the Incarnation or prior to God's revelation of Christ on this earth. All must start with Man on earth, in this world, for if one does not start at the bottom he can never get to the top. To ignore this fact, ignore this sequence in the revelation of Christ, is to miss Christ completely.

As it stands, according to Cyril and the "*Communication of Properties*", the Logos (God), the divine *person,* died – not the divine nature, but the divine *person.* And what, exactly, was the orthodox understanding of this divine person? It was the ***"one true subject of both natures"***, the one agent, the divine "I am", which was not *just* a human subject or self, mind you, but a *divine* subject, **Christ's one *true self.*** Thus it was not just the man Jesus who lost his *own* personal self, subject or "I am", it was also the divine person that lost **Its divine *metaphysical, ontological subject, "I am", "Who"*!** Christ's death, then, was the death of Jesus' *whole person*, his entire unitive life being one with God. Since they died as one, this left *no one, no person, either divine or human, to be resurrected* – and indeed, no *person* is resurrected. **Death is the end of all *persons,*** and this death is the true nature of everyone's death, the same mystery of Christ's death. Obviously the *true nature of death* has nothing to do with the body or the failure of its organs.

Death of the *person* Jesus was the *kenosis* necessary for *God's* human nature to return to its locus **in** God, whence it was conceived. This human kenosis is the loss of the *whole person,* not just Jesus' personal identity, but the **loss of God's personal identity,** which brings us to another aspect of Jesus' death that may help to better understand this loss, which is the part played by the Spirit in man's transformation.

The Spirit's particular *modus operandi* is transformation of the *soul*, whereas the Logos' *modus operandi* is transformation of the *body*. Unlike the Logos' *omnipresence* in creation (existential oneness with matter), the nature of the Spirit is to *indwell* in man, and this *indwelling* **is** man's experience of God ***within*** himself. It is because of the Spirit's *indwelling,* man experiences God as "personal". In comparison, the Logos and Transcendent do not *indwell,* but remain relatively *impersonal.* **It is the Spirit that makes God "personal" to man, yet,**

the Spirit is *only personal* because man is a *person.*

Those who have ever experienced the sudden infusion of the Spirit into the soul, can best understand how death is the *reverse* of this infusion. Thus, just as the Spirit is "*infused*" (*blown*) *into* the soul, so at death, the Spirit *blows out* – is "*defused*", we might say. (Needless to say, nothing can "blow out" that has not first "blown in".) So what is all this about? When the Spirit's interior transforming work is "*finished*", done, it leaves, literally "blows" out of body and soul just as it had once "blown in".

The Spirit's indwelling presence is to transform and enlighten, this is its "*modus operandi*". It is the Spirit, then, that transforms man's human nature into the Logos' *own incarnate* human nature – literally, transforms man into Christ. Just as in the incarnation the soul was created by the "power of the Spirit", by this same power It transforms all into Christ. This is why, on the cross, the Spirit's work in Jesus was done, "*finished*", and "went out" from Jesus. This left the *Logos* to be *revealed* as the true nature of the *body's eternal oneness with God* – the body, transformed into the Logos' *own eternal body*. This, of course, would be the *revelation* of the "Resurrection".

Man goes through his life thinking he is one with God *within* himself, one with the "indwelling" Spirit, yet this is not man's *eternal* oneness with God. This divine indwelling is only transformative, but is not the end Itself. Man's most *immediate* oneness is with the Logos, which, as said, is relatively "impersonal" compared to the "personal" Spirit *within himself*. Thus, where the **Logos' *operandi* is for the "*body*", the Spirit's *operandi* is for the soul, each playing its part in man's transformation.** The reason the *indwelling* Spirit is *personal-God* is *because* man is a *person* – we could say the Spirit is specifically present *because of* the *human person*. (Take away the *person* and there is no person **in** which to indwell.) This is why man's *self-awareness* is the same that gives him awareness of God, which, for many, is their most intimate rapport with God. No question, it is this indwelling Spirit man experiences as his union or oneness with God, and experiences the Spirit as the very source of his life and existence. Should the Spirit *leave* the body, however, there goes all experience of life and existence, all awareness of self and God – their union or oneness. There too, goes everything man calls "self" – which theology calls a "person". It is this *going out* of the Spirit that is the true experience of death – the only true "death" experience man will ever have. Why? Because God creates no *person* and saves no *person*. Keep in mind, *person is **not** the essence of human nature and human nature is not the essence of person.* Only a *person* can die, but *not* man's essential nature, which is, as

God ordained, transformed into the one eternal Christ.

As said, those who are not familiar with the *unitive oneness* in which Jesus was born, may never be able to have a true understanding of his death. For these people, Jesus' death was just the cessation of his bodily organs. But this is just another fallacy of the Alexandrian school – since God only took on *flesh,* then only the *flesh* could die – the *medical version* of death. This totally misses the true nature of Christ's death. What died was Jesus' entire *state of being in this world.* Those familiar with this state can imagine the shock of this *state of being* suddenly "blown out" – literally, the shock of death, yet, without being *physically* dead. No human being could plan on an event like this – all experience of divine and human life gone in one fell swoop? People tend to think some *experience* of life goes right on, which turns out not to be true. But now, without life, what is the true nature of *what is left*? *What* is the true nature of what remains beyond anything that could be called "life and being", beyond all self-identity human and divine? Beyond any experience but that of "the walking dead"?

As it turns out, the Spirit has no permanent or abiding union with the soul. The fact It "*indwells*" does not mean it can be *circumscribed* or *contained* in a soul – and certainly not *in* a physical body. The fathers believed all were created theocentric, God being the true **center** of one's being, with man, of course, being its **circumference.** Thus man depends on this divine Center for his life, and should this divine center go out, how can there be a circumference anymore? No Center = no circumference. So just as there cannot be one without the other, they die, disappear as one. This "blow out" is by no means the mere death of one's "me, myself and I", but the death of man's *earthly* oneness with God – Center and Circumference, gone forever. Thus the death of Christ was not the death of God *or* man, center or circumference, but *both* as one. Once the soul has been transformed into God's *own* eternal *human* soul, the Spirit's "work" is *finished* and goes out, taking with it man's entire experience of life, being, existence – even the awareness of *being* a body. With no experience of life or being, man is poised for a totally different life, but *not* one on this earth.

This death aligns with the fathers' understanding of death as the *final kenosis* or emptying required for eternal life. Just as the incarnation was the *initial kenosis* of the Logos' humanity entering into *earthly* existence, so too, the cross is the *final kenosis* or emptying (of earthly existence) in order to enter into the glory of *eternal life*.

With this death, man's union with God can no longer be localized ***in*** man. What remains to be revealed now, is what is called a "hypostatic union", which is not a union with Spirit, but first and foremost with the Logos. This eternal oneness with the Logos **can never be localized or experienced anywhere in man** – impossible. Remember, to "indwell" is *not* the Logos' *modus operandi.* This is why man's *eternal* oneness with God can only be **in** God and never **in** man. **One way to understand the difference: the Spirit in man is the *locus* of man's *earthly* union with God, whereas the Logos is the *locus* of man's *eternal* (or heavenly) union with God.**

It is only *after this* death (of Center and circumference) man is poised for the *revelation* of the true nature of "what remains" beyond all experience of life – beyond any person or being, human or divine – with nothing left but a *visible* body with *no experience of life*. Whatever the revelation, it will *not* be the revelation of any *person* or any *body*. It will be the revelation of a *personless* Christ – not "*who*" Christ is, but "*what*" Christ is – the eternal oneness of two disparate natures, God and man.

The true nature of death, then, is the loss of person – man's self-identity, "*who*" he is. God created no human person and saves no person because, obviously, no *person, subject or self* is capable of *participating* in God's eternal divine nature – impossible! (The "beatific vision" would be the end of a *person* anyway – "*See God and die*" is the truth of it.) Jesus' death was the loss of everything that can be defined as *person, a **particular*** human being. But as for his universal human nature – no different from any other human being – this will be infused with the glory of God. For those who think of Christ as a *divine* person, then there is only *one person* in heaven, not billions of Christs or billions of *persons,* but all transformed into Christ, God's *one* and *only* eternal human nature.

Obviously, the true nature of Christ's death is a *revelation* in itself, yet a revelation man may never be able to grasp this side of the grave. No getting around it, the crucified Christ is a powerful icon, its power being the *mystery of the true nature of death.* Its mystery is so profound it transcends all man's ideas of "death", all conjectures of the thinking mind – because its true nature is *unthinkable*. One reason it will always remain a mystery, however, is because if people knew the truth, they wouldn't believe it anyway.

It seems most people only consider the *purpose* of Christ's death – connect it with the notion of salvation. They give no thought to the *true nature of Christ's death,* which, for the fathers, was the question "*Who* really died?" – was it *just* the man Jesus, or was it a divine *person* – God? No question Jesus physically died, and no question a *divine person* could ***not*** die, the whole issue rested on how it could honestly be **said** a divine person died. As all the fathers knew and believed, God in essence and person is impassible and immutable, not subject to any human experiences or changes. Just the fact Jesus was subject to the whole human experience *nullifies* any idea he was impassible and immutable – that he was God, that is. How the proverbial party-line thought it could get away with saying "**God died**" indicates its dependency on the **un**thinking naiveté of "simple folk". This is not so much irrational as it is false. To my knowledge, however, apart from Cyril and some of his later followers, none ever countenanced the idea "God died", nor ever went along with the conspiracy called "*The Communication of Properties*".

What absolutely nullifies the truth and reality of Christ's death, however, is the belief that *whatever* died, after a few hours it just came back to life anyway – was resurrected. Given this view, then who honestly cares what or who died? Since it all *came back*, the issue is totally inconsequential. Why all the fuss when nothing and nobody really *died or* ceased to *exist*? The general Christian view is that Jesus physically died, and after a few hours, was miraculously revivified. So apart from the soul's leaving the body for a few hours, there was no real change, nothing happened of any import. That the soul's temporary absence from the body is what most Christians understand of Jesus' death and resurrection – and no doubt their own – is the usual party-line presentation of these events. But such a belief so completely misses the revelation of Christ, it makes belief in Christ absolutely meaningless. (That God forgives everyone's sins, has nothing to do with the true nature of death and resurrection – the revelation of *Christ*.)

It is because Christians have never honestly let the man Jesus die, they miss the whole revelation of Christ. In their view, the man Jesus, the same that walked this earth 2000 years ago, is the same that arose, the same that ascended, and the same now seated in some heavenly chair waiting to come back to earth. This utterly simplistic, static view, however, totally misses "*Christ*". If they honestly understood God creates *no person* – not even the *person Jesus* – and that in heaven there is *no person "Jesus"*, this would certainly stir the pot! "*What*" God created eternally one with Itself was *no person,* but solely man's common human nature – "**what"** is common to all and *particular* to none.

As to why Christians cannot accept that the person Jesus is gone, is because they cannot let go their *own person* – their own subject, "I am", *who* they are, their own personal identity. It is because they do not want to lose *their identity* they hang on to Jesus' historic identity. They could never countenance Jesus having to give up his personal identity lest "following Jesus" they too, would have to surrender their personal identity. But then, who really "follows Jesus" by *recapitulat-*

ing his same oneness with God? True followers may be rare indeed!

As to the loss of his own personhood, Jesus was on to this inevitability. This was the issue of his "agony in the garden". The question "*To be or not to be*" is not do **'I'** continue to exist or do **'I'** cease to exist? The question was how, with *no self-awareness* there could be *any awareness of God.* In the unitive condition, the loss of self-awareness is equally loss of awareness of God, loss of the whole experience of oneness with God. This is when one's *trust* in God has to ***exceed*** any *awareness-of-God-and-self.* Ultimately, however, man will have no choice in this matter. Just as man had no choice *to exist*, so too, he has no choice to *not exist*. It is all up to God. Even those who *think* they would be willing to give up their identity, have no choice in this matter anyway. It is because Jesus knew this, all he could say was "*Not my will, but Thine be done*".

Anyone whose goal is to lose his self-identity (*person)* or thinks he can get rid of his "self", is totally mistaken – that self can get rid of self is a logical contradiction. There is probably no greater fear man can have than loss of his self-identity – end up with no awareness of himself at all. This is because there is no greater **sense of *self-security* than *self-awareness*,** without it, man cannot imagine *his own* existence. In many respects, self-awareness, one's own identity, locks man in himself, which is why God is the only one that can ever get him *out of himself* – unlock this door, so to speak.

The theologian, Karl Rahner, regards Jesus' consciousness of his oneness with God as the *Hypostatic Union – big mistake here!* Jesus' consciousness of oneness with God was the *Unitive state* of *Theosis* and not the **person-less** *Hypostatic Union.* The fathers, of course, say nothing about Jesus' *consciousness of oneness* with God – called "*theosis*" in the *East,* and "mystical union" or "unitive state" in the West. The nature of unitive consciousness is that *one is as aware of God as he is of himself,* the two, given in the same autonomic reflexive movement of the mind. This abiding consciousness is neither solely awareness of self or God, but of the two – center and circumference – seen and known as one, yet distinct, for one is not the other. Barring a particular revelation, however, people would not understand nor recognize this *union* as "Christ" – Christ, that is, prior to death and resurrection. This is neither the revelation of God, self, Jesus, or of anyone, rather, it is the revelation of *Christ as the union of the two, revelation that **the true nature of this union is Christ**.* Christ is not God or any *person*, but the oneness of two disparate natures, God and man.

After describing Jesus' consciousness of oneness with God, however, Rahner goes on to say there is further growth, development, and experience of this consciousness. And then Rahner hits the nail on the head – he says this consciousness grew and then was "*absolutely handed over to the Logos*". In other words, Christ's death was handing over his whole unitive consciousness to God, which, on the cross, God obviously *took*. This "hand-over" was what Jesus' agony in the garden was about, the agony **"to be or not to be". If all consciousness of himself died, he would also lose his consciousness-of-God, of being one with God,** for without self-awareness "*who*" is there to be aware of God? **No one!** This is why loss of person, one's self-identity or self-consciousness is equally the loss of all consciousness of God. But who wants to live that way? No one could ever choose this, and knowing this, what did Jesus say? "*Not my will, but thy will be done*", and so it was! The whole person, the man Jesus, died *forever*. Beyond the grave there is no unitive consciousness or experience of oneness with God. Man's *earthly* unitive condition does not "carry over" to being his eternal life in and with God. Man's eternal life is a person-less "*hypostatic union*" eternally participating in the essence of God's own life, a life that has nothing in common with anything man experiences *on earth* – nothing in common with *theosis* or a "*unitive life*".

The idea that after the death of self-awareness there remains only the awareness-of-God is a myth – no truth to it at all. ***Who*** (person) is left to be aware of God? Some think when self or a person dies, this leaves only a *divine person aware* ***of Itself*** – no different than man's awareness of *his own* human self! God's Infinite Knowing is not remotely akin to human consciousness or any form of human knowing – God is *not* a *person*. All this is just another case of man making God into his own image. When people think of God as a "person" all they do is capitalize the "P" of a human person. There is no such revelation of God as a person, self, I am, me, who – and all the rest of it. This is why redefining *hypostasis* as *person,* not only falsified the true nature of the Trinity, but falsified the true nature of Christ. Get the Trinity wrong = get Christ wrong.

There is another view of Christ's death, one based on the fathers' view that everyone is created in the "image" of God. Since God, however, has no *image*, the Incarnate Christ is the "image" in which every man was created and destined to **become.** The moment this transformation is complete the image disappears, Christ disappears! Somewhere Maximus says this "*mirror*" (image or reflection of Christ) *is "broken*", which "breaking" is the death of Christ's image in man – the true nature of Jesus' own death in fact. Now there is no one left to be an *image* of Christ, and what *remains* is the imageless eternal Christ. So with no mirror or reflection remaining, there is no longer any *reflec-*

tion (consciousness) of *either* self, God, or Christ. Instead, what remains beyond all reflection and image is the Reality of which the image had been but the archetype – Christ, that is. In truth, the heavenly, *eternal* Christ can never **be** an *image*.

While the Logos' *own* incarnate human nature was *always* person-less, yet, to function on this earth it had to *become* its *own* person. Thus Jesus was fully aware of himself and never thought of himself as some divine "*person*". It was **his** will that was one with God, **his** own mind aware of God, **his** own life he gave to God, everything defined as a *person,* this was the person Jesus – until his death. The true nature of his death was the loss of his *whole person* – ***his personal*** oneness with God. But then, God was never one with the *person* Jesus – nor with any person. *Person* is man's *earthly* identity, "*who*" he is in the world, but heaven, however, is *not* in this world. There are no "who's" in man's eternal life **in** God. There is only the oneness of *what* man is and *what* God is – *Christ, that is.*

The true nature of Christ's death, then, had nothing to do with the cessation of Jesus' physical organs. It was a *spiritual death* that preceded his physical death. And just as the true nature of Christ's death was of a spiritual nature, so too, the true nature of resurrection is of a spiritual nature – and *not* a physical nature. (It is not the revivification of a dead body as many seem to think.) To find a real meaning for Jesus' death, one father (I think Irenaeus) said, "*If he had not died there would have been no resurrection*" – and indeed, Resurrection is not only the *only* reason for "death", but for Eternal Life!

* * * * * * * * *

There remains much more to say about the death of Christ, but since this could go to great lengths, we will only mention the following rather enlightening realities of death.

I. *Only Christ dies and only Christ rises*.

The meaning of this refers to the death of man's *earthly oneness* with God (which **is** Christ) and the *eternal, heavenly* Christ that rises. Where in this life it is an individual *person who* is one with God, **in** God, however, there is **no** individual person at all, for in *eternity* there is only the *person-less Christ.* Between the *earthly* Christ (man's oneness with God) and the *heavenly* Christ (man's eternal oneness with God) there is a huge difference. On earth, man is his *own* human nature (his own person), whereas in heaven, man is solely *God's own* eternal human nature – and no one else's! **Thus it is the earthly person *who* dies, and the person-less Christ that arises.** A more subtle meaning is that the moment man's earthly transformation is completely transformed into *God's own incarnate human nature,* this is the same moment Christ dies to become the heavenly Christ. Just as Jesus' *earthly* oneness with God died in order to become the *eternal* Christ, so too, is the way it goes for every human being. Thus, there comes a "point" when the *earthly* human nature of Christ is transformed into God's *own eternal* human nature. It's **not, then, "*we who*" die and rise – me, myself and I – but the *earthly* Christ that dies, and the *eternal* Christ that rises.**

For those who think Christ was "punished" *in their stead,* it should also follow that Christ died in *their stead,* arose and ascended *in their stead.* There is only one Christ, one same human nature, one same death and resurrection, there are not multiple human natures, multiple Christs, multiple deaths and resurrections. Thus Christ is man's *surrogate* in death, a *vicarious* death in that Christ dies in man's stead. **Just as in the case of Jesus, it was *God's own human nature* that died, not the human nature of Jesus or of any other *person.*** The Incarnation, being God's oneness with man's *universal human nature,* Christ's death was the surrogate for the death and resurrection of *every human being.* Yet who could possibly believe this – or even grasp it?

It is interesting that Christians can believe Christ *takes the place* of man's *punishment* for sin, but cannot believe Christ *takes the place* of man's death, resurrection and ascension. **How is it that Christ can *only* take man's place in punishment, but not Christ's place in eternal glory**? There's something mean-spirited about this – heaping sins on one man so every man can be glorified!? If someone *merited* eternal life for mankind, then **only this "one" is** the glory of mankind.

What gets in the way of understanding how all this works, is thinking it was only ***Jesus' individual* humanity that** died, whereas it was solely the ***Logos' own earthly universal humanity that died – Christ in this world, that is. In the incarnation the Logos not only took on the life of all mankind, but took on man's death and eternal glory as well.*** Another way to put it, when the soul, in its oneness with God, has reached that same stage as the man on the cross, death is its *final transformation* into Christ – i.e., God's *own human nature,* and no longer the human nature of Jesus, Mary, Joseph, Fred, Sally, or anyone. Just as Jesus' transformation into God's own human nature was not complete until his death-resurrection-and-Ascension, so it goes for every human being. And just as there is only one *earthly* Christ that dies, so too, there is only one *glorified* Christ that rises.

II. The Proverbial Mundane Question "*What if someone does not* *reach Jesus' unitive state before he dies, what if he did not finish his spiritual journey in this world? Does he go straight to heaven anyway?"*

Answer: Death is the end of the world for everyone – forever out of time and space. But when has God ever depended on time and space to do anything? Never! Does man think he is the one who transforms his own soul and reveals God to himself? Of course not! So what, beyond space and time, could prevent God from transforming man's human nature? Absolutely nothing! Besides, did God ever inform anyone that to be holy he had to arrive at some high mystical estate in this world? **Never**! (The idea is even silly.) Just remember, **what man can never do, God can do in no time at all.**

The only reason for speaking of the "unitive state" in this book is because this was Jesus' condition at the time of **his** death – even at the time of his birth. Until we can understand *the death of this unitive condition as the death of* ***a whole person***, no one can ever have the whole story on the Real Christ – or even on the man Jesus. None of us, of course, were born in this state and none of us will die on a cross. Still, birth and death is how it goes for everyone. As to "how many" people die in Jesus' same unitive state, it matters not. All that matters is that ***you, as a person*** will be no more "saved" as a *person* than was the man Jesus. God saves only human nature, not persons. Besides, "**who"** is concerned about arriving at some exalted state? ***Who else but your self*** **– a person!** Once this person is gone, God transforms human nature without further ado.

Some people seem to think at death the soul pops out of the body and later, pops back into a body – or *some* body. Following death, however, the soul is *out of time and space,* so how, exactly, can it ever get back in? Does man think he can bring his self back? Remember, after Jesus died he **never** lived on earth again – and neither will anyone else. The idea people are born into this world with "warmed-over souls" is a ridiculous myth. Christ's revelation of resurrection buried this idea once and for all.

III. Does a "person" (or self) really exist, or is it just a term to express differences between people? Somewhere, the idea is afoot that "person" – subject, self, I am, self-awareness, etc. – never really existed in the first place, it is all an "illusion". The human "person", however, exists as truly as the heart beats and the lungs breathe. Man is a conscious, self-reflecting being, and this consciousness (man's personal self-identity) is **the** major function (faculty) of the human soul, no different than his functional intellect and will-power. **Man is first and foremost a conscious self-aware being, and only secondarily, a "rational soul"** – for which (rational soul) there is little evidence anyway. So *consciousness*, which is *self-awareness, subject, agent, I am, who*, this is **the major *function or faculty*** of the human soul – not an animal soul and not God's soul. At death, however, all these *functions* cease because they cannot possibly function in man's eternal life in God. These faculties only function for the span of man's earthly life, without which, he could not *live* an earthly life. These, however, could never function in God's divine life – nor are they needed. The glory of God would only overwhelm them – stun them for all eternity.

Although most people think "person" refers to the totality of their being (everything they are), when they die, however, they will learn otherwise. Defined as a "property" of human nature, it is not human nature itself. Besides *person*, however, what else is not saved are those properties of the body called "genes" – gender, race, and God knows what else – these have no "eternal life" either. God does not transform man's *differences,* only what all share in common. The reason "transformation" is necessary is because man's earthly life is *incompatible* with eternal life in God. Indeed, the only reason there is a "heaven" (God's eternal Life) is *because* eternal life is **not** man's earthly life, is not life in this world – nor in any "place", but solely *in* God.

So "person" defined as the soul's *agent, subject, self-identity or "I am*", is a *function* of the soul, but not, in essence, the soul itself. Just as a body can cease to function, so too the soul can cease to function. All these *functions*, however, are not the ultimate *essence* of body and soul – indeed, only God knows the true essence of man, of human nature – of all that God creates, in fact.

IV. No separation of body and soul.

Beyond death of the unitive condition, there is no experience of any *separate* body or soul, in fact, no experience of either one. There is neither division, union, or anything that could be called "*one*" or the *oneness* of any "two". Strictly speaking, human nature can no longer be defined as "body *and* soul". Obviously this duality is man's view of *his own* human nature, which is *not*, however, *God's own human nature.* In God, the glory of body and soul are indistinguishable, no duality whatsoever. This is where only the term "*Christ*" can define man's deified, *eternal human nature* – God's *own* human nature, that is.

Since all man knows about death is the cessation of bodily organs, based on this, the belief seems to be that since the soul was responsible for the life of the body, when the organs cease to function, the soul *leaves* the body – abandons it. But why would it leave? Is this all the soul is about – to make the body work? As the *cause* of the body's function, **the cessation of bodily function could only mean the *cessation* of the soul's functions. So just as the body does not disappear when it ceases to function, neither does the soul *leave* when it ceases to function.** As totally indistinguishable, body and soul move to a different dimension of existence – only *not* of this earth. There is *never* any separation of body and soul, both are simultaneously "transformed" and indistinguishable in the glory of God. Besides, an *immaterial soul* can *never* be enclosed in *matter* anyway, it cannot be *locked* into a physical body – ever. As the cause of the body itself, its priority governs both the body's initial and final estate. Body and soul can be no more separated than creation can be separated from its Creator. The idea that at death the soul *leaves* the body and then later, re-creates it (or re-enters it), is pure myth. There is probably nothing anyone could say, however, that would ever convince people there is no duality or separation of body and soul. This false idea has been around so long – maybe from the beginning of man – that there is no foreseeing any change in this false view. This is too bad, because **there is no truth to it whatsoever.**

V. Death of the soul

In one sense it could be said the human *soul* actually dies. If the soul is the "life of the body", then how could the body die *unless* the soul died? *Why would* (or *how could*) the body die if its *life* did *not* die? How could the body's *life* go right on living without its body? **Either the soul is the life *of* the body or it is not –** we can't have it two ways at once. If a soul can function without a body, then it does not need one. And so too, if the soul is *not* the life of the body, then the body also does not need a soul to live.

Right here we could launch into the philosophical understanding of man as a composition of three souls – vegetative, sensory, and *rational.* But there is more to human nature than these three souls. Indeed, Paul defined man as "body-soul-*spirit*" – which we will go over later. If we remember, in the *unitive state*, man's experience of his *soul* or *life,* is no different from his experience of God. There is no drawing a line between the experience of God as *one's life* and that of one's *soul*. While One is not the other, still, there is only ***a single experience of Life and Being.*** When completely transformed, however, this One Life (*God and soul*), leave the body forever and are never ***experienced* again. Thus the body lives on, but with *no experience* of "life" – none!** Either the body has a life of its own (is soul-less) or man's definition of the soul as "life of the body" is *not true.*

To avoid any anxiety about the soul's *dying* (ceasing to exist), let us remember that the "soul" man experiences during *his earthly life* is *not* his deified soul in eternal life – i.e., *in God.* What man experiences as a "soul" on this earth is no longer recognized or experienced as such in eternal life.[2] So those who think "loss of soul" means going to hell, had better think again – death of the soul would leave *no one* to go to hell!

---

[2] It was the belief of some theologians (Duns Scotus, to name but one) that the soul is identical with its faculties (or functions) and that these functions *are* the true nature of the "soul". On a purely *experiential* basis this seems to be true, for without its functions (especially will and intellect) what is left to call a "*human soul*"? So when Maximus affirms that in the end these faculties *cease to function* – since once in God they are no longer needed – this would mean death of the soul. Scotus believed, however, that the "will", as the faculty of love-of-God, could only be perfectly fulfilled in eternal life *as God's own love.* So just as the Spirit's Love is the fulfillment of the will, the Logos' divine Knowing is the fulfillment of the intellect, and the Transcendent, the fulfillment of the Ground and Glory of all Being.

RESURRECTION

"Christ died in order to reveal the resurrection, took to himself a human body so that what was mortal might be transformed into immortality and what was passible into impassibility". (Irenaeus)

It should be an embarrassment to Christianity to think Jesus' resurrection was nothing more than his body coming back to life – as if his soul left for a few hours and then returned. To think this is proof of life after death or means that physical bodies will live forever, misses the mark completely. For one thing, after death, Jesus never lived on earth again – nor will anyone else.

The Egyptians are the first to be credited with belief in resurrection. The reason for mummifying bodies was belief the soul, at some undisclosed time, would return to its same body. It is said the Israelites adopted this belief during their captivity in Egypt, thus belief in resurrection was around centuries before Christ. Like everyone else, however, Jesus and his apostles put no "time" on it, had no idea when "resurrection of the body" would occur. Like their peers, they may have assumed there was a "waiting period" after death (the Judaic understanding of "Sheol") before some future event took place, a new earthly kingdom, the end of the world, (I do not know what), at which time, all would rise.

Since Jesus' resurrection revealed no new belief, what obviously surprised the Apostles was its "timing". That Jesus was resurrected almost immediately after death – less than 48 hours – is what made it so extraordinary, even incredible. Obviously, resurrection does not wait on some cataclysmic event, end of the world, or calculated in any *earthly time*. The importance of noting the short time-lapse between Jesus' death and resurrection is because ***as it went for the incarnate Christ, so it goes for everyone.*** Thus, just as Christ arose right after death, so it goes for everyone. Resurrection is not thousands of years down the road or awaits some particular event in this world.

Waiting for resurrection was the Jewish idea, but as we know, Jesus never fit the Judaic mold. Though Jesus tried to fulfill the Judaic notion of "Messiah", his efforts obviously came to naught. Like everyone else, he had to learn God's *plans* are not man's plans. Anything man thinks he has accomplished will only come to naught. Jesus' "*Thy will be done*" was this recognition, he had to give up all expectations of what he thought was his mission, leave it to God not knowing what would become of it or how it would all end. Most people only surrender themselves to God if they believe something good will come of it, but Jesus *agonized* over this surrender because he couldn't see how any possible good could come from his untimely death – his unfulfilled mission. But here again, Jesus didn't fit the Judaic mold of *waiting* for some indefinite time in Sheol to rise. That he arose *hours* after death evidently means there's really nothing to *wait for*.

Some people believe Christ's resurrection was *proof* that man's belief in "resurrection" was true, yet what Christ resurrection revealed was *not* proof of either the Egyptian or Judaic understanding of resurrection. The ancient belief was that following the soul's return to bodily life, it then lived *eternally* in *this world,* after all, a ***material*** **body can only live in a *material* world – how could it not?** That Jesus never lived on earth again tells us eternal life in God is *not* a physical world with physical bodies and that the "resurrection" God *revealed,* was *not* in accord with the Egyptian and Judaic belief system. Yet, because the term "in-carnation" *only* refers to a *physical* body, resurrection was thought to refer *only* to a physical body. So given the Christian understanding of *incarnation* and *resurrection*, God put on a human body and when it died, God left it for a few hours, then returned and took it on again. This scenario seems to be the common Christian belief of incarnation and resurrection. But how utterly naive and meaningless is this? Certainly Paul's idea of a "new creation" never meant returning to the old creation. On the contrary, it meant a whole new beginning of life, a totally different life, not the one man knows on this earth or in his present earthly body.

Because Jesus never lived on earth again, those who expect to live *forever* on some physical planet, only deceive themselves. Also, because the revelation of Christ did not accord with the Judaic belief system, its scriptures can never yield the True Christ – in fact, these scriptures may even inhibit a true understanding of Christ. While the revelation of Christ by no means nullifies the Truth in Judaism, yet Judaism does not encompass the revelation of Christ. (Jews have never found "Christianity's Christ" in their ancient scriptures, whereas for Christians it all *foreshadows* Christ.)

But before going over what Christ's resurrection revealed, we must first say what it did **not** reveal. It was not a revelation of God, not the revelation of Jesus, not the revelation of a soul's return to revivify a dead body, and not the revelation of an earthly body's eternal life. Resurrection is **not** the "return" of anything – for anything that can *return,* never *died* in the first place. It is only what did *not* die that lives on. So strictly speaking, resurrection was not the revelation of any "body". Above all, it was not the revelation of man's final heavenly estate – the nature of man's *eternal life in God.*

There can never be an understanding of resurrection unless there is first an understanding of the true nature of *death*. Since whatever is immortal cannot die, and since the body man knows now on this earth can die, then the body man knows now is *not immortal*. Thus no "body" man knows now is immortal, lives on, returns or is "resurrected". Interestingly, Paul's reference to a "new body" is to *Christ's resurrected* body, not to the "body" prior to its death and transfiguration. This *new body* belongs to no particular man, because it is solely *Christ's* one *body – the* same body everyone will have. **So those who think their own particular body will rise, have it wrong. No "body" arises, only *Christ* rises.** As for the true nature of Christ's risen and ascended **body**, they need only look to the Eucharist. This is not just the risen Christ, but the *body* into which all men will be "re-created", "resurrected", this is everyman's eternal body. There is absolutely nothing eternal about the body such as man knows it in this earthly life. In fact, no **earthly** body could ever **be** "eternal" – nor was it ever created to be – because life in God is not on some material planet somewhere.

Resurrection is really not about the "body". Rather, resurrection is pure *revelation,* the revelation of the *real Christ* – the same revelation ***given to the man Jesus* that is given to all that "arise".** This was not the revelation that he, Jesus, was Christ, but that Christ is everyman's "resurrection". Remember, it was the ***person*** Jesus that died, leaving no "me, myself, or I" *to be* Christ. Christ is not "who" some particular individual person is, rather, Christ is everyman's eternal oneness with God.

Because a *person* is "*who*" one is, and not man's common human nature, then death of a *person* is not the death of man's human nature. This is why **the *only* question that can arise after death of a "*person*" is *not* "*who*" *remains*", but "*what*" remains?** Another way to put the question: **"*What* is the *true nature* of *what* remains *beyond any experience of bodily and spiritual life?*"** Whatever it is, it is certainly nothing man ever thought it was. Thus the reason for the question, "what remains?" is due to the fact *life* goes right on without any **experience of life, being, soul, energy – no "*experience*" at all.** (If the bodily *senses* did not remain, then there could be no verification that a physical *body* remains at all – or even exists.)

Had it not been for Jesus' terrible physical condition, following the death of his *whole person,* he could have continued to live on earth – though totally changed. No longer having any *experience* of life, soul or God, his experience would have been that of the "*walking dead*" – which may well have been his experience. It is because the body continues to exist, however, there is the question of its true nature – how does it live on with no *experience of life, a soul, God, or anything known.* If man had any idea of the true nature of what remains beyond death, there would be no question to ask and no need for any *revelation* to answer the question. As long as man thinks he knows the answer, then he truly never died. The true nature of "*what*" remains (goes on existing) can only be *revealed*, and it is this revelation that **is** the "Resurrection". Without this revelation, there is no answer to *what* exists beyond death, what life this may be, nor any knowledge of the true *essence* of human nature in its *eternal* oneness with God.

So the *revelation* we know as *Resurrection* is the answer to the true nature of "*what remains*" beyond death, beyond all *experience* of life and being. *Resurrection is one thing and one thing only* – ***it is the revelation of the Real Christ.*** Christ is not "**who**" remains, but the true nature of "***what***" remains. At the same time, however, it is equally the revelation of the Incarnation, for the two, *Resurrection* and *Incarnation*, can never be separated, they are two sides of the same coin. Thus Resurrection is the ultimate revelation of the *whole mystery of Christ*, revelation of the Truth of God's eternal oneness with Man, how it works, how it even exists. So first and foremost, *Resurrection* is a totally unique, one-of-a-kind "***revelation", and this revelation of the real Christ* is exactly *what* Resurrection is – and all it is.** This is not the revelation "I am Christ", or "Jesus is Christ", it is not the revelation of any *person*, but of man's one essential nature eternally one with God. So now let us go over what is learned from this revelation.

1. It reveals there is "something" in man that goes right on living only *without any experience of life or being,* thus, strictly speaking, apart from death of a "person", there is no such thing as "death". Once the body's physical senses have ceased to function, however, then there is no way to *see* or *feel* any physical body whatsoever. While people think a "soul" remains, yet with no experience of life or being, there is no experience of a body or soul. Basically, the *experience* of body and soul can never be disconnected, without one there could be no experience of the other. The body that lives on – or remains beyond person – is *not* the body people think they know or experience on this earth. As non-experiential, it could be regarded as a "formless body" – having no earthly form. To understand this, it might be helpful to recall the epithet "*Cosmic Christ*" – the Logos' oneness with matter – in this case, oneness with man's body. Resurrection, then, is not the *revelation* of the soul's eternal life, but of the *body's eternal oneness with God* – though not the "body" man knows and sees on this earth.

2. The resurrection also reveals there *is no separation of body and*

soul. There's no soul popping out of a body and later popping back in, this ancient myth is false. John of Damascus had it right – "*when Christ died, the Logos was never separated from either the body or soul of Christ, but maintained their oneness in the Logos*" – maintained the oneness not only of God and man, but of body and soul, neither of which can be separated from God. One reason there is no separation of body and soul is because the Logos and Spirit cannot be separated – the Logos one with the body, the Spirit, one with the soul.

3. Resurrection also reveals it is not an event that takes place down the road hundreds or thousands of years after one dies. Following death of the sensory body, man is immediately out of space-and-time, has no awareness and experience of it. Thus resurrection can never be an event or revelation "in time and space" – no "time element" can be attached. That it *directly follows* death of the body, is what Christ revealed – *Christ* being the "*Way*" it goes for every human being.

Death, of course, is the *end of the world* for everyone. Should there ever be some cataclysmic ending, no one will be around to talk about it anyway, so there is no use conjecturing about such an event. Just as death was the end of this world for Jesus, so it will be for everyone. Resurrection has never meant a return to earthly life.[1] As said, the resurrection Christ revealed, was **not** the Egyptian or Jewish understanding of it. The idea there can be any kind of "eternal life" in a material world – and thus in a physical body – is just another grim fairy tale. To think trillions of people are now waiting to get their bodies back is, quite frankly, bizarre – absurd. If souls are with God already, then **who needs a sensory body that cannot see God anyway?** Since nothing so distracts from seeing God as the senses, what possible good would they be in heaven?

And it is not just the senses that cannot see God, neither can the intellect – attached as it is to the senses. While some think the higher intellect is the "eye" of the soul, all this "eye" sees is **itself**. It is only the "*eye of the spirit*" that can see and know God – "*the eye with which I see God is the same eye with which God sees me*". (Recall Aristotle's "*other soul*" that he defined as "*that*" which eternally "*contemplates*" God – the "*Beatific Vision*". This is no eye of the intellect!)

The true nature of death, then, is not *just* the cessation of bodily functions – the medical definition of death – but also, the cessation of the soul's functions or faculties. While these functions were needed to

---

[1] In Jesus' lifetime, those God brought back to life all died again anyway. This fact should alert us that resurrection is other than a body's regaining normal functions – this is *not* the true nature of *resurrection*.

live an earthly life, they were never created for eternal life in God – where they are of no use whatsoever. Maximus the Confessor affirms as much – "*Our deification, our mystical resurrection, is the complete stripping away of the* ***natural actions of sense and mind*** *by the presence of the Spirit who directly transfigures the entire body altogether into something more divine"*. The senses serve only to perceive *material* objects, and material objects *do not exist in heaven,* thus they would be useless in heaven (eternal life in God.) If the senses cannot see God in this life, what makes people think they will see God in the next? People who think they can *eternally* see God and still live on earth, have never seen God – "See God and die" is the Truth of it. To think eternal life is anything remotely like man's mortal life on earth, is not just naive, but absolutely *impossible!*

4. Altogether, Resurrection is far more than the revelation of a formless body's oneness with the eternal "Form of God" (Logos), more than the inseparable oneness of body and soul, even more than man's eternal life with God. Above all, resurrection is the revelation of the whole mystery of God's eternal oneness with man, and how God brought it about – the Incarnation, that is. **Resurrection is equally the revelation of the Incarnation in that one is the *reverse* of the other. Both begin and end at the same point – in God, thus both are the same revelation – the Eternal *Form of God* (Logos), eternally one with the "*form of man*", this is the Truth of Christ.** So Resurrection is the *revelation* of a great Truth – the Truth of God and Man and how even man's body partakes in the eternal Form of God. But just as God's divine Form (Logos) cannot be categorized as *either* matter or spirit, so too, the eternal "form of man" cannot be so categorized. When it comes to *eternal life,* all man's categories, ideas and definitions become meaningless.

Although it is ***through*** **the Logos** man is eternally one with God, yet man is not just united to the Logos, but rather with the whole Trinity. Where the Incarnation was Christ's *human descent* from the glory of the Transcendent, Resurrection heralds Christ's *human ascent* back to the glory of the Transcendent. Thus, the Resurrection is the reverse of the Incarnation.

As a very *specific revelation,* it could be said Resurrection is the *sole* revelation of the Real Christ. Perhaps no one could have been more surprised with this revelation than the man Jesus, this same Truth, same revelation of *Christ*, however, is the *inevitable* revelation of every human being. But unless one can put himself in Jesus' shoes as a human being – a human nature no different than his own – there is no possibility of knowing the True Christ. As we have been pointing out, it was not the ***person*** Jesus "who" was Christ, rather, it is solely man's universal (***person-less***) human nature (one with God) *that is Christ.* The ultimate revelation of this Truth **is** "*Resurrection*", what *Resurrection* **is**. The man Jesus was the recipient of this revelation just as it will be for every human being. So long as people think only the man Jesus is *Christ*, they can never grasp or know the *real Christ* – not in this life at least. **So long as Jesus *points* to Christ (and not to himself), there is no obstacle to knowing the true nature of Christ, but to think only one man – Jesus himself – *is* Christ, and one does *not* know the *real Christ.***

The fathers believed Jesus was not deified *until* his resurrection and ascension. Thus Jesus only reached the earthly fulfillment of God's Incarnate humanity at the ***end* of his human journey.** Hilary affirms this when he says it was only at the *end of Its human journey* the *incarnate Logos* became "*perfect man and perfect God*" – and not ***before***. So even in the case of Jesus, man's creation is not over until it is over – until it reaches the end for which it was created in the first place. And when it is over, all those human properties *needed* for earthly existence that are incompatible with *eternal existence*, all these **are gone forever**. With his death, the man Jesus, as a particular human "*person*" no longer exists, and what exists, **is God's own transfigured, glorified human nature**. Now there is *only Christ*, the eternal oneness of God's ***own* divine and human natures**.

Hilary also cautions – "*Do not confuse the time and natures in the mystery of the dispensation (Incarnation), for according to the attributes of his different natures he must speak of himself in relation to the mystery of his (Christ's) humanity in one way before his birth, in another while he was yet to die, and in another as eternal*". Thus Jesus' saying "*I am the resurrection*" was said *prior* to his death, not *after*. Had he said this *after* his resurrection he would have said, "*Christ **is** the resurrection*" – "*no longer "I", but only Christ rises*". Christ alone is man's eternal life, not someone's "me, myself and I". So *after* Jesus' death he could *not* have said "I am" – because there is no "I am" anymore. Nor *before* he died could he have said, "*Christ is the Resurrection*", **because** the *true nature* of resurrection had not yet been *revealed* to him.

We rarely hear any commentary on Jesus' saying "*I am the resurrection*". Most people seem to think this was foreknowledge of *his own* resurrection. Yet he never said, "I will be resurrected" – or "you will be resurrected" – rather, the implication was that **he is *what* resurrection *is* – not just *his*, but *everyone's*.** Now if we take this as

Jesus referring to *Hilary's third or final estate of Christ* – i.e., a *post–* resurrection statement – then the reference is to his resurrection being the Truth and Reality of *everyone's* resurrection and not just his own. **Thus it is the eternal heavenly Christ that is the true nature of everyman's resurrection – in the end, everyone, the same one Christ.**

That after resurrection the Apostles visibly saw and talked to Jesus, does not tell us the true nature of resurrection. Thus Paul, who never saw "Jesus in the flesh", claims to have seen the resurrected Christ – but *what* did he see? A blinding Light! Indeed, it is because Paul *saw no one,* he asked, "Who are you?" And since Paul knew nothing of "Christ", the only answer he could have understood was, "I am Jesus" – the *person* Paul had only *heard* about. We have already gone over what this message meant to Paul – namely, ***the universality of man's common human nature.*** What does it matter "who" you persecute when human nature is the same for all? To persecute Jesus, Paul, Sally or Ted, is all the same, at least in the eyes of God. As said, God is no respecter of "persons". This, of course, was the big eye-opener for Paul, without it, he could never have understood the *real Christ.* As he tells us – "*Even if we **once** knew Christ **in the flesh**, that is not how we know him **now**.*"

Paul is not just pointing out the difference between the past *visible* man Jesus, and the eternal *invisible* Christ, but pointing out the change that took place between the two, past and present, old and new – "*for everyone who is in Christ there is a new creation, the old creation is **gone** and now the new creation is here" (2 Cor.5:16.)* Following Jesus' death a radical change took place, one that could not have occurred prior to the completion of his earthly mission, a change required because man's heavenly life is *incompatible* with his earthly existence. So between the old and new creation there was not merely a change from the transitory to the eternal, but a radical transfiguration of body and soul. With this transfiguration the old creation (Jesus) is gone, and now, only the new creation, Christ, remains. If people do not let the old visible Jesus die they will never know the invisible eternal Christ. This is why clinging to the old man "*we once knew in the flesh*" is to miss the living Christ.

Because Paul's revelation of the Resurrected Christ was not "Jesus in the flesh", he regarded the resurrected body of Christ as a "spiritual body". Had it been a sensory body, then he would have seen "Jesus in the flesh". So while the Apostles saw a sensory body, what they did ***not*** see was Christ's "spiritual body" – no one can visibly see a spiritual body anymore than they can visibly see God.

This is why the apostles who knew "Jesus in the flesh", saw the visible man Jesus, and Paul only saw a blinding light. If the resurrected Jesus is no different in heaven than on earth, then why didn't Paul see "Jesus in the flesh"? It goes without saying, the apostles would not have believed Jesus was resurrected had they *not* seen him "in the flesh". Merely to see a "blinding light" would not have *proved* any resurrection to them! Keep in mind the Apostles' Judaic mind-set according to which, resurrection was to be the restoration to an *earthly physical body*. This was not, however, Paul's understanding of "resurrection" – based on his revelation of the resurrected Christ. It is because he saw no one "in the flesh" he regarded the true nature of resurrection as a "spiritual body" and not a visible, material body. Obviously, what it takes for one man to believe, is not what it takes for another man.

It could be said, the only reason Jesus was *seen in the flesh* after his death was to satisfy people's lowly senses – after all, "*seeing-is-believing*". The Apostles, like most people in this world, would not have believed had they not seen. If Jesus had died alone someplace and not in public view, no one would have believed he even died, much less been resurrected. This is why his death had to be dramatized for all time, publicly witnessed, and also, why his resurrected body had to be seen to be believed. As for the saying, "Blessed are those who believe and do *not see*", obviously, the Apostles were not yet among those so blessed.

The Apostles' *sensory seeing*, of course, misleads if one thinks resurrection means *eternal* life is a material, sensory body – a body that can only exist in some *material* world. At most, physically *seeing* Jesus might at least prove to an erstwhile disbeliever there is life after death, or that there is such a thing as "resurrection", but this is as far as it goes. The sole purpose of all God's miracles is to affirm one's faith – the Truth – which is why making a big theological, doctrinal or scientific issue out of miracles, is to miss the message completely. **People who rely on their senses for any *eternal truth* can only be regarded as *spiritually* dysfunctional.**

That Christ's *eternal body* is *not* a visible body attests to the limits of the senses, limited as they are to *material* objects. Somewhere St. Augustine noted that when speaking to "simple people" of anything invisible or purely spiritual, to their minds it was as good as non– existent. For this reason he had to assure them heaven was a physical "place" where their senses would see God – just as they might see a tree or a frog. "*In learning that in the end there will be no time or space or physical body, simple people would* **be alarmed** *thinking there would be nothing at all. Easier to think the body will be turned into the ethe-*

real than have no body at all." (Augustine.) No question, Truth is all but guaranteed to "alarm" people – which is why they rarely hear any. My conviction is that the Truths of Christianity have always been watered down – practically from the beginning – not only to avoid "alarming" people, but to actually make them feel good, especially as regards man's end or afterlife. Nothing that alarms people, after all, could attract converts, much less keep sheep in the fold.

It was just such a condescension to "simple folk", however, that, unfortunately, the notion of heaven as a *physical* place with *physical* bodies remains the notion of most people – after all, how could a physical body live in a non-physical dimension? Inconceivable! Just as Augustine said, what man cannot verify with his senses has no reality for him – which is another reason people cling to the sensory image of the historical man Jesus. Evidently, this is sufficient to make belief possible – at least on a sensory level.

To think the resurrected body is the same as man's present earthly body, flies in the face of the event we know as the "Ascension". Without the Ascension, man's understanding of Resurrection remains incomplete. If the body the Apostles saw was *eternal*, then the man Jesus would still be around. The fact that almost immediately after resurrection Jesus disappeared from this earth, tells us the body the Apostles saw was *not* eternal – which is *why* it disappeared. Then too, if the resurrected body can live an earthly life, then why die at all? As said, those who think eternal life or heaven is full of physical bodies can only envision heaven as a planet somewhere – and who knows, maybe someday NASA will find it. Heaven, however, is not a "place", but a totally different dimension of existence – God's own dimension of Existence. Earthly life and eternal life are totally *incompatible*. Nothing created has any eternal life of its own, and for God to grant eternal life to anything created, God has to transform it into Its Own *dimension of existence* – what "other" ***eternal life*** is there? Since God alone is Eternal Life, unless man can somehow *participate* in God's eternal life, there is no other "*way*" man could have *any eternal* life – none.

Paul explains his view of the "resurrected body" as a "spiritual body", this way – "*The thing (body) that is sown is perishable, but what is raised is glorious. When it is sown, it* ***embodies the soul****, when it is raised, it* ***embodies the spirit****. If the soul has its own embodiment, so does the spirit have its own embodiment. The first man Adam, as scripture says, became a living soul, but the last Adam has become a life giving spirit. That is, first the one with the soul, not the spirit, and after that, the one with the spirit. The first man being from earth is earthly by nature, the second man is from heaven. As this earthly man*

***was**, so are we on earth, and as the heavenly man **is (now)**, so are we in heaven. And we who have been molded on the earthly man, will be molded on the heavenly man"* (I Cor. 5: 35-53.)

To understand this, we have to remember Paul's view of man was as a composite of *body-soul-spirit.* He was not stuck with the later Aristotelian dictum of man as solely a body and soul. For Paul, then, besides having a rational soul, man also has a "spirit". Thus where the soul has its own *earthly form* or embodiment, the spirit also has its own *formless spiritual* embodiment, *different* from that of the soul. Perhaps this is what Jesus meant when he said "*unless a man lose his soul he cannot enter into the Kingdom of God"* – meaning it is man's "spirit" that "arises" and not his soul. (The terms *life* and *soul* were often used interchangeably.) Thus where the *soul* is man's *earthly* life and experience, his *spirit* is his *eternal* life. This, at least, seems to be Paul's understanding of man, his resurrection and eternal life. (Still, no one can *bodily see* either a soul or spirit.)

So if the soul, then, is only the life of the *flesh* (which is all the *animal* soul is) and it dies, this leaves the "spirit" with its own type of "spiritual embodiment". This type of "embodiment", of course, no one knows ahead of time or until they are dead. But since the *essence* of flesh or matter is also saved, we need only recall the Logos' *existential union* with matter – the "cosmic" Christ – that enjoys the same glorious estate in the Transcendent as does the eternal "spirit".

As for the difference between a *spiritual* and a *physical* body, the major difference is that a physical body *experiences* a "soul", whereas a spiritual body experiences **no** soul at all. These are totally different realities and ways of existing, so different in fact, the only way to account for the difference is to negate every possible comparison.

Paul's view of a "spiritual body", however, is not out of line with Athanasius' understanding of the Logos as solely one with the body, whereas the Spirit is one with the soul. Thus the *Spirit* transforms the soul and the *Logos* transforms the body. If one has a handle on the Trinity, this is perfectly understandable – Spirit and Logos, the essence of God, one with soul and body, and all, in the glory of the Transcendent. If we think of Christ as the *threshold* uniting the created and Uncreated, we can understand the divine essence (or Trinity) on one side, and man's transformed nature on the other, and **Christ** being the **line** uniting the two. The only reason man's human nature has to be radically transformed or changed is because eternal life with God is *not* a material life in a material world. But then, anyone who has seen God knows that.

It is well to remember Paul's understanding of Christ came from no biblical account – which had not yet been written – but solely from *his own personal experiences of Christ.* When he said "*If Christ has not been raised, then our preaching is in vain, and your faith is also in vain*", his reference was to *his* having seen the resurrected Christ, the blinding Light, this was the Christ in which Paul put his Faith. **His faith never rested on seeing the man Jesus "in the flesh", nor did it rely on any scripture, nor on anything he had been told, instead, he relied solely on the resurrected Christ *revealed* to him.** This experience, the blinding Light of the resurrected Christ, this *was the sole source of Paul's faith.* Had he relied on anything else, then, indeed, his faith would have been **in vain**. So too, those who rely on seeing the man Jesus "in the flesh", who rely on scripture or anything they've been told, **their faith *is* in vain**.

There is another important lesson we can learn from Paul. When rapt to the high heavens, he said he did not know if he was "*in the body or out of the body*". It seems Paul had a taste of eternal life, yet didn't know if he had a body or not. What does this tell us about man's final estate? If man comes to a state where it makes no difference if he is *in* a body or not, then what possible benefit would it be to have a body at all? How could one miss their body if they didn't even know they had one?

Though the bible says nothing about it, there was the Judaic notion that immediately after death, Jesus' soul went to "hell" and back – "*he descended into hell and on the third day he arose again*" (the Apostles Creed.) The Jews, of course, never believed in "eternal punishment" or the Christian notion of "hell", they believed, however, that after death the soul descends to "Sheol", a place of "waiting" until heralded by some great event when all would arise – be resurrected. Thus it was thought Christ descended to Sheol to release all those waiting souls – Adam, Eve, Abraham, Moses and others – so they could rise with him. This notion was based on the idea that prior to the revelation of Christ, there was no one in heaven (no one had yet been "saved"), but now, with the coming of Christ, there was no more "waiting" period between death and resurrection. Thus all those "waiting" arose at the *same time* as Christ, not later or down the road sometime. This seems to mean that now there is no more "waiting period", and everyone's resurrection immediately follows his death – exactly as it did for Jesus. If Jesus did not reveal the "way" it goes for everyone, then his life revealed nothing to no one.

Since no one actually witnessed the resurrection, no one knows the time it occurred. Knowing Jesus, however, it was probably on the Sabbath. The Apostles, of course, did not find out until Sunday morning when they discovered the empty tomb. Just as no one witnessed Jesus' resurrection, so too, no one will witness anyone's resurrection – why? Because it has nothing to do with a physical body coming back to life. Resurrection is solely the revelation of the Real Christ, the same given to the man Jesus that will be given to everyone. As already said, resurrection is not the revelation of Jesus, but the revelation Christ is no *particular* human being or *person,* but is *everyone's* eternal oneness with God. Remember, "person" was the subject, the "I am", and this "person" is dead. And whether we think of the one "*who*" died on the cross as the "person" of God or man, it makes no difference because *whoever that person* was, he is now *dead and gone – forever*. The resurrection is the revelation of the true nature of "*what*" remains when all "persons" or "*who's*" die. After all, man's *eternal* oneness with God is the only revelation *to die for.*

So what is it that gets in the way of having a true understanding of resurrection? The only answer is "false beliefs". It seems people judge the soul by its bodily functions, and when these functions give out, they think the soul is gone out. Thus all man takes for a soul is a living, breathing body, and where they see no breathing body they assume the soul has left and gone "somewhere" – as if the body had somehow "contained" or imprisoned a soul! The body, however, never "contained" a soul, just the opposite, the soul contains the body. An immortal soul is far more than the body's "*sensory*" soul, which, after all, is just an *animal* soul and *not* immortal anyway. The soul, however, is not the true principle of bodily life, God alone is the principle of all life, material and immaterial. So too, God alone knows the true nature of man and how he works. For our part, we divide up everything – body, soul, psyche, faculties, properties, higher and lower – you name it. This reminds us of Heraclitus 2600 years ago accusing the philosophers of dividing up everything under the sun, while he saw the *oneness* of it all.

Think of all the philosophical views and religious beliefs man could have been spared had he never postulated a dualism of body and soul in the first place. This dualism was obviously based on the visible body going back to the earth – ever in flux and change – while the immortal soul was thought to be beyond all such flux and change. The soul, however, is no static ghost in a machine, on the contrary, it is ever in the process of transformation. It is *because* there is no separation of body and soul the body partakes in the soul's eternal life in God. This is why the notion of the soul's "getting back" into a visual body is so absurd – there is no going back to what never left in the first place. This fallacious idea of resurrection illustrates how man clings to earthly life because he honestly does not trust God with his *eternal life*. Man's beliefs always rest on his own fictional, comforting terms, not on God's revealed Truth.

In this matter, we might recall Cyril's analogy of the "hypostatic union" (of God and man) as similar to the inseparable oneness of body and soul, an analogy that is actually true, in that there is no separation possible. Not only is this "oneness" beyond the experience of any duality, but even beyond the experience of any "one" – i.e., one entity, one being, one individual – no "one" that could be pointed to or put one's finger on. This is not only the true nature of the resurrected body, but the oneness of Christ's two natures – *no separation* or *division* possible between God and man, nor between body and soul.

Death brings about a radical change from the awareness of "having a body" or "being a body" to having no awareness of any body. While the material body remains unchanged, yet it is a body without an "owner" or any *person* (self) to experience it. Beyond death, the true nature of the body or "what remains", is unknown. The revelation of this "*unknown*" is the true nature of *Resurrection.* It is the revelation of Christ as the true nature of "what" remains *beyond* any owner, any *subject or person* (be it divine or human), beyond any center or circumference (within or without), beyond all experiences of life and being, beyond any experience of a soul, and the experience of any *body*. **Resurrection is the revelation of the true nature of Christ, the eternal oneness of the Form-of-God (Logos) with the eternal form-of-man.**

To say the true nature of resurrection is the revelation of the Real Christ sounds simple enough, yet to grasp this revelation one must first be dead, otherwise the enormity of this revelation may never be truly understood. Resurrection is not the revelation of God, the Trinity, the man Jesus, your "self", or any "one" being. To say any more about this, however, the background required would entail writing several books of *introduction*. It would entail truly knowing and identifying the Trinity in one's own life; and second, it would mean having lived the entire spiritual journey from beginning to end – which end begins with death. The revelation of Resurrection and Incarnation is the revelation of the Alpha and Omega of Christ – meaning, man ends where Christ began and Christ begins where man ends. All that can be made clear here, is that the true nature of resurrection is the particular, one-of-a-kind revelation of Christ. In fact, the very definition of "Resurrection" ***is*** "Christ". Resurrection has nothing to do with any revivification of a dead body, a soul's return to a body, or any form of earthly existence – temporary or eternal. Anyone who plans on any of this, is just living in Sheol waiting for something that will never happen.

Eternal life or heaven, is life with and in God's eternal dimension of existence, and just as God is not a *place*, so too, heaven is not a place. As for God being a "place", Philo of Alexandria says this, "*God himself is called* **place**, *from the fact that he contains all, but is contained by nothing, and that he is a place of refuge for all, and because he is his own space being contained in himself alone. As for me, I am not a place, but* ***in*** *a place, and every existent likewise, for that which is contained is different from that which contains it, and the Godhead, being contained by nothing, is necessarily itself* ***its own place.***" No question, this is a beautiful understanding of God as a "Place". But since the **place** of creation *already* exists *in* God, then what is the difference between man's *present life* **in** this world and his *eternal life* **in** God? If death and resurrection make no difference, then what is it about? Those who think it possible for man to live eternally in this world – on this or any planet – are incapable of having any understanding of death and the true nature of "resurrection".

Since *outside* or *apart* from God nothing exists, and that by reason of its existence everything is "existentially" one with God – i.e., depends on God for its existence – does not mean anything that exists **is** God or ***is*** eternal life. Because God alone is eternal life, for man to have eternal life means he must be granted *more* than his mere existence, *more* than an "*existential union*" with God. Man's *eternal life* is what is called a *"hypostatic union"*, a union *not* in man, not in creation, and not even livable in this world. So although all creation is in God, by no means does it have any eternal life of its own, nor is it guaranteed any eternal life at all. **So the "place" of Eternal life is *not* in the created, but in the Uncreated.**

Because God's heavenly dimension is not subject to time and space, it is not "spatially distant" from man's present dimension. On the contrary, God is closer to man than he is to himself. When earthly life is over, man moves into this divine dimension of existence, and if people wonder what they will be doing in heaven, they have no idea of God's Infinite Existence in which they will partake. Having been transformed into oneness with God's Wisdom (Logos) he will know as God knows (*have the same mind as Christ*), and through the Logos, share a oneness with the glorious Transcendent, as well as the fiery love and power of the Spirit. It is not what man will **do** in heaven, but what man will **be**.

In this world, man only knows God as *God is* ***in his own self,*** whereas in eternal life, there is only **God-in-Itself** and no longer in (or for) man himself. Thus death is the transition from earthly to eternal life, from an earthly dimension to God's dimension of existence. To think there is any resemblance or that this transition does not require a radical change in human nature, is an illusion. Life on earth and eternal life are not remotely compatible, in fact, life in and with God negates everything man knows and experiences of earthly existence – even the way he knows God.

A question that might be asked about the revelation of Resurrection is "to *whom* is this revelation given?" Since death is the loss of *person* (one's self-identity), then "**who**" is the resurrection revealed to?" Needless to say, if there is no "who" **to be** revealed, and no "who" to reveal it to, the question cannot even be asked. To understand the true nature of resurrection, people have to get beyond "who" someone is, otherwise they can never understand the real Christ and their own eternal life with God.

Yet there is an answer to the above question, even though it can never be *intellectually* grasped. In this matter we might recall Irenaeus' noting the difference between the Logos *ad extra* and *ad intra. Ad extra,* the *manifest* Logos is cosmic (the *"Cosmic Christ"),* but *ad intra,* the *immanent* Logos is *"God's Wisdom".* While resurrection is the body's eternal oneness with the Cosmic Logos, far more important, however, resurrection is a "*participation*" in the **Logos' Wisdom – God's divine knowing.** *So the revelation that* **is** *the resurrection, is not a revelation* **to** *someone* of *someone, it is simply* ***God's own knowing, own Wisdom,*** **indeed, God's Truth.** As long as this revelation is associated with any human person, it is *somebody's* wisdom, and *not God's.* It is God's Wisdom that lies the other side of the grave beyond all persons and anything that can be defined as *person.* This Wisdom belongs to no person, nor can ever be known by any person.

God's divine Knowing is non-experiential, non-intellectual, It is not a presence, is not *in* or above anything, has no connection to the mind, can never be localized anywhere or grasped. A bad analogy of Its "revelation" might be compared to simply drawing a curtain aside, or lifting a fog no one ever knew existed. It is just a divine Knowing of which nothing more can be said.[2]

In summary: the one who died was the unique human *person*, Jesus. The one that arose was Christ – *no human or divine* ***person***. **The**

---

[2] Many years ago there was a radio program called "*The Shadow*" – a man becoming invisible in order to catch crooks. Seeing no one around, the crooks would ask, "*Who knows this*?" The only answer they got – "*The Shadow knows!*" Looking back, there may be some profound truth here – just the word "*shadow*" has long had a mystical connotation. If the answer had been "*God knows*", it would have been meaningless, but "*The shadow knows"* is enough to make one's hair stand on end.

Resurrection is the revelation of Christ – not Jesus and not God, but the Real Christ. Remember, it was not *Jesus' own* human nature that was eternally one with God, but *God's own human nature,* and the revelation of this Truth **is** the "Resurrection".

A wonderful way to understanding how man becomes Christ, is Paul's analogy, *"Christ is the yeast that raises the whole lump"* – human nature is the dough, the Logos is the yeast, and all rise to *become* Christ, the Whole Loaf.

End Note

From earliest days to this, there has always been the issue of whether the "resurrected body" is a *physical* body – such as man knows it here on earth – or if it is a *spiritual* body, such as man does *not* experience here on earth. The argument, however, is fatuous since no one can actually define either one – the true nature of a physical body or a spiritual body. Let us consider the following notions:

1. To my knowledge, all the old Greek philosophers regarded matter as *eternal.* I am not aware any of them probed the real nature or essence of *matter*. Although they regarded it all as subject to flux and change, yet none really regarded *prime matter* (the origin of all this impermanence) as anything but eternal – having no origin.

2. In Genesis, it says nothing at all of God creating *prime matter* or matter itself. That "God created heaven and earth" is all we get – this "earth" being a "formless void", seemingly nothing but water.

3. Origen states that no man knows the true nature of matter – and, indeed, man is *still* looking for this!

4. Several of the fathers – Gregory of Nyssa for one – thought the true nature of matter was "spiritual" in nature.

5. The Stoics, of course, regarded the universe as the "manifestation" of the divine Logos and never really separated matter from the Logos or the physical from the spiritual (the eternal Logos.)

Put together, what is to be said of the true nature of matter – the essence of man's physical body? The controversy can be pinpointed to the discrepancy between the apostles affirming Jesus *appeared* to them in a *physical* body – which then disappeared forever – and Paul's seeing the resurrected Christ as ***not*** "*Jesus in the flesh*" and thus regarded the resurrection as a *spiritual* body. Neither deny a "body", what is at odds is its *eternal nature.*

The bottom line is that man neither knows the true nature or essence of either matter or spirit – much less its **eternal** nature. Although man can choose to believe whatever he will, in the end, however, his beliefs will come to naught in the Face of the Truth.

ASCENSION

"We rise in his body, it is to this body we shall ascend, in it shall we repose in the glory of God".
(One of the Fathers)

It would be hard to imagine a more extraordinary phenomenon than seeing someone suddenly disappear before your eyes. No one witnessed the resurrection, no one *saw* Jesus' body restored to life, but here, the apostles see Jesus literally vaporized before their eyes. This is like no other miracle, yet it is totally down-played, not only in the biblical account, but in Christianity as a whole. Traditionally, Jesus' death and resurrection is celebrated as having more import for mankind than anything Christ revealed. Regarded as the major victory and truth of Christ, Resurrection is treated as if it were Christ's ultimate revelation. But Resurrection is not the final or ultimate revelation of Christ, nor the end God destined for all human beings.

Without the "Ascension", man's understanding of Christ can never be complete. Stopping with the "Resurrected Christ" has not only generated erroneous views of Christ, but of everyman's final estate. That resurrection is man's end, has led to all kinds of absurd, mythical and false ideas as to the true nature of man's eternal life *in* God. The true nature of Christ's *heavenly* life as God revealed it, is no "resurrected" earthly life.

Had resurrection implied that "eternal life" required a physical body – which requires life on some physical planet – there could be no way to explain the bodily disappearance of Jesus. If heaven could have been lived in his resurrected body, then why did he disappear? And to *where* did he ascend? Also, why did Jesus tell his apostles that for them to become enlightened – know the Truth – it was necessary he *leave* them, **be *visibly* seen no more**? Obviously, to see God and the incarnate Logos (or Real Christ) one must let go all physical images. While we are entitled to the icons of the historical Jesus, let us not mistake these for God or the incarnate Logos. Even during the Logos' incarnate life on earth, Christ was never available to the senses – as Jesus said, only God could reveal "Christ" because "flesh and blood" could not do this. That Jesus had to leave for the Eternal Christ to be revealed, means that the man the Apostles *saw* was *not* Christ.

Between resurrection and ascension we only have five accounts of Jesus appearing to his apostles, unusual accounts in that no one recognized him. Mary thought he was the gardener; and on "*that same day*", on the way to Emmaus, Jesus showed himself "*under another form*" and was only identified in the breaking of the bread. What John records as his "third appearance" was on the shore of Galilee where again, he was only recognized after the miracle of the fishes. On "*that same evening*" Jesus appeared to the disciples, who also did not recognize him – Thomas wouldn't even believe it was him until he showed him his wounds. These four appearances were on the same day as his resurrection, and according to one account, it was on this same evening he took them to the Mount of Olives where, according to Luke's Gospel, "*he withdrew from them and was carried up to heaven*". In *Acts*, Luke says, "*while they looked on, he was raised up and a cloud received him out of their sight*". Neither John or Matthew record this event, and Mark only says, "*after he had spoken to them, was taken up into heaven and sitteth on the right hand of God*". These are the only accounts we have of Jesus' Resurrection and Ascension. It could be said, Jesus Ascended on the same day he was Resurrected, the two events being consecutive and not disconnected in time, in days or weeks. In other words, "resurrection" keeps going with no interval between. Jesus' appearances, of course, were due to the Apostle's need "***to see** in order to believe*".

Luke's saying Jesus "appeared" for "forty days" after his resurrection, was only symbolic (according to some scholars) and not factual. So too, we wonder how Paul could say Jesus appeared to "*more than 500 of the brethren at the same time*", when Peter tells us "*God allowed him to be seen, not by the whole people, but only by certain witnesses God had chosen beforehand*". But whatever the biblical discrepancies, Jesus' physical appearance had so changed that his identity could only be ascertained by reference to his pre-resurrected life. Given that his own apostles did not recognize him, one wonders if Jesus "appeared" today in a supermarket, if anyone would recognize him. The lesson, of course, is to be polite to one's neighbor because it just might be Jesus!

Possibly, if the apostles had immediately recognized Jesus – as they had previously known him – they might have doubted he really died, in which case, they would have doubted the resurrection. It is interesting, however, they knew him *despite* not seeing the man they knew, which tells us there is more to "knowing" someone than what *appears*.

Altogether, only three short sentences recount the Ascension. After the many pages of Jesus' Passion building up to the surprise and wonder of the Resurrection, the sparse account of the Ascension is anti-climactic, even given short shrift. Thus the final and glorious revelation of God's *own* transfigured and glorified *human nature* has never been understood as *strategic* to the whole revelation of Christ. What threw water on this glorious event was Luke's story of "*two men in white*" (Acts1:10) who asked the witnesses why they were standing, looking at the clouds? When told they were looking for a man in-the-clouds (Jesus), what could these "men-in-white" have said to comfort these bereft men? Being psychologically astute, they reassured them, "*This Jesus who was taken up from you into heaven, will come back the same way you have seen him go there*". These words have so comforted Christians for over two thousand years, people are still waiting to see Jesus appear in the clouds. What is so incredible, is that this remark from two unidentified "men in white" could so throw Christianity off course. What Luke had in mind, of course, was Jesus' allusion to Daniel's dream (7:13) where he saw "*coming on the clouds of heaven, one like a son of man*" who would establish an earthly "*empire*" or "*kingdom*" that would never be destroyed. But if the messiah was to *come* on a cloud, who expected him to *leave* on a cloud – and *without* establishing an empire or kingdom? Jesus' untimely Ascension obviously threw a wet blanket on Daniel's expectations.

The problem with interpreting Jesus according to the Judaic scriptures, is the attempt to keep the revelation of Christ in a *scriptural box.* It were as if God ***had** to stick* to the Judaic scriptures and could not reveal anything different or outside of them. That Christ can never be put in any scriptural box, seems not to have crossed the minds of the Apostles and Paul – or possibly, even Jesus himself. The "Christ" God revealed, however, cannot be found in the Judaic scriptures that nowhere affirm man's destiny to be *eternally one with God, or Yahweh.* That Jesus came into this world fully conscious of his oneness with God, means he knew he did **not** fit into his own scriptures, and thus he predicted an early death. Obviously no "book" can prove the revelation of Christ. In truth, neither God nor Christ can be *revealed* in or through any book. Those who have to rely on a book only do so because they really do not know God – or Christ.

It is thanks to the "men in white", however, the problem of Jesus leaving without fulfilling the expectations of the Messiah, was resolved. Jesus would re-appear later, "come again" in order to fulfill the messianic expectation – an idea called a "second coming". And what was he to come for? According to scripture, to establish the "*Kingdom of Israel"* on this earth. Since establishing a Jewish kingdom was the ultimate *proof* required to prove he was the promised messiah, and since he did *not* fulfill this role, then he had to "come back" to do it. Remember, the apostles based their belief in Jesus on his being the "*messiah"*, God's "*anointed*", and if he did *not* fulfill this role, it would mean their belief in him had been in vain, totally misplaced – they had been *wrong* about him. Rather than admit such a thing, however, they readily postponed his messianic role to a later date. So, according to the "men in white", his "return" was the solution to the apostles' dilemma.

So one reason Jesus' Ascension has always been downplayed – its imperative revelation never honestly grasped – is because it threw a wet blanket on all the expectations the Resurrection had set in motion. Since it was expected Jesus would *then* fulfill his messianic mission, his unexpected *Ascension* was not only disconcerting, it was a "letdown". As recorded, the last thing the apostles asked him on earth was when he was going to establish Israel's earthly kingdom? Jesus simply told them he knew nothing about any such *time* – obviously, Christ's "*kingdom is not of this world"*. But then, what possible meaning could a small "Jewish Kingdom" have for the rest of mankind anyway? Jesus' followers only understood him according their Judaic mind-set, certainly not the mind-set of the rest of the world. Yet the revelation of Christ was never intended to be so limited. It should have been obvious God has no intention of resolving the political dilemmas man creates for himself. Anyone anticipating any kind of political rescue or some earthly Edenic "kingdom" is waiting in vain.

So, based on the words of the "men in white", what the Ascension means to most people is that just as a "cloud" carried Jesus' *physical* body to some *physical* place (with "seating" facilities, no less), just so, he will return. (Where else could a *material* body live but in a *material* place?) So now Jesus is "sitting" next to his bearded father waiting for a signal to come back in a cloud again. If there is anything unbelievable about this scenario, it is that some people actually believe it – take it literally. This was not, however, what the Ascension was about, not what God revealed. The reason the Ascension was the final disappearance of the *visible human body* of the man Jesus is **because "*Christ*" is *not* a *visual* human body**, in fact, the real Christ was **never the "*appearance*" of any visible body, not even that of the man Jesus.** Whatever the essence of Man created in God eternally one with God, this is not the visible body and soul of any individual human being. The Logos' *own* eternal body belongs to no man, is no man's individual body. To visually see the individual body of anyone is *not* to see the essential form (or body) that the Logos created for Itself alone. This truth, of course, is too dire for Christians to accept because they need to *see* (at least in their own minds) in order to believe. People simply cannot believe the man Jesus left this earth *forever* and will never be *seen* "in the flesh" again. If this is what the Ascension portends or means, then what is there to "celebrate" or even to think about? If people believed Jesus disappeared *forever*, they would not have spent these several thousand years waiting for his return. As said, for Christians the *end* has *never* been the "Ascension," it has only been a "Resurrection" – man's return to his former body. **This is why the tremendous reality and Truth that God revealed in the Ascension, has been totally lost on Christianity.**

People like the idea of a glorious *physical* body, but *not* if it disappears on them – or they couldn't tell if they had one or not. Yet, if there is any revelation that speaks to the body's final or heavenly *reality*, it is the Ascension. Every cell of the body *infused* with divine air, the body literally dissolved in this glorious air, seemingly becoming the air itself. **This is the end of any *experience* of having or being a body. And it is not *someone's* experience, rather, it is solely the *body's own experience*! Every cell of it becoming totally formless with no boundaries, nothing left of any discrete form or entity.** Though we use the term "*air*", this is not, of course, any "air" man knows, all that is known is that it is divine and glorious, an infusion that seemingly dissolves the body in Itself. What is amazing is that God even *revealed* a thing like this – the Ascension – by having Jesus' body literally vaporized before the eyes of his disciples. They had no knowledge of what Jesus' body experienced, yet God *visually demonstrated* this *experience* by its disappearing from this earth. What other "way" could God have revealed the truth that man's ultimate existence is **no** *earthly* existence? God *manifested* this experience by having Jesus' body disappear as if in a cloud – in air. This way, God let man know what his *body* can expect to *experience.* Thus Jesus' disappearance merely *manifested* an otherwise *un-seeable* and unknowable bodily experience. Indeed, it was to *demonstrate* the great truth of man's *eternal life* that the Incarnation was all about.

No bystander, of course, can "see" this *experiential* event, it is not a *visible* phenomenon. It is because the apostles could *not* see this that God *manifested* it – the Truth of man's final estate – by simply having Jesus "disappear" before their eyes. What should have alerted them to the ultimate nature of the *body's* eternal oneness with God, they thought, instead, it was just another of Jesus' temporary disappearances. This, at least, is exactly how Christianity understands the Ascension. Jesus' "return" or second coming will be just another of those post-resurrection appearances, such as the apostles had witnessed. This, of course, totally misses the revelation and true nature of "Ascension".

The sole purpose of the Incarnation was to manifest man's journey to God – his transformation into Christ. All the early fathers believed

Christ was the revelation of everyman's journey and that Jesus was an "instrument" of this revelation – the example of someone who became the eternal Christ. Man's transformation, of course, is totally *experiential,* and while no one knows Jesus' own *experiences*, yet, if one can relate to his transformation, one will understand that what God *manifested is what every human being will experience.* This is not to say everyone has the same *experiences*, it means everyone will encounter the same *truth* and *reality* God revealed as his "way" to eternal life. Thus for example, everyone can relate to Jesus' death, yet no man will have Jesus' *same experience* of it, even though its *true nature* and reality will be the *same* for every human being. And so too, resurrection and ascension. These events – and many others – are the same *experiential* events that reveal the same truth every human being will encounter. In fact, anything man cannot *experience,* he will never know. Mere *intellectual* knowing – on which many base their "beliefs" – is not the truth of anything. Think of this: if Jesus had not *experienced* his oneness with God why would he have ever died for merely *believing* this to be true? He died because he knew it first-hand *experientially*, and not because he "believed it". The point is this: unless man can relate to Jesus' own *experience* of being assumed into God's divine and glorious dimension of existence, then the Ascension is no more than just another of his disappearances – his taking a seat beside his father to wait out time until he returns. But there is no truth to this whatsoever – and besides, there are no chairs in heaven.

If people could ever grasp the Truth God revealed in the "Ascension" they would come upon the most unbelievable of all God's revelations to man. That man's final experience of existence on this earth is the physical body's experience of being assimilated, seemingly dissolved into God's own glorious dimension of existence, who can believe this? Because no on-looker sees this, he will never believe it – remember, like the apostles, man only *believes what he can see*. But if one can get beyond this naiveté and take his cue from Jesus' own "ascension" *experience*, he can expect this same experience for his own body. While man's body will not visibly disappear – such as God *manifested* in the ascension – yet his *body* forever dwells in God's divine and glorious existence. But then, of course, here come the undertakers! The body is buried, the Reverend prays for the body's resurrection while family and friends wipe their eyes. Who would believe that this decaying body dwells in unutterable glory? No body – because **they don't see it!**

Although **Jesus' *experience* of "ascension" is the way it goes for everyone,** yet *outsiders* looking at a dead body would *never* believe a thing like this. Because **the senses are incapable of witnessing any eternal Truth,** people know absolutely nothing about what a so called "dead body" actually *experiences* – indeed, who knows what the trees or animals actually experience? Yet, this is the body's whole experience of the **revelation called the "Ascension", and to think man has missed it completely!** Missed the most astounding revelation God ever gave to mankind, but one man may never be able to believe. Indeed, **Truth is unbelievable** – like Jesus said, **"***I tell you the Truth, which is why you do not believe it"*. Fortunately, however, it will not be long before every ***body*** verifies this Truth for itself.

It seems that early on, Christians must have had some understanding of the true nature of the Ascension as a reality for every man. Nothing else explains the Christian's reverence for the bodily relics of its martyrs, saints and holy people. Granted, the rush for these relics can seem bizarre at times, yet, there was something holy, almost sacred about '*dem bones'*. What was behind this reverence was not the thought of their resurrection – God putting humpty-dumpty back together again – but that this human being, body and soul, now lived in God's own heavenly dimension. All they saw, of course, were bones (or whatever), yet they *knew* what they could *never visually see* was the eternal glory in which this body and soul now existed.

The term *"heaven"*, of course, is just another name for man's eternal life in God. Thus "heaven" is not a *place* anymore than God is a *place*. Like God, heaven is nowhere in space and time, yet, like God, heaven is available to man in a nanosecond, a tiny step, even closer than man is to himself. So when people die they are really going *nowhere*, no ***place,*** that is. What people *see* is only in time and space, what they can *never see,* however, is man's true *life* in God's eternal dimension of existence. So while the so called "dead" no longer experience earthly existence, they *experience* and *know* God's dimension of existence, their eternal oneness with God being "*Christ*" – the ultimate goal of his journey. Man does not become God and God never became a man, it is the oneness of the two that ***is*** Christ.

The reason man tends to *look* upward or toward the sky when he thinks of "heaven", or even prays to God, is the recognition of God's utter transcendence, God beyond man. No question, the Uncreated, the whole Trinity transcends all creation, **but** there is more to God than being "transcendent" to creation. Were it not for the divine Logos – one of *God's triune modes of existence* – there would be no creation at all. Because nothing can come from nothing, *everything* must come from *something,* some *source* or *cause*. The Greek philosophers regarded matter as eternal – *prime matter* being its original source. They disputed, of course, as to the true nature of this *prime matter* – what element could this be, water, air, ether, fire, earth, or what? For the Stoics, this eternal element was not just fire, it was the dynamic divine intelligence governing the whole of the universe, ever present in it, and the sole *reason for its being.* This divine omnipresent source they called "Logos". After all, without a material body what is there for a soul to *in-form* or for a *Spirit* to *indwell?* No question, the *prime* Source and Cause of the physical body **is** the Logos. While Its purely existential oneness with matter need *not* be eternal, yet God can and has made this to be an eternal oneness, a oneness, however, unknown in man's earthly dimension of existence, but known in God's eternal dimension. So although man does not know the body's *eternal form* on earth, yet *the body will know this in God.* It is the body's movement into God's *eternal* dimension that is the *true nature of the Ascension.*

Although Resurrection is incomplete without Ascension, the two, however, have nothing in common. Resurrection is the revelation of the true nature of the *earthly incarnate Christ*, whereas Ascension is the revelation of the true nature of the *eternal, heavenly Christ.* Although Luke did not witness the Ascension, his description was in accord with Jesus' quote from Daniel (7:13) – i.e., Jesus appearing in a "cloud". The biblical understanding of "cloud" has always had a "mystical" meaning used in descriptive accounts of man's immediate experiences of God – e.g., Moses' encounter with God on Sinai, God's "overshadowing" Mary, and many other accounts. It is always indicative of how the revelation of God "shrouds" (or "clouds") the intellectual mind, leaves it in a state of "unknowing" void of images, concepts – literally, stops the mind. That Jesus ascended to heaven in this mystical, non-material "cloud", means heaven is a totally *different dimension of existence* than this material world. And since heaven is "where" God is ("Everywhere", in fact), Christ is no "place", but dwells eternally *in* God's glorious *dimension of existence* – a dimension *closer* to man than he is to himself.

Since every major event in Christ's life is a revelation of Man and how it will go for everyone, we might go over what this particular event reveals.

I. That the body *disappears* in the glory of God (heaven) tells us there are **no *visible* bodies in God (in heaven)** and that "heaven" is no material, physical "place".

II. Both resurrection and Ascension reveal there is **no separation of body and soul,** the whole of man arises and ascends as one. Thus body and soul experience the *same* glorious existence in God – there is no duality at all.

III. A *glorified body* is **not a visible body,** thus it is not what man sees and experiences in this life. Just as it was necessary for the soul to be transformed in order to share God's eternal life, so too, the body. Where Resurrection is the soul's final transformation, Ascension is the body's final transformation. Where Resurrection is not beyond an earthly physical body, the Ascension ***is beyond*** an earthly living body.

IV. The Ascension reveals that **resurrection is *not* man's final heavenly estate**, not his eternal life with and in God. Just as resurrection was not the end of Christ's journey, so too, it is not the end of man's journey. Though the *resurrected* body is a "formless body", it is not yet a "glorified body", which glorification was Jesus' Ascension. While resurrection assures man of life after death, the Ascension assures man eternal life is ***not*** in or of this world, not on this earth or any "place", but solely in and with God.

V. The ascension is **not some "out of the body" experience – but its *opposite!*** It **is** the bodily experience of every cell filled and dissolved in a *glorious air* – and the true nature of this "air"? The glory of the Logos, God. This "air" puts an end to the senses and *their experience of a body.* There is no *leaving* the body nor anything "*rising*" and floating around in space! Just as death is the end of the *experiential* soul, Ascension is the end of the *experiential* body, for just as the Spirit transforms the soul, the Logos transforms the body. In the end, then, Spirit and Logos, soul and body, are one in the glory of the Transcendent. This is the eternal heavenly Christ – "Universal man", the *one* and *only* glorious body of Christ in the glory of the Trinity.

So death, resurrection, ascension, are the great realities the Incarnation revealed, each mystery a further revelation of its true nature – only in reverse. In the beginning, overshadowed by the glorious Most High, the Spirit, creates the soul and the Logos becomes one with the body; and in the end – the Spirit claims the soul and the Logos the body, both overwhelmingly infused with the Glory of the Transcendent. This is the "way" God transforms all into one Christ – as Paul put it: "*He will transform the body of our lowliness that it may be one with the body of His glory...**He will make us Sons of God as He was made Son of man***". For those who can grasp this, its Truth is beyond belief. While people choose their beliefs, they can never choose the Truth because Truth is beyond belief.

Speaking of man's heavenly estate, Maximus the Confessor says, "*Through the bodies we shall have, in every body that we shall see wherever we direct our eyes, we shall behold God Himself with perfect clarity". "Only God will appear in them when they transcend the limits of their own nature."* The reason the Stoics did not believe in a detached soul is because they were certain the physical body was one with the divine Logos as well. That the divine Logos can change all into its own glorious "body" is Paul's understanding – "*He will transform the body of our lowliness that it may be one with the body of His glory".* Thus the body participates in the Logos' same divine existence.

Origen regarded the true nature of matter as *invisible* with no qualities, it was the substrate for everything created, both intellectual and corporeal – "*Matter, the meaning of which"*, he said, "*they themselves have not succeeded in understanding*". (Today scientists are still trying to figure out the true nature of matter.) Gregory of Nyssa regarded matter as basically "*spiritual*" and said that in the end the body is "*transelemented",* becomes spiritual or immaterial, and changed into its invisible elemental structure. He and others believed that at bottom, matter was essentially invisible, spiritual or non-material – a "formless body", in other words. Gregory also compared deification to a drop of wine swallowed up in the sea, the body or flesh being so assimilated to the divine Logos none of its natural characteristics – weight, form, color, spatial or visible properties – remained. Because some of the fathers regarded the true nature of matter as unknowable or "spiritual", does not mean, however, they were pantheists or thought matter *was* God. They simply regarded its true nature as *beyond* the senses and intellect to know.

The importance of the Ascension has been totally overlooked as man's ultimate estate. As it stands, the Ascension is treated as a phenomenon of no relevance for Man – but only for the man Jesus. The bible nowhere spells out the tremendous change and transformation necessary to become *eternal*, to live *unendingly* in God's infinite dimension of existence. Eternal life is incompatible with an earthly physical body ever in the process of change, impermanence and flux. Those who believe an *earthly* body can become eternally *immutable, static or unchangeable,* are only fooling themselves. They have no idea of *eternal life* or what is required to live eternally one with God.

The reason people may never have a true understanding of resurrection and ascension is because they have "time" on their hands and judge everything accordingly. Because the mind cannot imagine anything not subject to time and space, the great truths Christ revealed may only be understood when they happen – when people are no longer subject to space and time. All talk, conjectures and paradigms in the world are a waste-of-time when it comes to the experiential realities of these great Truths. One good thing, at least – in a short "time" everyone will experience these truths first hand.

The importance of the Ascension as the ending of *the incarnate Logos'* earthly life is that it is the revelation of how it will go for every human being. Like the Resurrection, the Ascension is its own one-of-a-kind *revelation,* yet, due to the "men in white", Christianity missed it – are waiting to see Jesus in the clouds! This goes to show how little it takes to cover up and obscure a great Truth. Taking words literally and relying on sensory data for Truth is the major problem. A true understanding of Christ, however, requires a far more mystical mindset than anything perceived by the senses, or even conceived by the intellect. The fact the true nature of death, resurrection and ascension can never be *seen* for the looking, is why Christianity has always stressed *Faith* (which is ***not*** belief) as the only "way-of-knowing" Truth. If Faith – that "*truth sensor*" in every human being – is not recognized, then it is as Heraclitus said – "You already *know* (Truth), only you don't know that you know!"

As for the apostles, we are not aware they believed anything they couldn't see for themselves. If they hadn't seen Jesus *disappear* in a cloud, they would have thought Jesus was still on earth some *place.* When he left, they honestly believed he'd be back soon – Christians, of course, are still waiting, waiting **because they have never understood the true nature of the Ascension.**

As matters stand, there is little indication the full implication of the Ascension has ever been grasped. It seems its sole import was to set the stage for what followed – namely, Pentecost, a celebration that has always overshadowed the great truth the Ascension revealed.

PENTECOST

We know "Pentecost" ("fifty days") was a Jewish feast day and that many came to Jerusalem to celebrate it. The followers of Jesus evidently gathered for their own celebration of the day. As best I understand it, this Jewish feast, held fifty days after the Passover, marked the time it took the Israelites to travel from Egypt to the foot of Mount Sinai where, it seems, they reaped the first harvest of the wheat they had sown. It was, then, a celebration of the "first fruits" or harvest. Being at the foot of Mt. Sinai, however, and knowing the revelation about to be revealed at its summit, this feast was also an anticipation of God's revealing the "Torah" or "Law" to them.

Given this background, it is significant that as this feast anticipated the revelation of God to the Israelites, this would become the feast day when God revealed Christ to Jesus' followers. What is interesting about the Christian Pentecost is that it was not the revelation of anything new, but the revelation of what the disciples already knew. It was like waking up to the fact they already knew the truth, only had not recognized it. Probably everyone has had the experience of knowing something, yet unable to be clear as to its real meaning, its why's and wherefore's. Since the apostles already had all the knowledge they needed, the grace of Pentecost was the wonderful realization when it all came together, *was seen in a whole new Light.* This was knowing Christ in the Light of God, instead of through the human medium, Jesus. Now they had absolute certitude of what they knew, knew its Truth without a doubt, and on this Truth they staked their lives – indeed, with the exception of John, like Jesus, they gave their lives for this Truth. Pentecost, then, is tied up with the revelation of the *incarnate Logos* – the true Christ.

This experience of Pentecost is not unknown to Christians or to others. Thus for Elias it was like a gentle "breeze", for Moses like "fire" and a "cloud", for many, a "light" above the head, and so on. But whether striking or subtle, it is always a moment of *absolute knowing* – always unexpected and unforgettable. Because the nature of *revelation* stays with one forever, it changes one forever, there is *no going back.*

That this enlightenment came to the apostles like "tongues of fire" over their heads, is highly symbolic, not of the Spirit, but of the Logos. Remember, for the Stoics prime matter was *fire* – the Logos' first primal *manifestation,* Itself being the "*reason* for being". Philo and the Christians linked this with the biblical account of the Logos as *God's Wisdom – God's own knowing.* Though Pentecost is usually associated with the Spirit, yet the Spirit was only the *Cause* of the enlightenment, not its content, which as said, the Apostles already had, but didn't know they had. This "content" or *knowledge* enlightened by the Spirit, was the *whole mystery of Christ.*

Where the Ascension is a revelation of the cosmic dimension of the Logos, Pentecost is the revelation of the Logos as God's Wisdom or divine knowing. We do not like to call this divine knowing "omniscience" because the term is misunderstood as having all kinds of petty scientific, intellectual, or psychic connotations. God's *Knowing,* however, is *not* available to the human mind or intellect. Though more akin to "unknowing" or "no-mind", even this is *not* God's knowing. Because it is the certitude of Truth not available to the mind, there is no way to explain this "Knowing". As close as we can come is to say it is that "Truth-Sensor" in every human being – that *mystery* we call

"*Faith*". (As said before, however, Faith is *not* belief, nor is belief, Faith – the two are even opposites.)

Pentecost, then, is not the revelation of the Spirit, but rather, *how* the Spirit works to reveal Christ –and not Itself. Christ does not reveal itself, only the Spirit reveals Christ. And just so, the Spirit reveals the Logos and the Logos reveals the Spirit, both revealing the Transcendent, that, in turn, reveals the others. It is because God, the Trinity, has no *self* (or *person*) to reveal, that *each reveals the other*. This is how the Trinity works, this is God's *modus operandi.* There is no such revelation as "I am this one", or "He (or She) is that one", or "I am God", all these subjective human labels or ideas indicate **no** authentic revelation of God.

The Spirit, then, being the power of God, is not enlightenment, but the *Enlightener*. The Logos, on the other hand, **is** divine *Knowing* – Sophia, God's Wisdom. The saying that in the end "*we shall have the mind of Christ*" was not a reference to the *human mind* of the man Jesus, but to the Mind of Christ – *God's own Wisdom* (divine Knowing.) So where Resurrection is the revelation of Christ as the Logos' eternal oneness with Man, and the Ascension, the revelation of the *body* of Christ in the glory of the Transcendent; Pentecost is the revelation of the Logos' divine Knowing – Wisdom. This is how the Trinity works, and how, from birth to death to heaven, man's entire journey is bound up in Christ's eternal oneness with and in the Trinity.

For an understanding of the Trinity as God's *modus operandi*, there is nothing like the part each plays in man's Death, Resurrection, Ascension and Pentecost, each a particular revelation of "how" the Trinity works to bring man to the eternal life God planned and willed for one and all.

DEIFICATION

It is said the term "*deification*" ("to become god" or "being made divine") originated in Egypt. The Greeks took it from there, and from the Greeks it entered the Christian vocabulary. For neither Egyptian, Greek or Christian, however, was the term used in the Monotheistic sense of someone "becoming" Almighty God. Even as it was used by the philosophers, a "god" never meant the "One", "Source", "Logos", etc. Instead, "god" was a title of honor bestowed on an individual for some "super-human" accomplishment. Among the philosophers there was no goal of becoming the "One". For Plato it was the divine image or *form* "participating" in the One; for Aristotle, his "other soul" would eternally "contemplate the One"; the Stoics' goal was to be one with the Logos; and for Plotinus as well, it was to be "one with the One". Judaism, of course, never had the goal of becoming one-with-the-*One.* So altogether, the term "deification" is misleading when applied to man's spiritual life. Nobody believed that anyone *became* the Absolute One. As a title, however, "god" can be found in the Old Testament – even Jesus said, *"I have said you are gods and all of you children of the Most High*". But whatever its mythical origin and various usage, its use in a Christian context is the present focus.

Prior to the revelation of Christ, the goal of some of the Greek religious cults, was "deification", which meant "become one with the One". In their view, the ascent to this goal entailed a process of *purgation, illumination*, and *union,* three stages that, it seems, Origen adopted and bequeathed to the Christian spiritual tradition. Whatever the Gentiles' understanding of this path, however, it was given a Christian understanding. So having defined Christ as the eternal *union* of God and man, to attain this same *union,* to *become* Christ, entailed purgation, illumination and union. Thus a standard formulation of this process are three stages – *katharsis* or purification, *theoria* or illumination, and *theosis* or *deification* – also referred to as "*union with God"*.

Referring to man's transformation as "deification" first entered the Christian vocabulary with Clement of Alexandria (150 – 215), a convert from Stoicism. Although he said Jesus was *born* in a state of *apatheia,* it is doubtful this ever meant "deification" in the Stoic sense of the term. Although Irenaeus (125 – 202) is said to have defined "deification" as "*theosis*", we are not sure if by this he meant Clement's "apatheia" – the state in which Jesus was **born** – or Jesus' final, glorified state following resurrection and ascension. To my knowledge, for the fathers, the term "deification" referred to Jesus' heavenly estate *after* his resurrection and not before. In general, however, the term "*deification*" referred to the "process" of becoming one with God which meant *to become* Christ – eternally one with God. No father, of course, believed Jesus or any human being "became" God – such a belief falls outside Monotheism.

For the fathers, man's transformation and deification was the rock-bed of Christ's revelation and what the Incarnation was about. As one author put it, "***Salvation was always defined as deification***", *this was the whole theme of Christian faith and the whole, true, biblical message.* Thus for Irenaeus, Athanasius and all the early fathers, the purpose of God becoming man was man's *deification* – "*God became man that man might become God*" – become Christ, that is, eternally one with God.

As someone not familiar with either the term "*deification*" or "*theosis*", researching their specific Christian usage was not helpful because these terms could refer to either of Hilary's 2nd or 3rd states in the life of Christ. Thus "*Theosis*" can mean anything from a "mystical union" to the ultimate absorption of the soul into God. So as the original reference to Christ, "theosis" simply referred to the oneness of God and man, with *no distinction* between Christ's *earthly* or *heavenly* life – and herein lies a problem.

With the exception of Hilary, the fathers never pointed out or articulated any difference between Christ's *earthly* and *heavenly* (*eternal*) life, yet all regarded Jesus' death, resurrection and ascension as his ultimate or final "*deification*". So while they assumed a difference, they never pinned it down, emphasized or articulated it. Between these two states however – man's *earthly life with God* in this world, and Christ's *eternal life in God,* there is such a huge difference, that a *chasm* literally exists between the two. As for the nature of this *chasm,* this is obviously the true nature of "*death-resurrection-ascension*". But if Hilary (300 – 368) pointed out a difference (between his 2nd and 3rd states) it was not until the 400's that Cyril of Alexandria articulated the Incarnation as a "*Hypostatic Union*". Prior to this time, man's oneness with God was simply called "*theosis*" – which term, we might add, remains the only term theologians use to this day.

The terms "*deification*" and "*theosis*", however, are not familiar terms used in Western Spirituality – such as they are used in Eastern Spirituality. It seems the Eastern Church retained the term "*Theosis*" for the state of being one with God, while the Western Church would refer to this as a "Unitive State" or "Mystical Union". What is rare in both vocabularies, however, is any mention of "*Hypostatic Union*". We have already gone over why Cyril's original *Monophysitic* understanding was rejected, and yet, no other term was ever used to refer to the true nature of the *Incarnate Christ.* One reason "*Hypostatic Union*" is set off from *"theosis"* is because all the fathers regarded "*Theosis*" as a state that *every* human being could attain – and ideally, in this life. Thus the state in which Jesus was born into this world (*Theosis*), every man could attain. Still, all believed Jesus' human nature was only "transfigured" and "glorified" *after* his death, this final "*deification*" being the nature of Resurrection and Ascension. Obviously this postulates a difference between man's oneness with God in *this world* and his oneness in *God's eternal life,* yet, the fathers never articulated any difference, and with the exception of Hilary, never really pointed this out.

Since Hilary lived *before* Cyril (376 – 444), we could not expect him to refer to any "*hypostatic union".* As he pointed out, prior to the Incarnation there was only the divine Logos – and no Christ. It is when the Logos created and united human nature eternally with Itself we have *Christ* – Cyril's *hypostatic union.* The second state was God *revealing* this oneness (Christ), which was the *earthly incarnation* (conception and birth) of the man Jesus, who came into this world one with God – the state of *theosis*. The third state, "*after*" his earthly life was over, Hilary says Christ was then "*perfect Man and perfect God*" – basically a *hypostatic union.* Note that Hilary did not say the "*eternal Christ"* was "***a***" perfect man, but uses the generic "***man***" – "*perfect Man*". Where his 2nd state refers to a *particular* man, his 3rd state refers to *Universal* Man.

That the human nature of Jesus was not glorified or "deified" until the time of his resurrection and ascension means **Jesus only reached the fullness or final estate of the Incarnate Logos' humanity at the *end* of his human journey and not before**. What is astounding about this understanding, is that it was *not* a reference to *Jesus'* own human nature, but a reference to ***God's own human nature,*** **yet a nature not yet perfect as long as it remained on this earth!** That human nature only achieves perfection in its final "deified" heavenly estate, is the recognition that no man (no human nature) this side of heaven, is perfect. Thus even during Jesus' earthly life this was not yet the "perfect man". Though born into the world as perfect as man can be in *this world,* this still was not man's ultimate perfection. Christ's 2nd or "unitive" state, then, was not yet the perfection of human nature – not Christ's heavenly estate.

Obviously, there is a great difference between the 2nd and 3rd states of Christ – one, earthly and imperfect, the other, heavenly and perfect. Although the fathers recognized a difference, yet none spelled it out. Though some grasped the difference, others, it seems, were so eager to *deify* the man Jesus, they either never "got it" or never wanted to point it out. For an understanding of Christ, however, the difference between these two states is strategic. The state in which the historical man Jesus lived, was not the heavenly estate of Christ, as said, the two are incompatible. Were they compatible, the historical person, Jesus, had no reason to die or leave this earth – nor would anyone else. Nothing *created* has any eternal life of its own – which is all flux and change – only the Uncreated **is** *eternal life*. While on earth, man can have various degrees of oneness with God, yet no earthly union or oneness is comparable to his *eternal* oneness with and *in* God. These two unions actually belong to opposing dimensions of existence. Earthly oneness is meant for this life, and is as far as man can go this side of death. Eternal oneness, however, is *in* God's *own* immanent dimension of existence.

The implication, of course, is that there is no *perfect man* this side of eternal life. At the same time, it also means the state of *theosis* (man's oneness with God *in this world*) is not man's *eternal* heavenly state in God – not yet a "*hypostatic union*". As said, the fathers recognized a difference between Christ's earthly and heavenly life in that Jesus "grew in Wisdom" – implying there was further growth (or transformation) in his life with God. Without this *spiritual growth,* Jesus would not have been fully human – after all, it makes no sense Jesus was born as one who had ***finished*** the human journey ***before*** he ever lived it! This is why his death and Resurrection was a revelation of the **eternal Christ beyond** the man Jesus *as he was known in this world.* It is by change and transformation man ceases to be what he is *now,* in order to become what God destined him *to be or become.* No doubt this is why the fathers held *"man was created to be **more** than he is now*", for just as the man Jesus became **more** than he was on this earth, so too, all are destined to become more than they are now.

Where man starts this *ascent* from his human condition, the incarnate Logos, however, started Its *descent* from the divine condition – the *hypostatic union.* Because the Logos' human nature was never in need of *purgation* and *illumination*, it began its human condition in *union* with God. Thus the Logos' human nature came into this world fully aware of its oneness with God, and lived out this "unitive condition" during its earthly life. This "unitive condition", then, can be regarded as Hilary's 2nd state in Christ's life – the man, Jesus, knowing no other human condition but his oneness with God.

Having entered this world fully aware of its oneness with God, Jesus' human nature was that of a ***whole* human person,** in that no human being on this earth is ***whole*** until fully aware of his abiding union with God. Until such time, man is in conflict with himself, divided, and ever seeking fulfillment. This is why it could be said the historical

Jesus is the archetype of a ***whole human being*** – actually the true state in which God intended every man is to live his earthly life. The view that man was created a static entity, a *completed* human being from the beginning, is a wrong view of man – and of the whole of creation – because man's end is nothing like his beginning. Until man attains eternal life, his existence has not reached the end for which it was created. Even for Jesus, his human nature was not complete until it reached its eternal life in God.

So for every human being, then, what is called a "*unitive state of being*" is their *earthly* oneness with God – no different than Jesus' experience of oneness with God **in this life**. Barring a particular revelation of this oneness as "*Christ*", however, nobody could possibly know this, which is why Christ can only be *revealed,* and not "figured out" in some rational, philosophical, theological or scriptural way. Jesus himself never revealed Christ – as he said, only God could do this – *because* Christ is *not "who"* any individual person is. (Keep in mind, in Jesus' own lifetime the term "Messiah" or "anointed" was *not* a reference to man's eternal oneness with God. In fact, the Greek term "Christ", was not even around or used in the time of Jesus.) It seems, however, Paul is the one who saw *his* oneness with God as "Christ" – "No longer, I, but Christ lives in me". Had this been Jesus' understanding of "Christ", he could have said the same thing – "It is not I, but Christ lives in me".

At any rate, because no specific terms or definitions were given to account for Hilary's two different states, the result has been much confusion, not only as regards the man Jesus, but the true nature of everyman's earthly journey and final estate. In the literature, at least, the confusion has been mistaking the 2nd state in which Jesus was born ("theosis" or "unitive state") for as far as any man can go or *ever* attain, which, obviously, is not true. This is not what Christ revealed. What was not true for Jesus' spiritual life with God, is not true for any man's life with God. The issue, however, is not "what you call it" (the 2nd and 3rd estates), but clarity as regards the *difference between them.* As said, for a true understanding of Christ, this difference is **strategic**. We might think of this as the difference between the icon of the "man Jesus on the cross" – the temporary *earthly* Christ – and the icon of the "Eucharist", the *eternal* heavenly Christ. There is a huge difference!

While a Christology based on the Eucharistic ***heavenly*** *Christ* is on the mark, unfortunately, there exists no Christology based on the ***earthly*** *existence* of Christ. While the Eucharist is the consummate or final nature of Christ's *glorified human nature* – the "*hypostatic union*" – this was *not* Christ's *earthly* human existence. Those who think there is no difference between man's earthly and eternal existence, have missed Christ completely.

The single most noteworthy difference – earthly and heavenly – is that **in** God the "*hypostatic union*" is "*personless*", whereas man's *earthly* union with God is **in** man himself, in his *own* self or *person.* (*Who*, after all, knows and experiences *his* union with God but man *himself?)* The *hypostatic union*, on the other hand, is not a union or oneness of God with any person, self or individual human being. Rather, this union is solely God's oneness with the *essence* of Man's common human nature, an *essence and union solely* ***in*** *God, and thus, known only* ***to*** *God.*

This eternal union in God is not a union with any "property" (person or self), or with any "accident" extrinsic to the *essence* of human nature – none of which could possibly exist in *eternal life* anyway. People who think they can see God, live in the glory of God, *participate* in God's divine nature, and at the same time, maintain any form of earthly existence – such as they know it now – do not honestly know God. To think God's *own* human nature retains someone's *earthly identity* is absurd. The sole identity of God's *own* human nature, ***is "Christ".***

It was because human nature cannot live simultaneously *in* God's glorious dimension of existence, and at the same time, function in this world, this necessitated the "kenosis" of the Logos' *human nature.* As far as human nature can descend from its glorious estate in God without relinquishing the *hypostatic union* altogether, this was Hilary's 2nd state – the *union* of God and man *in this world,* a union man knows and experiences *within himself.* So where the hypostatic union is solely ***in*** *God,* in contrast, man's *earthly union* with God is **in himself**.

It is because God is no "person" and *saves* no person, that the *hypostatic union* is totally person-less. Thus man's eternal oneness with God is impersonal and impartial – which is the measure of *Truth* anyway, because God is not into man's "partialities". **So what is imperative to point out is that a *hypostatic union in* God, and a *mystical union* in man, denote two totally *different unions.*** These are **not** just two different *"experiences*", but rather, two different *realities*, two different dimensions of existence. As the revelation of the *Real Christ,* the *hypostatic union* is totally *non-experiential* – since there is no *experiencer* – and thus man's eternal union with God is absolutely *personless* and *impersonal.*

On earth, Jesus, as a human person, knew and experienced *his* oneness with God (certainly this was not *God's* experience!) What Jesus (or any person) *experiences* and *knows* as *his* oneness with God is *not* a *hypostatic union.* Before this final union can even be revealed, all man knows and experiences of *his own* union with God has to be **void-ed, cease to exist** – why? Because this was **his** union with God, **his** individual personal oneness with God which is **not,** however, God's oneness with ***Its own universal*** **human nature**. So the difference is between: 1) the individual or particular, and the common or universal; 2) between the common essence of human nature and one individual human being; 3) between an individual *person* and *no person;* 4) between God's *own* human nature and man's *own* human nature; 5) between man's earthly oneness with God **in** *himself* and man's eternal oneness solely **in** *God*; 6) between man's experience of oneness with God and *no experience* of oneness in God. These two different unions (earthly and eternal) are unalike, even *incompatible.* As long as any person, subject or self remains, man's *eternal* union cannot be revealed or ever known. Indeed, it was the *loss of* ***his experience*** *of oneness with God* – loss of his *person* – that was the true nature of Jesus' death – seemingly "God" left him. The Resurrection, however, is the *revelation* of the *hypostatic union* – i.e., the *essence* of man's *one universal human nature* God created for Itself alone, and did not create for any particular human being, this is the "*Eternal Christ".*

Obviously, the idea that God *revealed* one individual being or particular person as "*Christ*", is a wrong understanding of Christ – no Truth to this whatsoever. Christ is **not** a particular person – in fact, God *creates no person* and thus, there is **no person *to be*** Christ. Where people think of Christ as "other" to themselves, yet **Christ is neither *"other", nor one's self;*** Christ is God's *own* **common** *human nature.* Man's eternal union with God then, is neither *his* experience nor *God's experience* (God is *impassible* anyway), yet this union or oneness **is** *God's own Knowing,* for to have the "mind of Christ" is to have (or participate in) God's (Logos') Own Wisdom. As Truth Itself, God's revelation of Christ is the Truth of all Mankind and not merely one particular human being or person. As to whether man believes this or not, understands it or not, this is not God's problem. Christ is *man's problem* and a universal *challenge* to one and all.

But now, then, if the term "*hypostatic union*" designates the ultimate revelation of Christ in the Trinity, what are we to call man's knowing and experiencing *his own* union with God here on earth – just as Jesus did? While Clement called the state in which Jesus was born a state of "*apatheia",* this only articulates the more psychological dimension of this union, but not its deeper mystical dimension. On the other hand, if, for Irenaeus and others, the term "*theosis*" referred to the deification of Jesus' human nature, then the question is how we are to distinguish Christ's earthly life of union with God from Christ's eternal union with God in the Trinity? Obviously, the term "*theosis*" is inadequate to point out any difference between these two different unions – with God ***in*** *this* world, and eternal life ***in*** God.

As said, if we can define the notion of "deification" as a *process of transformation*, the term "*theosis*" can be confusing if it refers to *both* man's earthly and heavenly oneness with God – which are **not** the same. Thus the only term Christianity has to set off this difference is "*hypostatic union*". The reason we rarely hear of "*hypostatic union*", however, is because it is both ***post*** death and resurrection as well as a reference to the Incarnation – prior to Jesus' life in this world. It was to reveal this eternal oneness that required a *kenosis* – a coming down from a *hypostatic union* in God – to the earthly state of *theosis* in which Jesus lived his *earthly* union with God. With his death, however, there begins the Ascent to the *hypostatic union in God.*

All we are pointing out here is the *difference* between man's *earthly* state of oneness with God (call it *theosis*, a *unitive state* or whatever), and man's *eternal or heavenly* oneness with and in God. This difference applies to every human being. Jesus' earthly oneness with God was not a *hypostatic union,* not man's eternal and glorious estate in God. Those who maintain man's earthly and heavenly oneness with God are the same, with no radical change, really do not know what they are saying. These are two totally different dimensions of existence – earthly and heavenly – so different, that a virtual *chasm* lies between the two.

Man, then, can look forward to two major turning points in his spiritual ascent. First, coming to the same "unitive state of being" (*theosis*) in which the Logos' human nature was born into this world, and second, going forward to recapitulate Jesus' same death, resurrection and ascension that ends in the "*hypostatic union*". Since the whole purpose of the Incarnation was to reveal that as it went for the man Jesus is "the Way" it goes for every human being, this is why the revelation of Christ is the revelation of *Man* – the "way" of everyman's life in union with God. This was the meaning of Irenaeus' "recapitulation"– i.e., Christ as the principle of everyman's *transformation* ("deification" or "salvation".) There is no other **"Way"** to eternal life.

With his death, Jesus as a particular "person" died – is no more – and what remains is solely the **Logos' *own*** glorified human nature. Resurrection and Ascension is the revelation of the ***Logos'*** *glorified humanity,* not the glorified humanity of any particular *person*. Keep in mind, for Athanasius, Cyril and the Alexandrians, the Logos never assumed the human nature of *any particular human being or person* in the first place. Add to this, Nazianzus' dictum, "*what the Logos did not assume is not saved,*" means neither the *person* of Jesus, nor any human *person,* is saved – God creates no person and saves no person. Add to this, God does not create a *particular* human nature (there is no such thing), means God also does not save any *particular* human being. In the end, it is only man's one common *universal human nature* – the Logos' *own* human nature – this is the *eternal* oneness of God and Man, **this is Christ**.

That the fathers regarded transformation into Christ as the Christian goal or end, means every human being is to **recapitulate** Christ's incarnate life and come to Christ's same glorious heavenly estate. Thus *"Each individual must reproduce what took place in Christ, each must die to his former life and receive the Logos in himself, thus Christians are so many Christs, or rather* ***they are but one Christ for the Logos unites Itself with them all*** *"* Methodius (d. 311.)

For Cyril, "*Christ possesses us himself since he took over our nature and made of our body the body of the Logos.*" This is the view expressed by the fathers – Hilary, Gregory of Nyssa, John Chrysostom, and many others – "*If God can become man, then surely he can deify mortals*".

That the Incarnation was about anything other than "salvation **is** deification", was *not* the understanding of the fathers. Although they believed Christ came, lived and died for mankind, the *sacrifice* involved was never focused on the cross, but on the Incarnation. God taking on human nature was the *real* sacrifice, not death of a man's body – as Irenaeus put it, "*The purpose of the Incarnation was the deification of man*". The purpose was not saving man in or for this world, but transforming them to participate in God's *eternal life* – that is *not* in this world.

The *process* of transformation is no *sideline* to Christianity, rather, it is its *essence*. This is not – as some would have us think – a kind of "mysticism" that infiltrated Christianity from the outside or some pagan source. Man's transformation is exactly what the Incarnation was about – the revelation of everyman's life transformed into the end God destined for all. Any understanding of the Christian "way" as other than a radical transformation of human nature, is *not* authentic Christianity.

The only reason people think some particular knowledge is "*mystical*" is because it defies their *wrong* views. Thus, when man discovers he has the wrong view or understanding, then, of course, the Truth he learns always strikes him as "mystical". The Truth, however, is not mystical, it is only "mystical" relative to man's wrong views in the first place. If people could start out with the Truth, their experiences would only *confirm* this Truth, and would not be regarded as some kind of "mystical knowledge".

Maximus the Confessor asked, "*If the dogma of 'salvation as deification' belongs to the mystery of the faith of the Church, why was it not included with the other dogmas in the symbols expounding the pure faith of Christians composed by our holy and blessed fathers?*" Indeed, would that this had been declared a *dogma,* Christians would have a very different understanding of Christ! The notion that to be saved one had to *believe* this or that, is too naive for words – as Jesus said, those who say "Lord, Lord" can't save anyone. God's plan of saving man and creation has nothing to do with people's different beliefs or disbeliefs. For one and all, the only way of salvation is man's *transformation* and ultimate deification, this is the "Way" Christ revealed.

The overriding concern of the fathers was what the Incarnation meant for all humanity, certainly not just for the man Jesus. The deification of Jesus' human nature was the model of everyman's deification – the "*way*" of all human beings. For many, the question was whether this transformation was actually an *ontological transformation* into something *other* than what man is now, and if so, what could this be? "*It does not yet appear what we shall be...*"; "*transfiguration is the revelation of what we* ***are to be*** *when deified by him*". "*What he was by nature we become by grace*". Since only the Creator knows the true nature of *what* It creates – knows *what* "man" really is – then only God knows *what* man will be transformed into or *become*. All we know is what God revealed – namely, that *however it went for the incarnate Christ is how it will go for all men. "For the union of God and man accomplished absolutely in Christ is to be fulfilled in due measure in each Christian as Christ made it possible. His work is efficacious for the consummation of humanity"* (Origen 185 – 254.)

Created *theocentric* (God-centered), the fathers believed man's deification was rooted in his creation – God's plan from the beginning. According to Paul, *Adam* filled his "divine center" with his own desires and gratifications, thus aborting his ultimate deification. So for Paul, Christ came to restore man's *original nature* in order to go forward to his ultimate destiny. Christ, then, was the *corrective* to the idea Adam had ruined it for mankind, for Christ revealed man was created to be *more* than he is *now* anyway – more, that is, than Adam *ever was* – which means a radical change and transformation into what *man is **not now***. He must undergo Jesus' same death (*of his personhood*) to come to the revelation of the true, eternal Christ – which is the Resurrection. From here man ascends into the glory of God to "*share in God's own* *divine nature"* (2 Peter 1:4) and, having the "*mind of Christ"*, participate in God's own divine Knowing. This and much more is how it will go. Obviously it is a mistake to think there is anything eternal about "human nature" *as man knows it* ***now.*** Maximus defined this beautifully, "*Like a wheel, Christ at the center, all people have the same center into which Christ draws back to himself the distinct elements of their being which he brought into existence, one body, one mind, one glory"*.

Long before the revelation of Christ, among the eclectic religious sects, there developed various paths and disciplines by which they sought the goal of "deification" – to become one with the *One.* (An interesting epithet of one cult's motto was: "*I was not, I was, I am not, I don't care"* – no one left to care, that is. In Latin, I think it reads, "was not, was, am not, don't care".) Because the Stoics regarded the "One" as *impassible*, *immovable* and *unchangeable* – in sharp contrast to man's ever changing *passibility* – the ultimate goal was to become as immovable, impassible and unchangeable as the "One". Since the "*logoi*" present in everyone was the "*impassible stillpoint*" or *center* of his being, one must conform himself to this inner *logoi* and learn to live from this silent center, ever mindful of it.

Maximus refers to this *divine center of being* – "*A clean heart might be said to be one which has not at all* ***any natural movement*** *in any way whatsoever. The Lord comes to it in perfect simplicity and as on a beautifully clean tablet writes his own laws on it"*. Those who know what is called a "unitive state" know by experience the *divine center of being* is *impassible*, nothing can ever touch it, neither fear, bliss or anything in-between. God is the soul's impassible *divine center* and we (ourselves) its *passible circumference.* This fact is much akin to the Stoics' understanding of a state they called "apatheia" where no passions or emotions reach to the center. So any idea God is subject to man's human experiences, defies man's *experience of God as impassible.* This is why the Stoics taught that man must live by reason (logos) and not by his passions and emotions – which only lead to suffering. Although some thought it impossible to *permanently* attain this Stoic's goal ("apatheia") in this life, yet, all regarded it as man's eternal oneness with the divine Logos. We will not go into other notions of *deification* such as *gnosis* and *contemplation* as the ultimate goal, but stick to the particular path of transformation bequeathed to the Christian tradition by the fathers.

While today we think of achieving a state of "apatheia" as a kind of psychological discipline, for the fathers, achieving a state of "*theosis"* could only be done by *supernatural grace.* Thus for Irenaeus,

Christ was the "Way" of transformation – "*Christ became what we are in order to cause us to be what he is Himself,* ***deification comes about through baptism and the Eucharist.***" Baptism and the Eucharist, then, were the grace-giving "*mysteries*" of Christ's transformative "Way". (Though originally "Baptism" and "Eucharist" were called the "*Mysteries of Christ*", the Western Church later called these "*sacraments*" – an unfortunate misnomer.)

Cyril's definition of *hypostatic union* as the oneness of Christ's dual natures, never meant becoming "one with the One", of *attaining* union, theosis or deification. The uniqueness of Cyril's term is pointing out this was no union that man could ever attain or affirm of himself – it was not *his* union with God, but rather, God's eternal union with Its *own* human nature. This is *not* a union with any particular human being or person, but a union solely with the bare essence of Mankind. As a union formed and found solely *in* God, it is beyond man's own knowing and experiencing. Anything man can *experience* he can describe, locate, affirm and define to some extent, yet, a oneness solely *in* God defies all this – which is why it can only be "*revealed.*" *Hypostatic union",* then, is the only term that defines the eternal *oneness* of Christ and sets it apart from all other known types of union man can know or experience.

The reason for going over this is to point out the difference between the 2nd and 3rd estates in the life of Christ. If the 2nd is as much as has been defined "*theosis*" (or in the West, "*mystical union*"), this is obviously not man's final estate or as far as man is destined to go. This was solely Christ's *earthly* oneness with God – the same every Christian can experience on earth – a state, however, that must undergo a radical change to become Christ's 3rd or final estate in God. Death, resurrection and ascension usher in a whole new and different *existence*, one no one could possibly grasp ahead of time – and anything said of it, would not be welcomed anyway. For most people, man's final estate would be either unthinkable or frightening *because* it is *nothing like* man's earthly existence or his childish expectations of *eternal life*. In truth, man's eternal life in God is literally "unthinkable".

The deification of human nature, then, means its ultimate transcendence, a radical ontological change. Body and soul are elevated beyond all its known earthly properties and faculties, beyond its own person or self, even beyond everything the human mind can think of. Man will lose all he knew, be left with nothing known to hang on to. Anyone who thinks in God man will have his same body and soul, same mind, will, consciousness – in short, everything he has or is *now*, couldn't be more mistaken. One purpose of the revelation of Christ was to allay people's fears of death and affirm the Truth and Reality of their "eternal life". Christ was God saying to man, "see how it went for this man Jesus, this is how it will go for every human being". And look at all Jesus went through, he gave his whole life to God and ended up with nothing – on a cross, hated by some, not believed by most, yet, where did he end up? In the unutterable glory of God! This is the good news of Christ.

The idea of being transformed beyond all self-identity terrifies people – theologians especially. Not only is the idea of losing one's ID frightening to people, but losing any part of themselves is unthinkable. People want to keep their same mind, same will, same self-consciousness, same body – nothing really changed, but only made "better". Anyone who thinks man would *never* choose his *self* over God or *choose **himself** instead of God*, is mistaken – everybody wants to eat his cake and keep it too. This brings to mind the saying of the Hindu sage Ramakrishna, "*I would rather taste sugar than **be** sugar*" – i.e., experience and know God, rather than *be* God. Even though Christ is not God (but the eternal oneness of man *and* God), Christians would say the same thing – they would rather **know** Christ than **be** Christ, that way, they can know Christ and **keep themselves too**. Yet, beyond *their self*, "*who"* would be left *to be* or *become* Christ? No one! Without self, no one could ever know ***themselves*** as God, or as Christ – or as sugar! This is why, if one *were* God, *were* Christ, or *were* sugar, *they* (**their self**) would never know it! There is no such thing as "I am God", "I am Christ", or "I am sugar" – ridiculous! But this is exactly why "***you"*** will be nothing, and *Christ will be All*.

The point is – those who think they can give their self to God and **keep it too,** only fool themselves. People claim they want to give their selves to God, yet, what they really mean is that they will give God everything **but** their ID. As they see it, without an ID "*who*" would there be to know and love God? No one! *God, then, is man's excuse for hanging on to his ID, **he** wants to know and love God for **himself** and **not** for God's sake.* Using God as an excuse to hang on to one's ID is symptomatic of wanting one's *own* way – which is *never* God's way. That out of fear, people dread loss of their identity – i.e., their very consciousness of themselves – is symptomatic of a lack of perfect trust in God, for where there is lack of trust, there is *fear*. Man is convinced that if *he himself* ceased to exist, God would cease to exist ***for him*** – which is true, God exists *for no one*. It is man who exists for God, God does not exist for man – indeed, God can go right on without man. But this is why the revelation of "Christ" is greater than the revelation of God – so God exists, what is that to man? Christ, however, is the revelation of *man's eternal oneness with God,* so now, let God go right on because man is *going with God* – and for all eternity.

It is because people think reference to their "self" is reference to their whole being or existence, they think annihilation of "self" is the annihilation of their whole existence. Although it turns out "self" is *not* man's *being or existence,* yet the fact people *think* so, is all the better since it will be **their very existence, *their whole being*** that must be surrendered to God. To surrender anything less, counts for nothing. This surrender was exactly Jesus' predicament in the garden, this was the ultimate *kenosis of Christ's* ***human*** *nature.* It was not just surrendering body and soul to God, but rather, if God so willed, giving up his very **existence.** Since *God* was Jesus' deepest experience of *life* and *being,* for him to lose his experience of *life* and *being* would be to lose God! (In the unitive state there is no separating one's *own* experience of *life* from one's experience of God's *life.)* **This human kenosis, then, was not just giving up his *own* ID, but *God's* ID as well!**

The perplexity of this forfeiture is that without awareness of *one's own* existence, ***who*** is left to be aware of God's existence? Nobody! And there's the rub, there is the "fine-line" between God and man. No one, however, will come to this **line – "to be or not to be"** – without being able to face complete annihilation – i.e., if it be God's will, to *cease to exist,* forever. Unless one trusts God that "*all will be well*", he will never encounter this *line* – **because on this line no one knows what God *will or will not do.*** This is why Jesus' only possible answer to this, was **"***Thy will be done*"! The choice "to be or not to be" is *not* man's to make, but God's alone.

Sooner or later, everyone will come to the "fine line" between God-for-himself and God-without-himself (really, ***God-in-Itself.)*** This *line* is between *one's own* existence and non-existence. Death of self is the cut-off line between all man knows of himself and God, a line between the created and the Uncreated, between two different dimensions of existence, a line where there is no way of knowing whether man will ultimately cease to exist or not. Thus, all one can say is **"so be it!"** What Jesus "sweat-out" in the garden was not fear of *physical* death, but the cessation of his very "self", his whole life with God – the only life he ever knew. Although Jesus sweat and prayed over this terrible possibility, yet he faced it squarely, dealt with it, and finally said "*Not my will, but thine be done*".

But there is no use worrying ahead of time about this cut-off line. Even if one thinks he is willing to give up his ID to God, all he can do is offer, for of himself, he can never give it up. Until and unless God removes the line and takes man's ID from him, it remains intact. It takes a lot of living (testing) before there is the perfect love and trust necessary to squarely face this line – "to exist or not to exist" – without the slightest movement of fear absolutely necessary for a genuine "*So be it*"! (People unprepared for this particular confrontation (the fine line) can react anywhere from sheer terror to such a debilitating fear they spend the rest of their life avoiding any thought or remembrance of such a possibility.) Nobody, however, will ever be in this position who does not know God like the back of their hand, have lived with God through the ups and down of earthly existence. This is why it takes a lot of living with God before ever being faced with the fine-line of personal extinction and an *unmovable* "*so be it*".

Human nature does not dissolve or vanish. The only *one* gone forever is a particular individual being, a person – why? Because Christ was never any particular being or *person* (*subject* or *self*) in the first place. **God's own human nature is no man's *own* being, own person or self.** Remember, for the fathers, *person* was a subject or self that, in the Incarnation, **the Logos *never* assumed or ever *became.*** And since what the "*Logos did not assume is not saved*", then no person, subject or self is saved. But who can take this truth? As Jesus said, "*Let those who can take it, take it*"!

Man's final transformation, then, entails no loss of human nature, but only loss of "person" – subject or self. Remember, in the "unitive condition" self-awareness is equally awareness of God, thus, the loss of self-awareness is equally the loss of awareness of God. That *faculty-of-soul* man experiences as "*consciousness*" (self-awareness) has *ceased to* function *forever.*[1] Consciousness, after all, is but a *function* of the mind. Following this cessation, the revelation of "***what***" remains (not "*who*" remains) is not only beyond all consciousness (subject, who, person), but beyond all awareness, knowing, thinking – the *mind itself.* Thus the revelation of the *true nature of* **what** *remains* beyond any "person" – self or consciousness – is the oneness of the *bare essence* of two disparate natures – **Christ.** Just as Jesus had no "Christ" to believe in or depend on, the revelation of "Christ" – which *is* the resurrection – is the revelation of the eternal oneness of God and man, a Truth that lies beyond all man's "beliefs", ideas and expectations. This is the revelation of man's eternal oneness with God ***beyond himself***,

---

[1] According to Maximus, God doesn't take away the will and mind, they simply *cease their activity,* cease because they have attained their end in God. It is their perfect fulfillment that causes the cessation of all man's faculties of body and soul – for apart from God, what would be left to want or know? Since body and soul have been transformed and perfectly fulfilled in the vision and glory of God, what need is there for any "agent" or "subject" (*person*) "who" couldn't even *function* in God's eternal life.

beyond all individuality and person, beyond all man's mundane definitions of "human nature", and certainly, beyond all earthly existence. Indeed, this is the revelation of the *Real Christ* – *man's Eternal Life.*

Resurrection is not the revelation that any "one" is Christ. Christ is beyond all such individuality of being and person. Christ is no "one" in particular and "everyone" in general – the **one and only "Christ"**. So no *person*, then, *becomes* the Logos' (God's) glorified *human* nature. According to Maximus, man's transformation entails a *"**Loss of individual personhood in union with God**"*. Of this he says, *"Having God through prayer as its mystical and only Father by grace, the soul will center on the oneness of its hidden being by a distraction from all things, and it will experience, or rather, know divine things, all the more as **it does not want to be its own, or able to be recognized from, or by itself, or anyone else's, but only all of God,** who takes it up becomingly and fittingly as only He can, penetrating it completely without passion and deifying all of it and transforming it unchangeably to Himself".*

According to the "proverbial party-line", however, the ultimate Christian goal is only to be "one ***with*** Christ", be ***united to*** Christ, everyone "one-**in**-Christ". ***To be Christ*** has never been the *stated* goal of the proverbial party-line – even though this was the belief of the fathers – i.e., to *become* the *image* (Christ) in which man was created. Thus, when Paul said "*No longer I, but Christ lives in me*", he never said he was one ***with*** Christ, *united **to*** Christ, was **in** Christ, nor that ***he* was** Christ. Paul knew that the **true nature** of *his own oneness with God **was Christ,*** for such was *revealed* to him – and indeed, has been revealed to many ever since! Christ is neither Jesus, Paul nor any*one,* Christ is simply the oneness of God and man's bare essential nature. Without this particular revelation, however, it is doubtful people could ever understand the Truth that the **true nature of every man's oneness with God *is Christ.* It is only man's oneness *with God,*** *and not with Christ,* **that transforms man into Christ** – into God's *own eternal* human nature.

Paul never said he was *united to* Christ – much less to the man Jesus. Since Paul and Jesus had the same human nature, how could Paul be united to *what* he is already? Two human beings do not constitute two human natures anymore than a million human beings constitutes a million human natures. Furthermore, Christ is not the union of *persons* – divine or human (nor of two human persons) – but the union of *natures*. Man's singular human nature can only be one with God and never one with some *other* human nature – which doesn't even exist. Absolutely, all talk of being united **to** Christ is mere sentiment. However, should one think of Christ as Almighty God, then of course, to be united to Christ means being united to God – **which union IS Christ and not a union WITH Christ.**

So just as the man Jesus was ***not one with Christ***, neither is anyone else. Although the real Christ is no particular human person, yet, in this life, we *supply* the human *person* of the *personless Christ,* just as Jesus did. So this side of the grave, at least, everyone is called to supply the human personhood of God's **personless** human nature. This might be Paul's notion of "*putting on Christ*" – meaning, like Jesus, everyone is to supply ("put on" or be) the *human person* of Christ in *this world.* With the death of this *person,* however, man's common human nature becomes the heavenly, glorified (*personless*) Christ in the Trinity – God's *own* human nature, that is.

Since Christ is neither "I", "You" or "some *other* person", it could be said that once transformed into Christ, man is left without Christ. (Jesus, after all, *had* no Christ.) Though this may be difficult to understand, it is strategic. Where man goes through life knowing Christ as "other" than himself, an object to himself, in the end, however, not only is there **no *objective* Christ, but without self, there is also no *subjective* Christ.** There is no such person as "I am Christ" because there is **no "I am", person or self, *to be* Christ.** What this means is that the Real Christ has *always* been beyond both *object* and *subject – always been personless,* that is.

This is what Maximus says about the "subject-object" business: *"Anyone who does not transcend himself and all thought and settle into silence beyond all thought, is absolutely incapable of being free from* ***mutability****. Every thought expresses a duality of aspects, the thinker and the object of thought, neither of the two can completely retain simplicity (non-duality.) For the thinker is a subject who bears the power of thinking of himself. And what is thought of is a subject having inherent in it the capacity of being thought of – or else the essence whose faculty it is which* ***formerly existed****. For there is no being at all which is by itself a simple essence or thought, to the extent of also being an undivided monad. As far as God is concerned, if we say he is an essence,* ***he has not naturally inherent in him the possibility of being thought, because he is not composed, his essence is not capable of being a subject of thought.*** *He is entirely above essence and entirely above thought, thus the one who still in some way possesses any thought has not yet left the dyad (duality); but the one who has completely abandoned it, arrives in some fashion into the monad in having supremely relinquished the power of thinking".* Where man's knowing is a "*dyad*", God's Infinite Knowing is beyond all thinking, all consciousness (a *dyad)* and even beyond a *monad.* God's Infinite Knowing is none of this.

We have consistently pointed out that all the fathers believed God creates no particular *person,* and that the Incarnation was not God uniting Itself to any particular human being or person, but solely to *man's common human nature*. Thus God only creates human nature while each individual creates his own person. This means that as a human "*person*" (self or I am), Jesus was *not* united to God, only his common, universal human nature was united to God – a human nature, however, the fathers never regarded as *Jesus' own*, but as *God's own.* So just as Jesus' human nature was *not his,* but God's, so too, the Christian goal is the transformation of *his* human nature into God's *own incarnate* human nature.

To think that all "Christ" means **is** man's earthly oneness with God, doesn't define Christ at all. The fact God is existentially united with *everything* that exists, is *not* Christ. Reference to Christ is solely to *God and Man* – "man" being God's *own* created human nature. While *theosis* (a supernatural state of union with God) may define Jesus' *earthly* oneness with God, without further growth in Wisdom, Jesus could not have revealed man's ultimate transformation into Christ's eternal ***hypostatic oneness with and in God.*** No "union" less than this **is** the eternal *Real Christ.* The ultimate Christian goal is **transformation *into* Christ, *not*** oneness ***with*** **Christ**. Strictly speaking –

It is impossible to be one with Christ.

I. *Just as the man Jesus was* ***not*** *one* ***with*** *Christ, neither is any human being* ***one with*** *Christ.* Though, like Jesus, every man experiences *his* oneness with God, this is *not a* oneness **with** Christ. As said, since Christ's human nature is everyone's same human nature, there can be **no "union" with *what one is already.*** The incarnate Logos (God) is not united with billions of *human natures* – that do not even exist. Because there is only *one* human nature there is only *one* Christ.

II. And just as man cannot be united to what he is already, so too, **he cannot be united to *what* he is to *become* or be transformed into.** While Christ's *deified human nature* is the goal of all human nature, yet human nature cannot be *united* to its *finished product* ahead of time. Just as the newborn cannot be *united* to what it will be 10, 30, or 50 years down the road, so too, man can never be *united* to what he is to *become.* Obviously, the goal or end is not to *become united* to Christ, but be transformed *into* Christ.

III. Another reason man can never be united to Christ is because, created *in* the image of Christ, no one can be "one" with his own image. While an image *reflects* Christ, the *reflection* itself is *not* the one *reflected* – one need only look in a mirror to understand this. Since the one looking is not the one reflected, there is no way one can be *united* to his own image in a mirror. Just so, neither Christ nor man is united to his own image – impossible – man can only *become* that of which he **is** an image – Christ. The moment man *becomes* this image, Maximus refers to this as the "*broken mirror*" – no mirror or image remaining. Thus the moment one *becomes* "that" of which he had only been an image, no *self-reflection is ever again possible.* [2]

So on this journey, the reason no one experiences *themselves becoming* Christ is because no one honestly knows Christ ahead of time. While man thinks he knows Christ, it is *because* he also knows *himself* he sees no affinity – and rightly so. He does not know what transformation into Christ really means, how it goes, where it might take him, or what drastic change it might entail. So, until man's transformation is complete, he honestly does not know *what* he is being transformed into. But when this is a *fait accompli*, all images and intellectual ideas ultimately fall by the wayside. Those who think they know all there is to Christ only know ***about*** Christ – what they have heard, read, or may have been taught – yet none of this is the **Real Christ**. In truth, no one can possibly know the fullness of Christ prior to *becoming* Christ, for Christ **is neither one's self nor some other.**

Obviously there is much more to Christ than can be known from any Council's doctrines or dogmas, a knowing that transcends man's theologies and formulations. The Incarnation, however, demonstrated these truths without theologizing or dogmatizing, because it is only by experientially recapitulating *(re-living) Jesus' own spiritual life with God* that is the "*Way*" one comes to the Real Christ. So while stated dogmas are changeless and static, the experience of Christian truths is always dynamic, unanticipated and unexpected. So just as Jesus gave his whole life to God – and *not* to Christ – so too, every man gives his life to God alone. Christ is really the Alpha and Omega of man's existence. "*As Creator, the Logos stands at the* ***beginning*** *of creation, and as the* ***incarnate*** *Christ, He stands as its* ***end*** *when all things will exist not only through Him* (Logos) *but in Him* (God.) *In order to be in Christ, creation had to be assumed by God, made God's own, this is the final glorification of man"* (Maximus.)

The goal of man's journey, then, is to become the Logos' *own hu-*

---

[2] For more reasons why there is "No Oneness with Christ", see Chapter 28, ***Eucharist***.

man nature – Christ. As created, man begins with his *own being*, his own individual person or self, but in the end, is transformed into *God's own human nature*. Based on the notion of the Trinity as three "persons", Maximus says the divine *person* of the Logos is ultimately "substituted" for man's own person – "*What must be deified in us is our* ***entire nature*** *belonging to* ***our*** *person, which must enter into union with God, and become "****a divine Person****" created in two natures, a human nature which is deified, and a nature that deifies."* Without being a *human person*, then, man is nobody in particular and everybody in general. When speaking of a *particular person,* the reference is to a particular human being, one of a particular gender, race, religion, language, culture and so on, **yet God (Logos) neither creates or unites any of this to Itself. So while Jesus *was* a particular person, the *Logos' human nature, however, was no person, no particular human being.*** To understand this, however, requires a totally different understanding of Christ than the traditional "party-line" portrays. Christ is **not** the *particular* man Jesus, but God's eternal oneness with man's universal, common human nature. As the oneness of two natures, then, Christ is not "*who*" anyone is, but "*what*" Christ is.

So all God intends to *save* is "that" in man capable of eternal existence – capable of "bearing the vision" and "participating" in God's own Infinite Existence. The whole purpose of transformation is to make this heavenly or Godly existence possible. Because eternal life in God is not earthly life, whatever made earthly life possible has to go – be transformed or ultimately eliminated – because eternal life in God is nothing like earthly existence. In God, man has no need for a sensory body or those earthly faculties of soul that made for rational choices, desires, energies, self-awareness, and all the rest of it. In God there is no need for these earthly functions because in God, man participates in God's own *modus operandi* that utterly transcends all man's earthly *modus operandi.* Many of the fathers believed there was no end of going ever deeper into the Godhead, and that beyond the grave, in and with the Infinite, there was no staid "end" to the human "journey". So while man has a beginning, yet in God, he has no end.

A Note on Transformation

Genuine "transformation" is purely supernatural, and its effect so subtle that no one experiences that it is even happening. It is only when it reaches some critical point there is an abrupt change that, at first, man does not understand at all. Only when the "effects" of this change are experienced in daily living, one begins to understand it – though hard put to say *exactly how* he has changed. Transformation has nothing to do with any change of mind, heart or personality, it is not some therapeutic restoration or rehabilitation, rather it is a **change in "being" itself, a change at the very core of one's being.**

The reason for stressing the true nature of transformation is because the term ("transformation") has been used so loosely and ineptly as to become meaningless. Thus some Christians think all it takes to be "transformed **in** Christ" is the mere *belief* that "*Jesus saves*", and that their soul will be made as sinless as that of the man Jesus. A mere change of mind or heart, however, is not genuine transformation, at best this is mere *persuasion*. It seems some people take their *beliefs* as self-fulfilling – as if *truth depended* on whatever they believed it to be. And indeed, one's beliefs are *self-fulfilling* in that they strengthen one's *self,* make it invulnerable and securely *boxed* in. It is only the gift of **Faith, which is *not* belief,** that can release man from all his *self-fulfilling* beliefs. Jesus' saying "*It is because I tell you the Truth, you don't believe me*" means Truth is *not* believable *because* Truth is not a matter of *belief!* **Faith**, on the other hand, which is neither in or of the mind, is *that* ungraspable, indefinable "*Truth-Sensor*" in man which alone will take him where he would otherwise *never **think*** to go – or even think to *believe*.

God has never revealed what man wants to *believe* – most people only believe what comforts them anyway.[3] Not a single revelation of God was ever intended to be in accord with any of man's belief systems, religions or scriptures – the idea God has to stick to man's "scriptures", is patently absurd. God is beholden to no man or any of his beliefs – God does not *depend* on man for anything, and certainly not for the Truth. Actually, a genuine revelation of God can even ruin man's beliefs – why? Because Eternal Truth is beyond his belief-boxes. But if beliefs are fickle, the ever Present Truth-Sensor (Faith) in man, will reveal everything he needs to know, which alone, will carry him to his destined end in God.

Another loose use of "transformation" is the comforting idea that it only means a "change for the better" and certainly not the *permanent* "loss", "cessation", or "death" of something. To think transformation is only a "change for the better", obviously generates no anxiety. The proverbial example is that of the caterpillar that does not *die* to become a butterfly, rather, it is only "transformed". The truth, however, is that

---

[3] Once an 8 yr. old hollered to his 5 year old sister in another room, "Do you believe in Santa Claus?" She answered, "I don't know". He said, "Well, if you don't, then you won't get any presents!" She shouted back, "Oh, then, yes I do!" This is a perfect example of *belief* and how it works – people believe in order to get something thinking that if they don't believe, they'll get nothing.

to become a butterfly the caterpillar had to lose everything it means *to be* a caterpillar, for had it not *ceased to exist* as a caterpillar it could *never* have become a butterfly. This is somewhat analogous to the difference between man's *earth bound* life with God, and his being freed, as Paul put it, *"to meet Christ in the clouds"*. This example, however, is only analogous to transformation into a "unitive state of being", whereas the *ultimate end* of the unitive state is *death* of the butterfly – not the caterpillar.

Yet, the ultimate transformation of man works much the same way in that unless he first *ceases to exist* as a caterpillar, and later, *ceases to exist* as a butterfly – what he is *now* – he can never become what God destined him to *become.* It is this eternal loss of *what man is now* that people fear most, and why man has invented all kinds of comforting scenarios and beliefs rather than face any permanent loss or the finality of death. Yet there is no going "backwards", transformation is an irreversible *forward* movement, always toward God's destined end. Thus, what man is at the beginning, is *not what* he is at the end.

As said, *transformation* is solely God's doing. No man can transform himself, he neither knows how nor knows ahead of time where he is going or where it will all end. That he *thinks* he knows – how it goes and how it ends – only creates problems for himself because all his expectations will come to *naught.* He cannot know the end until he gets there, and the sooner he admits he doesn't know, the better off he is with this *truth.* The true nature of transformation is a mystery, its movement so subtle it is virtually undetectable. Thus man really does not know *where* he is in the whole process – how far he has come or how far he has to go.

The only time he is alerted to this process, is when some critical point is reached – unknown to him – when, abruptly, something is *lost,* gone forever, dies and can *never* be experienced again. Initially, it is not always evident that this loss is a gain, but down the road, this will be understood as all to the good. Transformation, then, is the subtle process of dying, dying to man's present life with absolutely no *resurrection* of his former life possible. Man will lose everything in *this* life *because* this is *not* his *eternal* life. Christ, as the revelation of everyman's spiritual journey, entails the death of man's *earthly* oneness with God (the earthly Christ) in order to live *eternally* with and in the Trinity, for this alone is the *heavenly eternal Christ.*

GOD WILL BE ALL IN ALL

"Then shall the Son himself too, be subjected to him that subjected all things to him, in order that God may be all in all."
(1 Cor. 15:28)

The understanding of this statement by Paul, was the cause of much dissention and anathemas among the fathers. It seems they had given little thought to Christ's existence in the future life, never questioned Christ's *eternal* status and whether or not the "*Son*" would *remain* "incarnate" for all eternity. Since the Incarnation had accomplished its mission of salvation, then what further need was there for an "incarnate" *Son* – for "Christ"?

According to Paul, once the Son had "subjected" (saved and returned) all things to God, the Son would likewise be "subjected" (or returned) to God. But if the Son ***is*** God, how can God be "subjected" or returned to God? Evidently Paul's understanding of "Son" was only a reference to the "incarnate Christ" or man Jesus, it was *not* a reference to God, the eternal Logos/Spirit. His was still the Judaic understanding of the Spirit (or Logos) as God's created "instrument" in creation and that, despite its exalted status, it was *not* God. Obviously, Paul had no grasp of God's Trinitarian nature, not, at least, as the fathers would come to understand it. In his view, when all had been created and saved by the Spirit/Logos' incarnation, there was no further need for any instrumental Logos/Spirit and thus, in the end, God would be "all in all".

Paul's view of the "end" is based on two assumptions. 1. At some *time* God *began* creating, and 2. There is a **time** when God is done creating – decides never to create anything again. Thus, as a "Creator", God is finished. But who can say there was any *time* God did **not** create or any time God will no longer create? God is not *sometimes* a creator and *sometimes* not a creator. All man can rightly assume is that *created* "things" have a beginning and an end, he cannot presume more than that.

The fathers had no simplistic understanding of Paul's statement – as if he only meant in the *end* God would be *in* everything and everything would be *in* God. Since this is how creation exists *right now,* this is obviously not the end Paul envisioned. (Since "outside" God nothing exists, all existence is *in* God already, this is why God is "omnipresent" *in* all that exists – right *now.*) If the fathers had this simplistic understanding, it would never have become the rancorous issue it did. Paul was not addressing either the beginning or the present, but the future, the ending of all creation. He did not just say God would be *present in* all things, he said, God will "***Be All***" – all that is left of "things". Paul's view of the end became an issue that would forever color people's understanding of Christianity, its purpose and ending.

Many different interpretations can be given to Paul's idea of the "end", and, of course, the fathers had them all. What this meant to them is reflected in their different Christologies and paradigms of Christianity that had to do with either the *eternal* or *temporary* status of Christ. If the sole purpose of the incarnation was the salvation of man (and creation), and this purpose had been accomplished once and for all, then what need would God, man or creation, have for Christ anymore? With nothing left to save, with no further need for "Christ", what, in the end, would become of Christ?

Once again, the whole issue harks back to the question of just "*who*" was the Son? "Who" in the end would be "subjected" to God? Was Paul's reference to "Son" a reference to the man Jesus, or to God – the eternal Logos, or "Son" as the later fathers maintained? In light of the fathers' understanding of God as "Trinity", Paul raised the issue of the "Son's" final, subjugated status. Obviously, Paul's reference was to "Christ" – be it the *incarnate* Spirit/Logos **or** the man Jesus. In his Judaic view, Christ was the incarnation of God's *created* medium in creation, the Spirit/Logos. When creation was over and this "medium" had saved and returned all to God, then there would be no further reason for this "medium". Since Paul did not regard Spirit/Logos as the *immanent essence* of God (the Trinity), we can discount his use of "son" as reference to the Logos/Spirit as Almighty God – God, after all, cannot be "subjected" to God. But since as a mere human being, Jesus could not have "saved" creation, then Paul's reference to "son" could only be to "Christ" as the *incarnate* Spirit/Logos. Thus, in the end, the one *subjected* to God was the incarnate Spirit/Logos – Christ.

As we know, some of the fathers regarded the eternal Uncreated Logos as a "*Son*", the same one (of the Trinity) that took on human nature and became "Christ". Once the mission of salvation had been accomplished and all returned to God, in light of the Trinity, this could only mean all creation was returned (or subjected) to the *Transcendent-Logos-Spirit* with no *incarnate* "*Christ*" remaining. Since God (Logos/Spirit) cannot be *subject* to God – which makes no sense – then "who" was Paul's "Son" that became "subject" to God? In light of the Trinity, this could only be the created man Jesus. Was Jesus, then, the "Son" Paul was referring to, or was it God – the eternal Logos or Spirit?

No one spelled out the answer to this question more boldly than

Marcellus of Ancyra (d. 374), he said, "*The relationship of Sonship will disappear; it is limited to the Incarnation and the purposes for which the Logos became incarnate, and the Logos will again become what he was from eternity, immanent in the Father.*" So when all is saved, the Logos returns to what it had always been *prior* to the incarnation – namely, God, the eternal Logos. This was by no means solely Marcellus' understanding, it was that of Origen, Tertullian, Novatian, Irenaeus, and Gregory of Nyssa – to my knowledge, just about all the fathers. Marcellus tells us this was also the view of Julius and Athanasius – the chief bishops of Rome and Alexandria at that time. Like Marcellus, many of the fathers believed "Father and Son" were only temporary titles, "relational terms", temporary and transient that no longer applied when the work of Christ is finished, or when, in the end, the "*Logos will again become what he was from eternity immanent in the Father.*"

To my knowledge, the dispute over Paul's comment did not arise until the time of Marcellus. Prior to this, there seemed to be no question Paul's reference was to all creation ultimately returning to God – certainly *not* returning to some *earthly* "kingdom". There also seemed to be the understanding the "incarnate son" would return to Its former *non-incarnate* existence so that in the end, there would be no "incarnate Logos" – **no Christ, that is**. Prior to Marcellus, however, it seems no one had articulated this view so boldly or succinctly. We can imagine, then, how upsetting this must have been for those concerned for the "simple folks" understanding of this. If the Christian's whole focus is on the **incarnate** Logos or **Christ,** and it turns out that in the end Christ no longer exists, then what becomes the focal point of Christianity? Christ as a temporary savior exists no more, is not eternal, only the Logos/Spirit/Father are eternal. Were people, then, only worshiping and praying to someone **who was,** and not to the **One that Is**? It seems Paul and Marcellus' views of the end was like dropping a bomb on the traditional party-line depiction of Christ. Despite all the attempts to vilify Marcellus' understanding of Paul, and despite Marcellus being exonerated, to this day, the party-line sticklers continue to besmirch him.

Regarding Paul's statement, there are two issues we can immediately put aside: 1.) For Paul, the immanent essence of God was *not* a Trinity – which had yet to be formulated or pinned down. His was still the Judaic view of the Spirit or Logos as God's *created mediums* in the work of creation – the same *incarnate* Spirit/Logos being the medium for its salvation. 2.) There is also no use resurrecting the whole Arian issue of just "*who*" was God's "Son" – the eternal Logos or the man Jesus? These issues only came up after Paul's time anyway.

One issue we must not forget, however, is Paul's understanding that Christ, or the Messiah, would immediately return to finish his mission and establish an earthly "kingdom" – the "Kingdom of Israel", that is. Even though Jesus said *his* "kingdom" was *not* of this world, still, his Jewish Apostles and disciples expected him to *first* fulfill the Judaic Messianic promise. When this never happened, however, changes had to be made regarding this expectation. (And let's face it, the Gentile population had no invested interest in the establishment of a Kingdom of Israel in their midst.) Since Paul's "end" mentions no "kingdom", but solely addresses man's final, heavenly estate *in* God, for some fathers, he raised the question of Christ's "kingdom" being either *in* God (as Paul had it) or *in* this world, as the Jewish Apostles expected.

For many, it seems, the expectation was that Christ would "come again" to establish peace on earth for a thousand years, followed by the end of the world – *Armageddon,* as some people think. As for Jesus saying "*my kingdom will have no end*" (be *eternal,* that is), was this a reference to some kingdom in *this* world or to the "kingdom of *heaven*"? I think we can say for all the fathers, the only *eternal life* they anticipated was *in heaven* with God – certainly not on this earth! As to how some Christians derived the view Christ's *eternal* kingdom is an *earthly* kingdom, a "*new creation*", I have no idea.[1] The Nicene Creed is not clear, "*he will come again to judge the living and dead, and his kingdom will have no end*" – exactly *what (or where) is this kingdom* that will have no end?

As to why this issue (of a "kingdom") had any importance for the fathers, it was due to Paul's saying that in the end **the Son** (be it Christ, Jesus, or Spirit/Logos) **had no "eternal kingdom", but would hand over everything, including himself, to be eternally "subjected" to God alone**. In other words, the "Son" (whoever that was) had no *eternal* kingdom at all! So what, then, does it mean "*his kingdom will have no end*"? Needless to say, the consistent effort to somehow make *scripture true* to the word, has always proved a pain. Different interpretations have been the cause of endless dissensions and condemnations, people going off to start their own churches – virtually their own religions. Scripture has never provided man with any peace or truth. For Truth, man can only rely on God alone. (And God is no book. God

---

[1] The Stoics thought after the Logos (Divine Fire) had consumed the world (with fire), everything would be "*re-created*", all being a "*new creation*" of the Logos – a notion no doubt picked up by Paul. With Christ, the "old creation" had passed away, for Christ **was** the "*new creation*" in which everyone would be "*re-created*" – made new.

never said or wrote a single word.)

Instead of going after Paul for making his statement about the "end" of Christ, some of the fathers went after Marcellus – who actually agreed with Paul. For Marcellus, the "Son" was only the man Jesus, *not* God or the Logos. Thus he affirms that in the end, when the "son" (Jesus) had accomplished his mission of salvation, "*the Logos will again become what he was from eternity, immanent in the Father*." So while the Logos remains eternal, it is Its incarnation, the "son" Jesus that will become "subjected" to God – along with the rest of creation. This is not, however, just the end for the man Jesus, but the end for Christ as well – end of the eternal *oneness* of God and man. We can understand why some of the fathers did not agree with this, and why they added to the Nicene Creed, "*and his* (Christ's) *kingdom will have no end*". After all, if the "Son" **is** God, then of course, the Son's (or God's) heavenly kingdom has no end – just as it also had no *beginning*.

But putting aside the absurd issue of some "kingdom" and who will rule it, the real issue is the final or eternal status of the Logos' human nature. This is important because the motto adopted throughout this book has been – "*however it goes for Christ is how it goes for all men*". But here now, Paul poses this question: following the deification of the Logos' human nature, did the Logos (God) *remain Incarnate* for all eternity, or did *the Logos again become what he was from eternity, immanent in the Father*? The issue is not Christ's *human nature* being subjected to the Logos (God) – which we take for granted anyway – but the *eternity of Christ,* the *incarnation itself* – the eternal oneness of God and man. This is the question: "Is God (Logos) *stuck* with Its human nature for all eternity – or not?" Since the Logos became incarnate to save man, and this mission is now accomplished, why would the Logos **remain** *incarnate* (one with human nature) for all eternity? That there would be an end to the *incarnate* Logos or Christ, did not sit well with some of the fathers. On the other hand, that *after* the Incarnation the Logos now **had** to remain incarnate for all eternity, this was also problematic. If the purpose of the Incarnation is done and over with, why remain Incarnate?

Though we know the Logos (God) is eternal, yet, do we know the *incarnate* Logos or *Christ* – God's oneness with man – is eternal? If not, then what becomes of the Logos' *own* human nature and consequently, everyone else's? It goes without saying, if human nature could become as "eternal" as God, then human nature can *become* God. But did any of the fathers actually believe this?

The answer to this question brings up a subject so far avoided in this book, which is the answer – "*Yes*". The fathers did believe man could become God, in fact, their over-riding motto was "*God became man in order that man might become God*" (Irenaeus). Though that truth was explained away for later generations, no one could read the fathers and not encounter their belief in this matter. For my part, I have stuck with their view that man, created in the *image* of Christ, the goal was to *become* that image – *become* Christ, that is. But there comes a point at which we cannot ignore the fathers' having gone beyond this to affirm that just as God became man, man can become God. One can find many such statements in the fathers' works. Although we have explained these statements as their references **not** to God, but to Christ, the fact is, many of the fathers referred to *Christ* **as** God, and thus, to be transformed into Christ is to be transformed into God. Some were not even as good as Cyril when it came to pointing out the distinctions in Christ's dual natures – the divine and human. In this matter of "Christ-is-God", many fathers could be accused of *Monophysitism* – the belief Christ was totally divine – because in the end his human nature had been deified.

For those who believed man's nature would be ultimately deified or transformed **into God,** there was no problem with Paul's view that in the end there would be only the Logos (God) and no human nature. But if human nature is made God, then there is no "*Christ*" any more, the Incarnation (God's oneness with man) would be over and "*God is All*". So just as creation came from God, it returns to God. Since the mission of the *incarnate* Logos (Christ) had been accomplished, what need was there for the Logos to *remain* incarnate?

If one thinks the Logos remains *eternally* one with Its human nature, then the Trinity could be formulated "Father-Christ-Spirit", making *man's human nature* the *essence* of the Trinity! But to think the *Uncreated* Logos is *also* a *created* human being (Christ), would not be a true understanding of the Trinity – certainly none of the fathers accepted this. Only the Logos is eternally *Uncreated,* whereas "Christ" is the Logos' oneness with *created* nature. That in the end, Christ is *not* eternal, is the problem raised by Paul. The fathers had a choice to either ignore this problem (as most people do), not admit there is a problem (as theologians do), or face it squarely, which the fathers did. That God's *own* human nature ultimately *becomes* God's divine nature was the issue Paul raised. This was not just the final heavenly status of Christ's human nature, but the final heavenly status of *everyman's eternal human nature.*

Since it would not do to preach Christ and, at the same time, admit that in the end there will be no Christ, out of consideration for what the "common people" envisioned as their eternal life, there was inserted into the creed "*and his* (Christ's) *reign* (or kingdom) *will have no end*" – recited to this day. The notion of Christ as a king eternally reigning over some kingdom would at least assure people of an *eternal Christ*. This addition to the creed, however, was not Paul's view nor the majority of the fathers. Eventually, Paul's understanding that in the end *"God would **be all** in all"* had to be ignored or explained away. In this case, "his kingdom will have no end" was the end of the hot blooded dissension among the early fathers, and how "Christ's kingdom" became another lock-step doctrine of the proverbial *party-line.*

That in the end, there would be solely the Logos (God) and no Christ, or **no incarnate human nature,** seems to have been acceptable to all the fathers. Origen put it this way: *"It is the simple sort of Christians who are attached to Christ's manhood, but the true gnostic, the man of real spiritual advancement and insight strains upward to the Logos, **the soul's authentic life**. The mediator between God and man is not, in the last analysis, the God-man Jesus Christ, but the Logos who **bridges** the gulf between the Godhead and creatures".* For Origen, the Logos was the Trinity's bridge that unites God and man, it was not the man-God, Jesus Christ. Indeed, prior to the Logos' incarnation, the man-God Jesus Christ never existed. In his view, Jesus' human nature was increasingly deified until, after the resurrection, his material body disappears and his soul is filled and *fused* with the Logos. Thus, he says, "*We become divinely possessed, transformed into Him (the Logos) is how we participate in the divine nature*". For Origen, resurrection and ascension was the end of "Christ", in the end there is only the Logos. As we know, this was the same view as the later Cappadocian fathers who did not believe the Logos' human nature was retained after its glorification. We'd go as far as to say that for all the early fathers, the *incarnate* Logos or "Christ" was temporary and not eternal.

Their understanding of "transformation" never ended with man's transformation **into** Christ, but transformation **into** the Logos, one of the Trinity – the divine Son. All those for whom "Son of God" was the Logos (the Son's incarnation, being "Christ"), tell us that by grace and "adoption", man becomes God's *same Son* – the Logos. To them, Jesus' saying "*You are all sons of God"* meant that just as he, following his resurrection and ascension, returned to heaven as the divine Son (or Logos), so too, every man.

In the fathers' stated view, the Logos or "Son" was the ***uncreated image*** of the Father, while the Logos' or Son's *human nature* was the ***created image*** of the Logos. Thus *human nature* is created in the image of the Logos (or Son), and *not* just the image of *Christ*. This means that in the end, for man to be transformed into the *image* in which he was created, he becomes, *not* Christ, but the "*adopted Sons of God*" – **becomes the Logos, that is**.[2] Thus Cyril referred to the eternal Logos as the "natural" Son of God, and to man, as *becoming* the "adopted Sons of God". All references to "adopted Sons" were references to *becoming* the *uncreated divine Logos* or Son, they were never references to *becoming Christ*. Since the man Jesus was created in the same *image* of the Logos as every other human being, then, like Jesus, man must become "that" of which he is but an image – become the Logos – God. For Paul, then, to say in the end there would be no Christ, and God would *be* All, was in keeping with the fathers' view – only, unlike Paul, their ending was totally Trinitarian. **Where Paul would have the son (Spirit/Logos) ultimately "subjected" to God, for the fathers all was subjected to the uncreated Logos – God, the whole Trinity.**

Depending on the understanding of "Son" as either God (Logos) or as the man Jesus, there are two views of Christ's ending. For the fathers, the deification of the Logos' (or Son's) human nature was its transformation into the Logos or Son. But if the "son" was the man Jesus, then the deification of human nature was that of the transfigured, glorified *incarnate* Logos – Christ, that is. Where in the first view, the end is solely the Logos (God or "Son"), in the second view, the end is the eternal *incarnate* Logos – the heavenly Christ, that is.

But either way Christ is defined (as God or as the *Incarnation* of God) the fathers, going with Paul seemed to agree that in the end, all men will become God's *Son*. This was the purpose of the incarnation – the "*Logos (or Son) became man that man might become the Logos (or Son)*". The end of man, then, is not transformation into the *incarnate* Logos or Christ, but into the Logos Itself – "God's (so called) begotten Son".) Indeed, it was Cyril's view that *what the Son was by Its divine "nature", man becomes by "grace" or "adoption"*. This goes beyond man's transformation into Christ (the eternal union of God and man), but ends with man's transformation into the Logos – God.

As to how created human nature can be transformed into the Uncreated divine nature, the terms used were "transelemented", "absorbed", "dissolved" ("like a drop of water in the sea"), "possessed", or so "fused" and "in-fused" with God it could no longer be known as other than the divine Logos. Another view was that human nature was "overshadowed" by the glorious Logos, yet remained as a *spiritual*,

---

[2] This view of the Logos or Son as the "image of the Father" was in keeping with Plato's *archetypal images* as reflections of the absolute "One" – images of God, in Christian terms. Plato never regarded these archetypal images as the One, but only as "*reflections*" of It.

invisible body. No one ever suggested the annihilation of human nature, on the contrary, this was its ultimate transformation – we might say its "transubstantiation". This is why the fathers had no trouble with Paul's view there would be no *incarnate* Son or Christ when all would be transformed into the same "Son" or Logos.

Even Origen, who regarded the "son" as the man Jesus, wrote, "*Happy are they who no longer need the Son of God as a physician who helps the sick, nor as shepherd, nor as redemption, but as Wisdom, and as Logos and as righteousness. Like St. Paul, the mature Christian does not need the historical Jesus*". For him, the truth of Christ transcended the purely historical understanding of Christ; the *union* of the human and divine was not eternal or permanent, but solely intended for the sake of salvation. Since man was now saved, what need was there for the *incarnate* Son or Christ anymore?

For Maximus the Confessor, the change of human nature into the divine nature meant neither its destruction nor its survival, what is destroyed are all its properties (non-essentials) while its "naked" or basic nature survives. Thus for Maximus, that in the end "God will be all in all" means God alone will **appear** in all – "*Through the bodies we shall have, in every body that we shall see wherever we direct our eyes, we shall behold God Himself with perfect clarity*"; "*Only God will appear in them when they transcend the limits of their own nature, not in such a way that their nature will perish, but so that only* ***He who truly has being*** *will appear in them*"; "*The transcendence of nature is the* ***non-appearance*** *of nature, just as air when filled with light is not apparent since only the light dominates*". In other words, if there was *perpetual daylight*, then no one would ever know the stars existed, their existence is only known in *darkness*. In God or heaven, however, there is no darkness, All is Light – so who knows what exists? But then, after seeing God, what else would anyone want to see? People do not understand, the glory of God will blind them to this world and everything in it. As Paul says – "*We all, with faces unveiled, reflecting as in a mirror the glory of the Lord, are being transformed into his very image from glory to glory as through the Spirit of the Lord*" (2 *Cor. 3:18.)* This is why, in heaven, the senses no longer function and would be of no use whatsoever. Those who think they can both see God and other people (or things) obviously have never "seen" God. So too, those earthly faculties of soul that generated desires, intellectual knowing – all its functions and energies – will be of no use since they will have achieved their end, *know* all Truth with nothing more to be desired or known. In the end, then, because human nature will *participate* in God's own *modus operandi,* there is no further need for anything that made earthly existence possible.

Since Paul's ending was *after* all had been saved (or transformed into Christ), *then* the Uncreated Logos would transform Its created human nature into Itself. Some people, of course, object to this view, thinking it means Christ's humanity was *absorbed* into the Logos or became, as Gregory of Nyssa put it – like a drop of vinegar in water. These people forget, however, the Logos' humanity was "deified", made divine, and **who knows what a *deified* humanity is**? Since only God knows the reality of human nature, only God knows what its deification is. So rather than useless speculations in this matter, we leave the end to God.

We would suggest, however, that one way the created could "disappear" in God, would be for God to *consume* it, thus making it part and parcel of Its own existence. The problem with the Stoic's idea of the Logos as a consuming Fire, is that once there is nothing left to consume, the Fire Itself goes out – in which case, the Stoic's "Logos" would be no more. But there is another way God can "consume" the created, a way suggested by the "Eucharist" – the heavenly Christ. Like eating bread that becomes part and parcel of a created body, eating God's heavenly manna (the Eucharist) man becomes part and parcel of God's heavenly "body" – the "Form of God" was Paul's term for the Logos. **The Eucharist is not man *consuming* God, but the divine Logos consuming man.** Could God actually do this? Is there anything God could not possibly do?

One thing we know, God is not eternally *stuck* with anything created, and if everything ends up being *eternal,* this is the next thing to *being* God anyway. God, after all, is the only eternal life there is, the only *true or real existence "that is".* If man got his existence from "nothing" then the only place he can "go" is back to nothing. All things, however, get their existence solely from God – there is no "other" *Existence*. And since no one knows *how* God creates anything, or *how* the Logos became Incarnate, then we should not expect to know *how* Christ and all creation can *become* the divine Logos – after all, one mystery is as good as another. **All we need know is that *however in the end it goes for Christ, this is how it goes for all men.* So if in the end Christ's human nature is consumed by God, then so be it for every human being.**

The bottom line is that this whole issue is basically meaningless. The revelation of Christ is everyman's eternal oneness with God, and if all *become* Christ, and then God *consumes* Its *own* human nature, there will be no one left to even think about it! So if beyond transformation into Christ, the "end" is the Logos' consummating human nature so

God (Trinity) will **"Be All"**, then ***So Be It*** – **no** one will be around to give a care!

A NEW CHRISTOLOGY

The New Testament view and understanding of Christ is *not* premised on God as Trinity. It was only when the early fathers grappled with the *mystery of Christ,* the Trinity emerged as necessary for a true understanding of Christ. So what is most remarkable about the early development of the understanding of Christ, is how the Trinity, almost of Itself, emerged as an essential requirement for this understanding. Obviously, it is not Christ that reveals the Trinity, rather, it is the Trinity that reveals Christ. If the Trinity was not strategic for this understanding, the Trinity can be taken (and has been) as merely a way to deify the man Jesus. This is why, without an *experiential* recognition of the Trinity in one's own life, It remains little more than a theological construct, a so called "mystery", imaged and spoken of as three discrete beings – more especially, two anthropomorphic beings.

The stated premise of this book has been the impossibility of having a true understanding of Christ without *first* having a true grasp and understanding of the Trinity. Thus one must first recognize the Trinity in his *own spiritual life* before he can ever come upon the place of Christ in his life. To think one can know Christ first and *then* know God (Trinity), is not how it works or can ever work. Those who think "God" ("Trinity") and "Christ" mean the same thing, miss them both and know neither God nor Christ. It is only in light of the Trinity one is poised for the revelation of Christ as the true nature of his (and everyone's) eternal oneness *with and in the Trinity.*

So one problem with the present day Christology is its purely *theological-intellectual* approach that attempts to account for the Trinity, but which, in truth, can only be recognized by man's distinct (different) triune revelations and *experiences* of God. Prior to this *personal encounter with God* no one really cares about his eternal life with God anyway – and why should he? It is only *after he* encounters God, he then questions his eternal life with God, at which point he is poised for the revelation of Christ as *his eternal life with and in the Trinity.* This is why there can be no true understanding of Christ without first being able to identify man's **triune experience(s) of God.** As it stands, however, given the "proverbial party-line" rendition of the Trinity, no one could ever recognize the Real Trinity, nor, consequently, the real Christ.

It is well to remember that neither Jesus, John, Paul or their disciples, understood "Christ" in Light of the Trinity. In Judaism the "Spirit" (and/or "Logos") was God's *created medium* in creation, and never regarded as God. This fit Paul's view that Christ was the "Spirit made visible", whereas for John, it was the "Logos" that "became flesh", in-

carnated. It seems even after John's Gospel appeared, the "incarnation" was premised solely on the *Logos,* and *not* on the Trinity. But any Christology based solely on the Logos goes no further than accounting for the *material body* of the man Jesus, and *not* man's complete human nature.

Pages and pages could be quoted where the view of the Trinity is presented as three individual entities or beings – beings of the same essence, of course. This view or way of speaking of the Trinity – especially "father and son" as individual beings – is so pervasive, it makes one wonder if the writer (some authoritative theologian) really thinks the Trinity **is,** in fact, three *individual entities.* Even though we are constantly assured God is not three beings, yet the theological language seems incapable of reflecting this truth. This is why man conjures up images of the Trinity as an old man, a younger man and a dove. Father and son are *consistently* spoken of as if they were two discrete individuals, even two *embodied* beings. As it stands, the proverbial language of the Trinity only *abets tri-theism.*

The Real Trinity, however, also brings up the true nature of the eternal *union or oneness* of God and man. That the immanent *essence* of God is *eternally* united to the *essence* of human nature can *only* be a union of the *whole Godhead (Trinity)* with man's *whole human nature.* Thus the "incarnation" cannot be only a union of the Logos with the physical body or "flesh", but rather, an eternal union of everything God **is** with everything man **is** – *a union of essences or natures.* There is no union of "parts to parts", no union of man solely with the Logos as if It were separate from the Spirit's oneness with the soul – and all being *in* the Transcendent. That the union of *natures* or *essences* is *only in* and *with* the Logos' hypostasis, is not even possible. There is no such thing as being united with only "one" of the Trinity and not the others. Yet the proverbial *language for Christ* is that *only* the body or *flesh* is united to God (Logos.)

The reason we cannot say Christ is the "*in-carnation*" of the Trinity, however, is because neither the Spirit nor Transcendent have any *existential* union with *matter* – with the *physical body,* that is. God's *existential union* with matter or the body is solely the prerogative of the Logos, *not* the Spirit or Transcendent. That only the body is united to the Logos, however, does not account for the rest of human nature. It is because the term "*in-carnation*" only applies to the *Logos* we have been handed a view of *Christ's humanity as just a physical body (flesh) united to God.* A ***wrong*** view of *human nature*, however, can only promote a wrong view of Christ. No true understanding of Christ can be based solely on the Logos, but must be premised on the entire Godhead. As the eternal oneness of God and human nature, Christ's place (and man's own destiny) is *centered in* the Trinity and *not just* in the Logos.

So one obvious deficit in the proverbial understanding of Christ is the consistent, unrelenting reference to Christ's humanity as no more than a *body or flesh.* No Christology *was ever* premised on Christ's human nature as an authentic, whole human being – no different than any other human being. Though we are assured God's humanity was a human *soul* ("*psyche*" in Greek), this admission is a mere formality with no evidence of having any impact on any Christology, theology, doctrine, or understanding of Christ. From the beginning to this day, at least 95% of all references to Christ's humanity are solely to his body or flesh. Even the Eucharist is regarded as solely the *flesh* or *body* of Christ; and Paul, referring to the end-times, says everyone will be "one *body*" in Christ's *body*. Although writers tell us what the fathers meant by "flesh" or body, was a total human nature – body and soul – there is no evidence they ever understood an "individual" human soul. Even the Antiochenes, who insisted against the Alexandrians that Jesus had a human soul, consistently refer to his "flesh." It seems their understanding of a soul went no further than "*life* of the *body*", which did not include the faculties of the soul – the will, mind, consciousness or subject (self-identity.) After all, plants and animals have a "soul" defined as "life". Certainly man's "soul" is more than the life of a physical body!

Apart from a physical body, however, Christ's human nature is treated as if it were totally deified, divine, "taken over" by God – or even as God Itself. No one familiar with the language of the party-line or theological-speak, can miss this fact, it is everywhere. While everyone "assumes" Jesus had a "rational" soul, no authentic account is taken of this whatsoever. **Always, Jesus is just the *visible material body* of God**.

A possible explanation for this is that, apart from the Apostles, neither their disciples nor Paul ever knew the man Jesus. Thus the understanding of Jesus was not premised on a living human being, but on a man now living a heavenly, glorified life with God. This Christology, however, leaves a chasm between the reality of man's earthly existence and his eternal or heavenly existence. No one can relate to man's heavenly eternal, transfigured and glorified human nature in God – for who honestly knows what that is, or how it goes? Until man *gets there*, he'll never know. If, however, man cannot relate to Christ's earthly *human nature no different than his own,* then he has missed the very purpose and revelation of the Incarnation. Christ revealed everyman's earthly journey to God and his eternal destiny in and with God.

Another reason that may account for the narrow, literal understanding of "in-carnation" as "flesh", is that John's use of "Logos" was the Stoics' notion of the Logos as the "*soul*" of the universe, Its *material* manifestation being Its "**body**". So this view may account for why some of fathers assumed the Logos was the **divine *soul* of Christ and that his *body*, was Its "*visible manifestation*".** Though Paul tells us Jesus was as human as ourselves, "*like us in every way*", he also says he based his Christology *not* on the man Jesus who he **never saw "*in the flesh*"**, but based his faith on the *resurrected, glorified* Christ revealed to him. Obviously, no one's faith rests on someone they can see and know "in the flesh" – thousands of people saw the man Jesus – but instead, rests on the divine Christ as "revealed" to them. Thus, like Paul's revelation, the early fathers' Christologies were premised on the eternal *heavenly* Christ and not on the *earthly* existence of the man Jesus – who they never knew or saw. This may account for why, apart from "flesh", no true human being is recognizable in their Christologies. Though affirming Jesus was a complete human being, yet this is not reflected in their language, creeds or doctrines, nor, seemingly, in their own mind-sets. As said before, they had no real grasp of an "individual soul" such as every human being is created, a human soul with all its faculties no different than anyone else's.

With regard to the genesis of the "individual soul", we have gone over the false belief held at that time, that there was but one original universal soul passed on via the male seed from one generation to the next. Aristotle compared this to "passing on the flame of life *from one candle to another*". Though Judaism believed God created Adam's soul, it did *not* believe God created ***every* individual soul – created just as innocent and unflawed as that of Adam.** (God, of course, cannot create "flawed" or "sinful" souls.) One of the most overlooked revelations of the Incarnation was that God *alone* creates *every* individual soul One-on-one – just as God created Jesus' own soul One-on-one. For both Jew and Gentile, however, whatever the genesis of the *first* human soul, it was from this *original* soul that all subsequent souls were generated. In the case of Judaism, however, all generations were thereafter tainted with Adam's fallen soul. It is because Jesus had no human father from which to acquire a "fallen soul", Paul likened him to the first, original (sinless) soul God created – a "second *adam*" ("mankind" in Hebrew.) From here, it was but a step to the notion Jesus' mission was to restore man to the soul's *original* sinless state – which Paul linked to the Judaic "purifying rite of baptism".

There was also the view, since God alone created Jesus' soul and was one with it, his soul had to be different from the rest of mankind.

Where some thought God took the place of his soul, the Alexandrians believed God was the sole agent or subject of Jesus' soul – God literally "possessed" Jesus' soul. Add all this to the Platonic view that the universal soul of man was divine, and we have the format for all the early Christologies. Given these facts, let us go over some of the problems inherent in a Christology constructed on these aberrant beliefs.

1. Since God alone creates souls One-on-one, souls are not "hand-me-downs" – no human being creates a soul or passes theirs along.

2. Since God cannot create sin, no soul is created with sin. (The idea man can inherit, or even be tainted with another's sin, is too bizarre for words.) Man is not born with sin, but with free will. How man uses this freedom, *alone* accounts for sin, accounts for all the evil man knows of – because *he does it.*

3. From Paul onwards, all Christologies were premised on the belief Jesus was the *only* sinless human being ever born – the rest of mankind was born with sin (apart from Adam.) Thus it was assumed Jesus' human nature was *different,* a human nature so elevated it couldn't possibly be like that of another human being. While sin can certainly affect human nature, it does **not change** it. If sin actually changed human nature there would be no possibility of reform, which we know is not true. **The truth that no man is born with sin, however, would certainly have changed Paul's, and all subsequent, Christologies.** There is no underestimating the implications of Jesus' sinlessness for Paul and the fathers – indeed, the whole of Christianity. According to Paul, without sin, what would "Christ" mean to most Christians?

4. Another Platonic view Paul adopted was the notion that *flesh* was responsible for all man's problems – sins. Thus in taking on flesh, Paul says God "*made him sin*". (Notice, Paul says "*made him*" – created him.) The flesh, however, has no mind or free-will, it is innocence itself – a dead body cannot sin, only the soul's free-will can sin. It is how man uses or abuses his body that can be sinful. Paul's Platonic view, then, totally ignores the *soul's* free-will as responsible for sin. Man's blaming the body for sin, however, is all but proverbial – and Platonic. Like the devil, the body is another scapegoat for man's refusal to accept responsibility for his willing, thinking, and evil doing. The problem of sin is on the soul, not on the body. It is because of this false Platonic view of the flesh, however, Jesus' sinless flesh or body

was given all precedence, and his soul's free-will *given none.* (There was a big fight over whether or not Jesus even had a human will – the heresy of *Monotheletism* or "one will".)

5. Since God created the human soul of the man Jesus no different than that of any other human being, what God had to supply in the Incarnation was only the body's *physical genes* – such as every human parent must supply. Mary, of course, supplied her own as well. This *fleshly, genetic factor* is the very meaning of "*incarnate*" – **genes, of course, belong to the *flesh* and not to the *soul*.** So the miracle of the Incarnation was God supplying a father's genes – **God literally being the *biological* father of Jesus.** That God created a human soul was no miracle. As said, one of the *revelations* of the incarnation is that ***God alone creates each human soul*** – which was *not* the belief at that time. This fact, however, has been totally overlooked as a major Truth God revealed in Jesus' miraculous conception – God alone creating every individual soul, *no human father or mother involved whatsoever.* What parents supply are the physical genes, whereas life, existence, being itself, all come directly from God and not from the parents.

6. So while the biblical understanding "*the Logos became flesh*" (*incarnation*) accounts for a physical body, it does not account for a soul. That a divine *Form* (or *Soul*) took on *flesh* is a Platonic view. This is why the biblical saying "*became flesh*" raises the question of whether the Logos united itself *only* to the flesh or to a human soul as well? (For a Platonist, of course, this would have been inconceivable.) The fathers, however, in their creeds and formulations changed the biblical saying "*became flesh*" to "*became man*", this way, a human soul could be included – and rightly so.

7. But this still leaves us the deceptive, misleading word "*became*" – the Logos *became* flesh or *became* man. Now anything that *becomes* something else ceases to be what it was. Thus if a tree becomes an animal, it is no longer a tree, if an animal became a man, it is no longer an animal, so too, if God *became* man, It is no longer God. It goes without saying, however, God did not, cannot, *become* anything or anyone. There is no place in monotheism for the **Uncreated *becoming* created** – it's an oxymoron, and none of the fathers believed this. As Cyril put it, anyone who believes God can *become* a human being "*has a deranged mind*". So to say "God *became flesh* or *man*" is blatantly false. **God cannot become what God is *not*, and God is *not* a human being.** The term *became* should be eliminated from all creeds, doctrines and Christologies, the term has deceived enough people already. What is meant by "Incarnation" is God *creating and uniting to Itself* man's human nature. **God never *became* human nature or *became* a human being. *God IS, God does not "become".***

8. Something else the fathers' Christologies never accounted for was the divine Spirit's "indwelling" Jesus' human soul. If he had no soul, then, of course, there could be no "indwelling" Spirit. So if for Paul, Jesus was the "*Spirit made visible*" (in the flesh), then how could the Spirit "*indwell*" in Jesus' soul? For some, the Spirit *was* the divine Soul of the man. This is why, for the fathers, the Spirit's "indwelling" posed the question of whether or not it was the Spirit or *solely* the Logos that was "united" to human nature – more especially, united to the *soul* of Jesus. This was another big issue among the fathers and one that would affect all subsequent Christologies. It raised the question: "Is human nature *only* united to the Logos, or is human nature not also united to the Spirit?" Anyone who referred to the Spirit's "indwelling" in Jesus, Cyril accused of denying it was the **Logos** that was united to human nature. In his view, since the Spirit indwelled in every holy or spiritual person, to say It "indwelled" in Jesus, implied he was no different than some holy soul, or that he was only God's "adopted son" and not his "only begotten" son. So are we supposed to believe the Holy Spirit **did not *dwell* in Jesus?** What nonsense is this? No truth to it at all!

So this was *another* reason why the *soul* of Jesus was put to the side – the Spirit does not "indwell" in the *flesh,* and for Jesus, evidently, not even his *soul!* The Spirit's oneness with the human soul, then, **had no place in the fathers' Christologies.** Christ's human nature could *only* be united to the Logos and *not* to the Spirit – nor even to the Transcendent ("Father".) In light of this view, since the term *in-carnate* is solely a prerogative of the Logos, then Christ could **not** be considered the incarnation of *God* (the whole Trinity), but only the incarnation of the "individual" Logos. Obviously, the term "in-carnation" gives a narrow, limited view of Christ's humanity. **In truth, however, God's *whole* humanity is eternally one with God's *whole* divinity and not just 1/3rd of God's divinity.**

And how about the Transcendent (or "Father")? Jesus, of course, said he was united to the "Father" – not to the Spirit or Logos. The Transcendent is not **in** any man or **in** anything created, rather, all creation is **in** the Transcendent. The Transcendent is literally the Ground of all being. So this is the question: "is man's ultimate oneness with God *only* a oneness with the Logos, or is it a oneness with the whole Trinity?" A true answer to this would yield a **New Christology,** one centered in the Trinity and not just in the Logos. The Logos-Spirit-Transcendent, after all, can never be separated, there cannot be one without the others. Man's complete human nature can never be separated from the complete Godhead – Trinity.

9. There is only *one divine essence or nature* (not three natures or essences), and if human nature is united to the divine nature of the Logos it is also united to the divine nature of Spirit and Transcendent – how could it be otherwise? The divine nature of the Logos is no different from the Spirit and Transcendent, it is only their distinct *modus operandi* that differs. As said, the reason the Logos is the *medium* for the union of disparate natures is because only Its "modus operandi" (*divine mode of existence*) is "existentially" united with matter – the body. Without this "existential" union, nothing created could exist. So it is only *through* the Logos man could come to an "eternal" oneness with the Spirit and Transcendent. Indeed, it is this *initial "existential union*" that the *"indwelling" Spirit transforms into an "eternal union" of God's complete nature with man's "completed" nature.* Christ is the union of man's **entire human nature** with God's **entire divine nature,** and not *just* united to the divine Logos as if the Logos was a **part** of the Trinity. Yet, there exists no Christology that takes any of this into consideration.

And let us repeat, it was *not* the Trinity that became "incarnate" – impossible. As said, it is only because the Logos' *modus operandi* is *existentially* united to *matter* that union with the Trinity is even possible. **The Spirit and Transcendent are never united to matter, this is not their *modus operandi*.** This is also why, when it comes to the immaterial *soul,* we have to look to the Spirit for a more complete understanding of Christ's human nature. And by the same token, look to the Transcendent for the ultimate glorification of human nature **in** God.

10. Some of the fathers regarded the *soul* as the *locus* or seat of the union of the two natures. Where they differed was their understanding of the true nature of the *soul.* Was it the Platonic *divine*, or did the divine "*Form of God"* overwhelm the "human form" (soul) of man? Or was Jesus' individual human soul like every other human being? Obviously there was no agreement on this issue. Of all the fathers, however, there is only one who resolutely denied the soul as the true *locus* of the union of natures. This was Cyril – to his credit – only for the wrong reasons. (Remember, apart from lip-service, he granted the man Jesus no soul of *his own*.) Cyril said the *locus* of this union was not ***in*** any human soul, nor ***in*** the body – anybody. Rather, the union of natures was solely ***in*** God, this was the meaning of his "Hypostatic Union", and in this matter, Cyril was absolutely correct.

To locate this union solely **in** the Logos, however, only accounts for an "existential union" with matter, and to locate this union in the Spirit only accounts for a union with the soul, to locate this union in the whole Trinity, however, is the meaning of "hypostatic union". Obviously we are speaking of "different unions", one *earthly*, the other, *eternal.* While the earthly is *in* man, the eternal or heavenly is *in* God – big difference! As Hilary reminds us, we must not mix up Christ's *earthy life* with Christ eternal *heavenly life*.

That the locus of "hypostatic union" is *in* the essence of the *whole* Trinity was side-tracked when they made the Logos, *instead of the man Jesus,* an "*individual person*" – a discrete being, no less. With this "switch" from a human person to a divine person, the **locus of union** would not be *in* the divine essence or nature of God, but instead, solely ***in*** **the divine *person* of the Logos.** Keeping in mind the difference between *person* and *nature*, how it is possible for two disparate *natures* to be united **in** a *property* of nature – in the "owned" and not *in* the *owner* – who can figure this out? This is not a "mystery", it is senseless.

Christ is the union of natures *in* the *essence* of the Godhead (Trinity) and not ***in*** **any "person".** We know that locating this union in the Logos' *person* was done in order to make the Logos "*who*" (in person) the man Jesus was – but to make Jesus one of the Trinity? **Unbelievable**! *Who,* after all, can think of a "**person"** that is ***not*** **an *individual being*** – *a human being?* No one! But if God is no "individual being" then how can God be an individual "person"? **Impossible!** While Jesus was an individual being, the Logos, neither in nature or in person, is an individual being. It was the switch of persons, however – from Jesus to God – that made the Logos (God) to be an *individual being* – **pure tri-theism!**

We know the sole purpose of the term "person" was to serve as a way to define Christ as "one being", "one entity", "one individual", which is just what "*person*" implies – a single being. The union of two natures, however, does not make "*one person*" or make a *single being.* Many of the fathers complained that Christ as "one person" not only "mixed up" the natures, but tended to make Christ a single nature instead of two – *Monophysitism,* a heresy. But this is how the notion of "one person" opened the door to mistaking a divine person for a human person and vice versa. Mistaking man for God, however, is the meaning of *anthropolatrism*.

Locating the union of *natures* in a divine "*person*" has been the cause of much confusion. Some theologians have even denied the union of "natures" or "essences" – denied human nature could *ever* be united to the divine nature or essence of God. Instead, they hold human nature is *only* united **to** a divine person and *not* to the essence of God – as if a person was somehow independent of its nature! (This is the *ontological switch* from nature to person we have already gone over.) To hold there is only the union of *human nature* with a *divine person,* however, flies in the face of Chalcedon. It is also irrational because person and nature are not a "union". Person is a *property* of nature and not "united" to nature.

Also, according to the fathers, the incarnate Logos was *not* united to any human "person" – because God never created a human *person.* Thus God can *only* be united to man's nature or essence and *not* to any "person". No question, there are elements in Christian theology that defy clear thinking. And there is no use sloughing this off as a piece of "mystical theology" when it actually works *against* any authentic "mysticism". It is because the proverbial Christian party-line does *not* present a true understanding of the Trinity or Christ that Christian mystics – who have seen the truth for themselves – are often regarded as the "odd man out". It is not the mystics who are out of line, but rather, the party-line rendition of Christianity that skews the truth of the Trinity and Christ.

11. That the *locus* of the *hypostatic union* was solely *in* God and not in man, does not nullify the Spirit's being one with the human soul. Since we have said little of the Holy Spirit and Its particular *modus operandi* experienced by man, we might say something of It here.

a.) First, it is not the nature of the Transcendent or Logos to "indwell" in anything or anyone, it is solely the nature of the Spirit to "indwell". Thus the saying "*The kingdom of God is **within** you*" points to the Spirit, not to the Logos. The Logos, on the other hand, is omnipresent *throughout* creation, and can never be pointed to or localized anywhere. Also, the Transcendent, as the "Ground of all being", can never be pointed to or localized – man can never point to "what" he is *in*, he can only point to "what" is *in himself,* and the only divine *within* himself is the Spirit. So man will not find the Logos or Transcendent dwelling "within" himself, nor for that matter, find the *eternal* Christ within himself – as said before, one can only *be* Christ, never one *with* Christ.[1] (To be one with Christ would make *two* human natures,

[1] Christ revealed within one's self is revealed as one's own union or oneness with God. The Trinity revealed within one's self, however, is not only to see and know how the

whereas there is only *one* human nature. That "*all are* **one** *in Christ*" implies *multiple* human natures.)

b.) We know Jesus experienced the Spirit "within" himself. On one occasion he experienced Its "power" go *out* from him – when the sick woman touched his garment. Obviously, the Spirit acts solely on Its Own, *totally* independent of man. The Spirit cured the woman, did all the miracles in fact, for no man governs the Spirit. This does not mean the "indwelling Spirit" was Jesus' sole experience of God or that this Spirit's "indwelling" is all man can know and experience of God – by no means! God's "Indwelling" is but *one* of innumerable experiences man can have of the Trinity. This poses the question of whether or not Jesus regarded his experience of the "indwelling Spirit" as the seat or *locus* of *his soul's oneness with God?* Since no one can answer for another, we'll never know what he thought. What we do know, however, is that most people seem to regard God experienced "within" themselves as the *locus* of *their* personal union or oneness with God. But is this the true *locus* of man's *eternal* union with God, or is this only man's *earthly* experience of union with God? Remember, the mystery of Jesus' death was his experience of God abandoning him – God leaving him, *going out* of him. Since neither the Logos or Transcendent *indwelled* in him, this could only have been the Spirit going out – leaving him. **(Only what can *come in* can *go out*.)** The Resurrection was the revelation of the Logos' eternal oneness with the *material body* or *flesh,* without which, man's *whole* human nature (body and soul) could neither exist nor be *made* eternal.

This tells us that the *modus operandi* of the indwelling Spirit is that of transformer, purifier, enlightener – indeed, It is man's deepest, most dynamic and personal experience of God. The irony is that man's most "personal" experience of God is *not* a "person" (a father or son), but a "Spirit"! No one calls the Spirit "a person" – but then, the Logos and Transcendent are also not "persons" because their nature is also "spirit". When the Spirit's transformation of human nature is complete, It "goes out" – leaves the body – because Its soteriological *modus operandi* (transformative work) is "finished".[2]

---

triune Godhead works in Man, but, how it works in Its *own* inner *modus operandi*.

[2] In man's heavenly *eternal life in* the Trinity, there is no "indwelling Spirit" – because there is no "person" for It to *indwell*. The Spirit only "indwells" in man's *earthy* form as his experiences of God's abiding presence **in** him**self**. Once **in** God (eternal life), however, man's oneness with God is ***in*** God and God is no longer **in** him**self** – in man.

In terms of the Trinity, then, what Jesus experienced *within* himself was neither the Logos nor the Transcendent (those so called "persons", father and son), but rather, experienced *God's indwelling Spirit.* Christology, however, holds human nature was *only* united to the Logos and not to the Spirit and Transcendent. Granted, it is only *through* (or *because of*) the Logos, the Spirit *indwells* in Christ's humanity; yet Christology takes no recognition of this fact. There is no recognition that human nature is united to the Trinity's *divine essence,* and not **solely to the essence of the Logos** – as if the Logos had a *separate* essence!

While all things exist *in* the Transcendent, and the Spirit "*indwells*" as the soul's personal enlightener and transformer, yet the Logos' *omnipresence* throughout existence ("*closer to man than he is to himself*") is the *locus* of man's *eternal* oneness in and with the Trinity. After all, the oneness of body and soul is *only due* to the oneness of Spirit and Logos – in the Transcendent. There can be no "dividing up" the Trinity, in fact, referring to It as a "*unity*", is not really on the mark.

* * * * * *

From what has been said so far, it should be obvious the early Christologies adopted as "orthodox" are not conducive to an honest grasp of the Trinity, and, consequently, of Christ. To account for a Christology based solely on the Logos and not on the Trinity, we should remember that, initially, there was no comprehensive understanding of the Trinity. The philosophical history of the Logos was always understood as Its being one with *matter*, while the Judaic understanding of Spirit was solely Its connection with the *soul* – not with matter. **Thus the soul was the prerogative of "Spirit", and matter or flesh the prerogative of "Logos".** Even after John's Gospel appeared (around 100 or so) and named the "Logos" as the "one" that became *incarnate*, the distinction between Logos and Spirit still was not clear. This lack of clarity is reflected in the fathers' understanding the Logos only became one with flesh, and not also, the Spirit as one with the soul. It accounts for their consistent use of "flesh" when speaking of Christ's humanity, and ignoring the Spirit's "indwelling" union with the soul.

As Luke tells us, the incarnation only came about by the "overshadowing of the Most High" (the Transcendent) and by the "power of the Spirit" coming upon Mary. This accounts for the Spirit's creation of a human soul *in-forming* Mary's *flesh* – Mary's flesh being *already existentially one* with the Omnipresent Logos. Without the Spirit's *informing* the flesh (or matter) with a created human soul, there is *no* human nature. It is the "composite" of the two, body and soul, that is human nature – which *composite*, Aristotle held, was "greater" than its parts. So just as the Logos was one with the body and the Spirit one with the Soul, the "composite" nature was Grounded in the Transcendent – literally one with the entire Trinity, the Trinity being the "composite" of God's *one divine nature*.

Given the early problem of the relationship between Logos and Spirit and their union with body and soul, may account for why Christology has always been based on the Logos taking on flesh (*in-carnate*) with no account of the soul's union with the Spirit. Obviously, what is required is a more comprehensive understanding of the Trinity, and thus, a Christology based on the Trinity, not just on the Logos.

It can be said that up to Chalcedon (451), at least, all the disputes and different Christologies were due, not to any dispute over Christ as the union or oneness of God and man, but to an insufficient grasp of the Trinity. John's view of Christ was solely the *Logos became flesh*, in Paul's view, "*the Spirit became visible*", while Jesus regarded himself as "one with the *Transcendent"* (Father.) While verbally, at least, we have a Trinity here, yet this is a long way from people being able to grasp the Trinity in the immediacy of their *own lives and experiences of God,* and, consequently, in the life of the man Jesus. Without this immediacy, however, or without recognizing how the Trinity works in the life of every human being, there is no possibility of having a true understanding of the real Christ.

In summary:

The reason there is need for an entirely new Christology is because of the number of **false assumptions** on which both the old and present Christologies are based. **Thus no Christology can be based on:**

a) The idea God created one original soul that the male seed passed on from one generation to the next, and that because this original soul fell or sinned, all subsequent souls were born deficient or with sin. **There is no truth to this at all**.

b) Based on this false assumption, because Jesus had no human father, he was regarded as sinless while everyone else was born with sin. Thus it was assumed the purpose of the Incarnation (Christ) was to restore man to his original sinless nature. But t**here's no truth to this as well.** (Since God cannot create a soul with sin, perhaps someone could research to see if he has a *gene* for sin.)

c) Based on the Platonic notion matter was responsible for "individuating" one Universal Form (or Soul) into multiple bodies, and that matter or the flesh "entombed" a divine form or soul, is no definition of mankind. That to *be human* was no more than to be "enfleshed" or an *incarnated* body, implies a radical dualism that defies the human experience. Certainly it gives no place to any *individual human soul.*

d) The idea God ***became*** flesh or *became* a human being **is obviously false**. For the Uncreated to ***be*** or ***become*** anything created is an oxymoron and totally outside monotheism. (Also, God **cannot** "*beget*" God, and whatever God *creates* is **not** God.)

e) Since "*person*" both requires and implies an individual *being*, to say that God is three individual persons is ***tri-theism*** **– false.**

f) Denying Jesus' *human personhood* left the door open to the idolatrous notion he was God-in-person and thus, one of the Trinity – an eternal mode of God's existence. Since no one knows what God as a *person* is, to think the *human person* Jesus is a *divine person* **makes *God* (not Jesus) an individual being or entity.** (Everyone assumes a "person" is an individual being or entity.) **This is why father-and-son as "persons" are treated as individual beings – the worst case of *tri-theism* possible.** But where did people get this idea? It is all in the theology, the proverbial language and presentation of Christianity, this is what people have been taught. Jesus, however, was as *human a person* as ever born in this world. **It is mistaking his human person for God, that is the definition of *anthropolatry*.**

Earlier (in Chapter 17) we went over some of the *wrong turns* made in the early development of the understanding of Christ. The major wrong turn, of course, was applying the notion "*person*" to God – God, after all does not ***own*** a Trinity or three persons; God **is** Trinity and the owner of all It creates which is ***not Itself!*** In this chapter, however, we have pointed out the peculiar mindset and some mistaken beliefs prevalent in the early centuries of Christianity. But how it is possible for informed people today, to stick to some of these old, false, scriptural ideas? **How can any theology or Christology be premised on what is so obviously false**?

Few people realize that promoting "scripture" as the ultimate *Truth* is actually a way to keep man's mind stuck in a B.C. mentality – a totally "patriarchal", masculine mentality. All the scriptural terms and theological assumptions are premised on God, the Logos and Christ, as **males** – to mention but one error. It is not a matter of being "modern", it is a matter of the **Truth.** The bible not only takes people back to a

B.C. mentality, but tends to keep it there hankering after the old, revering the old, seeking inspiration from the old, following old views and rules, sticking to the old as if God had not moved on, as if God was *there* and not *here now*. The bible breeds an antiquated mentality. It is a historical document that incorporates all kinds of false, mythical, and anthropomorphic views of Almighty God. Anyone who takes it at face value will never know the Truth – ever! Scripture is just another mental "box" man must learn to transcend.

Having pointed out the inadequacies of our present Christologies, the imperative need for a new Christology should be obvious. Although this means starting over from the beginning, this cannot be done without knowing the fathers' previous struggles and concerns in this matter. We must learn from them by going over all their pros and cons, disputes and battles, for much that got thrown out should never have been thrown out, and much that was "devised" should never have been let in. **We should also remember, there was a great deal that many of fathers *never accepted* so long as they lived!** To think they were all of one mind-set as regards Christ, is false. Considering their present heavenly estate, however, all would no doubt welcome a new Christology. Being now in eternal life, Christ is no longer a *mystery,* all are now privy to the one True Christ, for such they were destined to *be,* and such they have become.

End Note

Nothing so suggests the need for a new Christology than researching the early development of Christianity's understanding of Christ. Regarding the true nature of Christ, the views presented by the Gospels, Paul, John and their early successors, were never of one accord. While all seemed to agree on Christ's "saving mission", the true nature of Christ, however, was elusive, problematic, even contentious. Despite all the synods and councils of the first five centuries, there was never any agreement across the board. Everyone had their own particular view of Christ, and while some fought for their view, others simply dropped out – or had their works destroyed.

What remains puzzling, however, is exactly *who* wrote up the "final decisions" adopted at the various councils. Those familiar with this background know it is naive to think its views were based on the majority *vote* of the bishops in attendance. We need not go into the political intimidation, coercion and threats often behind these votes – loss of one's bishopric and reputation was always at issue. As one author noted, "*Doctrine often seemed to be the victim – or product – of Church politics and conflicts of personality*". Terrible to say, those who made all the decisions and wrote the documents were the few who wielded the most power; not only as regards Church *authority*, but beginning in the 300's, those who wielded the most power with the Emperor and his family.

What is so inconceivable, however, is how anyone could think the *true nature of Christ* could *ever* be reduced to a *vote* in the first place. That a few people could decide what all Christians are to believe, claim themselves the ultimate authority, is utterly naive, as the early centuries give evidence, it cannot work – has never worked. No truth or belief can ever be premised on the authority "he said or we say" – the human mind does not work this way. To assume everyone has the same mind and understanding is to believe in the "*herd-mentality*". Thus someone talking about *Jesus, Christ, God, etc.* can never assume his meaning or understanding is the same as another – impossible! There are as many different mind-sets as there are human beings, no two can ever be identical. This is why "belief" can only be one's free *choice* and never coerced by any *authority,* or black-mailed by threats of going to hell if one does not believe! *Faith,* on the other hand, is the Presence of God's *Truth-Sensor* in every man, a *Knowing* that can never be intellectually grasped, nor, for that matter, ever be made a matter of *choice or belief.* **Truth is beyond belief.**

The point is that what has been handed down as the "traditional party-line" understanding of Christ, was **not** the result of any *agreement* among those responsible for the development of the "Christology" we have today. For the sake of peace and a semblance of unity perhaps, the language had to be compromised to free everyone (as much as possible) to give it their own "interpretation". This is why, to rely solely on the words and terms of the "party-line" is to become "boxed in", inured in a narrow mind-set. To take it literally, is the next thing to being unconsciously "brain washed" – which can be *tested* by the *fear* of ever thinking "outside-the-box". This is why it is somewhat comforting to know there was never any definitive agreement among the early fathers as to the true nature of the Incarnation or Real Christ. As said before, each had their own understanding, their own Christology, some on the mark, others, off the mark. Yet, it is well to keep in mind that ***Christ*** is the *greatest mystery* ever revealed to man, a mystery so profound one wonders why God ever entrusted this *mystery* to man at all.

The point is that *ideally* a new Christology would be free of any boxed-in narrow understanding of the Trinity and Christ. Just as the Trinity is the summation of all God's revelations to man, so too, Christ is the summation of Man and all man means to God. The Truth of God and man can never be narrowed down to the exclusive prerogative and revelation called "*Christianity*". The revelation of God and Man belongs to nobody, to no particular religion or sect, but belongs to God alone.

EUCHARIST

"The Eucharist is a continuation of the Incarnation".
Irenaeus (125 – 202)

Some people forget that before there were any Gospels and Epistles, even before there were any people called "Christians", the followers of Jesus met together to do the one thing he commanded of his Apostles – "*Do this in remembrance of me*". Following Pentecost, Jesus' Jewish followers met and did as Christ commanded – re-enact their last supper together. They called their little group "*The Way*" and never regarded themselves as other than a Jewish community – the last thing on their minds was to start a new religion. Their understanding of Christ was totally Jewish, wholly within their own religion and its revelation. Since the Jews were already widely dispersed around the civilized world, the Apostles traveled to these communities to tell them about "The Way". There was never a "wholesale" Jewish rejection of "The Way", individual communities simply felt no need to adopt this particular brand of Judaism. But if initially regarded as a sect of Judaism, everything began to change when its particular "way-of-life" became noticeable to the Gentile world. Given the various philosophical-religious sects already in practice, *The Way* attracted some of these Gentiles, and from here, the history of what came to be called "Christianity" began to take root.

From the beginning, however, what was the one, enduring, *central practice* of this new sect? It was *"Do this in remembrance of me*". Everything was built around this one practice, it was the sole reason for "getting together". Around this practice there arose particular prayers, talks, feasts, a whole form of participation (or protocol), what today we might call its particular "rites". All this was in place and practiced *before* the Epistles and Gospels appeared – and at least 60 years before John's Gospel. This "tradition", then, was in effect long before there was a "New Testament". Christianity never depended on any Christian Bible, was never founded on it, never spread or took root because of it. These writings were "after the fact", after the "tradition" had been established.

Nobody, perhaps, can understand the meaning of "tradition" better than the Jewish people. For them, "tradition" is basically on a par with their "sacred" Scriptures. This same Jewish understanding of "tradition" came along with the people of "*The Way*" and was handed down the ages. No one familiar with the early fathers could miss their constant reference to "tradition". Although, personally, I found this somewhat disconcerting and even questionable, nevertheless, it is not only *there,* but remains *here* today. The reason for pointing this out or speaking of this background, is to ask the following question: "*Without* **tradition,** *would there ever have been the religion we know as "Christianity?"*

On what basis did the first followers of Jesus ever decide to get together, to periodically meet, pray together, join their lives, as it were, in a common bond? Was it not to keep alive, to recall and share their "remembrance" of the man Jesus – now, the heavenly Christ? There was no other reason. And how did Jesus tell them to "remember" him – by talking or writing about him, by merely "recalling" past events? He told them *exactly* how to remember him, "*Do* ***this*** *in remembrance of me*" – **do what?** Take bread and wine and repeat his words, "*This is my body*". To do this, to repeat this act, was the sole reason the Apostles and followers came together. This act was the ***center*** of their meetings, everything else was built around it. It was ***doing*** this, Jesus' one commandment – re-enacting his last "supper" on earth – that **was "The Way" – the way of keeping Christ present among them,** and why they called themselves "people of the Way". Without this "re-enactment", there would never have been what later became called, *"Christianity"*. So this was how, why and where, it all got started – by *doing* exactly the one thing Jesus ever told them to do, this was "The Way" *Christ* would be with them *always* – even to the end of time.

* * * * * * *

"*Eucharist*" is Greek for the Hebrew term "*Thanksgiving*", the term used in the blessing of the bread at the Jewish Passover meal. The "Passover", of course, is the central Jewish celebration, a "remembrance" of God's saving his people from years of enslavement in Egypt. The Seder meal, however, is not just any meal or family get-together to read the biblical account, it is actually a condensed "re-enactment" of this deliverance. The only one I attended could hardly be called a "meal", every item had a symbolic meaning and we followed a booklet detailing the meaning behind every tidbit. There were also certain roles people played or acted out. By no means was this merely "recalling" some past historical event, this was a "re-living" of it. In Judaism, to "*remember*" is to "*make present*". One of the best sermons I ever heard was by a Jewish Priest (a convert of course) who told us what "remembrance" meant to his Jewish people. He told us of sitting on his grandfather's lap listening to his dramatic and hazardous account of escaping Czechoslovakia during the Jewish persecution. He heard it over and over to where he could give the same dramatic account as if it had happened to him. In short, he virtually "re-lived" what his grandfather went through, it became part of him, a part of his own history, his ancestry – heritage. So the Jewish understanding of "remembrance" has nothing to do with merely "recalling" some past event, rather it means to *re-live* it, *re-create* it, *make it present*, make it part of yourself, because this is your heritage – literally, where you came from, even, *who* you are.

A major part of this Seder meal is bread specially blessed to become, as it were, God's *own* bread, the *Manna* sent from heaven, not only to save them from starvation, but to nourish their spirits as well. This was *not* ordinary bread made by human hands, but bread from heaven *made* or created by God. It was one thing for God to save them from slavery, but another to save them from sure death. There can be no underestimating what this gift of God's "Manna" meant to the Jewish people, it was literally the "means" by which they lived to tell the story. It is only against this background of Judaic history one can understand what the term "*remembrance*" meant to the Jews, to Jesus and the apostles at their own Passover meal together. When Jesus pointed to the bread – **not to his own physical body** – blessed it and said, "*This is my body*", everyone understood this as the heavenly bread *made by God* sent down to earth by God for man to live by, to be nourished and saved. As the Jewish mystic (Philo of Alexandria) put it, "*The Logos is the divine agent in creation and also the daily Bread from Heaven whereby man's spiritual life is fed.*" The apostles obviously never understood this bread as Jesus' present physical body – as usual, he was speaking of something other than meets the eye. Jesus told them when they *did this*, they were to "remember him" – remember, not the *person* that died and is no more – but rather, the eternal one that arose. Whatever the *heavenly nature* of this Manna, Jesus pointed to it as to the *heavenly (glorified) nature* of his body. This was the "Bread from heaven" God had created to be the *spiritual* nourishment and eternal life of one and all. Thus God's "gifts" of bread and wine came to be understood as the true nature of **Christ's *heavenly body*, the eternal Christ, "*thanksgiving*" ("*Eucharist*") being the term used for the *eternal Christ.***

Jesus never thought of anyone eating his visible, physical body – as he said, "*The flesh profiteth nothing*", "*the flesh has nothing to offer*". His reference was to his invisible heavenly body – i.e., *after* his death, resurrection and Ascension – a transfigured, glorified body, this was the "Bread from Heaven", neither earthly bread nor earthly body. Just so, it is Christ's heavenly spiritual body and soul that gives life and transforms man's earthly body and soul into God's *own* glorified body and soul. "*Just as a little bit of leaven changes all of the dough into itself, so too, that body which was brought to death by God, once it enters into us transforms and changes all* ***into itself*** " (Gregory of Nyssa.)[1]

It seems wine was symbolic of blood, the ancient belief being blood was the *life* of the body, virtually, the "*soul*" of the body – "*The soul of every flesh is the blood"* (Lev.17:11.) Take away the blood and the body is truly dead. In blessing the wine, Jesus' reference to it as *his* blood was a reference to his life-giving soul. Thus, bread and wine, body and soul, is everyone's definition of "human nature", in this case, a reference to the Logos' incarnate human nature that would be "transfigured" and utterly changed with its resurrection and ascension. This same transfigured Christ would become the "Way" Christ fulfilled the promise – "*I will be with you always till the end of time*". Thus, as God's Heavenly Manna, Christ remains with man, not merely as a "Presence", but as bread from heaven to be eaten in order to transform *our* body and soul into Christ's *own* heavenly body and soul. So just as the Seder meal of Passover was central to Jewish life, so too, this same "Supper" would become central to Christian life. This meal was the only *command* Jesus ever gave his apostles, "*remembrance*" being understood in the Jewish sense – to *re-live, re-create.*[2]

From the time of Pentecost, this Eucharistic meal was the heart and center around which all believers gathered, the one "practice" shared in common, and the same maintained down the centuries to this day. All the fathers either speak directly of the Eucharist or refer to it in some form, and from these accounts they obviously believed this to be Christ's presence with them. The fathers had no "theology" of the Eucharist, so there was never a dissenting word about it. Later, of course, theologians would split hairs and pick bones over every word of their descriptions and accounts. If the mystery of Christ – the oneness of God and man – is the great Christian mystery, how much more so the Eucharist? It is incredible that Christians can claim to understand the Incarnation (and believe it) and yet have no understanding of the Eucharist (and don't believe it.) The two mysteries, however, cannot

---

[1] The Stoics would have seconded Jesus referring to his body as the "manifest" Logos. Recall Zeno striking his breast and saying "*This is the Logos*!" That Jesus held up bread and said, "*This is my body"* (the *manifest* Logos) would not have fazed a Stoic. While the Apostles were not Stoics, their converts would be. In this case, however, it was *Jesus* who said it, and not Zeno.

[2] This brings to mind Paul's reference to Christ as a "new creation" – Christ *re-creating* everyone anew.

be separated, there is only one Christ, and to know the mystery of one is to know the other – no difference whatsoever.

It is my view that initially, the Apostles' re-enacting the last supper was done with its Judaic understanding in mind. They never had in mind what today we think of as "transubstantiation" or a miraculous change in the very *essence* (or *substance*) of the bread and wine. What they gradually came to *experience*, however, were its *effects* on them, that in some way they knew – and perhaps *experienced* outright – Christ's "presence" with and in themselves. It was in the actual doing and receiving that this occurred, an *effect* that went beyond their initial intent of merely bringing Christ to mind or keeping his memory alive. This was bringing Christ's *Presence* right into their midst, a wonder they had not expected, nor could have ever conceived of. By sharing their *experiences,* however, they came to realize that what they had in hand was not just bread and wine, but the living *presence* of Christ – in them, with them, among them. There is nothing Jesus ever said or did that so cemented their faith in Christ as this. No longer an earthly, but a heavenly *presence*, Christ remained with them, *in* them.

While the term "transubstantiation" might be one way to put it – to satisfy the intellectuals – there is no way to explain "how" God does anything. When we think about it, the whole universe is one big miracle, everything being the "effect" of an Uncaused Cause. Yet *the Cause is* ***in*** *the effect,* and just so, God is the Cause and Christ the *effect* – the "Eucharist" effecting and transforming all who receive It.

Who most succinctly defined the Eucharist was Irenaeus (125 – 202), "*The Eucharist is a continuation of the Incarnation*", i.e., the divine Logos *becoming incarnate* in all of us, deifying our body and soul into its own heavenly and glorious estate. The fathers also noted how this transformation takes place by the power of the Holy Spirit – just as it happened at the incarnation. Thus to become *what* Christ is, everyone undergoes Christ's same incarnation – first God *unites* all to Itself by the *Incarnation*, and then, "*deifies"* all in the *Eucharist*. The fathers regarded the Eucharist not only as the deified heavenly Christ, but the "means" and "Way" man is transformed into Christ.

The incarnation, then, is not a one-time event, but how it works in every soul. The Eucharist recapitulates the Incarnation in that the same way the Logos became incarnate is the same "way" everyone becomes Christ. "*It is no less a feat to* ***give*** *things their original nature than to* ***change*** *their nature. If God can change bread and wine into Christ's heavenly glorified body, so too God can change our own body into Christ's heavenly glorified body"* (Ambrose, d.397.)

So just as the original Incarnation occurred, so too, the divine

Logos – already *existentially present* in one and all – by the power of the Spirit *becomes* incarnate in man, transforming human nature (body and soul) into *Its own* glorified human nature.

Augustine explains it this way – just as the ordinary bread we eat is transformed into our body, in similar fashion, when we eat the Bread of Life, we are transformed into Christ's Body. It is not we who "consume" Christ, but Christ that consumes us – transforming and incorporating our human nature into Its own glorified human nature. Distributing the Eucharist to others, St. Augustine is reported to have said, "*Receive what you are to become*", a truth so tremendous who can believe it? Just as bread becomes inseparable from the body, our body becomes inseparable from Christ's heavenly body – a body, however, that is not Christ's *historical* body prior to death, resurrection, and Ascension, but Christ's transformed, glorious, transfigured, heavenly body. As to how God could make anything "created" become eternal or one with the Uncreated, the only way is for God to "consume" the created, incorporate it into Itself. This is just what the Eucharist reveals, the "How-To" of God consuming and transforming man's nature to become part of Itself, and even, share in Its Uncreated life – the Trinity. [3]

It has been said Irenaeus is the first father to say "how" bread and wine *became* this glorified Christ, he says, "*We offer to him the things that are his own, consistently announcing and confessing the unity of flesh and spirit. For as the bread taken from the earth, when it* ***has received the consecration from God,*** *is no longer common bread but is the Eucharist, which consists of* **two realities, earthly and heavenly,** *so also our bodies, when they receive the Eucharist, are no longer corruptible, but have the hope of the resurrection into eternal life.*" While Irenaeus uses the term "consecration", earlier than this, however, Ignatius (35 – 110) used the term "transmutation", and Justin Martyr (100 – 165) said the bread was "eucharized". For Tertullian it was a "re-presentation", a "making present" of the incarnate Christ, while others used the term "transformation". Although there was no standard vocabulary, all believed the bread and wine had become Christ's living presence.

For Irenaeus, this "*consecration from God*" was likened to the incarnation when the Logos, by the "**power of the Spirit**" took on human

---

[3] In one of his letters to me, Fr. Raimundo Panikkar (a renowned theologian, recently deceased) wrote: "*The mahayana tradition* (of Buddhism) says, '*If you see the Buddha, kill him!' My Christian translation is: 'If you see the Christ,* ***eat*** *him!' What else is the Eucharist? He disappears in us!*"

nature (in Mary.) So too, by this same *Power*, bread and wine takes on the *glorified* body and soul of Christ. Where, in the incarnation the Logos *took on matter and "appeared" in human form*, in the Eucharist, the heavenly Christ *takes on matter and "appears" in the form of bread and wine*. Thus the Logos, present in all creation was in Mary *prior* to the incarnation, it was by the *power of the Spirit*, however, the Logos took on Mary's flesh and became incarnate. Just so, it works in every man – the Power of the Spirit transforming the Logos in every man into God's *own human nature.* This is the "way" the Logos becomes incarnate in everyone, the same mystery as the original incarnation. It is from this point of *union* man goes forward to Christ's same end – death, resurrection, ascension – literally, a "*recapitulation*" of Christ's life from beginning to end.

It is important, then, to remember the Incarnation was effected by the transforming Spirit – "*the Spirit will come upon you*" – and that it is the Spirit that *effects* this transformation, just as it did in the man Jesus. The Eucharist, then, is both the Logos *re-creating* and uniting human nature to Itself, as well as the Spirit *effecting* this transformation, all being **in** the glorious Transcendent. So just as the incarnation was on the part of the whole Trinity, so too, man's Eucharistic transformation is an act of the whole Trinity. The Eucharist, then, is the incarnational means or "way" man's transformation works, the end being body and soul (human nature) ultimately transformed into Christ's same heavenly Eucharistic body and soul. As someone said, "*a divinized Christian is a living Eucharist*". Indeed, the Eucharistic Christ ***is*** man's *final heavenly estate.*

For Irenaeus, the Eucharist was the only basis for a true understanding of Christ – ***"Our way of thinking is attuned to the Eucharist, and the Eucharist in turn confirms our way of thinking".*** Thus, if one's whole understanding of Christ is bound up in the Eucharist, one will know the Real Christ. The Eucharist not only confirms Its own truth, but confirms man's Knowing It. The mystery of Christ **is** no different from the mystery of the Eucharist, to know one is to know *the same one*. Any other approach to understanding Christ is purely conceptual, theological, philosophical, biblical, hearsay – and so on. But throwing all this aside, one need only "**attune**" himself to the Eucharist and one will know the Real Christ. The reason the Eucharist is the *way* of knowing Christ is because **It is** the heavenly Christ.

We have already gone over the fathers' dilemma trying to find a way to present and define Christ's dual natures as "one" Christ – one being, one individual, one nature, one person – yet none of these worked, they only promoted Monophysitism, tri-theism – created an ontological can of worms. The answer, however, was with the fathers all the time. All knew the Eucharist as the "one Christ", the Eucharist being the true, perfect and *only* presentation of the *oneness* of Christ's dual natures – body, soul and divinity, this is the *One Christ* – the Eucharist. All theological-philosophical speculations fall away in the presence of this one and only Christ. Though re-*presented* millions of times over, yet it is ever the same *one* Christ – same *one* Eucharist. When we think of the centuries of disputes, accusations, animosities and exiles, yet, the *one* heavenly Christ was with them all the time!

If everyone heeded Irenaeus' – *"Our way of thinking is attuned to the Eucharist, and the Eucharist in turn confirms our way of thinking"* – they would find the Eucharist has a way of resolving all the issues regarding the real Christ. Any resolution apart from the Eucharist is solely conceptual, a matter of interpretation, a piece of someone's theology and thus, forever disputable. The Eucharist has a way not only of resolving all issues concerning Christ, but one will find there the answer to all man's perennial questions. Just as the Incarnation answers all man's proverbial questions as regards God, man, and their relationship, so too, the Eucharist answers equally profound questions. Let us give a few examples:

1. The great philosophical question was finding a way to account for how the one could become many, and the many could be become "one". Thus, how could *one universal* human nature become innumerable *individuals*? The Eucharist is the answer to this quandary – the one *universal* Eucharistic Christ multiplied infinitely. The many *individual* hosts being the one same *universal* Christ. And then reverse this, if the same "One" is many, then the many are the same "One" – the One Christ, that is.

2. How is it that the "real" actually "appears", and yet, what appears is not the real? What appears is no illusion, but truly exists – it could *not* exist were it not *real*. So how does this work? The senses are only capable of apprehending what *appears* of the real, this is as far as they go. It takes the "eye of the soul" to see the *real beyond the senses – beyond* what only *appears.* So while what we see with the senses is *not* "It", yet, in reality, it **is** "It". Just so, in the Eucharist all the senses see is bread and wine (only what *appears*), while in reality, beyond the senses, It **is** the great Reality. The Eucharist thus illustrates how what the senses see *is,* in fact, the very same Reality they *do not* see.

It seems some theologians believe there are two Christs, one "*visi-*

ble" in heaven, the other, "*invisible*" in the Eucharist. Hearing of this, Gregory of Nazianzus would have added this to his list of absurdities – the way people have *split up* Christ (see his quote on p. 146.) There is only one Christ, the same "*on earth as in heaven*".

3. So "where" is this place we call "heaven"? We know Christ "ascended into heaven", thus "where" Christ is, is "where" is heaven. Because heaven **is** Christ's heavenly dimension of existence, the Eucharist is "where" heaven is – right here and right now.

Since Christ was *not* visible on earth – as Jesus said, "Christ" could *only* be *revealed* by God – and since man's sensory eyes are incapable of "seeing" Christ, what makes one think Christ is *visible* in heaven? It makes no sense. (Who can "see" the eternal *union* or *oneness* of God and man?) Here again, people are hung up on the idea heaven is some "physical, sensory, place". God, however, cannot be confined to any physical *place*, nor can Christ. The Eucharistic Christ informs us *heaven* is not a "place", for "where" God **is, is** "where" God and man *are eternally one.* Thus the Eucharist – Christ's heavenly glorious state of being – is "where" heaven is, heaven being a *dimension of existence* beyond space and time. So **just as in the Incarnation the Logos came *into* space and time in order to "appear", so too, in the Eucharist, the eternal Christ now "appears" *in space and time* as bread and wine.** But if *sensory objects* take up "space", *spiritual realties* do not – cannot. The Eucharist, then, is God's way of informing man that the Reality of what only *appears* is actually beyond space and time. Thus the Reality of the Eucharistic Christ that "*appears*" is actually beyond space and time. That this Reality belongs to God's *eternal dimension (or state) of existence,* this **is** "*heaven*" – closer to man than he is to himself.

Following the resurrection, all the apostles saw was a *sensory* body, not Christ's transformed spiritual body. So too, in the Eucharist, the *senses* only see bread and wine and do not see Christ's eternal, transfigured body and soul. Yet, the Eucharist is Christ's same resurrected spiritual body, the same Christ in the here-and-now with man, in this earthly life, as the source of his spiritual nourishment and transformation. Hilary refers to the Eucharist as our *assumption* into Christ – "*We are assumed in Him, just as the fullness of divinity is present in Him, so we too are filled in Him.*" Like most of the fathers, Hilary made no distinction between what is true of Christ and what is true of every human being.

4. The Eucharist is a revelation of the ultimate transfiguration of

man's body and soul, literally his heavenly estate. Thus his body will be transubstantiated just like the elements of bread and wine, and just as bread and wine "appear" unchanged to the senses, so too his body will "appear" unchanged to the senses – even though it has been totally transformed into Christ, no different from Christ. No one knows the **essence of matter nor has ever *seen* it,** yet, it was this very essence of man's body that, in the Incarnation, God eternally united to Itself. This is why the whole mystery of creation, the universe and man, is "summed up" in Christ, literally summed up in the mystery that **is** the Eucharist. The Eucharistic Christ actually reveals how all this works, *works beyond all appearances,* works to reveal man's eternal life with God. Indeed, the true nature of the Eucharist ***is*** man's eternal life in God.

5. People often ask if Christianity has any "technique" to offer that enables man to both know and become one with God? Are there teachers to show us the way? What can we *do* to be transformed into Christ? In short, exactly what does Christianity have to offer in this matter? Strictly speaking, it has nothing to offer but the Eucharist – Christ Itself. The Eucharist is the sole "technique" or "Way" Christianity has to offer, it is the teacher and transformer, the "means to the end", the Alpha and Omega of Christianity. This is the living Christ, the "way" God works in the here and now, and the only "Way" Christianity has ever had to offer.

An interesting phenomenon of the Eucharist is that one can either focus *outward* on the Eucharist – Christ's *presence* in the Blessed Sacrament – or, on receiving the Eucharist, one can focus *inward* on Christ *within* oneself. To focus inward is to focus on the presence of God *in* oneself, whereas to focus outward is *to be* ***in*** that Presence. Where in the former, we seem to encompass God – like the temple housed the Ark – in the latter, however, it is we who are encompassed by the Presence – even, *pervaded* by it. So these are two very different ways the Eucharist works – **God's Presence within us, or we, in God's Presence.** Strictly speaking, of course, Christ cannot be "contained", rather, it is Christ that contains us. But however we think of it, the Eucharist is the only "technique" God ever revealed to man. [4]

So keep in mind this heavenly bread is not a symbol of anything,

---

[4] Interestingly, the controversy called "*Iconoclasm*" or "smashing images" (725 – 843) outlawed all images of Christ **but** the Eucharist, which alone, it held, was appropriate to "venerate". The come-back was that the Eucharist was **not** an icon or image of Christ, but was, Itself, the Real Christ.

but is a *living Presence.* While the mind can focus on a symbol, it can never focus on a *Presence*. A Presence not only radiates, but engulfs, this is the meaning to be ***in** the Presence,* and this Presence is *what* the Eucharist is. The bread does not "contain" God – nothing can "contain" God – so too, the bread does not "contain" Christ, rather it is Christ's Presence that contains the bread. Though man experiences God *in* himself, he certainly does not "contain" God! Like God's *omnipresence* in the cosmos, the cosmos does not "contain" God, rather, God contains the cosmos.

Some people have mixed up the "Eucharistic Christ" with what they call the "Cosmic Christ", but the two are not the same. Where the cosmos only has an *existential oneness* with the Logos, Christ, however, is *not* the *eternal oneness* with the elements, but a oneness with man's entire *human nature.* While God's oneness with the cosmos is beautiful and uplifting, yet what is that to man? Man is not the sky, the sea, a flower or a frog. The "Cosmic Christ" doesn't address man's unique life and human condition. The Eucharist, however, does this, addresses One-on-one every *human being's* oneness with God. Man is not transformed into the sun or stars, but into Christ's glorified *humanity*. The Eucharist is the heavenly *incarnate* Christ, body and soul that through the Holy Spirit, transforms the essence of human nature into God's *own* **incarnate human nature – Christ.** So while the omnipresent Logos is throughout man's whole being, this cosmic Logos is *not* the *incarnate Christ.* The Eucharist is more than cosmic, it is God's eternal oneness with mankind.

6. Something else about the Eucharist, is the way it *equalizes* all human beings. God doesn't care *who* one is, whether Pope or a despicable human being, Christ is the same for all and "belongs" to no one. Christ not only levels the playing field in *this* world, but in the *next*: heaven, eternal life. There are no "levels" of Christ, no "holier-than-thou's", no first, last or middle class, no hierarchy, no "*who's-who*" – no differences across the board. There is only one Christ and all will *be Christ* – no more, no less.

7. And what is this thing called "eschatology"– "last things" or Christ's "second coming"? How can Christ come again when Christ is already here? It makes no sense. This notion is for people who think Jesus is sitting on a throne on some planet waiting to fly back to earth. The Eucharist, however, contradicts this whole idea. Transcending all time and space (heaven as some physical place) Christ is ever with us here-and-now, and not *waiting some place* to be "with us". Obviously,

only those who do *not* know Christ is already "with us" are the ones who are "waiting". God, however, waits for no one; so those waiting around for Christ have already missed Christ completely.[5]

No Oneness with Christ

It would seem that according to the traditional party-line, the Christian goal is to become ***one with*** Christ, or ***one in*** Christ. But what, exactly, does this mean? How does this work – or *does* it work? Let us see:

1.) If the term "Christ" means "God", then oneness with Christ would mean oneness with God – which is what it means ***"to be" Christ*** and not one ***"with" Christ***.

2.) So too, if someone thought the man Jesus was God, then to be one with Jesus would also mean to be one with God – a **oneness *that is* Christ and *not* a union *with* Christ.**

3.) If, on the other hand, someone believed *Jesus was a human being,* then the notion of being one with another human being would *not* be a union with God – since God is not a human being – but a union in which there is no God and no Christ! And as to being one with a particular *person* – say the historical Jesus – this would be two persons with the same human nature and no divine nature to speak of. (The man Jesus had no divine nature.) That the *same* human nature can be a "union" of two persons, is inconceivable.

4.) If, however, "Christ" means the oneness of God and man – God's divine nature united with man's human nature – then how could one human nature *be one with what it is already*? Impossible! There is no such thing as a union of *two human natures* – because there is only "one" human nature. Given Christ's dual natures, to be one with Christ would make a threesome – the Philosopher's *"Third Man"* – one divine and *two* human natures. (No such thing as two human natures.)

5.) If one thinks there is a difference between the essence of one human being and another, then "*Christ*" would be the union of God with different human natures. In this case, there would be countless,

---

[5] Vatican II changed the Mass so that right after the consecration – when Christ became "Present" – everyone was to say "*Christ has died, Christ is risen,* ***Christ will come again***". Now how can Christ **come *again*** when Christ is already with us ***right now*?** It makes no sense! I have never recited this, but regard it is a statement of *unfaith*, of *unbelief* in Christ's true presence with us **right here and now**. (Probably this is where some theologians got the idea of two *living* Christ – one in heaven and one on earth.)

innumerable "Christs" – as many Christs as human beings in fact! This is not, however, the *revelation of Christ.* There is *one* God, *one* human nature, and the eternal *oneness* of the two is *one Christ.* All this is pointing out is the *impossibility* of ever being *one with Christ's* dual natures, and why one can only *be or become Christ.*

6.) No man, of course, can be united to **"what" he is to *become* – a caterpillar, for example, cannot be *united* to a butterfly, it can only *become* a butterfly.** So too, man cannot be *united* to **what he is to become – Christ, that is.** No matter how one tries to make a case for it, there is no such thing as "*union with Christ*". That one can only **be or become Christ** is obviously the *Way* God made it to be.

7.) When Paul said "No longer I but Christ lives in me", he did not mean he was united to Christ. With no "I", how could "I" be united to Christ? He also did not say he was **in** Christ or **with** Christ. No, Christ was in Paul as *his* human nature's oneness with God – which oneness **is** Christ. So what the Eucharist reveals is that those who receive Christ are one with God and that their oneness with God **is** Christ. Of course this oneness will further develop and be transformed, for this is the "Way" the Eucharist works to transform all into the eternal Christ.

8.) Keep in mind that Christ's *hypostatic oneness* is *personless*, so if there is no person, "*who*" is there to be united to? **The Eucharist is not a *person* –** either divine or human – indeed, whoever referred to the Eucharist as a "*person*"? No one. And who would think of referring to the Eucharist as a "*him*" or a "*her*"? No one. It is only man's *person-less* human nature that is one with God and *becomes Christ.*

What the Eucharist does, is to inform man he is *one **with God**.* How many people are *seeking* to be one with God yet doubt if they really are – or ever could be? The Eucharist assures all that they are one with God, for the *Eucharistic Christ* **is the oneness they seek!** As said, however, this is not a oneness **with** Christ, rather, it is **man's oneness with God that *is* Christ.** To forget this is to *mistake* oneness with God for oneness with Christ. The saying, "*Receive what you are to become*" is, perhaps, the most profound truth man could ever realize. As difficult as it may be for some to believe, yet to realize this truth is to know the Real Christ, know God's eternal destiny for mankind – which **is** Christ.

So the notion that the Christian goal is to be "one-*with*-Christ" is not possible because it doesn't work – cannot work. Man's oneness with God is neither a oneness with the man Jesus, nor a oneness with Christ's dual natures, it is solely a oneness with God's divine nature. Like the man Jesus ***who was never one with Christ*** – man can only be "one with God". Thus, the Christian end or goal is to be transformed *into* Christ – the eternal union of God with Its one and only *human nature,* this alone *is Christ.*

Something else, if the Christian goal was only to be *one* with Christ, then all one would have to do is receive the Eucharist and the goal would be achieved – simple as that! So what is wrong with this understanding? To *receive* Christ one can say, like Paul, "Christ is *in* me" – not "Christ is united to me" or "Christ and I are one". So, merely to receive the Eucharist is *not the end,* but the "way and means" to the end – which end is to be transformed into *God's* own *heavenly human nature* – no different from Christ.

There can be no "union", then, with *Christ's human nature* – no different than one's own – there can only be a union with *Christ's divine nature* (*God.*) It is this union that transforms one's human nature into *God's own* human nature. It is only *after* one's *own* human nature is one with God's divine nature that one can then go forward to be transformed into *God's **own** glorious, human nature* – this is how it works. No one can be "united" to either Jesus' human nature or Christ's dual natures, he can only be one with God's divine nature. To honestly understand Christ, then, is also to understand the impossibility of being united ***to*** Christ and why one can only *become* or *be* Christ.

To say **"there is no such thing as being united to Christ"** pretty much flies in the face of the proverbial party-line understanding that people have been given. Always we hear we are one *with* Christ, united *to* Christ, one *in* Christ and so on. Yet all this is impossible – there is no such thing as becoming one with *what* one *is to become.* Nor is it possible to be one with *what* one is already – human nature, that is. (Remember – there is no such thing as different human natures, there are only different persons!)

So even though we constantly hear about being united **to** Christ (and I certainly would not anathematize this sincere but mistaken desire), this is not how it works. The reason this is difficult to understand is because self – a particular person – is always getting in the way. Remember, *God never united Itself to any "person" or any self, but only to human nature.* This is why it is a mistake to think it is **we**, **ourselves** "***who***" are one with God, for "*that*" in man one with God is not one's self (his own person), but is no one in *particular* – Christ, that is. It takes a particular revelation, however, to see that "**that**" in man united to God, is **not** one's self, but is the **mystery of *Christ.***[6] Only God

[6] A major *revelation* in the Christian spiritual journey is the revelation that the true nature of one's union with God ***is not himself, but is Christ*** – *a* revelation I have good reason to believe is not rare.

knows the true essence of human nature, and it is this unknown *universal* nature that is one with God. If one could only understand it is not **his** human nature (or person) that is one with God, they could also understand why it was not **Jesus'** human nature or person that was one with God. The one universal human nature God created and united to Itself was not the human nature of this or that human being or person. The point is that it is not we *ourselves* (me, myself and I) *who* are one with God, rather, *Christ alone is man's oneness with God. Christ, being no person* – not even Jesus, Mary or Joseph – is man's one, universal *personless* (hypostatic) union with God.

So it is not Sally, John or Jesus' human nature that is one with God, but **God's** human nature that is one with God. Miss this "difference" – between somebody's human nature and God's human nature – and you miss Christ completely. God's oneness with man is *personless* – no persons or selves (divine or human) have any place in this eternal oneness. This is why, to understand the true nature of *Christ* is to understand the true nature of every man's oneness with God and why no one can be one **with** Christ, but can only ***become*** or ***be*** **Christ. In truth, *man has no other oneness with God than Christ.***

The Eucharist, then, informs man he is one with God. Yet how many people are seeking to be one with God yet doubt if they really are – or ever could be? The Eucharist assures all that they are, indeed, one with God. While this is not a oneness with Christ, the Eucharist is a *oneness with God that is Christ.* As mentioned, the saying, "*Receive what you are to become*" is, perhaps, the most profound truth man could ever realize. As difficult as it may be for some to believe, yet, to realize this truth is to know the Real Christ – this is the way the Eucharist works, or how God makes it work.

Perhaps we could explain man's transformation this way. As man comes from the hand of God, his human nature is *existentially* one with the Logos. It is from here – his existential or essential union with God – he begins his transformation into Christ – the Eucharist being the Logos' "**incarnating**" in man. Just as in the Incarnation it was not Jesus' *own* human nature that was one with God, so too, the Logos' incarnation in every man is not one's *own* human nature, but *God's own human nature* that is one with God. So it is not "me, myself or I" who am one with God – a particular person or human being – rather, it is solely God's *own* incarnate human nature one with God. The Eucharist, then, is not only the Logos becoming incarnate in man, but transforming man's human nature into *Its own* eternal human nature. This is how, in the end, man's human nature *becomes* God's own glorified human nature – eternally one in the Trinity.

The Eucharistic Christ, then, is simultaneously the "way'' this transformation works, it is both the Way and, in the End, *what* all will *become.* While the Eucharist is Christ *present* both within and without (man), this "Presence" does not constitute any eternal union or oneness *with* Christ. The Eucharistic Christ is the *means* by which God *first* effects an abiding oneness with man's *own human* nature, and *thereafter,* begins the transformation into *God's own* incarnate human nature. Needless to say, this transformation will entail a radical change in human nature itself – but then, man was created to become *more* than he is now. This becoming *more* is a transformative process that has no "quick-fixes". This is not the place to go into this process, we are only pointing out how the Eucharist works to make this a reality. We could even say **this is what the Eucharist is all about and why God made it so.** One way or another, it seems God is determined **to be** All in All!

So in the end, then, it is not ***we*** (some *person* or other) ***who** become* Christ, rather, it is solely man's common **human nature** transformed into **God's *own* incarnate human nature** – this oneness of natures *being* "Christ". While Christ is the image of God in man, the Eucharist, however, is no "image" but the Reality Itself. Once transformed into this Reality, there is *no image* of Christ, there is solely Its Reality.

The Eucharist, then, is the revelation of man's *end* – the definitive end of his human journey. The Incarnation is but the beginning – after all, there can be no "end" *before* man has lived the human experience. Had God revealed the Eucharistic Christ at the *beginning*, no one could possibly have understood it – witness all the disciples that left Jesus over this "eucharistic" issue. And not only these disciples, but much of Christianity debunks the "bread and wine" as a mere symbol, a kind of ritualistic "remembrance". Somehow their Christian "Faith" never included the Truth God reveals in the Eucharistic Christ. The Eucharist is actually the final estate of Christ's glorified, transformed human nature in its eternal oneness with and in God. So too, the Eucharistic Christ is the end estate for every human being – one Christ, one eternal human nature one with God in the Trinity.

So the Eucharist is not only the principle or *means* of transformation, but the *end* itself – not only the Alpha and Omega but the "Way" between. While in his earthly life Jesus *pointed* the "way" to God, now, however, it is the *heavenly Christ* that **is** the "Way". The Eucharist imparts a knowledge of Christ quite apart from anything said or found in the gospels. While the bible only recounts three years of Jesus' "public" life, the Eucharist is the *living Christ with us now* – and not the historical man who lived 2000 years ago. One of the early

Popes remarked that we are more fortunate today than in Jesus' historical life-time, because then, only few people knew Christ, whereas now, in the Eucharist, Christ can be known by everyone.

While the Eucharist seems utterly "other" than *what* man is *now*, yet it is the *same* human nature, only ***not* the "human nature" man knows *now*.** Nothing we know of man's nature *on this earth* is recognizable in the Eucharist because no one knows the *essence* of man that God united to Itself. But whatever its essence, we know the Eucharist as man's ultimate *essence* united eternally to the *essence* of God. The *mystery of the Eucharistic Christ* is not only the true nature of man's oneness with God, but the mystery of man's *final heavenly estate.*

In Truth, the mystery of Christ is bound up in the Eucharist, and so too, the mystery of man's final oneness with God. While the cross is the fitting icon of man committing his very *existence* to God, the Eucharist is the icon of the glorified "person-less" Christ – man's final oneness with God. The Eucharist is not only Christ's promise to be with man always, but the fulfillment of the whole purpose of the Incarnation – that all may be eternally one with and in God. As one of the fathers put it – "*We shall pass from the grace of faith to the grace of vision when Christ will indeed transform us into himself*".

A Personal Note:

Preparing for First Holy Communion (age 6 or 7), I would always recall a priest telling us "*the Host only becomes Christ after you consume it*". I do not recall the context, but his words stuck. Since we had been taught the Eucharist was *already* Christ, what did he mean it only *became* Christ *after* we received it? Although I had no knowledge of Christ, yet, because I already knew God and knew God was **no human being**, I decided the Eucharist **was** God and that I provided Christ's humanity. Thus, put together – me and God – this is *what made* the Eucharist "Christ". Though I certainly never thought this made *me* Christ – I couldn't figure Christ out – yet I definitely experienced the Eucharist as the "*Presence of God*" which, for me, was enough. Even later, *after* Christ had been revealed, my initial understanding of the Eucharist never appreciably changed.

APPENDIX I
CHRISTIAN ONTOLOGY

The concern of "*ontology*" is not *that* some "thing" exists, but *what* it is that exists, what is its essential or real nature. It is also the inquiry into what causes a thing to be what it is and how things differ according to genus and species. What are called "ontological categories" are the basic divisions into which everything can be divided – its major divisions: being, element, plant, animal, and human natures. Although God transcends all possible ontological categories, yet the existence, essence (or nature) of God, has always been the object of inquiry.

What we want to point out in this chapter is the difference between a Platonic and Aristotelian view of man and its impact on Christology. The difference between the two would bring about another strategic "switch" from the earlier more Platonic understanding of Christ, to the much later medieval understanding that would come to dominate Christology. From medieval times to this day, all orthodox Christologies would be premised on what the Scholastics regarded as Aristotle's view of man. So just as the general mind-set at the time of the early fathers was basically Platonic, the medieval mind-set of the Scholastics would become Aristotelian. This, then, was another of those "switches" that can be pointed out when chasing down the devolution of Christianity into a Jesus-cult.

It would be possible to divide Christianity into two major Christologies – that of the early fathers and the later medieval group called the "scholastics". It is because the Eastern Orthodox Church adheres mainly to the early fathers its Christology is regarded as representing a more *mystical* understanding of Christ, and the Western Church, the more *rational* or *intellectual* understanding. Although both share more in common than not, yet with different backgrounds, their theology of Christ and the Trinity is presented quite differently. While we do not want to go over the pros and cons of their differences, we must make clear the early fathers were not students of philosophy such as we find in the later Western Church. In the Eastern Church, if one did not know God, the Trinity or Christ *experientially,* then they could not be regarded as authentic "theologians". Thus, if one does not, himself, *experientially* know God and Christ, then he really should not say anything.

To recognize this "switch" from the original understanding of Christ, however, would entail some knowledge of these two philosophies and their ontological view of reality. Where Plato presents us with a broad based *universal* as the ontologically real, Aristotle narrows it down to the *individual* as the ontologically real. **Thus Christ, origi-**

nally regarded as "*Universal Man*", is narrowed down to being an *Individual Man* – Jesus, that is. This was a big switch. As to how the ontological reality of "*being*" went from Plato's *universal* to Aristotle's *individual* was by defining "*individual*" *as* "*person*". Aristotle, of course, never defined *individual* as *person*, it was Christianity that *used* Aristotle to back up its own idea of *person*, give it some philosophical rationale – or cover its tracks, we might say. This is why they latched onto Boethius' definition of "*person*" as an "*individual*" being.

While the fathers had no immediate concern with the philosophical notion of "ontological being", this concern turned out to be the result of their centuries of disputes over the true meaning of the term "*hypostasis*" – and in the West, the term "*substance*". Was this a reference to the *one* nature (essence) of God, or a reference to the Trinity as *three particular individuals* – three "*persons*" as this would be defined? Is the Trinity "*what*" God is, or is the Trinity "*who*" God is? As a result of this dichotomy between nature and person, swords were drawn on both sides.

It could be said the major concern of *scholastic philosophy* was to find some philosophical rationale to underpin or prop up its doctrinal dictums and beliefs. Although the Eastern Church scoffs at Western Scholasticism – as so much intellectual confusion – do not think for a minute the East did not take anything from it. It is quite possible to show how Aristotelianism impacted the East, show what the East took from the scholastics that it would have been best to reject. In the era of the fathers, Platonism and Stoicism were the leading philosophies, this was the *educated* mind-set in which their understanding of Christ took root. It would be a thousand years before the Scholastic Aristotelians took over the Christian "mind-set" we have today. What is unfortunate, however, is those who write the history of the early development of Christian thought and doctrine, consistently rely on the present day Aristotelian rendition of it. It could be said this is a deliberate attempt to eliminate any possible "Platonic" understanding of Christ as a ***universal*** in order to make Christ solely one ***particular*** man – Jesus, of course.

It has been said that in the early centuries, Aristotle's works – namely "*Physics*" (much later re-named "*Metaphysics*") and *Psyche* (later re-named "*De Anima*" or "*The Soul*") – were virtually unknown. Yet, there is no evidence for this. Given the religious fervor of the times, Aristotle's works simply had nothing to offer. He had no impact in the early centuries taken up with Plato and Stoicism, he was renowned as a scientist and logician, not as a metaphysician. It remains a mystery why his original book titles were changed, because everything he wrote of any "metaphysical" significance can probably be reduced to ten pages or so. Like everyone else, however, he has undergone various translations, and like everyone else, there is no end to various interpretations. There can be no question, however, when Western Christianity discovered Aristotle in the 12th century or so, he was given a Christian understanding, and this, of course, is our sole concern. So what we want to point out here, is another one of those major theological (or Christological) "switches" that came about with the discovery of Aristotle, a *change in the ontological definition of man.*

Taken from Boethius' *rendition* of Aristotle's definition of man as "*an individual substance of a rational nature",* the Christian ontological definition of man became "*person*". Thus the essence of man or "what" man is, is now a *person* – a person who owns (or has) a body and soul. So the switch is from the ontological essence of "what" man is (human nature) to "who" a man is – *a person.* This, of course, is Boethius' definition of man and *not* Aristotle's. Concern with "who" some particular individual or *person* is, was not part of the Greek agenda, and looking for any philosophical back-up for the much later Christian notion of "person", is a waste of time.

To pinpoint this ontological switch – from nature to person – let us go over Aristotle's basic view of "things". For him, nothing had any **real or actual being** that was not *embodied* in matter, or could not be verified, first and foremost, by the *senses.* He debunked Plato's "Idea" of the existence of a *divine universal Form (soul)* in which *individual* forms "*participate in some exemplary Form that constitutes its perfection*" (Plato.) Aristotle debunked this because Plato's *universal* was not *materially* embodied, thus its very existence could *not* be verified by any sensory data. He also debunked Plato's notion of "*participation*" – a term that had great meaning for the fathers and, indeed, for the whole of Christianity.

Aristotle did not deny the existence of a human soul, but until it was embodied in matter, it only had "potential" existence as a human being. For him, *real being* was neither matter nor soul, but the two as a single "unit", a *concrete* individual. In his own words – "***the unit (individual) is something whose essence it is to be one.***" The human genus, however, is more than the sum of its parts, for the *union* of its two substances (body and soul) makes it a "*third substance*", this third substance being *a composite of the two.* As to just what this third substance is, Aristotle doesn't say. All we know is that it is the result of a *union* of two different substances – matter and non-matter (soul.) So the nature of man is a composition of "three" substances – body, soul, and a mixture of the two. "*If then, **matter** is one thing and **form** is an-*

other, the ***compound*** *of these is a* ***third****, and both matter and form and the compound are substances"* (his own words.)

For Aristotle, *substance* is always a universal – as he says, "*substance means a* ***one and a "this"*** *as we maintain"*. Since everything that exists is *one individual thing*, and everything *is* a substance (without which it could not exist), therefore, **"that"** a thing is, is **"what"** it is. **"What is meant by "individual" is a "numerical one"** – a physical, "numerical one*"*. So while "***matter only has the potential for individuality*"** it was **"*form* (soul) *that gave matter its actual or real existence*".** Where, for Plato, "matter" was the *cause* of "*individuation*", for Aristotle, it was "form" ("soul" or "psyche") that was the *cause* of individuation. His reference to an "individual", then, is neither to *just* a material substance or *just* an immaterial substance, but to the composite of the two, which composite he calls a "unit" or "individual". A human being, then, is a composite of matter "in-formed" by a rational form or soul. That Aristotle does not separate the existence of a thing from the essence (or nature) of a thing, pinpoints the major difference between his and Plato's understanding of "**real**" being. Thus:

Plato = "that" a thing is (exists) is **not** "what" it *really* is.
Aristotle = "that" a thing is (exists) **is** "what" it *really* is.

As this regards the ontological reality of man, for Plato, man's *real* nature was a *universal* (divine) soul ***minus*** a material body, for Aristotle, it was an *individual* soul ***plus*** a material body. That **"*the unit (individual) is something whose essence it is to be one*",** means "what" man is, is an individual "unit" of body and soul – a unit that, in his view, can *never* possibly be separated. So instead of Plato's soul being some eternal *universal,* for Aristotle the "soul" is solely one **embodied** "individual" – a "*numerical one*". It was not just matter alone, however, that was a "numerical one", rather, it was the form or soul that was – *universally* – **a "numerical one".** The only reason man is always an "individual" being is because it is the *nature of the soul* ***to be*** *one* – the **same** one soul however. So just as Plato held to one universal soul, Aristotle held to one *universal* ***individual*** *soul.* Strictly speaking, there is no *real* difference whether the soul is a *universal* one or *universally* one "individual", either way, there is no getting away from its *universality*. As to "where" this "individual soul" came from, **Aristotle tells us it comes from one's own father!** For Aristotle, it is the father's *same one original soul* that is handed down from father to offspring, one generation after another – like **"*a flame passed from one candle to another*"** (his own words.) Nothing really "individual" about

Aristotle's "soul", it is the *same one individual soul* as one's father, grandfather – on down the line.

He tells us what he means by "soul" is "life", the nature of which is "active movement". "Form as the principle of life is the primary actualization of a natural organic body, and the type of soul or form makes some organic body "what" it is, gives it its essence". Soul (form or psyche), then, was actual being and the cause of the body's life and movement. He definitely gives priority to essence or "what" something is over its material existence – that "the **actual** is prior to the **potential**" means the soul (or form) is actual being, whereas matter only has **potential** being. The essence of man, then, is actual life even prior to being a physically embodied "individual" – which is not too different from Plato's view.

So for Aristotle, the soul is the ***cause*** of the body, and as to where the soul comes from, he tells us – "*A father begets a "such" out of a "this", and when it has been* ***begotten*** *it is a "this such".* ("*Such*" means ***what*** something is, "*this*" means ***that*** it is.) *The begetter is of the* ***same kind*** *as the begotten (****not****, however, the same* ***one in number, but in form)****"* – his own words. Thus **human beings are multiple in number, but one in soul.** The soul a father begets is not a *different* soul, it only has a different body. Fathers, then, hand down their souls "*like candles passing on the same flame candle after candle".* The *flame* or soul is the same, it is the *candles* (bodies) that differ. The *flame,* of course, does not make or create the candle, on the contrary, the candle is created for the *flame.* And what other function does a flame have but to **burn** something? If there was nothing to burn, there would *be* no flame. And we know, of course, what happens when the flame consumes the candle – the flame goes out! As to the origin and cause of the first or *original soul,* Aristotle logically chased this down to a dead-end where he had to admit the existence of an "Uncaused Cause", an "Unmoved Mover" – this is what started everything going.

That there is only one soul passed down from father to father – from Adam to Cain on down the line – means every soul passed on is the *same one soul.* No new flame was lit, this was a father's same flame, same life, same soul, it only lit a new candle. **So there are multiple candles, but only one flame.** As said, however, if the soul is no different from that of the father, then despite the "multiplicity" of bodies (candles), this view is not appreciably different from Plato's one *universal soul,* and in places, Aristotle even intimates the existence of one ***original*** (individual) *universal* soul. While *quantifying* material bodies is no problem, quantifying immaterial souls (or any soul) has always been a philosophical problem.

How to get from a *universal* to the *particular* – from the "one" to the many – is the proverbial philosophical problem, and the difference between Plato and Aristotle (universal and individual) is just an example of this. In a Christian context, this was the same problem the fathers confronted in their understanding of whether "*hypostases*" referred to the One essence of God, or to the *individual distinctions* in the one essence. How were they to explain that in the Incarnation "*the Logos assumed man's* ***universal*** *human nature, yet a nature that appeared (was seen) in one* ***individual****"?* The relation between the One (universal) and the many (individuals) is **a** problem that can be found in all man's philosophies and religions.

Given the prevailing belief that a father *begets* the soul of his offspring, we can understand why the Incarnation – where *God* (and not a man) was the *biological father* of a particular man – would be hard to fit into either Aristotle or Plato's paradigm. At best, for Plato the Incarnation might be the revelation of the *Original Universal Soul* as the divine *Image* of the *One*. For the Stoics, the "Incarnation" would be the manifestation of the eternal Logos "*embodying*" the whole universe. (The Stoics regarded the Logos as the "Soul of the Universe".) For Aristotle, however, God-the-father could only *beget* his *own same soul,* thus, just as a *human* father begets a *human soul*, so too, a *divine* father begets a *divine* soul – and do not think for a minute this was not the understanding of the some of the fathers, i.e., God took the place of Jesus' human soul!

Unlike Aristotle, for Plato, material existence was not the essence or reality of anything. All "*individual* things" were impermanent, ever changing, material objects of the senses, they were mere appearances, dim shadows of some immutable essences or intelligible realities (*forms* or *ideas*) the true knowledge of which, could only be known through intellectual cognition and *never through the senses*. For Plato, whatever man knows or learns via his senses is no more than "opinion", whereas only the intellect has true knowledge of the "real". (The senses, remember, only apprehend material, physical things, they know nothing of anything immaterial such as a *soul*.) At best, he says, "*single objects only "participate" in some exemplary form (or soul)"*. Plato only granted *real* being to essences – his divine Ideas or Forms regarded as "*Images*" of the *One*.

For Plato, then, everything that existed was a copy or *image* of some perfect Form or archetypal ideal. Thus all men were images or "shadowy" copies of one original Form. Plato's view that the eternal Form of man was an "image" of the "*One*" (or "*Good*") had a special meaning for the fathers. Not only was man "*made in the image of*

God", but the divine Logos was referred to as the "Image of the Father" and man was the image of the *incarnate* Logos – Christ. For the fathers, then, Plato's original and perfect Form was Christ – "*the Form of God*" as Paul put it – and everyone made in Its image was the image all human beings were created to be or become. All the fathers' Christologies incorporated this Platonic view of the *Universal* Christ, every individual to *become* this incarnate image of God – Christ. Thus it is no *one individual* that is Christ, but rather, everyone's true *original* nature or image ***is*** Christ – no place in this scenario (*image*) for any "individual identities".

For Plato, then, the one "original human soul" or "Image of the One", was the divine archetypal Form of every human soul. Entrapped in a physical body, however, it is only a shadow or image of Itself, which man must *know* in order to get out of the shadow – recall the cave-man coming out into the sun light. As to how this divine Soul could ever be "entrapped" in a physical body, in his view, it was due to man's *ignorance.* Man is entrapped by his ignorant senses, lives by his senses instead of by his higher intellect, thus he mistakes material things for the Real. In contrast, Aristotle placed great store on sensory data, but then, he was a scientist, not a metaphysician. (Anyone who relies on sensory data for any abiding *reality* is not, in my view, a "metaphysician".) For him, anything you *can't* see has no true existence – after all, how could one know the existence of anything if it was not embodied in matter? Why believe in something you can't see? While he did not deny the existence of an immaterial form or soul, yet without a body it only had "*potential"* existence – potential reality.

In this matter we might remember Aristotle's affirming that the union of body and soul (two different "substances") results in a "third substance" which, he says, is "greater than its parts". It would seem Christianity took this "third substance" to mean a "*subsistent*", a *person*, and thus the union of body and soul results in a *person.* This, however, would not make *person* the ontological reality of man, rather, it would make *body-soul-person* the ontological reality. (Without body and soul there couldn't be a *person* anyway.)

Some have compared this triad to Paul's – and the fathers' – belief that man was a composite of *body-soul-spirit*, making the case that "*spirit*" **is** the *person* made in God's image. Others have made the case that body-soul-spirit is how man reflects the Trinity – and, indeed, it is too bad the Incarnation was not premised on the Trinity instead of solely focused on the Logos.

While Aristotle affirms the soul has *actual* existence whether embodied or not, yet it does not constitute *human nature until* or unless, it takes on a body. This poses the question of what happens to the soul when the body dies – without a body does the soul have any eternal existence? Evidently not! Solely by themselves, neither matter nor form (soul) have *true being,* only the *composite* of the two has real human existence. Aristotle said that if anything in man survived death it could only be "***another kind of soul***".

He says – "*But nothing is yet clear on the subject of the intellect and the* ***contemplative*** *faculty. However, it seems to be* ***another kind of soul****, and this alone admits of* ***being separated, as that which is eternal from that which is perishable****, while it is clear from these remarks that the other parts of the soul are* ***not separable****, as some assert them to be, though it is obvious that they are* ***conceptually distinct***".

For Aristotle, then, neither body or soul are eternal, only "**another kind of soul**" – the "*contemplative faculty*" – is eternal.[1] As to what this faculty "contemplates", it was the "*Uncaused Cause*", "*Unmoved Mover*" – it contemplates the "***One, the supreme object of all knowledge and the ultimate object of all desire***". He also tells us this *One* eternally "contemplates Itself". Evidently, Aristotle's "other soul" – the one that contemplates God – was *not* included in his *ontological reality* of man. To this, Plato, however, might say, "*that*" in man that contemplates God, **is** God.

Actually, to *contemplate* the "One" was considered the highest goal a gnostic or spiritual person could attain. In Christianity, this might be why "heaven" is regarded as a "Beatific Vision" – the contemplation of God. For Aristotle, however, there is no eternal form or soul, no eternal body – no *eternal human nature.* The only thing eternal in man is ***another kind of soul*** that can eternally contemplate God. Although he links this contemplative *faculty* to the intellect, yet he says it is ***separable*** from the intellect. So while there is nothing eternal about the intellect itself, somehow this *other* contemplative *soul* or faculty is *temporarily* linked to the intellect and is all that survives man's ontological being – since **there is nothing else eternal about man.**

Needless to say, the Scholastics were not too happy about this, but then, they were not contemplatives. Their interest in Aristotle's "faculties of the soul" must have come to a rather abrupt end when (according to Aristotle) these faculties all died and ceased to exist. Aquinas, of course, made Aristotle's "other soul" to be the highest point of the in-

---

[1] It was not possible to find the origin of Aristotle's (384 – 322 B.C.) understanding of "*contemplation*". In the mystical sense it meant "*the partial or complete identification of the knower with the object of knowledge and the consequent loss of one's own individuality*". As we know, "*contemplation*" became a central tenet of Christian spirituality and remains so to this day.

tellect, *a passive intellect* – though he treats the whole intellect as eternal.

It was a mistake, however, for Aristotle and Aquinas to link this "contemplative soul" to the intellect for there is nothing "intellectual" about "contemplation". The *contemplative* faculty is not only *beyond* reach of the intellect, but the intellect actually gets in its way. **"Contemplation" is not an intellectual activity, it is just the opposite.** But at least Aristotle granted there was *something* in man that was *eternal* – since nothing else he defined as *human nature* was eternal – only man's "contemplation" of God is "saved". So where did Aristotle's *human nature* or "*numero uno*" end up? Nothing left but the contemplation of God! Really, not a bad ending.

Because Christians did not believe in Plato's "pre-existent" soul, they would say the soul existed in the "mind of God" prior to its being given concrete reality. Thus Meister Eckhart tells us we must get back to where we were before we existed – back to the mind of God, that is. The "mind of God" was Plotinus' *nous* – the intellectual principle and first emanation of the One. This *nous* was equivalent to the Logos that the fathers referred to as the "only *begotten* Son of the Father". Both Origen and Plotinus regarded the *nous* (or Logos) as "eternally generated" from the One. Thus the Logos, as God's Wisdom or divine *Knowing* is the "mind" of God, and "to get back to the mind of God before we existed" would mean getting back to the Logos – "*to have the (*same*) mind of Christ*", *to be* that of which man is only now an image.

Needless to say, there is no way one could make a case that Plato or Aristotle would ever have agreed with the Christian notion of "person" as the true essence or nature of *anything* – or that it had any *real being*. Aristotle even tells us why not – "*Bare matter", he says, "underlies essence or form, and the complete individual underlies **accidents***" – i.e., quality, quantity, place, characteristics, properties, etc. He says the reason these "accidents" or "properties" cannot define true being is because *"no universal attribute is a **substance**, this is plain from the fact that no common predicate indicates a "this" (*existence*), but rather a "such" (*essence or "*what*".) *If not, many difficulties follow, especially the **third man***". In other words, since no property (such as *person*, say) **is a substance** (or of the *essence),* then it cannot constitute the ontological reality of anything. To hold that a mere *property* is an ontological essence is the dilemma he calls the "*third man*" – a logical paradox, an unthinkable proposition.

This "third man" (*tritos anthropos),* however, is interesting. The attempt to pass from one *thing* to another, or even relate one concept to another, there is the necessity of a *third* intervening thing. We might put the dilemma this way: how can an attribute, characteristic or *property of a substance be, or ever become,* the *what or* substance of *that* (a thing)? To make the case that a *property* or *characteristic* **is** an ontological reality there would have to be some intervening "thing" that transforms it into the essential substance. In Christian terms, where body and soul are ***substances***, yet a *person* or *subject* **is not a *substance*** and thus, cannot constitute any ontological reality.

A better example of a "third man", however, is Plato's belief man *"participates"* in the *essence of the "One".* Aristotle debunked this view – a view, however, that would take on a particular meaning for the fathers regarding the soul's ultimate "participation" in God's divine nature. As to how, or to what extent, the soul "participates" in the divine, no one spelled out – to my knowledge, even Plato never spelled it out. Aristotle dismissed the idea because to "participate" in something would require some kind of *third* intervening party, in this case, a **"third man" – one that is neither God nor man**. To pass from one thing to another necessitates a "third" *intervening* thing to make this "pass– over" possible. After all, if man *was really* God, then how is one to account for *man*? Whatever could "intervene" between man and God would have to be a "*third man*" – and who can imagine what that would be? So "third man" indicates some necessary "intermediary" or "bridge" between man and God. In the light of Christianity, it would be hard to find a more beautiful understanding of Christ – the "intermediary", the "bridge" between God and man. Christ is truly the unknown *Third Man* – indeed, Christ **is** God ***and*** man.

Since, for Aristotle, only a composite of body and soul constitutes the ontological reality of man and that the *two can never be separated,* it would seem the Christian belief in a body's *resurrection* might confirm his view. **But not so!** As we have seen, for Aristotle, there was nothing eternal about body or soul. When the flame (soul) has burnt up the candle, when there is nothing left to burn, the flame goes out. For Plato, of course, and more especially for the Stoics, this was an "*Eternal Flame*", one that had no beginning and no end.

The problem this created for the Scholastics, however, was not Aristotle's view that body and soul were *not* eternal or could never be separated – after all he was not a Christian – the problem was their view of human nature as a "person". (Remember, person was a *property* of nature, which, according to Aristotle, cannot constitute any ontological reality – because it is not a *substance.)* But if body and soul are separated at death – which Aristotle *never* believed – what **becomes of the *person***? Aquinas held that since the soul alone did *not* constitute a complete human being or *person,* then after death there could be no "persons" in heaven. Only when the soul's former body was restored (resurrected) would someone be a complete person. The only *persons* presently in heaven with a resurrected physical body are Jesus and his Mother, and until the resurrection, no other *person* is in heaven – *because human nature* is not complete without a physical body. Where Paul and the fathers regarded Jesus' resurrected body as a "spiritual body", according to Aquinas, this is false. Until the resurrection, the souls in heaven are "not all there"! This means that the *souls* presently in heaven are totally person-less, *subject-less, self-less,* no "I am" or self-identity whatsoever – **actually the Truth of things!** So there is no use praying to St. John, Peter or any saintly person, because *he* is not there yet – nor is Aquinas himself. Only when everyone is resurrected can anyone in heaven be *identified* – **be a person.** This is the conclusion one gets when making *person* the *ontological reality* of man *instead* of *human nature* – no **real** human beings in heaven yet! (This has to be the last *straw* on Aquinas' theology.)

Aquinas' obvious implication is that heaven can only be on some *physical* planet, one big enough for trillions and trillions of *material bodies.* God help us! But this is what we get when "person" is taken to be man's ontological reality. But if the *soul* already in heaven is eternally enjoying the *Beatific Vision* – which is the Christian orthodox belief – then what could a material body add to this? Why would a body be necessary when the physical senses cannot see God anyway?

In this matter Aristotle said something interesting. Material substances, he said, not only had the *potential* for actuality, but the "***potential to change, to be in a more completed state***". So what might this *more completed or final state* be? Apart from God, nothing begins without an *end,* so who knows the end God has destined for *matter*? As to its final state, Aristotle held **the true nature of matter was "*unknowable*"** – the same view as those who hold the essence of God is *unknowable.* And who knows the *eternal connection* of these ***unknowables***? The divine Logos, of course, immediately comes to mind. For the Stoics at least, the Logos and matter were never disconnected in the first place. No doubt this is why the fathers regarded the "*incarnation*" as the union of man's *body* or flesh with the divine Logos.

Although all the philosophers regarded some *original* form of *prime matter* as eternal, yet Aristotle agreed with Plato that material substances were not real or "*actual being*". For Aristotle, real or actual being was "active movement" – "life" in other words. So where, for Plato, ontological reality was the *underlying essence or nature* of material "things", for Aristotle, ontological reality did not "*underlie*" anything, but was the "individual unit" (or unity) of matter and form.

Where Plato held forms or universals were *independent* of the material objects that imperfectly manifested them, Aristotle held neither material objects nor immaterial forms were independent, but together, formed the unity of *real* being. Sensible objects, he says, are the *first realities* – as apprehended by the senses – and only after that, via the intellect, can man know the essences (Forms or Ideas) of the "*secondary realities*" – such as a soul.

While Plato did not deny material reality, yet the *essence* of something is **not** what *appears* to exist, rather, it was the essence or *what* does *not appear* that had real existence. Matter was always in flux, impermanent – "things" here today and gone tomorrow – he didn't see any abiding reality in this – but then, neither did Aristotle. For him, the only *eternal* thing in man was his "other soul" – "*that*" in man that could eternally contemplate the One. Both philosophers, however, agreed that all knowledge begins with the senses, and that the intellect gets its knowledge of created "things" via the senses. But while *material* substances were perceived by the senses, *immaterial* substances could only be known when the intellect "was added". So while the senses can affirm something *exists*, only the intellect knows *"what"* it is that exists. As said, for Plato, to base any intellectual knowledge of ultimate truth on any sensory data nets man nothing more than speculation and *opinion* – for him, pure ignorance. To this, however, we would add that no true knowledge of *God* enters through *either* the senses ***or*** the intellect, for *neither* one is the *route* of God's *transcendent revelation* to man.

So let us not pretend we can justify any notion of God or Truth based on man's sensible or intellectual *modes of knowing*. "*That*" in man capable of encountering the truth and reality of God is no known faculty, but "something" that probably doesn't even belong to man, but rather, to *God **in** man*. Thus what we call the "eye-of-the-spirit" is, at bottom, God's own seeing and knowing. That Paul defined human nature as *body-soul-spirit* might account for this mysterious "spiritual" faculty, for in themselves, body and soul seem to lack this capacity. So Aristotle rightly postulated that whatever this faculty is, it must be "*another kind of soul*", a "*contemplative faculty*" he calls it.

As for "person", Aristotle never went beyond genus and species to ponder "*who*" some individual human being might be. As much as he said was: "*To speak of the soul of Socrates or Coriscus* (or Jesus, let's say) *simply means **this particular soul and this particular body,** the **individual is analogous to the universal in its composition***". Since being "individual" is a universal, then reference to Socrates or Coriscus is solely a reference to a ***particular*** individual – a "***person***" according to the Christian understanding of "person". Aristotle's understanding of a "subject" was primarily grammatical – a "subject" could be any "thing" about which something could be predicated – said about or attributed to. Thus the fact Socrates, Coriscus and Jesus are all *particular individuals* do not really differ. It is when *predicating* "something" **about them,** they are referred to as "***who***", pointing to whatever differentiates them. It is pointing out *differences* that defines "who" one is – a person in other words. As for these *differences,* Aristotle put these down to different *physical properties, attributes, accidents, characteristics,* etc. The difference was **not** the fact each was an "individual" human being, but that each candle (body) had different *accidental properties,* characteristics, etc.

Also worthy of note, his understanding was that '*primary substance*' (**sensible matter**) **was the seat of the *subject*** as well as all its individual properties and modifications (changes.) His "secondary substance" – form or soul – on the other hand, *has no subject* – he says **"*the subject is* <u>*not*</u> *present in the form or soul, but only in its embodied material substance*" –** his own words. Thus, because form or soul is *subject– less,* nothing can be predicated of it or attributed to it that is any different from any other soul. This means that anything that could be said about Socrates refers to his *properties,* (*accidents*) and not his individual human nature. A *subject*, then, does not refer to the *nature* of a thing (its *ontological being)*, but to something said about it – i.e., its particular properties or characteristics that are *not* of its essence. **In short, person, subject, "I am", self, is *not* the *essence* of human nature.**

That a "secondary substance" (soul) is *not expressed by any subject*, but only expressed by "primary substance" (a material body) means that a *subject* only inheres in a material substance and *not* in the secondary substance – the soul or form. So, for Aristotle, man's soul constitutes no subject, **is no person, self or I am.** And because no *immaterial essence or form constitutes a subject,* then nothing can be predicated of it. That man's common soul is *subject-less* means that without a material body there is no subject to speak of – no "*who*" to be a subject. So for Aristotle, a human *subject* is mere skin and bones – this is his physical "primary substance" or some individual "thing".

Interestingly, references to consciousness, self-awareness, or even the term "self" (or "ego") are never mentioned by the ancient philosophers. It seems self-awareness is never taken into consideration in their philosophies, but taken for granted as the "thinking mind". Even today, the theological outline of the faculties of the human soul give no consideration to man's self-awareness, consciousness or self, which is why "thinking" that a *subject* or *person* ("who") constitutes ontological reality, is so fallacious. Existence (of anything) does not depend on "thinking" or a "thinking subject" (person.) Those who think so are only putting *De-cart* before the horse.

Aristotle says this: *"The act of thinking cannot be the best of things. Therefore it must be **itself** that thought thinks (since it is the most excellent of things) and its thinking is a thinking on thinking. **Divine thinking** will be one with the object of its thought... so throughout eternity is the thought which has itself for its object."* What he calls "thinking on thinking" seems as close as what, today, we would call "consciousness" or "self-awareness" – without which there would **be** no subject, no one *who* is aware of himself.

He seems to imply man's *contemplative faculty* (or "*other soul*") spends eternity *contemplating* God – the Christian notion of the "Beatific Vision". On the other hand, it would seem the Divine spends Its eternity contemplating Itself! This is reminiscent of the Hindu view of the divine Brahman – "*being-consciousness-bliss*" – the assumption being when the *subject* **is** the sole *object of itself* this is some kind of *final estate* – even God's eternal estate. This, however, is a failure to recognize that ***subject-as-object is* the very nature of everyman's *human consciousness*** from birth to death. There is no other way to be aware of one's self but as object-to-one's-self. **Without a subject (self) there is no "object" (self), and without an "object" (self), there is no such subject (self.)** To think that realizing "self" *is* its *own* object (and is the nature of eternal life), is too naive for words, rudimentary at best and totally false at worst. (For some people, of course, the mistake is thinking *sensory objects* are objects-of-consciousness when they are **only objects-of-the-senses.)**

Since the object of consciousness is always itself (**subject**), take away one or the other (subject- as-object or object-as-self) and **both are gone** – neither subject nor object exist anymore because ***consciousness* has ceased to *function***. To think that beyond subject-**as**-object (or vice versa) is *another* subject – some divine subject – is mere speculation and *opinion* – "ignorance" Plato would call it. Man simply has to stop making God into his own image. As someone put it, "*Man creates God and then wonders why he can't find Him*". God's divine *Knowing* is of a totally different nature than man's knowing and consciousness. God is no person – subject, self, consciousness, *who*, "I am" – **this is *man*, not God.**

Aristotle's notion of "thinking", or consciousness as subject-object, is difficult to reconcile with his view a *subject* only inheres in a *material body,* when neither body or soul are eternal. All one can do is postulate some *eternal* link between his idea of "thinking", "consciousness" and his eternal "contemplative faculty", which, it would seem, Aquinas did. As said, Aquinas made this *eternal* faculty the "highest point" of the intellect. (I believe he referred to this as the "passive intellect".) For those who believe the soul is immortal or eternal, Aristotle's placing the *subject, self or "who" you are,* in the *material* body, would be problematic. Still, a Christian granting eternal life to the body would at least ensure the immortality of the body's *subject* or self. As for Plato, who regarded the "universal soul" as eternal, who could honestly say what he thought about any "immortal" subject or self?

The reason for pointing out some of the major differences between Plato and Aristotle is to point out the different possibilities they presented for an understanding of Christ. We do not know what either philosopher would say about the Incarnation, but obviously Plato had the greater influence on the earliest understanding of Christ. It seems, however, it was Aristotle's understanding of human nature – as an *individual material body and soul* – that would come to dominate Christian theology. By making Aristotle's "***individual** embodied being*" a ***person***, and then making the Trinity three (non-embodied) *individual persons or beings,* the original use of "*hypostasis*" was redefined as "***person***" in order to define Christ as ***one (individual) "embodied" divine person or being.*** This is how the *individual* man, Jesus, was made to be *one* ***divine "embodied" being or person – Christ.*** Since "person", however, implies some "*individual* being" we have a "*Monophysitic Christ*" – one individual being of one nature. This is basically the party-line presentation of Christ and as such, is every Christian's understanding of Christ as one ontological **being**. Yet only the man Jesus was one ontological being.

Needless to say, because the Trinity is not three individual beings, the Trinity cannot be three individual persons – after all, **without an *individual being* "who" is there to be an *individual person?*** To say Jesus was the embodiment of a *divine being or person* not only *assumes* the Trinity is three beings or persons, but assumes human nature can be a divine person. *This makes a human being God's own self or person.* There is no truth to this whatsoever – as said, it is a piece of Hinduism.

Once the Logos was made the one divine *person* of Christ, Jesus **could not** be regarded as a human person lest it make Christ the union of two persons. But this is how "Christ" was made to be God's *own* embodied *individual divine person.* But to say Jesus was not a human person, implies he was not an individual human being – as said, **without a "person" there is *no individual being* (divine or human) to**

speak of. Furthermore, to make *person* the *property* of Almighty God and at the same time the property of human nature – as in the case of Christ – either makes God a human being, or makes a human being God. There's no getting around this piece of *anthropolatry.*

If this seems hard to follow, this is the result of making God a person – or three persons. Take away God as persons and nothing is easier to understand than **Christ as the eternal oneness of God and Man – literally, the end of the subject.** All we are pointing out is how the term "person" applied to God, skewed a true understanding of Christ. To account for *Christ* ***as*** *one individual person* there had to be an *ontological switch* from *nature* as *real being* to ***person*** **as** ***real being*** **– from "what" man is, to "who"** ***a*** **man is – more especially, "who" the man Jesus was.** It is because his human nature was no different than anyone else's, it had to be "**who**" he was, that made all the difference. **The only problem – it is not "who" God is that makes people different, it is the** ***human person*** **himself that makes for differences.**

To say a *person* is *incommunicable* means no one can be *who* someone else is. For Plato, however, about the only thing really "incommunicable" was the fact that physical bodies could not occupy the same space at the same time. For Aristotle, on the other hand, the mere fact of being a material individual (a "numerical one") accounts for being "incommunicable" – while the flame (soul) is the same, the *material candles* (bodies) differed. Thus by reason of their different *bodies,* father and son were incommunicable – one could never **be** the other. As for what Christianity would regard as "person", for Aristotle these were "accidentals" of an individual that did not constitute his essential nature. Remember, he thought the "subject" was in the body and not in the soul. In Christianity, of course, neither body or soul is incommunicable, it is the soul's *agent* or *subject* (person) that is *incommunicable* – can never be anyone else.

It is rare for any Christian theologian or writer on the subject of Christ, to ever point out the *ontological switch* from essence to person as the ontological reality of human nature. Yet it is all implied in the proverbial party-line as if taken for granted. Perhaps the earliest writer to articulate this *switch* was Leontius of Byzantium, a sixth century monk credited with coining the term "*enhypostasia*" (**in** the person) as a definition of Christ's two natures "**in** one person". His definition was a clear shift from *nature* to *person* as the ontology of being. Thus he concludes his somewhat discombobulated book – "*The ontological foundation of being is not nature but person. Nature is not self-subsistent, nature does not exist* except ***in*** *a* ***hypostasis (an individual being.)*** *It is hypostasis – person, individual or personal subject – that*

results *in the union of essences. Christ is the whole "person" and Its natures are parts of the whole. The Logos was the personal divine subject of his divinity and his humanity. Thus the person "I" of Christ was that of the Logos – which "I" includes its own human nature."* Since the *nature* (essence) of both God and man can only exist **in** a person, then "*person*" or "*who*" one is, *is* the whole foundation of **being** – of *real* existence, that is.[2]

The first problem with this view is that Leontius **defines person or hypostasis as an "individual being";** he assumes *person* and *individual* are identical and that both reference a concrete individual being. But did hypostasis *ever* mean "individual being"? If it did, then we have the Trinity's triune hypostases as three *individual* beings – *tritheism.* But if the nature and person of God (Logos) is **not** a single individual being, **then how could the divine *person* of Christ be a single being?** To make either the nature (essence) or persons of the Logos- Spirit-Transcendent *individual beings*, is a false understanding of the Trinity and, consequently, a false understanding of Christ.

Leontius goes on to say, *"Hypostasis* (individual or person) *is the* ***one reality*** *in which the two natures are united without separation and confusion, the composite natures in the whole, that is the end product of the union of the two natures and two natures are parts of the whole"* – the *whole* Christ, that is. He then adds, *"Whereas in all other men, person and nature are indissolubly fused, yet they are totally distinct in Christ".* Thus only the man Jesus is not a human person, whereas for everyone else, person and nature are "fused". Leontius is really postulating different *kinds of human natures,* one *with* person and one *without* person. But then, theology has never honestly agreed with Paul that Christ's human nature was "like ours in every way but sin".

Leontius' other glaring error was saying hypostasis or *person* was the "*product of the union of the two natures"* – this is somewhat reminiscent of Aristotle's "third substance" as the unitive *product* of body and soul – the *whole* being greater than its parts. However, to hold that the *product* or *composite* of the union (of two natures) makes a single person, is just a step from "*Monophysitism*" – i.e., "one composite na-

---

[2] Hinduism would have no problem with Leontius' view of person – subject or self – as the ontological reality of Brahman or God. This explains the consistent Hindu question "*Who* am I?" in search of one's true identity – the answer, of course, "I am Brahman", or "I am God". Hinduism, however, is more generous than Christianity in that Brahman is the true *subject* of *every human being* and not *just* the man Jesus, "who", Christianity claims, is the *only human being in all of history eternally one with God.* This explains why Christians are making paths to India, it seems they have many Christs there.

ture". There are so many problems with this view, it would be pointless to go into them at length. We only quoted Leontius as an example of the Christian *switch* in the "*ontology of being*" from nature to person. Strictly speaking, God (Trinity) and Christ fit no category of ontological being, and trying to categorize them as such, is no more than "*forcing-the-fit*".

From a purely philosophical point of view, the *ontological reality* of Christ is totally unique and does not fall into any known philosophical category. Since God is not ***a*** being and the Trinity, not three beings, it follows that without "individual beings" there can be no "*person*" or "*persons*". **Since the notion of *person* is wholly premised on "individual being", and since the Trinity is not three individual beings, then God is not three persons.** Anyone who holds "person" to be an *ontological reality,* holds the Trinity to be three ontological *beings* – "*tri-theism*" (three gods.) As Infinite Existence, God transcends all categories of "ontological being". God is the Source of all being and not **a** being.

Should anyone think Christianity made no such *ontological switch,* let him see how far he gets in Christian theology with no reference to the term "person" – and all it means. Thus, eliminate: *God is three persons; the "son" is second person of the Trinity; "hypostasis" is a person; individual is a person; Christ is one divine person (or two natures in one divine person); self or subject is a person; Jesus is no-person* – and so on. This is not merely dropping a *particular word*, but eliminating a whole theological understanding of the Trinity, Christ, and man, **all premised on *person*.** There is no getting around the fact that the major **keystone** of Christian theology is "*person*". To eliminate the whole notion of *person* used to define the Trinity and Christ, and this whole Christian paradigm implodes.

The result of theology's ontological switch from nature (essence) to person, presents an entirely different understanding of the Trinity and Christ than would be otherwise. Where the essential nature of man was universally the same for all, now the *essential* nature of man is each individual *person – different* persons. How any *ontology of being* could be premised on human *differences,* defies all logic – but then, there has never been much evidence for defining man as a "rational" being in the first place. Man is better defined as an *emotional being,* for at bottom, his feelings probably govern 99% of all his judgements and behaviors. This is why the Stoics held that unless man could get beyond being governed by his emotions and feelings he could never live "rationally". Until such time, man hasn't a clue what it means to **be** a "rational being". The Stoics got their view from their understanding of the divine Logos (*reason*) as the transcendent Intelligence governing all things – the ultimate *Reason-for-being*. Thus the Stoic goal of *right living* was to be *at one* with *divine Intelligence* – at one with the Logos. This "reason for being" (Logos) was why and how man was created a *rational* being – which, obviously, he is not now – but which he should strive to *become*.

It goes without saying, none of the Greek philosophers were prepared to deal with Christian Monotheism, the Trinity, Christ, or even the man Jesus, and to think these truths can ever be premised on anyone's philosophical views is an error in itself. But unfortunately, this is what happened. Certain elements of philosophy became as sacrosanct as dogma, even perpetuated as the "right understanding" of Christian Truths. It was to defend a "right understanding" these philosophical elements were used to provide the *rationale* for the orthodox Christian position. The problem is not philosophy, but Christianity's questionable adaptation of certain philosophical ideas and positions. When a theologian can find no *philosophy* to cover his tracks, he then proclaims it a "divine mystery" – a mystery of his own making that is. The one great mystery of Christ is the eternal union of two totally disparate natures. God only knows how this works, or even what this "union" actually means as far as man's human nature is concerned. Yet it is this eternal oneness of God and man **in** the Trinity that is the central mystery of Christianity and the *sole keystone* of its Faith.

End Note

Since the major concern of this book has been going over the earliest understanding of Christ, we have avoided getting into any of the later medieval scholastic debates and theologies of the Western Church. The purpose of this chapter was to point out some of the relevant aspects of the philosophical milieu in which Christianity was born, and the educated mind-set of its times. Though it has been many years since I went over the works of Duns Scotus (1266 – 1308), it is my view that of all the medieval "scholastics", he was closer to the early fathers' understanding of Christ than those who came after them. What is particularly unique about Scotus is that he never bought into the present day *dogmatic* Aristotelian view of man – nor did he buy Plato's view. Where for Plato, matter is the cause of individuation (what makes something an *individual* being), for Aristotle, (and basically Aquinas), the soul was the cause of individuation – responsible for "individual" being – Scotus however, had an entirely different view.

For Scotus, a "universal" is only an *intellectual abstraction* whereas what is ***real** is the "commonality" of **what** is **one** in the many.*

Thus the *real* essence of man's *common* human nature has the *potential* to be or *become* many individual "ones". "*The singular (nature)*", he says, "*which is predicated of many, has to be some single essence which many can be, otherwise, a singular nature over (or apart from) its many applications to different particulars would "evaporate"*. In other words, were it not for man's *common human nature* there could be no *particulars* (individuals or persons), they would simply *evaporate* – because they had no *reality* at all. Scotus is only affirming that **real being is *not the individual,*** but "***what" is common in many individuals* – "essence", that is.** Scotus is just putting the horse (reality of essence) *before* the cart (individuality or particularity.)

He said the *essence* (**real** nature) of man, has the *potential* to *become* an individual. Thus individuation is the *actualization* of nature's *potential*. An "individual" is a "mode" or "actuality" of the essence, but the individual is **not itself the real essence of being.** While he holds this *actualization* does not change the essence, he holds the essence is *more* real than the individual and the individual *less* real than the essence. Needless to say, this was like throwing a bomb on the Scholastic's (and Aquinas') notion that only an embodied *individual* was "real being" – the true essence of human nature. What Scotus is pointing out, however, is the same as Cyril – "*The Logos did not assume some particular human being* (individual), *but man's* ***common*** *human nature, yet a nature that appeared (was seen) in one individual*". So which came first, the essence of man or an *individual* man? Scotus is just pointing out the view of all the early fathers – essence is prior to the individual.

Scotus pulls the rug out from under the Scholastic notion that only the ***individual*** man Jesus was the ***essence*** of God's human nature – and hence, only he, the individual man Jesus, was Christ. But if an *individual* is the *essence* of man, then God's uniting itself to the individual essence of mankind would mean every *individual* is Christ – innumerable Christs, that is. Were this the case, the one Real Christ "*evaporates*". The *essential reality* of mankind is no one *individual* – or any individual. That Scotus' essence ("*commonality*") of human nature **is prior to the individual,** is certainly the prescribed understanding of Christ that this book (*The Real Christ*) espouses. So if anyone thinks this understanding of Christ is off-the-beat of Christian theology, they need only study Blessed Duns Scotus. In my view, his understanding of Christ is the best representative of the early fathers' understanding of Christ – certainly better than the whole of "scholasticism" put together. It was a bleak day when Aquinas, instead of Scotus, was declared the "official" theologian of the Western Church. This was another wrong turn, one that has ended just as Aquinas said – as so much "straw".

APPENDIX II
THEOLOGY OF NO-SELF

It has been said that complete loss-of-self is not in the Christian tradition, that it has no theological or orthodox foundation – it is *not Christian*. One can expect to find this denunciation in just about every commentary on the Christian spiritual life, some statement assuring the reader no one *ever* loses their self-identity, not in this life, and certainly not in the next. This has *not* been said by the totally unqualified, but by otherwise respected writers in the field of Christian spirituality – though usually by a "commentator".

While there is no question these people believe what they say, what is questionable is whether their belief is based on "orthodox" Christianity or if it is just a gut-reaction to their own personal fears – afraid it might be true. Actually, nothing could be easier to account for, nothing more theological and orthodox than the ultimate loss of *all* self – one's own personal identity. Not only is no-self orthodox, but Christian theology *depends* on this Truth. It could be said *no-self is* the major premise of the Christian Faith, fundamental to it. So let us briefly state the key theological premises.

1. "*Person*" is defined as the soul's *agent*, *subject*, "*I am*", "*self-identity*", everything meant by "*self*". Orthodox theology holds the man **Jesus was *not a human person***, he had (or owned) **no subject, no-self, no personal "I am", this was not his "self-identity".** It is a fundamental teaching, then, that Jesus was not a *human person,* that he, a human being, **had *no-self. This is the orthodox teaching!***

No theologian would dare deny Jesus had **no-self,** or say he was a "*human* person", for if he did, he'd be thrown out as a Nestorian – a heretic. So anyone who says **no-self** is not fundamental to Christianity, its tradition and theology, or thinks it is **not basic** to its understanding of "*Christ*", has no knowledge of Christianity and should be ignored completely.

2. Orthodoxy holds that in the Incarnation, God (Logos) never assumed (or created) any human *person* – any human subject or agent of the soul, any self, or "I am", thus **God never created the self-identity of any human person, not even the man Jesus**. God only creates human nature, whereas man freely creates his own unique *person,* his own unique self and all this means. **It is because God never created the human person or self of the man Jesus, that Jesus is said to be *no-person, no-self. This is orthodox!***

3. Add to this – the dictum of all the fathers, as stated by Gregory of Nazianzus – "*What the Logos did not assume (or unite to Itself) in the Incarnation is not saved*", *only "**what**" the Logos assumed is saved*". **Since God did not assume or create any human *person* or *self*, this means no self or "person" is saved**. If this is not *orthodox*, then Gregory and all the fathers were wrong. In truth, however, they had it right – ***they were orthodox!***

What this means is that anyone who intends to "follow Jesus" had better **lose his self** as soon as possible. Those who think they can give their self to God and **not** lose it, are only fooling themselves – want to eat their cake, but keep it too. *Loss of self is the very foundation of Christianity.*

4. Premised on the Western Church's understanding of "hypostasis" as "person", and that the Trinity is three persons, some people may argue that the reason Jesus was not a *human* person is because he was a *divine* person instead. But this is ***not orthodox.*** The divine "person" of Christ was ***not*** **the man Jesus**, the **divine person was *God*** (the Logos) – ***this is orthodox.*** **Think of it this way**:

God is man's true being, but man is *not God's* being

God is man's true self, but man is *not God's* self.

(So too, one could say **God is man's true person, but man is not God's person**.)

5. Another piece of (Alexandrian) orthodoxy is that instead of Jesus as a human person or self, God's person or self **acted in Jesus' stead** – acted as the divine agent or subject of Jesus' soul, thus God's person was substituted for Jesus' human person or self. This means that the one "***who***" died on the cross, was *not* the self-less person Jesus, rather, it was ***God's own divine self – subject, "I am", God's "ontological self", that died on the cross. So now, even God has no self!*** No subject or agent, no "I am"! If God did *not* die, then "**who**" did? Remember, Jesus had no-self anyway – **thus it was God, *Jesus' true divine self* "*who*" died. So the one that arose, of course, was the totally *self-less "Christ"*.** So everything defined as God's *person* or self-identity died, is gone forever – why? Because, i**n truth, God is no self and no person**. That it was God *in person*, a divine self that died, this is **perfectly *orthodox*.**

The real *mystery* of the cross is that no one really understands it. The fathers never thought there was any "salvation" in the death of a mere human person. **Only the death of a *divine person or self* constitutes man's eternal salvation, and in this, the fathers were absolute-**

ly correct. This is the truth of the cross, yet no one can even conceive of it, and if they could, they wouldn't accept it anyway. **The human mind cannot get hold of anyone, divine or human, with *no self-identity.*** Yet it is the death of this divine "metaphysical self or person" that effects man's eternal life in and with God – his salvation, that is. That not only was Jesus self-less, but **God is self-less –** this is the foundation of Christianity's whole understanding of *salvation.* Those who deny that death of a *divine self* is the keystone of Christianity's understanding of salvation, are simply "***not orthodox***".

If the one "*who*" died did not lose its self-identity, then all that died on the cross was a physical body. God, however, did not *dramatize* Christ's death for all time just to reveal someone's organs had stopped functioning. Christianity is founded on the *true nature of Christ's death,* based on ***"who" truly died,*** **it was not founded on the death of a human person or self, but a *divine* person, a divine self.** This is why the cross is literally the icon of *no-self,* its mystery being the death of God as a divine person, a divine self – a divine subject "I am", and all this means.

* * * * *

None of this, of course, is *my* theology or orthodoxy, I never made any of it up. It's all in the books and has been for over 1500 years now, and if orthodox theologians do not like it, they will just have to eat crow. But so much for anyone who says complete loss of self or person is unorthodox or un-theological, they had better go back to their books.

But if the orthodoxy of **no-self** is plain as day, yet who in Christianity ever points this out or even talks about it? Obviously, it is not something theologians would wish to discuss or even think about, they couldn't handle it – but then, few people can. Those who deny this truth, merely spend time searching for ways to circumvent it – as theologians do. **Remember, the definition of "*person*" as "subject", "I am", "who" or "self", dates from 4th century writings and is *not* a product of modern psychology – as some authors would like us to believe.**

The three strategic ways **my theology** differs from the going orthodox theology is **1**) God is no person(s) or self – never was, this is absolutely false.[1] **2**) The historical Jesus was a *whole human person.* **3**)

[1] That God is a divine subject, self, "I am" is **orthodox Hinduism – God, made in the image of man.** This is why people are flocking East to find out, like Jesus, "**who**" they really are, discover they are really God *in person* – absolute anthropolatry.

Self – the agent of the soul, its subject, "I am", and *who* one is (self-identity), is everything man calls "consciousness", and as such, it is **the *major faculty* of the human soul.** Without self-awareness there could be no development (or function) of the mind and will. Self or consciousness, then, is not only the cause and source of self-identity, it is ***the* major *faculty (function) of the soul itself.*** Should consciousness cease to function, so would all the faculties of the soul.[2] This is the truth, this is how it goes.

Since it is human consciousness or self-awareness that sets man off from animals, with the cessation of the faculties or functions (of the human soul), man would become either less than he is now, or *more* than he is now. Since, by definition, "transformation" can only be a forward movement, the cessation of the soul's faculties is but another step (perhaps the most major step) toward man's eternal destiny in and with God. The point – **everything man calls "self" – self-awareness, I am, who, etc. – is the soul's *function* called "consciousness".**

People tend to mistake reference to "self" as a reference to "being". "Self", however, **is *not* an *entity* or a *being* – it is a *function!*** Self is always a reference to "*who*" some *particular* being is, while "being" is a reference "*that something exists*" – or "**is**", and is not a reference to "*who*" exists. This is why any attempt to make *self* (*person, or who* someone is) an "ontological *being*" (*real being*) is consummate ignorance.

In this book I have gone along with the proverbial definition of *person* as it refers to *human beings,* but consistently affirmed that the idea God is a *person* is **absolutely false**. The reason for going along with the definition of *man* as a *person,* is because theology has no other term or way of accounting for *self, subject, I am, who – or one's personal self-identity* – thus it served my purpose to use the proverbial term "person". In truth, however, nothing man calls *person* is the true nature of human consciousness or self-awareness – man's subjective self or "I am". The fact everyone is an "I am", a subject and agent, is how it works for *every* human being and does not constitute any real *difference* between them. **While *use of the soul's faculties* will not**

---

2 "Consciousness" is the reflexive mechanism of the mind bending on itself to know itself – thus "I exist", "I am myself and no other", "I think, I desire, I will, I say", etc. The power or energy that runs this mechanism is located in the very center of man's being – man only has one *true center* – and if this power or energy should *cease*, there would be no reflexive mind – no *experience* of energy, power, or even the experience of "*being*" in fact. There is nothing eternal about the functions or faculties of the soul. Maximus the Confessor, however, is the only one I know who says this outright, and he was absolutely right – *orthodox*!

make for differences as regards man's *eternal life,* yet the term "person" includes many *non-eternal* factors as well, factors, that in this life at least, can account for just about all the differences people can see or take note of. God is the only One that has access to the soul and knows "*what*" in man is destined for eternal life. Thus "person" only points to a "*particular*" human being, points to *observable* differences – best called a "personality" – that has no *eternal* life at all.

Eternal life has nothing to do with "who" one is, but "what" one is – a human being. Because Eternal life in God is not in *this* world, human nature as man knows it *now,* on this earth, is not God's *own* ***eternal*** *human nature*. It is God's *own* human nature – as only God knows it – that is the ***eternal Christ,*** Man's eternal oneness with God. We would do well to keep in mind the overlooked saying of Gregory of Nazianzus in one of his *Orations* – "***in Christ we have two "what's"*** **(natures),** ***not two "who's", two "I am's" or "two persons".*** We are not transformed into "who" Christ is, because Christ is **not** a "*who*". We are transformed into "*what*" Christ is – i.e., the essence of God and Man eternally one. It could not be put more simply than this.

There is much more that could be said here, but we only wish to point out *no-self* (as no-*person*) is not only *orthodox*, but *foundational* to the entire Christian paradigm. None of this, however, is *my theology*. And as for *my theology* being orthodox, let's just say it is "***more*** *orthodox than the orthodox"*.

APPENDIX III
THEOTOKOS

We want to go over the theology of Mary as it bears on a true understanding of Christ. Just as an understanding of Christ depends on a right understanding of the Trinity, so too, an understanding of Mary depends on a right understanding of Christ. The Trinity, Christ, Mary, these can never be separated, for **without Mary there would have been no revelation of Christ, no man Jesus and no Christianity.** She was as necessary for the revelation of Christ as was Almighty God – indeed, what would God have done without her?

In all books recounting the development of Christianity (its understanding of the Trinity and Christ) "*Theotokos*" is the name given to one of the major issues that would forever impact a true understanding of Christ. Although Mary's exalted status had been recognized from the beginning, it only became an "issue" in the year 428, and as to how this came about is a story in itself, so let us briefly go over it.

To list all the titles given to God, to Christ and Jesus, would take many pages. Thus Christ is "King", "Prince of peace", "Lamb of God", "Good Shepherd" – the list goes on and on. It was just a matter of time before Mary would also have her own litany of titles. We know from the earliest writings she was always referred to as the "holy" or "blessed" virgin. It seems that by the third century "*Theotokos*" or "god-bearing" (*Mater Dei* or *Mother of God)* had become a popular epithet for Mary. Although it is said Origen (185 – 254) first used this epithet, by 324 it had become a popular term, and by 428 "*Theotokos*" was used in the *official liturgy* of the Church.

It is not hard to understand how Mary came to be called "Theotokos". We can point out a number of reasons. If one believed *Jesus* was God, then, of course, his mother Mary was the "Mother of God". Also, if God *begot* the Son-of-God, and no child has but one parent, then Mary was the Mother of the Son-of-God. Then too, unless one is a "polytheist" who divides gods into male and female, referring to God as a "father" is no different than referring to God as "mother" – what could be the difference apart from gender? If, however, God is *not* at once *mother-father*, then God must have had a spouse equally divine, which spouse was "Mary".

Another possible reason for "Theotokos" is that women were not too happy about worshiping two males in the Trinity – a father and son. Thus "Mother of God" might have been a statement of feminine one-upmanship. But whatever the thinking behind the term, "***Theotokos*" points out that without a *woman* there could have been no "Incarnation" or revelation of "Christ" – and this is *the truth.*** So to reveal the Incarnation, then, while a *human* male was obviously *dispensable,* a human female was *indispensable*.

Since Christ is the union or oneness of God and man, the title "Mother of God" raises the question of whether Mary is the mother of Christ's *divine nature* or only the mother of Christ's *human nature*? **This question was the whole issue of the "Theotokos".** Incredibly, the answer to this question amounted to a schism in the Church, a schism that had not a thing to do with Mary or the title "Mother of God".

The only reason it became an "issue" was due to Church politics, particularly the rivalry between the Sees of Alexandria and Constantinople. As the story goes, there was a plot afoot to have the Patriarch of Constantinople recognized as having the same authority as the Pope in Rome – recognized as an ecclesiastical equal. Since Alexandria was the older, larger and more prestigious See, there was dissention among the Bishops over which See should head the Eastern Church – to say nothing of the horror this plot caused the Pope in Rome.

Before the issue of the *Theotokos* came up, Cyril had inherited the See of Alexandria from his uncle. If his See was declared the greater, this would make him Patriarch of all the Eastern Churches. So this, then, was the political background at the time the Patriarch of Constantinople died and was replaced by a monk, someone not a Bishop and not into Church politics, but renowned, however, for his wise counsel, austere life, and for being a stickler on "orthodoxy".

We can only imagine what a shock it must have been for this monk to move from his routine monastic life into a den of ecclesiastical conspiracies. As we know, those who cannot play this political game are not going to last very long – and thanks to Cyril, this monk was ostracized.

So here enters into Christian history the monk Nestorius, a priest whose biography is impeccable, and whose heroic feat of spreading Christianity to foreign lands is unrivaled by *any* of the fathers. In contrast to his life, the biography of Cyril reads like a list of crimes and misdemeanors. For thousands of persecuted people, Cyril was the devil incarnate.

As the story goes, as Patriarch, some of Nestorius' underlings brought up the question of the *orthodoxy* of the Church's official use of the epithet *Theotokos* in its liturgy. Since, like Christ, Mary had a litany of epithets, it is hard to believe *Theotokos* ever upset Nestorius, particularly if it was already used in some liturgical prayer – even Patriarchs don't change liturgical prayers with a mere *fiat*!

Evidently, he told one of his assistants at next Sunday's Mass, to explain to the people *God had no mother*, and that Mary was the "Mother of Christ" – "*Christotokos*".

Now, for people who believed the man Jesus was God, to deny Mary was his mother, was as good as denying God Himself. This was heresy, and if this was the Patriarch's view, then he was a heretic – so down with him! It is reported that after this announcement by the "assistant" – I think his name was something like "Anthanasius" – everyone ran out of Church and rioted. If one studies the history of the times, however, and knows the prevailing social unrest, they would discover these riots were not infrequent. It seems people would use any excuse to riot, and "Theotokos" was as good as any. To think they rioted, burned, looted, injured and destroyed property **out of love for Mary,** is ludicrous.

If the people were angry with Nestorius for denying Jesus was Almighty God, they were correct. Nestorius never believed any human being was God. He was an Antiochene who believed Jesus was a complete human being – a human *person*. His was the *orthodox* belief of Christ as the union of two complete and disparate natures, God and man. Christ was not *just* the man Jesus, nor *just* God, but the union of two *natures, not* the union of two *persons* – as Cyril **falsely** accused Nestorius. It was Nestorius' orthodox Antiochene view of Christ that flew in the face of Cyril's *unorthodox* ***Monophysitic*** view (Christ had *one divine nature)* that was the real issue at hand.

News of the riot spread fast, and when Cyril (in Alexandria) heard of it, he first wrote to Nestorius and then to Pope Celestine, telling him to condemn Nestorius, which, without further ado, or even giving Nestorius a chance to respond, the Pope did – condemn Nestorius. Everyone knows why he did this. It had nothing to do with *Theotokos*, but with the threat of the Eastern Churches setting up their own "second pope" at Constantinople. This was a chance for Rome to get rid of any threat a Patriarch of Constantinople might become, and also, to get the Alexandrians on his side.

No need to recount the quick synod Cyril put together among his Alexandrian cohorts to condemn Nestorius – as Celestine told him to do. It was at the behest of Nestorius, however, the Emperor called the Council of Ephesus (431) to decide the issue. This Council was a face-off between the Alexandrian understanding of Christ's human nature as so much *flesh*, and the Antiochene understanding of Christ as a complete human being – a human *person*. Since Nestorius represented the Antiochene understanding, at issue was not *his* condemnation, but a condemnation of the whole Antiochene understanding of Christ.

As to how the Alexandrians got their way, when even the Emperor was behind Nestorius, there is only one explanation. Since the Pope had already ordered Nestorius' condemnation, what Council would now decide *against* the Pope? Whatever Celestine came to understand as Nestorius' Antiochene view of Christ, no Pope is going to condemn a man one day and exonerate him the next. Celestine had to save face lest "papal authority" – the last word on the faith – should be compromised.

Shortly after the Council of Ephesus, however, Celestine died (432), and the new Pope, Xystus III, was basically in accord with the Antiochenes. His goal, however, was to bring the two sides together and, knowing this, the Antiochenes pleaded with him to exonerate Nestorius – back in his monastery at Ephesus. To do this, however, would have been for one Pope to declare another Pope wrong – admit his predecessor had been mistaken. But for one Pope to declare another Pope wrong, to my knowledge, has never happened. This illustrates the absolute authority of a Pope – be he right or wrong! So even though everyone recognized Celestine was wrong, from here on, every Pope would take Nestorius, *instead* of Celestine, as the one who was wrong – *incredible*! Strange how politics can triumph over truth.[1]

Obviously, the issue of *Theotokos* as a legitimate title for Mary was never the real issue. The whole issue was the truth of Christ – was Jesus a genuine human being (a "*person*") or, under the facade of flesh, was he Almighty God walking, talking, suffering and dying? It was all about Cyril claiming a victory for his **"one natured Christ"** – ***Monophysitism.*** He took the term "incarnation" literally, God took on "flesh", but never united Itself to man's complete human nature. There is no human nature in Cyril's Christology or in any of the Alexandrians', what they call "human nature" is simply "flesh". (Actually, it is much easier to "deify" Jesus if a man is only "flesh", than if he is a genuine human *person.*)

This issue could never have come up, of course, were it not for the

---

[1] In this matter I might interject an incident when I was 12 or so. Having read a book, *Pageant of the Popes,* recounting the historical facts of the Popes' lives, after reading of the utter debauchery, nepotism, even murder on the part of so many of them, I asked my dad, "How could anyone trust anything a Pope ever said to be the truth?" His reply, *"Notice, despite the immoral lives of some of them, none ever tried to change the Church's teaching on faith or morals."* This at least, separates a Pope's personal beliefs and morals from the "traditional" teaching of the Church – and there is something to be said for that. But when a Pope *officially* condemns as false what is actually true – as in the case of Nestorius' understanding of Christ – this is beyond a matter of personal belief, it is a matter of the true Faith. What was condemned was the understanding of the man Jesus as a true human being, a *real human person!* If this was *not* the truth, then what is left is Monophysitism, polytheism and anthropolatry.

idea God "*begot*" God. Thus it would never have occurred to anyone Mary was the "Mother of God" had it not been for the biblical idea God "*begot*" God (a son, of course.) **If God did *not* "beget" God (a son) then God could not be called "father-of-God" nor Mary be called "mother-of-God".** It makes sense, after all, if God (a son) has a father, then God (a son) also has a mother. What makes *no sense* is that God *only* had a father and **no** mother – why would anyone choose between God having *only* a father **or** *only* a mother? It is pretty obvious why this choice was made, and *who* made it. God can only be a **male**, and God can only beget a **male**, that's just the way it went – so say **males**, at least. All this, of course, is utter nonsense and totally polytheistic. But keep in mind, the belief in those days was that fathers passed on their *own* souls to their offspring. It was because *God* was the father of Jesus, that Jesus' soul (or life) was regarded as God's *own* divine life. Thus all Mary supplied was Jesus' "humanity" – his flesh, that is. **This was (and remains) the proverbial belief – God supplied Jesus' divine nature (God's *own* soul or life), while Mary supplied his human nature – flesh.**

Needless to say, Cyril never countenanced any notion the Godhead or Trinity had a beginning, was ever "born", or had a *mother* or a *father*. His reference was solely to **God being born into *this world* – the *incarnation,*** that is. This, however, posed the same old question of "***who***" was the "**son**" – was it the divine Logos (God) or the man Jesus? Was Mary, then, the mother of the divine Logos ("son"), or was she only the mother of the human "son" – the man Jesus? It is the answer to this question that raises the question of "who" was the son's *mother* – was she mother of the eternal Logos (God) or only the mother of the human being Jesus?

Given Cyril's "Monophysitic" resolution that Christ had **one divine nature,** Mary, as the mother of Christ's *one divine nature,* is what made her the "Mother of God". As we know, he had a fit if anyone tried to speak of Jesus as if he was *distinct* from God, for him, this simply blew apart his understanding of the union or oneness of God and man. So too, he allowed no distinction between Mary as "mother of God" and Mary as "mother of the man Jesus", for this too, would have blown his view of Christ as *one divine being.* Although Mary provided the flesh or "individual appearance" of Christ, yet, because Christ had *one divine nature*, *Christ* was *God,* and Mary, the "Mother of God". His understanding of *Theotokos* was obviously premised on his *Monophysitic* understanding of Christ's one divine nature.

While some have lauded Cyril as a champion of Mary, the truth is, she was **his excuse** to champion the idea of Christ's *one divine nature*.

Cyril never took his understanding of Christ from Mary, rather he took his understanding of Mary from his *own idea* of Christ. Since the term *Theotokos* was in place long before Cyril and Nestorius came on the scene, the fact it was never an "issue" prior to this time, points to its being *used* as a way for Cyril to promote *his* idea of Christ. He also used it as a way to resolve the conflict between which See, Alexandria or Constantinople, best represented the "orthodox" Church. Nestorius' reminding people Almighty God *had no mother*, was all Cyril needed to attack the Patriarch of Constantinople as "unorthodox" – attack the whole Antiochene understanding of Christ, of which Nestorius was its "authoritative" spokesperson at the time.

It was in the course of this dispute, however, both Nestorius and Cyril articulated two different "theologies of Mary". First, Nestorius pointed out to Cyril, "*To say she was the mother of God means she was* ***consubstantial*** *with the Father*". Cyril countered with his view that, since Mary "*bore in the flesh, God, who was united* ***hypostatically*** (in essence) *with flesh, for that reason we* ***call*** *her Mother of God"*. While neither one gave any credence to Nestorius' view, **both views, however, suggest a theology of Mary worthy of consideration.**

First of all, both views were based on the notion God "**begot**" a Son "*consubstantial*" with God (*of the same nature or essence of God),* thus it is solely God's "begetting" that makes God a "Father". (Keep in mind, if God did *not beget*, then God is not a "father" and the Logos is not a "son" – and Mary is not God's "Mother".) **Second**: Both the terms *hypostases* (essence) used by Cyril, and *consubstantial* (of the same essence) used by Nestorius, mean the same thing – both terms were used by the fathers. But where Cyril's reference is simply to *God being one with the "flesh"*, Nestorius' reference was *specifically* to the "*Father*" being *one with Mary.* All Nestorius is pointing out is that for Mary to be "Mother of God" (Logos or son), she would have to be of the same *essence* as the Father. So let us see how these two views would work.

Understanding Nestorius' View

a) Just like the divine Son (Logos) is "consubstantial" (of one essence) with the Father, so too, Mary is of one essence (consubstantial) with the Father. This would not be a *fourth* divine Person of the Trinity, but rather, Father-Mother would be **one and the *same* divine hypostasis or person**. Thus the Trinity would be "*Father/Mother-Logos (son)-Spirit*". "Mother" is not a *separate* hypostasis or person of the Trinity any more than Jesus is a separate hypostasis or person of the Trinity. **If we think in terms of God as three "*persons*", then *fa-***

ther/mother* constitute a single divine *person,* just as the God-man (Christ) constitutes a single divine *person. So just as we say Christ is the oneness of two natures *in the one person of the Logos*, so too we can say God and Mary are two natures in the *one person of the Father.*

b) What Nestorius seems to be saying, **if** Mary is, in truth, the "Mother of God", then God is not just a father, but a "mother/father". The two could no more be separated than Cyril could separate the Logos and Jesus. From this we might also infer that just as Jesus was the incarnation of the divine son (God), so too, Mary was the incarnation of the divine mother (God.) **Any objection to Mary as the incarnation of God-the-Mother would be the same objection to *Jesus* as the incarnation of God-the-Son!** In this matter of Mary and Jesus, be they human, divine, or the union of divine and human, *mother* and *child* either stand or fall together.

So given Nestorius' understanding of ***prosopon,*** he could have understood Cyril as saying Mary was of the same *prosopon* (*or person*) as the Father. (Remember, it was only *after* Ephesus – after Nestorius had been condemned – Cyril changed his mind from *hypostasis* as "essence" to *hypostasis* as "*prosopon*" or "person".) So if *hypostasis* means "*prosopon*", then Mary being *hypostatically* one with God, meant she was one ***in* the *prosopon* or person of the Father, just as Jesus' human nature was one *in* the *prosopon* or person of the *Son* – the Logos.** The difference? Mary is one with the *Father* and Jesus, one with the *Logos* (son.) Thus Mary, being one with the Father, she is, in truth, the "Mother of God". *Father/Mother, then, are One Divine Person,* and the *one* that "begot" the Logos was not just "Father", but also "Mother". And just as in the Incarnation, God acted as the ***human father*** of Jesus, so too, Mary acted as the *human mother* of Jesus. So, if God *begot* God (a son or Logos), God is not just a divine father, but equally, a divine mother. And so too, for the earthly conception of the man Jesus, just as Mary acted as the human mother of Jesus, God acted as the human father of Jesus. So this is how it goes – the Logos (God or son) was divinely "begotten" by the one divine person (Father/Mother), and later *humanly* conceived (made incarnate) by the divine Father/Mother acting as Jesus' *natural* father and mother – egg and sperm, that is.

That the one *person* of the Trinity called "Father" is really "Father/Mother", would be the true theology of *Theotokos* as "Mother of God". Nestorius makes this all theologically correct – it is Mary's *consubstantial* oneness with the Father that *really defines* Mary as "*Theotokos".* **The distinction "father" and "mother", however, are only *metaphoric titles* and not "*hypostatic distinctions*". As *consubstan-***

***tial* "progenitors", there is no "hypostatic distinction" between mother/father.**

Although neither Nestorius or Cyril gave any consideration to Christ's mother being "consubstantial" (of one nature) with God-the-father, they should have. What it means is that God is no more a "father" than a "mother" and, by the same token, God is no more a "son" than a "daughter". That the title for God as **only** a "father" and **only** a "son", belongs to polytheism's pantheon of *gendered* gods.

Since there exists no revelation of God as either a "father", "mother", "son" or "daughter", why **call** God a "father" rather than a "mother"? Unless people are hung up on the Trinity as *gendered* beings, God is no more a father than a mother, nor is the Logos more a son than a daughter. So just as God's *divine* nature was *hypostatically* one with man's human nature, **both** Mary and Jesus' human nature were *consubstantially* one with God's divine nature. This, at least, was Nestorius' view **based** on *Cyril's* understanding of the *Theotokos.*

But let us now consider Cyril's understanding of *Theotokos* – *"Mary bore in the flesh, God, who was hypostatically united to the flesh, for that reason **we call her** Mother of God".* Right off, Cyril admits *Theotokos* is just a "title" or what Mary is "**called".** Unlike Nestorius, who went straight to the *truth* of what *Theotokos* really means or implies, Cyril sidesteps the **real** issue. His Monophysitic reasoning is this: because Mary "*bore in the flesh, God*", and God "*was united hypostatically with the flesh*", this makes her the "Mother of God". His view raises two important questions: 1) *Whose* flesh was God united to – Mary's flesh or *only* Jesus' flesh? And 2) Was it the Father or the Logos that was "*hypostatically united to the flesh"?* (Remember, Cyril's view of "human nature" was only "*flesh*".)

1. Cyril's view that *human* nature (flesh) is "*hypostatically*" ***one in essence* with divine nature**, is his *Monophysitic* understanding of Christ. (That human nature is united *to* God's divine essence, however, does not make the two "one essence".) But this is why Cyril insisted it was **not** Jesus' human nature that was conceived and born, rather, it was *God's **own** human nature* that was conceived and born, and for this reason, Mary was the *"Mother of God*" and ***not** just* the mother of the man Jesus. Since the two natures of the "*hypostatic union*" could not be separated, and Christ's *divine nature was God,* then "Christ" was of one divine nature. Continually dividing up Christ as God and/or man, was anathema to him.

That the essence of God was united to the essence of man – his understanding of "hypostatic union" – was absolutely correct. Only keep in mind, for Cyril, *hypostasis* was solely a reference to nature or *essence,* it was **not** a reference to *prosopon* or *person*. It was only *after* Ephesus (441) he was corrected for not pointing out the union of natures or essences was **in** the distinct *person* (or *prosopon*) of God (the Logos or "son".) Once others had decided *hypostasis* meant *prosopon* or *person,* then Cyril's use of "*hypostatic union*" fell short of being a union ***in*** the "*one person*" (or *hypostasis*) of the Logos.

As to whether or not Cyril honestly "changed his mind" in this matter, or subsequent authors did it for him, is a moot question. The use of *prosopon* or *person,* however, did not solve the problem of *Monophysitism* anyway, it only made it *inevitable* – everyone assumes "*one person*" refers to some "*individual*" *being* of an individual nature. Interestingly, however, unlike Cyril who regarded hypostasis as "essence", **Nestorius definitely understood *hypostasis* as *prosopon* – the *orthodox* view, in other words.** It is *because* Cyril missed this completely (mistook *hypostasis* as *essence* and not *prosopon* or person), he accused everyone else of saying Christ was a union of two *prosopa* or persons. (To my knowledge, no father ever said Christ was the union of two persons. Some held, however, there were "two births" – first, the divine nature from the Father, and then, the human nature from Mary.)

2. But apart from the issue of whether or not "hypostasis" means nature or person, it is difficult to follow Cyril's reasoning. He says because Mary *bore* God *in the flesh,* this made her "mother of God"– made her mother of the Uncreated, eternal Logos? Who can figure this out? Then too, at the moment of incarnation, when the Logos "took on flesh", *whose* flesh was it? **Whose** flesh did the Logos unite to Itself **in order** to become incarnate? It could **not** have been the flesh of the man Jesus ***who did not yet exist!*** In order to conceive the man Jesus, God *had* to became one with ***her flesh – "hypostatically one" with Mary's flesh*!** For there to ***be*** an incarnation, then, God had *first* to become one with Mary's flesh, literally become ***in-carnate*** **in Mary**. ("*In-carnate*" means to take on flesh – God's uniting flesh to Itself.) How else could she have conceived Jesus if God had not supplied the Y chromosome, and she, the X? For this, Mary had to be one *in flesh* with God – egg and sperm, no less. God literally, even physically, had to become one with her flesh, Jesus being *after* the fact – its *product.* **Absolutely, Mary was as *hypostatically united to God in the flesh* as Jesus ever was.** In more ways than one, then, Mary was, indeed, the "Spouse" of God. In truth, Jesus was only one with God **because** God made Mary one with Itself. So putting first things first, Jesus' union with God came *after* Mary's union with God.

Now of course, Jesus could have just "appeared" out of the blue –

with no father or mother – but this would not have been an "*incarnation*". Since Jesus' soul came from God (as it does for everyone) and his flesh from God's oneness with Mary, then it was *her* flesh, *her* body that was one with God *before* it could ever have become one with *Jesus'* flesh. So it was **she and God *together*** that conceived the one that would reveal **"Christ" as an individual being in this world.**

If "flesh" is all the Logos took on in order to be incarnate – as all the fathers imply – then God, being one with Mary's flesh, **how is she not also Christ?** Since it was her flesh the Logos was united to, then she can be regarded as the "feminine" representative of Christ – if one needs a gender – just as Jesus is regarded as the "male" representative of Christ. (God, of course, being *genderless*, is the sole "divinity" of Christ.) **Since the human nature of Mary and Jesus were no different, and since God (the *divine* Christ) has no gender, then both Mary and Jesus are equally Christ.** (Recall Paul's saying, "*in Christ there is neither male nor female*" – neither son nor daughter, father nor mother.)

It was, then, only because of God's oneness with Mary's flesh the revelation of the "incarnation" was possible. So first, Mary **is** the "incarnate" Christ, and *through her* flesh made one with God, the man Jesus was conceived. Without her X and God miraculously supplied the **Y,** there would have been no conception or earthly "incarnation". (Without the Y, the child born of Mary would have been her *clone.*) So just as the Y chromosome gave us the masculine icon of Christ, the X chromosome gave us the feminine icon of Christ. That God created the human soul of Jesus, was no miracle – God creates every soul, and every soul is genderless, only *flesh* has *genes.* So the miracle of Christ's earthly incarnation was first and foremost God's *union* with Mary, this was the "miraculous conception" of Christ's human nature.

In those days, of course, no one knew anything about genes and chromosomes. We now know, however, Mary could not have conceived a male child without a Y chromosome. But since the human ovum (eggs) necessary for conception was not discovered until the 19th century,[2] how has this scientific fact changed the Christian understand-

---

[2] Karl Ernst von Baer proved that mammals, including humans, developed from eggs. Baer concludes *"every animal which springs from the coition of male and female is developed from an ovum and none from a simple formative liquid"* (semen) – the belief for thousands of years. No unfertilized human ovum can produce a Y chromosome (male), nor can any human male sperm produce XX – a female. Though there had been *theories* about a female ovum, there is nothing like *seeing to believe*. This discovery was a huge breakthrough that explains why society as a whole, and man's religions in particular, were Patriarchal and male dominated, and how, following this scientific break-though, the status of women in society has subsequently taken a major turn for

ing of the "Incarnation"? It has never been given the slightest consideration – absolutely, it would up-set the traditional "party-line" understanding of Christ.

Obviously, the Logos did **not** take Its flesh or body **solely** from Mary, rather, the physical body of the Logos came from the **union** of Mary and God, ovum and sperm no less – after all, without ovum and sperm there would be no-*body* for a soul. It was this *union* that "conceived" a human body for a human soul. So it was not *just* Mary – as the fathers thought – that supplied the "flesh" (or human nature) of the Incarnate Christ, **it was the *union* of God and Mary that formed the physical body of Christ.** Because the revelation of Christ depended on Mary's oneness with God, and because this oneness came *before* there could have been an earthly Incarnation, her eternal status is as great as Christ, and no less than Christ. The earthly Incarnation of God, then, took place ***in*** Mary, it was she and God supplying the flesh, and the Holy Spirit providing the soul, this is the way it went.

No one denies God became incarnate **in** Mary's womb and used **her flesh.** So if Jesus is Christ ***because*** God was one with *his* **flesh** ("*and the Logos became flesh*"), **then how is Mary *not* Christ since God became one with *her* flesh?** To deny God became one with **her flesh** is to deny the revelation of Christ – because there wouldn't have been one. **God literally became "incarnate" *in* Mary *before* God ever became incarnate in Jesus –** remember, prior to God's becoming incarnate in Mary, Jesus never existed. So if we define "Christ" as *God-flesh* – the Alexandrian belief the Incarnation was only God uniting Itself to flesh – then **how is Mary not Christ**? This is not an attempt to make Christ into a female image of Christ, on the contrary, to understand Mary **as** Christ, points out that the immanent nature of God is **not gendered,** and that the *immanent essence of human nature* is also not gendered. There are not "two Christs", one female and one male. These gendered *distinctions* do not, and cannot, ever define God, mankind, or Christ. Christ is the single Archetype of *all mankind,* and if the man Jesus represents the male species, Mary represents the female species, neither one transcending the other because the *real Christ*

---

the better. Thinking men were the sole procreators, is why children were regarded as the father's property with no genetic relationship to the woman or mother. This is also why male offspring were essential if the family, clan, tribe or monarchy, was to survive, and why only the male in the family could inherit in order to carry on the family. There were no women listed in the family tree, it was solely the line-up of father and sons. And so too, because God was a "Creator", God had to be a male and always referred to as "He". Given this belief system is why, if God had begot a "daughter" and not a "son", there would have been no Christianity. **Incredible!**

is gender-less. Jesus, then, is no more the masculine icon of the incarnate Logos than Mary is the feminine icon. Those who have a problem with Mary as an icon of Christ obviously have a "gender" problem. But then, no one *stuck* with any gender problem can ever have a true understanding of Christ anyway!

This Alexandrian (God-flesh) view, of course, is based on the idea the Incarnation was God only uniting Itself to *flesh*. But what about the (God-Man) – Antiochene belief God was equally one with the soul – with man's whole human nature? When the angel told Mary "*The Spirit will come upon you*", in Judaism, this meant she was specially "*anointed*" by God – chosen to be one with God, one with the "indwelling" Spirit (in the soul.) And what does "*anointed*" mean in Greek? It means "*christos*", the same term used to express Jesus' oneness with God. It was only *after* Mary's "fiat", however, Jesus was conceived. Thus, at the Annunciation, Mary was anointed (was *christos*) prior to the term ever being used to refer to Jesus as the "anointed" or "*christos*". In body and soul, then, she was as one with God as Jesus ever was – **who can deny this**? And who can deny that without Mary, the man Jesus would **never have been conceived or born**? God depended on Mary just as Jesus depended on them both.

As for God's choice of Mary, to think God looked over all the Jewish women and picked one out of the crowd, this is not the way God works. God doesn't pick-and-choose, God plans, creates, fashions, and endows according to "the plan", thus God could not have planned the incarnation without planning Mary. That her name was "Mary" is no more important than her son's name was "Jesus" – what's in a name after all? But let us consider her own "miraculous" conception "born without sin", no different than Jesus.

While some people may point out Mary had a *human* father whereas Jesus had no human father, keep in mind, Paul and the fathers believed lack of a human father is what made Jesus "sinless", yet, since both (Jesus and Mary) were born without sin, **the difference of "fathers" makes no difference!** Reference to Mary's "Immaculate Conception" meant she had been exempt from "inheriting" any sin from her human father. What was miraculous about her birth, however, is that her mother Anne – according to the story – was over the child-bearing age, yet God told her father, Joachim, his wife would conceive a child. **So Mary is a case where God supplied the female X (since Anne had none to give) instead of the male Y – as in the case of Jesus.** And don't think Anne and Joachim didn't regard their little girl as God's miracle! Absolutely, her conception was no less "miraculous" than that of Jesus. But just as the female "ovum" wasn't discovered until the 19th century, so too, **the *true nature* of Mary still remains to be discovered.**

Apart from Mary's "sinless" birth, however, her "Assumption" actually reveals the true nature of resurrection as the "revelation" of Christ – which was **not** a soul coming back to a body, such as people think of "resurrection". That Jesus and Mary Ascended to the **same** glorious estate God willed for all mankind, illustrates that beyond man's hang-up with gender, in heaven there is only one (genderless) "Christ". Then too, given Christianity's view of the merits of redemptive suffering, the fact Mary suffered more than Jesus, makes *him* "*Co-redeemer*" with her. All this points out is that Mary *preceded* Christ, that she was one with God before there was the man Jesus. If this is what Cyril meant by "Theotokos", then he did, indeed, have a very exalted understanding of Mary. Both his view and that of Nestorius, have a logic of their own – an *unexplored* theology however.

Needless to say, to recognize Mary is no less Christ than Jesus, may take many centuries before the male mentality could even conceive such a thing – after all, God is supposed to be **male**, the Son is **male**, Christ a **male**, Jesus a **male – totally a male mentality!** Just as it took centuries before the female ovum was discovered, it may take centuries before the true nature of the revelation of Christ is recognized. Mary was as equally en-fleshed as was the man Jesus – her flesh as one with God as was the flesh of the man Jesus – **who can deny this**?

To think Christ is female is no less justifiable than thinking Christ is male. To know that Mary is also Christ is a step in the right direction because it counters those who think Christ is solely a male man. Also, that Mary was no less Christ than Jesus, opens the door for the rest of mankind. For in truth, Christ is not only more than the man Jesus and more than the woman Mary, Christ is everyman's eternal oneness with God.

Christianity, of course, has never been ready for this understanding of Mary – and it may never be ready. To this point in history, utterly dependent as it is on the male species, few people are ready for any profound change in their staid understanding of human nature – or even their understanding of God. But just as the true nature of the divine Christ utterly transcends the human Jesus, so too, it utterly transcends the human Mary. So just as there is far more to the man Jesus than his being an "historical" person, so too, there is far more to Mary than her being an "historical" person.

When the truth of Mary is finally discovered – realized, revealed, or better understood – only then will the true nature of the "Mother of God" be given its true place in Christian doctrine and theology. Since the fathers wouldn't hear of Mary being understood as any other than "Mother of God", imagine their delight to have it finally proclaimed ***"God was hypostatically united to her flesh just as God was hypostatically united to Jesus' flesh".*** (Cyril's view.) In one voice they'd second this proclamation. Anyone who objected, of course, would be labeled a "Nestorian" and thrown out. But where Cyril's theology of Mary goes no further than **flesh** (basically "*Christotokos*"), Nestorius is the one who actually defined the *real Theotokos* as ***"consubstantially one with the Father" just as Jesus was consubstantially one with the Son (Logos.)*** **God, after all, being genderless, is no less a mother than a father!**

No question, Christianity depended on a woman for its key-revelation – Christ. It took a woman to reveal God's utter love and bond with mankind, a woman through whom God revealed man's eternal oneness with God. Unfortunately, not even in this day and age would Christians, especially men, be able to accept Mary as God-incarnate or the feminine icon of Christ. Christian society, even in the 21st century, has a long way to go before it could ever countenance a truth like this – no theologian, of course, would touch it. For them, "*Theotokos*" is just a *high sounding epithet and nothing more.*

Perhaps there is no better way to understand God becoming incarnate **in** Mary than the Eucharist – the "*continuation of the Incarnation*" as Irenaeus said, or the "*birth of Christ in the soul*" as Origen put it. All the fathers believed the Eucharist was the Logos' transforming human nature into *Its own* human nature – into Christ, that is. So just as God became Incarnate in Mary, so too, the Eucharist is the Logos becoming Incarnate in every human being. **If the Logos becoming Incarnate in Mary did not transform her into Christ, then God transforms no one!** How is it, then, the fathers passed her by as if only the man Jesus was the incarnate Christ? **If the Logos took on *her flesh, her body* and made it one with Its divine nature, then she is no less the incarnate Christ than Jesus.** And if one asks how the Eucharistic Christ can give "birth to Christ" in the soul, this ***is*** the mystery of the Eucharist – Christ multiplied infinitely, yet *only One Christ.*

So how did this *Theotokos* business all end up? We know Nestorius had no problem with *Theotokos* and continued to use the term without apologies or corrections. Cyril, however, took refuge in the "Communication of Properties" (which Nestorius rejected) that said it was "*permissible to* ***say"*** Mary was the "Mother of God". So, like Cyril, one can **call** her "Mother of God". Yet, it was Nestorius, concerned for orthodoxy or truth, who said if she is *truly* "mother of God" (or mother of the "Son-of-God") then she was **"consubstantially one"**

with the Father – meaning, Mary was as one with the Father as Jesus was one with the Son. So there you have it, the final word on the *correct* theology of Mary – the "Mother of God".

* * * * * *

A Personal Note

It has been a joy to write this on Mary. It expresses what she has meant in my own life from as early as I remember – even before I knew God. It is tempting to give some account of life with Mary, but since this is not the place, I will only say that from birth, for me, Mary has always been of a totally "transcendent" nature. My understanding of her can be summed up with an incident when I was either 2 or 3 helping my mother set up the Christmas crèche. She would unwrap the figures and hand them to me to position in the crèche. Unwrapping one figure she said, "Oh, here is Mary, the mother of Jesus", and when I looked at that statue, the words instantly came to mind, "*Is that **all** she is?*" Never for a second in my life did I believe a thing like that – that she was just the mother of Jesus. Even when *having* to admit she was once an "historical" figure, I dismissed this out of hand as irrelevant. I could never relate to the "biblical figure" of Mary. For me, not only did Christ utterly transcend the biblical figure of Jesus, so too, Mary transcended the biblical figure of Mary.

As it turned out, in my life I never found God to be merciful, caring, kind, considerate, or remotely comforting. As a youngster, God let me know It had a *work* to do in me, so forget anything I wanted, anything going on in my personal life mattered nothing to God. I learned early, God was no respecter of "persons", absolutely, God never cared "who" I was, God's work is concerned with "*what*" we are, not "who" we are. Mary, on the other hand, is the one who cares for "*who*" we are as human "persons", cares for what is going on in our mundane lives. She is the essence of divine compassion, understanding, mercy, caring, everything human – she was not revealed as "mother" for nothing.

Mary cares more for man than does the Trinity Itself, she is the only "heart" of God. She is the conduit of every miracle and grace, even the conduit of every prayer to God. As said, I learned early (age seven) it was useless to pray to God; God's sole concern was with some "work" It had to do in me – couldn't imagine what that was, and didn't even like the idea of God interfering with my freedom and choices. The most terrible mistake I ever made was, at age nine, physically ill and at the bottom of the barrel, in desperation I turned to God – an aura of light in the center of my being – and begged It for some help. And what did God do? That light faded to a pinpoint, and in Its going out, suddenly exploded into a black hole that took over just about all the space in my being. I totally collapsed, mentally, physically, there was never an incident in my life comparable to this cruelty. If this taught me any lesson, it was never, ever, pray to God for anything – and I never did. So much for God's "work" in man! The only good thing God ever did for man was reveal Its Own Immanent "Mother". I do not know what God would do without Her; for myself, I'd have been totally lost.

Something else I learned from this horrible mistake of turning to God for help. This is the conviction that if someone really sees God, sees and knows the Trinity like the back of their hand, it does not cross their mind to ask God for this and that, nor to complain or praise as if God was some object of worship or devotion – or one's valet. It is not a matter of this seeming "inappropriate", rather, it is just how this *experiential* reality works. God is not "there" for "me, myself and I", rather, "me, myself and I" are "there" for God. God and man are in "business", we are God's business and God is our business. But this is why those who make a big issue about God as either "personal or impersonal" don't know what they are talking about. God transcends this meaningless dichotomy.

The point is this: while God's *work* is transforming man's human **nature** – transforming all into Christ – Mary is the one who cares for the ***person*** and everything going on in their mundane day-to-day life. So while God takes care of ***what*** we are (human nature), Mary takes care of ***who*** we are. If God had not planned it this way, then, of course, it wouldn't be true. Although God's transformation of nature can be called a "grace", yet grace is God's ordinary "*operandi*" and not an answer to prayer, nor is grace for the benefit of any *person,* but only for man's *nature*. So as marvelous as God's transforming work in human *nature*, Mary's prerogative is care for the individual *person* – "who" one is. Because her particular function in God is seeing to the mundane concerns in people's lives, this is why she has been revealed as "Mother". Where God's concern is with man's *essential nature*, Mary's concern is with the individual *person(s.)*

I have heard it said some people fear having a devotion to Mary lest it subtract from their devotion to Christ – or to God. Mary, however, can only lead one to God because the two are inseparable. She even has a way of "fading" into Christ as if she was the other side of the same coin. Just like true love of God is not a "devotion", so too, true love of Mary is not a "devotion. (I've always had an aversion to the term "devotion" because it smacks of sentiment and *feelings.)* True love of God and Mary, however, can never be called a "devotion", they are too intrinsic to one's life to ever to be associated with "devotion." I'd even go so far as to say, unless people can get beyond their "devotions" – even their devotion to the man Jesus – they will never develop a deep spiritual life. Devout feelings are fickle and tend to keep one on the surface of a spiritual life. To depend on mere "devotion" is the death knell of any abiding spiritual life.

Considering Christianity *depends* on Mary, it is important to understand not merely "*who*" she was, but *"what"* she **is**. If we can imagine the Trinity as a triangle, Its Center is the true nature of everything we call "Mary". At the very heart of the Trinity, the transcendent nature of Mary is part and parcel of the essence of God. For me, at least, this was never a mere "belief", but an experiential Truth. Where everyone is free to "take this or leave it", if they leave it, they miss out on the only other meaningful revelation (beside Christ) God revealed to mankind. As the heart of God, Mary is as utterly divine and transcendent as the Trinity Itself. Of all the terms for the extraordinary *mystery* of Mary, "Theotokos" best epitomizes the true nature of her eternal (and maternal) transcendence in God.

ACKNOWLEDGEMENTS

It has taken over five years to write this book. The only uninterrupted time for writing, however, has been my retreats at the Camaldolese Hermitage on the Big Sur, California. Although a regular retreatant at the Monastery for almost 40 years, yet several years ago, when their suggested donations went up to $95 a day – and then $110 – I knew it would be financially impossible to go there anymore. But as happened before in my life, God wonderfully provided the "way", this time, through the generosity of an unusual contemplative community in Austin, Texas, by the name of "*The Church of Conscious Harmony*". When its pastor and founder, Tim Cook, along with its administrator, Don Genung, heard of my writing and need for some uninterrupted time, they offered to pay for my retreats at the monastery, which they have done these last four years. My stays at the monastery, however, have never been "just to get some work done", but more importantly, to get into the whole rhythm of the eremitic monastic life into which I know I was born. When I tell my kids, "I'm going home", they know exactly where I am going.

How can I ever express my thanks to the Austin community? All I can do here, is point them out as a rare model of a *monastic community in the world.* About the only thing Fr. Thomas Keating and I have ever agreed on, was the extraordinary uniqueness of this particular community. Nobody is accepted as a "parishioner" who is *not* a dedicated Christian contemplative, its lifestyle as demanding as any form of monastic life. I first met its pastor, Tim Cook, in 1985 at the *Omega Institute* in New York – before he started this community. With Tim, then, I can say I have watched this community form and grow – grow beyond everyone's expectations even. It is a phenomenon in itself, a testimony to God's calling people to live a contemplative life no different than their ordinary daily lives – and not as something apart from it. At any rate, I thank Tim, Don, and the whole community for sponsoring my time at Camaldoli. It has been my finding that God's *grace* always has a way of *spreading Itself around* and is never really intended for just one individual. Thus I see the gift of the Austin community as benefiting many, and not just myself.

In a totally different way, I received help for this book from Dr. Joseph Conti, Department of Comparative Religion, *California State University, Fullerton, CA.* Since I do not own more than ten books and have no access to the internet, he not only provided all the books listed in the Bibliography, but a four foot stack of individual articles we never bothered to keep track of. Although I requested all the books listed, Dr. Conti would come across books he thought I might be interested in, thus I looked through many books not listed here. Unfortunately, not all the writings of the early fathers are available in English. (Recently, however, I heard some company is presently working on this project.) For sure, however, I could not have done the research for this book without Dr. Conti's help. He had instant access to religious libraries not possible at any local library – to say nothing of the extended time periods he was afforded due to his university status. So many thanks to Dr. Conti.

I must also thank another long standing friend, Pat Masters, who will be the book's final proof reader. Should anyone come across any "typos", it is because of my penchant to keep changing things *after* her corrections. Apart from Pat's editorial experience, she also manages the blog site "*Bernadette's Friends*", set up by our mutual friend, Dr. Ramesh Balakrishnan, founder of the *Thrasys Inc Co*., San Francisco. There is no expressing my gratitude to Pat and Ramesh for all their help over the years.

I am especially grateful to Ramesh for the time we spent discussing the many issues in this book, his feed-back has been invaluable. Though not an "editor" – I could never trust a "professional editor" – it is his intelligent grasp of the book's thesis and content I have relied on. Where many readers only see the forest, he is one who can also see the trees. It is not just his acute mind, but as a Catholic contemplative, it is his "mystical aptitude" that has never ceased to amaze me. So my special thanks to Ramesh for his time and interest.

Another friend is Dr. Nancy Baker, Professor of Philosophy, *Sarah Lawrence College*, N.Y. Despite her own projects and busy schedule, I am grateful for the time and interest she has given to this book, her comments and criticisms have been much appreciated. Though an Anglican, she credits her extensive Zen Buddhist background for her understanding of the Real Christ.

I've been blessed to have the choice of publishers for this book. I chose **ContemplativeChristians.com** because I trusted its founder, Rev. Peter Traben Haas, to make no changes to the original text. My appreciation for his work knows no bounds. On the back-cover I've asked him to leave us an account of his credentials, the title of his books, and his present ministry.

Although everyone mentioned here are long-standing friends, this does not mean they all agree with everything in this book, much less "like" some of my comments. Yet there is something about enduring friendship that transcends all the details and meeting of minds. For all of us, I think I can say, we see God's grace in our friendship, somehow it works for all of us, and for this I am truly grateful to God.

POSTSCRIPT

If this book has been difficult to read, it is because it was extremely difficult to write. This difficulty can be compared to young David confronting Goliath and his powerful army with nothing more than a little rock in hand. This little rock is the revelation of Christ (in the Trinity) given me by God at age 15, and across the river is Goliath, the "Proverbial Christian Party-line" now some 2000 years old. Throwing a rock at Goliath won't do any good, all one can do is open one's hand, offer the rock, and "*let those who can take it, take it*".

As said at the beginning, the sole reason for this writing is my conviction the true revelation of Christ has been lost to Christianity. What goes by the name "Christian" is not what God revealed, but a theological *spin* on the greatest of God's revelations to Mankind. In my view, Goliath's army will be its own undoing, and the few Christians left will be on the other side of the river with the "rock" in the palm of their hand.

It is one thing to trace the early development of Christian doctrine, but another to pin-point and explain its wrong turns. To thoroughly explain or go into some of the issues would have taken several volumes, which is why, being mindful of the complexities and implications involved, the attempt to simplify was especially difficult. Whole chapters were eliminated lest people, without the same background, find these issues tedious and of no real interest to their personal spiritual pursuits. (Some people love the forest, but have no interest in the trees.) This book, however, was never intended to be a "spiritual treatise", a catechism, much less a criticism of the Christian Faith. Written by an "insider", it merely reflects a genuine concern of one of its faithful. If it gets people thinking, examining their beliefs, then it can only be to the good. It makes no difference if people agree or disagree with anything in the book, while people may share the same Faith, the bottom line, each is responsible for his *own* intellectual and spiritual integrity, and not that of another. One is only responsible for what God has directly given him to know, he can never be responsible for what other people know.

BIBLIOGRAPHY

All books listed in this Bibliography follow the traditional "party-line" and reflect today's acceptable Christology.

Adam, James, *The Religious Teachers of Greece,* Edinburgh: T. T. Clark, 1923.

Anton, John P. with George L. Kustas, eds., *Essays in Ancient Greek Philosophy*, Albany, NY: State University of New York Press, 1971.

Aristotle, *Complete Metaphysic,* Revised Oxford translation, Princeton, Princeton University, 1984.

_____, *Dei Anima: On the Soul*, Hugh Lawson Trancred, Harmondsworth, New York, NY: Penguin Books, 1986.

Arnold, E. Vernon, *Roman Stoicism*, New York: Humanities Press, 1958.

Balthasar, Hans Urs von, *Cosmic Liturgy: The Universe According to Maximus the Confessor*, San Francisco, CA: Ignatius Press, 2003.

Bathrellos, Demetrios, *The Byzantine Christ*, New York: Oxford University Press, 2004.

Beeley, Christopher A., *Gregory of Nazianzus on the Trinity and the Knowledge of God: In Your Light We Shall See Light*, New York: Oxford University Press, 2008.

Bellitto, M. Christopher, *The General Councils,* N.Y. Paulist Press.

Berthold, George C., ed., *Maximus Confessor: Selected Writings*, New York: Paulist Press, 1985.

Bethune- Baker, James Franklin, *An Introduction to the Early History of Christian Doctrine*, London: Methuen Company, 1903.

_____, *Nestorius and His Teaching: a Fresh Examination of the Evidence, with Special Reference to the Newly Recovered Apology of Nestorius, in The Bazaar of Heraclides*, Cambridge: The University Press, 1908.

Boethius, *De Topicis Differentiis*, Eleonore Stump, trans., Ithaka and London: Cornell University Press, 1978.

Bourke, Vernon J., ed., *The Essential Augustine*, New York: New American Library, 1964.

Brown, Raymond E., *Jesus, God and Man: Modern Biblical Reflections*, Milwaukee: Bruce, 1967.

Buonaiuti, Ernesto, "The Ethics and Eschatology of Methodius of Olympus", *The Harvard Theological Review*, Vol. 14, No. 3, July 1921.

Cherniss, Harold F., *The Platonism of Gregory of Nyssa*, New York: B. Franklin, 1971.

Christensen, Michael J., and Jeffery A. Wittung, eds., *Partakers of the Divine Nature: the History and Development of Deification in the Christian Traditions*, Imprint, Madison WI: Fairleigh Dickinson University Press, 2007.

Chroust, Anton–Hermann, "Aristotle and the 'Philosophies of the East'", *The Review of Metaphysics*, Vol. 18, No. 3, March 1965, pp. 572–580.

Cooper, Adam G, *The Body in St. Maximus the Confessor: Holy Flesh, Wholly Deified*, New York: Oxford University Press, 2005.

Cyril, Saint, *Patriarch of Alexandria*, Norman Russell, trans., New York: Imprint, London: Routledge, 2000.

Cross, Richard, *The Metaphysics of the Incarnation: Thomas Aquinas to Duns Scotus*, Oxford, New York: Oxford University Press, 2002.

Damascene, St. John, *Barlaam and Ioasaph*, Rev. G R. Woodward, trans., Cambridge, MA: Harvard University Press, 1962.

Damascus, St. John, *On the Divine Images*, David Anderson, trans., New York: Crestwood, 1980.

Davis, Leo Donald, *First Seven Ecumenical Councils (325–787); Their History and Theology*, Imprint, Wilmington, DL: M. Glazier, 1987.

Demetrius of Rostov, Saint, *The Life of Our Holy Monastic Father Maximus the Confessor and Martyr, from The Great Collection of the Lives of the Saints,* Volume 5, House Springs, MO: Chrysotom Press, 2002.

Dowling, Maurice James, *Marcellus of Ancyra: Problems of Christology and the Doctrine of the Trinity*, Belfast (UK): Queen's University, 1987.

Dunn, James D. G., *Christology in the Making: A New Testament Inquiry into the Origins of the Doctrine of the Incarnation*, Philadelphia: The Westminster Press, 1980.

Durant, Will, *The Story of Civilization: Part II – The Life of Greece*, New York: Simon and Schuster, 1939.

Eriugena, Joannes Scotus, *Periphyseon: On the Division of Nature*, Indianapolis: Bobbs–Merrill, 1976.

Evagrius of Ponticus, *The Greek Ascetic Corpus*, Sinkewicz, Robert E., trans., New York: Oxford University Press, 2005.

_____, *The Praktikos: Chapters on Prayer,* Spencer, MA: Cistercian Publications, 1970.

Evans, David Beecher, *Leontius of Byzantium: An Origenist Christology,* Dumbarton Oaks Center for Byzantine Studies, Washington,

Trustees for Harvard University, available through J. J. Augustin, Locust Valley, New York: 1970.

Finan, Thomas, and Vincent Twomey, eds., *The Relationship between Neoplatonism and Christianity*, Imprint Kill Lane, Blackrock, Co. Dublin: Four Courts Press, 1992.

Flemington, W. F., *The New Testament Doctrine of Baptism*, London: S.P.C.K., 1953.

Florovsky, George, *The Eastern Fathers of the Fourth Century*, Catherine Edmunds, trans., Belmont, MA: Notable Academic Books, 1987.

Friedman, Maurice, *Martin Buber's Life and Works*, Wayne State University Press, 1988.

Gaudoin–Parker, Michael L, *The Real Presence Down Through the Ages*, Staten Island, NY: Alba House, 1993.

Gilbert, Peter, trans., *On God and Man: The Theological Poetry of St. Gregory of Nazianzus*. Crestwood, NY: St. Vladimer's Seminary Press, 2001.

Gregory of Nazianzus, *Nicene and Post–Nicene Fathers*, Vol. 7. Peabody, MA: Hendrickson, 1994.

Gregory of Nyssa, *The Soul and the Resurrection*, New York: St. Vladimir's Seminary Press, 1993.

Gross, Jules, *The Divinization of the Christian According to the Greek Fathers*, Anaheim, CA: A C Press, 2002.

Hardy, Edward Rochie, ed., *The Christology of the Later Fathers*, Philadelphia: Westminster Press, 1977.

Harnack, Adolf von, *History of Dogma*, Volumes 1,2,3, 4 and 5, New York: Dover Publications, 1961.

Harris, R. Baine, ed., *The Significance of Neoplatonism*, Norfolk, VA: International Society for Neoplatonic Studies, Old Dominion University, Distributor: Albany, NY: State University of New York Press, 1976.

Hilary of Poitiers, Saint, *De Trinitate*, E.P. Meijering, trans., Leiden: E.J. Brill, 1982.

Irenaeus, Saint, "Against the Heresies", *Scandal of the Incarnation*, selected texts by Hans Urs von Balthasar, San Francisco: Ignatius Press, 1981.

Kelly, J.N.D., *The Athanasian Creed*, New York: Harper Row, 1964.

_____, *Early Christian Creeds*, New York: D. McKay, 1966.

_____, *Early Christian Doctrines*, New York: Harper Row, 1978.

Lee, Michelle V., *Paul, the Stoics, and the Body of Christ*, New York: Cambridge University Press, 2006.

Lightfoot, J., *The Apostolic Fathers*, Grand Rapids, MI: Baker Book House, 1973.

Lossky, Vladimir, *Mystical Theology of the Eastern Church*, New York: St. Vladimir's Seminary Press, 1976.

_____, *The Vision of God*, Moorhouse, Ashleigh, trans., Crestwood, New York: St. Vladimir's Seminary Press, 1983.

Louth, Andrew, *Early Christian Writings: The Apostolic Fathers*, London: Penguin Books, 1987.

_____, *Maximus the Confessor*, London, New York: Routledge, 1996.

_____, *The Origins of the Christian Mystical Tradition: From Plato to Denys*, Oxford: Clarendon Press, 1983.

Lubac, De Henri, *Origen on First Principles*, Glouchester, Mass, Peter Smith, 1975.

Maloney, George, *The Cosmic Christ; from Paul to Teilhard*, New York: Sheed and Ward, 1968.

Maximus the Confessor, Saint, *Maximus the Confessor,* Classics of Western Spirituality, New York: Paulist Press, 1985.

_____, *The Ascetic Life: The Four Centuries on Charity*, New York: Newman Press, 1955.

McKeon, Richard, Ed., *The Basic Works of Aristotle*, The Modern Library, N.Y. 2001.

Meyendorff, John, *Byzantine Theology: Historical Trends and Doctrinal Themes*, New York: Fordham University Press, 1974.

_____, *Christ in Eastern Christian Thought*, New York: St. Vladimir's Seminary Press, 1987.

Milas, Rick R, *The Correspondences of Clement of Alexandria's View of Apatheia to that of the Stoic Philosophers*, written as a partial fulfillment for a Masters of Divinity Degree at Concordia Theological Seminary, Fort Wayne, Indiana, 1978.

Min, Anselm K., *Paths to the Triune God: An Encounter between Aquinas and Recent Theologies*, Notre Dame, IN: University of Notre Dame Press, 2005.

Musurillo, Herbert, ed., *From Glory to Glory: Texts from Gregory of Nyssa's Mystical Writings,* Crestwood, NY: St. Vladimir's Seminary Press, 1979.

Nikodimos of the Holy Mountain, Saint, and St. Makarios of Corinth, *The Philokalia: The Complete Text*, London, Boston: Faber and Faber, 1979.

Nielson, J.T., *Adam and Christ in the Theology of Irenaeus of Lyons*, Nevada:Van Gorcum Co., 1968.

O'Meara, Dominic J., ed., *Neoplatonism and Christian Thought*, Albany, NY: State University of New York Press, 1982.

Origen: *On First Principles,* G.W. Butterworth, trans., New York: Harper and Row, Harper and Row Torchback reprinted Gloucester, MA, 1973.

_____, *The Song of Songs: Commentary and Homilies*, translated and annotated by R.P. Lawson, ACW, Westminster, MD: Newman Press, 1957.

Parvis, Sara, *Marcellus of Ancyra and the Lost Years of the Arian Controversy, 325–345*, Oxford, New York: Oxford University Press, 2006.

Patterson, L. G. *Methodius of Olympus: Divine Sovereignty, Human Freedom, and Life in Christ*, Washington, D.C.: Catholic University of America Press, 1997.

Pauck, Wilhelm, *Harnack and Troeltsch: Two Historical Theologians*, New York: Oxford University Press, 1988.

Pelikan, Jeroslav, *Jesus Through the Centuries: His Place in the History of Culture*, New Haven: Yale University Press, 1985.

_____, *The Emergence of the Catholic Tradition (100–600),* Volume 1, Chicago: University of Chicago Press, 1971.

_____, *The Spirit of Eastern Christendom (600–1700),* Volume 2, Chicago: University of Chicago Press, 1974.

_____, *The Growth of Medieval Theology (600–1300),* Volume 3, Chicago: University of Chicago Press, 1971.

Philo of Alexandria, *Philo of Alexandria*, Classics of Western Spirituality, New York: Paulist Press, 1981.

Pollard, Evan T., "Marcellus of Ancyra: A Neglected Church Father", *Epiktasis*, 1972, pp. 187–196.

Power, David N., *Irenaeus of Lyons on Baptism and Eucharist: Selected texts and Introduction,* Bramcote Nottingham: Grove Books Limited, 1991.

Rahner, Karl, *Theological Investigations,* Volume XIII, New York: Seabury Press, 1975.

_____, *Theological Investigations,* Volume V, Baltimore: Helicon Press, 1966.

_____, *Foundations of Christian Faith, An Introduction to the Idea of Christianity*, New York: Seabury Press, 1978.

Rahner, Karl and Wilhelm Thüsing, *A New Christology*, New York: Seabury Press, 1980.

Reid, Duncan, *Energies of the Spirit,* "Trinitarian Models in Eastern Orthodox and Western Theology", Atlanta, GA: 1979.

Reith, Herman, *The Metaphysics of St. Thomas Aquinas*, Imprint, Milwaukee, WI: Bruce, 1958.

Rorem, Paul, *Eriugena's Commentary on the Dionysian Celestial Hierarchy*, Toronto: Pontifical Institute of Mediaeval Studies, 2005.

Russell, Norman, *The Doctrine of Deification in the Greek Patristic Tradition*, Imprint, Oxford, New York: Oxford University Press, 2004.

Schaff, Philip, ed., *Nicene and Post-Nicene Fathers of the Christian Church*, Second Series Volume V, of *Gregory of Nyssa: Dogmatic Treatises*, New York: Cosimo Classics, 2007.

Schaff, Philip and Henry Wace, eds., *Nicene and Post–Nicene Fathers of The Christian Church*, Second Series, Volume VII: S. Cyril of Alexandria, S. Gregory Nazianzus, Peabody, MA: Hendrickson Publishers, 1994.

Scotus, John Duns, Early *Oxford Lecture on Individuation,* The Franciscan Institute, St. Bonaventure, N.Y. 14778. 2005.

Sherwood, Polycarp, *The Earlier Ambigua of Saint Maximus the Confessor and his Refutation of Origenism*, Imprint, Rome: Orbis Catholicus, 1955.

_____, *Of St. Maximus the Confessor and his Refutation of Origenism*, Rome: Orbis Catholicus, 1955.

Theodore, The Studite, *On The Holy Icons,* St. Vladimir's Seminary Press, N.Y. 1981.

Thorsteinsson, Runar M., "Paul and Roman Stoicism: Romans 12 and Contemporary Stoic Ethics", *Journal for the Study of the New Testament*, 29.2, 2006.

Thunberg, Lars, *Microcosm and Mediator: The Theological Anthropology of Maximus the Confessor,* Chicago, IL: Open Court, 1995.

U.S. Catholic Church, *Catechism of the Catholic Church*, 2nd edition, Publisher: Image, 1995.

Vinson, Martha, trans., *St. Gregory of Nazianzus: Select Orations*, Washington, DC: The Catholic University Press of America, 2003.

Verdenius, W. J. *Parmenides*, Amsterdam: Adolph M. Hakkert, Publisher, 1964.

Wallis, Robert Ernest, *Gregory of Nyssa's Against Eunomius*, New York: Oxford University Press, 2007.

Wawrykow, Joseph Peter, *The Westminster Handbook to Thomas Aquinas*, Louisville, KY: Westminster John Knox Press, 2005.

Wickham, Lionel R., *Cyril of Alexandria: Select Letters*, ed. and trans., New York: Oxford University Press, 1983.

Winston, David, trans., *Philo of Alexandria: The Contemplative Life, the Giants, and Selections*, New York: Paulist Press, 1981.

Wislow, Donald F., *The Dynamics of Salvation: A Study in Gregory of Nazianzus*, Cambridge, MA: North American Patristic Society, 1979.

Williams, A.N., *The Ground of Deification in Aquinas and Palamas,* New York: Oxford University Press, 1999.

Wolfson, Harry Austryn, *The Philosophy of the Church Fathers*, Cambridge: Harvard University Press, 1970.

+ + +

Also by Bernadette Roberts

The Experience of No-Self: *A Contemplative Journey*

The Path to No-Self: *Life at the Center*

What is Self? *A Study of the Spiritual Journey in Terms of Consciousness*

Made in the USA
Lexington, KY
26 May 2018